Roman Society from Nero to Marcus Aurelius

Roman Society

FROM NERO TO MARCUS AURELIUS

by Samuel Dill

Meridian Books
THE WORLD PUBLISHING COMPANY
Cleveland and New York

A MERIDIAN BOOK
Published by The World Publishing Company
2231 West 110th Street, Cleveland 2, Ohio
First Meridian printing July 1956.
Sixth printing December 1964.
Library of Congress Catalog Card Number: 56-10024
Printed in the United States of America. 7WP67

PREFACE

There must always be something arbitrary in the choice and isolation of a period of social history for special study. No period can, from one point of view, be broken off and isolated from the immemorial influences which have moulded it, from the succession of coming ages which it will help to fashion. And this is specially true of the history of a race at once so aggressive, yet so tenacious of the past, as the Roman. The national fibre was so tough, and its tone and sentiment so conservative under all external changes, that when a man knows any considerable period of Roman social history, he may almost, without paradox, be said to know a great deal of it from Romulus to Honorius.

Yet, as in the artistic drama there must be a beginning and an end, although the action can only be ideally severed from what has preceded and what is to follow in actual life, so a limited space in the collective history of a people may be legitimately set apart for concentrated study. But as in the case of the drama, such a period should possess a certain unity and intensity of moral interest. It should be a crisis and turning-point in the life of humanity, a period pregnant with momentous issues, a period in which the old order and the new are contending for mastery, or in which the old is melting into the new. Above all, it should be one in which the great social and spiritual movements are incarnate in some striking personalities, who may give a human interest to dim forces of spiritual evolution.

Such a period, it seems to the writer of this book, is that

which he now presents to the reader. It opens with the self-destruction of lawless and intoxicated power; it closes with the realisation of Plato's dream of a reign of the philosophers. The revolution in the ideal of the principate, which gave the world a Trajan, a Hadrian, and a Marcus Aurelius in place of a Caligula and a Nero, may not have been accompanied by any change of corresponding depth in the moral condition of the masses. But the world enjoyed for nearly a century an almost unexampled peace and prosperity, under skilful and humane government. The civic splendour and social charities of the Antonine age can be revived by the imagination from the abundant remains and records of the period. Its materialism and social vices will also sadden the thoughtful student of its literature and inscriptions. But if that age had the faults of a luxurious and highly organised civilisation, it was also dignified and elevated by a great effort for reform of conduct, and a passion, often, it is true, sadly misguided, to rise to a higher spiritual life and to win the succour of unseen Powers. To the writer of this book, this seems to give the Antonine age its great distinction and its deepest interest for the student of the life of humanity. The influence of philosophy on the legislation of the Antonines is a commonplace of history. But its practical effort to give support and guidance to moral life, and to refashion the old paganism, so as to make it a real spiritual force, has perhaps hardly yet attracted the notice which it deserves. It is one great object of this book to show how the later Stoicism and the new Platonism, working in eclectic harmony, strove to supply a rule of conduct and a higher vision of the Divine world.

But philosophy failed, as it will probably fail till some far-off age, to find an anodyne for the spiritual distresses of the mass of men. It might hold up the loftiest ideal of conduct; it might revive the ancient gods in new spiritual power; it might strive to fill the interval between the remote Infinite

Spirit and the life of man with a host of mediating and succouring powers. But the effort was doomed to failure. It was an esoteric creed, and the masses remained untouched by it. They longed for a Divine light, a clear, authoritative voice from the unseen world. They sought it in ever more blind and passionate devotion to their ancient deities, and in all the curiosity of superstition. But the voice came to them at last from the regions of the East. It came through the worships of Isis and Mithra, which promised a hope of immortality, and provided a sacramental system to soothe the sense of guilt and prepare the trembling soul for the great ordeal on the verge of another world. How far these eastern systems succeeded, and where they failed, it is one great purpose of this book to explain.

The writer, so far as he knows himself, has had no *arrière pensée* in describing this great moral and spiritual movement. As M. Boissier has pointed out, the historian of the Antonine age is free to treat paganism apart from the growth of the Christian Church. The pagan world of that age seems to have had little communication with the loftier faith which, within a century and a half from the death of M. Aurelius, was destined to seize the sceptre. To Juvenal, Tacitus, and Pliny, to Plutarch, Dion Chrysostom, Lucian, and M. Aurelius, the Church is hardly known, or known as an obscure off-shoot of Judaism, a little sect, worshipping a "crucified Sophist" in somewhat suspicious retirement, or more favourably distinguished by simple-minded charity. The modern theologian can hardly be content to know as little of the great movement in the heathen world which prepared or deferred the victory of the Church.

It will be evident to any critical reader that the scope of this book is strictly limited. As in a former work on the Society of the later Empire, attention has been concentrated on the inner moral life of the time, and comparatively little space has been given to its external history and the machinery of government. The relation of the Senate to the Emperor in the first century, and the organisation of the municipal towns have been dwelt on at some length, because they affected profoundly the moral character of the age. On the particular field which the writer has surveyed, Dean Merivale, Dr. Mahaffy, Professor Bury, and Mr. Capes have thrown much light by their learning and sympathy. But these distinguished writers have approached the period from a different point of view from that of the present author, and he believes that he has not incurred the serious peril of appearing to compete with them. He has, as a first duty, devoted himself to a complete survey of the literature and inscriptions of the period. References to the secondary authorities and monographs which he has used will be found in the notes. But he owes a special obligation to Friedländer, Zeller, Réville, Schiller, Boissier, Martha, Peter, and Marquardt, for guidance and suggestion. He must also particularly acknowledge his debt to M. Cumont's exhaustive work on the monuments of Mithra. Once more he has to offer his warmest gratitude to his learned friend, the Rev. Charles Plummer, Fellow of C.C.C., Oxford, for the patience and judgment with which he has revised the proof sheets. His thanks are also due to the Messrs. R. and R. Clark's reader, for the scrupulous accuracy which has saved the author much time and labour.

September 19, 1904.

Roman Society from Nero to Marcus Aurelius

CONTENTS

BOOK I

CHAPTER I

THE ARISTOCRACY UNDER THE TERROR

CHAPTER II

THE WORLD OF THE SATIRIST

CHAPTER III

THE SOCIETY OF THE FREEDMEN

BOOK II

CHAPTER I

THE CIRCLE OF THE YOUNGER PLINY

CHAPTER II

MUNICIPAL LIFE

CHAPTER III

THE COLLEGES AND PLEBEIAN LIFE

BOOK III

CHAPTER I

THE PHILOSOPHIC DIRECTOR

CHAPTER II

THE PHILOSOPHIC MISSIONARY

CHAPTER III

THE PHILOSOPHIC THEOLOGIAN

BOOK IV

CHAPTER I

SUPERSTITION

CHAPTER II

BELIEF IN IMMORTALITY

CHAPTER V

ISIS AND SERAPIS

CHAPTER VI

THE RELIGION OF MITHRA

BOOK I.

INFESTA VIRTUTIBUS TEMPORA

CHAPTER I

THE ARISTOCRACY UNDER THE TERROR

THE period of social history which we are about to study is profoundly interesting in many ways, but not least in the many contrasts between its opening and its close. It opens with the tyranny of one of the worst men who ever occupied a throne; it ends with the mild rule of a Stoic saint. It begins in massacre and the carnage of civil strife; it closes in the apparent triumph of the philosophic ideal, although before the end of the reign of the philosophers the shadows have begun to fall. The contrast of character between the two princes is generally supposed to find a correspondence in the moral character and ideals of the men over whom they ruled. The accession of Vespasian which, after a deadly struggle, seemed to bring the orgies of a brutal despotism to a close, is regarded as marking not only a political, but a moral, revolution. It was the dawn of an age of repentance and amendment, of beneficent administration, of a great moral revival. We are bound to accept the express testimony of a contemporary like Tacitus,[1] who was not prone to optimist views of human progress, that along with the exhaustion of the higher class from massacre and reckless extravagance, the sober example of the new emperor, and the introduction of fresh blood and purer manners from the provinces, had produced a great moral improvement. Even among the old noblesse, whose youth had fallen on the age of wild licence, it is probable that a better tone asserted itself at the beginning of what was recognised by all to be a new order. The crushed and servile, who had easily learnt to

[1] *Ann.* iii. 55; xvi. 5; cf. Suet. *Vesp.* ix. xii.

imitate the wasteful vices of their oppressors, would probably, with equal facility, at least affect to conform to the simpler fashions of life which Vespasian inherited from his Sabine ancestors and the old farm-house at Reate.[1] The better sort, represented by the circles of Persius, of Pliny and Tacitus, who had nursed the ideal of Stoic or old Roman virtue in some retreat on the northern lakes or in the folds of the Apennines, emerged from seclusion and came to the front in the reign of Trajan.

Yet neither the language of Tacitus nor the testimony from other sources justify the belief in any sudden moral revolution. The Antonine age was undoubtedly an age of conscientious and humane government in the interest of the subject; it was even more an age of religious revival. But whether these were accompanied by a corresponding elevation of conduct and moral tone among the masses may well be doubted. On the other hand the pessimism of satirist and historian who had lived through the darkness of the Terror has probably exaggerated the corruption of the evil days. If society at large had been half as corrupt as it is represented by Juvenal, it would have speedily perished from mere rottenness. The Inscriptions, the Letters of the younger Pliny, even the pages of Tacitus himself, reveal to us another world from that of the satirist. On countless tombs we have the record or the ideal of a family life of sober, honest industry, and pure affection. In the calm of rural retreats in Lombardy or Tuscany, while the capital was frenzied with vicious indulgence, or seething with conspiracy and desolated by massacre, there were many families living in almost puritan quietude, where the moral standard was in many respects as high as among ourselves. The worst period of the Roman Empire was the most glorious age of practical Stoicism. The men of that circle were ready, at the cost of liberty or life, to brave an immoral tyranny; their wives were eager to follow them into exile, or to die by their side.[2] And even in the palace of Nero there was a spotless Octavia, and slave-girls who were ready to defend her honour at the cost of torture and death.[3] In the darkest days, the violence of the bad princes spent itself on

[1] Suet. *Vesp.* ii. quare princeps quoque et locum incunabulorum assidue frequentavit, manente villa, qualis fuerat olim, etc.

[2] Tac. *Ann.* xv. 23; xvi. 21, 34; *Agric.* 2, 45; Plin. *Ep.* iii. 16, § 10; vii. 19, § 3; iii. 11, § 3; ix. 13, § 3.

[3] Tac. *Ann.* xiv. 60.

their nobles, on those whom they feared, or whom they wished to plunder. The provinces, even under a Tiberius, a Nero, or a Domitian, enjoyed a freedom from oppression which they seldom enjoyed under the Republic.[1] Just and upright governors were the rule and not the exception, and even an Otho or a Vitellius, tainted with every private vice, returned from their provincial governments with a reputation for integrity.[2] Municipal freedom and self-government were probably at their height at the very time when life and liberty in the capital were in hourly peril. The great Stoic doctrine of the brotherhood and equality of men, as members of a world-wide commonwealth, which was destined to inspire legislation in the Antonine age, was openly preached in the reigns of Caligula and Nero. A softer tone—a modern note of pity for the miserable and succour for the helpless—makes itself heard in the literature of the first century.[3] The moral and mental equality of the sexes was being more and more recognised in theory, as the capacity of women for heroic action and self-sacrifice was displayed so often in the age of the tyranny and of the Stoic martyrs. The old cruelty and contempt for the slave will not give way for many a generation; but the slave is now treated by all the great leaders of moral reform as a being of the same mould as his master, his equal, if not his superior, in capacity for virtue.

The peculiar distinction of the Antonine age is not to be sought in any great difference from the age preceding it in conduct or moral ideals among the great mass of men. Nor can it claim any literary distinction of decided originality, except in the possession of the airy grace and half-serious mockery of Lucian. Juvenal, Tacitus, and the younger Pliny, Suetonius and Quintilian, Plutarch and Dion Chrysostom, were probably all dead before Antoninus Pius came to the throne. After Hadrian's reign pure Roman literature, in any worthy sense, is extinct; it dies away in that Sahara of the higher intellect which stretches forward to the Fall of the Empire. There is no great

[1] Tac. *Ann.* iv. 6; i. 80; xiii. 50, 51; xi. 24; Suet. *Nero*, x.; *Dom.* viii.; cf. Merivale, vii. 385; Renan, *Apôtres*, p. 308 sqq; Gréard, *Morale de Plut.* p. 200.

[2] Suet. *Vitell.* v.; *Otho*, iii. provinciam administravit moderatione atque abstinentia singulari.

[3] Sen. *Ep.* 47; *De Ira*, i. 5; iii. 24; *De Benef.* iv. 11, § 3; *De Brev. Vit.* xiii. § 7; Plin. *Ep.* iv. 22; Juv. xiv. 15 sqq.; xv. 131; D. Cass. lxvi. 15; *Or. Henz. Inscr. Lat.* 7244, Bene fac, hoc tecum feres; Denis, *Hist. des Idées Morales*, ii. 156, 172, 181.

historian after Tacitus; there is no considerable poet after Statius and Juvenal, till the meteor-like apparition of Claudian in the ominous reign of Honorius.

The material splendour and municipal life of the Antonine age are externally its greatest glory. It was pre-eminently a sociable age, an age of cities. From the wall of Hadrian to the edge of the Sahara towns sprang up everywhere with as yet a free civic life. It was an age of engineers and architects, who turned villages into cities and built cities in the desert, adorned with temples and stately arches and basilicas, and feeding their fountains from the springs of distant hills. The rich were powerful and popular; and never had they to pay so heavily for popularity and power. The cost of civic feasts and games, of forums and temples and theatres, was won by flattery, or extorted by an inexorable force of public opinion from their coffers. The poor were feasted and amused by their social superiors who received a deference and adulation expressed on hundreds of inscriptions. And it must be confessed that these records of ambitious munificence and expectant gratitude do not raise our conception of either the economic or the moral condition of the age.

The glory of classic art had almost vanished; and yet, without being able to produce any works of creative genius, the inexhaustible vitality of the Hellenic spirit once more asserted itself. After a long eclipse, the rhetorical culture of Greece vigorously addressed itself in the reign of Hadrian to the conquest of the West. Her teachers and spiritual directors indeed had long been in every family of note. Her sophists were now seen haranguing crowds in every town from the Don to the Atlantic. The influence of the sophistic discipline in education will be felt in the schools of Gaul, when Visigoth and Burgundian will be preparing to assume the heritage of the falling Empire.[1] From the early years of the second century can be traced that great combined movement of the Neo-Pythagorean and Platonist philosophies and the renovated paganism which made a last stand against the conquering Church in the reigns of Julian and Theodosius. Philosophy became a religion, and devoted itself not only to the private direction of character and the preaching of a higher life, but

[1] Sid. Apoll. *Ep.* viii. 6, § 5.

to the justification and unification of pagan faith. In spite of its rather bourgeois ideal of material enjoyment and splendour, the Antonine age, at least in its higher minds, was an age of a purified moral sense and religious intuition. It was, indeed, an age of spiritual contradictions. On the one hand, not only was the old ritual of classical polytheism scrupulously observed even by men like Plutarch and M. Aurelius, but religious imagination was appropriating the deities of every province, almost of every canton, embraced by the Roman power. At the same time the fecundity of superstition created hosts of new divinities and genii who peopled every scene of human life.[1] On the other hand syncretism was in the air. Amid all the confused ferment of devotion a certain principle of unity and comprehension was asserting itself, even in popular religion. The old gods were losing their sharp-cut individuality; the provinces and attributes of kindred deities tended to fade into one another, and melt into the conception of a single central Power. The religions of Egypt and the remoter East, with their inner monotheism, supported by the promise of sacramental grace and the hope of immortality, came in to give impetus to the great spiritual movement. The simple peasant might cling to his favourite god, as his Neapolitan descendant has his favourite saint. But an Apuleius, an Apollonius, or an Alexander Severus[2] sought a converging spiritual support in the gods and mysteries of every clime.

Platonist philosophy strove to give rational expression to this movement, to reconcile cultivated moral sense with the worships of the past, to find a bond between the vagrant religious fancies of the crowd and the remote esoteric faith of the philosophic few. On the higher minds, from whatever quarter, a spiritual vision had opened, which was strange to the ancient world, the vision of One who is no longer a mere Force, but an infinite Father, Creator, Providence and Guardian, from whom we come, to whom we go at death. Prayer to Him is a communion, not the means of winning mere temporal blessings; He is not gratified by bloody sacrifice; He is dishonoured by immoral legend.[3] He cannot be imaged in gold or ivory graven

[1] *Or. Henz.* iii. Ind. p. 27 sq.

[2] Apul. *Apol.* c. 55, sacrorum pleraque initia in Graecia participavi, et plurimos ritus . . . didici; Lamprid. *Alex. Sev.* c. 29, 43.

[3] Max. Tyr. *Diss.* viii.; xi. § 3; xvii.; D. Chrys. *Or.* xii. § 83.

by the most cunning hand, although the idealised human form may be used as a secondary aid to devotion. These were some of the religious ideas current among the best men, Dion Chrysostom, Plutarch, Maximus of Tyre, which the Neo-Platonic school strove to harmonise with the rites and legends of the past. The means by which they tried to do so, and the measure of their success, it is one purpose of this book to explain.

The Antonine age saw for a brief space the dream of Plato realised, when kings should be philosophers, and philosophers should be kings. Philosophy had given up its detached and haughty reserve, or outspoken opposition to imperial power. In the second century it lent all its forces to an authority which in the hands of the Antonine princes seemed to answer to its ideals.[1] The votaries of the higher life, after their persecution under the last cruel despot, rose to an influence such as they had never wielded save in the Pythagorean aristocracies of southern Italy. Philosophy now began to inspire legislation and statesmanship.[2] Its professors were raised to the consulship and great prefectures. Above all, it was incarnate, as it were, in the ruler who, whatever we may think of his practical success, brought to the duties of government a loftiness of spiritual detachment which has never been equalled by any ruler of men. Whether there was any corresponding elevation of conduct or moral tone in the mass of men may well be doubted by any one who has studied the melancholy thoughts of the saintly emperor. Lucian and M. Aurelius seem to be as hopeless about the moral condition of humanity as Seneca and Petronius were in the darkest days of Nero's tyranny.[3] Such opinions, indeed, have little scientific value. They are often the result of temperament and ideals, not of trustworthy observation. But it would be rash to assume that heightened religious feeling and the efforts of philosophy had within a hundred years worked any wide-spread transformation of character. It was, however, a great step in advance that the idea of the principate, expounded by Seneca, and the younger Pliny, as a clement, watchful, infinitely

[1] Renan, *Les Évangiles*, p. 382.

[2] Friedl. *Sittengesch.* iv. 420; Denis, *Idées Morales*, ii. 200 sqq.; Renan, *M. Aurèle*, p. 24 sqq.

[3] Luc. *Som.* 32; *Traj.* 15; *Charon*, 15, 20; *Tim.* 14, 36; M. Aurel. v. 10, 33; ix. 29; 34; x. 19: cf. Sen. *De Ira*, ii. 8; *Ad Marc.* ii. 17, 20, 22; Petron. *Sat.* 88.

laborious earthly providence had been realised since the accession of Trajan. It was easier to be virtuous in the reign of M. Aurelius than in the reign of Nero, and it was especially easier for a man of the highest social grade. The example of the prince for good or evil must always powerfully influence the class who are by birth or office nearest to the throne. And bad example will be infinitely more corrupting when it is reinforced by terror. A fierce, capricious tyranny generates a class of vices which are perhaps more degrading to human dignity, and socially more dangerous, than the vices of the flesh. And the reign of such men as Caligula, Nero, and Domitian not only stimulated the grossness of self-indulgence, but superadded the treachery and servility of cowardice. In order to appreciate fully what the world had gained by the mild and temperate rule of the princes of the second century, it is necessary to revive for a moment the terrors of the Claudian Caesars.

The power of Seneca as a moral teacher has, with some reservations, been recognised by all the ages since his time. But equal recognition has hardly been given to the lurid light which he throws, in random flashes, on the moral conditions of his class under the tyranny of Caligula and Nero. This may be due, perhaps, to a distrust of his artificial declamation, and that falsetto note which he too often strikes even in his most serious moments. Yet he must be an unsympathetic reader who does not perceive that, behind the moral teaching of Seneca, there lies an awful experience, a life-long torture, which turns all the fair-seeming blessings of life, state and luxury and lofty rank, into dust and ashes. There is a haunting shadow over Seneca which never draws away, which sometimes deepens into a horror of darkness. In whatever else Seneca may have been insincere, his veiled references to the terrors of the imperial despotism come from the heart.

Seneca's life almost coincides with the Julio-Claudian tyranny. He had witnessed in his early manhood the gloomy, suspicious rule of Tiberius, when no day passed without an execution,[1] when every accusation was deadly, when it might be fatal for a poet to assail Agamemnon in tragic verse, or for a

[1] *Ep.* 108, § 22; cf. Suet. *Tib.* lxi. nullus a poena hominum cessavit dies.

historian to praise Brutus and Cassius,[1] when the victims of delation in crowds anticipated the mockery of justice by self-inflicted death, or drank the poison even in the face of the judges. Seneca incurred the jealous hatred of Caligula by a too brilliant piece of rhetoric in the Senate,[2] and he has taken his revenge by damning the monster to eternal infamy.[3] Not even in Suetonius is there any tale more ghastly than that told by Seneca of the Roman knight whose son had paid with his life for a foppish elegance which irritated the tyrant.[4] On the evening of the cruel day, the father received an imperial command to dine. With a face betraying no sign of emotion, he was compelled to drink to the Emperor, while spies were eagerly watching every expression of his face. He bore the ordeal without flinching. "Do you ask why? He had another son." Exiled to Corsica in the reign of Claudius,[5] Seneca bore the sentence with less dignity than he afterwards met death. He witnessed the reign of the freedmen, the infamies of Messalina, the intrigues of Agrippina, and the treacherous murder of Britannicus; he knew all the secrets of that ghastly court. Installed as the tutor of the young Nero, he doubtless, if we may judge by the treatise on Clemency, strove to inspire him with a high ideal of monarchy as an earthly providence. He probably at the same time discovered in the son of Cn. Domitius Ahenobarbus and Agrippina the fatal heritage of a vicious blood and the omens of a ghastly reign. The young tiger was held on leash for the famous quinquennium by Burrus and Seneca. It seemed only the device of a divine tragic artist, by a brief space of calm and innocence, to deepen the horror of the catastrophe. And, for Seneca, life darkened terribly towards its close. With high purposes for the commonweal, he had probably lent himself to doubtful means of humouring his wayward pupil, perhaps even to crime.[6] His enormous wealth, whether won from imperial favour, or gained by usury and extortion,[7] his power, his literary brilliance, aroused

[1] Suet. *Tib.* 61; Tac. *Ann.* iv. 34.

[2] D. Cass. lix. 19; Suet. *Calig.* 53.

[3] *Nec. Inj.* xviii.; cf. Suet. *Calig.* 50; Sen. *De Ira*, i. 20; iii. 18; *De Tranq.* xiv.; *Ad Polyb.* xiii. xvii.; *Ad Helv.* x. 4; *De Benef.* iv. 31.

[4] Sen. *De Ira*, ii. 33.

[5] Tac. *Ann.* xii. 8; D. Cass. 60. 8; 61. 10; Sen. *Ad Polyb.* 13. 2; *Ad Helv.* 15. 2.

[6] For the worst charges *v.* D. Cass. lxii. 2; lxi. 10; Tac. *Ann.* 13. 13.

[7] D. Cass. *l.c.*; Tac. *Ann.* 13. 42. But cf. Seneca's reply, Tac. *Ann.* 14. 53, and 15. 62.

a host of enemies, who blackened his character and excited the fears or the jealousy of Nero. He had to bear the unenviable distinction of a possible pretender to the principate.[1] He withdrew into almost monastic seclusion, and even offered to resign his wealth.[2] He strove to escape the evil eyes of calumny and imperial distrust by the most abject renunciation. But he could not descend from the precipice on which he hung; his elevation was a crucifixion.[3] Withdrawn to a remote corner of his palace, which was crowded with the most costly products of the East, and surrounded by gardens which moved the envy of Nero,[4] the fallen statesman sought calm in penning his counsels to Lucilius, and bracing himself to meet the stealthy stroke which might be dealt at any moment.[5] In reading many passages of Seneca, you feel that you are sitting in some palace on the Esquiline, reading the *Phaedo* or listening to the consolations of a Stoic director, while the centurion from the palace may at any moment appear with the last fateful order.

Seneca, like Tacitus, has a remarkable power of moral diagnosis. He had acquired a profound, sad knowledge of the pathology of the soul. It was a power which was almost of necessity acquired in that time of terror and suspicion, when men lived in daily peril from seeming friends. There never was a period when men more needed the art of reading the secrets of character. Nor was there ever a time when there were greater facilities for the study. Life was sociable almost to excess. The Roman noble, unless he made himself deliberately a recluse, spent much of his time in those social meeting-places of which we hear so often,[6] where gossip and criticism dealt mercilessly with character, where keen wits were pitted against one another, sometimes in a deadly game, and where it might be a matter of life or death to pierce the armour of dissimulation.[7] Seneca had long shone in such circles. In his later years, if he became a recluse, he was also a spiritual director. And his Letters leave little doubt that many a restless or weary spirit laid bare its secret misery to him, for advice or

[1] Tac. *Ann.* 15. 65.
[2] Sen. *Frag.* 108.
[3] Sen. *De Tranq.* x. 6.
[4] Sen. *Ep.* i. 18; Tac. *Ann.* 14. 52.
[5] *Ep.* 70, § 14; 88, § 17; *Ep.* 77; *De Ira*, iii. 15; *Ad Helv.* 5, § 4.
[6] Mart. vii. 27, 11; Juv. xi. 4; Sen. *Dial.* 1, 5, 4; *De Benef.* vii. 22, 2; Friedl. *Sittengesch.* i. 281.
[7] Sen. *De Ira*, ii. 33; *De Tranq.* xii. 7.

consolation. Knowing well the wildest excesses of fantastic luxury, all the secrets of the philosophic confessional, the miseries of a position oscillating between almost princely state and monastic renunciation, the minister of Nero, with a self-imposed cure of souls, had unrivalled opportunities of ascertaining the moral condition of his class.

Seneca is too often a rhetorician, in search of striking effects and vivid phrase. And, like all rhetoricians, he is often inconsistent. At times he appears to regard his own age as having reached the very climax of insane self-indulgence. And yet, in a calmer mood, he declares his belief that the contemporaries of Nero were not worse than the contemporaries of Clodius or Lucullus, that one age differs from another rather in the greater prominence of different vices.[1] His pessimism extends to all ages which have been allured by the charm of ingenious luxury from the simplicity of nature. In the fatal progress of society, the artificial multiplication of human wants has corrupted the idyllic innocence of the far-off Eden, where the cope of heaven or the cave was the only shelter, and the skin-clad savage made his meal on berries and slaked his thirst from the stream.[2] It is the revolutionary dream of Rousseau, revolting from the oppression and artificial luxury of the *Ancien Régime*. Seneca's state of nature is the antithesis of the selfish and materialised society in which he lived. Our early ancestors were not indeed virtuous in the strict sense.[3] For virtue is the result of struggle and philosophic guidance. But their instincts were good, because they were not tempted. They enjoyed in common the natural bounties of mother earth.[4] Their fierceness of energy spent itself on the beasts of the chase. They lived peaceably in willing obedience to the gentle paternal rule of their wisest and best, with no lust of gold or power, no jealousy and hatred, to break a contented and unenvious harmony. The great disturbers of this primeval peace were avarice and luxury.[5] The moment when the first nugget flashed its baleful temptations on the eyes of the roaming hunter was the beginning of all human guilt and misery.[6] Selfish greed, developing into insatiable appetite, is

[1] Sen. *Ep.* 97, § 2; Sen. *De Benef.* i. 10, § 1. Cf. *De Ira*, ii. 8; *Ep.* 95, § 20; *Ep.* 115, § 10.

[2] Sen. *Ep.* 90, § 42.

[3] *Ep.* 90, § 40.

[4] *Ib.* 90, § 38.

[5] *Ib.* 90, § 5, § 36, avaritia atque luxuria dissociavere mortales.

[6] *Ib.* 90, § 12.

the original sin which turned the garden into wilderness. In individualist cravings men lost hold on the common wealth of nature. Luxury entered on its downward course, in the search for fresh food and stimulus for appetite, till merely superfluous pleasures led on to those from which untainted nature recoils.[1] Man's boasted conquests over nature, the triumphs of his perverted ingenuity, have bred an illimitable lust, ending in wearied appetite; they have turned those who were brothers into cunning or savage beasts.

Such a theory of society has, of course, no value or interest in itself. Its interest, like that of similar *à priori* dreams, lies in the light which it sheds on the social conditions which gave it birth. Like the Germany of Tacitus, and the Social Contract of Rousseau, Seneca's theory of the evolution of humanity is an oblique satire on the vices of his own age. And not even in Tacitus or Suetonius are to be found more ghastly revelations of a putrescent society, and the ennui and self-loathing which capricious sensualism generates in spirits born for something higher. It may be worth noting that the vices which Seneca treats as most prevalent and deadly are not so much those of sexual impurity, although they were rife enough in his day, as those of greed, gross luxury, treacherous and envious cruelty, the weariness of jaded nerves and exhausted capacities of indulgence.[2] It is not the coarse vices of the Suburra, but the more deadly and lingering maladies of the Quirinal and the Esquiline which he is describing. There is a universal lust of gold:[3] riches are the one ornament and stay of life. And yet in those days a great fortune was only a splendid servitude.[4] It had to be guarded amid perpetual peril and envy. The universal greed and venality are worthily matched by the endless anxiety of those who have won the prize. Human life has become a scene of cruel and selfish egotism, a ferocious struggle of beasts of prey, eager for rapine, and heedless of those who go down in the obscene struggle.[5] It is an age when men glorify the fortunate and trample on the fallen. The cunning and cruelty of the wild beast on the throne have taught a lesson of dissimulation to the subject.

[1] Sen. *Ep.* 90, § 19.

[2] *De Brev. Vit.* xvi. tarde ire horas queruntur; *Ep.* 77; *Ep.* 104, § 15.

[3] *Ep.* 115, § 10; *De Ira*, iii. 33; *Ep.* 60; *Ep.* 74.

[4] *Ad Polyb.* vi. 5, magna servitus est magna fortuna.

[5] *De Ira*, ii. 8.

At such a court it is a miracle to reach old age, and the feat can only be accomplished by accepting insult and injury with a smiling face.[1] For him who goes undefended by such armour of hypocrisy there is always ready the rack, the poisoned cup, the order for self-murder. It is characteristic of the detachment of Seneca that he sees the origin of this hateful tyranny. No modern has more clearly discerned the far-reaching curse of slavery.[2] Every great house is a miniature of the Empire under a Caligula or Nero, a nursery of pretenders capable of the same enormities. The unchecked power of the master, which could, for the slightest faults, an ill-swept pavement, an unpolished dish, or a sullen look, inflict the most brutal torture,[3] produced those cold hearts which gloated over the agony of gallant men in the arena, and applauded in the Senate the tyrant's latest deed of blood. And the system of household slavery enervated character while it made it heartless and cruel. The Inscriptions confirm Seneca's picture of the minute division of functions among the household, to anticipate every possible need or caprice of the master.[4] Under such a system the master became a helpless dependent. There is real truth, under some ludicrous exaggeration, in the tale of a Roman noble, taking his seat in his sedan after the bath, and requiring the assurance of his slave that he was really seated.[5]

It is little wonder that on such lives an utter weariness should settle, the disgust of oversated appetite, which even the most far-fetched luxuries of the orient, the most devilish ingenuity of morbid vice, could hardly arouse. Yet these jaded souls are tortured by an aimless restlessness, which frets and chafes at the slow passing of the hours,[6] or vainly hopes to find relief in change of scene.[7] The more energetic spirits, with no wholesome field for energy, developed into a class which obtained the name of "Ardeliones." Seneca,[8] Martial,[9] and the younger Pliny[10] have left us pictures of these idle

[1] *De Ira*, ii. 33.
[2] *Ib.* iii. 35, deinde idem de republica libertatem sublatam quereris quam domi sustulisti.
[3] *Ib.* iii. 24, 32; Petron. *Sat.* 49, 53; Sen. *Ep.* 47, § 10; Juv. vi. 490; Sen. *De Clem.* i. 18.
[4] Boissier, *Rel. Rom.* ii. 353; Marq. *Priv.* i. 142; Wallon, *L'Escl. dans l'Ant.* ii. 146.
[5] Sen. *De Brev. V.* xiii.
[6] *Ib.* xvi. transilire dies volunt.
[7] Id. *Ep.* 104, § 15; 89, § 20; *Ep.* 28.
[8] Id. *De Tranq.* xii. § 7.
[9] Mart. ii. 7, 8 (*v.* note on the word in Friedländer's ed.); iv. 78.
[10] Sen. *Ep.* i. 9; cf. Friedl. *Sittengesch.* i. 271.

busybodies, hurrying round the forums, theatres, and great houses, in an idle quest of some trivial object of interest, waiting on patrons who ignore their existence, following some stranger to the grave, rushing pell-mell to the wedding of a much-married lady, or to a scene in the law courts, returning at nightfall, worn out with these silly labours, to tread the same weary round next day. Less innocent were they who daily gathered in the *circuli*,[1] to hear and spread the wildest rumours about the army on the frontier, to kill a woman's reputation with a hint, to find a sinister meaning in some imperial order, or to gloat in whispers over the last highly-coloured tale of folly or dark guilt from the palace. It was a perilous enjoyment, for, with a smiling face, some seeming friend was probably noting every hint which might be tortured into an accusation before the secret tribunal on the Palatine, or angling for a sneer which might cost its author a fortune, or send him to the rocks of Gyarus.

In reading Seneca's writings, especially those of his last years, you are conscious of a horror which hardly ever takes definite shape, a thick stifling air, as it were, charged with lightning. Again and again, you feel a dim terror closing in silently and stealthily, with sudden glimpses of unutterable torture, of cord and rack and flaming tunic.[2] You seem to see the sage tossing on his couch of purple under richly pannelled ceilings of gold, starting at every sound in the wainscot,[3] as he awaits the messenger of death. It is not so much that Seneca fears death itself, although we may suspect that his nerves sometimes gave the lie to his principles. He often hails death as welcome at any age, as the deliverer who strikes off the chain and opens the prison door, the one harbour on a tempestuous and treacherous sea.[4] He is grateful for having always open this escape from life's long torture, and boldly claims the right to anticipate the executioner. The gloom of Seneca seems rather to spring from a sense of the terrible con-

[1] Juv. xi. 4; Mart. vii. 97; Quintil. vi. 3, 105; Sen. *De Tranq.* xii. § 7; *De Ben.* vii. 22, 2; *De Prov.* i. 5, 4; Boissier, *L'Opp.* p. 201 sqq.

[2] *Ad Marc.* xx.; *De Tranq.* x.; *Ep.* 94 *ad fin.*; *Ep.* 70.

[3] *Ep.* 90, § 43, at vos ad omnem tectorum pavetis sonum et inter picturas vestras, si quid increpuit, fugitis attoniti.

[4] *Ep.* 70, § 14; *Ep.* 88, § 17, malis paratus sum; *Ep.* 24, § 11; *Ad Polyb.* ix. nullus portus nisi mortis; *Ad Marc.* xx. mors quae efficit ut nasci non supplicium sit.

trast between wealth and state and an ignominious doom which was ever ready to fall. And to his fevered eye all stately rank seems at last but a precipice overhanging the abyss, a mark for treacherous envy or the spitefulness of Fortune.[1] "A great fortune is a great servitude,"[2] which, if it has been hard to win, is harder still to guard. And all life is full of these pathetic contrasts. Pleasure is nearest neighbour to pain; the summer sea in a moment is boiling in the tempest; the labour of long years is scattered in a day; there is always terror lurking under our deepest peace. And so we reach the sad gospel of a universal pessimism; "nothing is so deceitful and treacherous as the life of man."[3] No one would knowingly accept such a fatal gift, of which the best that can be said is that the torture is short, that our first moment of existence is the first stage to the grave.[4] Thus to Seneca, with all his theoretical indifference to things external to the virtuous will, with all his admiration for the invulnerable wisdom, withdrawn in the inner citadel of the soul, and defying the worst that tyrants or fortune could inflict, the *taedium vitae* became almost unendurable. The interest of all this lies, not in Seneca's inconsistency, but in the nightmare which brooded on such minds in the reign of Nero.

Something of the gloom of Seneca was part of the evil heritage of a class, commanding inexhaustible wealth and assailed by boundless temptations to self-indulgence, which had been offered by the conquest of East and West. The weary senses failed to respond to the infinite sensual seductions which surrounded the Roman noble from his earliest years. If he did not succeed in squandering his fortune, he often exhausted too early his capacity for healthy joy in life, and the nemesis of sated appetite and disillusionment too surely cast its shadow over his later years. Prurient slander was rife in those days, and we are not bound to accept all its tales about Seneca. Yet there are passages in his writings which leave the impression that, although he may have cultivated a Pythagorean aceticism in his youth,[5] he did not

[1] *Ad Marc.* x.
[2] *Ad Polyb.* vi.
[3] *Ad Marc.* xxii. § 3.
[4] *Ad Polyb.* ix.; *Ep.* 77; *Ad Marc.* xxi. § 7.
[5] *Ep.* 108, § 17. He adopted the Pythagorean discipline under the influence of Sotion, a pupil of Sextius, but gave it up on the proscription of suspected rites in the reign of Tiberius, cf. Suet. *Tib.* 36; cf. Zeller, *Die Phil. der Gr.* iii. 1, 605.

altogether escape the taint of his time.[1] His enormous fortune did not all come by happy chance or the bounty of the emperor.[2] His gardens and palace, with all its priceless furniture, must have been acquired because at one time he felt pleasure in such luxuries. A soul so passionate in its renunciation may, according to laws of human nature, have been once as passionate in indulgence. In his case, as so often in the history of the Church, the saint may have had a terrible repentance.

It is probable, however, that this pessimism is more the result of the contrast between Seneca's ideal of the principate, and the degradation of its power in the hands of his pupil Nero. Seneca may have been regarded once as a possible candidate for the throne, but he was no conspirator or revolutionary.[3] He would have condemned the visionaries whose rudeness provoked even the tolerant Vespasian.[4] In a letter, which must have been written during the Neronian terror, he emphatically repudiates the idea that the votaries of philosophy are refractory subjects. Their great need is quiet and security. They should surely reverence him who, by his sleepless watch, guards what they most value, just as, on a merchantman, the owner of the most precious part of the cargo will be most grateful for the protection of the god of the sea.[5] Seneca would have his philosophic brethren give no offence by loud self-assertion or a parade of superior wisdom.[6] In that deceitful dawn of his pupil's reign, Seneca had written a treatise in which he had striven to charm him by the ideal of a paternal monarchy, in the consciousness of its god-like power ever delighting in mercy and pity, tender to the afflicted, gentle even to the criminal. It is very much the ideal of Pliny and Dion Chrysostom under the strong and temperate rule of Trajan.[7] Addressed to one of the worst emperors, it seems, to one looking back, almost a satire. Yet we should remember that, strange as it may seem, Nero, with all his wild depravity, appears to have had a strange charm for many, even to the end. The men who trembled

[1] D. Cass. 62. 2 ; 61. 10. Zeller, iii. 1, 641, n. 1.
[2] D. Cass. *l.c.*
[3] *Tac. Ann.* xv. 55.
[4] Suet. *Vesp.* 15.
[5] Sen. *Ep.* 73, § 3.
[6] *Ib.* 103, § 4.
[7] *De Clem.* i. 19 ; Plin. *Paneg.* i. 72 ; D. Chrys. *Or.* ii. § 77 ; iii. § 39 ; 70 sqq.

under the sombre and hypocritical Domitian, regretted the wild gaiety and bonhomie of Nero, and each spring, for years after his death, flowers were laid by unknown hands upon his grave.[1] The charm of boyhood, with glimpses of some generous instincts, may for a time have deceived even the experienced man of the world and the brooding analyst of character. But it is more probable that the piece is rather a warning than a prophecy. Seneca had watched all the caprices of an imperial tyrant, drunk with a sense of omnipotence, having in his veins the maddening taint of ancestral vice,[2] with nerves unstrung by maniacal excesses, brooding in the vast solitudes of the Palatine till he became frenzied with terror, striking down possible rivals, at first from fear or greed,[3] in the end from the wild beast's lust for blood, and the voluptuary's delight in suffering. The prophecy of the father as to the future of Agrippina's son [4] found probably an echo in the fears of his tutor. But, in spite of his forebodings, Seneca thought the attempt to save him worth making. He first appeals to his imagination. Nero has succeeded to a vicegerency of God on earth.[5] He is the arbiter of life and death, on whose word the fortunes of citizens, the happiness or misery of whole peoples depend. His innocence raises the highest hopes.[6] But the imperial task is heavy, and its perils are appalling. The emperor is the one bond by which the world-empire is held together;[7] he is its vital breath. Man, the hardest of all animals to govern,[8] can only be governed long by love, and love can only be won by beneficence and gentleness to the frowardness of men. In his god-like place, the prince should imitate the mercy of the gods.[9] Wielding illimitable power, he is yet the servant of all, and cannot usurp the licence of the private subject. He is like one of the heavenly orbs, bound by inevitable law to move onward in a fixed orbit, unswerving and unresting. If he relies on cruel force, rather than on clemency, he will sink to the level of the tyrant and meet

[1] Suet. *Dom.* 23, *Nero,* 57; cf. Tac. *Hist.* i. 7, ipsa aetas Galbae irrisui ac fastidio erat adsuetis juventae Neronis et imperatores forma ac decore corporis . . . comparantibus.

[2] Suet. *Calig.* 50; cf. Sen. *Nec. Inj.* 18; *De Ira,* i. 20; ii. 33; iii. 18; *De Ben.* ii. 12, 21.

[3] Suet. *Calig.* 38.

[4] Id. *Nero,* 6.

[5] *De Clem.* i. 1, § 2, electusque sum qui in terris deorum vice fungerer.

[6] *Ib.* i. § 5.

[7] *Ib.* i. 4, 1, ille vinculum per quod respublica cohaeret, ille spiritus vitalis.

[8] *Ib.* i. 17, 1.

[9] *Ib.* i. 7, 2.

his proper fate.[1] Cruelty in a king only multiplies his enemies and envenoms hatred. In that fatal path there is no turning back. The king, once dreaded by his people, loses his nerve and strikes out blindly in self-defence.[2] The atmosphere of treachery and suspicion thickens around him, and, in the end, what, to his maddened mind, seemed at first a stern necessity becomes a mere lust for blood.

It has been suggested that Seneca was really, to some extent, the cause of the grotesque or tragic failure of Nero.[3] The rhetorical spirit, which breathes through all Seneca's writings, may certainly be an evil influence in the education of a ruler of men. The habit of playing with words, of aiming at momentary effect, with slight regard to truth, may inspire the excitable vanity of the artist, but is hardly the temper for dealing with the hard problems of government. And the dazzling picture of the boundless power of a Roman emperor, which Seneca put before his pupil, in order to heighten his sense of responsibility, might intoxicate a mind naturally prone to grandiose visions, while the sober lesson would be easily forgotten. The spectacle of "the kingdoms of the world and all the glory of them" at his feet was a dangerous temptation to a temperament like Nero's.[4] Arrogance and cruelty were in the blood of the Domitii. Nero's grandfather, when only aedile, had compelled the censor to give place to him; he had produced Roman matrons in pantomime, and given gladiatorial shows with such profusion of cruelty, as to shock that not very tender-hearted age.[5] The father of the emperor, in addition to crimes of fraud, perjury, and incest, had, in the open forum, torn out the eye of a Roman knight, and deliberately trampled a child under his horse's feet on the Appian Way.[6] Yet such is the strange complexity of human nature, that Nero seems by nature not to have been destitute of some generous and amiable qualities. We need not lay too much stress on the innocence ascribed to him by Seneca.[7] Nor need we attribute to Nero's initiative the sound or benevolent measures which characterised the beginning of his reign. But he showed

[1] *De Clem.* i. 12.

[2] *Ib.* i. 13, 2, scelera enim sceleribus tuenda sunt.

[3] Renan, *L'Antéchr.* p. 125.

[4] *De Clem.* i. 1, § 2, egone ex omnibus mortalibus placui electusque sum qui in terris deorum vice fungerer?

[5] Suet. *Nero*, c. 4.

[6] *Ib.* c. 5.

[7] Sen. *De Clem.* i. 1, § 5.

at one time some industry and care in performing his judicial work.[1] He saw the necessity, in the interests of public health and safety, of remodelling the narrow streets and mean insanitary dwellings of Rome.[2] His conception of the Isthmian canal, if the engineering problem could have been conquered, would have been an immense boon to traders with the Aegean. Even his quinquennial festival, inspired by the Greek contests in music and gymnastic,[3] represented a finer ideal of such gatherings, which was much needed by a race devoted to the coarse realism of pantomime and the butchery of the arena. Fierce and incalculably capricious as he could be, Nero, at his best, had also a softer side. He had a craving for love and appreciation[4]; some of his cruelty was probably the revenge for the denial of it. He was singularly patient of lampoons and invective against himself.[5] Although he could be brutal in his treatment of women, he also knew how to inspire real affection, and perhaps in a few cases return it. He seems to have had something of real love for Acte, his mistress. His old nurses consoled him in his last hour of agony, and, along with the faithful Acte, laid the last of his race in the vault of the Domitii.[6] Nero must have had something of that charm which leads women in every age to forget faults, and even crimes in the men whom they have once loved. And the strange, lingering superstition, which disturbed the early Church, and which looked for his reappearance down to the eleventh century, could hardly have gathered around an utterly mean and mediocre character.[7]

When Nero uttered the words "Qualis artifex pereo,"[8] he gave not only his own interpretation of his life, he also revealed one great secret of its ghastly failure. It may be admitted that Nero had a certain artistic enthusiasm, a real ambition to excel.[9] He painted with some skill, he composed verses not without a certain grace. In spite of serious natural defects, he took endless pains to acquire the technique of a singer. Far into the night he would sit in rapt enthusiasm listening to

[1] Suet. *Nero*, c. 15; cf. *Dom.* c. viii.

[2] *Nero*, c. 16.

[3] *Ib.* c. 12, instituit et quinquennale certamen primus omnium Romae more Graeco triplex, etc.

[4] *Ib.* c. 20; 53; Renan, *L'Antéchr.* p. 132.

[5] Suet. *Nero*, c. 39.

[6] *Ib.* c. 50.

[7] Renan, *L'Antéchr.* p. 316.

[8] Suet. *Nero*, c. 49; Renan, *L'Antéchr.* 130. sqq.

[9] Suet. *Nero*, c. 24, 49, 52, 55; Tac. *Ann.* xiv. 16; cf. Macé, *Suétone*, p. 179; Boissier, *L'Opp.* p. 265.

the effects of Terpnus, and trying to copy them.[1] His artistic tour in Greece, which lowered him so much in the eyes of the West, was really inspired by the passion to find a sympathetic audience which he could not find at Rome. And, in spite of his arrogance and vanity, he had a wholesome deference for the artistic judgment of Greece. Yet it is very striking that in the records of his reign, the most damning accusation is that he disgraced the purple by exhibitions on the stage. His songs to the lyre, his impersonation of the parturient Canace or the mad Hercules, did as much to cause his overthrow as his murders of Britannicus and Agrippina.[2] The stout Roman soldier and the Pythagorean apostle have the same scorn for the imperial charioteer and actor. A false literary ambition, born of a false system of education, was the bane of Roman culture for many ages. The dilettante artist on the throne in the first century had many a successor in the literary arts among the grand seigneurs of the fifth. They could play with their ingenious tricks of verse in sight of the Gothic camp-fires. He could contend for the wreath at Olympia when his faithful freedman was summoning him back by the news that the West was seething with revolt.[3]

Nero's mother had dissuaded him from the study of philosophy; his tutor debarred him from the study of the manly oratory of the great days.[4] The world was now to learn the meaning of a false artistic ambition, divorced from a sense of reality and duty. Aestheticism may be only a love of sensational effects, with no glimpse of the ideal. It may be a hypocritical materialism, screening itself under divine names. In this taste Nero was the true representative of his age. It was deeply tainted with that mere passion for the grandiose and startling, and for feverish intellectual effects, which a true culture spurns as a desecration of art.[5] Mere magnitude and portentousness, the realistic expression of physical agony, the coarse flush of a half-sensual pleasure, captivated a vulgar taste, to which crapulous excitement and a fever of the senses took the place of the purer ardours and visions of the

[1] Suet. *Nero*, c. 53, c. 20, cf. c. 24.

[2] Philostr. *Apoll. Tyan.* iv. 36, 39; Tac. *Ann.* xiv. 15, 16; xv. 67, odisse coepi postquam parricida matris et uxoris, auriga et histrio et incendiarius extitisti; Suet. *Nero*, c. 21; D. Cass. 63. 9, 10.

[3] Suet. *Nero*, c. 23.

[4] *Ib.* c. 32.

[5] Merivale, viii. p. 70 sq.; Schiller, *Gesch. der Röm. Kaiserzeit*, i. p. 467.

spirit.[1] Nero paid the penalty of outraging the conventional prejudices of the Roman. And yet he was in some respects in thorough sympathy with the masses. His lavish games and spectacles atoned to some extent for his aberrations of Hellenism. He was generous and wasteful, and he encouraged waste in others,[2] and waste is always popular till the bill has to be paid. He was a "cupitor incredibilium." [3] The province of Africa was ransacked to find the fabled treasure of Dido.[4] Explorers were sent to pierce the mysterious barrier of the Caucasus, and discover the secret sources of the Nile. He had great engineering schemes which might seem baffling even to modern skill, and which almost rivalled the wildest dreams of the lunatic brain of Caligula.[5] His Golden House, in a park stretching from the Palatine to the heights of the Esquiline, was on a scale of more than oriental magnificence. At last the master of the world was properly lodged. With colonnades three miles long, with its lakes and pastures and sylvan glades, it needed only a second Nero in Otho to dream of adding to its splendour.[6] To such a prince the astrologers might well predict another monarchy enthroned on Mount Zion, with the dominion of the East.[7] The materialist dreamer was, like Napoleon I., without a rudimentary moral sense. Stained with the foulest enormities himself, he had a rooted conviction that virtue was a pretence, and that all men were equally depraved.[8] His surroundings gave him some excuse for thinking so. He was born into a circle which believed chiefly in "the lust of the eye and the pride of life." He formed a circle many of whom perished in the carnage of Bedriacum. With a treasury drained by insane profusion, Nero resorted to rapine and judicial murder to replenish it.[9] The spendthrift seldom has scruples in repairing his extravagance. The temples were naturally plundered by the man who, having no religion, was at least honest enough to deride all religions.[10] The artistic treasures of Greece were carried off by the votary of Greek art; the gold and silver images of her shrines were

[1] Petron. *Sat.* 8, where the decay of artistic sense is traced to the grossness of evil living; at nos vino scortisque demersi ne paratas quidem artes audemus cognoscere.

[2] Suet. *Nero*, c. 11, 12.

[3] Tac. *Ann.* 15. 42.

[4] *Ib.* 16. 1; Suet. *Nero*, 31.

[5] *Ib.* 16, 31.

[6] *Ib.* c. 31; cf. *Otho*, 7.

[7] Suet. *Nero*, c. 40.

[8] *Ib.* c. 29 *ad fin.*

[9] *Ib.* c. 32; D. Cass. 63. 17.

[10] Suet. *Nero*, c. 56.

sent to the melting-pot.[1] Ungrateful testators paid their due penalty after death; and delation, watching every word or gesture, skilfully supplied the needed tale of victims for plunder. It is all a hackneyed story. Yet it is perhaps necessary to revive it once more to explain the suppressed terror and lingering agony of the last days of Seneca.

The impressions of the Terror which we receive from Seneca are powerful and almost oppressive. A thick atmosphere of gloom and foreboding seems to stifle us as we turn his pages. But Seneca deals rather in shadowy hint and veiled suggestion than in definite statement. For the minute picture of that awful scene of degradation we must turn to Tacitus. He wrote in the fresh dawn of an age of fancied freedom, when the gloom of the tyranny seemed to have suddenly vanished like an evil dream. Yet he cannot shake off the sense of horror and disgust which fifteen years of ignoble compliance or silent suffering have burnt into his soul. Even under the manly, tolerant rule of Trajan, he hardly seems to have regained his breath.[2] He can scarcely believe that the light has come at last. His attitude to the tyranny is essentially different from that of Seneca. The son of the provincial from Cordova views the scene rather as the cosmopolitan moralist, imperilled by his huge fortune and the neighbourhood of the terrible palace. Tacitus looks at it as the Roman Senator, steeped in all old Roman tradition, caring little for philosophy, but caring intensely for old Roman dignity and the prestige of that great order, which he had seen humbled and decimated.[3] The feeling of Seneca is that of a Stoic monk, isolated in a corner of his vast palace, now trembling before the imperial jealousy, which his wealth and celebrity may draw down upon him, and again seeking consolation in thoughts of God and eternity which might often seem to belong to Thomas à Kempis. The tone of Tacitus is sometimes that of a man who should have lived in the age of the Samnite or the Carthaginian wars, before luxury and factious ambition had sapped the moral strength of the great aristocratic caste, while his feelings are divided between grim anger at

[1] Suet. *Nero*, c. 32; D. Cass. 63. 11.

[2] Tac. *Agric.* c. 3, sic ingenia studiaque oppresseris facilius quam revocaveris.

[3] Peter, *Gesch. Litt.* ii. 53 sqq.

a cruel destiny, and scornful regret for the weakness and the self-abandonment of a class which had been once so great. The feelings of Seneca express themselves rather in rhetorical self-pity. The feelings of Tacitus find vent in words which sometimes veil a pathos too proud for effusive utterance, sometimes cut like lancet points, and which, in their concentrated moral scorn, have left an eternal brand of infamy on names of historic renown.

More than forty years had passed between the date of Seneca's last letters to Lucilius and the entry of Tacitus on his career as a historian.[1] He was a child when Seneca died.[2] His life is known to us only from a few stray glimpses in the Letters of Pliny,[3] eked out by the inferences of modern erudition. As a young boy, he must have often heard the tales of the artistic follies and the orgies of Nero, and the ghastly cruelties of the end of his reign. As a lad of fifteen, he may have witnessed something of the carnival of blood and lust which appropriately closed the régime of the Julio-Claudian line. He entered on his *cursus honorum* in the reign of Vespasian, and attained the praetorship under Domitian.[4] A military command probably withdrew him from Rome for three years during the tyranny of the last Flavian.[5] He was consul suffectus in 97, and then held the proconsulship of Asia. It cannot be doubted from his own words that, as a senator, he had to witness tamely the Curia beset with soldiery, the noblest women driven into exile, and men of the highest rank and virtue condemned to death on venal testimony in the secret tribunal of the Alban Palace. His hand helped to drag Helvidius to the dungeon, and was stained with the blood of Senecio. He lived long enough under a better prince to leave an unfading picture of the tragedy of solitary and remorseless power, but not long enough to forget the horrors and degradation through which he had passed.

The claim of Tacitus to have been uninfluenced by passion

[1] Seneca died in 65 A.D. The *Histories* of Tacitus were published *circ.* 106-107; cf. Plin. *Ep.* vii. 20; Peter, *Gesch. Litt.* ii. 42.

[2] Tacitus was born about 55 A.D. (Peter, ii. 43; Macé, *Suétone*, p. 35, 81; Momms. *Plin.* p. 51). He was, perhaps, fifteen years older than Suetonius, and seven years older than Pliny.

[3] Plin. *Ep.* i. 6, 20; iv. 13; vi. 9, 16, 20; vii. 20, 33; viii. 7; ix. 10, 14.

[4] *Hist.* i. 1; *Ann.* xi. 11. This latter important passage fixes the date of his praetorship, 88 A.D.; cf. Teuffel, ii. p. 165 n. 6; Peter, ii. 43.

[5] *Agric.* c. 45.

or partiality[1] has been disputed by a modern school of critics.[2] Sometimes, from a love of Caesarism and strong government, sometimes from the scholarly weakness for finding a new interpretation of history, the great historic painter of the Julio-Claudian despotism has been represented as an acrid rhetorician of the Senatorial reaction, a dreamer who looks back wistfully to the old Republic, belonging to one of those haughty circles of the old régime which were always in chronic revolt, which lived in an atmosphere of suspicion and poisonous gossip, and nourished its dreams and hatreds till fiction and fact melted into one another in gloomy retrospect.[3] He is the great literary avenger of the Senate after its long sanguinary conflict with the principate, using the freedom of the new order to blacken the character of princes who had been forced, in the interests of the world-wide empire, to fight and to crush a selfish and narrow-minded caste.[4]

The weakness of all such estimates of Tacitus lies in their failure to recognise the complex nature of the man, the mingled and crossing influences of training, official experience, social environment, and lofty moral ideals[5]; it lies even more in a misconception of his aims as a historian. Tacitus was a great orator, and the spirit of the rhetorical school, combined with the force and dexterity of style which it could communicate, left the greatest Roman historians with a less rigorous sense of truth than their weakest modern successors often possess.[6] No Roman ever rose to the Thucydidean conception of history. Moreover Tacitus, although originally not of the highest social rank,[7] belonged to the aristocratic class by sympathy and associations. Like Suetonius, he necessarily drew much of his information from the memories of great houses and the tales of the elders who had lived through the evil days.[8] He acquired thus many of the

[1] *Hist.* i. 1, sed incorruptam fidem professis, neque amore quisquam et sine odio dicendus est; Nipperdey, *Einl.* xxvi.

[2] Merivale, viii. 84; Schiller, *Gesch. der Röm. Kaiserzeit*, i. 140, 586. According to Schiller, Tacitus has no research, no exactness of military or geographical knowledge, no true conception of the time. He is an embittered aristocrat and rhetorician. For a sounder estimate *v.* Peter, ii. 43, 60, 63; Nipperdey, *Einl.* xxv. For the influence on the work of Suetonius of the Senatorial tradition, *v.* Macé, *Suétone*, p. 84; Peter, *Gesch. Litt.* ii. 69.

[3] Peter, *Gesch. Litt.* ii. 66.

[4] Merivale, viii. 95 sqq.

[5] Peter, ii. 46 sqq.

[6] *Ib.* ii. 188, 200.

[7] His father was probably a Roman Eques, procurator in Belgium; Plin. *H. N.* vii. 16, 76.

[8] Macé, *Suétone*, p. 83, Peter, ii. 69 sqq.

prejudices of a class which, from its history, and still more from its education, sought its ideals in the past rather than in the future. He mingled in those circles, which in every age disguise the meanness and bitterness of gossip by the airy artistic touch of audacious wit, polished in many social encounters. He had himself witnessed the triumph of delation and the cold cruelty of Domitian. He had shared in the humiliation of the Senate which had been cowed into acquiescence in his worst excesses. And the spectacle had inspired him with a horror of unchecked power in the hands of a bad man, and a gloomy distrust of that human nature which could sink to such ignoble servility.[1] Yet on the other hand Tacitus had gained practical experience in high office, both as soldier and administrator, which has always a sobering effect on the judgment. He realised the difficulties of government and the unreasonableness of ordinary men. Hence he has no sympathy with a doctrinaire and chimerical opposition even under the worst government.[2] However much he might respect the high character of the philosophic enthusiasts of the day, he distrusted their theatrical defiance of power, and he threw his shield over a discreet reserve, which could forget that it was serving a tyrant in serving the commonwealth.[3] Tacitus may at times express himself with a stern melancholy bitterness, which might at first seem to mark him as a revolutionary dreamer, avenging an outraged political ideal. Such an interpretation would be a grave mistake, which he would himself have been the first to correct. The ideal which he is avenging is not a political, but a moral ideal.[4] The bitter sadness is that of the profound analyst of character, with a temperament of almost feverish intensity and nervous force. The interest of history to Thucydides and Polybius lies in the political lessons which it may teach posterity. Its interest to Tacitus lies in the discovery of hidden motives and the secret of character, in watching the stages of an inevitable degeneracy, the moral preparation for a dark, inglorious end. And the analyst

[1] Tac. *Ann.* i. 7; xv. 71; *Agr.* 45; Peter, ii. 62.

[2] *Ann.* xiv. 12, 57; *Hist.* iv. 6; *Agr.* 42; Peter, ii. 47.

[3] *Agr.* 42.

[4] *Ann.* iii. 65, praecipuum munus annalium reor, ne virtutes sileantur, utque pravis dictis factisque ex posteritate et infamia metus sit; cf. Peter, ii. 46; Nipperdey, *Einl.* xxvi.

was a curiously vivid painter of character, the character of individuals, of periods, and of peoples. His portraits burn themselves into the imaginative memory, so that the impression, once seized, can never be lost. Tiberius and Claudius and Nero, Messalina and Agrippina, in spite of the most mordant criticism, will live for ever as they have been portrayed by the fervid imagination of Tacitus. Nor is he less searching and vivid in depicting the collective feeling and character of masses of men. We watch the alternating fury and repentance of the mutinous legions of Germanicus,[1] or the mingled fierceness and sorrow with which they wandered among the bleaching bones on the lost battlefield of Varus,[2] or the passion of grief and admiration with which the praetorian cohorts kissed the self-inflicted wounds of Otho.[3] Or, again, we follow the changing moods of the Roman populace, passing from anger and grief to short-lived joy, and then to deep silent sorrow, at the varying rumours from the East about the health of Germanicus.[4] In Tacitus events are nearly always seen in their moral setting. The misery and shame of the burning of the Capitol by the Vitellians are heightened by the thought that the catastrophe is caused by the madness of civil strife.[5] In the awful conflict which raged from street to street, the horror consists in the mixture of cruelty and licence. The baths and brothels and taverns are crowded at the very hour when the neighbouring ways are piled with corpses and running with blood; the rush of indulgence paused not for a moment; men seemed to revel in the public disasters. There was bloodshed enough in the days of Cinna and Sulla, but the world was at least spared such a carnival of lust.[6] Even in reporting or imagining the speech of Galgacus to his warriors on the Grampians,[7] even in the pictures of the German tribes,[8] the ethical interest is always foremost. The cruel terror of the prince, the effeminacy and abandoned adulation of the nobles, the grossness and fierceness of the masses, contrasted with the loyalty, chastity, and hardihood of the German clans, seem to have dimly foreshadowed to Tacitus

[1] Tac. *Ann.* i. 39, 41.
[2] *Ib.* c. 61, 62.
[3] *Hist.* ii. 49.
[4] *Ann.* ii. 82.
[5] *Hist.* iii. 72.
[6] *Ib.* iii. 83.
[7] *Agr.* 32.
[8] *Germ.* 17, 19, 20, 23, 25.

a danger from which all true Romans averted their eyes till the end.[1]

The key to the interpretation of Tacitus is to regard him as a moralist rather than a politician. And he is a moralist with a sad, clinging pessimism.[2] He is doomed to be the chronicler of an evil time, although he will save from oblivion the traces and relics of ancient virtue.[3] He has Seneca's pessimist theory of evolution. The early equality and peace and temperance have been lost through a steady growth of greed and egotistic ambition.[4] It is in the past we must seek our ideals; it is from the past we derive our strength. With the same gloomy view of his contemporaries as M. Aurelius had,[5] he holds vaguely a similar view of cycles in human affairs.[6] And probably the fairest hope which ever visited the mind of Tacitus was that of a return to the simplicity of a long gone age. He hailed the accession of Vespasian and of Trajan as a happy change to purer manners and to freedom of speech.[7] But the reign of Vespasian had been followed by the gloomy suspicious despotism of Domitian. Who could be sure about the successors of Trajan? Tacitus hardly shared the enthusiasm and exuberant hopes expressed by his friend Pliny in his *Panegyric*. It was a natural outbreak of joy at escaping from the dungeon, and the personal character of Trajan succeeded in partially veiling the overwhelming force of the emperor under the figment of the freely accepted rule of the first citizen. Tacitus no doubt felt as great satisfaction as his friend at the suppression of the informers, the restored freedom of speech, the recovered dignity of the Senate, the prince's respect for old republican forms and etiquette.[8] He felt probably even keener pleasure that virtue and talent had no longer to hide themselves from a jealous eye, and that the whole tone of society was being raised by the temperate example of the emperor. But he did not share Pliny's illusions as to the prince's altered position under the new régime. The old Republic was gone for ever.[9] It was still the rule of one man, on whose character

[1] *Germ.* 33, *ad fin.*

[2] *Hist.* i. 3; ii. 38; iii. 72; Peter, ii. 62. Yet this should be qualified by such passages as *Ann.* iii. 55; *Agr.* i.; cf. Nipperdey, *Einl.* xxvii.

[3] *Ann.* iii. 65.

[4] *Ib.* iii. 26.

[5] M. Aurel. ix. 29, 34; x. 19.

[6] Tac. *Ann.* iii. 55; M. Aurel. vii. 1; ix. 4; x. 23; ix. 28.

[7] *Agr.* 3.

[8] Plin. *Paneg.* 35, 53, 54, 66; cf. Tac. *Hist.* i. 1.

[9] *Hist.* i. 1, omnem potentiam ad

everything depended. He would never have joined Plutarch and Dion in exalting the emperor to the rank of vicegerent of God. With his experience and psychologic skill, he was bound to regard all solitary power as a terrible danger both to its holder and his subjects.[1] "Capax imperii, nisi imperasset" condenses a whole disquisition on imperialism. In truth, Tacitus, like many thoughtful students of politics, had little faith in mere political forms and names.[2] They are often the merest imposture: they depend greatly on the spirit and social tone which lie behind them. In the abstract, perhaps, Tacitus would have given a preference to aristocracy. But he saw how easily it might pass into a selfish despotism.[3] He had no faith in the people or in popular government, with its unstable excitability. He admitted that the conquests of Rome, egotistic ambition, and the long anarchy of the Civil Wars had made the rule of one inevitable. But monarchy easily glides into tyranny, and he accepts the Empire only as a perilous necessity which may be justified by the advent of a good prince. The hereditary succession, which had been grafted on the principate of Augustus, had inflicted on the world a succession of fools or monsters. The only hope lay in elevating the standard of virtue, and in the choice of a worthy successor by the forms of adoption.[4] The one had in his own time given the world a Domitian, and was destined within three generations to give it a Commodus. The other secured to it the peace and order of the age of which Tacitus saw the dawn.[5]

The motive of Tacitus was essentially ethical, and his moral standard was in many respects lofty. Yet his standard was sometimes limited by the prejudices of his class. He cherished the old Roman ideal of "virtus" rather than the Stoic gospel of a cosmopolitan brotherhood of man.[6] Like Pliny, he felt little horror at gladiatorial combats,[7] although he may have had a certain contempt for the rage for them. He had probably far less humane feelings than Pliny on the subject of slavery.[8]

unum conferri pacis interfuit; cf. *Hist.* i. 16; ii. 38.

[1] *Ann.* xiv. 47; *Hist.* iv. 8, bonos imperatores voto expetere, qualescumque tolerare.

[2] *Ann.* xv. 46; vi. 42; iv. 33; iii. 27; *Hist.* ii. 38.

[3] Peter, ii. 53; *Ann.* vi. 42.

[4] *Hist.* i. 16; Peter, ii. 61.

[5] Tac. *Agr.* i.

[6] Peter, ii. 48.

[7] Tac. *Ann.* i. 76; quanquam *vili* sanguine nimis gaudens. Cf. *Dial. de Or.* 29; Plin. *Ep.* vi. 34, 1.

[8] *Ann.* xiv. 43; *Germ.* 20.

While he admired many of the rude virtues of the Germans, he prayed Heaven that their tribal blood-feuds might last for ever.[1] He has all the faith of Theognis in the moral value of blood and breeding. He feels a proud satisfaction in recording the virtues of the scion of a noble race, and degeneracy from great traditions moves his indignant pity.[2] He sometimes throws a veil over the degenerates.[3] The great economic revolution which was raising the freedman, the petty trader, the obscure provincial, to the top, he probably regarded with something of Juvenal's suspicion and dislike. The new man would have needed a fine character, or a great record of service, to commend him to Tacitus.[4] But, with all these defects of hard and narrow prejudice, Tacitus maintains a lofty ideal of character, a severe enthusiasm for the great virtues which are the salt of every society.

Of the early nurture of Tacitus nothing is directly known. But we may be permitted to imagine him tenderly yet strictly guarded from the taint of slave nurses [5] by a mother who was as unspotted as Julia Procilla, the mother of his hero Agricola.[6] What importance he attached to this jealous care of a good woman, what a horror he had of the incitements to cruelty and lust which surrounded the young Roman from his cradle, are to be traced in many a passage coming from the heart. His ideal of youthful chastity and of the pure harmony of a single wedded union, reveals to us another world from the scene of heartless, vagrant intrigue, on which Ovid wasted his brilliant gifts. His taste, if not his principles, revolted against the coarse seductions of the spectacles and the wasteful grossness of the banquets of his time.[7] He envies the Germans their freedom from these great corrupters of Roman character, from the lust for gold, and the calculating sterility which cut itself from nature's purest pleasure, to be surrounded on the deathbed by a crowd of hungry, shameless sycophants. While Tacitus had a burning contempt for the nerveless cowardice and sluggishness which degraded so many of his order,[8] he may have valued

[1] *Germ.* 33. Cf. his contempt for the Christians and devotees of Eastern cults, *Ann.* ii. 85 ; xv. 44.

[2] *Ann.* i. 53 ; iv. 3 ; iii. 39 ; vi. 29 ; xii. 12 ; iii. 24 ; xvi. 16. Cf. Peter, ii. 51.

[3] *Ann.* xiv. 14.

[4] *Ann.* ii. 21 ; vi. 27 ; iv. 3.

[5] *De Or.* 29.

[6] *Agr.* 4.

[7] *Germ.* 19, saepta pudicitia agunt, nullis spectaculorum inlecebris . . . corruptae ; *De Or.* 29.

[8] *Hist.* iii. 37; *Ann.* i. 7; xv. 57, 71.

even to excess, although it is hardly possible to do so, the virtues of the strenuous soldier. Proud submission to authority, proud, cold endurance in the face of cruel hardship and enormous odds, readiness to sacrifice even life at the call of the State, must always tower over the safe aspirations of an untried virtue. The soldier, though he never knows it, is the noblest of idealists. The ideal of Tacitus, although he sees his faults of temper,[1] was probably the character of his father-in-law, Agricola, grave, earnest and severe, yet with a mingled clemency, free from all vulgar avarice or ostentation of rank, from all poisonous jealousy, an eager ambitious warrior, yet one knowing well how to temper audacious energy with prudence.[2] Tacitus would probably have sought his ideal among those grey war-worn soldiers on a dangerous frontier, half warrior and half statesman, just and clement, stern in discipline, yet possessing the secret of the Roman soldier's love, the men who were guarding the Solway, the Rhine, and the Danube, while their brethren in the Senate were purchasing their lives or their ease by adulation and treachery. Yet, after all, Tacitus was too great for such a limited ideal. He could admire faith and courage and constancy in any rank.[3] With profound admiration and subdued pathos, he tells how the freedwoman Epicharis, racked and fainting in every limb with the extremity of torture, refused to tell the secret of the Pisonian conspiracy, and by a voluntary death shamed the knights and nobles who were ready to betray their nearest kin.[4] The slave girls of the empress, who defiantly upheld her fair fame, under the last cruel ordeal, are honoured by a like memorial.[5]

The deepest feeling of Tacitus about the early Empire seems to have been that it was fatal to character both in prince and subject. This conviction he has expressed with the burning intensity of the artist. He could never have penned one of those laborious paragraphs of Suetonius which seem transcribed from a carefully kept note-book, with a lifeless catalogue of the vices, the virtues, and the eccentricities of the subject. For Tacitus, history is a living and real thing, not a matter of mere antiquarian interest. He has seen a single

[1] *Agr.* 22. [2] *Ib.* 40.
[3] *Ann.* xv. 60. [4] *Ib.* xv. 57. [5] *Ib.* xiv. 60.

lawless will, unchecked by constitutional restraints or ordinary human feeling, making sport of the lives and fortunes of men. He has seen the sons of the proudest houses selling their ancestral honour for their lives, betraying their nearest and dearest, and kissing the hand which was reeking with innocent blood.[1] When he looked back, he saw that, for more than fifteen years, with brief intervals, virtue had been exiled or compelled to hide itself in impotent seclusion, and that power and wealth had been the reward of perfidy and grovelling self-abasement.[2] The brooding silence of those years of humiliating servitude did not extinguish the faith of Tacitus in human virtue, but it almost extinguished his faith in a righteous God. Tacitus is no philosopher, with either a reasoned théodicée or a consistent repudiation of faith.[3] He uses popular language about religion, and often speaks like an old Roman in all things touching the gods.[4] He is, moreover, often as credulous as he is sceptical in his treatment of omens and oracles.[5] But, with all his intense faith in goodness, the spectacle of the world of the Caesars has profoundly shaken his trust in the Divine justice. Again and again, he attributes the long agony of the Roman world to mere chance or fate,[6] or the anger of Heaven, as well as to the madness of men.[7] Sometimes he almost denies a ruling power which could permit the continuance of the crimes of a Nero.[8] Sometimes he grimly notes its impartial treatment of the good and the evil.[9] And again, he speaks of the Powers who visit not to protect, but only to avenge. And so, by a curse like that which haunted the Pelopidae in tragic legend, the monarchy, cradled in ambition and civil strife, has gone on corrupting and corrupted. The lust of despotic power which Tacitus regards as the fiercest and most insatiable of human passions, has been intensified by the spectacle of a monarchy commanding, with practically unlimited sway, the resources and the fortunes of a world.

[1] *Ann.* xv. 71.

[2] *Hist.* i. 2.

[3] *Agr.* 4, memoria teneo solitum ipsum narrare se studium philosophiae acrius, ultra quam concessum Romano ac Senatori, exhausisse. Cf. Fabian, *Quid Tac. de num. Div. judicaverit*, p. 1.

[4] *Hist.* v. 5; Nipperdey, *Einl.* xiv.

[5] *Hist.* i. 22; ii. 78; i. 86. But cf. *Ann.* xii. 43, 64; xiv. 32; xv. 8; *Hist.* i. 3; ii. 50; and Fabian, pp. 17-19.

[6] *Ann.* iv. 20; cf. vi. 22.

[7] *Hist.* ii. 38.

[8] *Ann.* xiv. 12; Fabian, p. 23.

[9] *Ann.* xvi. 33, aequitate deum erga bona malaque documenta.

It was a dazzling prize, offering frightful temptations both to the holder and to possible rivals and pretenders. The day on which a Nero or a Caligula awoke to all the possibilities of power was a fateful one. And Tacitus, with the instinct of the tragic artist, has painted the steady, fatal corruption of a prince's character by the corroding influence of absolute and solitary sway. Of all the Caesars down to his time, the only one who changed for the better was the homely Vespasian. In Tiberius, Caligula, and Nero, some of this deterioration of character must be set down to the morbid strain in the Julio-Claudian line, with its hard and cruel pride, and its heritage of a tainted blood, of which Nero's father knew the secret so well. Much was also due to the financial exhaustion which, in successive reigns, followed the most reckless waste. It would be difficult to say whether the emperors or their nobles were the most to blame for the example of spendthrift extravagance and insane luxury. Two generations before the foundation of the Empire, the passion for profusion had set in, which, according to Tacitus, raged unchecked till the accession of Vespasian.[1] Certainly, the man who would spend £3000 on a myrrhine vase, £4000 on a table of citrus-wood, or £40,000 on a richly wrought carpet from Babylon, had little to learn even from Nero.[2] Yet the example of an emperor must always be potent for good or evil. We have the testimony of Pliny and Claudian,[3] separated by an interval of three hundred years, that the world readily conforms its life to that of one man, if that man is head of the State. Nero's youthful enthusiasm for declamation gave an immense impulse to the passion for rhetoric.[4] His enthusiasm for acting and music spread through all ranks, and the emperor's catches were sung at wayside inns.[5] M. Aurelius made philosophy the mode, and the Stoic Emperor is responsible for some of the philosophic imposture which moved the withering scorn of Lucian. The Emperor's favourite drug grew so popular that the price of it became almost prohibitory.[6] If the model of Vespasian's homely habits had such an effect in reforming society, we may be sure that

[1] *Ann.* iii. 55; cf. xvi. 5.
[2] Friedl. *Sittengesch.* iii. pp. 80, 81.
[3] Plin. *Paneg.* 45; Claudian, *In Cons. Hon.* 299, componitur orbis Regis ad exemplum.
[4] Suet. *De Clar. Rhet.* c. 1.
[5] Id. *Nero*, 21; Philostr. *Apoll. Tyan.* iv. 39.
[6] Friedl. *Sittengesch.* i. 54.

the evil example of his spendthrift predecessors did at least as much to deprave it.

And what an example it was! The extravagance of the Claudian Caesars and the last Flavian has become a piece of historic commonplace. Every one has heard of the unguent baths of Caligula, his draughts of melted pearls, his galleys with jewel-studded sterns and gardens and orchards on their decks, his viaduct connecting the Palatine with the Capitoline, his bridge from Bauli to Puteoli, and many another scheme of that wild brain, which had in the end to be paid for in blood.[1] In a single year Caligula scattered in reckless waste more than £20,000,000.[2] Nero proclaimed that the only use of money was to squander it, and treated any prudent calculation as meanness.[3] In a brief space he flung away nearly £18,000,000. The Egyptian roses for a single banquet cost £35,000.[4] He is said never to have made a progress with less than a thousand carriages; his mules were shod with silver.[5] He would stake HS.400,000 on a single throw of the dice. The description of his Golden House is like a vision of lawless romance.[6] The successors of Galba were equally lavish during their brief term. Otho, another Nero, probably regarded death in battle as a relief from bankruptcy.[7] Within a very few months, Vitellius had flung away more than £7,000,000 in vulgar luxury.[8] Vespasian found the exhaustion of the public treasury so portentous[9] that he had to resort to unpopular economies and taxation on a great scale. Under Domitian, the spectacles and largesses lavished on the mob undid all the scrupulous finance of his father,[10] and Nerva had to liquidate the ruinous heritage by wholesale retrenchment, and the sale even of the imperial furniture and plate,[11] as M. Aurelius brought to the hammer his household treasures, and even the wardrobe and jewels of the empress, in the stress of the Marcomannic war.[12]

But the great imperial spendthrifts resorted to more

[1] Suet. *Calig.* 37; Sen. *Ad Helv.* x.
[2] Suet. *Calig.* 37.
[3] Suet. *Nero,* c. 30.
[4] *Ib.* c. 27.
[5] *Ib.* c. 30.
[6] *Ib.* c. 31; Tac. *Ann.* xv. 42.
[7] Suet. *Otho,* 5, nihilque referre, ab hoste in acie, an in foro sub creditoribus caderet.
[8] Id. *Vitell.* c. 13.
[9] Id. *Vesp.* 16; D. Cass. 66. 2, 8, 10.
[10] D. Cass. 67. 5; Suet. *Dom.* 12.
[11] D. Cass. 68. 2, συστέλλων ὡς οἷόν τε τὰ δαπανήματα.
[12] Capitol. *M. Aurel.* c. 17, in foro divi Trajani auctionem ornamentorum imperialium fecit vendiditque aurea pocula et cristallina, etc.

simple and primitive methods of replenishing their coffers. Self-indulgent waste is often seen linked with meanness and hard cruelty. The epigram of Suetonius on Domitian, *inopia rapax, metu saevus*,[1] sums up the sordid history of the tyranny. The cool biographer of Caligula, Nero, and Domitian, when in his methodical fashion, he has recorded their financial difficulties, immediately proceeds to describe the unblushing rapine or ingenious chicanery by which the needy tyrants annexed a coveted estate. The emperors now generally protected the provinces from plunder,[2] but they applied all the Verrine methods to their own nobles. It was not hard with the help of the sleuth hounds who always gather round the despot, to find plausible grounds of accusation. The vague law of majesty, originally intended to guard the security of the commonwealth, was now used to throw its protection around the sacrosanct prince in whom all the highest powers of government were concentrated.[3] The slightest suspicion of disloyalty or discontent, the most insignificant act or word, which a depraved ingenuity could misinterpret, was worked up into a formidable indictment by men eager for their share of the plunder. To have written the memoir of a Stoic saint or kept the birthday of a dead emperor, to possess an imperial horoscope or a map of the world, to call a slave by the name of Hannibal or a dish by that of Lucullus, might become a fatal charge.[4] "Ungrateful testators" who had failed to remember the emperor in their wills had to pay heavily for the indiscreet omission.[5] The materials for such accusations were easily obtained in the Rome of the early Caesars. Life was eminently sociable. A great part of the day was spent at morning receptions, in the Forum, the Campus Martius, the barber's or bookseller's shops, or in the colonnades where crowds of fashionable idlers gathered to relieve the tedium of life by gossip and repartee. It was a city, says Tacitus, which knew everything and talked of everything.[6] Never was curiosity more eager or gossip more reckless. Men were almost ready to risk their lives for a *bon mot*. And in the

[1] Suet. *Dom.* iii.

[2] Suet. *Otho*, iii.; *Vitell.* v.; *Dom.* viii.; Bossier, *L'Opp.* p. 170.

[3] Tac. *Ann.* i. 72; ii. 50; xiv. 48. For a clear account of this *v.* Boissier, *L'Opp.* p. 165.

[4] Suet. *Dom.* x.; cf. xii. satis erat obici qualecunque factum dictumve adversus majestatem principis.

[5] *Ib.* xii.

[6] Tac. *Ann.* xi. 27; xiii. 6, in urbe sermonum avida; *Hist.* ii. 91; Mart. v. 20; Friedl. *Sittengesch.* i. p. 280.

reign of Nero or Domitian, the risk was a very real one. The imperial espionage, of which Maecenas in Dion Cassius recognised at once the danger and the necessity,[1] was an organised system even under the most blameless emperors. It can be traced in the reigns of Nerva, Hadrian, and Antoninus Pius.[2] But under the tyrants, voluntary informers sprang up in every class. Among the hundreds of slaves attached to a great household, there were in such times sure to be spies, attracted by the lure of freedom and a fortune, who might report and distort what they had observed in their master's unguarded hours. Men came to dread possible traitors even among their nearest of kin, among their closest friends of the highest rank.[3] Who can forget the ignominy of those three Senators, one of them bearing the historic name of Cato, who, to win the consulship from Sejanus, hid themselves between the ceiling and the roof, and caught, through chinks and crannies, the words artfully drawn from the victim by another member of the noble gang? The seventh book of the *Life of Apollonius* by Philostratus is a revelation of the mingled caution and truculence of the methods of Domitian. Here at least we have left the world of romance behind and are on solid ground. We feel around us, as we read, the hundred eyes of an omnipresent tyranny. We meet in the prison the magistrate of Tarentum who had been guilty of a dangerous omission in the public prayers, and an Acarnanian who had been guilty of settling in one of the Echinades.[4] A spy glides into the cells, to listen to the prisoners' talk, and is merely regaled by Apollonius with a description of the wonders he has seen in his wanderings. When we are admitted to the secret tribunal on the Palatine, after Domitian has paid his devotion to Athene, we have before us a cruel, stealthy despot, as timid as he is brutally truculent. In spite of all scepticism about Philostratus, we are there at the heart of the Terror.

Compared with this base espionage, even the trade of the delator becomes almost respectable. Like everything in Roman social organisation, delation had a long history, too

[1] D. Cass. 52. 37.

[2] Mart. x. 48, 21; cf. Friedl. *Chronologie der Epigr. Mart.* p. 62; Friedl. *Sittengesch.* i. p. 285; Epict. *Diss.* iv. 13, 21, 5; Aristid. *Or.* ix. 62.

[3] Tac. *Ann.* iv. 69.

[4] Philostr. *Apoll. Tyan.* vii. 24.

long to be developed within the space of this work. The work of impeachment, which might be wholesome and necessary under the Republic, in exposing the enormities of provincial government, became the curse of the Empire. The laws of Augustus for the restoration of social morality gave the first chance to the professional delator. The jealous, secretive rule of Tiberius welcomed such sinister support,[1] and although the dark, tortuous policy of the recluse of Capreae might punish the excess of zeal in the informers, it was also ready to reward them for opportune displays of energy.[2] The open and daring tyranny of Caligula and Nero often dispensed with the hypocrisy of judicial forms of assassination. It was reserved for the last Flavian to revive the methods of Tiberius.[3] Domitian was at once timid and cruel. He was also a pedant who concealed from himself his own baseness by a scrupulous devotion to ancient forms even in religion. The obscene libertine, who chose the Virgin Goddess as his patroness,[4] could easily make the forms of old Roman justice a cloak for confiscation and massacre. In theory the voluntary accuser, without a commission from authority, was a discredited person. And successive emperors punished or frowned upon the delators of a previous reign.[5] Yet the profession grew in reputation and emolument. It is a melancholy proof of the degradation of that society that the delator could be proud of his craft and even envied and admired. Men of every degree, freedmen, schoolmasters, petty traders, descendants of houses as old as the Republic, men from the rank of the shoemaker Vatinius[6] to a Scaurus, a Cato, or a Regulus, flocked to a trade which might earn a fabulous fortune and the favour of the prince. There must have been many a career like that of Palfurius Sura, who had fought in the arena in the reign of Nero, who had been disgraced and stripped of his consular rank under Vespasian, who then turned Stoic and preached the gospel of popular

[1] Tac. *Ann.* i. 72, 74, Crispinus formam vitae iniit quam postea celebrem miseriae temporum et audaciae hominum fecerunt, etc.; cf. iii. 25; Sen. *De Ben.* iii. 26; Suet. *Tib.* lxi.

[2] Tac. *Ann.* iv. 20.

[3] Suet. *Dom.* xx. praeter commentarios et acta Tiberii nihil lectitabat; Plin. *Paneg.* 42, 48.

[4] Suet. *Dom.* xv.

[5] Tac. *Hist.* ii. 10; Plin. *Paneg.* 35; D. Cass. 68. 1; Jul. Capitol. *Ant. P.* c. 7; id. *M. Aurel.* c. 11; Meriv. vii. 370.

[6] Tac. *Ann.* xv. 34; iii. 66; *Hist.* iv. 42.

government, and, in the reign of Domitian, crowned his career by becoming a delator, and attempting to found a juristic theory of absolute monarchy.[1]

The system of Roman education, which was profoundly rhetorical, became a hot-bed of this venal oratory. It nourished its pupils on the masterpieces of free speech; it inflamed their imaginations with dreams of rhetorical triumph. When they went forth into the world of the Empire, they found the only arena for displaying their powers to be the dull court of the Centumviri, or the hired lecture hall, where they might dilate on some frigid or silly theme before a weary audience. It was a tempting excitement to exert the arts learnt in the school of Quintilian in a real onslaught, where the life or liberty of the accused was at stake. And the greatest orators of the past had never offered to them such a splendid material reward. One fourth of the estate of the condemned man had been the old legal fee of the accuser.[2] But this limit was left far behind in the judicial plunder of the early Caesars. Probably in no other way could a man then so easily make himself a millionaire. The leading accusers of Thrasea and Soranus in the reign of Nero received each £42,000 as their reward.[3] These notorious delators, Eprius Marcellus and Vibius Crispus, accumulated gains reaching, in the end, the enormous amount of £2,400,000. The famous, or infamous, Regulus, after the most prodigal expenditure, left a fortune of half a million.[4] His career is a striking example of the arts by which, in a debased society, men may rise to fortune, and the readiness with which such a society will always forgive anything to daring and success. Sprung from an illustrious but ruined race,[5] Regulus possessed shameless audacity and ruthless ambition,[6] which were more valuable than birth and fortune. He had every physical defect for a speaker, yet he made himself an orator, with a weird power of strangling his victims.[7] He was poor, but he resolved to be wealthy, and he reached the fortune which he proposed to himself as his goal. He was vain, cruel, and insolent, a slave of superstition,[8]

[1] Schol. ad Juv. iv. 53; Duruy, iv. 660.

[2] Tac. *Ann.* iv. 20.

[3] *Ib.* xvi. 33; Boissier, *L'Opp.* p. 186.

[4] Plin. *Ep.* ii. 20, 13; iv. 2; cf. Tac. *Hist.* iv. 42; Mart. vii. 31.

[5] Boissier, *L'Opp.* p. 193.

[6] Plin. *Ep.* ii. 11, 22.

[7] *Ib.* iv. 7; i. 20, 15.

[8] *Ib.* ii. 11, 22; ii. 20.

stained with many a perfidious crime. He was a peculiarly skilful and perfectly shameless adept in the arts of captation.[1] Yet this cynical agent of judicial murder, who began his career in the reign of Nero, lived on in peace and wealth into the reign of Trajan. He even enjoyed a certain consideration in society.[2] The humane and refined Pliny at once detested and tolerated him. The morning receptions of Regulus, in his distant gardens on the Tiber, were thronged by a fashionable crowd.

The inner secret of the imperial Terror will probably always perplex the historian. The solution of the question depends, not only on the value which is to be attached to our authorities, but on the prepossessions and prejudices which are brought to their interpretation. To one critic Tacitus, although liable to the faults which spring from rhetorical training and fervid temperament, seems fairly impartial and trustworthy.[3] Another treats the great historian as essentially a partisan who derived his materials from the memoirs and traditions of a class inflamed with reactionary dreams and saturated with a hatred of monarchy.[4] Some regard the tragedy of the early Empire as the result of a real peril from a senatorial conspiracy which perpetually surrounded the emperor. Others trace it to the diseased brains of princes, giddy with the sense of omnipotence, and often unstrung by vicious excesses, natures at once timorous and arrogant, anticipating danger by a maniacal cruelty which ended in creating the peril that they feared. Is it not possible that there may be truth in both theories? It may be admitted that there probably was never a powerful opposition, with a definitely conceived purpose of overthrowing the imperial system, as it had been organised by Augustus, and of restoring the republican rule of the Senate. It may be admitted that, while so many of the first twelve Caesars died a violent death, the violence was used to rid the world of a monster, and not to remodel a constitution; it was the emperor, not the Empire, that was hated. Yet these admissions need to be qualified by some reservations. The effect of the rhetorical character of Roman education in moulding the temper and ideals of the upper classes, down to the very end

[1] Plin. *Ep.* ii. 20, 2.

[2] *Ib.* iv. 7.

[3] *E.g.* Boissier, *L'Opp.* p. 296; Peter, *Gesch. Litt.* ii. p. 65: Teuffel, § 328, 15; Mackail, *Lat. Lit.* p. 215.

[4] Schiller, i. pp. 140, 586; Meriv. viii. 89 sqq.

of the Western Empire, has hardly yet been fully recognised. It petrified literature by the slavish imitation of unapproachable models. It also glorified the great ages of freedom and republican government; it exalted Harmodius and Aristogeiton, Brutus and Cassius, to a moral height which might suggest to generous youth the duty or the glory of imitating them. When a rhetor's class, in the reign of Caligula or of Nero, applauded the fall of a historic despot, is it not possible that some may have applied the lesson to the reigning emperor? Although it is evident that philosophic debates on the three forms of government were not unknown, yet probably few ever seriously thought of a restoration of the republic. None but a maniac would have entrusted the nerveless, sensual mob of Rome with the destinies of the world. As a matter of fact, the mob themselves very much preferred the rule of a lavish despot, who would cater for their pleasures.[1] But the Senate was still a name of power. In the three or four generations which had passed since the death of the first Caesar, men had forgotten the weakness and perfidy which had made senatorial government impossible. They thought of the Senate as the stubborn, haughty caste which had foiled the strategy of Hannibal, which had achieved the conquest of the world. The old families might have been more than decimated; new men of doubtful origin might have filled their places.[2] But ancient institutions possess a prestige and power which is often independent of the men who work them. Men are governed largely through imagination and mere names. Thus the Senate remained an imaginative symbol of the glory of Roman power, down to the last years of the Western Empire. The accomplished Symmachus cherishes the phantasm of its power under Honorius. And although a Caligula or Nero might conceive a feverish hatred of the assembly which they feared,[3] while they affected to despise it, the better emperors generally made almost a parade of their respect for the Senate.[4] The wisest princes had

[1] Suet. *Claud.* x.; *Calig.* lx.; D. Cass. 60. 1. On the assassination of Caligula, the Senate debated the question of abolishing the memory of the Caesars, and restoring the Republic; but the mob outside the temple of the Capitoline Jupiter demanded "one ruler" of the world.

[2] Tac. *Ann.* xi. 25; xiii. 27.

[3] Suet. *Calig.* xxx.; xxvi.; *Nero*, xxxvii. eumque ordinem sublaturum quandoque e republica . . .; cf. xliii. creditur destinasse senatum universum veneno per convivia necare. . . . D. Cass. 63. 15, 17.

[4] Plin. *Paneg.* 54, 62, 64; Spart. *Hadrian*, 6, 7, § 4; 8, § 6.

a feeling that, although they might have at their back the devotion of the legions, and an immense material force, still it was wiser to conciliate old Roman feeling by a politic deference to a body which was surrounded by the aureole of antiquity, which had such splendid traditions of conquest and administration.

The Senate was thus the only possible rival of the Emperor. The question is, was the Senate ever a dangerous rival? The true answer seems to be that the Senate was dangerous in theory, but not in fact. There can be little doubt that, in the reigns of Caligula and Nero, there were men who dreamed of a restored senatorial power.[1] It is equally certain that the Senate was incapable of asserting it. Luxury, self-indulgence, and conscription had done their work effectually. There were many pretenders to the principate in the reign of Nero, and even some in the reign of Vespasian.[2] But they had not a solid and determined Senate at their back. The world, and even the Senate, were convinced that the Roman Empire needed the administration of one man. How to get the one man was the problem. Hereditary succession had placed only fools or monsters on the throne. There remained the old principle of adoption. An emperor, feeling that his end was approaching, might, with all his vast experience of the government of a world, with all his knowledge of the senatorial class, with no fear of offence in the presence of death,[3] designate one worthy of the enormous charge. If such an one came to the principate, with a generous desire to give the Senate a share of his burdens and his glory, that was the highest ideal of the Empire, and that was the ideal which perhaps was approached in the Antonine age. Yet, outside the circle of practical statesmen, there remained a class which was long irreconcilable. It has been recently maintained with great force that the Stoic opposition was only the opposition of a moral ideal, not the deliberate propaganda of a political creed.[4] This may be true of some of the philosophers: it is certainly not true of all. Thrasea was a genial man of the world, whose severest censure expressed itself in silence and absence from the Senate,[5] who could even, on occasion, speak with deference of Nero. But his son-in-law,

[1] Suet. *Claud.* x.

[2] D. Cass. 66. 16; Suet. *Vesp.* xxv.

[3] See the speech of the dying Hadrian to the Senators, D. Cass. 69. 20.

[4] Boissier, *L'Opp.* 102.

[5] Tac. *Ann.* xvi. 21; xv. 23; xiv. 48, id *egregio* sub principe . . . senatui statuendum disseruit.

Helvidius Priscus, seemed to exult in flouting and insulting a great and worthy emperor such as Vespasian.[1] And the life of Apollonius by Philostratus leaves the distinct impression that philosophy, in the reign of Nero and Domitian, was a revolutionary force. Apollonius, it is true, is represented by Philostratus as supporting the cause of monarchy in a debate in the presence of Vespasian.[2] But he boasted of having been privy to conspiracies against Nero,[3] and he was deeply involved with Nerva and Orfitus in a plot against Domitian.[4] He was summoned before the secret tribunal to answer for speeches against the emperor delivered to crowds at Ephesus.[5] It may be admitted that the invective or scorn of philosophy was aimed at unworthy princes, rather than at the foundations of their power. Yet Dion Cassius evidently regards Helvidius Priscus as a turbulent agitator with dangerous democratic ideals,[6] and he contrasts his violence with the studied moderation, combined with dignified reserve, displayed by Thrasea in the reign of Nero. The tolerant Vespasian, who bore so long the wanton insults of the philosophers, must have come at length to think them not only an offence but a real danger when he banished them. In the first century there can be little doubt that there were members of the philosophic class who condemned monarchy, not only as a moral danger, but as a lamentable aberration from the traditions of republican freedom. There were probably some, who, if the chance had offered itself, might even have ventured on a republican reaction.

With a gloomy recognition of the realities of life, Domitian used to say that conspiracy against an emperor was never believed till the emperor was killed.[7] Of the first twelve Caesars seven died a violent death. Every emperor from Tiberius to M. Aurelius was the mark of conspiracy. This was often provoked by the detestable character of the prince. But it sometimes sprang from other causes than moral disgust. The mild rule of Vespasian was generally popular; yet even he had to repel the conspiracy of Aelianus and Marcellus.[8] The

1 Suet. *Vesp.* xv.; cf. xiii., where Demetrius is guilty of similar rudeness; D. Cass. 66. 12.

2 Philostr. *Apoll. Tyan.* v. 35.

3 *Ib.* vii. 3, 4.

4 *Ib.* vii. 8, 33; cf. D. Cass. 67. 18.

5 Philostr. *Apoll. Tyan.* vii. 9.

6 D. Cass. 66. 12, *βασιλείας τε ἀεὶ κατηγόρει καὶ δημοκρατίαν ἐπῄνει.*

7 Suet. *Dom.* xxi.

8 D. Cass. 66. 16.

blameless Nerva, the emperor after the Senate's own heart, was twice assailed by risings organised by great nobles of historic name.[1] The conspiracy of Nigrinus against Hadrian received formidable support, and had to be sternly crushed.[2] M. Aurelius had to endure with sad resignation the open rebellion of Avidius Cassius.[3] The better emperors, strong in their character and the general justice of their administration, might afford to treat such opposition with comparative calmness. But it was different in the case of a Nero or a Domitian. The conspiracy of Piso and the conspiracy of Saturninus formed, in each case, a climax and a turning-point. Springing from real and justified impatience, they were ruthlessly crushed and followed up with a cruel and suspicious repression which only increased the danger of the despot. "Scelera sceleribus tuenda" sums up the awful tale, in the words of Tacitus, "of the wrath of God and the madness of men."

There were many causes which rendered the tragedy of the early Empire inevitable. Probably the most potent was the undefined position of the prince and the dreams of republican power and freedom which for ages were cherished by the Senate. Carefully disguised under ancient forms, the principate of Augustus was really omnipotent, through the possession of the proconsular imperium in the provinces, and the tribunician prerogative at home.[4] In the last resort there was no legal means of challenging the man who controlled the legions, nominated the magistrates, and manipulated a vast treasury at his pleasure. The fiction of Augustus, that he had restored the Republic to the hands of the Senate and people, is unlikely to have deceived his own astute intellect.[5] The hand which, of its grace could restore the *simulacra libertatis*, might as easily withdraw them. The Comitia lost even the shadow of constitutional power in the following reign.[6] Henceforth the people is the army.[7] The holders of the great republican magistracies are mere creatures of the prince and obedient ministers of his power. The Senate alone retained some vestiges of its old

[1] D. Cass. 68. 3.
[2] Spart. *Hadr.* 7, § 15.
[3] Jul. Capitol. *M. Ant.* 24, 25.
[4] Momms. *Staatsr.* ii. 787-821; Professor Pelham has given a luminous account of the Principate in *Encycl. Brit.* vol. xx. p. 769.
[5] Suet. *Octav.* xxviii.
[6] Tac. *Ann.* i. 15.
[7] Suet. *Claud.* x.; D. Cass. 60. 1; where the soldiers plainly close the impotent debates in the Senate, and by hailing Claudius as emperor.

power, and still larger pretensions and antiquarian claims. In theory, during a vacancy in the principate, the Senate was the ultimate seat of authority, and the new emperor received his prerogatives by a decree of the Senate. In the work of legislation, its decisions divided the field with the edicts of the prince,[1] and it claimed a parallel judicial power. But all this was really illusory. The working of such a system manifestly depends on the character and ideas of the man who for the time wields the material force of the Empire. And "the share of the Senate in the government was in fact determined by the amount of administrative activity which each emperor saw fit to allow it to exercise." [2]

The half-insane Caligula had really a clearer vision of the emperor's position than the reactionary dreamers, when he told his grandmother Antonia, "*Memento omnia mihi in omnes licere.*"[3] He did not need the lessons of Agrippa and Antiochus to teach him the secret of tyranny.[4] Yet institutions can never be separated from the moral and social forces which lie behind and around them. The emperor had to depend on agents and advisers, many of them of social rank and family traditions equal to his own. He had by his side a Senate with a history of immemorial antiquity and glory, which cast a spell on the conservative imagination of a race which recoiled from any impiety to the past. Above all, he was surrounded by a populace which took its revenge for the loss of its free Comitia by a surprising licence of lampoon and epigram and mordant gossip and clamorous appeal in the circus and theatre.[5] And even the soldiers, who were the sworn supporters of the prince, and who often represented better than any other class the tone of old Roman gravity and manly virtue, could sometimes make their Imperator feel that there was in reserve a power which he could not safely defy. Hence it was that, with the changing character of the prince, the imperial power might pass into a lawless tyranny, only to be checked by assassination, while again it might veil its forces under constitutional forms, adopt the watchwords of the Republic, exalt the Senate to a place beside the throne, and make even accomplished statesmen fancy for the time that the days of ancient liberty had returned.

1 Momms. *Röm. Staatsr.* ii. 839.
2 *v.* Pelham, *Encycl. Brit.* xx. p. 779.
3 Suet. *Calig.* xxix.
4 D. Cass. 59. 24.
5 *Ib.* 56. 1; Tac. *Ann.* vi. 13; Suet. *Dom.* xiii.; Plut. *Galba*, 17.

Such a dream, not altogether visionary, floated before Pliny's mind when he delivered his *Panegyric* in the presence of Trajan. That speech is at once an act of thanksgiving and a manifesto of the Senate. The tone of fulsome extravagance is excused by the joy at escaping from a treacherous tyranny, which drove virtue into remote retreat, which made friendship impossible, which poisoned the security of household life by a continual fear of espionage.[1] The confidence which Pliny expresses in the majestic strength, mingled with modesty and self-restraint, which Trajan brought to the task of the principate, was amply justified. The overwhelming force of the emperor seemed, in the new age, to pass into the freely accepted rule of the great citizen.[2] Pliny indeed does not conceal from himself the immense actual power of the emperor. He is the vice-gerent of God, an earthly Providence.[3] His power is not less than Nero's or Domitian's, but it is a power no longer wielded wildly by selfish or cruel self-will; it is a power inspired by benevolence, voluntarily submitting itself to the restraints of law and ancient sentiment.[4] Founded on service and virtue, it can fearlessly claim the loving support of the citizens, while it recalls the freedom of the old Republic. A prince who is hedged by the devotion of his people may dispense with the horde of spies and informers, who have driven virtue into banishment and made a crowd of sneaks and cowards. Free speech has been restored. The Senate, which has so long been expected to applaud with grovelling flattery the most trivial or the most flagitious acts of the emperor, is summoned to a share in the serious work of government.[5] A community of interest and feeling secures to it a free voice in his counsels, without derogating from his dignity.[6] All this is expressed by a scrupulous observance of old republican forms. The commander of conquering legions, the Caesar, Augustus, Pontifex Maximus, has actually condescended to take the oath of office, standing before the consul seated in his chair![7] Here we seem to have the key to the senatorial position. They were ready to recognise the overwhelming power of the prince, if he, for his part, would only respect in form, if not in substance, the ancient dignity of the Senate. Tolerance, affability,

[1] Plin. *Paneg.* 43, 44, 35.
[2] *Ib.* 24, 62, 63, 66.
[3] *Ib.* 80.
[4] *Ib.* 62, 63, 64.
[5] *Ib.* 66.
[6] *Ib.* 72.
[7] *Ib.* 64.

politic deference to a great name, seemed to Pliny and his kind a restoration of the ancient freedom, almost a revival of the old Republic. Fortunately for the world a succession of wise princes perceived that, by deference to the pride of the Senate, they could secure the peace of their administration, without diminishing its effective power.

Yet, even from Pliny's *Panegyric*, we can see that the recognition of the prerogatives, or rather of the dignity, of the Senate, the coexistence of old republican forms side by side with imperial power, depended entirely on the grace and tolerance of the master of the legions. Nothing could be more curious than Pliny's assertion of the senatorial claims, combined with the most effusive gratitude to Trajan for conceding them. The emperor is only *primus inter pares*, and yet Pliny, by the whole tone of his speech, admits that he is the master who may equally indulge the constitutional claims or superstitions of his subjects or trample on them. In the first century a power, the extent of which depended only on the will of the prince, and yet seemed limited by shadowy claims of ancient tradition, was liable to be distrustful of itself and to be challenged by pretenders. In actual fact, the prince was so powerful that he might easily pass into a despot; in theory he was only the first of Roman nobles, who might easily have rivals among his own class. Pliny congratulates Trajan on having, by his mildness and justice, escaped the terror of pretenders which haunted the earlier emperors, and was often justified and cruelly avenged.[1] In spite of the lavish splendour of Nero or Caligula, the imperial household, till Hadrian's reorganisation, was still modelled on the lines of other great aristocratic houses. Nero's suspicions were more than once excited by the scale of establishments like that of the Silani, by wealth and display like Seneca's, by the lustre of great historic traditions in a gens like the Calpurnian.[2] The loyalty of Corbulo could not save him from the jealousy aroused by his exploits in eastern war.[3] And the power of great provincial governors, in command of great armies, and administering realms such as Gaul or Spain or Syria, was not an altogether imaginary danger. If Domitian seemed distrustful of Agricola

[1] Plin. *Paneg.* 69.

[2] Tac. *Ann.* xiii. 1; xiv. 52; xv. 48.

[3] D. Cass. 63. 17, πᾶσι γὰρ παρ' αὐτῷ δημόσιον ἔγκλημα ἦν ἀρετή τε καὶ πλοῦτος καὶ γένος: Tac. *Hist.* ii. 76.

in Britain, we must remember that he had in his youth seen Galba and Vindex marching on Rome, and his father concentrating the forces of the East for the overthrow of Vitellius in the great struggle on the Po.

The emperor's fears and suspicions were immensely aggravated by the adepts in the dark arts of the East. The astrologers were a great and baneful power in the early Empire. They inspired illicit ambitions, or they stimulated them, and they often suggested to a timorous prince the danger of conspiracy. These venal impostors, in the words of Tacitus, were always being banished, but they always returned. For the men who drove them into temporary exile had the firmest faith in their skill. The prince would have liked to keep a monopoly of it, while he withdrew from his nobles the temptation which might be offered to their ambition by the mercenary adept.[1] Dion Cassius and Suetonius, who were themselves eager believers in this superstition, never fail to record the influence of the diviners. The reign of Tiberius is full of dark tales about them.[2] Claudius drove Scribonianus into exile for consulting an astrologer about the term of his reign.[3] On the appearance of a flaming comet, Nero was warned by his diviner, Bilbilus, that a portent, which always boded ill to kings, might be expiated by the blood of their nobles.[4] Otho's astrologer, Seleucus, who had promised that he should survive Nero,[5] stimulated his ambition to be the successor of Galba. Vitellius, as superstitious as Nero or Otho, cruelly persecuted the soothsayers and ordered their expulsion from Italy.[6] He was defied by a mocking edict of the tribe, ordaining his own departure from earth by a certain day.[7] Vespasian once more banished the diviners from Rome, but, obedient to the superstition which cradled the power of his dynasty, he retained the most skilful for his own guidance.[8] The terror of Domitian's last days was heightened by a horoscope, which long before had foretold the time and manner of his end.[9] Holding such a faith as this, it is little wonder that the emperors should dread its effect on rivals who were equally

[1] Tac. *Ann.* ii. 32; xii. 52; D. Cass. 49. 43; D. Cass. 66. 10, 9; Suet. *Tib.* lxiii.

[2] Suet. *Tib.* xiv. lxix.

[3] Tac. *Ann.* xii. 52.

[4] Suet. *Nero,* xxxvi.

[5] Id. *Otho,* iv.

[6] Id. *Vitell.* xiv.

[7] *Ib.* ne Vitellius Germanicus intra eundem kalendarum diem usquam esset.

[8] D. Cass. 66. 10, 9.

[9] Suet. *Dom.* xv.

credulous, or that superstition, working on ambitious hopes, should have been the nurse of treason. Thus the emperor's uncertain position made him ready to suspect and anticipate a treachery which may often have had no existence. The objects of his fears in their turn were driven into conspiracy, sometimes in self-defence, sometimes from the wish to seize a prize which seemed not beyond their grasp. Gossip, lampoon, and epigram redoubled suspicion, while they retaliated offences. And cruel repression either increased the danger of revolt in the more daring, or the degradation of the more timorous.

In the eyes of Tacitus, the most terrible result of the tyranny of the bad emperors was the fawning servility of a once proud order, and their craven treachery in the hour of danger. He has painted it with all the concentrated power of loathing and pity. It is this almost personal degradation which inspires the ruthless, yet haughtily restrained, force with which he blasts for ever the memory of the Julio-Claudian despotism. It was in this spirit that he penned the opening chapters of his chronicle of the physical and moral horrors of the year in which that tyranny closed. The voice of history has been silenced or perverted, partly by the ignorance of public affairs, partly by the eagerness of adulation, or the bitterness of hatred. It was an age darkened by external disasters, save on the eastern frontier, by seditions and civil war, and the bloody death of four princes. The forces of nature seemed to unite with the rage of men to deepen the universal tragedy. Italy was overwhelmed with calamities which had been unknown for many ages; Campania's fairest cities were swallowed up; Rome itself had been wasted by fire; the ancient Capitol was given to the flames by the hands of citizens. Polluted altars, adultery in high places, the islands of the sea crowded with exiles, rank and wealth and virtue made the mark for a cruel jealousy, all this forms an awful picture.[1] But even more repulsive is the spectacle of treachery rewarded with the highest place, slaves and clients betraying their master for gain, and men without an enemy ruined by their friends. When the spotless Octavia, overwhelmed by the foulest calumnies, had been tortured to death, to satisfy the jealousy of an adulteress, offerings were voted to the

[1] Tac. *Hist.* i. 2.

temples.[1] And Tacitus grimly requests his readers to presume that, as often as a banishment or execution was ordered by Nero, so often were thanksgivings offered to the gods. The horrors of Nero's remorse for the murder of Agrippina were soothed by the flatteries and congratulations of his staff, and the grateful sacrifices which were offered for his deliverance by the Campanian towns.[2] Still, the notes of a funereal trumpet and ghostly wailings from his mother's grave were ever in his ears,[3] and he long doubted the reception which he might meet with on his return to the capital. He need not have had any anxiety. Senate and people vied with one another in self-abasement. He was welcomed by all ranks and ages with fawning enthusiasm as he passed along in triumphal progress to return thanks on the Capitol for the success of an unnatural crime.

The Pisonian conspiracy against Nero was undoubtedly an important and serious event. Some of the greatest names of the Roman aristocracy were involved in it, and the man whom it would have placed on the throne, if not altogether untainted by the excesses of his time, had some imposing qualities which might make him seem a worthy competitor for the principate.[4] But, to Tacitus, the conspiracy seems to be chiefly interesting as a damning proof of the degradation of the aristocracy under the reign of terror. Epicharis, the poor freedwoman of light character, who bore the accumulating torture of scourge and rack and fire, and the dislocation of every limb, is brought into pathetic contrast with the high-born senators and knights, who, without any compulsion of torture, betrayed their relatives and friends.[5] Scaevinus, a man of the highest rank, knowing himself betrayed by his freedman and a Roman knight, revealed the whole plot.[6] The poet Lucan tried in vain to purchase safety by involving his own mother. But Nero was inexorable, and the poet died worthily, reciting some verses from the *Pharsalia*, which describe a similar end.[7] The scenes which followed the massacre are an awful revelation of cowardly sycophancy. While the streets were thronged with the funerals of the victims,

[1] Tac. *Ann.* xiv. 64.
[2] *Ib.* xiv. 10, 12.
[3] *Ib.* xiv. 10; Suet. *Nero*, xxxiv.
[4] Tac. *Ann.* xv. 48.
[5] *Ib.* xv. 57.
[6] *Ib.* xv. 54.
[7] *Ib.* xv. 70; probably Lucan, *Phars.* iii. 638.

the altars on the Capitol were smoking with sacrifices of gratitude. One craven after another, when he heard of the murder of a brother or a dear friend, would deck his house with laurels, and, falling at the emperor's feet, cover his hand with kisses.[1] The Senate prostrated themselves before Nero when, stung by the popular indignation, he appeared to justify his deed. The august body voted him thanksgivings and honours.[2] The consul elect, one of the Anician house, proposed that a temple should be built with all speed to the divine Nero! Tacitus relieves this ghastly spectacle of effeminate cowardice by a scene which is probably intended, by way of contrast, to save the tradition of Roman dignity. Vestinus, the consul of that fatal year, had been a boon companion of the emperor, and had shown contempt for his cowardice in dangerous banter. Nero was eager to find him implicated in the plot, but no evidence of his guilt could be obtained. All legal forms at length were flung aside, and a cohort was ordered to surround his house. Vestinus was at dinner in his palace which towered over the Forum, surrounded by guests, with a train of handsome slaves in waiting, when he received the mandate. He rose at once from table, and shut himself in his chamber with his physician, lancet in hand, by his side. His veins were opened, and, without a word of self-pity, Vestinus allowed his life to ebb away in the bath.[3]

Vestinus, after all, only asserted, in the fashion of the time, his right to choose the manner of a death which could not be evaded. But Tacitus, here and there, gives glimpses of self-sacrifice, courageous loyalty and humanity, which save his picture of society from utter gloom. The love and devotion of women shine out more brightly than ever against the background of baseness. Tender women follow their husbands or brothers into exile, or are found ready to share their death.[4] Even the slave girls of Octavia brave torture and death in their hardy defence of her fair fame.[5] There is no more pathetic story of female heroism than that of Politta, the daughter of L. Vetus. He had been colleague of the emperor in the consulship, but he had the misfortune to be father-in-law

[1] Tac. *Ann.* xv. 71.
[2] *Ib.* xv. 73.
[3] *Ib.* xv. 68, 69.
[4] Plin. *Ep.* iii. 16; Tac. *Ann.* xv. 63.
[5] Tac. *Ann.* xiv. 60.

of Rubellius Plautus, whose lofty descent and popularity drew down the sentence of death, even in distant exile.[1] Politta had clasped the bleeding neck of Plautus in her arms, and nursed her sorrow in an austere widowhood.[2] She now besieged the doors of Nero with prayers, and even menaces, for her father's acquittal. Vetus himself was of the nobler sort of Roman men, who even then were not extinct. When he was advised, in order to save the remnant of his property for his grandchildren, to make the emperor chief heir, he spurned the servile proposal, divided his ready money among his slaves, and prepared for the end.[3] When all hope was abandoned, father, grandmother, and daughter opened their veins and died together in the bath. Plautius Lateranus met his end with the same stern dignity. Forbidden even to give a last embrace to his children, and dragged to the scene of servile executions, he died in silence by the hand of a man who was an undiscovered partner in the plot.[4] Even the mob of Rome, for whose fickle baseness Tacitus has a profound scorn, now and then reveal a wholesome moral feeling. When Octavia, on a trumped-up charge of adultery, was divorced and banished by Nero, the clamour of the populace forced him to recall her for a time, and the mob went so far in their virtuous enthusiasm as to overthrow the statues of the adulteress Poppaea, and crown the images of Octavia with flowers.[5] Perhaps even more striking is the humane feeling displayed towards the slaves of the urban prefect, Pedanius Secundus. He had been murdered by a slave, and the ancient law required, in such a case, the execution of the whole household. The proposal to carry out the cruel custom drove the populace almost to revolt. And it is a relief to find that a strong minority of the Senate were on the side of humanity.[6] But the army, above all other classes, still bred a rough, honest virtue. It was left, amid the general effeminate cowardice, for a tribune of a pretorian cohort to tell Nero to his face that he loathed him as a murderer and an incendiary.[7] Again and again, in that terrible year, when great nobles were flattering the Emperor, whom in a few days or hours they meant to desert, the common soldiers remained true to the death of

[1] Tac. *Ann.* xiv. 22, 57.
[2] *Ib.* xvi. 10.
[3] *Ib.* xvi. 11.
[4] *Ib.* xv. 60.
[5] *Ib.* xiv. 61.
[6] *Ib.* xiv. 42, senatusque obsessus in quo ipso erant studia nimiam severitatem aspernantium.
[7] *Ib.* xv. 67.

their unworthy chiefs. When Otho redeemed a tainted life by a not ignoble end, the pretorians kissed his wounds, bore him with tears to burial, and many killed themselves over his corpse.[1] In the storming of the pretorian camp by the troops of Vespasian, the soldiers of Vitellius, outnumbered and doomed to certain defeat, fell to a man with all their wounds in front.[2]

To these faithful, though often bloodthirsty, warriors the senators and knights of those days offered a contemptible contrast. Often the inheritors of great names and great traditions, the mass of them knew nothing of arms or the military virtue of their ancestors.[3] Sunk in sloth and enervated by excess, they followed Otho to the battlefield on the Po with their cooks and minions and all the apparatus of luxury.[4] In the rapid changes of fortune, from Galba to Otho, from Otho to Vitellius, from Vitellius to Vespasian, the great nobles had one guiding principle, the determination to be on the winning side. It was indeed a puzzling and anxious time for a calculating selfishness, when a reign might not last for a month, and when the adulation of Otho or Vitellius in the Senate-house was disturbed by the sound of the legions advancing from East and West. But the supple cowards of the Senate proved equal to the strain. They had the skill to flatter their momentary master without any compromising word against his probable successor. They soothed the anxieties of Vitellius with unstinted adulation, yet carefully refrained from anything reflecting on the Flavianist leaders.[5] Within a few months, full of joy and hope, which were now at last well founded, they were voting all the customary honours of a new principate to Vespasian.[6] The terror of Tiberius, Caligula, and Nero had done its work effectually. And its worst result was the hopeless self-abandonment and sluggish cowardice of a class, whose chief *raison d'être* in every age is to maintain a tradition of gallant dignity. It is true that many of the scions of great houses were mere mendicants, ruined by confiscation or prodigality, and compelled to live on the pension by which the emperor kept them in shameful dependence,[7] or on the meaner dole of some

[1] Tac. *Hist.* ii. 49.
[2] *Ib.* iii. 84.
[3] *Ib.* i. 88, segnis et oblita bellorum nobilitas, etc.
[4] *Ib.* i. 88.
[5] *Ib.* iii. 37, nulla in oratione cujusquam erga Flavianos duces obtrectatio; cf. i. 90; of the Acta of the Arval College, *C.I.L.* vi. 2051 sq.
[6] *Ib.* iv. 3.
[7] Suet. *Nero*, x.; *Vesp.* xvii.; Spart. *Hadr.* 7, § 9.

wealthy patron.[1] A Valerius Messala, grandson of the great Corvinus, had to accept a pension from Nero.[2] A grandson of Hortensius had to endure the contempt of Tiberius in obtaining a grant for his sons.[3] Others were unmanned by the voluptuous excesses of an age which had carried the ingenuity of sensual allurement to its utmost limits. The hopelessness of any struggle with a power so vast as that of the emperor, so ruthless and wildly capricious as that of the Claudian Caesars, reduced many to despairing apathy.[4] And while, from a safe historic distance, we pour our contempt on the cringing Senate of the first century, it might be well to remind ourselves of their perils and their tortures. There was many a senatorial house, like that of the Pisos, whose leading members were never allowed to reach middle age.[5] Much should be forgiven to a class which was daily and hourly exposed to such danger, so sudden in its onsets, so secret and stealthy, so all-pervading. It might come in an open circumstantial indictment, with all the forms of law and the weight of suborned testimony; it might appear in a quiet order for suicide; the stroke might descend at the farthest limits of the Empire,[6] in some retreat in Spain or Asia. The haunting fear of death had an unnerving effect. But not less degrading were the outrages to Roman, or ordinary human dignity to which the noble order had to submit for more than a generation. They had seen their wives defiled or compelled to expose themselves as harlots in a foul spectacle, to gratify the diseased prurience of the emperor.[7] They had been forced to fight in the arena or to exhibit themselves on the tragic stage.[8] Men who had borne the ancient honours of the consulship had been ordered to run for miles beside the chariot of Caligula, or to wait at his feet at dinner.[9] Fathers had had to witness without flinching the execution of their sons, and drink smilingly to the emperor on the evening of the fatal day.[10] The only safety at such a court lay in calmly accepting insults with affected gratitude. The example of Nero's debauchery, and the seductive charm which he undoubtedly possessed, were

[1] Juv. i. 100.
[2] Tac. *Ann.* xiii. 34.
[3] *Ib.* ii. 37, 38.
[4] Tac. *Hist.* i. 35.
[5] Sen. *De Ira*, ii. 33 ; cf. iii. 19.
[6] Tac. *Ann.* xiv. 58.
[7] Suet. *Nero*, xxxvii.
[8] Tac. *Ann.* xiv. 14 ; Juv. viii. 193 ; Suet. *Calig.* xviii. xxx. ; D. Cass. lix. 10.
[9] Suet. *Calig.* xxvii.
[10] Sen. *De Ira*, ii. 33.

probably as enfeebling and demoralising as the Terror. He formed a school, which laughed at all virtue and made self-indulgence a fine art. Men who had shared in these obscene revels were the leaders in the awful scenes of perfidy, lust, and cruelty which appropriately followed the death of their patron.[1] Some of them, Petronius, Otho, Vitellius, closed their career appropriately by a tragic death. But others lived on into the age of reformation, to defame the stout Sabine soldier who saved the Roman world.[2]

In spite of the manly virtue and public spirit of Vespasian, the Roman world had to endure a fierce ordeal before it entered on the peace of the Antonine age. Even Vespasian's reign was troubled by conspiracy.[3] His obscure origin moved the contempt of the great senatorial houses who still survived. His republican moderation gave the philosophic doctrinaires a chance of airing their impossible dream of restoring a municipal Republic to govern a world. His conscientious frugality, which was absolutely needed to retrieve the bankruptcy of the Neronian régime, was despised and execrated both by the nobles and the mob. Another lesson was needed both by the Senate and the philosophers. Society had yet to be purged as by fire, and the purging came with the accession of Domitian.

The inner secret of that sombre reign will probably remain for ever a mystery. There is the same question about Domitian as there is about Tiberius. Was he bad from the beginning, or was he gradually corrupted by the consciousness of immense power,[4] and the fear of the great order who might challenge it? Our authorities do not furnish a satisfying answer. We know Domitian only from the narrative of men steeped in senatorial traditions and prejudices,[5] and, some of them, intoxicated by the vision of a reconciliation of the principate with the republican ideals. The dream was a noble one, and it was about to be partially realised

[1] Tac. *Ann.* xiii. 12; xvi. 18; Suet. *Vitell.* iv.

[2] Renan, *Les Év.* p. 140. Some of their anonymous sneers may be traced in Suet. *Vesp.* xvi. xxiii. xiv.; cf. Duruy, iv. 653.

[3] D. Cass. 66. 16, *ἐπεβουλεύθη μὲν ὑπό τε τοῦ 'Αλιηνοῦ καὶ ὑπὸ τοῦ Μαρκέλλου.* Cf. Suet. *Vesp.* xiv.; Macé, *Suétone*, p. 86.

[4] Cf. Boissier, *L'Opp.* p. 169 sqq.; Bury, *Rom. Emp.* p. 395.

[5] On the sources of the history of the Flavians, *v.* Krause, *De C. Sueton. Tranq. Fontibus*; Macé, *Suétone*, p. 364, 376; Peter, *Gesch. Litt. d. Kaiserzeit*, ii. 69, 70. For the senatorial attitude to Domitian, *v.* Plin. *Paneg.* 48; Tac. *Agr.* 3, 41, 42, 45; *Hist.* iv. 51; iv. 2; Suet. *Dom.* xxiii.

for three generations, under a succession of good emperors. But the men inspired with such an ideal were not likely to be impartial judges of an emperor like Domitian. And even from their narrative of his reign, we can see that he was not, at least in the early years of his reign,[1] the utter monster he has been painted. Even severe judges in modern days admit that he was an able and strenuous man, with a clear, cold, cynical intellect,[2] which recognised some of the great problems of the time, and strove to solve them. He was indefatigable in judicial work.[3] In spite of the sneers at his mock triumphs,[4] his military and provincial administration was probably guided by a sound conception of the resources and the dangers of the Empire. His recall of Agricola, after a seven years' command in Britain, was attributed to jealousy and fear.[5] It is more probable that it was dictated by a wish to stop a campaign which was diverting large sums to the conquest of barren mountains. Domitian was an orator and verse writer of some merit, and he gave his patronage, although not in a very liberal way, to men like Quintilian, Statius, and Martial.[6] Like Nero, he felt the force of the new Hellenist movement, and, under forms sanctioned by Roman antiquarians, he established a quinquennial festival in which literary genius was pompously rewarded.[7] He had the public libraries, which had been devastated by fires in the previous reigns, liberally restocked with fresh stores of MSS. from Alexandria.[8] He gave close attention, whatever we may think of his science, to the economic problems of the Empire. And his discouragement of the vine, in favour of a greater acreage of corn, would find sympathy in our own time, as it was applauded by Apollonius of Tyana.[9] The man who decimated the Roman aristocracy towards the end of his reign, advanced to high positions some of those who were destined to be his bitterest defamers. Pliny and Tacitus and Trajan's father rose to high office in the

[1] Nagel, *Imp. T. Flav. Domitianus iniquius dijudicatus.*

[2] Meriv. vii. 356.

[3] Suet. *Dom.* viii.

[4] Tac. *Agr.* 39; cf. 41, tot exercitus in Moesia . . . amissi. D. Cass. 67. 4, 7; cf. Stat. *Silv.* iv. 3, 153; Mart. ix. 102; vii. 80, 91, 95; Meriv. vii. 347.

[5] Tac. *Agr.* 39.

[6] Quintil. iv., proem. 2; Statius, *Silvae*, iv. 2, 13; iii. 1, 1; Mart. ii. 91; iv. 27; iii. 95. For the flattery of Martial, *v.* esp. v. 19, 6; ix. 4; *Spectac.* 33.

[7] Suet. *Dom.* iv.

[8] *Ib.* xx.

[9] *Ib.* vii.; Philostr. *Apoll. Tyan.* vi. 42; *Vit. Soph.* i. 12.

earlier part of Domitian's reign.[1] He designated to the consulship such men as Nerva, Trajan, Verginius Rufus, Agricola, and the grandfather of Antoninus Pius.[2] This strange character was also a moral reformer of the antiquarian type. He punished erring Vestals, *more majorum*. He revived the Scantinian law against those enormities of the East, of which Statius shows that the emperor was not guiltless himself.[3] Yet a voluptuary, with a calm outlook on his time, may have a wish to restrain vices with which he is himself tainted. A statesman may be a puritan reformer, both in religion and morals, without being personally severe and devout. Domitian may have had a genuine, if a pedantic, desire to restore the old Roman tone in morals and religion. He was, after all, sprung from a sober Sabine stock,[4] although he may have sadly degenerated from it in his own conduct. And his attempt to reform Roman society may perhaps have been as sincere as that of Augustus.

But there can be little doubt that Domitian, although he was astute and able, was also a bad man, with the peculiar traits which always make a man unpopular. He was disloyal as a son and as a brother. He was morose, and he cultivated a suspicious solitude,[5] around which evil rumour is sure to gather. The rumour in his case may have been well-founded, although we are not bound to believe all the tales of prurient gossip which Suetonius has handed down. It is the penalty of high place that peccadilloes are magnified into sins, and sins are multiplied and exaggerated. It was a recognised and effective mode of flattering a new emperor to blacken the character of his predecessors; Domitian himself allowed his court poets to vilify Caligula and Nero.[6] And Pliny in his fulsome adulation of Trajan, finds his most effective resource in a perpetual contrast with Domitian. Tacitus could never forgive the recall and humiliation of his father-in-law. The Senate as a whole bore an implacable hatred to the man who carried to its furthest point the assertion of imperial prerogative.[7]

[1] Pliny was probably Quaestor in 90 A.D.; Trib. Pleb. 92; Praetor 93. Cf. Momms. (Morel), p. 61. Tacitus says, *Hist.* i. 1, dignitatem a Domitiano (81–96) longius provectam non abnuerim. From *Ann.* xi. 11 it appears that he was Praetor in 88. Cf. Peter, *Gesch. Litt.* ii. 43.

[2] Duruy, iv. 697 n.

[3] *Silv.* iii. 4, 37.

[4] Meriv. vii. 354.

[5] D. Cass. 67. 14; Suet. *Dom.* xiv.

[6] Mart. iv. 63; vi. 21, crudelis nullaque invisior umbra.

[7] Suet. *Dom.* xxiii.

Still the authorities are so unanimous that we are bound to believe that Domitian, with some strength and ability, had many execrable qualities. He shows the contradictions of a nature in which the force of a sturdy rural ancestry has not been altogether sapped by the temptations of luxury and power. He had a passionate desire to rival the military glory of his father and brother, yet he was too cautious and self-indulgent to attain it. He had some taste for literature, but he kept literature in leading-strings, and put one man to death for his delight in certain speeches in Livy, and another for a too warm eulogy of Thrasea and Helvidius Priscus.[1] He threw his whole strength into a moral and religious reaction, while he was the bitterest enemy of the republican pretensions and dreams of the Senate. Great historical critics have called him a hypocrite.[2] It may be doubted whether any single phrase or formula could express the truth about such a twisted and perverse character. Probably his dominant passion was vanity and love of grandiose display. He assumed the consulship seventeen times, a number quite unexampled.[3] His pompous triumphs for unreal victories were a subject of common jest. He filled the Capitol with images of himself, and a colossal statue towered for a time over the temple roofs.[4] The son and brother of emperors, already exalted to divine honours, he went farther than any of his predecessors in claiming divinity for himself, and he allowed his ministers and court poets to address him as "our Lord God."[5] His lavish splendour in architecture was to some extent justified by the ravages of fire in previous reigns. But the £2,400,000 expended on the gilding of a temple on the Capitol,[6] was only one item in an extravagance which drained the treasury. Its radiance, which dazzled the eyes of Rutilius in the reign of Honorius,[7] was paid for in blood and tears. The emperor, who was the ruthless enemy of the nobles, like all his kind, was profusely indulgent to the army and the mob. The legions had their pay increased by a fourth. The populace of Rome were pampered

[1] Suet. *Dom.* x.

[2] Renan, *Les Évang.* p. 291, Domitien, comme tous les souverains hypocrites, se montrait sévère conservateur.

[3] Suet. *Dom.* xiii.

[4] Mart. viii. 65.

[5] Suet. *Dom.* xiii. ; Mart. v. 8, 1 (*v.* Friedländer's note), vii. 2 and 34; viii. 2, 6 ; Stat. *Silv.* v. 1, 37 ; Meriv. vii. 375.

[6] Suet. *Dom.* v ; Gregorov. *Gesch. St. Rom.* i. 41.

[7] Rutil. Namat. i. 93.

with costly and vulgar spectacles,[1] as they were to the end of the Western Empire. Domitian's indulgence of that fierce and obscene proletariat was only a little more criminal than that of other emperors, because it ended in a bankruptcy which was followed by robbery and massacre. While the rich and noble were assailed on any trivial accusation, in order to fill an empty treasury, the beasts of Numidia were tearing their victims, gladiators were prostituting a noble courage in dealing inglorious wounds in the arena, and fleets of armed galleys charged and crashed in mimic, yet often deadly, battle in the flooded Flavian amphitheatre.[2]

To repair this waste the only resource was plunder. But Domitian was a pettifogger as well as a plunderer; he would fleece or assassinate his victims under forms of law. The law of majesty, and the many laws for restoring old Roman morality, needed only a little ingenuity and effrontery to furnish lucrative grounds for impeachment.[3] The tribe of delators were ready to his hand. He had punished them for serving Nero; they were now to reap a richer harvest under Domitian. Every fortune which rose above mediocrity, every villa with rich pastures and woodlands in the Apennines, or on the northern lakes, was marked for plunder.[4] Domitian was the first and only emperor who assumed the censorship for life.[5] The office made him absolute master of the lives and fortunes of his nobles. A casual word, a thoughtless gesture, might be construed into an act of treason; and the slave households furnished an army of spies. Nay, even kindred and near friends were drawn into this vast conspiracy against domestic peace and security. It may be admitted that Domitian had to face a real peril. The rebellion of Antonius Saturninus was an attempt which no prince could treat lightly, and the destruction of the correspondence in which so many men of rank were involved, may well have heightened Domitian's alarm.[6] He struck out blindly and savagely. He compelled the Senate to bear a part in the massacre, and Tacitus has confessed, with pathetic humiliation, his silent share in the murder of the upright and innocent.[7] Yet the imperial

[1] Suet. *Dom.* v. *ad fin.*; iv.

[2] D. Cass. 67. 8.

[3] Suet. *Dom.* xii.

[4] Pliny, *Paneg.* 50.

[5] Dion Cass. 67. 4, *τιμητὴς δὲ διὰ βίου πρῶτος δὴ καὶ μόνος καὶ ἰδιωτῶν καὶ αὐτοκρατόρων ἐχειροτονήθη*: Momms. *Röm. St.* ii. 1012.

[6] D. Cass. 67. 11.

[7] *Agr.* 45.

inquisitor was himself racked with terror in his last hours. He walked in a corridor where the walls were lined with mirrors,[1] so that no unseen hand might strike him from behind. On his last morning he started in terror from his bed and called for the diviner whom he had summoned from Germany.[2] But, amid all his terror, Domitian had a deep natural love of cruelty. He was never more dangerous than when he chose to be agreeable;[3] he loved to play with his victims. What a grim delight in exquisite torture, what a cynical contempt for the Roman nobles, are revealed in the tale of his funereal banquet![4] The select company were ushered into a chamber draped from floor to ceiling in black. At the head of each couch stood a pillar like a tombstone, with the guest's name engraved upon it, while overhead swung a cresset such as men hang in vaults of the dead. A troop of naked boys, black as all around, danced an awful measure, and then set on the dismal meal which was offered, by old Roman use, to the spirits of the departed. The guests were palsied with terror, expecting every moment to be their last. And the death-like silence was only broken by the voice of the Emperor as he told a gruesome tale of bloody deaths. In such cynicism of lawless power, in such meek degradation of a once proud order, did the tyranny of the first century reach its close.

[1] Suet. *Dom.* xiv. parietes phengite lapide distinxit.
[2] *Ib.* xvi. [3] D. Cass. 67. 9. [4] *Ib.* 67. 4.

CHAPTER II

THE WORLD OF THE SATIRIST

JUVENAL and Tacitus, although they moved in different circles, and probably never met, have much in common. Both were released from an ignominious silence by the death of Domitian. Both were then at the age which combines the ripeness of experience and reflection with a fire and energy still unflagging.[1] They were, from different causes, both filled with hatred and disgust for the vices of their time, and their experience had engendered in both a pessimism which darkened their faith. Tacitus belonged to the senatorial order who had held high office, and had seen its ranks decimated and its dignity outraged under the tyranny. Juvenal sprang from the lower middle class, which hated alike the degenerate noble and the insolent *parvenu* far more than it hated even a Domitian. Yet both Juvenal and Tacitus are united in a passionate admiration for the old Roman character. Their standards and ideals are drawn from the half-mythical ages of the simple warriors and farmer-statesmen of the old Republic. And their estimate of their time needs to be scrutinised in the light both of their hatreds and of their ideals.

The life of Juvenal is wrapt in obscurity, although nine lives of him are extant.[2] Scholars are still at variance as to the date of his birth, the date of many of his satires, and especially as to the time and circumstances of his banishment, about which there is so uniform a tradition. But, for our purpose, some facts are clear enough. Juvenal was the son of

[1] Tacitus b. probably 55 A.D. *Dial. de Or.* 1, juvenis admodum in 75 or 76; cf. *Agr.* 9. He was betrothed in 77 A.D.; cf. Meriv. viii. 92; Peter, *Gesch. Litt.* ii. 43; Nipperdey, *Einl.* iv. Juvenal b. *circ.* 55 A.D. (Peter, ii. 77); decessit longo senio confectus exul Ant. Pio imp. Vit. iv.; Teuffel, § 326, 1.

[2] Nettleship, *Lectures and Essays*, pp. 118 sqq.

a well-to-do freedman of Aquinum, and rose to the highest magisterial office in his native town at some time of his career.[1] He carefully hides his personal history from us; but we might gather from his Satires that he belonged to the lower middle class,[2] that he was in temper and tone an old plebeian of the times of the Republic, although vividly touched by the ideas of a new morality which had been afloat for more than two generations. But, like Tacitus, he has little sympathy with the great philosophic movement which was working a silent revolution. He had the rhetorical training of the time, with all its advantages and its defects. And he is more a rhetorician than a poet. We can well believe the report that his early literary enthusiasm found vent in declamation on those mythical or frivolous themes which exercised the youth in the Roman schools for many centuries. Although he was hardly a poor man[3] in the sense in which Martial, his friend, was poor, yet he had stooped to bear the ignominy and hardships of client dependence. He had hurried in rain and storm in the early morning to receptions at great houses on the Esquiline, through the squalor and noises and congested traffic of the Suburra.[4] He had doubtless often been a guest at those "unequal dinners," where the host, who was himself regaled with far-fetched dainties and old crusted Alban or Setine wine, insulted his poorer friends by offering them the cheapest vintage and the meanest fare.[5] He had been compelled, as a matter of social duty, to sit through the recitation of those ambitious and empty Theseids and Thebaids, with which the rich amateur in literature in those days afflicted his long-suffering friends.[6] He may have been often elbowed aside by some supple, clever Greek, with versatile accomplishments and infinite audacity. He may have been patronised or insulted by a millionaire *parvenu*, like the Trimalchio of Petronius, tainted with the memories of a shameful servitude. He saw new vulgar wealth everywhere triumphant, while the stiff, yet, in many ways, wholesome conventionality of old Roman life was defied and trampled upon by an aggressive vulgarity. In such a world there was little room for the man whose wealth is

[1] *Or. Henz.* 5599, IIVir. Quinq. Flamen Divi Vespasiani.
[2] Boissier, *L'Opp.* p. 316.
[3] Juv. xi. 74, 150; cf. xiv. 322.
[4] Mart. xii. 18.
[5] Juv. v. 30 sqq.; cf. Mart. iii. 49; iii. 60.
[6] Juv. i. 52; Mart. x. 4; iv. 49.

in his genius, and who clings to the traditions of ages which believed that men had a soul as well as a body. A man like Juvenal, living in such a society, almost necessarily becomes embittered. Like Johnson, in his Grub Street days, he will have his hours when bitterness passes into self-abandonment, and he will sound the depths of that world of corruption which in his better moods he loathes. Some of the associates of Juvenal were of very doubtful position, and more than doubtful morals;[1] and the warmth of some of his realistic painting of dark sides of Roman life arouses the suspicion that he may have at times forgotten his moral ideal. He certainly knows the shameful secrets of Roman life almost as well as his friend Martial does. But his knowledge, however gained, was turned to a very different purpose from that which inspired Martial's brilliant prurience.[2]

The Satires of Juvenal were probably not given to the world till after the death of Domitian.[3] The date of the earliest is about 100 A.D., that of the latest probably 127. Juvenal cautiously disguises his attacks on his own time. He whets his sword against the sinners whose ashes have long reposed beside the Flaminian and the Latin ways.[4] Very few of his contemporaries appear in his pages,[5] and the scenery is often that of the reigns of Tiberius, Claudius, or Nero. But his deepest and most vivid impressions must have come to Juvenal in that period which has been photographed with such minute exactness by Martial. And there is a striking correspondence between the two writers, not only in many of the characters whom they introduce, but in their pictures of the whole state of morals and letters.[6] They both detested that frigid epic which laboriously ploughed the sands of conventional legend, and they turned with weariness from the old-world tales of Thebes or Argos to the real tragedy or comedy of Roman life around them. Although they were friends and companions, it is needless to

[1] Juv. vi. 43: v. 30 sqq.; ix. 10 sqq.; xi. 186.

[2] It has been remarked that Martial's Epigrams on Juvenal all contain some obscenity, vii. 24; vii. 91; xii. 18.

[3] Teuffel, § 326, 4; Peter, *Gesch. Litt.* ii. 77; Nettleship, *Lectures and Essays*, p. 122, brings together the indications of date from 96–127 A.D. He thinks that perhaps some of the earlier *Satires* belong to the last years of Domitian, and that the words, spes et ratio studiorum in Caesare tantum, in *Sat.* vii., may refer to that Emperor (p. 132).

[4] Juv. i. 170.

[5] Marius Priscus, Isaeus, Archigenes.

[6] See a comparison of passages in Nettleship, pp. 125 sqq.

assume any close partnership in their studies. Starting with the same literary impulse, they deal to a large extent with the same vices and follies, some of them peculiar to their own age, others common to all ages of Rome, or even of the world of civilisation. A long list might easily be compiled of their common stock of subjects, and their common antipathies. In both writers we meet the same grumbling of the needy client against insolent or niggardly patrons, the complaints of the struggling man of letters about the extravagant rewards of low vulgar impostors. Both are bored to death, like the patient Pliny, by the readings of wealthy scribblers, or by tiresome pleadings in the courts, measured by many a turn of the clepsydra. They feel an equal disgust for the noise and squalor of the narrow streets, an equal love for the peace and freshness and rough plenty of the country farm. In both may be seen the scions of great houses reduced to mendicancy, ambitious poverty betaking itself to every mean or disreputable device, the legacy-hunter courting the childless rich with flattery or vicious compliance. You will often encounter the sham philosopher, as you meet him sixty years afterwards in the pages of Lucian, with his loud talk of virtue and illustrious names, while his cloak covers all the vices of dog and ape. Both deal rather ungently with the character of women,—their intrigues with actors, gladiators, and slaves, their frequent divorces and rapid succession of husbands, their general abandonment of antique matronly reserve. Both have, in fact, with different motives, uncovered the secret shame of the ancient world; and, more even than by that shame, was their indignation moved by the great social revolution which was confusing all ranks, and raising old slaves, cobblers, and auctioneers to the benches of the knights.

Yet with this resemblance in the subjects of their choice, there is the widest difference between the two writers in their motive and mode of treatment. Martial, of course, is not a moralist at all; the mere suggestion excites a smile. He is a keen and joyous observer of the faults and follies, the lights and shades, of a highly complex and artificial society which is "getting over-ripe." In the power of mere objective description and minute portraiture of social life, Martial is almost unique. Through his verses, we know the society of Domitian as we know hardly any other period of ancient society. But this very vividness and truthfulness is chiefly due to the fact that Martial was almost without a conscience. He was indeed personally, perhaps, not so bad as he is often painted.[1] He knows and can appreciate a good woman;[2] he can love, with the simplest, unsophisticated love, an innocent slave-child, the poor little Erotion,[3] whom he has immortalised. He can honour a simple manly character, free from guile and pretence.[4] He has a genuine, exuberant love of the fresh joys of country life, sharpened, no doubt, by the experience of the client's sordid slavery, amid the mingled poverty and lavish splendour of the capital.[5] Where could one find a fresher, prettier idyll than his picture of the farm of Faustinus, with its packed granaries, and its cellars fragrant with the juice of many an old autumn vintage, the peacock spreading his jewelled plumage, and the ring-dove cooing overhead from the towers? The elegant slaves of the great house in the city are having a holiday, and busy, under the bailiff's care, with rural toils, or fishing in the stream. The tall daughters of the neighbouring cottages bring in their well-stocked baskets to the villa, and all gather joyously at evening to a plenteous meal.[6] Martial has, moreover, one great virtue, which is a powerful antidote for many moral faults, the love of the far-off home of his childhood, the rugged Bilbilis, with its iron foundries near the sources of the Tagus, to which he retreated from the crush and din of plebeian life at Rome, and where he rests.[7] But when charity or justice has done its best for Martial, and no scholar will repudiate the debt, it still remains true that he represents, perhaps better than any other, that pagan world, naked and unabashed, and feels no breath of inspiration from the great spiritual movement which, in paganism itself, was setting towards an ideal of purity and self-conquest.

Juvenal, at least in his later work, reveals a moral standard and motive apparently unknown to Martial.[8] It may

[1] He says of himself, i. 5, 8, lasciva est nobis pagina, vita proba est; cf. iii. 68; v. 2; Ausonius urges the same plea, cf. *Idyll.* xiii. Pliny finds a long series of examples to warrant his indulgence in loose verses, *Ep.* iv. 14; cf. v. 3. It was a bad tradition of literature; cf. Nettleship, *Lectures and Essays*, p. 39.

[2] i. 14; iv. 13, 75.

[3] v. 34, 37; x. 61.

[4] i. 79; vii. 52.

[5] iii. 58; i. 56; ii. 38; cf. iii. 38.

[6] iii. 58.

[7] i. 50; iv. 55; xii. 18.

[8] Especially *Sat.* xi. xiii. xiv. xv.; cf. Munding, *Über die Sat. Juv.* p. 12.

be admitted, indeed, that Juvenal did not always write under the same high impulse. He had the rhetorician's love of fine, telling phrases, and startling effects. He had a rare gift of realistic painting, and he exults in using it. He has also burning within him an old plebeian pride which looked down at once on the degenerate son of an ancient house, and on the *nouveaux riches,* whose rise seemed to him the triumph of vulgar opulence without the restraint of traditions or ideals. Conscious of great talents, with a character almost fierce in its energy, he felt a burning hatred of a society which seemed to value only material success, or those supple and doubtful arts which could invent some fresh stimulus for exhausted appetite. In Juvenal a great silent, sunken class, whom we hardly know otherwise than from the inscriptions on their tombs,[1] finds for once a powerful voice and a terrible avenger. But, along with this note of personal or class feeling, there is in Juvenal a higher moral intuition, a vision of a higher life, which had floated before some Roman minds long before his time,[2] and which was destined to broaden into an accepted ideal. Juvenal, indeed, was no philosopher, and he had, like Tacitus, all the old Roman distrust of the theories of the schools.[3] He had probably little respect for such teaching as Seneca's.[4] Yet in important points he and Seneca belong to the same order of the elect. Although, perhaps, a less spotless character than Tacitus, he is far more advanced and modern in his breadth of sympathy and moral feeling. He feels acutely for the conquered provinces which have been fleeced and despoiled of their wealth and artistic treasures, and which are still exposed to the peculation and cruelty of governors and their train.[5] He denounces, like Seneca, the contempt and cruelty often shown to slaves. The man whose ideal seems often to be drawn from the hard, stern warriors who crushed the Samnites and baffled the genius of Hannibal, in his old age has come to glorify pity and tenderness for suffering as the best gift of God, the gift that separates him most widely from the brute

[1] *v.* Bk. ii. c. 3 of this work. M. Boissier has thrown a vivid light on this class in his *Rel. Rom.* iii. 3.

[2] Boissier, *Rel. Rom.* ii. 198; Nettleship, *Lectures and Essays* p. 136.

[3] xiii. 120; ii. 1 sqq.; cf. Mart. ix. 48.

[4] He refers, however, with respect to Seneca, viii. 212.

[5] viii. 90 sqq.; cf. Boissier, *L'Opp.* p. 332.

creation.[1] He preaches sympathy and mutual help, in an age torn by selfish individualist passions. He denounces the lust for revenge almost in the tones of a Christian preacher.[2] What heathen moralist has painted more vividly the horrors of the guilty conscience, that unseen inquisitor, with sterner, more searching eyes than Rhadamanthus? Who has taught with greater power that the root of sin is in the evil thought?[3] Juvenal realises, like Tacitus and Quintilian, the curse of a tainted ancestry, and the incalculable importance of pure example in the education of youth.[4] He, who knew so well the awful secrets of Roman households, sets an immense value on the treasure of an untainted boyhood, like that of the ploughman's son, who waits at Juvenal's simple meal "and sighs for his mother, and the little cottage, and his playmates the kids."[5] Observation of character had also taught him the fatal law that the downward path in conduct, once entered on, is seldom retraced. And this moral insight seems to come to Juvenal not from any consciously held philosophic doctrine, nor from a settled religious faith. His faith, like that of many of his time, was probably of the vaguest. He scorns and detests the Eastern worships which were pouring in like a flood, and carrying away even loose women of the world.[6] He pillories the venal star-reader from the East and the Jewish hag who interprets dreams. But he has also scant respect for classic mythologies, and regrets the simple, long-gone age, before heaven became crowded with divinities, before Saturn had exchanged the diadem for the sickle, when Juno was still a little maid,[7] when the terrors of Tartarus, the wheel, the vulture, and the lash of the Furies had not taken the place of a simple natural conscience.[8]

Juvenal's moral tone then appears to unite the spirit of two different ages. In some of his later Satires you catch the accent of the age which was just opening when Juvenal began to write, its growing sense of the equality and brotherhood of man, its cosmopolitan morality, its ideals of spiritual culture. But there are other elements in Juvenal, derived from old Roman

[1] Juv. xv. 131; cf. Sen. *De Ira*, i. 5; ii. 10, 25; iii. 24.

[2] Juv. xiii. 190.

[3] xiii. 208, nam scelus intra se tacitum qui cogitat ullum Facti crimen habet.

[4] xiv. 30; Tac. *De Or*. 28, 29.

[5] xi. 153.

[6] vi. 510.

[7] xiii. 39.

[8] xiii. 208.

prejudice and conventionality, or the result of personal temperament and experience, which are quite as prominent. Juvenal is an utter pessimist about his time, more extreme even than Tacitus. His age, if we believe him, has attained the climax of corruption, and posterity will never improve upon its finished depravity.[1] His long practice as a declaimer had given him a habit of exaggeration, and of aiming rather at rhetorical brilliancy than truth. Whole passages in his poems read like declamatory exercises turned into verse.[2] A mere hanger-on of great society, one of the obscure crowd who flocked to the rich man's levée, and knowing the life of the aristocracy only by remote observation or the voice of scandalous gossip, he hardly deserves the implicit trust which has been often accorded to his indictments of the society of his day. His generalisations are of the most sweeping kind; the colours are all dark. He thinks that the number of decent people in his day is infinitesimally small. And yet we may reasonably suspect, from his own evidence, that he often generalised from single cases, that he treated abnormal specimens as types. His moral ideals cannot have been a monopoly of his own. In the palace of Nero in the worst days, there was a pure Octavia as well as a voluptuous Poppaea. The wife and mother of the gross Vitellius were women of spotless fame.[3] And in reading the fierce, unmeasured declamation of Juvenal, we should never forget that he knew nothing personally of Pliny or Tacitus, or of the circle which surrounded Verginius Rufus and Spurinna. He has the same pessimist theory of human declension which was held by Seneca and by Tacitus. Every form of crime and sensuality has been rampant since Rome lost the treasure of poverty, since the days when silver shone only on the Roman's arms.[4] Juvenal's ideal lies in that mythical past when a Curius, thrice consul, strode homeward from the hills, mattock on shoulder, to a meal of home-grown herbs and bacon served on earthenware.[5] It is the luxury of the conquered lands which has relaxed the Roman fibre, which has introduced a false standard of

[1] Juv. i. 87, 147; x. 172; cf. Sen. *Nat. Q.* vii. 31; *De Ira*, ii. 8 sq.

[2] *e.g.* the picture of Otho, ii. 99; of Messalina, vi. 114; Lateranus, viii. 146; Sejanus, x. 56; Cicero, etc., viii. 231.

[3] Tac. *Hist.* ii. 64; cf. Plin. *Ep.* iv. 19; iii. 16; D. Cass. 68. 5; Sen. *ad Helv.* xiv.

[4] Juv. xi. 109; iii. 152, 183.

[5] xi. 78.

life, degraded great houses, and flooded the city with an alien crew of astrologers and grammarians, parasites and pimps.

Modern criticism has laboured hard to correct some of the harsher judgments on the luxury and self-indulgence of the period of the early Empire. Perhaps the scholarly reaction against an indictment which had degenerated sometimes into ignorant commonplace, may have been carried here and there too far. The testimony of Tacitus is explicit that the luxury of the table reached its height in the hundred years extending from the battle of Actium to the accession of Vespasian.[1] It was a period of enormous fortunes spent in enormous waste. Seneca or Pallas or Narcissus had accumulated wealth probably three or four times greater than even the fortune of a Crassus or a Lucullus. The long peace, the safety of the seas, and the freedom of trade, had made Rome the entrepôt for the peculiar products and the delicacies of every land from the British Channel to the Ganges. The costly variety of these foreign dainties was vulgarly paraded at every great dinner-party. Palaces, extending almost over the area of a town, were adorned with marbles from the quarries of Paros, Laconia, Phrygia, or Numidia,[2] with gilded ceilings and curious panels changing with the courses of the banquet,[3] with hundreds of tables of citrus-wood, resting on pillars of ivory, each costing a moderate fortune, with priceless bronzes and masterpieces of ancient plate. Nearly a million each year was drained away to the remoter East, to purchase aromatics and jewels for the elaborate toilette of the Roman lady.[4] Hundreds of household slaves, each with his minute special function, anticipated every want, or ministered to every passion of their masters. Every picturesque or sheltered site on the great lakes, on the Anio, or the Alban hills, in the Laurentine pine forests, or on the bays of Campania, was occupied by far-spreading country seats. Lavish expenditure and luxurious state was an imperious duty of rank, even without the precept of an emperor.[5] The senator who paid too low a rent, or rode along the Appian or Flaminian Way with too scanty a train,

[1] Tac. *Ann.* iii. 55; Sen. *Ad Helv.* x. 3; *Ep.* 89, § 22.

[2] Statius, *Silv.* v. 36; ii. 85.

[3] Petron. c. 60; Sen. *Ep.* 95, § 9; Friedl. *Sittengesch.* iii. p. 67.

[4] Plin. *H.N.* vi. 26; ix. 58; xii. 41. Cf. Friedl. iii. p. 80; Marq. *Röm. St.* ii. 53.

[5] Suet. *Nero*, xxx. putabat sordidos ac parcos esse quibus ratio impensarum constaret, etc.

became a marked man, and immediately lost caste.[1] These things are the merest commonplace of the social history of the time.

Yet, in spite of the admitted facts of profusion and self-indulgence, we may decline to accept Juvenal's view of the luxury of the age without some reserve. It is indeed no apology for the sensuality of a section of the Roman aristocracy in that day, to point out that the very same excesses made their appearance two centuries before him, and that they will be lamented both by Pagan and Christian moralists three centuries after his death. But these facts suggest a doubt whether the cancer of luxury had struck so deep as satirists thought into the vitals of a society which remained for so many centuries erect and strong. Before the end of the third century B.C., began the long series of sumptuary laws which Tiberius treated as so futile.[2] The elder Pliny and Livy date the introduction of luxurious furniture from the return of the army in 188 B.C., after the campaign in Asia.[3] Crassus, who left, after the most prodigal expenditure, a fortune of £1,700,000, had a town house which cost over £60,000.[4] The lavish banquets of Lucullus were proverbial, and his villa at Misenum was valued at £24,000. It was an age when more than £1000 was given for a slave-cook or a pair of silver cups.[5] Macrobius has preserved the menu of a pontifical banquet, at which Julius Caesar and the Vestals were present, and which in its costly variety surpassed, as he says, any epicurism of the reign of Honorius.[6] And yet Ammianus and S. Jerome level very much the same charges against the nobles of the fourth century,[7] which satire makes against the nobles of the first. When we hear the same anathemas of luxury in the days of Lucullus and in the reign of Honorius, separated by an interval of more than five centuries, in which the Roman race stamped itself on the page of history and on the face of nature by the most splendid achievements of military virtue and of civilising energy, we are inclined to question either the report of our authorities, or the satirist's interpretation of the social facts.

[1] Sen. *Ep.* 87, § 4; Suet. *Tib.* xxxv.; Friedl. i. 196.

[2] Liv. xxxiv. 1; Tac. *Ann.* iii. 53, 54.

[3] Liv. xxxix. 6, 7; Marq. *Priv.* i. 62, 162; Momms. *R. Hist.* ii. 409.

[4] Momms. *R. Hist.* iii. 417.

[5] *Ib.* 418; cf. Plin. *H.N.* ix. 80, 81; x. 23; Plut. *Lucull.* c. 40; Macrob. *Sat.* iii. 13, § 1.

[6] Macrob. *Sat.* iii. 13, § 11.

[7] Hieron. *Ep.* 117, § 8; Amm. Marc. xiv. 6, 7; xxviii. 4.

The good faith of the elder Pliny, of Seneca and Juvenal, need not, indeed, be called in question. But the first two were men who led by preference an almost ascetic life. The satirist was a man whose culinary tastes were satisfied by the kid and eggs and asparagus of his little farm at Tibur.[1] And the simple abstemious habits of the south, which are largely the result of climate, tended to throw into more startling contrast any indulgence of superfluous appetite. It is true that the conquests which unlocked the hoarded treasures of eastern monarchies, gave a great shock to the hardy frugality and self-restraint of the old Roman character, just as the stern simplicity of Spartan breeding was imperilled by contact with the laxer life of the Hellespontine towns and the wealth of the Persian court.[2] The Roman aristocracy were for two centuries exposed to the same temptations as the treasures of the Incas offered to Pizarro,[3] or the treasures of the Moguls to Clive. In the wild licence, which prevailed in certain circles for more than a century, many a fortune and many a character were wrecked. Yet the result may easily be exaggerated. Extravagant luxury and self-indulgence is at all times only possible to a comparatively small number. And luxury, after all, is a relative term. The luxuries of one age often become the necessities of the next. There are many articles of food or dress, which free-trade and science have brought to the doors of our cottagers, which would have incurred the censure of the elder Pliny or of Seneca. There are aldermanic banquets in New York or the city of London in our own day, which far surpass, in costliness and variety, the banquets of Lucullus or the pontiff's feast described by Macrobius. The wealth of Pallas, Narcissus, or Seneca, was only a fraction of many a fortune accumulated in the last thirty years in the United States.[4] The exaggerated idea of Roman riches and waste has been further heightened by the colossal extravagance of the worst emperors and a few of their boon companions and imitators. But we are apt to forget that these were the outbreaks of morbid and eccentric character, in which the last feeble restraints were sapped and swept away by the sense of

[1] Juv. xi. 69.
[2] Thucyd. i. 95.
[3] Prescott, *Conquest of Peru*, i. 304.
[4] Tac. *Ann.* xii. 53 (Pallas); D. Cass. 60. 34 (Narcissus); Tac. *Ann.* xiii. 42; D. Cass. 61. 10; cf. Duruy, v. p. 598.

having at command the resources of a world. Nero is expressly described by the historian as a lover of the impossible;[1] and both he and Caligula had floating before their disordered imaginations the dream of astounding triumphs, even over the most defiant forces and barriers of nature. There was much in the extravagance of their courtiers and imitators, springing from the same love of sensation and display. Rome was a city of gossip, and the ambition to be talked about, as the inventor of some new freak of prodigality, was probably the only ambition of the blasé spendthrift of the time.

Yet, after all the deductions of scrupulous criticism, the profound moral sense of Juvenal has laid bare and painted with a realistic power, hardly equalled even by Tacitus, an unhealthy temper in the upper classes, which was full of peril. He has also revealed, alongside of this decline, a great social change, we may even call it a crisis, which the historian, generally more occupied with the great figures on the stage, is apt to ignore. The decay in the morale and wealth of the senatorial order, together with the growing power of a new moneyed class, the rise to opulence of the freedman and the petty trader, the invasion of Greek and Oriental influences, and the perilous or hopeful emancipation, especially of women, from old Roman conventionality, these are the great facts in the social history of the first century which, under all his rhetoric, stand out clearly to the eye of the careful student of the satirist.

The famous piece, in which Juvenal describes an effeminate Fabius or Lepidus, before the mutilated statues and smoke-stained pedigree of his house, rattling the dice-box till the dawn, or sunk in the stupor of debauch at the hour when his ancestors were sounding their trumpets for the march,[2] has, for eighteen centuries, inspired many a homily on the vanity of mere birth. Its moral is now a hackneyed one. But, when the piece was written, it must have been a powerful indictment. For the respect for long descent was still deep in the true Roman, and was gratified by fabulous genealogies to the end. Pliny extols Trajan for reserving for youths of illustrious birth the honours due to their race.[3] Suetonius recounts the twenty-eight consulships, five dictatorships, seven

[1] Tac. *Ann.* xv. 42. [2] Juv. viii. 10. [3] Plin. *Paneg.* 69.

censorships, and many triumphs which were the glory of the great Claudian house,[1] and the similar honours which had been borne by the paternal ancestors of Nero.[2] Tacitus, although not himself a man of old family, has a profound belief in noble tradition, and sometimes speaks with an undisguised scorn of a low alliance.[3] As the number of the "Trojugenae" dwindled, the pride of the vanishing remnant probably grew in proportion, and a clan like the Calpurnian reluctantly yielded precedence even to Tiberius or Nero.[4] It is a sign of the social tone that the manufacture of genealogies for the new men, who came into prominence from the reign of Vespasian, went on apace. A Trojan citizen in the days of Apollonius traced himself to Priam.[5] Herodes Atticus claimed descent from the heroes of Aegina,[6] just as some of the Christian friends of S. Jerome confidently carried their pedigree back to Aeneas or Agamemnon.[7] Juvenal would certainly not have accepted such fables, but he was no leveller. He had a firm belief in moral heredity and the value of tradition. Plebeian as he was, he had, like Martial, his own old Roman pride, which poured contempt on the upstarts who, with the stains of servile birth or base trade upon them, were crowding the benches of the knights. He would, indeed, have applauded the *mot* of Tiberius, that a distinguished man was his own ancestor;[8] he recalls with pride that one humble son of Arpinum had annihilated the hordes of the Cimbri, and another had crushed the rising of Catiline.[9] But he had the true Roman reverence for the Curii, Fabii, and Scipios, and would gladly salute any of their descendants who reproduced their virtues.

It is a melancholy certainty that a great many of the senatorial class in Juvenal's day had fallen very low in all things essential to the strength of a great caste. Their numbers had long been dwindling,[10] owing to vicious celibacy or the cruel proscriptions of the triumvirate and the four Claudian Caesars, or from the unwillingness or inability of many to support the

[1] Suet. *Tib.* i. Cf. the funeral oration of Julius Caesar over his aunt, quoted by Suet. *Jul. Caes.* 6.

[2] Id. *Nero*, i.

[3] Tac. *Ann.* vi. 33.

[4] *Ib.* xv. 48.

[5] Philostr. *Apoll. Tyan.* iv. 12.

[6] Philostr. *Vit. Soph.* ii. 1.

[7] Hieron. *Ep.* 108, § 4.

[8] Tac. *Ann.* xi. 21, Curtius Rufus videtur mihi ex se natus.

[9] Juv. viii. 285 sqq.

[10] Tac. *Ann.* xi. 25.

burdens of their rank. It was a rare thing in many great houses to reach middle age.[1] Three hundred senators and two thousand knights had fallen in the proscription of the second triumvirate.[2] The massacre of old and young of both sexes, which followed the fall of Sejanus, must have extinguished many an ancient line; not a day passed without an execution.[3] Three hundred knights and thirty-five senators perished in the reign of Claudius.[4] Very few of the most ancient patrician houses were left when Claudius revised the lists of the Senate, and introduced a fresh element from Gaul.[5] Who can tell the numbers of those who fell victims to the rage or greed or suspicion of Caligula, Nero, and Domitian? The list must have been enormously swelled by the awful year of the four emperors. Vespasian found it necessary to recruit the ranks of the aristocracy from Italy and the provinces.[6]

At the same time, prodigality or confiscation had rendered many of those who survived unable to maintain their rank, and to bear the social and official burdens which, down to the end of the Western Empire were rigorously imposed on the great order. The games of the praetorship in the first century, as in the fifth,[7] constituted a tax which only a great fortune could easily bear. Aristocratic poverty became common. As early as the reign of Augustus, the emperor had found it politic to subsidise many great families.[8] The same policy had been continued by Tiberius, Nero, and Vespasian.[9] Tiberius, indeed, had scrutinised and discouraged some of these claims on grounds which the treasury officials of every age would applaud.[10] A grandson of the great orator Hortensius once made an appeal in the Senate for the means of supporting the dignity of his name. He had received a grant from Augustus to enable him to rear a family, and four sons were now waiting at the doors of the Curia to second his prayer. Hortensius, who was the great rival of Cicero, had possessed immense wealth. He had many splendid villas, he used to give dinners in his park, around which the deer would troop

1 Sen. *De Ira*, ii. 33, § 2; Juv. iv. 96.
2 Appian, *B.C.* iv. 5.
3 Suet. *Tib.* 61, nullus a poena hominum cessavit dies.
4 Id. *Claud.* xxix.
5 Tac. *Ann.* xi. 25.
6 Suet. *Vesp.* ix.; cf. Tac. *Ann.* iii. 55.
7 Sym. *Ep.* ii. 78; Seeck, *Prol.* xlvi.
8 Suet. *Octav.* xli.
9 Id. *Nero*, x.; *Vesp.* xvii.
10 Tac. *Ann.* ii. 37, 38.

to the lute of a slave-Orpheus; he left 10,000 casks of old Chian in his cellars. His mendicant and spiritless descendant had to go away with a cold withering refusal from Tiberius, softened by a contemptuous dole to his sons. The revision of the senatorial roll by Claudius in 48 A.D., revealed a portentous disappearance of old houses of the Republic, and the gaps had to be filled up from the provinces in the teeth of aristocratic exclusiveness.[1] Among the boon companions of Nero there must have been many loaded with debt, like Otho and Vitellius. The Corvinus in Juvenal who is keeping sheep on a Laurentine farm, and his probable kinsman who obtained a subsidy from Nero, the Fabii and Mamerci who were dancing and playing the harlequin on the comic stage, or selling their blood in the arena, must represent many a wreck of the great houses of the Republic.[2] Among the motley crowd who swarm in the hall of the great patron to receive the morning dole, the descendants of houses coeval with the Roman State are pushed aside by the freedmen from the Euphrates.[3] But aristocratic poverty knew no lower depth of degradation than in the hungry adulation which it offered to the heirless rich. Captation became a regular profession in a society where trade, industry, and even professional skill, were treated as degrading to the men of gentle blood.[4] It is characteristic of Juvenal that he places on the same level the legacy-hunter, who would stoop to any menial service or vicious compliance, with the honest tradesfolk, in whose ranks, if we may judge by their funerary inscriptions, was to be found, perhaps, the wholesomest moral tone in the society of the early Empire.

In a satire written after Domitian's death,[5] Juvenal has described a scene of fatuous adulation which, if not true in fact, is only too true to the character of the time. A huge mullet, too large for any private table, had been caught in a bay of the Adriatic. Its captor hastens through winter storms to lay his spoil at the emperor's feet. The kitchen of the Alban palace had no dish large enough for such a monster, and

[1] Tac. *Ann.* xi. 25; D. Cass. lx. 29. The last revision of the Senate was in the reign of Augustus; D. Cass. lv. 13.

[2] Tac. *Ann.* xiii. 34; Juv. i. 107.

[3] Juv. i. 103.

[4] Petron. *Sat.* c. 116, 124; Plin. *Ep.* ii. 20; Juv. i. 37; iii. 31.

[5] Juv. iv.; i. 27.

a council of trembling senators is hastily summoned to consult on the emergency. Thither came the gentle Crispus, that Acilius, whose son was to be the victim of the despot's jealousy, Rubrius tainted with a nameless crime, the bloated Montanus, and Crispinus, once an Egyptian slave, now a vulgar exquisite, reeking with unguents. There, too, was the informer whose whisper stabbed like a stiletto, the lustful, blind Catullus, and the arch flatterer Veiento, who had revelled at the Gargantuan feasts of Nero from noon till midnight. These are worthy brethren of the assembly who stabbed Proculus to death with their stiles at the nod of the freedman of Caligula,[1] and led Nero home in triumphal procession after his mother's murder.[2]

Many things had contributed to the degradation of the senatorial character. The dark and tortuous policy of Tiberius tended, indeed, to absolutism; yet he still maintained a tone of deference to the Senate, and sometimes, with cold good sense, repelled a too eager adulation.[3] But, in the reigns of Caligula and Nero, the great order had to submit to the deepest personal degradation, and were tempted, or compelled by their masters to violate every instinct of Roman dignity. The wild epileptic frenzy of Caligula, who spared not the virtue of his sisters,[4] as he boasted of his own incestuous birth,[5] who claimed divine honours,[6] temples, and costly sacrifices, who, as another Endymion, called the Moon to his embraces, who dreamt of obliterating the memory of Homer and Virgil and Livy, was not likely to spare the remnant of self-respect still left in his nobles.[7] He gave an immense impetus to the rage for singing, dancing, and acting,[8] for chariot-driving and fighting in the arena, not unknown before, which Juvenal and Tacitus brand as the most flagrant sign of degenerate morals. There was indeed a great conflict of sentiment under the early Empire as to some of these arts. Julius Caesar had encouraged or permitted Roman senators and knights to fight in the gladiatorial combats, and a Laberius

[1] D. Cass. lix. 26.

[2] Tac. *Ann.* xiv. 12.

[3] Suet. *Tib.* lxvii.

[4] *Calig.* xxiii. xxiv.; cf. L. comitiali morbo vexatus, which explains much to a medical man.

[5] *Ib.* xxiii.

[6] *Ib.* xxii.; cf. Sen. *De Ira*, i. 20.

[7] Suet. *Calig.* xxxiv. xxxv. vetera familiarum insignia nobilissimo cuique ademit; xxii.

[8] *Ib.* liv. lv. quorum vero studio teneretur, omnibus ad insaniam favit.

to act in his own play.[1] But a decree of the Senate, not long afterwards, had placed a ban on these exhibitions by men of noble rank.[2] Tiberius, who was, beyond anything, a haughty aristocrat, at a later date intervened to save the dignity of the order.[3] But the rage of the rabble for these spectacles had undoubtedly caught many in the ranks of the upper class. And Caligula and Nero[4] found, only too easily, youths of birth and breeding, but ruined fortune, who were ready to exhibit themselves for a welcome *douceur*, or to gain the favour of the prince, or even to bring down the applause of the crowded benches of the amphitheatre or the circus. Yet the old Roman feeling must have been very persistent, when a man like Domitian, who posed as a puritan, found it politic to remove from the Senate one who had disgraced his order by dancing in the pantomime, and even laid his interdict on all public theatrical performances.[5] The revels and massacres and wild debauchery of Nero did not so much to hasten his destruction as his singing his catches to the lute, or appearing in the parts of the incestuous Canace and the matricide Orestes.[6] From every part of the world, in all the literature of the time, there is a chorus of astounded indignation against the prince who could stoop to pit himself against Greek players and singers at Delphi or Olympia. Juvenal has been reproached for putting the chariot-driving of Damasippus in the same category with the Verrine plunder of provinces.[7] He is really the exponent of old Roman sentiment. And it may be doubted whether, from the Roman point of view, Juvenal might not justify himself to his critics. Even in our own emancipated age, we might be pardoned for feeling a shock if an English prime minister rode his own horse at the Derby, or appeared in a risky part on the boards of the Gaiety. And the collective sense of senatorial self-respect was too precious to a Roman patriot and moralist, to be flung away for mere love of sport, or in a fit of spurious artistic enthusiasm. Nero, and in an even lower fashion Caligula, were rebels against old Roman conventional restraints,

[1] Suet. *Jul. Caes.* xxxix.

[2] D. Cass. xlviii. 43.

[3] Suet. *Tiberius*, xxxv.

[4] Id. *Calig.* xviii. nec ullis nisi ex senatorio ordine aurigantibus; D. Cass. 59. 10, 13; Suet. *Nero*, xii.

[5] Id. *Dom.* viii. vii.

[6] Id. *Nero*, xx. xxi.

[7] Juv. viii. 89, 147.

and it is possible that some of the hideous tales about them, which were spread in the "circuli," may have been the vengeance of Roman pride on shameless social revolutionaries, who paraded their contempt for old-fashioned dignity and for social tradition. Nero was never so happy as when he was deafened with applause, and smothered with roses at the Greek festivals. He had once predicted for him a monarchy in those regions of the East,[1] where he would have escaped from the tradition of old Roman puritanism, and combined all the ingenious sensuality of Syria with the doubtful artistic taste of a decadent Hellenism. The cold haughty refinement of senatorial circles of the old régime, and the rude honest virtue of the plebeian soldiery,[2] rightly mistrusted this false sensational artist on the throne of the world.

Art, divorced from moral ideals, may become a dangerous thing. The emperor might spend the morning with his favourites in patching up lilting verses which would run well to the lute.[3] But the scene soon changed to a revel, where the roses and music hardly veiled the grossness of excess. The "noctes Neronis" made many a debauchee and scattered many a senatorial fortune.[4] And amid all this elaborate luxury and splendour of indulgence, there was a strange return to the naturalism of vice and mere blackguardism. A Messalina or a Nero or a Petronius developed a curious taste for the low life that reeks and festers in the taverns and in the stews. Bohemianism for a time became the fashion.[5] Its very grossness was a stimulant to appetites jaded with every diabolical refinement of vicious ingenuity. The distinguished dinner party, with the emperor at their head, sallied forth to see how the people were living in the slums. Many a scene from these midnight rambles has probably been preserved in the tainted, yet brilliant, pages of the *Satiricon*. Petronius had probably often plunged with Nero after night-fall into those low dens, where slave minions and sailors and the obscene priests of the Great Mother were roistering together, or sunk in the slumber

1 Suet. *Nero*, xl.; *v.* Krause, *De Sueton. Fontibus*, pp. 57, 80; Peter, *Gesch. Litt.* ii. 69.

2 Tac. *Ann.* xv. 67.

3 *Ib.* xiv. 16; cf. Suet. *Nero*, lii., where Suetonius distinctly says that some of Nero's verses, which he had seen, bore all the marks of originality. Philostr. *Apoll. Tyan.* iv. 39; Macé, *Suétone*, p. 127; Boissier, *L'Opp.* p. 248.

4 Suet. *Nero*, xxvii.

5 *Ib.* xxvi.; cf. Juv. vi. 115.

of debauch.[1] These elegant aristocrats found their sport in rudely assaulting quiet citizens returning from dinner, or plundering some poor huckster's stall in the Suburra, or insulting a lady in her chair. In the fierce faction fights of the theatre, where stones and benches were flying, the Emperor had once the distinction of breaking a praetor's head.[2] It was nobles trained in this school, experts in vice, but with no nerve for arms, who encumbered the train of Otho on his march to the sanguinary conflict on the Po.[3]

The demoralisation of a section of the upper class under the bad emperors must have certainly involved the degradation of many women. And one of the most brilliant and famous of Juvenal's Satires is devoted to this unsavoury subject. The "Legend of Bad Women" is a graphic picture, and yet it suffers from a defect which spoils much of Juvenal's work. Full of realistic power, with an undoubted foundation of truth, it is too vehement and sweeping in its censures to gain full credence. It is also strangely wanting in balance and due order of idea.[4] The problem of marriage is illustrated by a series of sketches of female manners, which are very disconnected, and, indeed, sometimes inconsistent. Thorough depravity, superstition, and ignorant devotion, interest in literature and public affairs, love of gymnastic and decided opinions on Virgil—in fact, vices, innocent hobbies, and laudable tastes are all thrown together in a confused indictment. The bohemian man of letters had heard many a scandal about great ladies, some of them true, others distorted and exaggerated by prurient gossip, after passing through a hundred tainted imaginations. In his own modest class, female morality, as we may infer from the Inscriptions and other sources, was probably as high as it ever was, as high as the average morality of any age.[5] There were aristocratic families, too, where the women were as pure as Lucretia or Cornelia, or any matron of the olden days.[6] The ideal of purity, both in men and women, in some circles was actually rising. In the families of Seneca, of Tacitus, of Pliny and Plutarch, there were, not

[1] Juv. viii. 172.
[2] Suet. *Nero*, xxvi.
[3] Tac. *Hist.* i. 88.
[4] See some admirable criticism in Nettleship's *Lectures and Essays*, 2nd series, p. 141; cf. Munding, *Über die Sat. des Juv.* p. 7.
[5] Duruy, v. 673; Boissier, *Rel. Rom.* ii. 233 sqq.
[6] Plin. *Ep.* iv. 19; iii. 16; iii. 3; Sen. *Ad Helv.* xiv. xix.; D. Cass. lxviii. 5 *ad fin.*

only the most spotless and high-minded women, there were also men with a rare conception of temperance and mutual love, of reverence for a pure wedlock, to which S. Jerome and S. Augustine would have given their benediction. Even Ovid, that "debauchee of the imagination," writes to his wife, from his exile in the Scythian wilds, in the accents of the purest affection.[1] And, amid all the lubricity of his pictures of gallantry, he has not lost the ideal of a virgin heart, which repels and disarms the libertine by the spell of an impregnable purity.[2] Plutarch's ideal of marriage, at once severe and tender, would have satisfied S. Paul.[3] Favorinus, the friend and contemporary of Plutarch, thought it not beneath the dignity of philosophic eloquence to urge on mothers the duty of suckling and personally caring for their infants.[4] Seneca and Musonius, who lived through the reign of Nero, are equally peremptory in demanding a like continence from men and from women. And Musonius severely condemns concubinage and vagrant amours of every kind; the man guilty of seduction sins not only against another, but against his own soul.[5] Dion Chrysostom was probably the first of the ancients to raise a clear voice against the traffic in frail beauty which has gone on pitilessly from age to age. Nothing could exceed the vehemence with which he assails an evil which he regards as not only dishonouring to human nature, but charged with the poison of far spreading corruption.[6] Juvenal's ideal of purity, therefore, is not peculiar to himself. The great world was bad enough; but there was another world beside that whose infamy Juvenal has immortalised.

It is also to be observed that Juvenal seems to be quite as much under the influence of old Roman conventionality as of permanent moral ideals. He condemns eccentricities, or mere harmless aberrations from old-fashioned rules of propriety, as ruthlessly as he punishes lust and crime. The blue-stocking who is a purist in style, and who balances, with deafening

[1] Ov. *Trist.* iii. 3, 15—

Omnia cum subeant: vincis tamen omnia, conjux;
Et plus in nostro pectore parte tenes.
Te loquor absentem; te vox mea nominat unam:
Nulla venit sine te nox mihi, nulla dies.

[2] Id. *Amor.* iii. 4, 3; cf. *Ars Am.* ii. 599; iii. 440, 613; Denis, *Idées Morales*, ii. 124.

[3] Plut. *Consol. ad Uxor.* x.; *Conj. Praec.* iv. xliv. xlvii.

[4] A. Gell. xii. 1.

[5] Denis, ii. 134; Zeller, *Die Phil. der Griech.* iii. 1, p. 660.

[6] D. Chrys. *Or.* vii. 133.

volubility, the merits of Homer and Virgil,[1] the eager gossip who has the very freshest news from Thrace or Parthia, or the latest secret of a tainted family,[2] the virago who, with an intolerable pride of virtue, plays the household tyrant and delivers curtain lectures to her lord,[3] seem to be almost as detestable in Juvenal's eyes as the doubtful person who has had eight husbands in five years, or one who elopes with an ugly gladiator,[4] or tosses off two pints before dinner.[5] We may share his disgust for the great ladies who fought in the arena and wrestled in the ring,[6] or who order their poor tire-women to be flogged for deranging a curl in the towering architecture of their hair.[7] But we cannot feel all his contempt for the poor penitent devotee of Isis who broke the ice to plunge thrice in the Tiber on a winter morning, and crawled on bleeding knees over the Campus Martius, or brought a phial of water from the Nile to sprinkle in the fane of the goddess.[8] Even lust, grossness, and cruelty, even poisoning and abortion, seem to lose some of their blackness when they are compared with an innocent literary vanity, or a pathetic eagerness to read the future or to soothe the pangs of a guilty conscience.

The truth is that Juvenal is as much shocked by the "new woman" as he is by the vicious woman. He did not understand, or he could not acquiesce in the great movement for the emancipation of women, which had set in long before his time, and which, like all such movements, brought evil with it as well as good. There is perhaps nothing more striking in the social history of Rome than the inveterate conservatism of Roman sentiment in the face of accomplished change. Such moral rigidity is almost necessarily prone to pessimism. The Golden Age lies in the past; the onward sweep of society seems to be always moving towards the abyss. The ideal past of the Roman woman lay more than two centuries and a half behind the time when Juvenal was born. The old Roman matron was, by legal theory, in the power of her husband, yet assured by religion and sentiment a dignified position in the family, and treated with profound, if somewhat cold, respect; she was busied with household cares,

[1] Juv. vi. 436—
Committit vates et comparat; inde Maronem,
Atque alia parte in trutina suspendit Homerum.
Cedunt grammatici, vincuntur rhetores—

[2] Juv. vi. 400 sqq.

[3] *Ib.* 268.

[4] *Ib.* 108, 60.

[5] *Ib.* 427.

[6] *Ib.* 252.

[7] *Ib.* 493.

[8] *Ib.* 528.

and wanting in the lighter graces and charms, austere, self-contained, and self-controlled. But this severe ideal had begun to fade even in the days of the elder Cato.[1] And there is hardly a fault or vice attributed by Juvenal to the women of Domitian's reign, which may not find parallel in the nine or ten generations before Juvenal penned his great indictment against the womanhood of his age. The Roman lady's irritable pride of birth is at least as old as the rivalry of the two Fabiae in the fourth century.[2] The elder Cato dreaded a rich wife as much as Juvenal,[3] and satirised as bitterly the pride and gossip and luxury of the women of his time. Their love of gems and gold ornaments and many-coloured robes and richly adorned carriages, is attested by Plautus and the impotent legislation of C. Oppius.[4] Divorce and ghastly crime in the noblest families were becoming common in the days of the Second Punic War. About the same time began that emancipation of women from the jealous restraints of Roman law, which was to be carried further in the Antonine age.[5] The strict forms of marriage, which placed the wife in the power of her husband, fell more and more into desuetude. Women attained more absolute control over their property, and so much capital became concentrated in their hands that, about the middle of the second century B.C., the Voconian law was passed to prohibit bequests to them, with the usual futile result of such legislation.[6] Yet the old ideal of the industrious housewife never died out, and Roman epitaphs for ages record that the model matron was a wool-worker and a keeper at home. A senator of the reign of Honorius praises his daughter for the same homely virtues.[7] But from the second century B.C. the education of the Roman girl of the higher classes underwent a great change.[8] Dancing, music, and the higher accomplishments were no longer under a ban, although they were still suspected by people of the old-fashioned school. Boys and girls received the same training from the grammarian, and read their Homer and Ennius together.[9] There were women in the time of

[1] Momms. *R. Hist.* ii. 408 (Tr.).
[2] Liv. vi. 34.
[3] Plut. *Cato Maj.* c. xx.; Juv. vi. 165, 460.
[4] Val. Max. ii. 1, 5; Liv. xxxiv. 1, 3; Marq. i. p. 62.
[5] Momms. *R. Hist.* ii. 408.
[6] Cic. *in Verr.* i. 42, 107.
[7] Sym. *Ep.* vi. 67; cf. Suet. *Octav.* lxiv.; *Or. Henz.* 2677, 4629, 4629, lanifica, pia, pudica, casta, domiseda.
[8] Macrob. *Sat.* iii. 14, 11.
[9] Friedl. i. 312; Boissier, *Rel. Rom.* ii. 240.

Lucretius, as in the time of Juvenal, who interlarded their conversation with Greek phrases.[1] Cornelia, the wife of Pompey, was trained in literature and mathematics, and even had some tincture of philosophy.[2] The daughter of Atticus, who became the wife of Agrippa, was placed under the tuition of a freedman, who, as too often happened, seems to have abused his trust.[3] Even in the gay circle of Ovid, there were learned ladies, or ladies who wished to be thought so.[4] Even Martial reckons culture among the charms of a woman. Seneca maintained that women have an equal capacity for cultivation with men.[5] Thus the blue-stocking of Juvenal, for whom he has so much contempt, had many an ancestress for three centuries, as she will have many a daughter till the end of the Western Empire.[6] Even in philosophy, usually the last study to attract the female mind, Roman ladies were asserting an equal interest. Great ladies of the Augustan court, even the empress herself, had their philosophic directors,[7] and the fashion perhaps became still more general under M. Aurelius. Epictetus had met ladies who were enthusiastic admirers of the Platonic Utopia, but the philosopher rather slyly attributes their enthusiasm to the absence of rigorous conjugal relations in the Ideal Society.[8] Even in the field of authorship, women were claiming equal rights. The *Memoirs of Agrippina* was one of the authorities of Tacitus.[9] The poems of Sulpicia, mentioned by Martial,[10] were read in Gaul in the days of Sidonius.[11] Greek verses, of some merit in spite of a pedantic affectation, by Balbilla, a friend of the wife of Hadrian, can still be read on the Colossus of Memnon.[12] Calpurnia, the wife of Pliny, may not have been an author; but she shared all Pliny's literary tastes; she set his poems to music, and gave him the admiration of a good wife, if not of an impartial critic.

Juvenal feels as much scorn for the woman who is interested in public affairs and the events on the frontier,[13] as he feels for the woman who presumes to balance the merits of Virgil and Homer. And here he is once more at war with a

[1] Lucr. iv. 1160; Juv. vi. 192.
[2] Plut. *Pomp.* lv.
[3] Suet. *Gram. Ill.* 16.
[4] Ov. *Ars Am.* ii. 282.
[5] Mart. xii. 98, 3; cf. Sen. *Ad Helv.* xvii.; *Ad Marc.* xvi.
[6] Claud. *Laus Serenae*, 146.
[7] Sen. *Ad Marc.* 4.
[8] Epict. *Fr.* liii.
[9] Tac. *Ann.* iv. 53; cf. Plin. *H. N.* vii. 8, 46.
[10] Mart. x. 35; vii. 69.
[11] Sid. Apoll. *Carm.* ix. 261.
[12] *C.I.G.* 4725–31.
[13] Juv. vi. 403; cf. 434.

great movement towards the equality of the sexes. From the days of Cornelia, the mother of the Gracchi, to the days of Placidia, the sister of Honorius, Roman women exercised, from time to time, a powerful, and not always wholesome, influence on public affairs. The politic Augustus discussed high matters of state with Livia.[1] The reign of Claudius was a reign of women and freedmen. Tacitus records, with a certain distaste for the innovation, that Agrippina sat enthroned beside Claudius on a lofty tribunal, to receive the homage of the captive Caractacus.[2] Nero emancipated himself from the grasping ambition of his mother only by a ghastly crime. The influence of Caenis on Vespasian in his later days tarnished his fame.[3] The influence of women in provincial administration was also becoming a serious force. In the reign of Tiberius, Caecina Severus, with the weight of forty years' experience of camps, in a speech before the Senate, denounced the new-fangled custom of the wives of generals and governors accompanying them abroad, attending reviews of troops, mingling freely with the soldiers, and taking an active part in business, which was not always favourable to pure administration.[4] In the inscriptions of the first and second centuries, women appear in a more wholesome character as "mothers of the camp," or patronesses of municipal towns and corporations.[5] They have statues dedicated to them for liberality in erecting porticoes or adorning theatres or providing civic games or feasts.[6] And on one of these tablets we read of a *Curia mulierum* at Lanuvium.[7] We are reminded of the "chapter of matrons" who visited Agrippina with their censure,[8] and another female senate, under Elagabalus, which dealt with minute questions of precedence and graded etiquette.[9] On the walls of Pompeii female admirers posted up their election placards in support of their favourite candidates.[10] Thus Juvenal was fighting a lost battle, lost long before he wrote. For good or evil, women in the first and second centuries were making themselves a power.

[1] Suet. *Octav.* lxxxiv.

[2] Tac. *Ann.* xii. 37, novum sane et moribus veterum insolitum, feminam signis Romanis praesidere.

[3] D. Cass. lxvi. 14; cf. Suet. *Vesp.* xvi.; Krause, *De Suet. Fontibus*, p. 75.

[4] Tac. *Ann.* iii. 33; cf. i. 64; i. 69, sed femina [*i.e.* Agrippina] ingens animi munia ducis per eos dies induit, etc.

[5] *Or. Henz.* 6000, 4036, 5158, 4643, 5134, 3774, 2417, 4055, 4056, 7207, 3815.

[6] *Ib.* 3738, 3773, 6992.

[7] *Ib.* 3740.

[8] Suet. *Galba*, v.

[9] Lamprid. *Heliogab.* iv.; cf. Lamprid. *Aurelian.* xlix.

[10] Mau, *Pompeii* (Kelsey Tr.), p. 479.

Although he was probably a very light believer in the old mythology,[1] and treated its greatest figures with scant respect, Juvenal had all the old Roman prejudice against those eastern worships which captivated so many women of his day. And, here again, the satirist is assailing a movement which had set in long before he wrote, and which was destined to gain immense impetus and popularity in the two following centuries. The eunuch priests of the Great Mother, with their cymbals and Phrygian tiaras, had appeared in Italy in the last years of the Hannibalic War.[2] The early years of the second century B.C. were convulsed by the scandals and horrors of the Dionysiac orgies, which fell on Rome like a pestilence.[3] The purity of women and the peace of families were in serious danger, till the mischief was stamped out in blood. The worship of Isis found its way into the capital at least as early as Sulla, and defied the hesitating exclusion of Augustus.[4] At this distance, we can see the *raison d'être* of what the satirist regarded as religious aberrations, the full treatment of which must be reserved for another chapter. The world was in the throes of a religious revolution, and eagerly in quest of some fresh vision of the Divine, from whatever quarter it might dawn. The cults of the East seemed to satisfy cravings and emotions, which found no resting-place in the national religion. Their ritual appealed to the senses and imagination, while their mysteries seemed to promise a revelation of God and immortality. Their strange mixture of the sensuous and the ascetic was specially adapted to fascinate weak women who had deeply sinned, and yet occasionally longed to repent. The repentance indeed was often shallow enough; the fasting and mortification were compatible with very light morals.[5] There were the gravest moral abuses connected with such worships as that of Magna Mater. It is well known that the temples of Isis often became places of assignation and guilty intrigue.[6] An infatuated Roman lady in the reign of Tiberius had been seduced by her lover in the pretended guise of the god Anubis.[7] The Chaldaean seer or the Jewish hag might often

[1] Juv. ii. 31; iv. 34; xiii. 38; vi. 394; vii. 194.
[2] Liv. xxix. 14.
[3] *Ib.* xxxix. 8; cf. Lafaye, *Culte des Div. d'Alexandrie*, c. iii.
[4] Apul. *Met.* xi. 817; Suet. *Octav.* xciii.; D. Cass. liii. 2.
[5] Catull. x. 26; Tibull. i. 3, 23; cf. Juv. xiii. 93.
[6] Ov. *Ars Am.* i. 77.
[7] Friedl. *Sittengesch.* i. 347.

arouse dangerous hopes, or fan a guilty passion by casting a horoscope or reading a dream.[1] But Juvenal's scorn seems to fall quite as heavily on the innocent votary who was striving to appease a burdened conscience, as on one who made her superstition a screen for vice.

In spite of the political extinction of the Jewish race, its numbers and influence grew in Italy. The very destruction of the Holy Place and the external symbols of Jewish worship threw a more impressive air of mystery around the dogmas of the Jewish faith, of which even the most cultivated Romans had only vague conceptions.[2] The Jews, from the time of the first Caesar, had worked their way into every class of society.[3] A Jewish prince had inspired Caligula with an oriental ideal of monarchy.[4] There were adherents of Judaism in the household of the great freedmen of Claudius, and their growing influence and turbulence compelled that emperor to expel the race from the capital.[5] The worldly, pleasure-loving Poppaea had, perhaps, yielded to the mysterious charm of the religion of Moses.[6] But it was under the Flavians, who had such close associations with Judaea, that Jewish influences made themselves most felt. And in the reign of Domitian, two members of the imperial house, along with many others, suffered for following the Jewish mode of life.[7] Their crime is also described as "atheism," and Clemens is, in the old Roman spirit, said to have been a man of the most "contemptible inactivity." In truth, the "Jewish life" was a description which might cover many shades of belief and practice in religion, including Christianity itself. The secret worship of a dim, mysterious Power, Who was honoured by no imposing rites, a spirit of detachment and quietism, which shrank from games and spectacles and the scenes of fashion, and nursed the dream of a coming kingdom which was not of this world, excited the suspicion and contempt of the coarse, strenuous Roman nature. Yet, in the gloom and deep corruption of that sombre time, such a life of retreat and renunciation had a strange charm for naturally

[1] Juv. vi. 547.

[2] Tac. *Hist.* v. 2, 4; Juv. xiv. 97.

[3] Sen. *Fr.* 42 (in Aug. *De Civ. Dei*, vi. 11), victi victoribus leges dederunt.

[4] Cf. Meriv. vi. 6.

[5] Suet. *Claud.* xxv.

[6] Tac. *Hist.* i. 22; Duruy, iv. 505.

[7] Suet. *Dom.* xv.; D. Cass. lxvii. 14; Ren. *Les Év.* p. 228.

pious souls, especially among women. There were indeed many degrees of conformity to the religion of Palestine. While some were attracted by its more spiritual side, others confined themselves to an observance of the Sabbath, which became very common in some quarters of Rome under the Empire. The children, as Juvenal tells us, were sometimes trained to a complete conformity to the law of Moses.[1] But Juvenal is chiefly thinking of the mendicant population from Palestine who swarmed in the neighbourhood of the Porta Capena and the grove of the Muses, practising all the arts which have appealed in all ages to superstitious women. Thus the Judaism of the times of Nero or Domitian might cover anything from the cunning of the gipsy fortune-teller to the sad, dreaming quietism of Pomponia Graecina.[2]

Yet it must be admitted that, although Juvenal, in his attacks on women, has mixed up very real vice with superstition and mere innocent eccentricity, or the explosive energy of a new freedom, the real vices of many women of his time are a melancholy fact. The Messalinas and Poppaeas had many imitators and companions in their own class. It is true that even the licentious fancy of Ovid and Martial generally spares the character of the unmarried girl. She was, in the darkest times, as a rule, carefully guarded from the worst corruptions of the spectacles,[3] or from the reckless advances of the hardened libertine, although an intrigue with a tutor was not unknown.[4] Her marriage was arranged often in mere childhood, seldom later than her seventeenth year. A girl was rarely betrothed after nineteen.[5] Her temptations and danger often began on her wedding-day. That there was a high ideal of pure and happy marriage, even in the times of the greatest licence, we know from Pliny and Plutarch, and from Martial himself.[6] But there were serious perils before the child-bride, when she was launched upon the great world of Roman society. A marriage of convenience with some member of a tainted race, *blasé* with precocious and

[1] Juv. xiv. 96; vi. 544; iii. 15; Ren. *Les Év.* p. 234.

[2] Tac. *Ann.* xiii. 32.

[3] Friedl. *Sittengesch.* i. p. 332; cf. Plin. *Ep.* vii. 24.

[4] Suet. *Ill. Gram.* xvi.

[5] Friedl. i. 314; *Inscr. Or.* 2656, 2668, 4803.

[6] Mart. iv. 13—

Diligat illa senem quondam: sed et ipsa marito,
Tunc quoque cum fuerit, non videatur anus.

Plut. *Conj. Praec.* xliv. xxxiv.; Plin. *Ep.* iv. 19; vi. 4; vii. 5.

unnatural indulgence, and ready to concede the conjugal liberty which he claimed, was a perilous trial to virtue. The bonds of old Roman marriage had, for ages, been greatly relaxed, and the Roman lady of independent fortune and vigorous, highly trained intellect, could easily find consolation for marital neglect. From Seneca to S. Jerome, the foppish procurator of the great lady was a dangerous and suspected person,[1] and not always without good cause. Surrounded by an army of slaves and the other obsequious dependents of a great house, treated with profound deference, and saluted with the pompous titles of *domina* and *regina*, the great lady's lightest caprice became law.[2] Costly jewels and the rarest luxuries of the toilet poured in upon her from regions which were only visited by the captains of Red Sea merchantmen, or by some Pythagorean ascetic seeking the fountains of the wisdom of the East.[3]

The political life of Rome had been extinguished by a jealous despotism, but social life in the higher ranks was never so intense and so seductive, and women had their full share in it. Ladies dined out regularly with their husbands, even at the emperor's table;[4] and they were liable to be assailed by the artistic wiles of which Ovid taught the secret, or by the brutal advances of the lawless Caligula.[5] It was a time when people loved to meet anywhere, under the trees of the Campus Martius, in the colonnades of the theatre, or round the seats of the public squares. Everywhere were to be seen those groups which spared no reputation, not even the emperor's. And behind the chair of the young matron often hovered the dangerous exquisite, who could hum in a whisper the latest suggestive song from Alexandria or Gades,[6] who knew the pedigree of every racehorse and the secret of every intrigue. It is at such scenes that Tacitus is probably glancing when he says that in Germany no one makes a jest of vice, or calls the art of corruption the fashion of the world;[7] chastity is not sapped by the seductions of the spectacles.

[1] Sen. *Fr.* xiii. de Matrimonio, formosus assecla et procurator calamistratus, etc., sub quibus nominibus adulteri delitescunt; cf. S. Hieron. *Ep.* 54, § 13. S. Jerome is evidently imitating Seneca; cf. *Or.* 639; Mart. v. 61.

[2] Juv. vi. 460; Sen. *Fr.* 51.

[3] Philostr. *Apoll. Tyan.* iii. 35; Luc. *Alex.* 44.

[4] Tac. *Hist.* i. 81, erat Othoni celebre convivium primoribus feminis virisque. D. Cass. lx. 7.

[5] Suet. *Calig.* xxxvi.

[6] Ov. *Ars Am.* i. 67; Friedl. i. 281.

[7] Tac. *Germ.* 19, nec corrumpere et corrumpi saeculum vocatur.

Augustus had, indeed, set apart the upper seats for women in the theatre and amphitheatre,[1] but on the benches of the circus the sexes freely mingled. It was there, while the factions of the red and blue were shouting themselves hoarse, Ovid pointed out to his pupil in gallantry, that he had his fairest chance of making a dangerous impression.[2] Yet even Ovid is half inclined to be shocked at the scenes on the stage which were witnessed by women and young boys.[3] The foulest tales of the old mythology, the loves of Pasiphae or the loves of Leda, were enacted to the life, or told with a nakedness of language, compared with which even Martial might seem chaste.[4] Not less degrading were the gladiatorial shows, so lavishly provided by Augustus and Trajan, as well as by Caligula and Domitian, at which the Vestals had a place of honour.[5] It is little wonder that women accustomed to take pleasure in the sufferings and death of brave men, should be capable of condemning their poor slave women to torture or the lash for a sullen look, or a half-heard murmur. The grossness with which Juvenal describes the effect of the stage on the morals of women savours of the Suburra.[6] But of the poisonous character of these performances there can be no doubt. And actors, musicians, and gladiators became a danger to the peace of households, as well as to the peace of the streets. The artistes of the pantomime were sternly suppressed both by Tiberius and Domitian, and not without good cause.[7] One famous dancer had the fatal honour of captivating Messalina.[8] The empress of Domitian was divorced for her love of Paris.[9] And the scandals which darkened the fame of the younger Faustina, and impeached the legitimacy of Commodus, even if they were false, must have rested on a certain ground of probability[10] It is melancholy to hear that M. Aurelius had to restrain the excesses of Roman matrons even under the reign of the philosophers.[11] To all these perils must be added the allurements of household slavery. While a Musonius or a Seneca

[1] Suet. *Octav.* xliv.

[2] Ov. *Ars Am.* i. 139—
Proximus a domina, nullo prohibente, sedeto.

[3] *Trist.* ii. 503—
Nec satis incestis temerari vocibus aures:
Adsuescunt oculi multa pudenda pati.
Cf. 515.

[4] Mart. iii. 86 says of his poems—
Non sunt haec improbiora mimis: lege.

[5] Suet. *Octav.* xliv.

[6] Juv. vi. 62.

[7] Suet. *Dom.* vii.; *Tib.* xxxiv.

[8] D. Cass. lx. 22, 28.

[9] Suet. *Dom.* iii.; D. Cass. lxvii. 3.

[10] Capitol. *M. Anton.* xix.

[11] *Ib.* xxiii. mores matronarum composuit diffluentes, etc.

was demanding equal chastity in man and woman, the new woman of Juvenal boldly claims a vicious freedom equal to her husband's.[1] The testimony of Petronius is tainted by a suspicion of prurient imagination. But the student of other sources can hardly doubt that, in the first century, as in the fourth, the Roman lady of rank sometimes degraded herself by a servile *liaison.* A decree of Vespasian's reign, which his biographer tells us was called for by the general licence, punished the erring matron with the loss of her rank.[2]

These illustrations from other authorities may serve towards a judicial estimate of Juvenal's famous satire on women. That it is not a prurient invention is proved by the pages of Tacitus and Suetonius and the records of Roman morals for more than two centuries. On the other hand, it must be read with some reservations. Juvenal is a rhetorician with a fiery temperament, who will colour and exaggerate, if he will not invent. He is intensely prejudiced and conventional, a man to whom desertion of ancient usage is almost as bad as a breach of the moral law, a man incapable of seeing that the evils of a new social movement may be more than compensated by the good which it brings. Moreover, the graver vices which he depicts with so much realistic power were certainly not so general as he implies. It is to be suspected that single instances of abnormal depravity have swelled in his heated imagination till they have become types of whole classes of sinners. At the worst, these vices infected only a comparatively small class, idle, luxurious, enervated by the slave system, depraved by the example of a vicious court. The very scorn and indignation with which Juvenal pillories the aristocratic debauchee reveal the existence of a higher standard of virtue. Both the literature and the inscriptions of that age make us acquainted with a very different kind of woman. Over against the Hippia or Saufeia or Messalina of Juvenal we must set the pure and cultivated women whom we meet in the pages of Pliny or Tacitus, or the poor soldier's concubine in the Inscriptions, who has all the self-denying love and virtue of our own cottagers' wives.[3]

[1] Juv. vi. 281.

[2] Suet. *Vesp.* xi. auctor senatui fuit decernendi ut quae se alieno servo junxisset ancilla haberetur ; cf. Mart. vi. 39 ; *C. Th.* iv. 9, 1.

[3] *Or. Henz.* 2669, 4653, 7383.

Just as Juvenal misunderstood the movement of female emancipation, which was to culminate in the legislation of the Antonine age, so has he misconceived some other great social movements of his time. Two in particular, the invasion of the new Hellenism and the rise of the Freedmen, he anathematises with the scorn and old Roman prejudice of the elder Cato.

There was nothing new in the invasion of Hellenism in the time of Juvenal. Nearly three hundred years before his day, the narrow conservatism of ancient Rome was assailed by the cosmopolitan culture of Hellas, which it alternately hated and admired. The knowledge of Greek was widely diffused in Italy in the time of the Hannibalic war.[1] Almost the last Roman of the ancient breed stooped in his old age to learn Greek, in order to train his son in the culture of the world.[2] But there were two different aspects of Hellenism. There was the Hellenism represented by Homer and Plato and Chrysippus; and there was the Hellenism of the low comic stage, of the pimp and parasite. And there were reactions against the lower Greek influences long before the days of Juvenal. Cicero, who did more than any man of his race to translate Greek thought into Roman idiom, yet expressed as bitter a contempt as Juvenal's for the fickle, supple, histrionic Greek adventurer.[3] Juvenal is not waging war with that nobler Hellenism which had furnished models and inspiration to the great writers of the Augustan age, and which was destined to refashion Italian culture in the generation following his death. The emperors, from Julius Caesar to M. Aurelius, were, with few exceptions, trained in the literature of Greece, and some of them gave a great impetus to Greek culture in the West. Augustus delighted in the Old Comedy, entertained Greek philosophers in his house, and sprinkled his private letters to Tiberius with Greek quotations.[4] Tiberius, although he had lived at Rhodes in his youth, seems to show less sympathy for the genius of Greece.[5] Caligula also can hardly be claimed as a Hellenist. Although he had once a wild dream of restoring the palace of Polycrates, and one, more sane, of a canal through the Corinthian Isthmus, he also

[1] Momms. *R. H.* ii. 414 sqq.

[2] *Ib.* 469; cf. Plut. *Cato*, xxiii.

[3] Mahaffy, *Greek World under Roman Sway*, p. 127.

[4] Suet. *Octav.* 89; *Tib.* 21.

[5] Id. *Tib.* 71, sermone Graeco, quanquam alioquin promptus et facilis, non tamen usquequaque usus est.

thought of wiping out the memory of the poems of Homer.[1] Dr. Mahaffy is probably right in treating Claudius as the first really Hellenist emperor.[2] Like our own James I., Claudius was a learned and very ludicrous person. Yet he was perhaps not so contemptible a character as he is painted by Suetonius. He had, at any rate, the merit of being a lover of Greek literature,[3] and he heaped honour on the country which gave it birth.[4] He used to quote Homer in his speeches in the Senate, and he composed histories in the Greek language, which, by an imperial ordinance, were to be read aloud regularly in the Museum of Alexandria.[5] In spite of the vices and pompous follies of Nero, his phil-Hellenism seems to have been a genuine and creditable impulse. His visits to the Greek festivals, and his share in the competitions, were not all mere vanity. He had a futile passion for fame as an artist, and he sought the applause of the race which had a real artistic tradition.[6] When we reach the plebeian Flavian race, Hellenism is still favoured. The bluff soldier, Vespasian, had an adequate command of the Greek language, and was the first emperor who gave liberal endowments to Greek rhetoric.[7] His son Domitian, that puzzling enigma, the libertine who tried to revive the morality of the age of Cato, the man who was said, but most improbably, to confine his reading to the memoirs of Tiberius, founded a quinquennial festival, with competitions, on the Greek model, in music, gymnastic, and horsemanship. By drawing on the inexhaustible stores of Alexandria, he also repaired the havoc which had been wrought in the Roman libraries by fire.[8] Already in Juvenal's life the brilliant sophistic movement had set in which was destined to carry the literary charm of Hellenism throughout the West. From the close of the first century there appeared in its full bloom that ingenious technique of style, that power of conquering all the difficulties of a worn-out or trifling subject, that delicate command of all varieties of rhythm, which carried the travelling sophist through a series of triumphs wherever he wandered. Classical Latin literature about the same time came

[1] Suet. *Calig.* xxi. xxxiv.

[2] Mahaffy, *The Greek World*, p. 255.

[3] Suet. *Claud.* xlii.

[4] *Ib.* xxv.

[5] *Ib.* xlii.

[6] Id. *Nero*, lv. erat illi aeternitatis perpetuaeque famae cupido. Cf. xxiv.

[7] Id. *Vesp.* xviii.

[8] Id. *Dom.* xx.

to a mysterious end. The only authors of any merit in the second century wrote in both languages indifferently.[1] And the great Emperor, who closes our period, preferred to leave his inner thoughts to posterity in Greek.

Juvenal, however, was not thinking of this great literary movement. Like so many of his literary predecessors, who had been formed by the loftier genius of the Greek past, like Plautus and Cicero, he vented his rage on a degenerate Hellenism. His shafts were levelled at the suttlers and camp-followers of the invading army from the East. The phenomena of Roman social history are constantly repeating themselves for centuries. And one of the most curious examples of perpetuity of social sentiment is the hatred and scorn for the Greek or Levantine character, from the days of Plautus and the elder Cato to the days of the poet Claudian.[2] For more than 600 years, the Roman who had borrowed his best culture, his polish and ideas from the Greek, was ready to sneer at the "Greekling." The conquerors of Macedon could never forgive their own conquest by Greek knowledge and versatility, by which old Roman victories in the field had been avenged. And, as the pride of the imperial race grew with the consciousness of great achievements, the political degradation and economic decay of Greece and Greek-speaking lands produced a type of character which combined the old cleverness and keenness of intellect with the moral defects of an impoverished and subject race. Something of Roman contempt for the Greek must be set down to that national prejudice and difference of temperament, which made our ancestors treat the great French nation, with all its brilliant gifts and immense contributions to European culture, as a race of posturing dancing-masters.[3] Such prejudices are generally more intense in the lower than in the upper and the cultivated classes. Juvenal, indeed, was a cultivated man, who knew Greek literature, and had been formed by Greek rhetors in the schools. But he was also a Roman plebeian, with that pride of race which is often as deep in the plebeian as in the aristocrat. He gives voice to the

[1] And many in the first century, Plin. *Ep.* iv. 3; viii. 4, 1; Friedl. iii. 360; Martha, *Les Moralistes sous l'Empire Rom.* p. 267; Teuffel, *R. Lit.* § 342; Mackail, *R. Lit.* 232.

[2] Plut. *Cato*, c. xxii.; Claud. *In Eutrop.* ii. 137, 339.

[3] Juv. iii. 85.

feeling of his class when he indignantly laments that the true-born Roman, whose infancy has drunk in the air of the Aventine, should have to yield place to the supple, fawning stranger, who has come with the same wind as the figs and prunes. The Orontes is pouring its pollutions into the Tiber.[1] Every trade and profession, from the master of the highest studies down to the rope-dancer and the pander, is crowded with hungry, keen-witted adventurers from the East. Every island of the Aegean, every city of Asia, is flooding Rome with its vices and its venal arts.[2] Quickness of intellect and depravity of morals, the brazen front and the ready tongue are driving into the shade the simple, unsophisticated honesty of the old Roman breed. At the morning receptions of the great patron, the poor Roman client, who has years of honest, quiet service to show, even the impoverished scion of an ancient consular line, are pushed aside by some sycophant from the Euphrates,[3] who can hardly conceal the brand of recent servitude upon him. These men, by their smooth speech, their effrontery and ready wit, their infinite capacity for assuming every mood and humouring every caprice of the patron, are creeping into the recesses of great houses, worming out their secrets, and mastering their virtue.[4] Rome is becoming a Greek town,[5] in which there will soon be no place for Romans.

Much of this indictment, as we have said, is the offspring of prejudice and temperament. But there was a foundation of truth under the declamation of Juvenal. The higher education of Roman youth had for generations been chiefly in the hands of men of Greek culture, from the days of Ennius and Crates of Mallus, before the third Punic War.[6] The tutor's old title *literatus* had early given place to that of *grammaticus*.[7] And, of the long line of famous *grammatici* commemorated by Suetonius, there are few who were not by origin or culture connected with the Greek east. Most of them had been freedmen of savants or great nobles.[8] Some had

[1] Juv. iii. 62 sqq.
[2] *Ib.* iii. 69–77.
[3] *Ib.* i. 104.
[4] *Ib.* iii. 72, viscera magnarum domuum dominique futuri.
[5] *Ib.* iii. 60.
[6] Suet. *Ill. Gram.* i. ii. antiquissimi doctorum qui iidem et poëtae et semigraeci erant (Livium et Ennium dico), etc.; Strab. vi. 3, 5 ; A. Gell. xvii. 17, i.
[7] Suet. *Ill. Gram.* iv.
[8] *Ib.* xx. xix. xvi. xv.

actually been bought in the slave market.[1] The profession was generally ill-paid and enjoyed little consideration, and it was often the last resort of those who had failed in other and not more distinguished callings. Orbilius, the master of Horace, had been an attendant in a public office.[2] Others had been pugilists or low actors in pantomime.[3] Q. Remmius Palaemon, whose vices made him infamous in the reign of Tiberius and Claudius, had been a house-slave, and was originally a weaver.[4] He educated himself while attending his young master at school, and by readiness, versatility, and arrogant self-assertion, rose to an income of more than £4000 a year. Sometimes they attained to rank and fortune by being entrusted with the tuition of the imperial children.[5] But the grammarian, to the very end, as a rule never escaped the double stigma of doubtful origin and of poverty.

The medical profession, according to the elder Pliny, was a Greek art which was seldom practised by Romans.[6] Julius Caesar, by giving civic rights to physicians from Egypt and Hellenic lands,[7] while he raised the status of the medical calling, also stimulated the immigration of foreign practitioners. The rank and fortune attained by the court physicians of the early Caesars, Antonius Musa, the Stertinii,[8] and others, which almost rivalled the medical successes of our own day, seemed to offer a splendid prize. Yet the profession was generally in low repute.[9] It was long recruited from the ranks of old slaves, and men of the meanest callings. Carpenters and smiths and undertakers flocked into it, often with only a training of six months.[10] Galen found most of his medical brethren utterly illiterate, and recommends them to pay a little attention to grammar in dealing with their patients.[11] They compounded in their own shops, and touted for practice.[12] They called in the aid of spells and witchcraft to reinforce their drugs. We need not believe all the coarse insinuations of Martial against their morality, any more than the sneers of Petronius against

[1] Suet. *Ill. Gram.* xiii. Staberius . . . emptus de catasta.
[2] *Ib.* xiii.
[3] *Ib.* xviii. xxiii.
[4] *Ib.* xxiii.
[5] *Ib.* xvii.; cf. Quintilian, iv. Prooem. 2; cf. Juv. viii. 186-97.
[6] Plin. *H.N.* xxix. 17.
[7] Suet. *Jul. Caes.* xlii.
[8] D. Cass. liii. 30; Plin. *H.N.* xxix. 4; *Or. Henz.* 2983.
[9] Juv. x. 221; Petron. 42; D. Cass. lxxi. 33; lxix. 22; Mart. ii. 16; v. 9; vi. 31; vi. 53; Tac. *Ann.* xi. 31, 35.
[10] Mart. i. 31; i. 48; viii. 74.
[11] Friedl. *Sittengesch.* i. 231.
[12] Epict. iii. 23, 30, 27.

their skill. But we are bound to conclude that the profession held a very different place in public esteem from that which it enjoys and deserves in our own time.

Astrology, which was the aristocratic form of divination, and involved in many a dark intrigue of the early Empire, was a Greek as well as a Chaldaean art. The name of the practitioner often reveals his nationality. The Seleucus [1] and Ptolemaeus who affected to guide the fate of Otho, and the Ascletarion of Domitian's reign,[2] are only representatives of a nameless crowd. And their strange power is seen in that tale of a Greek diviner, Pammenes, in the last years of Nero, whose horoscopes led to the tragic end of P. Anteius and Ostorius Scapula.[3] In other countless arts of doubtful repute, which ministered to the pleasure or amusement of the crowd, the Greek was always an adept. But it was his success as a courtier and accomplished flatterer of the great, which chiefly roused the scornful hatred of Juvenal and his fellows. The "adulandi gens prudentissima," would hardly have been guilty of the simple and obvious grossness of flattery which the rhetoric of Juvenal attributes to them.[4] They knew their trade better than the Roman plebeian. It was an old and highly rewarded profession in Greece, and had often been the theme of Greek moralists. Plutarch wrote an elaborate treatise on the difference between the sycophant and the true friend, in which he seems almost to exhaust the wily resources of the pretender. Lucian, with his delicate irony, seems almost to raise the Greek skill in adulation to the level of a fine art.[5] And the polished and versatile Greek, with his lively wit, his delicate command of expression, his cool audacity, and his unscrupulousness, was a formidable rival of the coarser Roman parasite celebrated in Latin comedy. We can well imagine that the young Greek, fresh from the schools of Ionia, was a livelier companion at dinner than the proud Roman man of letters who snatched the dole and disdained himself for receiving it.

There is perhaps no phase of Roman society in Domitian's day which we know more intimately than the life of the client. It is photographed, in all its sordid slavery, by both Juvenal and Martial. And Martial himself is perhaps the best example

[1] Suet. *Otho*, iv. vi.
[2] Id. *Dom.* xiv. xv.; cf. *Tib.* xiv.; *Nero*, xxxvi.
[3] Tac. *Ann.* xvi. 14.
[4] Juv. iii. 100.
[5] Luc. *De Merc. Cond.* c. 16, 19.

of a man of genius submitting, with occasional intervals of proud rebellion,[1] to a degradation which in our eyes no poverty could excuse. The client of the early Empire was a totally different person from the client of Republican times. In the days of freedom, the tie of patron and client was rather that of clansman and chief; it was justified by political and social necessity, and ennobled by feelings of loyalty and mutual obligation. Under the Empire, the relation was tainted by the selfish materialism of the age; it had seldom any trace of sentiment. The rich man was expected to have a humble train of dependents to maintain his rank and consequence. There was a host of needy people ready to do him such service. The hungry client rushed to his patron's morning reception, submitted to all his coldness and caprice, or to the insolence of his menials, followed his chair through the streets, and ran on his errands, for the sake of a miserable alms in money or in kind.[2] The payment was sometimes supplemented by a cast-off cloak, or an invitation at the last moment to fill a place at dinner, when perhaps it could not be accepted.[3] In the train which the great man gathered about him, to swell his importance, were to be seen, not only the starving man of letters, the loafer and mere mendicant, but the sons of ruined houses "sprung from Troy," and even senators and men of consular rank who had a clientèle of their own.[4]

Nothing throws a more lurid light on the economic condition of Italy in the time of the early Empire than this form of pensioned dependence. The impression which we derive from Juvenal and Martial is that of a society divided between a small class of immensely wealthy people, and an almost starving proletariat.[5] Poverty seems almost universal, except in the freedman class, who by an industrial energy and speculative daring, which were despised by the true-born Roman, were now rapidly rising to opulence. The causes of this plebeian indigence can only be glanced at here. The agricultural revolution, which ruined the small freeholders and created the plantation system,[6] had driven great numbers of

[1] Mart. i. 104, ii. 68.

[2] Juv. i. 100; v. 17; Mart. xii. 18—
Dum per limina te potentiorum
Sudatrix toga ventilat, etc.;
iii. 7, 36; Suet. *Nero*, xvi; *Dom.* vii.

[3] Mart. ii. 79; Juv. v. 17.

[4] Juv. i. 100—
Jubet a praecone vocari
Ipsos Trojugenas.

[5] Mart. ii. 43; iii. 38, 12, pallet cetera turba fame; Juv. iii. 153, 161; xi. 40.

[6] Momms. *R. H.* ii. 374 (Tr.).

once prosperous farmers to the capital, to depend on the granaries of the State, or on the charity of a wealthy patron. Such men were kept in poverty and dependence by that general contempt for trade and industrial pursuits which always prevails in a slave-owning society. Many of the greatest families had been reduced to poverty by proscription and confiscation. A great noble might be keeping sheep on a Laurentine farm, if he could not win a pension from the grace of the Emperor. At the same time, from various causes, what we should call the liberal professions, with the doubtful exception of medicine, tortured those engaged in them by the contrast between ambitious hopes and the misery of squalid poverty. "Make your son an auctioneer or an undertaker rather than an advocate or a man of letters" is the advice of Martial and Juvenal, and of the shrewd vulgar guests of Trimalchio.[1] Any mean and malodorous trade will be more lucrative than the greatest knowledge and culture. The rich literary amateur, who should have been a Maecenas, in that age became an author himself, composed his own Thebaid or Codrid, and would only help the poor man of genius by the loan of an unfurnished hall for a reading.[2] The unabashed mendicancy of Martial shows the mean straits to which the genuine literary man was reduced.[3] The historian will not earn as much as the reader of the *Acta Diurna*.[4] It is the same with education. What costs the father least is the training of his son. The man who will expend a fortune on his baths and colonnades, can spare a Quintilian only a fraction of what he will give for a pastry cook.[5] The grammarian, who is expected to be master of all literature, will be lucky if he receives as much for the year as a charioteer gains by a single victory.[6] If the rhetor, weary of mock battles, descends into the real arena of the courts, he fares no better.[7] The bar is overcrowded by men to whom no other career of ambition is open, by old informers who find their occupation gone, by the sons of noble houses who parade the glory of their ancestors in order to attract vulgar clients. They are carried in a litter, surrounded by

[1] Mart. iv. 5; v. 56—
Artes discere vult pecuniosas?
Fac discat citharoedus aut choraules.
Si duri puer ingeni videtur,
Praeconem facias, vel architectum;
Juv. vii. 104; x. 226; Petron. 46, destinavi illum artificii docere, aut tonstreinum aut praeconem etc.

[2] Juv. vii. 38 sqq.

[3] Mart. ii. 43; iv. 40; v. 42, quas dederis, solas semper habebis opes.

[4] Juv. vii. 104.

[5] *Ib.* vii. 180.

[6] *Ib.* vii. ad fin.

[7] *Ib.* vii. 121 sqq.

slaves and dependents, down to the courts of the Centumviri. The poor pleader must hire or borrow purple robes and jewelled rings, if he is to compete with them. And in the end, he may find his honorarium for a day's hard pleading to be a leg of pork, a jar of tunnies, or a few flasks of cheap wine. In this materialised society all the prizes go to the coarser qualities; there is nothing but neglect and starvation before taste and intellect. And poverty is punished by being forced to put on the show of wealth.[1] That stately person in violet robes who stalks through the forum, or reclines in a freshly decorated chair, followed by a throng of slaves, has just pawned his ring to buy a dinner.[2] That matron, who has sold the last pieces of her ancestral plate, will hire splendid dress, a sedan chair, and a troop of attendants, to go in proper state to the games.[3] Thus you have the spectacle of a society divided between the idle, luxurious rich and the lazy, hungry poor, who imitate all the vices of the rich, and although too proud to work, are not ashamed to borrow or to beg.

In such a society, where the paths of honest industry seemed closed to the poor, or as yet undiscovered, the great problem was how to secure without labour a share of the wealth which was monopolised by the few. The problem was solved by the obsequiousness of the client, or by the arts of the will-hunter. Owing to celibacy and vice, childlessness in that age was extraordinarily common in the upper class. In a society of "ambitious poverty," a society where poverty was unable, or where it disdained, to find the path to competence through honest toil, the wealthy, without natural heirs, offered a tempting prey to the needy adventurer. Captation by every kind of mean flattery, or vicious service, became a recognised profession. In the Croton of Petronius there are only two classes, the rich and the sycophant, the hunters and the hunted.[4] Even men of high position, with no temptation from want, would stoop to this detestable trade.[5] And the social tone which tolerated the captator, made it almost an honour to be beset on a sick bed by these rapacious sycophants. One of the darkest and most repulsive features in that putrescent society was the

[1] Juv. iii. 182; Martha, *Moralistes sous l'Emp.* p. 400.
[2] Mart. ii. 57.
[3] Juv. vi. 353.
[4] Petron. 116, in hac urbe nemo liberos tollit . . . aut captantur aut captant.
[5] *e.g.* Regulus, Plin. *Ep.* ii. 20.

social value which attached to a vicious and shameful childlessness. A morose and unlovely old age could thus gather around it a little court of dependents and pretended friends, such as a career of great achievement would hardly attract. There have been few more loathsome characters than the polished hypocrite by the sick-bed of his prey, shedding tears of feigned sympathy, while with eager eyes he is noting every symptom of the approaching end.[1]

Juvenal and Petronius, the embittered plebeian, and the cynical, fastidious epicure of Nero's court, alike treat their age as utterly corrupted and vulgarised by the passion for money; "inter nos sanctissima divitiarum Majestas."[2] No virtue, no gifts, no eminence of service, will be noticed in the poor.[3] A great fortune will conceal the want of talent, sense, or common decency. Everything is forgiven to the master of money bags, even the brand of the slave prison.[4] In Juvenal and Martial probably the most resonant note is the cry of the poor —"How long." Yet, after all, it is not a fierce cry of revolt; against that highly organised and centralised society the disinherited never dreamed of rebellion, even when the Goths were under the walls. It is rather an appeal, though often a bitter and angry appeal, for pity and a modest share in a wasted abundance. In the poems of Juvenal and Martial, as in the sentiment of the colleges and municipalities for generations, the one hope for the mass of helpless indigence lay in awaking the generosity and charity of the rich. The rich, as we shall see in another chapter, admitted the obligation, and responded to the claim, often in the most lavish fashion. A long line of emperors not only fed the mob of the capital, but squandered the resources of the State in providing gross and demoralising amusements for them.[5] Under the influence of the Stoic teaching of the brotherhood of man and the duty of mutual help, both private citizens and benevolent princes, from Nero to M. Aurelius, created charitable foundations for the orphan and the

[1] Juv. xii. 100; i. 36; Mart. v. 39; Plin. *Ep.* ii. 20; Petron. 140.

[2] Juv. i. 112; Petron. 88, pecuniae cupiditas haec tropica instituit.

[3] Juv. iii. 164.

[4] *Ib.* 131, 103; i. 26; iv. 98; Mart. ii. 29; iii. 29; v. 13, 35.

[5] Suet. *Octav.* xliii.-v.; *Calig.* xviii.; *Claud.* xxi.; *Nero*, xi. xii.; *Titus*, vii.; *Dom.* iv.; D. Cass. 65. 25; Spart. *Hadr.* vii.; D. Cass. 68. 10, 15; Capitol. *M. Anton.* vi.; but cp. Suet. *Tib.* xlvii.; Tac. *Hist.* ii. 62; D. Cass. 66. 15; Suet. *Octav.* xliv.; D. Cass. 54. 2; 68. 2; Capitol. *Anton. P.* xii.

needy.[1] Public calamities were relieved again and again by imperial aid and private charity.[2] The love of wealth was strong, but a spirit of benevolence was in the air, even in the days of Juvenal; and the constant invectives of poet or philosopher against wealth and luxury are not so much the sign of a growing selfishness, as of a spreading sense of the duty of the fortunate to the miserable. Although the literary men seem never to have thought of any economic solution of the social problem, through the tapping of fresh sources of wealth from which all might draw, yet there can be no doubt that there was, at least in provincial cities, a great industrial movement in the Antonine age, which gave wealth to some, and a respectable competence to many. The opulent freedman and the contented artisan have left many a memorial in the inscriptions. Yet the movement had not solved the social problem in the days of Lucian, as it has not solved it after seventeen centuries. The cry of the poor against the selfish rich, which rings in the ears of the detached man of letters at the end of the Antonine age, will still ring in the ears of the ascetic Salvianus, when the Germans have passed the Rhine.[3]

The scorn and hatred of Juvenal for wealth and its vices is natural to a class which was too proud to struggle out of poverty, by engaging in the industries which it despised. And the freedman, who occupied the vacant field, and rose to opulence, is even more an object of hatred to Juvenal and Martial than the recreant noble or the stingy patron. He was an alien of servile birth, and he had made himself wealthy by the usual method of thinking of nothing but gold. These men, who were not even free Romans, had mastered the power which commands the allegiance of the world. The rise of this new class to wealth and importance probably irritated men of Juvenal's type more than any other sign of social injustice in their time. And the Trimalchio of Petronius, a man of low, tainted origin, the creature of economic accident, whose one faith is in the power of money, who boasts of his fortune as if it had been won by real talent or honourable

[1] Victor. *Epit.* 12; Spart. *Hadr.* vii. § 12; Capitol. *M. Anton.* xxvi.; *Ant. P.* viii.; D. Cass. 68. 5; *Orelli Henz.* 4365, 7244; Friedländer, *Petron. Einleit.* 49; Duruy, v. 429; iv. 787; Boissier, *Rel. Rom.* ii. 208; cf. Plin. *Ep.* ix. 30.

[2] Tac. *Ann.* xiv. 62; ii. 47, 48.

[3] Salv. *De Gub. Dei,* v. 30; *Ad Eccles.* iv. 22.

service, who expends it with coarse ostentation and a ludicrous affectation of cultivated taste, may be tolerated in literature, if not in actual life, for the charm of a certain kindly bonhomie and honest vulgarity, which the art of Petronius has thrown around him. Yet, after all, we must concede to Juvenal and Martial, that such a person is always a somewhat unpleasing social product. But the subject is so important that it claims a chapter to itself. And, fortunately for us and our readers, the new freedmen were not all of the type of Trimalchio.

CHAPTER III

THE SOCIETY OF THE FREEDMEN

THE historian, who is occupied with war and politics, and the fate of princes and nobles, is apt to lose sight of great silent movements in the dim masses of society. And, in the history of the early Empire, the deadly conflict between the Emperor and the Senate, the carnival of luxury, and the tragic close of so many reigns, have diverted attention from social changes of immense moment. Not the least important of these was the rise of the freedmen, in the face of the most violent prejudice, both popular and aristocratic. And literature has thrown its whole weight on the side of prejudice, and given full vent alike to the scorn of the noble, and to the hate and envy of the plebeian. The movement, indeed, was so swift and far spreading that old conservative instincts might well be alarmed. Everywhere in the inscriptions freedmen are seen rising to wealth and consequence throughout the provinces, as well as in Italy, and winning popularity and influence by profuse benefactions to colleges and municipalities. In almost every district of the Roman Empire the order of the Augustales, which was composed to a great extent of wealthy freedmen,[1] has left its memorials. "Freedman's wealth" in Martial's day had become a proverb.[2] Not only are they crowding all the meaner trades, from which Roman pride shrank contemptuously, but, by industry, shrewdness, and speculative daring, they are becoming great capitalists and landowners on a senatorial scale. The Trimalchio of Petronius, who has not

[1] On the Augustales *v. Orell. Henz.* ii. p. 197; iii. p. 427; Friedländer, *Cena Trim. Einl.* p. 39; Marq. *Röm. Staatsverw.* i. 513 sqq.; Nessling, *De Seviris Augustalibus.*

[2] v. 13, 6, et libertinas arca flagellat opes; cf. Sen. *Ep.* 27, § 5, patrimonium libertini.

even seen some of his estates,[1] if we allow for some artistic exaggeration, is undoubtedly the representative of a great class. In the reign of Nero, a debate arose in the Senate on the insolence and misconduct of freedmen.[2] And it was argued by those opposed to any violent measures of repression, that the class was widely diffused; they were found in overwhelming numbers in the city tribes, in the lower offices of the civil service, in the establishments of the magistrates and priests; a considerable number even of the knights and Senate drew their origin from this source. If freedmen were marked off sharply as a separate grade, the scanty numbers of the freeborn would be revealed. In the reigns of Claudius and Nero especially, freedmen rose to the highest places in the imperial service, sometimes by unquestionable knowledge, tact, and ability, sometimes by less creditable arts. The promotion of a Narcissus or a Pallas was also a stroke of policy, the assertion of the prince's independence of a jealous nobility. The rule of the freedmen was a bitter memory to the Senate.[3] The scorn of Pliny for Pallas expresses the long pent-up feelings of his order; it is a belated vengeance for the humiliation they endured in the evil days when they heaped ridiculous flattery on the favourite, and voted him a fortune and a statue.[4] Some part of the joy with which the accession of Trajan was hailed by the aristocracy was due to the hope that the despised interlopers would be relegated to their proper obscurity. Tacitus is undoubtedly glancing at the Claudian régime when he grimly congratulates the Germans on the fact that their freedmen are little above the level of slaves, that they have seldom any power in the family, and never in the State.[5]

It shows the immense force of old Roman conservatism and of social prejudice which is the same from age to age, when men so cultivated, yet of such widely different temperament and associations as Pliny and Tacitus, Juvenal and Martial [6] and Petronius, denounce or ridicule an irresistible social movement. We can now see that the rise of the

[1] Petron. *Sat.* 48.

[2] Tac. *Ann.* xiii. 27, si separarentur libertini manifestam fore penuriam ingenuorum.

[3] Plin. *Paneg.* 88.

[4] Id. *Ep.* vii. 29; viii. 6.

[5] Tac. *Germ.* 25, liberti non multum supra servos sunt, raro aliquod momentum in domo, nunquam in civitate.

[6] Mart. ii. 29; iii. 29; xi. 37; iii. 82; v. 14.

emancipated slave was not only inevitable, but that it was, on the whole, salutary and rich in promise for the future. The slave class of antiquity really corresponded to our free labouring class. But, unlike the mass of our artisans, it contained many who, from accident of birth and education, had a skill and knowledge which their masters often did not possess.[1] The slaves who came from the ancient seats of civilisation in the East are not to be compared with the dark gross races who seem to be stamped by nature as of an inferior breed. This frequent mental and moral equality of the Roman slave with his master had forced itself upon men of the detached philosophic class, like Seneca, and on kindly aristocrats, like Pliny.[2] It must have been hard to sit long hours in the library beside a cultivated slave-amanuensis, or to discuss the management of lands and mines and quarries with a shrewd, well-informed slave-agent, or to be charmed by the grace and wit of some fair, frail daughter of Ionia, without having some doubts raised as to the eternal justice of such an institution. Nay, it is certain that slaves were often treated as friends,[3] and received freedom and a liberal bequest at their master's death. Many educated slaves, as we have seen, rose to distinction and fortune as teachers and physicians.[4] But the field of trade and industry was the most open and the most tempting. The Senator was forbidden, down to the last age of the Empire, both by law and sentiment, to increase his fortune by commerce.[5] The plebeian, saturated with Roman prejudice, looking for support to the granaries of the state or the dole of the wealthy patron, turned with disdain from occupations which are in our days thought innocent, if not honourable. Juvenal feels almost as much scorn for the auctioneer and undertaker as he has for the pander, and treats almost as a criminal the merchant who braves the wintry Aegean with a cargo of wine from Crete.[6] His friend Umbricius, worsted in the social struggle, and preparing to quit Rome for a retreat in Campania, among the other objects of his plebeian scorn, is

[1] Suet. *Ill. Gram.* xiii., xvii., xx.; cf. Marq. *Priv.* i. 158.

[2] Sen. *Ep.* 47, § 1; *De Clem.* i. 18, 3; *De Ben.* iii. 21; *Ep.* 77, § 31; Plin. *Ep.* viii. 16, 1; iii. 19, 7; ii. 17, 9; cf. Juv. xiv. 16.

[3] Sen. *Ep.* 47, servi sunt, immo humiles amici. Cf. Macrob. *Sat.* i. 11, 12; Eurip. *Ion*, 854; *Helen.* 730; Wallon, *L'Esclav.* iii. 22.

[4] *v.* supra, p. 92.

[5] D. Cass. 69. 16; *C. Th.* xiii. 1, 21; Friedl. *Sittengesch.* i. 197.

[6] Juv. xiv. 270.

specially disgusted with the low tribe who contract for the building of a house, or who farm the dues of a port or undertake to cleanse a river-bed.[1] There is no room left in Rome for men who will not soil themselves with such sordid trades. Manifestly, if the satirist is not burlesquing the feeling of his class, there was plenty of room left for the vigorous freedman who could accept Vespasian's motto that no gain is unsavoury.[2] But those men had not only commercial tact and ability, the wit to see where money was to be made by seizing new openings and unoccupied fields for enterprise; they had also among them men of great ambitions, men capable of great affairs. It required no common deftness, suppleness, and vigilant energy for an old slave to work his way upwards through the grades of the imperial chancery, to thread the maze of deadly intrigue, in the reigns of Claudius or Nero, and to emerge at last as master of the palace. Yet one of these freedmen ministers, when he died, had served ten emperors, six of whom had come to a violent end.[3] That a class so despised and depressed should rise to control the trade, and even the administration of the Empire, furnishes a presumption that they were needed, and that they were not unworthy of their destiny.

Yet however inevitable, or even desirable, this great revolution may seem to the cool critic of the twentieth century, it is possible that, had he lived in the first, he might have denounced it as vigorously as Juvenal. The literary and artistic spirit, often living in a past golden age, and remotely detached from the movements going on around it, is prone to regard them with uneasy suspicion. It is moved by sacred sentiment, by memories and distant ideals, by fastidious taste, which expresses itself often with passionate hatred for what seems to it revolutionary sacrilege. It is also apt to fasten on the more grotesque and vulgar traits of any great popular movement, and to use a finished skill in making it ridiculous. It was in this way that literature treated the freedmen. They had many gross and palpable faults; they were old slaves and Orientals; as they rose in the world they were eager for money, and they got it; they were, many of them, naturally vulgar, and they paraded their new wealth with execrable taste, and

[1] Juv. iii. 32. [2] Suet. *Vesp.* xxiii. [3] Stat. *Silv.* iii. 3, 83, Tu toties mutata ducum juga rite tulisti Integer, etc.

trampled on better, though poorer, men than themselves. Juvenal and Martial, by birth and associations, have little in common with that accomplished exquisite of the Neronian circle who has painted with the power of careless genius the household of the *parvenu* Trimalchio. Yet they have an equal scorn or detestation for the new man who was forcing his way from the lowest debasement of servile life to fortune and power. But the embittered man of letters, humiliated by poverty, yet brimful of Roman pride, avenges his ideals with a rougher, heavier hand than the Epicurean noble, who had joined in the "Noctes Neronis" with a delicate, scornful cynicism, who was too disillusioned, and too fastidiously contemptuous, to waste anger on what he despised. Juvenal would blast and wither the objects of his hatred. Petronius takes the surer method of making these people supremely ridiculous. The feeling of men like Juvenal and Martial is a mixture of contempt and envy and outraged taste. The Grub Street man of letters in those days despised plodding industry because he dearly loved fits of idleness; he hated wealth because he was poor. The polished man of the world was alternately amused and disgusted by the spectacle of sudden fortune accumulated by happy chance or unscrupulous arts, with no tradition of dignity to gild its grossness, yet affecting and burlesquing the tastes of a world from which it was separated by an impassable gulf. There is more moral sentiment, more old Roman feeling, in the declamation of Juvenal than in the cold artistic scorn of the *Satiricon;* there is also more personal and class feeling. The triumph of mere money is to Juvenal a personal affront as well as a moral catastrophe. Poverty now makes a man ridiculous.[1] It blocks the path of the finest merit. The rich freedman who claims the foremost place at a levée is equally objectionable because he was born on the Euphrates, and because he is the owner of five taverns which yield HS.400,000 a year.[2] The impoverished knight must quit his old place on the benches to make way for some auctioneer or pimp, some old slave from the Nile who stalks in with purple robes and bejewelled fingers, and hair reeking with unguents.[3] The only refuge

[1] Juv. iii. 153, Nil habet infelix paupertas durius in se, Quam quod ridiculos homines facit; 164.

[2] Id. i. 104.

[3] Id. i. 26; iv. 108.

will soon be some half-deserted village on old-fashioned Sabine ground, where the country folk sit side by side in the same white tunics with their aediles in the grassy theatre.[1] It is evident from Juvenal, Martial, and Petronius that the popular hostility to the new men was partly the result of envy at their success, partly of disgust at their parade of it. Juvenal and Martial are often probably dressing up the rough epigrams of the crowd. We can almost hear the contemptuous growl as one of these people, suspected of a dark crime, sweeps by in his downy sedan. That other noble knight used to hawk the cheap fish of his native Egypt, and now possesses a palace towering over the Forum, with far-spreading colonnades and acres of shady groves.[2] A eunuch minister has reared a pile which out-tops the Capitol.[3] Fellows who used to blow the horn in the circus of country towns now give gladiatorial shows themselves.[4] Prejudice or envy may not improbably have invented some of the tales of crime and turpitude by which these fortunes had been won. Rome was a city of poisonous rumour. Yet slavery was not a nursery of virtue, and the *Satiricon* leaves the impression that the emancipated slave too often imitated the vices of his master. The poisoner, the perjurer, the minion, were probably to be found in the rising class. After their kind in all ages, they looked down with vulgar insolence on those less fortunate or more scrupulous. When they rose to the highest place, the imperial freedmen were often involved in peculation and criminal intrigue.[5] Yet, after all reservations, the ascent of the freedmen remains a great and beneficent revolution. The very reasons which made Juvenal hate it most are its best justification to a modern mind. It gave hope of a future to the slave; by creating a free industrial class, it helped to break down the cramped social ideal of the slave-owner and the soldier; it planted in every municipality a vigorous mercantile class, who were often excellent and generous citizens. Above all, it asserted the dignity of man. The vehement iteration of Juvenal is the best testimony to the sweep and force of the movement. And

[1] Juv. iii. 173.
[2] Id. iv. 5, 23; vii. 180.
[3] Id. xiv. 91, Ut spado vincebat Capitolia nostra Posides; cf. Suet. *Claud.* xxviii.; Plin. *H.N.* xxxi. 2.
[4] Juv. iii. 34 sqq.
[5] Tac. *Ann.* xi. 37; xii. 25, 65; xi. 29; Suet. *Octav.* lxvii.; D. Cass. lix. 29.

the later student of Roman society cannot afford to neglect a great social upheaval which, in an aristocratic society, dominated by pride of class and race, made an Oriental slave first minister of the greatest monarchy in history, while it placed men of servile origin in command of nearly all the industrial arts and commerce of the time.

The reign of the freedman in public affairs began with the foundation of the Empire, when Julius Caesar installed some of his household as officers of the mint.[1] The emperor in the first century was, theoretically at least, only the first citizen, and his household was modelled on the fashion of other great houses. In the management of those vast senatorial estates, which were often scattered over three continents, there was need of an elaborate organisation, and freedmen of education and business capacity were employed to administer such private realms. And in the organisation of a great household, there was a hierarchy of office which offered a career to the shrewd and trustworthy slave. Many such careers can be traced in the inscriptions, from the post of valet or groom of the bedchamber, through the offices of master of the jewels and the wardrobe, superintendent of the carriages or the vineyards, up to the highest financial control.[2]

During the first century the same system was transferred to the imperial administration. It suited the cautious policy of Augustus to disguise his vast powers under the quiet exterior of an ordinary noble; and the freedmen of his household carried on the business of the State. He sternly punished any excesses or treachery among his servants.[3] Tiberius gave them little power, until his character began to deteriorate.[4] Under Caligula, Claudius, and Nero, the imperial freedmen attained their greatest ascendency. Callistus, Narcissus, and Pallas rose to the rank of great ministers, and, in the reign of Claudius, were practically masters of the world. They accumulated enormous wealth by abusing their power, and making a traffic in civic rights, in places or pardons. Polyclitus, who was sent to compose the troubles in Britain in 61 A.D., travelled with an enormous train, and gave the provinces an exhibition of the arrogance of their servile masters.[5]

[1] Suet. *Jul. Caes.* lxxvi.; cf. Friedl. *Sittengesch.* i. 56 sqq.

[2] For such a career cf. *Or. Henz.* 6344.

[3] Suet. *Octav.* lxvii.

[4] Tac. *Ann.* iv. 6.

[5] *Ib.* xiv. 39.

Helius was left to carry on the government during Nero's theatrical travels, and the exhibitions of his artistic skill in Greece.[1] Galba put to death two of the great freedmen of Nero's reign, but himself fell under the influence of others as corrupt and arrogant, and he showered the honours of rank on the infamous Icelus.[2]

It is curious that it was left for Vitellius to break the reign of the freedmen by assigning offices in the imperial bureaux to the knights, the policy which was said to have been recommended by Maecenas,[3] and which was destined to prevail in the second century. But the change was very incomplete, and the brief tragic reign of Vitellius was disgraced by the ascendency for a time of his minion Asiaticus, whom the Emperor raised to the highest honours, then sold into a troop of wandering gladiators, and finally received back again into freedom and favour.[4] The policy of the Flavian dynasty in the employment of freedmen is rather ambiguous. Vespasian is charged with having elevated Hormus, a disreputable member of the class, and with having appointed to places of trust the most rapacious agents.[5] But this is probably a calumny of the Neronian and Othonian circle who defamed their conqueror. Under Domitian, the freedmen, Entellus and Abascantus, held two of the great secretaryships. But it is distinctly recorded that Domitian distributed offices impartially between the freedmen and the knights.[6] On the accession of Trajan, Pliny, in his Panegyric, exults in the fall of the freedmen from the highest place.[7] Yet Hadrian is said to have procured his selection as emperor by carefully cultivating the favour of Trajan's freedmen. Hadrian, in reorganising the imperial administration, and founding the bureaucratic system, which was finally elaborated by Diocletian and Constantine, practically confined the tenure of the three great secretaryships to men of equestrian rank. Among his secretaries was the historian Suetonius.[8] Antoninus Pius severely repressed men of servile origin in the interest of pure

[1] Suet. *Nero*, xxiii.

[2] D. Cass. lxiv. 3; Suet. *Galba*, xiv.; Plut. *Galba*, c. 17.

[3] D. Cass. lii. 25; Tac. *Hist.* i. 58, Vitellius ministeria principatus per libertos agi solita in equites Romanos disponit.

[4] Suet. *Vitell.* xii. [5] Id. *Vesp.* xvi.

[6] Id. *Dom.* vii. quaedam ex maximis officiis inter libertinos equitesque communicavit.

[7] Plin. *Paneg.* 88.

[8] Spart. *Hadr.* iv., xxi.; Macé, *Suétone*, p. 91.

administration;[1] but they regained some influence for a time under M. Aurelius, and rose still higher under his infamous son.

The position of freedmen in the imperial administration was partly, as we have seen, a tradition of aristocratic households. The emperor employed his freedmen to write his despatches and administer the finances of the Empire, as he would have used them to write his private letters or to manage his private estates. But, in the long conflict between the prince and the Senate, the employment of trusted freedmen in imperial affairs was also a measure of policy. It was meant to teach the nobles that the Empire could be administered without their aid.[2] Nor was the confidence of the Emperor in his humble subordinates unjustified. The eulogies of the great freedmen in Seneca and Statius, even if they be exaggerated, leave the impression that a Polybius, a Claudius Etruscus, or an Abascantus were, in many respects, worthy of their high place. The provinces were, on the whole, well governed and happy in the very years when the capital was seething with conspiracy, and racked with the horrors of confiscation and massacre. This must have been chiefly due to the knowledge, tact, and ability of the great officials of the palace. Although of servile origin, they must have belonged to that considerable class of educated slaves who, along with the versatility and tact of the Hellenic East, brought to their task also a knowledge and a literary and linguistic skill which were not common among Roman knights. The three imperial secretaryships, *a rationibus*, *a libellis*, and *ab epistulis*, covered a vast field of administration, and the duties of these great ministries could only have been performed by men of great industry, talent, and diplomatic adroitness.[3] The Polybius to whom Seneca, from his exile in Sardinia, wrote a consolatory letter on the death of his brother, was the successor of Callistus, as secretary of petitions, in the reign of Claudius, and also the emperor's adviser of studies. Seneca magnifies the dignity, and also the burden, of his great rank, which demands an abnegation of all the ordinary pleasures of life.[4] A man has no time to indulge a private grief who has to study and arrange for the Emperor's decision thousands of appeals,

[1] Capitol. *Ant. P.* vi., xi.
[2] Friedl. *Sittengesch.* i. 56.
[3] *Ib.* i. p. 83.
[4] Sen. *Ad Polyb.* vi. vii.

coming from every quarter of the world. Yet this busy man could find time for literary work, and his translations from the Greek are lauded by the philosopher with an enthusiasm of which the cruelty of time does not allow us to estimate the value.[1] The panegyric on Claudius Etruscus, composed by Statius, records an even more remarkable career.[2] Claudius Etruscus died at the age of eighty, in the reign of Domitian, having served in various capacities under ten emperors,[3] six of whom had died by a violent death. It was a strangely romantic life, to which we could hardly find a parallel in the most democratic community in modern times. Claudius, a Smyrniote slave,[4] in the household of Tiberius, was emancipated and promoted by that Emperor. He followed the train of Caligula to Gaul,[5] rose to higher rank under Claudius, and, probably in Nero's reign, on the retirement of Pallas, was appointed to that financial office of which the world-wide cares are pompously described by the poet biographer.[6] The gold of Iberian mines, the harvests of Egypt, the fleeces of Tarentine flocks, pearls from the depths of Eastern seas, the ivory tribute of the Indies, all the wealth wafted to Rome by every wind, are committed to his keeping. He had also the task of disbursing a vast revenue for the support of the populace, for roads and bulwarks against the sea, for the splendour of temples and palaces.[7] Such cares left space only for brief slumber and hasty meals; there was none for pleasure. Yet Claudius had the supreme satisfaction of wielding enormous power, and he occasionally shared in its splendour. The poor slave from the Hermus had a place in the "Idumaean triumph" of Vespasian, which his quiet labours had prepared, and he was raised by that emperor to the benches of the knights.[8] The only check in that prosperous course seems to have been a brief exile to the shores of Campania in the reign of Domitian.[9]

Abascantus,[10] the secretary *ab epistulis* of Domitian's reign, has also been commemorated by Statius. That great office which controlled the imperial correspondence with all parts of

[1] Sen. *Ad Polyb.* xi.
[2] Statius, *Silv.* iii. 3.
[3] *Ib.* 66, Tibereia primum Aula tibi —Panditur.
[4] *Ib.* 60.
[5] *Ib.* 70.
[6] *Ib.* 86.
[7] *Ib.* 100.
[8] *Ib.* 145.
[9] Mart. vi. 83; Stat. *Silv.* iii. 160.
[10] As to the form of his name *v.* Markland's *Statius*, p. 238.

the world, was generally held by freedmen in the first century. Narcissus, in the reign of Claudius, first made it a great ministry.[1] Down to the reign of Hadrian the despatches both in Greek and Latin were under a single superintendence. But, in the reorganisation of the service in the second century, it was found necessary, from the growing complication of business, to create two departments of imperial correspondence.[2] Men of rank held the secretaryship from the end of the first century. Titinius Capito, one of Pliny's circle, filled the office under Domitian; Suetonius was appointed by Hadrian.[3] And during the Antonine age, the secretaries were often men of literary distinction.[4] Abascantus, the freedman secretary in the Silvae, had upon his shoulders, according to the poet, the whole weight of the correspondence with both East and West.[5] He received the laurelled despatches from the Euphrates, the Danube, and the Rhine; he had to watch the distribution of military grades and commands. He must keep himself informed of a thousand things affecting the fortunes of the subject peoples. Yet this powerful minister retained his native modesty with his growing fortune. His household was distinguished by all the sobriety and frugality of an Apulian or Sabine home.[6] He could be lavish, however, at the call of love or loyalty. He gave his wife Priscilla an almost royal burial.[7] Embalmed with all the spices and fragrant odours of the East, and canopied with purple, her body was borne to her last stately home of marble on the Appian Way.[8]

Some of the great imperial freedmen were of less unexceptionable character than Claudius Etruscus and Abascantus, and had a more troubled career. Callistus, Narcissus, and Pallas, were deeply involved in the intrigues and crimes connected with the history of Messalina and Agrippina. Callistus had a part in the murder of Caligula, and prolonged his power in the following reign. Narcissus revealed the shameless marriage of Messalina with Silius, and, forestalling the vacillation of Claudius, had the imperial harlot ruthlessly struck down as she lay grovelling in the gardens of Lucullus.[9]

[1] Macé, *Suétone*, p. 91; cf. Tac. *Ann.* xi. 33.

[2] Macé, 92, 93; Friedl. *Sittengesch.* i. 86, 87.

[3] Plin. *Ep.* viii. 12; *C.I.L.* vi. 798; Macé, pp. 89, 115.

[4] Macé, pp. 90, 116.

[5] Stat. *Silv.* v. 1, 80.

[6] *Ib.* v. 118 sqq.

[7] *Ib.* v. 210.

[8] Friedl. *Sittengesch.* i. 88.

[9] Tac. *Ann.* xi. 30, 37, 38.

But he incurred the enmity of a more formidable woman even than Messalina, and his long career of plunder was ended by suicide.[1] Pallas had an even longer and more successful, but a not less infamous and tragic career.[2] Of all the great freedmen, probably none approached him in magnificent insolence. When he was impeached along with Burrus, on a groundless charge of treason, and when some of his freedmen were called in evidence as his supposed accomplices, the old slave answered that he had never degraded his voice by speaking in such company.[3] Never, even in those days of self-abasement, did the Senate sink so low as in its grovelling homage to the servile minister. At a meeting of the august body in the year 52, the consul designate made a proposal, which was seconded by a Scipio, that the praetorian insignia, and a sum of HS.15,000,000, should be offered to Pallas, together with the thanks of the state that the descendant of the ancient kings of Arcadia had thought less of his illustrious race than of the common weal, and had deigned to be enrolled in the service of the prince![4] When Claudius reported that his minister was satisfied with the compliment, and prayed to be allowed to remain in his former poverty, a senatorial decree, engraved on bronze, was set up to commemorate the old-fashioned frugality of the owner of HS.300,000,000! His wealth was gained during a career of enormous power in the worst days of the Empire. He was one of the lovers of Agrippina,[5] and, when he made her empress on the death of Messalina, two kindred spirits for a time ruled the Roman world. He gratified his patroness by securing the adoption of Nero by Claudius, and he was probably an accomplice in that emperor's murder. But his fate was involved with that of Agrippina. When Nero resolved to shake off the tyranny of that awful woman, his first step was to remove the haughty freedman from his offices.[6] Pallas left the palace in the second year of Nero's reign. For seven years he lived on undisturbed. But at last his vast wealth, which had become a proverb, became too tempting to the spendthrift prince, and Pallas was quietly removed by poison.[7]

[1] Tac. *Ann.* xii. 57; xiii. 1.
[2] *Ib.* xii. 25, 65.
[3] *Ib.* xiii. 23.
[4] *Ib.* xii. 53; Plin. *Ep.* viii. 6.
[5] Tac. *Ann.* xii. 25, 65.
[6] *Ib.* xiii. 14.
[7] *Ib.* xiv. 65; Suet. *Nero*, xxxv.; D. Cass. 62. 14.

The wealth of freedmen became proverbial, and the fortunes of Pallas and Narcissus reached a figure hardly ever surpassed even by the most colossal senatorial estates.[1] The means by which this wealth was gained might easily be inferred by any one acquainted with the inner history of the times. The manner of it may be read in the life of Elagabalus, whose freedman Zoticus, the son of a cook at Smyrna, piled up vast riches by levying a payment, each time he quitted the presence, for his report of the emperor's threats or promises or intentions.[2] In the administration of great provinces, in the distribution of countless places of trust, in the chaos of years of delation, confiscation, and massacre, there must have been endless opportunities for self-enrichment, without incurring the dangers of open malversation. Statius extols the simple tastes and frugality of his heroes Abascantus and Claudius Etruscus, and yet he describes them as lavishing money on baths and tombs and funeral pomp. The truth is that, as a mere matter of policy, these wealthy aliens, who were never loved by a jealous aristocracy, had to justify their huge fortunes by a sumptuous splendour. The elder Pliny has commemorated the vapour baths of Posides, a Claudian freedman, and the thirty pillars of priceless onyx which adorned the dining saloon of Callistus.[3] A bijou bath of the younger Claudius Etruscus seems to have been a miracle of costly beauty. The dome, through which a brilliant light streamed upon the floor, was covered with scenes in rich mosaic. The water gushed from pipes of silver into silver basins, and the quarries of Numidia and Synnas contributed the various colours of their marbles.[4] The gardens of Entellus, with their purple clusters which defied the rigours of winter, seemed to Martial to outrival the legendary gardens of Phaeacia.[5] In the suburbs, hard by the Tiburtine way, rose that defiant monument of Pallas, bearing the decree of the Senate, which aroused the angry scorn of the younger Pliny.[6]

The life of one of these imperial slave ministers was a strangely romantic career which has surely been seldom matched in the history of human fortunes. Exposed and sold

[1] Marq. *Röm. St.* ii. p. 55; Duruy, v. p. 598; Friedl. *Sittengesch.* i. p. 192; cf. Olympiod. *ap.* Phot. § 44 (Müll. *Frag. Hist. Gr.* iv.).

[2] Ael. Lamprid. *Heliogab.* x.; cf. Capitol. *Anton. P.* xi.; Suet. *Claud.* xxviii.

[3] Plin. *H.N.* xxxi. 2; xxxvi. 12.

[4] Statius, *Silv.* i. 5, 36; Mart. vi. 42, et certant vario decore saxa.

[5] Mart. viii. 68.

[6] Plin. *Ep.* vii. 29.

in early youth in the slave markets of Smyrna, Delos, or Puteoli, after an interval of ignominious servitude, installed as groom of the chambers, thence promoted, according to his aptitudes, to be keeper of the jewels, or tutor of the imperial heir, still further advanced to be director of the post, or to a place in the financial service, the freedman might end by receiving the honour of knighthood, the procuratorship of a province, or one of those great ministries which placed him in command of the Roman world. Yet we must not deceive ourselves as to his real position.[1] To the very end of the Empire, the fictions on which aristocratic power is largely based, retained their fascination. In the fifth century a Senate, whose ancestors were often originally of servile race, could pour their scorn on the eunuch ministers of the East.[2] And the decaying or *parvenu* Senate of the Flavians had, when they were free to express it, nothing but loathing for the reign of the freedmen.[3] These powerful but low-born officials are a curious example of what has been often seen in later times, the point-blank refusal, or the grudging concession, of social status to men wielding vast and substantial power. The younger Pliny, in his Panegyric on Trajan, glories in the preference shown under the new régime for young men of birth, and in his letters he vents all the long-suppressed scorn of his order for the Claudian freedmen. Even the emperors who freely employed their services, were chary of raising them to high social rank. Freedmen ministers were hardly ever admitted to the ranks of the Senate[4]; they were rarely present at its sittings, even at the very time when they were governing the world. Sacerdotal and military distinctions were seldom conferred upon any of them. They were sometimes invested with the insignia of praetorian or quaestorian rank.[5] A few were promoted to the dignity of knighthood, Icelus, Asiaticus, Hormus, and Claudius Etruscus[6]; but many a passage in Martial or Juvenal seems to show that ordinary equestrian rank was in those days a very doubtful distinction.[7] The emperors, as raised above all ranks, might not

[1] Friedl. *Sittengesch.* i. 75; *Or. Henz.* 6344.
[2] Claud. *In Eutrop.* ii. 137.
[3] Plin. *Paneg.* 88.
[4] Suet. *Nero*, xv. in curiam libertinorum filios diu non admisit.
[5] Tac. *Ann.* xi. 38; xii. 53.
[6] Suet. *Galba*, xiv.; Tac. *Hist.* ii. 57; iv. 39.
[7] Mart. iii. 29; v. 8, 14, 35, 23; cf. Friedl. *Sittengesch.* i. 212.

have been personally unwilling to elevate their creatures to the highest social grade.[1] But even the emperors, in matters of social prejudice, were not omnipotent.

Still, the men who could win the favours of an Agrippina and a Messalina, could not be extinguished by the most jealous social prejudice. The Roman Senate were ready, on occasion, to fawn on a Pallas or a Narcissus, to vote them money and insignia of rank, nor did they always refuse them their daughters in marriage. In the conflict which is so often seen between caste pride and the effective power of new wealth, the wealth and power not unfrequently prevail. The lex Julia prohibited the union of freedmen with daughters of a senatorial house.[2] Yet we know of several such marriages in the first century. The wife of the freedman Claudius Etruscus, was the sister of a consul who had held high command against the Dacians.[3] Priscilla, the wife of Abascantus, another minister of servile origin, belonged to the great consular family of the Antistii. Felix, the brother of Pallas, had married in succession three ladies of royal blood, one of them the granddaughter of Cleopatra.[4]

The women of this class, for generations, wielded, in their own way, a power which sometimes rivalled that of the men. These plebeian Aspasias are a puzzling class. With no recognised social position, with the double taint of servile origin and more than doubtful morals, they were often endowed with many charms and accomplishments, possessing a special attraction for bohemian men of letters. Their morals were the result of an uncertain social position, combined with personal attractions and education. To be excluded from good society by ignoble birth, yet to be more than its equal in culture, is a dangerous position, especially for women. Often of oriental extraction, these women were the most prominent votaries of the cults or superstitions which poured into Rome from the prolific East. Loose character and religious fervour were easily combined in antiquity. And the *demi-monde* of those days were ready to mourn passionately for Adonis and keep all the feasts of Isis or Jehovah, without

[1] Suet. *Claud.* c. xxviii.
[2] *Dig.* xxiii. 2, 44.
[3] Statius, iii. 3, 115.
[4] Id. v. 1, 53; Tac. *Hist.* v. 9; Suet. *Claud.* xxviii. Felicem . . . Judaeae proposuit—trium reginarum maritum.

scrupling to make a temple a place of assignation.[1] The history of the early Empire, it has been rather inaccurately said, shows no reign of mistresses. Yet some of the freedwomen have left their mark on that dark page of history. Claudius was the slave of women, and two of his mistresses lent their aid to Narcissus to compass the ruin of Messalina.[2] The one woman whom Nero really loved, and who loved him in return, was Acte, who had been bought in a slave market in Asia. She captured the heart of the Emperor in his early youth, and incurred the fierce jealousy of Agrippina, as she did, at a later date, that of the fair, ambitious Poppaea.[3] Acte was faithful to his memory even after the last awful scene in Phaon's gardens.[4] And, along with his two nurses, the despised freedwoman guarded his remains and laid the last of his line beside his ancestors. Caenis, the mistress who consoled Vespasian after his wife's death, without any attractions of youth or beauty, suited well the taste of the bourgeois Emperor. It was a rather sordid and prosaic union. And Caenis is said to have accumulated a fortune, and besmirched the honest Emperor's name, by a wholesale traffic in State secrets and appointments.[5] In the last years of our period a very different figure has been glorified by the art of Lucian. Panthea, the mistress of L. Verus, completely fascinated the imagination of Lucian when he saw her at Smyrna, during the visit of her lover to the East.[6] Lucian pictures her delicately chiselled beauty and grace of form by recalling the finest traits in the great masterpieces of Pheidias and Praxiteles and Calamis, of Euphranor and Polygnotus and Apelles; Panthea combines them all. She has a voice of a marvellous and mellow sweetness, which lingers in the ear with a haunting memory. And the soul was worthy of such a fair dwelling-place. In her love of music and poetry, combined with a masculine strength of intellect capable of handling the highest problems in politics or dialectic, she was a worthy successor of those elder daughters of Ionia whose

[1] Catull. x. 26; Tibull. i. 3, 33; Ov. *Ars Am.* iii. 635; cf. *Amor.* i. 8, 73; iii. 9, 33.

[2] Tac. *Ann.* xi. 29.

[3] *Ib.* xiii. 12, 46; xiv. 2; Suet. *Nero*, xxviii. Acten libertam paullum abfuit quin justo matrimonio sibi conjungeret.

[4] Suet. *Nero*, l.

[5] D. Cass. lxvi. 14.

[6] Luc. *Imag.* 10. See Croiset's *Lucien*, p. 273, on the *Imagines* as illustrating Lucian's power as a critic of art.

charm and strength drew a Socrates or a Pericles to their feet.[1] Surrounded by luxury and the pomp of imperial rank, and linked to a very unworthy lover, Panthea never lost her natural modesty and simple sweetness.

The great freedmen, who held the highest offices in the imperial service till the time of Hadrian with almost undisputed sway, are interesting by reason of the strangely romantic career of some of them. But these are very exceptional cases. In the bureaux of finance, it has been discovered from the inscriptions that the officials were all of equestrian rank. On the other hand, a great number of the provincial procurators were freedmen. And the agents of the Emperor's private fisc seem to have been nearly always drawn from this class. The lower grades of the civil service were full of them.[2] But to the student of society, the official freedmen are, as a class, not so interesting as their brethren who in these same years were making themselves masters of the trade and commercial capital of the Roman world. And the interest is heightened by the vivid art with which Petronius has ushered us into the very heart of this rather vulgar society. The *Satiricon* is to some extent a caricature. There were hosts of modest, estimable freedmen whose only record is in two or three lines on a funeral slab. Yet a caricature must have a foundation of truth, and a careful reader may discover the truth under the humorous exaggeration of Petronius.

The transition from the status of slave to that of freedman was perhaps not so abrupt and marked as we might at first sight suppose. It is probable that many a slave of the better and more intelligent class found little practical change in the tenor of his life when he received the touch of the wand before the praetor. Some, like Melissus, the free-born slave of Maecenas, actually rejected the proffered boon.[3] There was, of course, much cruelty to slaves in many Roman households, and the absolute power of a master, unrestrained by principle or kindly feeling, was an unmitigated curse till it was limited by the humane legislation of the second century.[4] But there must have been many houses, like that of the younger Pliny, where the slaves were treated, in Seneca's

[1] Xen. *Mem.* iii. 11; Plat. *Menex.* c. iv.

[2] Cf. Friedl. *Sittengesch.* i. 82.

[3] Suet. *De Ill. Gram.* xxi.

[4] Marq. *Priv.* i. 189; Denis, *Idées Morales*, ii. 208; Spart. *Hadr.* xvii.

phrase, as humble friends and real members of the family, where their marriages were fêted with general gaiety,[1] where their sicknesses were tenderly watched, and where they were truly mourned in death. The inscriptions reveal to us a better side of slave life, which is not so prominent in our literary authorities. There is many an inscription recording the love and faithfulness of the slave husband and wife, although not under those honoured names. And it is significant that on many of these tablets the honourable title of *conjunx* is taking the place of the old servile *contubernalis.* The inscriptions which testify to the mutual love of master and servant are hardly less numerous. In one a master speaks of a slave-child of four years as being dear to him as a son.[2] Another contains the memorial of a learned lady erected by her slave librarian.[3] Another records the love of a young noble for his nurse,[4] while another is the pathetic tribute of the nurse to her young charge, who died at five years of age. The whole city household of another great family subscribe from their humble savings for an affectionate memorial of their young mistress.[5] Seneca, in his humanitarian tone about slavery, represents a great moral movement, which was destined to express itself in legislation under the Antonines. And the energy with which Seneca denounced harsh or contemptuous conduct to these humble dependents had evidently behind it the force of a steadily growing sentiment. The master who abused his power was already beginning to be a marked man.[6]

Frequent manumissions were swelling the freedman class to enormous dimensions. The emancipation of slaves by dying bequest was not then, indeed, inspired by the same religious motive as in the Middle Ages. But it was often dictated by the natural, human wish to make some return to faithful servants, and to leave a memory of kindness behind. But without the voluntary generosity of the master, the slave could easily purchase his own freedom. The price of slaves varied enormously, according to their special aptitude and grade of service. It might range from £1700, in rare cases, to £10, or even less, in our money.[7] But taking the average price of

[1] Sen. *De Ben.* iii. 21; *Ep.* 47; Plin. *Ep.* ii. 17, 9; viii. 16; cf. Marq. *Priv.* i. 175.

[2] *Or.* 2808.

[3] *Ib.* 2874.

[4] *Ib.* 2816.

[5] *Ib.* 2862.

[6] Sen. *De Clem.* i. 18.

[7] Marq. *Priv.* i. 174.

ordinary slaves, one careful and frugal might sometimes save the cost of his freedom in a few years. The slave, especially if he had any special gift, or if he occupied a prominent position in the household, had many chances of adding to his *peculium*. But the commonest drudge might spare something from the daily allowance of food.[1] Others, like the cooks in Apuleius, might sell their perquisites from the remains of a banquet.[2] The door-keepers, a class notorious for their insolence in Martial's day,[3] often levied heavy tolls for admission to their master's presence. And good-natured visitors would not depart without leaving a gift to those who had done them service. It must also be remembered that the slave system of antiquity covered much of the ground of our modern industrial organisation. A great household, or a great estate, was a society almost complete in itself. And intelligent slaves were often entrusted with the entire management of certain departments.[4] The great rural properties had their quarries, brickworks, and mines; and manufactures of all kinds were carried on by servile industry, with slaves or freedmen as managers. The merchant, the banker, the contractor, the publisher, had to use, not only slave labour, but slave skill and superintendence.[5] The great household needed to be organised under chiefs. And on rural estates, down to the end of the Western Empire, the villicus or procurator was nearly always a man of servile origin.[6] In these various capacities, the trusted slave was often practically a partner, with a share of the profits, or he had a commission on the returns. Such a fortunate servant, by hoarding his *peculium*, might soon become a capitalist on his own account, and well able, if he chose, to purchase his freedom. His *peculium*, like that of the son *in manu patris*, was of course by law the property of his master. But the security of the *peculium* was the security for good service.[7] Thus a useful and favourite slave often easily became a freedman, sometimes by purchase, or, as often happened in the case of servants of the imperial house, by the free gift of

[1] Sen. *Ep.* 80, § 4, peculium suum quod comparaverunt ventre fraudato pro capite numerant.

[2] Apul. *Met.* x. 14; cf. Boissier, *Rel. Rom.* ii. 397.

[3] v. 22, 10, negat lasso janitor esse domi; Sen. *Nec. Inj.* xiv. cubicularii supercilium.

[4] Momms, *R. H.* ii. 380 (Tr.)

[5] Marq. *Priv.* i. 162 sq.

[6] *C. Th.* ix. 30, 2; ii. 30, 2.

[7] Marq. *Priv.* i. p. 163.

the lord. There are even cases on record where a slave was left heir of his master's property. Trimalchio boasted that he had been made by his master joint heir with the Emperor.[1]

The tie between patron and freedman was very close. The emancipated slave had often been a trusted favourite, and even a friend of the family, and his lord was under an obligation to provide for his future. The freedman frequently remained in the household, with probably little real change in his position. His patron owed him at least support and shelter. But he often gave him, besides, the means of an independent life, a farm, a shop, or capital to start in some trade.[2] In the time of Ovid, a freedman of M. Aurelius Cotta had more than once received from his patron the fortune of a knight, besides ample provision for his children.[3] A similar act of generosity, which was recklessly abused, is recorded by Martial.[4] By ancient law, as well as by sentiment, senators were forbidden to soil themselves by trade or usury.[5] But so inconvenient a prohibition was sure to be evaded. And probably the most frequent means of evasion was by entrusting senatorial capital to freedmen or clients, or even to the higher class of slaves.[6] When Trimalchio began to rise in the social scale, he gave up trade, and employed his capital in financing men of the freedman class.[7] These people, generally of Levantine origin, had the aptitude for commerce which has at all times been a characteristic of their race. And, in the time of the Empire, almost all trade and industry was in their hands. The tale of Petronius reveals the secret of their success. They value money beyond anything else; it is the one object of their lives. They frankly estimate a man's worth and character in terms of cash.[8] Keen, energetic, and unscrupulous, they will "pick a farthing out of a dung-heap with their teeth"; "lead turns to gold in their hands."[9] They are entirely of Vespasian's opinion that gold from any quarter, however unsavoury, "never smells." Taking the world as it was, in many respects they deserved to succeed. They were not, indeed, encumbered with dignity or self-respect. They

[1] Petron. *Sat.* 76.

[2] Marq. *Priv.* i. 165.

[3] *Ib.* p. 178, n.

[4] Mart. v. 70; cf. vii. 64.

[5] Liv. xxi. 63, quaestus omnis patribus indecorus visus; D. Cass. 69. 16; cf. *C. Th.* xiii. 1, 4; *v.* Godefroy's note.

[6] Plut. *Cat. Maj.* 21.

[7] Petron. 77, sustuli me de negotiatione et coepi libertos foenerare.

[8] Id. 77, assem habeas, assem valeas.

[9] Id. 43, paratus fuit quadrantem de stercore mordicus tollere:—in manu illius plumbum aurum fiebat.

had one goal, and they worked towards it with infinite industry and unfailing courage and self-confidence. Nothing daunts or dismays them. If a fleet of merchantmen, worth a large fortune, is lost in a storm, the freedman speculator will at once sell his wife's clothes and jewels, and start cheerfully on a fresh venture.[1] When his great ambition has been achieved, he enjoys its fruits after his kind in all ages. Excluded from the great world of hereditary culture, these people caricature its tastes, and imitate all its vices, without catching even a reflection of its charm and refinement. The selfish egotism of the dissipated noble might be bad enough, but it was sometimes veiled by a careless grace, or an occasional deference to lofty tradition. The selfishness and grossness of the upstart is naked and not ashamed, or we might almost say, it glories in its shame. Its luxury is a tasteless attempt to vie with the splendour of aristocratic banquets. The carver and the waiter perform their tasks to the beat of a deafening music. Art and literature are prostituted to the service of this vulgar parade of new wealth, and the divine Homer is profaned by a man who thinks that Hannibal fought in the Trojan War.[2] The conversation is of the true bourgeois tone, with all its emphasis on the obvious, its unctuous moralising, its platitudes consecrated by their antiquity.

It is this society which is drawn for us with such a sure, masterly hand, and with such graceful ease, by Petronius. The *Satiricon* is well known to be one of the great puzzles and mysteries in Roman literature. Scholars have held the most widely different opinions as to its date, its author, and its purpose. The scene has been laid in the reign of Augustus or of Tiberius, and, on the strength of a misinterpreted inscription, even as late as the reign of Alexander Severus.[3] Those who have attributed it to the friend and victim of Nero have been confronted with the silence of Quintilian, Juvenal, and Martial, with the silence of Tacitus as to any literary work by Petronius, whose character and end he has described with a curious sympathy and care.[4] It is only late critics of the lower empire, such as Macrobius,[5] and a dilettante aristocrat like Sidonius Apollinaris,[6] who pay any attention to this re-

[1] Petron. 76.
[2] Id. 50.
[3] *Or.* 1175; cf. Teuffel, *Rom. Lit.* ii. § 300, n. 4.
[4] Tac. *Ann.* xvi. 18, 19.
[5] Macrob. *Som. Scip.* i. 2, 8.
[6] Sidon. Apoll. *Carm.* ix. 268.

markable work of genius. And Sidonius seems to make its author a citizen of Marseilles.[1] Yet silence in such cases may be very deceptive. Martial and Statius never mention one another, and both might seem unknown to Tacitus. And Tacitus, after the fashion of the Roman aristocrat, in painting the character of Petronius, may not have thought it relevant or important to notice a light work such as the *Satiricon*, even if he had ever seen it. He does not think it worth while to mention the histories of the Emperor Claudius, the tragedies of Seneca, or the *Punica* of Silius Italicus.[2] Tacitus, like Thucydides, is too much absorbed in the social tragedy of his time to have any thought to spare for its artistic efforts. The rather shallow, easy-going Pliny has told us far more of social life in the reigns of Domitian and Trajan, its rural pleasures and its futile literary ambitions, than the great, gloomy historian who was absorbed in the vicissitudes of the deadly duel between the Senate and the Emperors. One thing is certain about the author of this famous piece—he was not a plebeian man about town, although it may be doubted whether M. Boissier is safe in maintaining that such a writer would not have chosen his own environment of the Suburra as the field for his imagination.[3] It is safer to seek for light on the social status of the author in the tone of his work. The *Satiricon* is emphatically the production of a cultivated aristocrat, who looks down with serene and amused scorn on the vulgar bourgeois world which he is painting. He is interested in it, but it is the interest of the detached, artistic observer, whose own world is very far off. Encolpius and Trimalchio and his coarse freedman friends are people with whom the author would never have dined, but whom, at a safe social distance, he found infinitely amusing as well as disgusting. He saw that a great social revolution was going on before his eyes, that the old slave minion, with estates in three continents, was becoming the rival of the great noble in wealth, that the new-sprung class were presenting to the world a vulgar caricature of the luxury in the palaces on the Esquiline. Probably he thought it all bad,[4] but the bad

[1] Sidon. Apoll. *Carm.* xxiii. 155, et te Massiliensium per hortos sacri stipitis, Arbiter, colonum Hellespontiaco parem Priapo, etc.

[2] Tac. *Ann.* xii. 8; xiii. 2; xv. 45, 60, 65; Tac. *Hist.* iii. 65.

[3] Boissier, *L'Opp.* p. 257, ce n'est pas la coutume qu'on mette son idéal près de soi.

[4] Petron. 88, at nos vino scortisque demersi ne paratas quidem artes audemus cognoscere, sed accusatores anti-

became worse when it was coarse and vulgar. The ignorant assumption of literary and artistic taste in Trimalchio must have been contrasted in the author's mind with many an evening at the palace, when Nero, in his better moods, would recite his far from contemptible verses, or his favourite passages from Euripides, and when the new style of Lucan would be balanced against that of the great old masters.[1] And the man who had been charmed with the sprightly grace of the stately and charming Poppaea may be forgiven for showing his hard contempt for Fortunata, who, in the middle of dinner, runs off to count the silver and deal out the slaves' share of the leavings, and returns to get drunk and fight with one of her guests.[2]

The motive of the work has been much debated. It has been thought a satire on the Neronian circle, and again an effort to gratify it, by a revelation of the corruptions of the plebeian world, the same impulse which drove Messalina to the brothel, and Nero to range the taverns at midnight.[3] It has been thought a satire on the insolence and grossness of Pallas and the freedmen of the Claudian régime which Nero detested, to amuse him with all their vulgar absurdities. Is it not possible that the writer was merely pleasing himself—that he was simply following the impulse of genius? Since the seventh century the work has only existed in fragments.[4] Who can tell how much the lost portions, if we possessed them, might affect our judgment of the object of the work? One thing is certain, its author was a very complex character, and would probably have smiled at some of the lumbering efforts to read his secret. Even though he may have had no lofty purpose, a weary man of pleasure may have wished to display, in its grossest, vulgarest form, the life of which he had tasted the pleasures, and which he had seen turning into Dead Sea fruit. He was probably a bad man in his conduct, worse perhaps in his imagination; and yet, by a strange contradiction, which is not unexampled in the history of character, he may have had dreams of a refined purity and temperance which tortured and embittered him by their contrast with actual life.

quitatis vitia tantum docemus et discimus. This rather applies to the higher cultivated class.

1 Petron. 118; cf. Boissier, *L'Opp.* 213.
2 Petron. 70, 67.
3 Juv. vi. 115; Suet. *Nero*, xxvi.
4 Teuffel. *Rom. Lit.* § 300, n. 1.

Out of the smoke of controversy, the conclusion seems to have emerged that the *Satiricon* is a work of Nero's reign, and that its author was in all probability that Caius Petronius who was Nero's close companion, and who fell a victim to the jealousy of Tigellinus. Not the least cogent proof of this is the literary criticism of the work. It is well known that Lucan, belonging to the Spanish family of the Senecas, had thrown off many of the conventions of Roman literature, and discarded the machinery of epic mythology in his *Pharsalia*. He had also incurred the literary jealousy of Nero. The attack in the *Satiricon* on Lucan's literary aberrations can hardly be mistaken. The old poet Eumolpus is introduced to defend the traditions of the past. And he gives a not very successful demonstration, in 285 verses, of the manner in which the subject should have been treated, with all the scenery and machinery of orthodox epic.[1] This specimen of conservative taste is the least happy part of the work.

Such evidence is reinforced by the harmony of the whole tone of the *Satiricon* with the clear-cut character of Petronius in Tacitus. There was evidently a singular fascination about this man, which, in spite of his wasted, self-indulgent life, was keenly felt by the severe historian. Petronius was capable of great things, but in an age of wild licence he deliberately devoted his brilliant talent to making sensuality a fine art. Like Otho, who belonged to the same circle, he showed, as consul and in the government of Bithynia, that a man of pleasure could be equal to great affairs.[2] After this single digression from the scheme of the voluptuary, he returned to his pleasures, and became an arbiter in all questions of sensual taste, from whose decision there was no appeal. His ascendency over the Emperor drew upon him the fatal enmity of Tigellinus. Petronius was doomed. It was a time when not even the form of justice was used to veil the caprices of tyranny, and Petronius determined not to endure a long suspense when the issue was certain. He had gone as far as

[1] Petron. 118, 119; cf. Boissier, *L'Opp.* p. 239. Other proofs of the date of the *Satiricon* are the occurrence of names like Apelles and Menecrates, c. 64, 73; cf. Suet. *Calig.* 33; *Nero*, 30; Friedl. *Cena Trim. Einl.* 9; the reflections on decline of oratory, *Sat.* 1; cf. Tac. *Dial. Or.* c. 35; the invention of a peculiar glass, which belongs to the reign of Tiberius, cf. Plin. *H. N.* xxxvi. 66; D. Cass. 57. 21 ad fin.

[2] Tac. *Ann.* xvi. 18, vigentem se ac parem negotiis ostendit.

Cumae to attend the Emperor. There he was stopped. He retired to his chamber and had his veins alternately opened and rebound, meanwhile conversing with his friends or listening to light verses, not, as the fashion then was, seeking consolation from a Stoic director on the issues of life and death. He rewarded some of his slaves; others he had flogged before his eyes. After a banquet he fell calmly into his last sleep. In his will there was none of the craven adulation by which the victim often strove to save his heirs from imperial rapacity. He broke his most precious myrrhine vase, to prevent its being added to Nero's treasures.[1] His only bequest to the Emperor was a stinging catalogue of his secret and nameless sins.[2]

The *Satiricon*, as we have it, is only a fragment, containing parts of two books, out of a total of sixteen. It is full of humorous exaggeration and wild Aristophanic fun, along with, here and there, very subtle and refined delineation of character. But, except in the famous dinner of Trimalchio, there are few signs of regular construction or closeness of texture in plot and incident. Even if we had the whole, it might have been difficult to decipher its motive or to unlock the secret of the author's character. We can only be sure that he was a man of genius, and that he was interested in the intellectual pursuits and tendencies of his time, as well as in its vices and follies. We may perhaps surmise that he was at once perverted and disillusioned, alternately fascinated and disgusted by the worship of the flesh and its lusts in that evil time. He is not, as has been sometimes said, utterly devoid of a moral sense. Occasionally he shows a gleam of nobler feeling, a sense of the *lacrimae rerum*, as in that passage where the corpse of the shipwrecked Lichas is washed ashore. "Somewhere a wife is quietly awaiting him, or a father or a son, with no thought of storm; some one whom he kissed on leaving. . . . He had examined the accounts of his estates, he had pictured to himself the day of his return to his home. And now he lies, O ye gods, how far from the goal of his hopes. But the sea is not the only mocker of the hopes of men. If you reckon well, there is

[1] Plin. *H. N.* xxxvii. 7 (20), T. Petronius consularis moriturus invidia Neronis, . . . trullam myrrhinam HS. $\overline{ccc}$ emptam fregit.

[2] Tac. *Ann.* xvi. 19, sed flagitia principis et novitatem cujusque stupri perscripsit atque obsignata misit Neroni.

shipwreck everywhere."[1] There is also a curious note of contempt for his own age in a passage on the decay of the fine arts. The tone is, for the moment, almost that of Ruskin. The glories of the golden age of art were the result of simple virtue. An age like the Neronian, an age abandoned to wine and harlotry, which dreams only of making money by any sordid means, cannot even appreciate what the great masters have left behind, much less itself produce anything worthy. Even the gods of the Capitol are now honoured by an offering of crude bullion, not by the masterpieces of a Pheidias or an Apelles. And the race which created them are now for us, forsooth, silly Greeklings![2]

Yet side by side with a passage like this, there are descriptions of abnormal depravity so coarsely realistic that it has often been assumed, and not unnaturally, that the writer rioted in mere filth. It should be remembered, however, that there was a tradition of immorality about the ancient romance,[3] and Petronius, had he cared to do so, might have made the same apology as Martial, that he provided what his readers demanded.[4] That Petronius was deeply tainted is only too probable from his associations, although Tacitus implies that he was rather a fastidious voluptuary than a gross debauchee. Yet a sensualist of the intellectual range of Petronius may have occasionally visions of a better world than that to which he has sunk. Is it not possible that the gay elegant trifler may sometimes have scorned himself as he scorned his time? Is it not possible that, along with other illusions, he had parted with the illusions of vice, and that in the "noctes Neronis" he had seen the adder among the roses? He has written one of the keenest satires ever penned on the vulgarity of mere wealth, its absurd affectations, its vanity, its grossness. May he not also have wished, without moralising in a fashion which so cultivated a trifler would have scorned, to reveal the abyss towards which a society lost to all the finer passions of the spirit was hurrying? In the half comic, half ghastly scene in which Trimalchio, in a fit of maudlin sentiment,

[1] Petron. 115, si bene calculum ponas, ubique naufragium est.

[2] Id. 88. For a favourable estimate of the *Satiricon*, cf. Schiller's *Gesch. röm. Kaiserzeit*, i. 469, 470.

[3] See Boissier's remarks, *L'Opp.* p. 228.

[4] Mart. v. 2; iii. 68; cf. Mahaffy, *Greek World under Roman Sway*, p. 298.

has himself laid out for dead, while the horns blare out his funeral lament, we seem to hear the knell of a society which was the slave of gold and gross pleasure, and seemed to be rotting before its death.

But it need hardly be said that the prevailing note of the *Satiricon* is anything but melancholy. The author is intensely amused with his subject, and the piece is full of the most riotous fun and humour. It belongs formally to the medley of prose and verse which Varro introduced into Roman literature on the model of Menippus of Gadara.[1] It contains disquisitions on literary tendencies of the day in poetry and oratory, anecdotes and desultory talk. But Petronius has given a new character to the old "Satura," more in the manner of the Greek romance. There probably was no regular plot in the complete work, no central motive, such as the wrath of Priapus,[2] to bind it together. Yet there is a certain bond of union in the narrative of lively, and often questionable, adventures through which Petronius carries his very disreputable characters. In this life and movement, this human interest, the *Satiricon* is the distant ancestor of *Gil Blas*, *Roderick Random*, and *Tom Jones*.

The scene of the earlier part, long since lost, may have been laid at Massilia.[3] In the two books partially preserved to us, it lies in southern Italy, at Cumae or Croton, in those Greek towns which had plenty of Greek vice, without much Greek refinement.[4] The three strangers, whose adventures are related, Encolpius, Ascyltus, and Giton, if we may judge by their names, are also Greek, with the literary culture of their time, and deeply tainted with its worst vices. At the opening of our fragment, Encolpius, a beggarly, wandering sophist, is declaiming in a portico on the decay of oratory.[5] He is expressing what was probably Petronius's own judgment, as it was that of Tacitus,[6] as to the evil effects of school declamation on musty or frivolous subjects. He is met by a

[1] Teuffel, *Rom. Lit.* i. p. 239; Friedl. *Cena Trim. Einl.* 5.

[2] *Ib.* p. 5.

[3] Sidon. Apoll. *Carm.* ix. 268; xxiii. 155.

[4] Petron. 81, cf. Friedl. *Cena Trim. Einl.* 6. Puteoli is excluded by the complaints of municipal decay in c. 44: Naples, by the fact that the town is a Roman colony (44, 57); Cumae was the only town in this region which had Praetors. Cf. *Or. Henz.* 1498, 2263; Petron. 65.

[5] Petron. *Sat.* 1, 2.

[6] Tac. *De Or.* c. 31, 35.

rival lecturer, Agamemnon, who urges, on behalf of the unfortunate teachers of this conventional rhetoric, that the fault lies not with them, but with the parents and the public, the same excuse, in fact, which Plato had long before made for the maligned sophist of the fifth century B.C.[1] But Encolpius and his companions, in spite of these literary interests, are the most disreputable adventurers, educated yet hopelessly depraved. They are even more at home in the reeking slums than in the lecture hall. Encolpius has been guilty of murder, theft, seduction. The party are alternately plunderers and plundered. They riot for the moment in foul excesses, and are tortured by jealousy and the miseries of squalid vice. Only those who have a taste for pornography will care to follow them in these dark paths. Reduced to the last pinch of poverty, they are invited to dine at the all-welcoming table of Trimalchio, and this is for us the most interesting passage in their adventures. But, on leaving the rich freedman's halls they once more pass into scenes where a modern pen cannot venture to follow them. Yet soon afterwards, Encolpius is found in a picture gallery discussing the fate of literature and art with Eumolpus,[2] an inveterate poet, as vicious as himself. Presently the party are on shipboard off the south Italian coast. They are shipwrecked and cast ashore in a storm near the town of Croton.[3] A friendly peasant informs them that, if they are honest merchants, that is no place for their craft. But if they belong to the more distinguished world of intrigue, they may make their fortune. It is a society which has no care for letters or virtue, which thinks only of unearned gain. There are only two classes, the deceivers and their victims. Children are an expensive luxury, for only the childless ever receive an invitation or any social attention. It is like a city ravaged by the plague; there are only left the corpses and the vultures.[4] The adventurers resolve to seize the rare opportunity; they will turn the tables on the social birds of prey. The pauper poet is easily translated into a millionaire with enormous estates in Africa.[5] A portion of his wealth has been engulfed

[1] *Rep.* vi. p. 492 A.

[2] Petron. *Sat.* 83.

[3] *Ib.* 114.

[4] *Ib.* 116, nihil aliud est nisi cadavera quae lacerantur aut corvi qui lacerant.

[5] *Ib.* 117.

in the storm, but a solid HS.300,000,000, with much besides, still remains. He has a cough, moreover, with other signs of debility. There is no more idiotic person, as our Stock Exchange records show, than a man eager for an unearned fortune. The poor fools flocked around Eumolpus, drinking in every fresh rumour about his will. He was loaded with gifts;[1] great ladies made an easy offer of their virtue and even that of their children.[2] Meanwhile he, or Petronius, plays with their follies or tortures their avidity. In one of his many wills, the heirs of the pretended Croesus are required not to touch their booty till they have devoured his remains before the people![3] The tales of barbarian tribes in Herodotus, the memories of the siege of Saguntum and Numantia, are invoked in brutal irony to justify the reasonableness of the demand. "Close your eyes," the cynic enjoins, "and fancy that instead of devouring human flesh, you are swallowing a million of money." Petronius could be very brutal as well as very refined in his raillery. The combined stupidity and greed of the fortune-hunter of all ages are perhaps best met by such brutality of contempt.

The really interesting part of their adventure is the dinner at the house of Trimalchio, a rich freedman, to which these rascals were invited. Trimalchio is probably in many traits drawn from life, but the picture of himself, of his wife and his associates, is a work of genius worthy of Fielding or Smollett or Le Sage. Petronius, it is clear, enjoyed his work, and, in spite of his contempt for the vulgar ambition and the coarseness and commonness of Trimalchio's class, he has a liking for a certain simplicity and honest good nature in Trimalchio. The freedman tells the story of his own career[4] without reserve, and with a certain pride in the virtue and frugality, according to his standards, which have made him what he is. He also exults in his shrewdness and business capacity. His motto has always been, "You are worth just what you have." "Buy cheap and sell dear." Coming as a little slave boy from Asia, probably in the reign of Augustus,[5]

[1] Petron. *Sat.* 124.

[2] *Ib.* 140.

[3] *Ib.* 141.

[4] *Ib.* 75, 76.

[5] *v.* Friedl. *Cena Trim. Einl.* p. 7. His cognomen Maecenatianus marks him as a slave of the friend of Augustus who died 8 B.C. Trimalchio would therefore be born *circ.* 18 B.C. (*Sat.* 71, 29, 75). He was perhaps over seventy at the time of the dinner (*Sat.* 27, 77), which may therefore be placed about 57 A.D.

he became the favourite of his master, and more than the favourite of his mistress. He found himself in the end the real master of the household, and, on his patron's death, he was left joint-heir to his property with the emperor. But he had ambitions beyond even such a fortune. He became a ship-owner on a great scale. He lost a quarter of a million in a single storm, and at once proceeded to build more and larger ships. Money poured in; all his ventures prospered. He bought estates in Italy, Sicily, and Africa. Some of his purchases he had never seen.[1] He built himself a stately house, with marble porticoes, four great banqueting-halls, and twenty sleeping-rooms.[2] Everything to satisfy human wants was produced upon his lands. He was a man of infinite enterprise. He had improved the breed of his flocks by importing rams from Tarentum. He had bees from Hymettus in his hives. He sent to India for mushroom spawn.[3] A gazette was regularly brought out, full of statistics, and all the daily incidents on his estates;[4] the number of slave births and deaths; a slave crucified for blaspheming the genius of the master; a fire in the bailiff's house; the divorce of a watchman's wife, who had been caught in adultery with the bathman; a sum of HS.100,000 paid into the chest, and waiting for investment—these are some of the items of news. Trimalchio, who bears now, after the fashion of his class, the good Roman name of Caius Pompeius, has risen to the dignity of Sevir Augustalis in his municipality;[5] he is one of the foremost persons in it, with an overwhelming sense of the dignity of wealth, and with a ridiculous affectation of artistic and literary culture, which he parades with a delightful unconsciousness of his blunders.

When the wandering adventurers arrive for dinner,[6] they find a bald old man in a red tunic playing at ball, with eunuchs in attendance. While he is afterwards being rubbed down with unguents in the bath, his servants refresh themselves with old Falernian. Then, with four richly dressed runners preceding him, and wrapped in a scarlet mantle, he is borne to the house in his sedan along with his ugly minion. On the wall of the vestibule, as you entered, there were frescoes, one of which represented the young Trimalchio, under the leadership

1 Petron. *Sat.* 48.

2 *Ib.* 77.

3 *Ib.* 38, scripsit ut illi ex India semen boletorum mitteretur.

4 *Ib.* 53.

5 *Ib.* 71; cf. Friedl. *Cena Trim.* p. 308.

6 Petron. *Sat.* 27.

of Minerva, making his entry into Rome, with other striking incidents of his illustrious career, while Fortune empties her flowing horn, and the Fates spin the golden thread of his destiny.[1] The banquet begins; Alexandrian boys bring iced water and delicately attend to the guests' feet, singing all the while.[2] Indeed, the whole service is accompanied by singing, and the blare of instruments. To a great, deafening burst of music, the host is at last borne in buried in cushions, his bare shaven head protruding from a scarlet cloak, with a stole around his neck, and lappets falling on each side; his hands and arms loaded with rings.[3] Not being just then quite ready for dinner, he, with a kindly apology, has a game of draughts, until he feels inclined to eat, the pieces on the terebinthine board being, appropriately to such a player, gold and silver coins.[4] The dinner is a long series of surprises, on the artistic ingenuity of which Trimalchio plumes himself vastly. One course represents the twelve signs of the Zodiac, of which the host expounds at length the fateful significance.[5] Another dish was a large boar, with baskets of sweetmeats hanging from its tusks. A huge bearded hunter pierced its sides with a hunting knife, and forthwith from the wound there issued a flight of thrushes which were dexterously captured in nets as they flew about the room.[6] Towards the end of the meal the guests were startled by strange sounds in the ceiling, and a quaking of the whole apartment. As they raised their eyes, the ceiling suddenly opened, and a great circular tray descended, with a figure of Priapus, bearing all sorts of fruit and bon-bons.[7] It may be readily assumed that in such a scene the wine was not stinted. Huge flagons, coated with gypsum, were brought in shoulder high, each with a label attesting that it was the great Falernian vintage of Opimius, one hundred years old.[8] As the wine appeared, the genial host remarked with admirable frankness, "I did not give as good wine yesterday, although I had a more distinguished company!"

The amusements of the banquet were as various, and some of them as coarse or fantastic, as the dishes. They are gross

[1] Petron. *Sat.* 29.
[2] *Ib.* 31.
[3] *Ib.* 32.
[4] *Ib.* 33.
[5] *Ib.* 35.
[6] *Ib.* 40.
[7] *Ib.* 60; cf. Sen. *Ep.* 90, § 15, laquearia ita coagmentat . . . ut totiens tecta quotiens fercula mutentur.
[8] *Sat.* 34; Cic. *Brut.* lxxxiii. The Consulship of Opim. was B.C. 121.

and tasteless exaggerations of the prevailing fashion. In a literary age, a man of Trimalchio's position must affect some knowledge of letters and art. He is a ludicrous example of the dogmatism of pretentious ignorance in all ages. He has a Greek and Latin library,[1] and pretends to have once read Homer, although his recollections are rather confused. He makes, for instance, Daedalus shut Niobe into the Trojan horse; Iphigenia becomes the wife of Achilles; Helen is the sister of Diomede and Ganymede.[2] One of the more refined entertainments which are provided is the performance of scenes from the Homeric poems, which Trimalchio accompanied by reading in a sonorous voice from a Latin version.[3] He is himself an author, and has his poems recited by a boy personating the Bacchic god.[4] As a connoisseur of plate he will yield to no one,[5] although he slyly confesses that his "real Corinthian" got their name from the dealer Corinthus. The metal came from the fused bronze and gold and silver which Hannibal flung into the flames of captured Troy. But Trimalchio's most genuine taste, as he naïvely confesses, is for acrobatic feats and loud horn-blowing. And so, a company of rope-dancers bore the guests with their monotonous performances.[6] Blood-curdling tales of the wer-wolf, and corpses carried off by witches, are provided for another kind of taste.[7] A base product of Alexandria imitates the notes of the nightingale, and another, apparently of Jewish race, equally base, in torturing dissonant tones spouted passages from the *Aeneid*, profaned to scholarly ears by a mixture of Atellan verses.[8] Trimalchio, who was anxious that his wife should display her old powers of dancing a *cancan*, is also going to give an exhibition of his own gifts in the pantomimic line,[9] when the shrewd lady in a whisper warned him to maintain his dignity. How far she preserved her own we shall see presently.

[1] Petron. 48; on private and public libraries, cf. Sen. *De Tranq.* c. ix.; Plin. *Ep.* i. 8, § 2; ii. 17, § 8; iii. 7, § 7; iv. 28, § 1; Suet. *Vit. Pers.*; Luc. *Adv. Indoct.* 1, 16; Mart. vii. 17, 1; Suet. *J. Caes.* xliv.; *Octav.* xxix.; Marq. *Priv.* i. 114; Gregorov. *Hadr.* (Tr.) p. 240; Macé, *Suétone*, p. 220; Sid. Apoll. ii. 9.

[2] Petron. 52.

[3] Id. 59.

[4] Id. 41; cf. Epict. iii. 23; Plin. *Ep.* i. 13; iii. 18, 4; vi. 15; Mart. iii. 44, 45; 50.

[5] Sen. *Brev. Vit.* xii. 2; *Or. Henz.* 3838; Mart. iv. 39; Marq. *Priv.* ii. 688; Friedl. *Sittengesch.* iii. 84.

[6] Petron. 53.

[7] Id. 62, 63; cf. Apul. *Met.* i. 8.

[8] Petron. 68.

[9] Id. 52.

The company at this strange party were worthy of their host. And Petronius has outdone himself in the description of these brother freedmen, looking up to Trimalchio as the glory of their order, and giving vent to their ill-humour, their optimism, or their inane moralities, in conversation with the sly observer who reports their talk. They are all old slaves like their host, men who have "made their pile," or lost it. They rate themselves and their neighbours simply in terms of cash.[1] The only ability they can understand is that which can "pick money out of the dung-heap," and "turn lead to gold."[2] These gross and infinitely stupid fellows have not even the few saving traits in the character of Trimalchio. He has, after all, an honourable, though futile, ambition to be a wit, a connoisseur, a patron of learning. His luxury is coarse enough, but he wishes, however vainly, to redeem it by some ingenuity, by interspersing the mere animal feeding with some broken gleams, or, as we may think, faint and distorted reflections, of that great world of which he had heard, but the portals of which he could never enter. But his company are of mere clay. Trimalchio is gross enough at times, but, compared with his guests, he seems almost tolerable. And their dull baseness is the more torturing to a modern reader because it is an enduring type. The neighbour of the Greek observer warns him not to despise his company;[3] they are "warm" men. That one at the end of the couch, who began as a porter, has his HS.800,000. Another, an undertaker, has had his glorious days, when the wine flowed in rivers;[4] but he has been compelled to compound with his creditors, and he has played them a clever trick. A certain Seleucus, whose name reveals his origin, explains his objections to the bath, especially on this particular morning, when he has been at a funeral.[5] The fate of the departed friend unfortunately leads him to moralise on the weakness of mortal men, mere insects, or bubbles on the stream. As for medical aid, it is an imaginary comfort; it oftener kills than cures.[6] The

[1] Petron. 38, 43.

[2] Id. 43, in manu illius plumbum aurum fiebat.

[3] Id. 38, Collibertos ejus cave contemnas, valde succosi sunt. *v.* Friedl. *Cena Trim.* p. 223.

[4] Petron. 38.

[5] Id. 42.

[6] Id. 42, medicus nihil aliud est quam animi consolatio. For similar opinions of the medical profession, cf. Petron. 56; D. Cass. lxix. 22; lxxi. 33; Mart. vi. 31; vi. 53; ii. 16; Epict. iii. 23, § 27; Juv. iii. 77; Luc. *Philops.*

great consolation was that the funeral was respectably done, although the wife was not effusive in her grief.[1] Another guest will have none of this affected mourning for one who lived the life of his choice and left his solid hundred thousand.[2] He was after all a harsh quarrelsome person, very different from his brother, a stout, kindly fellow with an open hand, and a sumptuous table. He had his reverses at first, but he was set up again by a good vintage and a lucky bequest, which he knew, by a sly stroke, how to increase; a true son of fortune, who lived his seventy years and more, as black as a crow, a man who lustily enjoyed all the delights of the flesh to the very end.[3]

But the most interesting person for the modern student is the grumbler about the management of town affairs; and here a page or two of the *Satiricon* is worth a dissertation. The price of bread has gone up, and the bakers must be in league with the aediles. In the good old times, when the critic first came from Asia, things were very different.[4] "There were giants in those days. Think of Safinius, who lived by the old arch, a man with a sharp, biting tongue, but a true friend, a man who, in the town council, went straight to his point, whose voice in the forum rang out like a trumpet. Yet he was just like one of us, knew everybody's name, and returned every salute. Why, in those days corn was as cheap as dirt. You could buy for an as a loaf big enough for two. But the town has since gone sadly back.[5] Our aediles now think only how to pocket in a day what would be to some of us a fortune. I know how a certain person made his thousand gold pieces. If this goes on, I shall have to sell my cottages. Neither men nor the gods have any mercy. It all comes from our neglect of religion. No one now keeps a fast, no one cares a fig for Jove. In old days when there was a drought, the long-robed matrons with bare feet, dishevelled hair, and pure hearts, would ascend the hill to entreat Jupiter for rain, and then it would pour down in

c. 21, 26; *Adv. Indoct.* c. 29; Marq. *Priv.* ii. 779. Sen. gives a higher idea of the craft, *De Ben.* vi. 16; cf. Apul. *Met.* x. 8, where the doctor rejects the base proposals made to him.

[1] Petron. 42, planctus est optime, etiam si maligne illum ploravit uxor.

[2] Id. 43.

[3] Id. 43, noveram hominem olim oliorum, et adhuc salax est. On the phrase olim oliorum *v.* Friedl. *Cena Trim.* p. 237.

[4] Petron. 44.

[5] Id. 44, haec colonia retroversus crescit tanquam coda vituli. This passage is used to prove that Puteoli cannot be Trimalchio's town. Friedl. *Cena Trim.* p. 239.

buckets."[1] At this point the maundering, pious pessimist is interrupted by a rag dealer[2] of a more cheerful temper. "Now this, now that, as the rustic said, when he lost his speckled pig. What we have not to-day will come to-morrow; so life rubs along. Why, we are to have a three days' show of gladiators on the next holiday, not of the common sort, but many freedmen among them. And our Titus has a high spirit; he will not do things by halves. He will give us cold steel without any shirking, a good bit of butchery in full view of the amphitheatre. And he can well afford it. His father died and left him HS.30,000,000. What is a paltry HS.400,000 to such a fortune?[3] and it will give him a name for ever. He has some tit-bits, too, in reserve, the lady chariot-driver, and the steward of Glyco, who was caught with his master's wife; poor wretch, he was only obeying orders. And the worthless Glyco has given him to the beasts; the lady deserved to suffer. And I have an inkling that Mammaea is going to give us a feast, where we shall get two denarii apiece. If she does the part expected of her, Norbanus will be nowhere. His gladiators were a wretched, weedy, twopenny-halfpenny lot, who would go down at a mere breath. They were all cut to pieces, as the cowards deserved, at the call of the crowd, 'give it them.' A pretty show indeed! When I applauded, I gave far more than I got. But friend Agamemnon, you are thinking 'what is all this long-winded chatter.'[4] Well, you, who dote on eloquence, why won't you talk yourself, instead of laughing at us feeble folk. Some day I may persuade you to look in at my farm; I daresay, though the times are bad, we shall find a pullet to eat. And I have a young scholar ripening for your trade. He has good wits and never raises his head from his task. He paints with a will. He has begun Greek, and has a real taste for Latin. But one of his tutors is conceited and idle. The other is very painstaking, but, in his excess of zeal, he teaches more than he knows. So I have bought the boy some red-letter volumes, that he may get a tincture of law for domestic purposes. That

[1] Petron. 44 *ad fin.* itaque statim urceatim plovebat.

[2] Id. 45. On the meaning of Centonarius *v.* Marq. *Priv.* ii. 585. They had a great number of Collegia, often leagued with the Fabri; *v. Henz. Ind.* pp. 171-72; *C. Th.* xiv. 8.

[3] For the cost of such shows, *v. Or.* 81; *C.I.L.* ii. *Suppl.* p. 1034; Friedl. *Cena Trim. Einl.* p. 58; Friedl. *Sittengesch.* ii. p. 136.

[4] Petron. 46, quid iste argutat molestus?

is what gives bread and butter. He has now had enough of literature. If he gives it up, I think I shall teach him a trade, the barber's or auctioneer's or pleader's,[1] something that only death can take from him. Every day I din into his ears, Primigenius, my boy, what you learn you learn for profit. Look at the lawyer Philero. If he had not learnt his business, he could not keep the wolf from the door. Why, only a little ago, he was a hawker with a bundle on his back, and now he can hold his own with Norbanus. Learning is a treasure, and a trade can never be lost."

To all this stimulating talk there are lively interludes. A guest thinks one of the strangers, in a superior way, is making game of the company, and assails him with a shower of the choicest abuse, in malodorous Latin of the slums, interlarded with proud references to his own rise from the slave ranks.[2] Trimalchio orders the house-dog, Scylax, to be brought in, but the brute falls foul of a pet spaniel, and, in the uproar, a lamp is overthrown; the vases on the table are all smashed, and some of the guests are scalded with the hot oil.[3] In the middle of this lively scene, a lictor announces the approach of Habinnas, a stone-cutter, who is also a great dignitary of the town. He arrives rather elevated from another feast of which he has pleasant recollections. He courteously asks for Fortunata,[4] who happens to be just then looking after the plate and dividing the remains of the feast among the slaves. That lady, after many calls, appears in a cherry coloured tunic with a yellow girdle, wiping her hands with her neckerchief. She has splendid rings on her arms, legs, and fingers, which she pulls off to show them to the stone-cutter's lady. Trimalchio is proud of their weight, and orders a balance to be brought in to confirm his assertions. It is melancholy to relate that, in the end, the two ladies get hopelessly drunk, and fall to embracing one another in a rather hysterical fashion. Fortunata even attempts to dance.[5] In the growing confusion the slaves take their places at table, and the cook begins to give imitations of a favourite actor,[6] and lays a wager with his master on the chances of the green at the next races. Trimal-

[1] Petron. 46 *ad fin.*; cf. Mart. v. 56; Juv. vii. 5, 176.

[2] Petron. 57.

[3] Id. 64.

[4] Id. 67.

[5] Id. 70.

[6] Id. Ephesum tragoedum coepit imitare—Sonst unbekannt, Friedl. *Cena Trim.* 306.

chio, who by this time was becoming very mellow and sentimental, determines to make his will, and to manumit all his slaves, with a farm to one, a house to another. He even gives his friend the stone-cutter full directions about the monument which is to record so brilliant a career. There is to be ample provision for its due keeping, in the fashion so well known from the inscriptions, with a fair space of prescribed measurements, planted with vines and other fruit trees. Trimalchio wishes to be comfortable in his last home.[1] On the face of the monument ships under full sail are to figure the sources of his wealth.[2] He himself is to be sculptured, seated on a tribunal, clothed with the *praetexta* of the Augustalis, with five rings on his fingers, ladling money from a bag, as in the great banquet with which he had once regaled the people.[3] On his right hand there is to be the figure of his wife holding a dove and a spaniel on a leash. A boy is to be graved weeping over a broken urn. And, finally, in the centre of the scene, there is to be a horologe, that the passer-by, as he looks for the hour, may have his eyes always drawn to the epitaph which recited the dignities and virtues of the illustrious freedman. It told posterity that "C. Pompeius Trimalchio Maecenatianus was pious, stout, and trusty, that he rose from nothing, left HS.30,000,000, and never heard a philosopher." The whole company, along with Trimalchio himself, of course wept copiously at the mere thought of the close of so illustrious a career. After renewing their gastric energy in the bath, the company fell to another banquet. Presently a cock crows, and Trimalchio, in a fit of superstition, spills his wine under the table,[4] passes his rings to the right hand, and offers a reward to any one who will bring the ominous bird. The disturber was soon caught and handed over to the cook for execution. Then Trimalchio excites his wife's natural anger by a piece of amatory grossness, and, in

[1] Cf. *Or. Henz.* 4070, 7321; Petron. 71, valde enim falsum est vivo quidem domos cultas esse, non curari eas ubi diutius nobis habitandum est.

[2] *v.* the monument of C. Munatius Faustus at Pompeii, *C.I.L.* x. 1030. But Mau, p. 415 (Tr.), interprets it differently from Friedl. *Cena Trim.* p. 307.

[3] See the monument of the surgeon oculist of Assisi, *Or.* 2983, who records the amount he gave for his freedom, his benefactions, and his fortune. *v. C.I.L.* v. 4482, the monument of Valerius Anteros Asiaticus, a Sevir Aug. of Brescia.

[4] Plin. *H.N.* xxvi. 2 (26); xxviii. 6 (57), plerique (suadent) anulum e sinistra in longissimum dextrae digitum transferre.

retaliation for her very vigorous abuse, flings a cup at her head. In the scene which follows he gives, with the foulest references to his wife's early history, a sketch of his own career and the eulogy of the virtues that have made him what he is.[1] Growing more and more sentimental, he at last has himself laid out for dead;[2] the horn-blowers sound his last lament, one of them, the undertaker's man, with such a good will, that the town watch arrived in breathless haste with water and axes to extinguish a fire. The strangers seized the opportunity to escape from the nauseous scene. Their taste raised them above Trimalchio's circle, but they were quite on the level of its morals. Encolpius and his companions are soon involved in other adventures, in which it is better not to follow them.

The lesson of all this purse-proud ostentation and vulgarity, the moral which Petronius may have intended to point, is one which will be taught from age to age by descendants of Trimalchio, and which will be never learnt till a far off future. But we need not moralise, any more than Petronius. We have merely given some snatches of a work, which is now seldom read, because it throws a searching light on a class which was rising to power in Roman society. We have now seen the worst of that society, whether crushed by the tyranny of the Caesars, or corrupted and vulgarised by sudden elevation from ignominious poverty to wealth and luxury. But there were great numbers, both among the nobles and the masses, who, in that evil time, maintained the traditions of old Roman soberness and virtue. The three following chapters will reveal a different life from that which we have hitherto been describing.

[1] Petron. 75, ad hanc me fortunam frugalitas mea perduxit.

[2] Id. 78; cf. Sen. *De Brev. Vit.* xx. 3, where a similar scene is described. Turannius—componi se in lecto et velut exanimem a circumstante familia plangi jussit.

BOOK II

RARA TEMPORUM FELICITAS

CHAPTER I

THE CIRCLE OF THE YOUNGER PLINY

It is a great relief to turn from the picture of base and vulgar luxury in the novel of Petronius to the sobriety and refinement of a class which has been painted by a less skilful artist, but a better man. The contrast between the pictures of Petronius and those of Pliny, of course, raises no difficulty. The writers belonged indeed to the same order but they were describing two different worlds. The difficulty arises when we compare the high tone of the world which Pliny has immortalised, with the hideous revelations of contemporary licence in the same class which meet us in Juvenal, Martial, and Tacitus. And historical charity or optimism has often turned the contrast to account. But there is no need to pit the quiet testimony of Pliny against the fierce invective of Juvenal. Indeed to do so would indicate an imperfect insight into the character of the men and the associations which moulded their views of the society which surrounded them. The friends of Pliny were for the most part contemporaries of the objects of Juvenal's wrath and loathing.[1] But although the two men lived side by side during the same years, and probably began to write for the public about the same date,[2] there is no hint that they ever met. They were socially at opposite poles; they were also as widely separated by temperament. Pliny was a charitable, good-natured man, an aristocrat, living among the *élite*, with an

[1] Some of Pliny's older friends, the elder Pliny, Quintilian, Suetonius, Verginius Rufus, go back to the age which Juvenal professes to attack (i. 170). But, although Juvenal mentions few names of his own generation, such as Isaeus and Marius Priscus, a comparison between his subjects and those of Martial shows that they were dealing with the same social facts. Cf. Teuffel, *R. Lit.* ii. § 326, n. 6; Nettleship, *Lectures and Essays*, p. 124 sqq.

[2] Mommsen, *Pline* (Morel), p. 77; Nettleship, *Lectures and Essays*, 131.

CHAPTER I

THE CIRCLE OF THE YOUNGER PLINY

It is a great relief to turn from the picture of base and vulgar luxury in the novel of Petronius to the sobriety and refinement of a class which has been elaborately painted by a less skilful artist, but a better man. The contrast between the pictures of Petronius and those of Pliny, of course, raises no difficulty. The writers belonged indeed to the same order, but they were describing two different worlds. The difficulty arises when we compare the high tone of the world which Pliny has immortalised, with the hideous revelations of contemporary licence in the same class which meet us in Juvenal, Martial, and Tacitus. And historical charity or optimism has often turned the contrast to account. But there is no need to pit the quiet testimony of Pliny against the fierce invective of Juvenal. Indeed to do so would indicate an imperfect insight into the character of the men and the associations which moulded their views of the society which surrounded them. The friends of Pliny were for the most part contemporaries of the objects of Juvenal's wrath and loathing.[1] But although the two men lived side by side during the same years, and probably began to write for the public about the same date,[2] there is no hint that they ever met. They were socially at opposite poles; they were also as widely separated by temperament. Pliny was a charitable, good-natured man, an aristocrat, living among the *élite*, with an

[1] Some of Pliny's older friends, the elder Pliny, Quintilian, Spurinna, Verginius Rufus, go back to the age which Juvenal professes to attack (i. 170). But, although Juvenal mentions few names of his own generation, such as Isaeus, Archigenes, and Marius Priscus, a comparison between his subjects and those of Martial shows that they were dealing with the same social facts. Cf. Teuffel, *R. Lit.* ii. § 326, n. 5; Nettleship, *Lectures and Essays*, p. 124 sqq.

[2] Momms. *Plin.* (Morel), p. 7; Peter, *Gesch. Litt.* ii. 77; Nettleship, *Lectures and Essays*, 131.

assured position and easy fortune—a man who, as he admits himself, was inclined to idealise his friends.[1] He probably shut his eyes to their moral faults, just as he felt bound in honour to extol their third-rate literary efforts. Juvenal was, as in a former chapter we have seen reason to believe, a soured and embittered man, who viewed the society of the great world only from a distance, and caught up the gossip of the servants' hall. With the heat of an excitable temperament, he probably magnified what he heard, and he made whole classes responsible for the folly and intemperance of a few. Martial, the friend of Juvenal, lived in the same atmosphere, but, while Juvenal was inspired by a moral purpose, Martial caters, unabashed, for a prurient taste.[2] Both the charitable optimist and the gloomy, determined pessimist, by limiting their view, can find ample materials for their respective estimates of pagan society towards the end of the first century. A judicial criticism will combine or balance the opposing evidence rather than select the witnesses.

The truth is that society in every age presents the most startling moral contrasts, and no single comprehensive description of its moral condition can ever be true. This has been too often forgotten by those who have passed judgment on the moral state of Roman society, both in the first age of the Empire and in the last. That there was stupendous corruption and abnormal depravity under princes like Caligula, Nero, and Domitian, we hardly need the testimony of the satirists to induce us to believe. That there were large classes among whom virtuous instinct, and all the sober strength and gravity of the old Roman character, were still vigorous and untainted, is equally attested and equally certain. Ingenious immorality and the extravagance of luxury were no doubt rampant in the last century of the Republic and in the first century of the Empire, and their enormity has been heightened by the perverted and often prurient literary skill with which the orgies of voluptuous caprice have been painted to the last loathsome details. Yet even Ovid has a lingering ideal of womanly dignity which may repel, by refined reserve, the audacity of libertinism.[3] He was forced, by old-fashioned scruple or imperial displeasure, to make an elaborate apology for the

[1] Plin. *Ep.* vii. 28. [2] Mart. iii. 68, 86; v. 2. [3] Ov. *Amor.* iii. 4, 2.

lubricities of the *Ars Amandi*.[1] The most wanton writer of the evil days shrinks from justifying adultery, and hardly ever fails to respect the unconscious innocence of girlhood. In the days when, according to Juvenal, Roman matrons were eloping with gladiators, and visiting the slums of Rome, Tacitus and Favorinus were preaching the duties of a pure motherhood.[2] In the days when crowds were gloating over the obscenities of pantomime, and aristocratic dinner-parties were applauding the ribaldry of Alexandrian songs, Quintilian was denouncing the corruption of youth by the sight of their fathers toying with mistresses and minions.[3] In an age when matrons of noble rank were exposing themselves at the pleasure of an emperor, the philosopher Musonius was teaching that all indulgence, outside the sober limits of wedlock, was a gross, animal degradation of human dignity.[4] And it is thus we may balance Juvenal and Martial on the one side and Pliny on the other. The gloomy or prurient satirist gives us a picture of ideal baseness; the gentle and charitable aristocrat opens before us a society in which people are charmingly refined, and perhaps a little too good. Yet it is said with truth that an age should be judged by its ideals of goodness rather than by its moral aberrations. And certain it is that the age of Pliny and Tacitus and Quintilian had a high moral ideal, even though it was also the age of Domitian. The old Roman character, whatever pessimists, ancient or modern, may say, was a stubborn type, which propagated itself over all the West, and survived the Western Empire. It is safe to believe that there was in Italy and Gaul and Spain many a *grand seigneur* of honest, regular life, virtuous according to his lights, like Pliny's uncle, or his Spurinna, or Verginius Rufus, or Corellius. There were certainly many wedded lives as pure and self-sacrificing as those of the elder Arria and Caecina Paetus, or of Calpurnia and Pliny.[5] There were homes like those at Fréjus,[6] or Como, or Brescia,[7] in which boys and girls were reared in a refined and severe simplicity, which even improved upon the

[1] Ov. *Trist.* ii. 212, 346, 353, Vita verecunda est, Musa jocosa mihi; 497.

[2] Tac. *De Or.* 28, non in cella emptae nutricis sed gremio ac sinu matris educabatur; A. Gell. xii. 1.

[3] Quintil. i. 2, 4, 8; nostras amicas, nostros concubinos vident.

[4] Stob. *Flor.* vi. 61; Suet. *Nero*, xxvii.; cf. Denis, *Idées Morales, etc.*, ii. p. 134.

[5] Plin. *Ep.* iii. 16; iii. 5; iv. 19; vi. 4; vii. 5.

[6] Tac. *Agric.* 4.

[7] Plin. *Ep.* i. 14.

tradition of the golden age of Rome. And, as will be seen in a later chapter, many a brief stone record remains which shows that, even in the world of slaves and freedmen, there were always in the darkest days crowds of humble people, with honest, homely ideals, and virtuous family affection, proud of their industries, and sustaining one another by help and kindness.

In this sounder class of Roman society, it will be found that the saving or renovating power was, not so much any religious or philosophic impulse, as the wholesome influence, which never fails from age to age, of family duty and affection, reinforced, especially in the higher ranks, by a long tradition of Roman dignity and self-respect, and by the simple cleanness and the pieties of country life. The life of the blameless circle of aristocrats which Pliny determined to preserve for the eyes of posterity, seems to be sometimes regarded as the result of a sudden transformation, a rebound from the frantic excesses of the time of the Claudian Caesars to the simpler and severer mode of life of which Vespasian set a powerful example. That there was such a change of moral tone, especially in the class surrounding the court, partly caused by financial exhaustion, partly by the introduction of new men from the provinces into the ranks of the Senate, is certified by the supreme authority of Tacitus.[1] Yet we should remember that men like Agricola, the father-in-law of Tacitus, or Verginius Rufus, or Fabatus, the grandfather of Pliny's wife, or the elder Pliny, and many another, were not converted prodigals. They knew how to reconcile, by quietude or politic deference, the dignity of Roman virtue with a discreet acquiescence even in the excesses of despotism. The fortunes of many of them remained unimpaired. The daily life of men like the elder Pliny and Spurinna, is distinguished by a virtuous calm, an almost painful monotony of habit, in which there seems to have been nothing to reform except, perhaps, a certain moral rigidity.[2] Above all, and surely it is the most certain proof and source of the moral soundness of any age, the ideal of

[1] Tac. *Ann.* iii. 55, sed praecipuus adstricti moris auctor Vespasianus erat; Suet. *Vesp.* ix.; cf. Schiller, *Gesch. Röm. Kaiserz.* ii. 506; Duruy, iv. 646; Renan, *Les Év.* 140, 381; *L'Antéchr.* 494.

[2] Pliny is pleased with the virtuous monotony, *Ep.* iii. i. § 2, me autem ut certus siderum cursus ita vita hominum disposita delectat, senum praesertim; cf. iii. 5.

womanhood was still high, and it was even then not seldom realised. There may have been many who justified the complaint of moralists that mothers did not guard with vigilant care the purity of their children. But there were women of the circle of Tacitus and Pliny as spotless as the half-legendary Lucretia, as they were far more accomplished, and probably far more charming. It is often said that women sink or rise according to the level of the men with whom they are linked. If that be true, there must have been many good men in the days of the Flavian dynasty.

The younger Pliny, whose name, before his adoption, was Publius Caecilius Secundus,[1] was descended from families which had been settled at Como since the time of the first Caesar.[2] They belonged to the local aristocracy, and possessed estates and villas around the lake. Pliny's father, who had held high municipal office, died early, but the boy had the great advantage of the guardianship of Verginius Rufus, for whose character and achievements his ward felt the profoundest reverence.[3] That great soldier had been governor of Upper Germany at the close of Nero's reign, and, with a deference to old constitutional principles, which Pliny must have admired, had twice, at the peril of his life, refused to receive the imperial place at the hands of his clamorous legions.[4] Pliny was born in 61 or 62 A.D., the time which saw the death of Burrus, the retirement of Seneca from public life, and the marriage of Nero with Poppaea.[5] His infancy therefore coincided with the last and wildest excesses of the Neronian tyranny. But country places like Como felt but little of the shock of these moral earthquakes. There was no school in Como till one was founded by Pliny's own generosity.[6] But the boy had probably, in his early years, the care of his uncle, the author of the *Natural History*, who, during the worst years of the Terror, was living, like many others, in studious retirement on his estates.[7] The uncle and nephew were men

[1] Momms. *Plin.* (Morel), p. 32.

[2] The Caecilii were probably established at Como from 59 B.C.; cf. Catull. 35; Plin. *Ep.* iv. 30, 1; vii. 32, 1; vi. 24, 5; ix. 7; Momms. *Plin.* p. 33 (Morel).

[3] Plin. *Ep.* ii. 1; vi. 10.

[4] Tac. *Hist.* i. 8, 52; ii. 49.

[5] Plin. *Ep.* vi. 20, 5. He was in his eighteenth year when the famous eruption of Vesuvius took place 79 A.D., D. Cass. lxvi. 21 sq.

[6] Plin. *Ep.* iv. 13, 3.

[7] Rendall, xiii. in Mayor's ed. Plin. *Ep.* iii.; Plin. *H. N.* ii. 85 (199)?

of very different temperament, but there can be little doubt that the character and habits of the older man profoundly influenced the ideals of the younger. The elder Pliny would have been an extraordinary character even in a puritan age; he seems almost a miracle in the age of the Claudian Caesars. He was born in 23 A.D., in the reign of Tiberius; and his early youth and manhood cover the reigns of Caligula and Claudius. He was only 32 when Nero came to the throne. He returned to Rome in 71 to hold a high place in the councils of Vespasian.[1] That more than monastic asceticism, that jealous hoarding of every moment,[2] that complete indifference to ordinary pleasures, in comparison with the duty, or the ambition, of transmitting to future ages the accumulations of learned toil, is a curious contrast to the Gargantuan feasts or histrionic aestheticism which were the fashion in the circle of the Claudian Emperors. The younger Pliny has left us a minute account of his uncle's routine of life, and justly adds that the most intense literary toil might seem mere idleness in comparison.[3] His studies often began soon after midnight, broken by an official visit to the emperor before dawn. After administrative work was over, the remainder of the day was spent in reading or writing. Even in the bath or on a journey, this literary industry was never interrupted. A reader or amanuensis was always at hand to save the moments that generally are allowed to slip away to waste. He tells Titus in his preface that he had consulted 2000 volumes for his *Natural History*.[4] The 160 volumes of closely written notes, which the austere enthusiast could have sold once for £3500, might have challenged the industry of a Casaubon or a Mommsen.

The laborious intensity of the elder Pliny was probably unrivalled in his day. But the moral tone, the severe self-restraint, the contempt for the sensual, or even the comfortable, side of life, the plain unspeculative stoicism, was a tone which, from many indications in the younger Pliny and in the other

[1] Plin. *Ep.* iii. 5; *Hist. Nat. Praef.* 3; Suet. *Vit. Plin.* He was 56 at his death in A.D. 79; cf. Peter, *Gesch. Litt.* i. 119, 420.

[2] Plin. *Ep.* iii. 5, § 13; Persius, who was eleven years younger than the elder Pliny, shows a character of the same type, cf. Pers. *Sat.* ii. 71-74; iii. 66 sqq.; cf. Martha, *Les Moralistes sous l'Emp.* p. 131 sqq.

[3] Plin. *Ep.* iii. 5.

[4] *Praef. H. N.* § 17; cf. § 18, profecto enim vita vigilia est.

literature of the time, appears to have been not so rare as the reader of Juvenal or Martial might suspect. A book like the Caesars of Suetonius, concentrating attention on the life of the emperor and his immediate circle, is apt to suggest misleading conclusions as to the condition of society at large. The old Roman character, perhaps the strongest and toughest national character ever developed, was an enduring type, and its true home was in the atmosphere of quiet country places in northern or central Italy, where the round of rural labour and simple pleasures reproduced the environment in which it first took form. We have glimpses of many of these nurseries or retreats of old-fashioned virtue in Pliny's Letters. Brescia and Padua, in the valley of the Po, were especially noted for frugality and severity.[1] And it was from among the youth of Brescia that Pliny suggested a husband for the daughter of the stoic champion, Arulenus Rusticus. There must have been many a home, like those of Spurinna, or Corellius Rufus, or Fabatus,[2] or the poet Persius, where, far from the weary conventionality of the capital, the rage for wealth, the rush of vulgar self-assertion, there reigned the tranquil and austere ideal of a life dedicated to higher ends than the lusts of the flesh, or the ghoul-like avarice that haunted death-beds. There are youths and maidens in the portrait-gallery of Pliny whose innocence was guarded by good women as pure and strong as those matrons who nursed the stern, unbending soldiers of the Samnite and Punic wars.[3]

The great struggle in which the legions of the East and West met again, and yet again, in the valley of the Po, probably did not much disturb the quiet homes on lake Como. The close of that awful conflict gave the world ten years of quiet and reformation, which were a genial atmosphere for the formation of many characters like Pliny's. The reign of the Flavians was ushered in by the mystery and glamour of Eastern superstition, by oracles on Mount Carmel and miracles at Alexandria.[4] But the plain Sabine soldier, who was the saviour of the Roman State, brought to his momentous task a clear unsophisticated good sense, with no trace of that

[1] Plin. *Ep.* i. 14; cf. Tac. *Agr.* iv.; Juv. iii. 165.
[2] Plin. *Ep.* iii. i; ii. 7; i. 12; v. 11.
[3] Cf. Pliny's letter to Calpurnia's aunt, *Ep.* iv. 19, quae nihil in contubernio tuo viderit nisi sanctum honestumque; cf. viii. 5; v. 16.
[4] Tac. *Hist.* ii. 78; iv. 81.

crapulous excitement which had alternated between the heroics of spurious art and the lowest bohemianism. Vespasian, although he was not a figure to strike the imagination, was yet, if we think of the abyss from which, by his single strength, he rescued the Rome world,[1] undoubtedly one of the greatest of the emperors. And his biographer, with an unusual tact, suggests what was probably one secret of his strength. Vespasian regularly visited the old farmhouse at Reate which was the cradle of his race. Nothing in the old place was ever changed. And, on holidays and anniversaries, the emperor never failed to drink from the old silver goblet which his grandmother had used.[2] The strength and virtue of the Latin race lay, not in religion or philosophy, but in the family pieties and devotion to the State. Vespasian found it urgent to bring order into the national finances, which had been reduced to chaos by the wild extravagance of his predecessors, and to recruit the Senate, which had been more than decimated by proscription, confiscation, and vicious self-abandonment.[3] In performing his task, he did not shrink from the charge of cheese-paring, just as he did not dread the unpopularity of fresh taxation.[4] But he could be liberal as well as parsimonious. He restored many of the ancient temples, even in country places.[5] He made grants to senators whose fortunes had decayed or had been wasted.[6] He spent great sums on colossal buildings and on amusements for the people.[7] But the most singular and interesting trait in this remarkable man is that, with no pretensions to literary or artistic culture, he was the first Caesar who gave a fixed endowment to professors of the liberal arts, and that he was the founder of that public system of education[8] which, for good or evil, produced profound effects on Roman character and intellect down to the end of the Western Empire. His motive was not, as some have suggested, to bring literature into thraldom to the State. He was really making himself the organ of a great intellectual

[1] Cf. *Or.* 746, 2364.

[2] Suet. *Vesp.* ii. locum incunabulorum assidue frequentavit, manente villa qualis fuerat olim, etc.

[3] *Ib.* viii. ix.

[4] D. Cass. lxvi. 8; Suet. *Vesp.* xvi.; cf. Meriv. vii. 274; cf. Schiller, *Gesch. röm. Kaiserzeit*, p. 515.

[5] Suet. *Vesp.* ix.; *Or.* 746, sacr. aedium restitutori, 1460, 1868, 2364; D. Cass. lxvi. 10.

[6] Suet. *Vesp.* xvii.

[7] *Ib.* xix.

[8] *Ib.* xviii.; continued by Hadrian, Spart. xvi.; by Ant. Pius, Capitol. xi.; by Alex. Severus, Lamprid. xliv; cf. *C. Th.* xiii. 3, 1, 2, 3; Eum. *Or. pro Scholis*, c. 11.

movement. For, while the vast field of administration absorbed much of the energy of the cultivated class, the decay of free institutions had left a great number with only a shadow of political interest, and the mass of unoccupied talent had to find some other scope for its energies. It found it for ages, till the end of the Western Empire, in fugitive and ephemeral composition, or in the more ephemeral displays of the rhetorical class-room.[1] Vespasian perhaps did a greater service in renovating the upper class of Rome by the introduction of many new men from the provinces, to fill the yawning gaps in senatorial and equestrian ranks. Spain contributed more than its fair share to the literature and statesmanship of this period.[2] And one of the best and most distinguished sons of that province who found a career at Rome, was the rhetor Quintilian.

The young Pliny, under his uncle's care, probably came to Rome not long after Quintilian entered on his career of twenty years, as a teacher of rhetoric.[3] While the elder Pliny was one of Vespasian's trusted advisers, and regularly visited the emperor on official business before dawn, his nephew was forming his taste and character under the greatest and best of Roman teachers. Quintilian left a deep impression on the younger Pliny.[4] He made him a Ciceronian, and he fortified his character. The master was one who believed that, in education, moral influence and environment are even more important than intellectual stimulus. He deplores the moral risks to which the careless, self-indulgent parent, or the corrupt tutor, may expose a boy in the years when the destiny of a life is decided for better or worse. Intellectual ambition is good. But no brilliancy of intellect will compensate for the loss of the pure ingenuous peace of boyhood. This is the faith of Quintilian, and it was also the faith of his pupil.[5] And it may be that the teaching of Quintilian had a larger share in forming the moral ideals of the Antonine age in the

[1] *v. Rom. Soc. in the Last Century of the Western Empire* (1st ed.), p. 355.

[2] Mommsen, *Rom. Prov.* (Tr.) i. p. 76.

[3] Pliny probably came to Rome about 72 A.D. Rendall, xiv.; in Mayor's Pliny, *Ep.* iii.; cf. Quintil. *Prooem.* i.

[4] Plin. *Ep.* ii. 14, 10; vi. 6, 3; vi. 32.

[5] Quintil. *Inst. Or.* i. 2, 6; cf. Plin. *Ep.* iii. 3, 4, cui in hoc lubrico aetatis non praeceptor modo sed custos etiam rectorque quaerendus est; cf. *Ep.* iv. 13, 4, ubi enim pudicius contineantur quam sub oculis parentum; cf. Tac. *Dial. de Or.* 28.

higher ranks than many more definitely philosophic guides, whose practice did not always conform to their doctrine.

Quintilian's first principle is that the orator must be a good man in the highest and widest sense, and, although he will not refuse to borrow from the philosophical schools, he yet boldly asserts the independence of the oratorical art in moulding the character of the man who, as statesman or advocate, will have constantly to appeal to moral principles.[1] This tone, combined with his own high example of seriousness, honour, and the purest domestic attachment,[2] must have had a powerful effect on the flower of the Roman youth, who were his pupils for nearly a generation. There are none of his circle whose virtues Pliny extols more highly than the men who had sat with him on the same benches, and who accompanied or followed one another in the career of public office. One of the dearest of these youthful friends was Voconius Romanus, who, besides being a learned pleader, with a keen and subtle intellect, was gifted with a singular social charm and sweetness of manner.[3] Another was Cornutus Tertullus, who was bound to Pliny by closer ties of sympathy than any of his friends, and for whose purity of character he had a boundless admiration. They were also united in the love and friendship of the best people of the time.[4] They were official colleagues in the consulship, and in the prefecture of the treasury of Saturn. For another academic friend, Julius Naso, who had been his loyal supporter in all his work and literary ambitions, he earnestly begs the aid of Fundanus, to secure him official advancement.[5] Calestrius Tiro, who rose to be proconsul of the province of Baetica, must be included in this select company. He had served with Pliny in the army of Syria, and had been his colleague in the quaestorship; they constantly visited one another at their country seats.[6] Such men, linked to one another by memories of boyhood and by the cares of the same official career, must have been a powerful and salutary element in social and political life at the opening of the Antonine age.

[1] Quintil. *Inst. Prooem.* i. 9-11; ii. 2, 15; xii. 1, 1; xii. 7, 7, non convenit ei, quem oratorem esse volumus, injusta tueri scientem.

[2] *Ib.* vi. *Prooem.* 4.

[3] Plin. *Ep.* ii. 13, hunc ego, cum simul studeremus, arte familiariterque dilexi, etc.

[4] *Ib.* v. 14; *Paneg.* 91, 92; cf. Momms. *Plin.* p. 64.

[5] Plin. *Ep.* vi. 6.

[6] *Ib.* vii. 16, 2; i. 10, 3; cf. Momms. p. 52. Pliny's service with the iii. Gallica was later than September, A.D. 81.

It is a curious thing that, while Pliny lived in the closest friendship with the Stoic opposition of Domitian's reign, and has unbounded reverence for its canonised saints, as we may call them, he shows few traces of any real interest in speculative philosophy. Indeed, in one passage he confesses that on such subjects he speaks as an amateur.[1] He probably thought, like his friend Tacitus, that philosophy was a thing to be taken in moderation by the true Roman. It was when he was serving on the staff in Asia that he formed a close friendship with Artemidorus, whom Musonius chose for his daughter's hand.[2] Pliny has not a word to say of his opinions, but he extols his simplicity and genuineness—qualities, he adds, which you rarely find in the other philosophers of the day. It was at the same time that he formed a friendship with the Stoic Euphrates. That philosopher, who is so studiously maligned by Philostratus, was a heroic figure in Pliny's eyes.[3] But what Pliny admires in him is not so much his philosophy, as his grave ornate style, his pure character, which showed none of that harsh and ostentatious severity which was then so common in his class. Euphrates is a polished gentleman after Pliny's own heart, tall and stately, with flowing hair and beard, a man who excites reverence but not fear, stern to vice, but gentle to the sinner. Pliny seems to have set little store by the formal preaching of philosophy. In a letter on the uses of sickness, he maintains that the moral lessons of the sick-bed are worth many formal disquisitions on virtue.[4]

Yet this man, apparently without the slightest taste for philosophic inquiry, or even for the homilies which, in his day, had taken the place of real speculation, had a profound veneration for the Stoic martyrs, and, true gentleman as he was, he risked his life in the times of the last Terror to befriend them. It needed both nerve and dexterity to be the friend of philosophers in those days. In that perilous year, 93 A.D., when Pliny was praetor,[5] the philosophers were banished from the city. Yet the praetor visited Artemidorus in his suburban retreat, and, with his wonted generosity, he helped the philo-

[1] Plin. *Ep.* i. 10, 4 ; cf. Tac. *Agr.* iv.

[2] Plin. *Ep.* iii. 11, 5.

[3] *Ib.* i. 10 ; cf. Philostr. *Apoll. Tyan.* v. 37, 40 ; vi. 8.

[4] Plin. *Ep.* vii. 26, 4.

[5] *Ib.* iii. 11, 2 ; Suet. *Dom.* x. ; D. Cass. lxvii. 10 ; cf. Momms. p. 59, where the date of Pliny's praetorship is fixed.

sopher to wipe out a heavy debt which he had contracted. One of Pliny's dearest friends was Junius Mauricus, the brother of Arulenus Rusticus, who had been put to death by Domitian for writing a eulogy on Thrasea the Stoic saint, the champion of the higher life in Nero's reign.[1] Junius Mauricus afterwards suffered exile himself in the same cause. He had charged himself with the care of his martyred brother's children, and Pliny helped him to find a worthy husband for the daughter of Rusticus.[2] With Fannia the widow of Helvidius, and the daughter of Thrasea, Pliny's intimacy seems to have been of the closest kind. From her he heard the tales, now too well worn, of the fierce firmness of the elder Arria in nerving her husband Paetus for death, and of her own determined self-immolation.[3] The mother of Fannia, the younger Arria, when Thrasea her husband was condemned to die in the reign of Nero, was only prevented from sharing his fate by the most earnest entreaties of her friends.[4] Fannia had followed Helvidius into exile in Nero's reign,[5] and again under Vespasian, when the philosopher, with a petulance very unlike the reserve of Thrasea, brought his fate upon himself by an insulting disregard of the emperor's dignity as first magistrate of the State, if not by revolutionary tendencies.[6] Fannia seems to have inherited many of the great qualities of her father Thrasea, the noblest and the wisest member of the Stoic opposition. He sprang from a district in Lombardy which was noted for its soundness and gravity of character. Unlike Paetus[7] and Helvidius, he never defied or intrigued against the emperor, even when the emperor was a Nero. And, though he belonged to the austere circle of Persius, he did not disdain to sing in tragic costume, at a festival of immemorial antiquity, in his native Patavium.[8] He performed his duties as senator with firm dignity, and yet with cautious tact. His worst political crime, and that which proved his ruin, was a severe reserve and a refusal to join in the shameful adulation of the matricide prince. He would not stoop to vote divine honours to the

[1] Suet. *Dom.* x.
[2] Plin. *Ep.* i. 14 ; cf. iii. 11, 3.
[3] *Ib.* iii. 16 ; cf. vii. 19 ; ix. 13.
[4] Tac. *Ann.* xvi. 34.
[5] Plin. *Ep.* vii. 19, 4 ; for the character of Helvidius Priscus, cf. Tac. *Hist.* iv. 5.
[6] Suet. *Vesp.* xv. ; D. Cass. lxvi. 12 ; cf. Peter, *Gesch. Litt.* ii. 98.
[7] Plin. *Ep.* iii. 16, 7.
[8] Tac. *Ann.* xvi. 21 ; D. Cass. lxii. 26.

adulteress Poppaea, and for three years he absented himself from the Senate-house.[1] Yet, when the end came, he would not allow the fiery Arulenus Rusticus to imperil his future, by interposing his veto as tribune.[2] His daughter Fannia was worthy of her illustrious descent. She showed all the fearless defiance of the elder Arria, when she boldly admitted that she had asked Senecio to write her husband's life, and she uttered no word to deprecate her doom. When all her property was confiscated, she carried the dangerous volume with her to her place of exile.[3] Yet this stern heroine had also the tenderer virtues. She nursed her kinswoman Junia, one of the Vestals, through a dangerous fever, and caught the seeds of her own death from her charge. With all her masculine firmness and courage, she had a sweetness and charm which made her not less loved than venerated. With her may be said to have expired the peculiar tradition of a circle which, for three generations, and during the reigns of eight emperors, guarded, sometimes with dangerous defiance, the old ideal of uncompromising virtue in the face of a brutal and vulgar materialism. It was the tradition which inspired the austere detachment of the poetry of Persius, with its dim solemnity and obscure depths, as of a sacred grove. These people were hard and stern to vicious power,[4] like our own Puritans of the seventeenth century. Like them too, they were exclusive and defiant, with the cold hauteur of a moral aristocracy, a company of the elect, who would not even parley with evil, for whom the issues of life and death were the only realities in a world hypnotised by the cult of the senses and the spell of tyranny. Their intense seriousness was a religion, although they had only the vaguest and most arid conception of God, and the dimmest and least comforting conception of any future life. They seemed to perish as a little sect of troublesome visionaries; and yet their spirit lived on, softened and sweetened, and passed into the great rulers of the Antonine age.

Before his formal period of military service as tribune of the 3rd Gallic legion in Syria, Pliny had, in his nineteenth year, entered on that forensic career which was perhaps the greatest

[1] Tac. *Ann.* xiv. 12; xvi. 21, 22; cf. D. Cass. 61. 15. [2] Tac. *Ann.* xvi. 26.
[3] Plin. *Ep.* vii. 19.
[4] Renan, *Les Évangiles*, p. 142, treats the philosophic opposition as a mere aristocratic reaction; cf. pp. 287, 382. Boissier, *L'Opp.* p. 103; Schiller, *Gesch. d. röm. Kaiserz.* pp. 509, 536.

pride of his life.[1] He practised in the Centumviral court, which was chiefly occupied with questions of property and succession. Occasionally he speaks with a certain weariness of the trivial character of the cases in which he was engaged. But his general estimate is very different. The court is to him an arena worthy of the greatest talent and industry,[2] and the successful pleader may win a fame which may entitle him to take rank with the great orators of the past. Pliny, inspired by memories of Quintilian's lectures, has always floating before him the glory of Cicero.[3] He will prepare for publication a speech delivered in an obscure case about a disputed will.[4] He is immensely proud of its subtlety and point, and the sweep of its indignant or pathetic declamation, and he is not unwilling to believe his legal friends who compared it with the *De Corona!* The suppression of free political life, the absence of public interests, and the extinction of the trade of the delator, left young men with a passion for distinction few chances of gratifying it. The law courts at any rate provided an audience, and the chance of momentary prominence. In the Letters of Pliny, we can see the young advocate pushing his way through the dense masses of the crowded court, arriving at his place with torn tunic, holding the attention of his audience for seven long hours, and sitting down amid the applause even of the judges themselves.[5] Calpurnia often arranged relays of messengers to bring her news of the success, from point to point, of one of her husband's speeches.[6] Youths of the highest social rank—a Salinator, or a Ummidius Quadratus—threw themselves eagerly into the drudgery which might make an ephemeral name.[7] Ambitious pretenders, with no talent or learning, and arrayed perhaps in hired purple and jewels, like Juvenal's needy lawyer, forced themselves on to the benches of the advocates, and engaged a body of claqueurs whose applause was purchased for a few denarii.[8] Pliny has such a pride in this profession, he so idealises what must have been often rather humdrum work, that he feels a personal pain at anything which seems to detract from the

[1] Plin. *Ep.* v. 8, 8; Momms. p. 52.
[2] Plin. *Ep.* vi. 1; iv. 16; vi. 23, 2.
[3] *Ib.* i. 20, 7.
[4] *Ib.* vi. 33, 8–11.
[5] *Ib.* iv. 16.
[6] *Ib.* iv. 19, 3, disponit qui nuntient sibi quem assensum, quos clamores excitarim, quem eventum judicii tulerim.
[7] *Ib.* vi. 11.
[8] *Ib.* ii. 14, 4.

old-fashioned, leisurely dignity of the court. In his day the judges seem to have been becoming more rapid and business-like in their procedure, and less inclined to allow the many *clepsydrae* which men of Pliny's school demanded for the gradual development of all their rhetorical artifices. He regrets the good old times, when adjournments were freely granted,[1] and days would be spent on a case which was now despatched in as many hours. It is for this reason that he cannot conceal a certain admiration for Regulus, in other respects, "the most detestable of bipeds" but who redeemed his infamy by an enthusiasm and energy as an advocate which rivalled even that of Pliny.

M. Aquilius Regulus, the prince of delators, and one of the great glories of the Roman bar in Domitian's reign, is a singular figure. His career and character are a curious illustration of the social history of the times. Regulus was the son of a man who, in Nero's reign, had been driven into exile and ruined.[2] Bold, able, recklessly eager for wealth and notoriety at any cost, as a mere youth he resolved to raise himself from obscure indigence, and soon became one of the most capable and dreaded agents of the tyranny. He gained an evil fame by the ruin of the great houses of the Crassi and Orfiti. Lust of blood and greed of gain drove him on to the wholesale destruction of innocent boys, noble matrons, and men of the most illustrious race. The cruelty of Nero was not swift enough to satisfy him, and he called for the annihilation of the Senate at a stroke. He rose rapidly to great wealth, honours were showered upon him, and, after a prudent retirement in the reigns of Vespasian and Titus, he reached the pinnacle of his depraved ambition under Vespasian's cruel son. He figures more than once in the poems of Martial, and always in the most favourable light. His talent and eloquence, according to the poet, were only equalled by his piety, and the special care of the gods had saved him from being buried under the ruins of a cloister which had suddenly fallen in.[3] He had estates at Tusculum, in Umbria and

[1] Plin. *Ep.* vi. 2, 6.

[2] For the career and character of M. Aquilius Regulus, *v.* Tac. *Hist.* iv. 42; Plin. *Ep.* i. 5; i. 20, 15; ii. 11; ii. 20; iv. 2; vi. 2; and Boissier, *L'Opp.* p. 193.

[3] Mart. i. 13, 83, 112, Cum tibi sit sophiae par fama et cura deorum, etc.

Etruria.[1] The courts were packed when he rose to plead.[2] Unfortunately, the needy poet furnishes a certain key to all this flattery, when he thanks Regulus for his presents, and then begs him to buy them back.[3] It is after Domitian's death that we meet Regulus in Pliny's pages. The times are changed, the delator's day is over, and Regulus is a humbler man. But he is still rich, courted, and feared; he is still a great power in the law courts. With a weak voice, a bad memory, and hesitating utterance,[4] by sheer industry and determination he had made himself a powerful speaker, with a style of his own, sharp, pungent, brutally incisive, ruthlessly sacrificing elegance to point.[5] He belonged to the new school, and sometimes sneered at Pliny's affectation of the grand Ciceronian manner.[6] Yet to Pliny's eyes, his earnest strenuousness in his profession redeems some of his vices. He insists on having ample time to develop his case.[7] He appears in the morning pale with study, wearing a white patch on his forehead. He has consulted the diviners as to the success of his pleadings.[8] It is a curious sign of the times that this great advocate, who already possessed an enormous fortune, was a legacy-hunter of the meanest sort. He actually visited, on her death-bed, Verania, the widow of that Piso, the adopted son of Galba, over whose murder Regulus had savagely gloated, and by telling her that the stars promised a hope of recovery, he obtained a place in her will. His mourning for his son displayed all the feverish extravagance and grandiose eccentricity of a true child of the Neronian age.[9] The boy's ponies and dogs and pet birds were slaughtered over his pyre. Countless pictures and statues of him were ordered. His memoir was read by the father to a crowded audience, and a thousand copies of it were sent broadcast over the provinces.[10] In Regulus we seem to see the type of character which, had fortune raised him to the throne, would have made perhaps a saner Caligula, and an even more eccentric Nero.

[1] Mart. vii. 31.
[2] *Ib.* vi. 38; vi. 64, 11.
[3] *Ib.* vii. 16.
[4] Plin. *Ep.* iv. 7, § 4.
[5] *Ib.* i. 20, 15; cf. references to the archaic literary taste of the day in Mart. v. 10.
[6] Plin. *Ep.* v. 12.
[7] *Ib.* vi. 2, 5.
[8] *Ib.* ii. 20.
[9] *Ib.* iv. 2.
[10] For the light which this throws on the production of books in that age, *v.* Haenny, *Schriftsteller u. Buchhändler*, pp. 39-41.

The struggles of the law courts were idealised by Pliny, and their transient triumphs seemed to him to match the glory of the Philippics or the Verrines. Yet, to do him justice, Pliny had sometimes a truer idea of the foundations of lasting fame. The secret of immortality, the one chance of escaping oblivion, is to leave your thought embalmed in choice and distinguished literary form, which coming ages will not willingly let die.[1] This, probably the only form of immortality in which Pliny believed, is the great motive for literary labour. The longing to be remembered was the most ardent passion of the Roman mind in all ages and in all ranks, from the author of the *Agricola* to the petty artisan, who commemorated the homely virtues of his wife for the eyes of a distant age, and made provision for the annual feast and the tribute of roses to the tomb. Of that immense literary ambition which Pliny represented, and which he considered it a duty to foster, only a small part has reached its goal. The great mass of these eager litterateurs have altogether vanished, or remain as mere shadowy names in Martial or Statius or Pliny.

The poems of Martial and Statius leave the impression that, in the reign of Domitian, the interest in poetical literature was keen and widely diffused, and that, besides the poets by profession, there were crowds of amateurs who dabbled in verse. The *Silvae* transport us into a charming, if rather luxurious world, where men like Atedius Melior or Pollius amuse themselves with dilettante composition among their gardens and marbles on the bays of Campania.[2] Martial has a host of friends similarly engaged, and the versatility of some of them is suspiciously wide. An old Ardelio is twitted by Martial with his showy and superficial displays in declamation and history, in plays and epigrams, in grammar and astronomy.[3] Canius Rufus, his countryman from Gades, Varro, Bassus, Brutianus, Cirinius, have all an extraordinary dexterity in almost every branch of poetical composition. Martial is too keen a critic not to see the fugitive character of much of this amateur literature. Like

[1] Plin. *Ep.* ii. 10, 4; iii. 7, 14, quatenus nobis denegatur diu vivere, relinquamus aliquid quo nos vixisse testemur; v. 5, 4; v. 8, 2, me autem nihil aeque ac diuturnitatis amor sollicitat; cf. vii. 20.

[2] Stat. *Silv.* ii. 2.

[3] Mart. ii. 7; v. 30; iii. 20; iv. 23; v. 23. For the same breadth of accomplishment in the fifth century, cf. Sidon. Apoll. *Carm.* v. 97; ii. 156; xxiii. 101; *Rom. Soc. in the Last Cent. of the Western Empire* (1st ed.), p. 375.

Juvenal, he scoffs at the thin talent which concealed its feebleness behind the pomp and faded splendour of epic or tragic tradition.[1] He roughly tells the whole versifying crowd that genius alone will live in coming ages. The purchased applause of the recitation hall merely gratifies for an hour the vanity of the literary trifler. It is a pity for his fame that Martial did not always maintain this tone of sincerity. He can at times sell his flattery to the basest and most stupid. He is capable of implying a comparison of the frigid pedantry of Silius Italicus to the majesty of Virgil.[2]

Pliny was a friend and admirer of Martial, and, with his usual generous hand, he made the poet a present when he left Rome for ever to pass his last years at Bilbilis.[3] The needy epigrammatist was only a distant observer, or hanger-on of that world of wealth and refinement in which Pliny was a conspicuous figure. But from both Pliny and Martial we get very much the same impression of the literary movement in the reign of Domitian. Pliny himself is perhaps its best representative. He is a true son of the Roman schools, as they had been revived and strengthened by Vespasian, for a life of many generations. Pliny does not think slightly of the literary efforts of his own day: some of them he even overrates. But already the Roman mind had bent its neck to that thraldom to the past, to that routine of rhetorical discipline, which, along with other causes, produced the combination of ambitious effort and mediocre performance that, for the last three centuries of the Empire, is the characteristic of all literary culture. From his great teacher Quintilian Pliny had imbibed a profound reverence for Cicero.[4] Alike in his career of honours and his literary pursuits, he loves to think that he is treading in the great orator's footsteps. In answer to a taunt of Regulus, he once boldly avowed his preference for the Ciceronian oratory to that of his own day. Demosthenes is also sometimes his model, though he feels keenly the difference that separates them.[5] Indeed his reverence for Greece as the mother of letters, art, and civic life was one of Pliny's sincerest

[1] Mart. vi. 60.
[2] *Ib.* iv. 14.
[3] Plin. *Ep.* iii. 21. This book is dated by Mommsen 101 A.D. (*Plin.* p. 14, Morel; *v.* App. C, p. 95); cf. Friedländer's *Martial*, "Chronologie der Epigr. Mart." p. 66.
[4] Plin. *Ep.* iv. 8, 4; v. 12, est mihi cum Cicerone aemulatio.
[5] *Ib.* vii. 30.

and most honourable feelings. To a man who had been appointed to high office in Greece he preaches, in earnest tones, the duty of reverence for that gifted race whose age was consecrated by the memories of its glorious prime.[1] Pliny's Greek studies must have begun very early. At the age of fourteen he had written a Greek tragedy, for which, however, he modestly does not claim much merit.[2] He had always a certain taste for poetry, but it seems to have been merely the taste created or enforced by the constant study of the poets under the grammarian. Once, while detained by bad weather on his way back from military service in Asia, he amused himself with composing in elegiac and heroic verse.[3] Later in his career, he published a volume of poems in hendecasyllabic metre, written on various occasions. But there was no inspiration behind these conventional exercises. He was chiefly moved to write in verse, as he naïvely confesses, by the example of the great orators who beguiled their leisure in this way. Among his published poems there were some with a flavour of Catullan lubricity, which offended or astonished some of his severer friends, who thought such doubtful lightness unworthy of a grave character and a great position.[4] No better illustration could be found of Pliny's incorrigible conventionality in such things than the defence which he makes of his suspected verses to Titius Ariston.[5] It is to Pliny not a question of morals or propriety. The ancient models are to be followed, not only in their elevated, but in their looser moods. The case seems to be closed when Pliny can point to similar literary aberrations in a long line of great men from Varro and Virgil and Cicero to Verginius Rufus and the divine Nerva.[6]

Pliny, however, though vain of his dexterity in these trifles, probably did not rate them very highly. It was to oratorical fame that his ambition was directed. He was dissatisfied with the eloquence of his own day, which, to use the words of Regulus, sprang at the throat of its subject, and he avowed himself an imitator of Cicero. His speeches, even for the centumviral court, were worked up with infinite care, although

[1] Plin. *Ep.* viii. 24, reverere gloriam veterem et hanc ipsam senectutem quae in homine venerabilis, in urbibus sacra.

[2] *Ib.* vii. 4, 2, Qualem? inquis. Nescio; tragoedia vocabatur.

[3] *Ib.* vii. 4, 3.

[4] *Ib.* iv. 14; cf. Ov. *Trist.* ii. 365, who makes pretty much the same excuse to Augustus.

[5] Plin. *Ep.* v. 3.

[6] Cf. Nettleship, *Lectures and Essays*, 2nd Series, p. 39.

with too self-conscious an aim to impress an audience. We can hardly imagine Cicero or Demosthenes coldly balancing their tropes and figures after the fashion of Pliny. When the great oratorical effort was over, the labour was renewed, in order to make the speech worthy of the eyes of posterity. It was revised and polished, and submitted to the scrutiny of critical readers for suggestions of emendation.[1] Pliny was probably the first to give readings of speeches to long-suffering friends. We hear with a shudder that the recital of the *Panegyric* was spread over three days![2] The other speeches on which Pliny lavished so much labour and thought, have perished, as they probably deserved to perish. The *Panegyric* was preserved, and became the parent and model of the prostituted rhetoric of the Gallic renaissance in the fourth century.[3] Pliny was by no means a despicable literary critic, when he was not paying the tribute of friendly flattery which social tyranny then exacted. He could sometimes be honestly reserved in his appreciation of a friend's dull literary efforts.[4] But in his ideals of oratory, he seems to be hopelessly wrong. There are some terse and epigrammatic sentences in the *Panegyric*, which redeem it by their strong sincerity. But Pliny's canons of oratorical style would have excited the ridicule of his great models, who were thinking of their goal, and not measuring every pace as they strained towards it. Pliny's theory that the mere length of a speech is a great element in its excellence, that swift directness is inartistic, that lingering diffuseness is an oratorical charm, that laboured manufacture of turgid phrases may produce the effect of the impetuous rush of Demosthenes and Cicero in their moments of inspiration, makes us rather glad, who love him, that we have not more of Pliny's oratory.[5]

It is by his letters that Pliny has lived, and will live on, so long as men care to know the inner life of the great ages that have gone before. The criticism, which is so quick to seize the obvious weaknesses of the author of a priceless picture of ancient society, seems to be a little ungrateful. We could forgive almost any failing or affectation in one who had left us a

[1] *Ep.* iii. 13, 5; vii. 17.
[2] *Ep.* iii. 18; cf. ii. 19.
[3] Teuffel, *R. Lit.* § 387; Mackail, *Lat. Lit.* p. 264; *Rom. Soc. in the Last Cent. of the W. Empire* (1st ed.), p. 357.
[4] Plin. *Ep.* iii. 15.
[5] *Ib.* 1, 20. It is curious that this praise of amplitude should be addressed to Tacitus; cf. Nipperdey, *Einleit.* xxxiv.

similar revelation of society when M. Aurelius was holding back the Germans on the Danube, or when Probus was shattering the invaders of the third century. The letters of Cicero offer an apparently obvious comparison, which may be used to the detriment of Pliny. Yet the comparison is rather inept. Cicero was a man of affairs in the thick of a great revolution, and his letters are invaluable to the student of politics at a great crisis in history. But in the calm of Trajan's reign, a letter-writer had to seek other subjects of interest than the fortunes of the state. Literature, criticism, the beauties of nature, the simple charm of country life, the thousand trivial incidents and eccentricities of an overripe society in the capital of the world, furnished a ready pen and a genial imagination, which could idealise its surroundings, with ample materials. Pliny is by some treated as a mediocrity; but, like our own Horace Walpole, he had the keen sense to see that social routine could be made interesting, and that the man who had the skill to do so might make himself famous. He was genuinely interested in his social environment. And intense interest in one's subject is one great secret of literary success. Pliny had also the instinct that, if a work is to live, it must have a select distinction of style, which may be criticised, but which cannot be ignored. He had the laudable ambition to put his thoughts in a form of artistic grace which may make even commonplace attractive. So good a judge as the late Mr. Paley did not hesitate to put the Latinity of Pliny on the level of that of Cicero. Pliny's Letters, perhaps even more than the masterpieces of the Augustine age, fascinated the taste of the fourth and fifth centuries. They were the models of Symmachus and Sidonius, who tried, but in very different fashion, to do for their age what Pliny did for his.[1]

Like his imitators, Sidonius and Symmachus, Pliny intended his Letters to go down to the future as a masterpiece of style, and as a picture of his age. We know that the letters of Symmachus were carefully preserved in duplicate by his scribes, probably by his own instructions, although they were edited and published by his son only after his death.[2] Pliny, like

[1] Macrob. *Sat.* v. 1, 7; Sidon. Apoll. i. 1, 1; iv. 22, 2, ego Plinio ut discipulus assurgo.

[2] Sym. *Ep.* v. 85. Seeck, *Prol.* xlv.

Sidonius, gave his Letters to the public in successive portions during his life.[1] Like Sidonius too, he felt that he had not the sustained power to write a consecutive history of his time, and the Letters of both are probably far more valuable. Pliny's first book opens with a kind of dedication to Septicius Clarus, who was the patron of Suetonius, and who rose to be praetorian prefect under Hadrian.[2] Pliny appears to disclaim any order or principle of arrangement in these books, but this is the device of an artistic negligence. Yet it has been proved by the prince of European scholars in our day that both as to date and subject matter, Pliny's Letters reveal signs of the most careful arrangement. The books were published separately, a common practice down to the end of Roman literary history. The same subject reappears in the same book or the next.[3] Groups of letters dealing with the same matter are found in their natural order in successive books. The proof is made even clearer by the silence or the express references to Pliny's family relations. Finally, the older men, who fill the stage in the earlier Letters, disappear towards the end; while a younger generation, a Salinator or a Ummidius Quadratus, are only heard of in the later. Men of Pliny's own age, like Tacitus or Cornutus Tertullus, meet us from first to last. The dates at which the various books were published have been fixed with tolerable certainty. It is enough for our present purpose to say that the earliest letter belongs to the reign of Nerva, and the ninth book was probably given to the world a year or two before the writer was appointed by Trajan to the office of imperial legate of Bithynia.[4]

It is easy, as we have said, and apparently congenial to some writers, to dwell on the vanity and self-complacency of the writer of these letters. By some he seems to be regarded chiefly as a *poseur*. To discover the weaknesses of Pliny is no great feat of criticism: they are on the surface. But "securus judicat orbis terrarum," and Pliny has borne the scrutiny of the great judge. Men of his own race and age, who spoke and wrote the most finished Latin, awarded him the palm of exquisite style. But Pliny has many qualities of

[1] Momms. *Plin.* (Tr.) p. 2; cf. Haenny, *Schriftsteller*, etc. p. 19.

[2] Plin. *Ep.* i. 1; vii. 28; i. 15; viii. 1; Macé, *Suétone*, p. 87.

[3] Momms. *Plin.* p. 4.

[4] *Ib.* pp. 7, 24; Teuffel, § 335, 1.

the heart, which should cover a multitude of sins, even more serious than any with which he is charged. He had the great gift of loyal friendship, and he had its usual reward in a multitude of friends. It has been regretted that Pliny does not deal with serious questions of politics and philosophy, that his Letters rather skim the surface of social life, and leave its deeper problems untouched. Pliny himself would probably have accepted this criticism as a compliment. The mass of men are little occupied with insoluble questions. And Pliny has probably deserved better of posterity by leaving us a vivid picture of the ordinary life of his time or of his class, rather than an analysis of its spiritual distresses and maladies. We have enough of that in Seneca, in M. Aurelius, and in Lucian. Of the variety and vividness of Pliny's sketches of social life there can never be any question. But our gratitude will be increased if we compare his Letters with the collections of his imitators, Symmachus and Sidonius, whose arid pages are seldom turned by any but a few curious and weary students. Martial, in his way, is perhaps even more clear-cut and minute in his portraiture. But Martial is essentially a wit of the town, viewing its vices, follies, and fashions with the eye of a keen, but rather detached observer. In reading Pliny's Letters, we feel ourselves introduced into the heart of that society in its better hours; and, above all, we seem to be transported to those quiet provincial towns and secluded country seats where, if life was duller and tamer than it was in the capital, the days passed in a quiet content, unsolicited by the stormier passions, in orderly refinement, in kindly relations with country neighbours, and amid the unfading charm of old-world pieties and the witchery of nature.

Pliny has also done a great service in preserving a memorial of the literary tone and habits of his time. Even in that age of fertile production and too enthusiastic appreciation, Pliny, like Seneca and Statius, has a feeling that the love for things of the mind was waning.[1] And he deemed it an almost religious duty, as Symmachus and Sidonius did more than three centuries after him, to arouse the flagging interest in letters, and to reward even third-rate literary

[1] Plin. *Ep.* iii. 18, 5; viii. 12, literarum senescentium reductor; Stat. *Silv.* i. Prooem.; *Petron.* 88; cf. Sidon. Apoll. *Ep.* viii. 8; ii. 14; vii. 15; ii. 10, 1.

effort with exuberant praise. He avows that it is a matter of duty to admire and venerate any performance in a field so difficult as that of letters.[1] Yet Pliny was not by any means devoid of critical honesty and acumen. He could be a severe judge of his own style. He expects candid criticism from his friends, and receives it with gratitude and good temper.[2] This is to him, indeed, the practical purpose of readings before final publication. He made emendations and excisions in the Histories of Tacitus, which the great author had submitted for his revision.[3] In his correspondence with Tacitus, there is a curious mixture of vanity along with a clear recognition of his friend's immense superiority of genius, and a sure prescience of his immortal fame. He is proud to hear their names coupled as chiefs of contemporary literature,[4] and he cherishes the hope that, united by loyal friendship in life, they will go down together to a remote future. When, in the year 106, Tacitus had asked him for an account of the elder Pliny's death, in the great eruption of Vesuvius, Pliny expressed a firm belief that the book on which Tacitus was then engaged was destined to an enduring fame.[5] He was not quite so confident as to the immortality of Martial's work,[6] although he appreciates to the full Martial's brilliant and pungent wit. On the other hand, writing to a friend about the death of Silius Italicus, he frankly recognises that the Epic of the Punic War is a work of industry rather than of genius.[7] Yet he cannot allow the author of this dull mechanical poem to pass away without some record of his career.[8] The death at seventy-five of the last surviving consular of the Neronian age, of the consul in whose year of office the tyranny of Nero closed, inspired a feeling of pathos which was probably genuine, in spite of the rather pompous and pedantic expression of it. And although he wrote the *Punica*, a work which was almost buried till the fifteenth century,[9] Silius was probably a not uninteresting person. He had been a delator under Nero, and

[1] Plin. *Ep.* vi. 17, § 5.
[2] *Ib.* vii. 17; v. 12.
[3] *Ib.* vii. 20; viii. 7.
[4] *Ib.* vii. 20; ix. 23, ad hoc illum "Tacitus es an Plinius?"
[5] *Ib.* vi. 16, 2.
[6] *Ib.* iii. 21, 6, at non erunt aeterna quae scripsit; non erunt fortasse; ille tamen scripsit tanquam essent futura.
[7] *Ib.* iii. 7, scribebat carmina majore cura quam ingenio.
[8] Mart. vii. 63; Tac. *Hist.* iii. 65.
[9] *v.* Teuffel, *R. Lit.* § 315, n. 5, and the opinions collected by Mayor, *Plin.* iii. p. 120.

had enjoyed the friendship of Vitellius, but he knew how to redeem his character under the Flavian dynasty, and he had filled the proconsulate of Asia with some credit.[1] Henceforth he enjoyed the lettered ease and social deference which were the privilege of his class for centuries. He retired finally to the shores of Campania, where, moving from one villa to another, and surrounding himself with books and gems of art, his life flowed away undisturbed by the agony of Rome in the last terror of the Caesars. Among his many estates he was the proud owner of one of Cicero's villas, and of the ground where Virgil sleeps. He used to keep the great poet's birthday with a scrupulous piety, and he always approached his tomb as a holy place. This apparently placid and fortunate life was, like so many in those days, ended by a voluntary death.[2] Silius Italicus, in his life and in his end, is a true type of a generation which could bend before the storm of despotism, and save itself often by ignominious arts, which could recover its dignity and self-respect in the pursuit of literary ideals, and, at the last, assert the right to shake off the burden of existence when it became too heavy.

Pliny's theory of life is clearly stated in the Letters, and it was evidently acted on by a great number of the class to which he belonged.[3] The years of vigorous youth should be given to the service of the state, in pursuing the well-marked and carefully-graduated career of honours, or in the strenuous oratorical strife of the law courts. The leisure of later years might be portioned out between social duty, the pleasures or the cares of a rural estate, and the cultivation of literary taste by reading and imitation of the great masters. The last was the most imperious duty of all, for those with any literary gifts, because charm of style gives the one hope of surviving the wreck of time;[4] for mere cultivated facility, as the most refined and creditable way of filling up the vacant spaces of life. Even if lasting fame was beyond one's reach, it was something to be able to give pleasure to an audience of cultivated friends at a reading, and to enjoy the triumph of an hour. There must

[1] Plin. *Ep.* iii. 7, 3.

[2] *v.* Mayor, *Plin.* iii. p. 114, for a learned note on suicide in the early Empire.

[3] Pliny, *Ep.* iv. 23, 3. For a similar ideal in the fifth century, *v. Roman Society in the Last Century of the Western Empire*, p. 165 (1st ed.).

[4] Plin. *Ep.* v. 8, § 1.

have been many a literary coterie who, if they fed one another's vanity, also encouraged literary ideals, and hinted gentle criticism,[1] in that polite delicacy of phrase in which the Roman was always an adept. One of these literary circles stands out in Pliny's pages. At least two of its members had held great office. Arrius Antoninus, the maternal grandfather of the Emperor Antoninus Pius,[2] had twice borne the consulship with antique dignity, and shown himself a model governor as proconsul of Asia.[3] He was devoted to Greek literature, and seems to have preferred to compose in that language. We need not accept literally Pliny's praises of his Atticism, and of the grace and sweetness of his Greek epigrams. But he seems to have had a facility which Pliny tortured his ingenuity in vain to imitate with the poorer resources of the Latin tongue.[4] Among the friends of Antoninus was Vestricius Spurinna, who had defended Placentia for Otho, who was twice consul under Domitian, and was selected by Trajan to command the troops in a campaign in Germany.[5] This dignified veteran, who had passed apparently untainted through the reigns of the worst emperors, varied and lightened the ordinary routine of his old age by the composition of lyrics, both in Greek and Latin, which seemed to his admirers to have a singular sweetness. Sentius Augurinus, a familiar friend of the two consulars, was also a brilliant verse writer,[6] who could enthral Pliny by a recitation lasting for three days, although the fact that Pliny was the subject of one of the poems may account for the patience or the pleasure. One of Pliny's dearest friends was Passennus Paullus, who claimed kindred with the poet Propertius, and, at any rate, came from the same town in Umbria. Passennus has been cruelly treated by Time, if his lyric efforts recalled, as we are asked to believe, the literary graces of his ancestor, and even those of Horace.[7] Vergilius Romanus devoted himself to comedy, and was thought to have reproduced not unworthily the delicate charms of Menander and Terence, as well as the scathing invective of older

[1] For a good example cf. Plin. *Ep.* iii. 15.

[2] Capitol. *Ant. P.* 1.

[3] Plin. *Ep.* iv. 3.

[4] *Ib.* iv. 18; cf. viii. 4.

[5] Tac. *Hist.* ii. 11; ii. 18, 36; Plin. *Ep.* i. 5; ii. 7; iii. 1, scribit et quidem utraqua lingua, lyra doctissima. Spurinna was 77, at the date of this letter, A.D. 101–102; Momms. p. 11.

[6] Plin. *Ep.* iv. 27; cf. ix. 8.

[7] *Ib.* vi. 15; ix. 22.

Greek masters of the art.[1] But there were others of Pliny's circle who essayed a loftier and weightier style. Probably the foremost of these was Titinius Capito, who, as an inscription records,[2] had held high civil office under Domitian, Nerva, and Trajan. He was an enthusiastic patron of letters, and readily offered his halls to literary friends for their recitations, which he attended with punctilious politeness. Cherishing the memory of the great men of the Republic, the Cassii, the Bruti, and the Catos, he composed a work on the death of the noble victims of the Terror.[3] He tried in vain to draw Pliny into the field of historical composition.[4] But the man who thought more of style and graceful charity than of truth, was not the man to write the history of such a time. He has done a much greater service in providing priceless materials for the reconstruction of its social history. Caninius Rufus was a neighbour of Pliny at Como.[5] He was one of those for whom the charms of country life had a dangerous seduction. His villa, with its colonnades, "where it was always spring," the shining levels of the lake beneath his verandah, the water course with its emerald banks, the baths and spacious halls, all these delights seem to have relaxed the literary energy and ambition of their master. Caninius meditated the composition of a Greek epic on the Dacian wars of Trajan.[6] But he was probably one of those lingering, dilatory writers who meet us in Martial,[7] waiting for the fire from heaven which never comes. The intractable roughness of barbarian names, which, as Pliny suggests, might have been eluded by a Homeric licence in quantity, was probably not the only difficulty of Caninius.

Among the literary friends of Pliny, a much more important person than Caninius was Suetonius, but Suetonius was apparently long paralysed by the same cautious hesitation to challenge the verdict of the public. A younger man than Pliny,[8] Suetonius was one of his most intimate friends. They

[1] Plin. *Ep.* vi. 21.

[2] *C.I.L.* vi. 798 ; *Or.* 801. He was Secretary (ab Epistulis) under Domitian, Nerva, and Trajan ; cf. Macé, *Suétone*, pp. 91, 93, 115.

[3] Plin. *Ep.* i. 17 ; viii. 12. Cf. C. Fannius, who wrote a history of the victims of Nero, Plin. *Ep.* v. 5. He died *circ.* 106, Macé, p. 82.

[4] Plin. *Ep.* v. 8. For similar unwillingness, cf. Sidon. Apoll. *Ep.* iv. 22.

[5] Plin. *Ep.* i. 3.

[6] *Ib.* viii. 4 ; ix. 33.

[7] Mart. iv. 33 ; vi. 14.

[8] Momms. *Plin.* p. 13, puts his birth in 77 A.D. ; but cf. Macé, p. 35, who places it in the year 69 ; see too Peter, *Gesch. Litt.* ii. 67. The indications in Suet. are *Domit.* xii. ; *Ill. Gramm.* iv. ; *Nero*, lvii.

both belonged to that circle which nursed the senatorial tradition and the hatred of the imperial tyrants.[1] The life of Suetonius was not very effectual or brilliant, from a worldly point of view. Although born within the rank to which every distinction was open,[2] he was a man of modest and retiring tastes, devoted to quiet research, and destitute of the eager ambition and vigorous self-assertion which are necessary for splendid success. He was probably for some years a professor of grammar.[3] He made a half-hearted attempt to gain a footing at the bar. In 101 A.D. he obtained a military tribunate, through Pliny's influence, but speedily renounced his command.[4] Henceforth he devoted himself entirely to that historical research, which, if it has not won for him any dazzling fame, has made historical students, in spite of some reservations as to his sources, his debtors for all time. Pliny had the greatest esteem for Suetonius, and was always ready to befriend him, whether it were in the purchase of a quiet little retreat near Rome,[5] or in obtaining for the childless antiquary the *Jus trium liberorum* from Trajan.[6] The two men were bound to one another by many tastes and sympathies, not the least strong being a curious superstition, which infected, as we shall see in a later chapter, even the most vigorous minds of that age. Suetonius had once a dream which seemed to portend failure in some legal cause in which he was engaged. He sought the aid of Pliny to obtain an adjournment. Pliny does not question the reality of such warnings, but merely suggests a more cheering interpretation of the vision.[7] Although devoted to research, and a most laborious student, the biographer of the Caesars was strangely tardy in letting his productions see the light. In 106, he had been long engaged on a work, which was probably the *De Viris Illustribus*.[8] Pliny assailed him with bantering reproaches on his endless use of the file, and begs him to publish without delay. From several indications, it appears that the lingering volume did not appear till 113.[9] It was not till the year 118, when Hadrian arrived

[1] Macé, p. 83; Peter, ii. 69; cf. Krause, *De Sueton. Fontibus*.
[2] For the authorities, *v.* Macé, p. 29.
[3] From 97 to 101 A.D., *ib.* pp. 53–57.
[4] Plin. *Ep.* iii. 8.
[5] *Ib.* i. 24; of the year 97. On the meaning of *contubernalis*, Suetonius being 28, and Pliny 35 years of age, *v.* Macé, p. 50.
[6] Plin. *Ad Traj.* 94; cf. Macé, p. 50.
[7] Plin. *Ep.* i. 18.
[8] Macé, p. 68; Plin. *Ep.* v. 10; Momms. *Plin.* p. 18.
[9] Macé, p. 69.

from the East after his accession, that Suetonius attained the rank of one of the imperial secretaryships.[1] Pliny in all probability had died some years before the elevation of his friend.

But although the dawn of a new age of milder and less suspicious government had, for the first time since Augustus, left men free to compose a true record of the past, and even to vilify the early Caesars,[2] the great mass of cultivated men in Pliny's time, as in the days of Ausonius and Sidonius, were devoted to poetry. The chief cause in giving this direction to the Roman mind was undoubtedly the system pursued in the schools. In the first century, as in the fifth, the formative years of boyhood were devoted almost entirely to the study of the poets. The subject-matter of their masterpieces was not neglected by the accomplished grammarian, who was often a man of learning, and sometimes a man of taste; and the reading of poetry was made the text for disquisitions on geography and astronomy, on mythology or the antiquities of religious ritual and constitutional lore.[3] But style and expression were always of foremost interest in these studies. The ear of the South has always felt the charm of rhythmical or melodious speech, with a keenness of pleasure generally denied to our colder temperament. And the Augustan age had, in a single generation, performed miracles, under Greek inspiration, in moulding the Latin tongue to be the apt vehicle of every mood of poetic feeling. That inspired band of writers, whose call it was to glorify the dawn of a world-wide empire and the ancient achievements of the Latin race,[4] rose to the full height of their vocation. They were conscious that they were writing for distant provinces won from barbarism, and for a remote posterity.[5] They discovered and revealed resources in the language, hitherto undreamt of. They wedded to its native dignity and strength a brilliancy, an easy grace and sprightliness, which positively ravished the ear of the street boys in Pompeii, or of the rude dweller on the Tanais or the Baetis.[6] In his own lifetime Virgil became a popular hero. His Eclogues were chanted on the stage;

[1] Macé, p. 90. For the disgrace of Suetonius, *v.* Spart. *Hadr.* xi. 2.

[2] Plin. *Paneg.* 53.

[3] See *Roman Society in the Last Century of the Western Empire*, p. 348 sq. (1st ed.).

[4] Virg. *Aen.* vi. 848 sq.

[5] Ov. *Trist.* iv. 128; Hor. *Carm.* ii. 20; Friedl. *Sittengesch.* iv. p. 299.

[6] Mau, *Pompeii* (Tr.), 486, 488; *C.I.L.* ii. 4967.

verses of the Aeneid can still be seen, along with verses of Propertius, scrawled on the walls of Campanian towns. Virgil, when he visited Rome, was mobbed by admiring crowds. When his poetry was recited in the theatre, the whole audience rose to their feet as if to salute the emperor.[1] He had the doubtful but significant honour of being recited by Alexandrian boys at the coarse orgies of a Trimalchio.[2] Never was a worthy fame so rapidly and splendidly won: seldom has literary fame and influence been so lasting.

The Flavian age succeeded to this great heritage. Already there were ominous signs of a decay of originality and force, of decadence in the language itself.[3] The controversy between the lovers of the new and the lovers of the archaic style was raging in the reign of Vespasian, and can be still followed in the *De Oratoribus* of Tacitus, or even in the verses of Martial.[4] Already the taste for Ennius and the prae-Ciceronian oratory had set in, for the dialect of the heroes of the Punic Wars, even for "the Latin of the Twelve Tables," [5] a taste which was destined to produce its Dead Sea fruit in the age of the Antonines. But whoever might cavil at Cicero,[6] no one ever questioned the pre-eminence of Virgil, and he and his contemporaries were still the models of a host of imitators. The mass of facile talent, thrown back on itself by the loss of free republican life and public interests, fascinated from earliest infancy by the haunting cadences of the grand style, rushed into verse-writing, to beguile long hours of idleness, or to woo a shadowy fame at an afternoon recital, with a more shadowy hope of future fame. The grand style was a charmer and deceiver. It was such a perfect instrument, it was so protean in its various power, it was so abundant in its resources, that a man of third-rate powers and thin commonplace imagination, who had been trained in skilful manipulation of consecrated phrase, might for the moment delude himself and his friends by faint echoes of the music of the golden age.

[1] Tac. *De Or.* 13, auditis in theatro Virgilii versibus surrexit universus populus, etc.

[2] Petron. *Sat.* 68.

[3] Plin. *Ep.* iii. 18, 4; viii. 12, 1; cf. Seneca's complaints of his time, *Ep.* 95, § 23; 100; Petron. 83–4.

[4] Tac. *Dial. de Or.* 20; Mart. v. 10; cf. Suet. *Octav.* 86, Cacozelos et antiquarios, ut diverso genere vitiosos, pari fastidio sprevit; Pers. i. 69 sq.; Sen. *Ep.* 114. For Hadrian's preference of Ennius to Virgil, etc., *v.* Spart. *Hadr.* c. 16; A. Gell. xii. 2; Macé, p. 96; Martha, *Les Moralistes sous l'Empire Rom.* p. 184.

[5] Sen. *Ep.* 114, § 13, duodecim tabulas loquuntur.

[6] Tac. *Dial. de Or.* 20.

The brilliancy of inherited phrase concealed the poverty of the literary amateur's fancy from himself. And, even if he were not deluded about his own powers, the practice in skilful handling of literary symbols, which was acquired in the schools, furnished a refined amusement for a too ample leisure. It is clear from the dialogue *De Oratoribus*, and from Pliny's Letters, that the meditative life, surrounded by the quiet charm of stream and woodland, far from the din and strife and social routine of the great city,[1] attracted many people much more than the greatest oratorical triumphs in the centumviral court, which, after all, were so pale and bourgeois beside the glories of the great ages of oratory. And although Aper, in the Dialogue of Tacitus, sneers at the solitary and unsocial toil of the poet, rewarded by a short-lived *succès d'estime*,[2] there can be no doubt that the ambition to cut a figure, even for a day, was a powerful inspiration at a time when the ancient avenues to fame had been closed.

It was to satisfy such ambitions that Domitian founded the quinquennial competition on the Capitol, in the year 86 A.D.,[3] as well as the annual festival in honour of Minerva on the Alban Mount. A similar festival, for the cultivation of Greek poetry, had been established at Naples in honour of Augustus, at which Statius had won the crown of corn-ears.[4] And Nero had founded another, apparently only for his own glorification.[5] The festival established by Domitian was more important and enduring. The judges were taken from the priestly colleges, and, amid a concourse of the highest functionaries of the state, the successful poet received his crown at the hands of the emperor. The prospect of such a distinction drew competitors from distant provincial parts. It is a curious illustration of the power and the skill of the literary discipline of the schools that, twice within a few years, the crown of oak leaves was won by boys under fourteen years of age. The verses of one of them may still be read upon his tomb.[6]

But these infrequent chances of distinction could not suffice

[1] Tac. *De Or.* 12.

[2] *Ib.* 9, 10.

[3] Suet. *Dom.* iv.

[4] Stat. v. 3, 225; cf. Suet. *Claud.* xi. A Greek comedy in honour of Germanicus was performed.

[5] Suet. *Ner.* xii. Suetonius says it was the first of the kind. It was called "Neronia."

[6] *Or.* 2603, to L. Val. Pudens, erected by his fellow-citizens in A.D. 110. He was only 13. *v.* Teuffel, § 314, n. 4; Friedl. *Sittengesch.* iii. p. 324.

for the crowd of eager composers. In those days, although the bookselling trade was extensive and vigorous, there was no organised publishing system by which a new work could be brought to the notice of the public.[1] The author had to advertise himself by giving readings, to which he invited his friends, and by distributing copies of his book. The mania for recitation was the theme of satirists from the days of Horace to the days of Epictetus.[2] Martial comically describes the frenzied poet torturing his friends day and night, pursuing them from the bath to the dining-room, and spreading a solitude around him.[3] Juvenal congratulates his friend on escaping to the country from the hoarse reciter of a frigid Theseid.[4] In the bohemian scenes of Petronius, the inveterate versifier, who will calmly finish a passage, after being cast ashore from a shipwreck, makes himself a nuisance by his recitations in the baths and porticoes of Croton, and is very properly stoned by a crowd of street boys.[5] No aspect of social life is more prominent in the Letters of Pliny than the reading of new works, epics, or lyrics, histories, or speeches, before fashionable assemblies. A liberal patron like Titinius Capito would sometimes lend a hall for the purpose. But the reciter had many expenses, from the hire of chairs to the fees to freedmen and slaves, who acted as *claqueurs*. In the circle of a man like Pliny, to attend these gatherings was a sacred duty both to letters and to friendship. In a year when there was a more than usually abundant crop of poets, the eager advocate could boast that he had failed no one, even in the month when the courts were busiest.[6] Doubtless, many of the fashionable idlers, who dawdled away their time in the many resorts devoted to gossip and scandal, were glad to show themselves in the crowd. Old friends would consider it a duty to support and encourage the budding literary ambition of a young aspirant of their set. Some sincere lovers of literary art would be drawn by a genuine interest and a wish to maintain the literary tradition, which was already betraying signs of weakness and decay. But, to a great many, this duty,

[1] Plin. *Ep.* vi. 2; ix. 11, 2; Mart. vii. 8. Cf. Haenny, *Schriftst. u. Buchh.* ii. p. 24 sqq.
[2] Epict. iii. 23, § 11.
[3] Mart. iii. 44, 45; iv. 81.
[4] Juv. i. 2; iii. 9.
[5] Petron. *Sat.* 90, 91, 115.
[6] Plin. *Ep.* i. 13; ii. 19; iv. 5; 27; v. 12; vi. 17, 21; viii. 21.

added to the endless round of other social obligations, was evidently becoming repulsive and wearisome.[1] Pliny could listen with delight and admiration to Sentius Augurinus reciting his poems for three long days.[2] He would calmly expect his own friends to listen for as many days to a whole volume of his poems, or to his *Panegyric* on Trajan.[3] Such was his high breeding, his kindliness, and such was his passion for literature in any form or of any quality, that he could hardly understand how what to him seemed at once a pleasure and duty should be regarded by others as an intolerable nuisance. The conduct of such people is treated with some disdain in one or two of the rare passages in which he writes of his circle with any severity. Some of these fashionable folk, after lingering in some place of gossip until the reading was well advanced, would enter the hall with ostentatious reluctance, and then leave before the end. Others, with an air of superiority, would sit in stolid silence and disguise the slightest expression of interest. This seemed to Pliny, not only grossly bad manners, but also neglect of a literary duty.[4] The audience should not only encourage honest effort; they should contribute their judgment to the improvement of style. Pliny, like Aristotle, has an immense faith in the collective opinion of numbers, even in matters of artistic taste.[5] He used to read his own pieces to successively wider circles, each time receiving suggestions for amendment. Many of Pliny's Letters, like the dialogue *De Oratoribus*, reveal the keenness with which in those days questions of style were debated. But, as in the circle of Sidonius, this very energy of criticism was perhaps due to a dim consciousness of waning force.[6] Pliny, with all his kindly optimism, lets fall a phrase here and there which betrays an uneasiness about the future of letters.[7] Enthusiasm is failing. Nay, there is a hardly veiled contempt for that eager mediocrity which Pliny and Titinius Capito made it a point of honour to encourage. We feel that we are on the edge of that arid desert of cultivated

[1] Plin. *Ep.* vi. 17.

[2] *Ib.* iv. 27.

[3] *Ib.* iii. 18; iv. 5.

[4] *Ib.* i. 13, 2; vi. 17; viii. 12, 1.

[5] *Ib.* vii. 17, 7, quia in numero ipso est quoddam magnum conlatumque consilium. Cf. Arist. *Pol.* iii. 11, διὸ καὶ κρίνουσιν ἄμεινον οἱ πολλοὶ καὶ τὰ τῆς μουσικῆς ἔργα καὶ τὰ τῶν ποιητῶν.

[6] Sidon. Apoll. *Ep.* ii. 14; vii. 15; i. 6.

[7] Plin. *Ep.* viii. 12. Seneca was even more pessimist, cf. *Ep.* 95, § 23; 100; *De Brev. V.* xiii. 1.

impotence in which the freshness and vigour of Roman literature was soon mysteriously to disappear.

Great as were the attractions of the capital, its gay social circles with their multifarious engagements, its games and spectacles, and literary novelties, yet the most devoted "Ardelio," in the end, felt the strain and the monotony to be oppressive.[1] Seneca and Pliny, Martial and Juvenal,[2] from various points of view, lament or ridicule the inanity and the slavery of city life. Roman etiquette was perhaps the most imperious and exacting that ever existed. Morning receptions, punctilious attendance at the assumption of the toga, at betrothals, or the sealing of wills, or the reading of some tedious epic, advice or support in the law courts, congratulations to friends on every official success, these duties, and many others, left men, who had a large circle of acquaintance, hardly a moment of repose. Hence the rapture with which Pliny escapes to the stillness of the Laurentine pine woods, or the pure cold breezes that blew from the Apennines over his Tuscan seat.[3] In these calm solitudes the weary advocate and man of letters became for a little while his own master, and forgot the din and crush of the streets, the paltry ambitions, the malevolent gossip and silly rumours of the great world, in some long-suspended literary task. There can be no doubt that an intense enjoyment was becoming more and more felt in country life. Its unbought, home-grown luxuries, its common sights and sounds, its antique simplicity, have a strange charm even for a hardened bohemian like Martial.[4] But Pliny, besides this commoner form of enjoyment, has a keen and exquisite feeling for beauty of scenery. He loves the amphitheatre of hills, crowned with immemorial forest that looks down on rich pastoral slope, or vineyard or meadow, bright with the flowers of spring, and watered by the winding Tiber; he loves the scenery of Como, where you watch the fishermen at his toils from some retreat on the terraced banks.[5] Where in ancient literature can you find a more sharp and clear-cut picture of a romantic scene than

[1] Plin. *Ep.* i. 9; quot dies quam frigidis rebus absumpsi! cf. the social life of Symmachus, *Roman Society in the Last Century of the Western Empire*, p. 128 sq. (1st ed.).

[2] Sen. *De Tranq.* xii.; Juv. iii. xi.; Mart. xii. 18.

[3] Plin. *Ep.* i. 9; iv. 1.

[4] Mart. iii. 58.

[5] Plin. *Ep.* v. 6, § 7, 8; i. 3; ix. 7, § 4.

in his description of the Clitumnus?[1] The famous stream rises under a low hill, shaded by ancient cypresses, and broadens into a basin in whose glassy ice-cold waters you may count the pebbles. Soon the current grows broader and swifter, and the barges are swept along under groves of ash and poplar, which, so vivid is their reflection, seem to be growing in the river-bed. Hard by, is a temple of the river-god, with many other chapels, and a seat of ancient augury; the magic charm of antique religious awe blends with the witchery of nature, and many a villa is planted on fair spots along the banks. There was plenty of sport to be had in the Apennines or the Laurentine woods. But Pliny was plainly not a real sportsman. He once tells his friend Tacitus, who seems to have rallied him on this failing, that although he has killed three boars, he much prefers to sit, tablets in hand beside the nets, meditating in the silent glade.[2] The country is charming to Pliny, but its greatest charm lies in the long tranquil hours which can be given to literary musing. Part of the well-regulated day of Spurinna, a man who had commanded armies and governed provinces, and who had reached his seventy-seventh year, is devoted to lyric composition both in Greek and Latin.[3] Pliny once or twice laments the mass of literary talent which, from diffidence or love of ease, was buried in these rural retreats.[4] There must have been many a country squire, like that Terentius, who, apparently lost in bucolic pursuits, surprised his guest by the purity of his taste and his breadth of culture. We often meet the same buried talent after nearly four centuries in the pages of Sidonius.[5]

The literature of the Flavian age has preserved for us many pictures of Roman villas. They occupied every variety of site. They were planted on rocks where the sea-foam flecked their walls,[6] or on inland lakes and rivers, embowered in woods, or on the spurs of the Apennines, between the ancient forest and the wealthy plain.[7] Some of these mansions were remote and secluded. But on the Bay of Naples, on the Laurentine shore or the banks of Lake Como,[8] they clustered thickly.

[1] *Ep.* viii. 8; cf. Virg. *Georg.* ii. 146; once visited by Caligula, Suet. *Calig.* 43.

[2] Plin. *Ep.* i. 6, solitudo ipsumque illud silentium quod venationi datur magna cogitationis incitamenta sunt.

[3] *Ib.* iii. 1, § 7.

[4] *Ib.* vii. 25.

[5] Sidon. Apoll. *Ep.* i. 6; ii. 14; vii. 15.

[6] Stat. *Silv.* ii. 2, 22, spumant templa salo.

[7] Plin. *Ep.* v. 6.

[8] *Ib.* ii. 17, § 27.

Building in the days of Domitian was as much the rage as it was in the days of Horace, and, just as then, all natural obstacles were defied in preparing a site to the builder's taste. In the grounds of Pollius Felix in the *Silvae,* whole hills had been levelled, and rocks had been cleared away to make a space for the house with its gardens and woodlands.[1] Manlius Vopiscus had built two luxurious seats on opposite banks of the Anio, where the stream glides silently under overarching boughs.[2] The villas pressed so close to the water that you could converse, and almost touch hands, across the interval between them. The love of variety, or the obligation imposed on senators to invest a third of their fortune in Italian land,[3] may account for the number of country seats possessed even by men who were not of the wealthiest class.[4] Pliny had villas at Laurentum, at Tifernum Tiberinum, at Beneventum, and more than two on Lake Como.[5] The orator Regulus had at least five country seats.[6] Silius Italicus had several stately abodes in the same district of Campania, and, with capricious facility, transferred his affections to each new acquisition.[7]

It is by no means an easy task, and perhaps not a very profitable one, to trace minutely the arrangement of one of these great houses. Indeed there seems to have been a good deal of caprice and little care for symmetry in their architecture. The builder appears to have given no thought to external effect. To catch a romantic view from the windows, to escape the sultry heat of midsummer, or woo the brief sunshine of December, above all to obtain perfect stillness, were the objects which seem to have dictated the plans of the Roman architect.[8] The Laurentine villa of Pliny and the Surrentine of Pollius Felix from their windows or colonnades gave glimpses of forest or mountain, or sea, or fat herds browsing on the meadow grass, or a view seaward to the islands off the Cam-

[1] Stat. *Silv.* ii. 2, 53 ; cf. iii. 1, 124.
[2] *Ib.* i. 3, 20–37.
[3] Imposed by Trajan on candidates for office, Plin. *Ep.* vi. 19. This was a repetition of former enactments, *e.g.* Suet. *Tib.* 48. It was revived again by M. Aurelius, Capitol xi. Exclusion from commerce necessitated investments in land. Plin. *Ep.* iii. 19, sum prope totus in praediis, aliquid tamen foenero. In A.D. 106 the price of land was rising ; *Ep.* vi. 19 ; but cf. iii. 19 (A.D. 101) ; see Friedl. i. p. 197.
[4] Sen. *De Benef.* vii. 10, 5 ; *Ep.* 89, § 20 ; Mart. v. 13, 7 ; Petron. *Sat.* 76, 77 ; Stat. *Silv.* ii. 6, 62.
[5] Plin. *Ep.* ii. 17 ; v. 6 ; ix. 7 ; iv. 1 ; iv. 13.
[6] Mart. vii. 31.
[7] Plin. *Ep.* iii. 7.
[8] Friedl. *Sittengesch.* iii. 64.

panian shore.[1] One room admits the morning sun, another is brightened by the glow of evening. Here is a colonnade where in winter you can pace up and down with shutters closed on the weather side, or in spring-time enjoy the scent of violets and the temperate sunshine.[2] In the mansions on the Anio, there is, according to Statius, an air of everlasting quietness, never broken even by wandering wind, or ripple of the stream.[3] Pliny has a distant room at Laurentum, to which even the licensed din of the Saturnalia never penetrates.[4] Thus these villas threw out their chambers far and wide, meandering in all directions, according to the fancy of the master, or the charms of the neighbouring scenery.

The luxury of the Roman villa consisted rather in the spaciousness and variety of building, to suit the changing seasons, than in furniture for comfort or splendour. There were, indeed, in many houses some costly articles, tables of citrus and ivory, and antique vases, of priceless worth.[5] But the chambers of the most stately houses would probably, to modern taste, seem scantily furnished. It was on the walls and ceiling and columns that the Roman of taste lavished his wealth. The houses of Pliny, indeed, seem to have been little adorned by this sort of costly display.[6] But the villa of Pollius Felix, like the baths of Claudius Etruscus, shone with all the glory of variegated marbles on plaque and pillar, drawn from the quarries of Phrygia, Laconia, and Syene, Carystus and Numidia.[7] Pliny confesses that he is not a connoisseur in art. He speaks with hesitation of the merit of a Corinthian bronze which he has acquired.[8] But he was surrounded in his own class by artistic enthusiasm, much of it, it is to be feared, pretentious and ignorant. The dispersion of the artistic wealth of Greek lands had flooded Italy with the works of the great masters. Collectors of them, like Silius Italicus, abounded. The fashion became so general and so imperious, that it penetrated even into the vulgar circle of people like Trimalchio, who, in interpreting the subject of the chasing on a cup, could confuse the Punic and the Trojan wars. In the villas described

[1] Plin. *Ep.* ii. 17 ; Stat. *Silv.* ii. 2, 76.

[2] Plin. ii. 17, § 16.

[3] Stat. *Silv.* i. 3, 29.

[4] Plin. *Ep.* ii. 17, § 24.

[5] Friedl. *Sittengesch.* iii. 87.

[6] Plin. *Ep.* v. 6.

[7] Stat. *Silv.* ii. 2, 85 ; i. 5, 36 ; Friedl. *Sittengesch.* iii. 65.

[8] Plin. *Ep.* iii. 6 ; cf. the taste of Silius Italicus, iii. 7, 8 ; Petron. *Sat.* 50, 88 ; Mahaffy, *Greek World*, etc., p. 139 sq.

by Statius, it would seem that the art of Apelles, Pheidias, Myron, and Polycletus adorned the saloons and colonnades.[1] It may be doubted, however, whether many of these works could claim such illustrious parentage. There was plenty of facile technique in those days which might easily deceive the vulgar collector by more or less successful reproduction.[2] The confident claim to artistic discrimination was not less common in the Flavian age than in later days, and it was probably as fallible. It is rather suspicious that, in the attempts at artistic appreciation in this period, attention seems to be concentrated on the supposed antiquity, rarity, or costliness of material. There is little in the glowing descriptions in the *Silvae* to indicate a genuine appreciation of real art.

It is possible that the great Roman country seat, in its vast extent, although not in the stateliness of its exterior, may have surpassed the corresponding mansions of our time. It was the expression in stone of the dominant passion of an enormously wealthy class, intoxicated with the splendour of imperial power, and ambitious to create monuments worthy of an imperial race. Moreover, the Roman's energy always exulted in triumphing over natural difficulties. Just as he drove his roads unswerving over mountain and swamp, so he took a pride in rearing his piles of masonry on the most obstinate and defiant sites, or even in the middle of the waves. But, in the extent of their parks, and the variety of floral display, the Romans of the most luxurious age seldom reached the modern English standard. The grounds of the villas which, in thick succession, lined the Laurentine or Campanian shore, cannot have been very extensive. Pliny has splendid views from his windows of forest, mountain, and meadow, but the scene lies plainly beyond the bounds of his demesne.[3] The gardens and shrubberies are very artificial, arranged in terraces or labyrinths close to the house, or with hedges of box clipped into shapes of animals along an open colonnade. The hippodrome at his Tuscan seat, for riding exercise, is formed by lines of box and laurel and cypress and plane tree. The fig and mulberry form a garden at the Laurentine villa.[4] The cultivated

[1] Stat. *Silv.* i. 3, 50; ii. 2, 63 sq.; Mart. iv. 39.

[2] Friedl. iii. 196; cf. Croiset, *Lucien*, c. ix. p. 265; Marq. *Priv.* ii. 611.

[3] Plin. *Ep.* v. 6, 7; cf. ii. 17, § 3.

[4] *Ib.* ii. 17, § 15; v. 6, § 33.

flowers are few, only roses and violets. But the Romans made up for variety by lavish profusion. In the Neronian orgies a fortune was sometimes spent on Egyptian roses for a single banquet.[1]

We might almost conjecture how the days passed amid such scenes, even without any formal diary. But Pliny has left us two descriptions of a gentleman's day in the country.[2] Pliny himself, as we might expect, awoke early, about six o'clock, and in one of those sleeping-rooms, so carefully shut off from the voices of nature or from household noise, with shutters still closed, he meditated some literary piece. Then, calling for his amanuensis, he dictated what he had composed. About ten or eleven, he passed into a shady cloister, opening on a bed of violets, or a grove of plane trees, where he continued his literary work. Then followed a drive, during which, according to his uncle's precept and example, his studies were still continued.[3] A short siesta, a walk, declamation in Greek and Latin, after the habit of Cicero, gymnastic exercise, and the bath, filled the space till dinner time arrived. During this meal, a book was read aloud, and the evening hours were enlivened by acting or music and the society of friends. Occasional hunting and the cares of a rural estate came in to vary this routine. The round of Spurinna's day, which excited Pliny's admiration by its rigid regularity, is pretty much the same as his own, except that Spurinna seems to have talked more and read less.[4]

To the ordinary English squire Pliny's studious life in the country would not seem very attractive. And his pretence of sport was probably ridiculed even in his own day.[5] But his Letters give glimpses of a rural society which, both in its pleasures and its cares, has probably been always much the same from one age to another in Europe. On his way to Como, Pliny once turned aside for a couple of days to his Tuscan estate, to join in the dedication of a temple which he had built for the people of Tifernum Tiberinum. The consecration was to be followed by a dinner to his good neighbours, who had elected him patron of their township, who were very proud of his career, and greeted him warmly whenever

[1] Suet. *Nero*, xxvii.; Friedl. iii. 77 sqq.
[2] Plin. *Ep.* ix. 36; iii. 1.
[3] *Ib.* iii. 5, § 15.
[4] *Ib.* iii. 1.
[5] *Ib.* ix. 36, § 6.

he came among them.[1] There is also the record of the restoration, in obedience to the warning of a diviner, of an ancient temple of Ceres on his lands, with colonnades to shelter the worshippers who frequented the shrine. And the venerable wooden statue of the goddess, which was much decayed, had to be replaced by a more artistic image. But the life of a Roman proprietor, of course, had its prosaic and troublesome side which Pliny does not conceal. There is an interesting letter in which he consults a friend on the question of the purchase of an estate.[2] It adjoined, or rather cut into his own lands. It could be managed by the same bailiff, and the same staff of labourers and artisans would serve for both estates. On the other hand, Pliny thinks, it is better not to put too many eggs into one basket. It is more prudent to have estates widely dispersed, and thus less exposed to a single stroke of calamity. Moreover this estate, however tempting, with its fertile, well-watered meadows, its vineyards and woods, is burdened by an insolvent tenantry, who, through faulty management, have been allowed to fall into arrear. Pliny, however, is tempted to buy at a greatly reduced price,[3] and, in order to meet the payment, although his wealth is nearly all in land, he can call in some loans at interest, and the balance can be borrowed from his father-in-law, whose purse is always at his disposal. Pliny was sometimes worried by the complaints of the people on his estates, and finds it very difficult to secure solvent tenants on a five years lease. He made liberal remissions of rent, but arrears went on accumulating, until the tenant in despair gave up any attempt to repay his debt. In this extremity, Pliny resolved to adopt a different system of letting. He substituted for a fixed rent a certain proportion of the produce,[4] in fact the métayer system, and employed some of his people to see that the returns were not fraudulently diminished. At another time he is embarrassed by finding that, owing to a bad vintage,

[1] Plin. *Ep.* iv. 1.

[2] *Ib.* iii. 19.

[3] *Ib.* § 7. This estate was once worth HS.5,000,000; it was now offered for HS.3,000,000, *i.e.* £25,000; cf. *Ep.* iv. 6; ii. 4, 3. The letter iii. 19 belongs to the year 101 A.D.; but in *Ep.* vi. 19 (106 A.D.) it appears that the price of land was rising, owing to competition, and Pliny advises Nepos to sell his Italian estates and buy others in the provinces; cf. vi. 3, 1.

[4] *Ep.* ix. 37, medendi una ratio, si non nummo sed partibus locem; cf. J. S. Mill, *Pol. Econ.* bk. ii. c. 8, 1; A. Young, *Travels in France*, p. 18.

the men who have bought his grapes in advance are going to be heavy losers. He makes a uniform remission to all of about twelve per cent. But he gives an additional advantage to the large buyers, and to those who had been prompt in their payments.[1] It is characteristic of the man that he says, quite naturally, that the landlord should share with his tenant such risks from the fickleness of nature.

So good a man was sure to be far more afflicted by the troubles of his dependents than by any pecuniary losses of his own. One year, there were many deaths among his slaves. Pliny feels this acutely, but he consoles himself by the reflection that he has been liberal in manumission, and still more liberal in allowing his slaves to make their wills, the validity of which he maintains as if they were legal instruments.[2] If Pliny shows a little too much self-complacency in this human sympathy, there can be no doubt that, like Seneca, he felt that slaves were humble friends, men of the same flesh and blood as the master, and that the master has a moral duty towards them, quite apart from the legal conventions of Rome.[3] When his wife's grandfather proposed to make numerous manumissions, Pliny rejoiced greatly at the accession of so many new citizens to the municipality.[4] When his favourite reader, Encolpius, was seized with hemorrhage, Pliny displayed a genuine and most affectionate concern for the humble partner of his studies.[5] Another member of his household, a freedman named Zosimus, suffered from the same malady. Zosimus seems to have been a most excellent, loyal, and accomplished man. He was very versatile, a comedian, a musician, a tasteful reader of every kind of literature.[6] His patron sent him to Egypt to recruit his health. But, from putting too great a strain upon his voice, he had a return of his dangerous illness, and once more needed change of air. Pliny determined to send him to the Riviera, and begs a friend, Paulinus, to let Zosimus have the use of his villa and all necessary attention, for which Pliny will

[1] Plin. *Ep.* viii. 2; ix. 37, 3.

[2] *Ib.* viii. 16; cf. the Lex Coll. Cultorum Dianae et Antinoi, *Or. Henz.* 6086. The slave member is permitted to dispose of his funeraticium by will. Marq. *Priv.* i. 189.

[3] Sen. *Ep.* 31; 47; 77; *De Clem.* i. 18, 3; *De Ben.* iii. 21; Juv. xiv. 16; D. Chr. *Or.* x.; Spart. *Hadr.* 18, § 7; Boissier, *Rel. Rom.* ii. 358; Denis, *des Idées Morales*, etc., ii. 208 sq.; Wallon, *L'Esclav.* i. c. 11; Marq. i. 189.

[4] *Ep.* vii. 32. Fabatus seems to have been a model country squire; cf. *Ep.* iv. 1; v. 11; vi. 12; vii. 11; viii. 10.

[5] *Ib.* viii. 1.

[6] *Ib.* v. 19; cf. Sen. *Ep.* 27, § 6; Friedl. *SG.* iii. 89; Marq. *Priv.* i. 158.

bear the cost.[1] In his social relations with his freedmen Pliny always shows himself the perfect, kindly gentleman. Juvenal and Martial poured their scorn on those unequal dinners, where the guests were graduated, and where poorer wine and coarser viands were served out to those of humble degree.[2] Pliny was present at one of these entertainments, and he expresses his contempt for the vulgar host in terms of unwonted energy.[3] His own freedmen, as he tells a fellow-guest, are entertained as equals at his table. If a man fears the expense, he can find a remedy by restraining his own luxury, and sharing the plain fare which he imposes on his company. Pliny's relations with his slaves and freedmen were very like those which the kindly English squire cultivates towards his household and dependents. The affectionate regret for a good master or mistress, recorded on many an inscription of that age,[4] shows that Pliny's household was by no means a rare exception.

Yet the Letters of Pliny, with all their charity and tranquil optimism, reveal now and then a darker side of household slavery. A man of praetorian rank named Largius Macedo, who forgot, or perhaps too vividly remembered, his own servile origin, was known as a cruel and haughty master. While he was enjoying the bath in his Formian villa, he was suddenly surrounded by a throng of angry slaves who, with every expression of hatred and loathing, inflicted on him such injuries that he was left for dead on the glowing pavement. He seemed, or pretended for a while, to be dead. A few who remained faithful took up the apparently lifeless corpse, amid the shrieks of his concubines, and bore him into the Frigidarium. The coolness and the clamour recalled him from his swoon. The would-be murderers meanwhile had fled, but many of them were caught in the end, and the outrage was sternly avenged.[5] In another letter, Pliny tells the tale of the mysterious disappearance of one Metilius Crispus, a citizen of Como, for whom Pliny had obtained equestrian rank, and made him a gift of the required HS.400,000. Metilius set out on a journey and was never heard of again.[6] It is

[1] Plin. *Ep.* v. 19.

[2] Mart. i. 44; iii. 49; Juv. v. 25 sqq.; cf. Sen. *De Ben.* vi. 33, § 4.

[3] Plin. *Ep.* ii. 6.

[4] *Or. Henz.* 2862, 2874, 6389.

[5] Plin. *Ep.* iii. 14.

[6] *Ib.* vi. 25; cf. the similar fate of Lampridius, at the close of the Western Empire in Gaul, Sid. Apoll. *Ep.* viii. 11. § 10.

significant that of the slaves who attended him no one ever reappeared. Amid such perils, says Pliny, do we masters live, and no kindness can relieve us from alarm. Seneca remarks that the master's life is continually at the mercy of his slaves.[1] And the cruel stringency of legislation shows how real was the peril.

Pliny was only an infant in the evil days when suicide was the one refuge from tyranny, when the lancet so often opened the way to "eternal freedom." Yet, even in his later years, men not unfrequently escaped from intolerable calamity or incurable disease by a voluntary death.[2] The morality of suicide was long a debated question. There were strict moralists who maintained that it was never lawful to quit one's post before the final signal to retreat. Men like Seneca regarded it as a question to be determined by circumstances and motives.[3] He would not palliate wild, impetuous self-murder, without a justifying cause. On the other hand, there might be, especially under a monster like Nero, cases in which it were mere folly not to choose an easy emancipation rather than a certain death of torture and ignominy. Eternal law, which has assigned a single entrance to this life, has mercifully allowed us many exits. Any death is preferable to servitude.[4] So, in the case of disease and old age, it is merely a question whether the remainder of life is worth living. If the mental powers are falling into irreparable decay, if the malady is tormenting and incurable, Seneca would permit the rational soul to quit abruptly its crumbling tenement, not to escape pain or weakness, but to shake off the slavery of a worthless life.[5]

Pliny was not a philosopher, and had no elaborate theory of suicide or of anything else. But his opinion on the question may be gathered from his remarks on the case of Titius Aristo, the learned jurist. To rush on death, he says, is a vulgar,

[1] Sen. *Ep.* 4, § 8 ; 107, 5.

[2] See a great mass of instances and authorities collected, with his unique learning, by Mayor, *Plin.* iii. pp. 114, 115 ; cf. Boissier, *L'Opp.* p. 212.

[3] Sen. *Ep.* 24, § 11 ; 58, § 36 ; 70, § 8 ; 117, § 22 ; *De Prov.* ii. 10 ; vi. 7 ; *De Ira*, iii. 15 ; Epict. i. 24 ; cf. ii. 15 ; iii. 24 ; M. Aurel. x. 8 ; x. 32 ; cf. Mommsen, *De Coll.* p. 100.

[4] Sen. *Ep.* 70, § 21, dum hoc constat praeferendam esse spurcissimam mortem servituti mundissimae.

[5] *Ib.* 58, § 36, non adferam mihi manus propter dolorem : hunc tamen si sciero perpetuo mihi esse patiendum, exibo ; non propter ipsum, sed quia impedimento mihi futurus est ad omne propter quod vivitur . . . prosiliam ex aedificio putri ac ruenti.

commonplace act. But to balance the various motives, and make a deliberate and rational choice may, in certain circumstances, be the proof of a lofty mind.[1] The cases of suicide described in the Letters are nearly always cases of incurable or prolonged disease. The best known is that of the luxurious Silius Italicus, who starved himself to death in his seventy-fifth year.[2] He was afflicted with an incurable tumour, almost the only trouble in his long and happy life. Corellius Rufus, who had watched over Pliny's career with almost parental care,[3] chose to end his life in a similar manner. Pliny was immensely saddened by the close of a life which seemed to enjoy so many blessings, high character, great reputation and influence, family love and friendship. Yet he does not question the last resolve of Corellius. In his thirty-third year he had been seized with hereditary gout. During the period of vigorous manhood, he had warded off its onsets by an extreme abstinence. But as old age crept on, its tortures, wracking every limb, became unendurable, and Corellius determined to put an end to the hopeless struggle. His obstinacy was proof against all the entreaties of his wife and friends, and Pliny, who was called in as a last resource, came only to hear the physician repelled for the last time with a single energetic word.[4] Sailing once on Lake Como, Pliny heard from an old friend the tragic tale of a double suicide from a verandah overhanging the lake. The husband had long suffered from a loathsome and hopeless malady. His wife insisted on knowing the truth, and, when it was revealed to her, she nerved him to end the cruel ordeal, and promised to bear him company. Bound together, the pair took the fatal leap.[5]

In spite of his charity and optimism,[6] it would not be altogether true to say that Pliny was blind to the faults and vices of his time. He speaks, with almost Tacitean scorn, of the rewards which awaited a calculating childlessness, and of the

[1] Plin. *Ep.* i. 22, 10; Aristo was a fine type of the puritan pagan, an "imago priscae frugalitatis."

[2] *Ib.* iii. 7, 1. For similar instances, *v.* Sen. *Ep.* 70, § 6; Tac. *Ann.* xi. 3; Suet. *Tib.* 53; Petron. 111; Epict. ii. 15.

[3] Plin. *Ep.* ix. 13, 6; cf. iv. 17, 4; vii.

[4] *Ib.* i. 12, 10. It is characteristic of the time that his last word was κέκρικα.

[5] *Ib.* vi. 24.

[6] Pliny boasts of idealising his friends; vii. 28, agnosco crimen. . . . Ut enim non sint tales quales a me praedicantur, ego tamen beatus quod mihi videntur.

eager servility of the will-hunter.[1] In recommending a tutor for the son of Corellia Hispulla, he regards the teacher's stainless character as of paramount importance in an age of dangerous licence, when youth was beset with manifold seductions.[2] He blushes for the degradation of senatorial character displayed in the scurrilous or obscene entries which were sometimes found on the voting tablets of the august body.[3] The decline of modesty and courteous deference in the young towards their elders greatly afflicted so courteous a gentleman. There seemed to be no respect left for age or authority. With their fancied omniscience and intuitive wisdom, young men disdain to learn from any one or to imitate any example; they are their own models.[4] Among the many spotless and charming women of Pliny's circle, there is one curious exception, one, we may venture to surmise, who had been formed in the Neronian age. Ummidia Quadratilla was a lady of the highest rank, who died at the age of eighty in the middle of the reign of Trajan.[5] She preserved to the end an extraordinary health and vigour, and evidently enjoyed the external side of life with all the zest of the old days of licence in her youth. Her grandson, who lived under her roof, was one of Pliny's dearest friends, a spotless and almost puritanical character. Ummidia, even in her old age, kept a troop of pantomimic artistes, and continued to enjoy their doubtful exhibitions. But her grandson would never witness them, and, it must be said, Ummidia respected and even encouraged a virtue superior to her own.

It has been remarked that, in nearly all these cases, where Pliny has any fault to find with his generation, the evil seems to be only a foil for the virtue of some of his friends. Even in his own day, there were those who criticised him for his extravagant praise of the people he loved. He takes the censure as a compliment, preferring the kind-heartedness which is occasionally deceived, to the cold critical habit which has lost all illusions.[6] Pliny belonged to a caste who were linked

[1] Plin. *Ep.* viii. 18; iv. 21; viii. 10, 11, neque enim ardentius tu pronepotes quam ego liberos cupio; cf. iv. 15, 3, fecunditate uxoris frui voluit eo saeculo quo plerisque etiam singulos filios orbitatis praemia graves faciunt.

[2] *Ib.* iii. 3, in hac licentia temporum.

[3] *Ib.* iv. 25, proximis comitiis in quibusdam tabellis multa jocularia atque etiam foeda dictu . . . inventa sunt.

[4] *Ib.* viii. 23, 3, ipsi sibi exempla sunt.

[5] *Ib.* vii. 24, she was born about A.D. 27, in the reign of Tiberius. Ummidia had the virtue of liberality; she built an amphitheatre and temple for Casinum, *Or. Henz.* 781.

[6] Plin. *Ep.* vii. 28, 2.

to one another by the strongest ties of loyalty and tradition.[1] The members of it were bound to support one another by counsel, encouragement, and influence, they were expected to help a comrade's advancement in the career of honours, to applaud and stimulate his literary ambition, to be prodigal of sympathy or congratulation or pecuniary help in all the vicissitudes of public or private life.[2] The older men, who had borne the weight of great affairs, recognised the duty of forming the character of their juniors by precept and criticism. In this fashion the old soldier Spurinna, on his morning drive, would pour forth to some young companion the wealth of his long experience. In this spirit Verginius Rufus and Corellius stood by Pliny throughout his official career, to guide and support him.[3] Pliny, in his turn, was always lavish of this kind of help, and deemed it a matter of pride and duty to afford it. Sometimes he solicits office for a friend's son, or commends a man to the emperor for the *Jus trium liberorum*.[4] Sometimes he applauds the early efforts of a young pleader at the bar, or gives him counsel as to the causes which he should undertake, or the discipline necessary for oratorical success.[5] He was often consulted about the choice of a tutor for boys, and he responded with all the earnestness of a man who believed in the infinite importance of sound influence in the early years of life.[6] To his older friends he would address disquisitions on style, consolations in bereavement, congratulations on official preferment, descriptions of some fair scene or picturesque incident in rural life. He often wrote, like Symmachus, merely to maintain the connection of friendly sympathy by a chat on paper. His vanity is only too evident in some of these letters. But it is, after all, an innocent vanity and the consuming anxiety to cherish the warmth and solidarity of friendship, and a high tone in the great class to which he belonged, might well cover even graver faults. If there was too much self-indulgence in

[1] Cf. *Ep.* v. 14, on his relations with Cornutus Tertullus: quae societas amicitiarum artissima nos familiaritate conjunxit.

[2] Plin. *Ep.* vi. 6; vi. 32; in which he offers a dowry to Quintilian's daughter in the most delicate way; cf. Juv. iii. 215; xv. 150; Sen. *De Benef.* ii. 21, 5; iv. 11, 3; Tac. *Ann.* iv. 62; yet cf. the judgment of D. Chrys. *Or.* vii. § 82; Denis, *Idées Morales*, ii. 175 sqq.

[3] Plin. *Ep.* viii. 23, 2; vi. 11, 3; i. 12, 12; ii. 1, 8 (of Verginius Rufus), sic candidatum me suffragio ornavit, etc., iii. 1, 6 (of Spurinna), quibus praeceptis imbuare!

[4] Plin. *Ad Traj.* 87, 94.

[5] Id. *Ep.* vi. 29.

[6] *Ib.* iii. 3.

that class, if they often abandoned themselves to the seductions of ease and literary trifling in luxurious retreats, it is also to be remembered that a man of rank paid heavily for his place in Roman society, both in money and in the observance of a very exacting social code. And no one recognised the obligation with more cheerful alacrity than Pliny.

Pliny felt a genuine anxiety that young men of birth should aim at personal distinction. Any gleam of generous ambition, any sign of strenuous energy, which might save a young aristocrat from the temptations of ease and wealth, were hailed by him with unaffected delight. He was evidently very susceptible to the charm of manner which youths of this class often possess. When to that was added strength of character, his satisfaction was complete. Hence his delight when Fuscus Salinator and Ummidius Quadratus, of the very cream of the Roman nobility, entered on the conflicts of the Centumviral Court.[1] And indeed these young men appear to have had many graces and virtues. Salinator, in particular, with exquisite literary culture, had a mingled charm of boyish simplicity, gravity, and sweetness.[2] Asinius Bassus, the son of Asinius Rufus, was another of this promising band of youth, blameless, learned, and diligent, whom Pliny commends for the quaestorship to Fundanus, then apparently designated as consul.[3] There is no more genuine feeling in the Letters than the grief of Pliny for the early death of Junius Avitus, another youth of high promise. Pliny had formed his character, and supported him in his candidature for office. He had helped him with advice in his studies, or in his administrative duties. Avitus repaid all this paternal care by a docility and deference which were becoming rare among the young men of the day. Winning the affection and confidence of his elders in the service, Avitus was surely destined to develop into one of those just and strenuous imperial officers, like Corbulo or Verginius Rufus, many of whom have left only a name on a brief inscription, but who were the glory and strength of the Empire in the times of its deepest degradation. But all such hopes for Avitus were extinguished in a day.

[1] Plin. *Ep.* vi. 11.

[2] *Ib.* vi. 26.

[3] *Ib.* iv. 15. Fundanus's consulship is mentioned in two inscriptions, *Or.* 1588, 2471. There is a difficulty about the dates which is discussed in Momms. *Plin.* p. 17, n. 3. Fundanus does not appear in the *Fasti*.

The upright and virtuous men of Pliny's circle, Corellius Rufus, Titinius Capito the historian, Pegasus the learned jurist, Trebonius Rufus the magistrate who suppressed the games at Vienne, Junius Mauricus, who would have denied them to the capital, and many others of the like stamp, have often been used to refute the pessimism of Juvenal. We have in a former chapter seen reason to believe that the satirist's view of female character needs to be similarly rectified. Even in the worst reigns the pages of Tacitus reveal to us strong and pure women, both in the palace and in great senatorial houses. In the wide philosophic class there was probably many an Arria and Plotina. In the *Agricola,* and in Seneca's letters to Marcia and Helvia, we can see that, even at the darkest hour, there were homes with an atmosphere of old Roman self-restraint and sobriety, where good women wielded a powerful influence over their husbands and their sons, and where the examples of the old Republic were used, as Biblical characters with us, to fortify virtue.[1] Seneca, in his views about women, as in many other things, is essentially modern. He admires indeed the antique ideal of self-contained strength and homely virtue. But he also believes in the equal capacity of women for culture, even in the field of philosophy, and he half regrets that an old-fashioned prejudice had debarred Helvia from receiving a philosophic discipline.[2] Tacitus and Pliny, who had no great faith in philosophy as a study for men, would hardly have recommended it for women. But they lived among women who were cultivated in the best sense. Pliny's third wife, Calpurnia, was able to give him the fullest sympathy in his literary efforts.[3] But her fame, of which she probably little dreamt, is founded on her purity and sweetness of character. Her ancestors, like Pliny's, belonged to the aristocracy of Como. Her aunt, Calpurnia Hispulla, who was a dear friend of Pliny's mother, had watched over her during the years of girlhood with a sedulous care which made her an ideal wife. What Calpurnia was like as a girl, we may probably picture to ourselves from the prose elegy

[1] Sen. *Ad Marc.* xiii. xiv.; *Ad Helv.* xvi.

[2] *Ad Marc.* xvi. par illis, mihi crede, vigor, etc. *Ad Helv.* xvii. 4, cf. Plut. *Conj. Praec.* xlviii. *φαρμάκων ἐπῳδὰς οὐ προσδέξεται (ἡ γυνὴ) τοῖς Πλάτωνος ἐπᾳδομένη λόγοις, κτλ.*; cf. Juv. vi. 450; Mart. vii. 69.

[3] Plin. *Ep.* iv. 19, § 4.

of Pliny on the death of the young daughter of Minutius Fundanus.[1] It is the picture of a beautiful character, and a fair young life cut off too soon. The girl had not yet reached her fourteenth year. She was already betrothed when she was seized with a fatal sickness. Her sweet girlish modesty, which was combined with a matronly gravity, charmed all her father's friends. She had love for all the household, her tutors and slaves, nurses and maids. A vigorous mind triumphed over bodily weakness, and she passed through her last illness with a sweet patience, encouraging her father and sister to bear up, and showing no shrinking from death.

Although we know of a good many happy wedded lives in that age,[2] there is no picture so full of pure devotion and tenderness as that which we have in Pliny's letters to Calpurnia. They are love-letters in the best sense and the most perfect style.[3] Pliny's youth was long past when he won the hand of Calpurnia, yet their love for one another is that of boy and girl. When she has to go into Campania for her health, he is racked with all sorts of anxiety about her, and entreats her to write once, or even twice, a day. Pliny reads her letters over and over again, as if they had just come. He has her image before him by night, and at the wonted hour by day his feet carry him to her vacant room. His only respite from these pains of a lover is while he is engaged in court. Pliny had frequent care about Calpurnia's health. They did not belong to the hideous class who preferred "the rewards of childlessness," but their hopes of offspring were dashed again and again. These griefs were imparted to Calpurnia's aunt, and to her grandfather, Calpurnius Fabatus, a generous old squire of Como, who was as anxious as Pliny to have descendants of his race. At the time of the old man's death, Calpurnia was with her husband in Bithynia, and she wished to hasten home at once to console her aunt. Pliny, not having time to secure the emperor's sanction, gave her the official order for the use of the public post on her journey back to Italy. In answer to his letter of explanation and excuse, Trajan sent his approval in his usual kind and courteous style. This is the last glimpse we have of Pliny and Calpurnia.[4]

[1] Plin. *Ep.* v. 16.

[2] Seneca and Paulina, Tac. *Ann.* xv. 64; Plutarch, *Ad Uxorem*, iv. v.

[3] Plin. *Ep.* vi. 4, 5, 7.

[4] Id. *Ad Traj.* 121, 122.

Pliny's character, as displayed in his Letters, is the embodiment of the finest moral tone of the great age which had opened when he died, in kindlier or juster treatment of the slave, in high respect for women, in conscientious care for the education of the young, in beneficent provision for the helpless and distressed. But it would be a mistaken view to regard these ideas as an altogether new departure. It is dangerous to assert that anything is altogether new in Roman social history. The truth is that the moral sentiment in which these movements took their rise had been for generations in the air. It was diffused by the Stoic preaching of the brotherhood and equality of men as fellow-citizens of one great commonwealth. The duty of redeeming the captive and succouring the poor had been preached by Cicero a century and a half before Pliny's Letters appeared.[1] Horace had, a few years later, asked the searching question, "Why should the worthy be in want while you have wealth?"[2] Seneca preaches, with the unction of an evangelist, all the doctrines on which the humane legislation of the Antonine age was founded, all the principles of humanity and charity of every age. He asserts the natural equality of bond and free, and the claim of the slave to kindness and consideration.[3] He brands in many a passage the cruelty and contempt of the slaveholder. He preaches tolerance of the froward, forgiveness of insult and injury.[4] He enforces the duty of universal kindness and helpfulness by the example of God, who is bounteous and merciful even to the evildoer.[5] Juvenal was little of a philosopher, but he had unconsciously drunk deep of the gospel of philosophy. Behind all his bitter pessimism there is a pure and lofty moral tone which sometimes almost approaches the ideal of charity in S. Paul. The slave whom we torture or insult for some slight negligence is of the same elements as we are.[6] The purity of childhood is not to be defiled by the ribaldry of the banquet and the example of a mother's intrigues or a father's brutal excesses.[7] Revenge is the pleasure of a puny soul.[8]

[1] Cic. *De Off.* ii. 18 (63), atque haec benignitas etiam reipublicae est utilis, redimi e servitute captos, locupletari tenuiores.

[2] Hor. *Sat.* ii. 2, 103—
Cur eget indignus quisquam, te divite?

[3] Sen. *Ep.* 47, § 1, 31; *De Benef.* iii. 21; *De Clem.* i. 18, 3; *De Ira*, iii. 24.

[4] Sen. *Ep.* 95, § 52.

[5] Sen. *Benef.* iv. 5; iv. 26; iv. 28, Di multa ingratis tribuunt.

[6] Juv. xiv. 16; vi. 219, 476.

[7] Id. xiv. 31.

[8] Id. xiii. 190.

The guilty may be left to the scourge of the unseen inquisitor. Juvenal regards the power of sympathy for any human grief or pain as the priceless gift of Nature, "who has given us tears."[1] It is by her command that we mourn the calamity of a friend or the death of the babe "too small for the funeral pyre." The scenes of suffering and pity which the satirist has sketched in some tender lines were assuredly not imaginary pictures. We are apt to forget, in our modern self-complacency, that, at least among civilised races, human nature in its broad features remains pretty much the same from age to age. On an obscure epitaph of this period you may read the words—*Bene fac, hoc tecum feres.*[2] Any one who knows the inscriptions may be inclined to doubt whether private benefactions under the Antonines were less frequent and generous than in our own day.

The duties of wealth, both in Greece and Rome, were at all times rigorously enforced by public opinion. The rich had to pay heavily for their honours and social consideration in the days of Cicero, and in the days of Symmachus, as they had in the days of Pericles.[3] They had to contribute to the amusement of the people, and to support a crowd of clients and freedmen. In the remotest municipality, the same ambitions and the same social demands, as we shall show in the next chapter, put an enormous strain on the resources of the upper class. Men must have often ruined themselves by this profuse liberality. In the reign of Augustus a great patron had several times given a favourite freedman sums of £3000 or £4000. The patron's descendant in the reign of Nero had to become a pensioner of the emperor. Juvenal and Martial reveal the clamorous demands by which the great patron was assailed.[4] The motives for this generosity of the wealthy class were at all times mixed and various. But in our period, the growth of a pure humane charity is unmistakable, of a feeling of duty to the helpless, whether young or old. The State had from the time of the Gracchi taken upon itself the immense burden of providing food for a quarter of a million of the proletariat of Rome. But in the

[1] Juv. xv. 133.

[2] *Or. Henz.* 6042.

[3] Cic. *De Off.* i. 14; Sym. *Ep.* ii. 78; ix. 126; Olympiod. § 44 (Müller, *Fr. H. Gr.* iv. p. 68); cf. Boeckh, *Public Ec. of Athens* (Trans. Lewis), pp. 458, 520, 578.

[4] Marq. *Priv.* i. 178 n. 10; cf. Juv. ii. 117; Mart. vii. 64, dominae munere factus eques; Tac. *Ann.* xiii. 34.

days of Pliny it recognised fresh obligations. The importance of education and the growth of poverty appealed powerfully to a ruling class, which, under the influence of philosophy, was coming to believe more and more in the duty of benevolence and of devotion to things of the mind. All the emperors from Vespasian to M. Aurelius made liberal provision for the higher studies.[1] But this endowment of culture, which in the end did harm as well as good, is not so interesting to us as the charitable foundations for the children of the poor. It was apparently the emperor Nerva, the rigid economist who sold the imperial furniture and jewels to replenish the treasury,[2] who first made provision for the children of needy parents throughout Italy. But epigraphy tells us more than literary history of the charity of the emperors. The tablet of Veleia is a priceless record of the charitable measures adopted by Trajan. The motive of the great emperor was probably, as his panegyrist suggests, political as much as benevolent.[3] He may have wished to encourage the rearing of children who should serve in the armies of the State, as well as to relieve distress. The provision was even more evidently intended to stimulate agriculture. The landed proprietors of the place, to the number of forty-six, received on mortgage a loan from the State of about £10,000 in our money, at an interest of five per cent, which was less than half the usual rate of that time.[4] The interest was appropriated to the maintenance of 300 poor children, at the rate of about £1 : 11s. a year for each male child, and £1 for each girl. The illegitimate children, who, it may be noted, were only two or three out of so many, received a smaller allowance. The boys were supported till their eighteenth year, the girls till fourteen. It was a bold and sagacious attempt to encourage Italian agriculture, to check the ominous depopùlation of Italy,[5] and to answer the cry of the poor. Hadrian continued and even added to the benefaction of Trajan.[6] Antoninus Pius, in

[1] Suet. *Vesp.* 18; Spart. *Hadr.* 16, § 8; Capitol. *Ant. P.* 11, § 3.

[2] D. Cass. 68. 2; Victor, *Epit.* 12.

[3] *Or. Henz.* 6664; Plin. *Paneg.* 28, hi subsidium bellorum, ornamentum pacis publicis sumptibus aluntur. Duruy, iv. 784; Boissier, *Rel. Rom.* ii. 211; Kratz, *De Benef., a Traj. collatis*, p. 11.

[4] Plin. *Ep.* x. 62. The letter reveals an unwillingness among the people of Bithynia to become debtors to the public treasury.

[5] Cf. Tac. *Ann.* iv. 27, minore in dies plebe ingenua; iii. 25; cf. Meriv. viii. 353.

[6] Spart. *Hadr.* 7.

honour of his wife Faustina, established a foundation for young girls who were to be called by her not altogether unspotted name.[1] A similar charity was founded in honour of her daughter by M. Aurelius.[2]

But, while the emperors were responding to the call of charity by using the resources of the State, it is clear, from the Letters of Pliny and from the inscriptions, that private benevolence was even more active. Pliny has a conception of the uses and responsibilities of wealth which, in spite of the teaching of Galilee, is not yet very common. Although he was not a very wealthy man, he acted up to his principles on a scale and proportion which only a few of our millionaires have yet reached. The lavish generosity of Pliny is a commonplace of social history. We have not the slightest wish to detract from the merited fame of that kindliest of Roman gentlemen. But a survey of the inscriptions may incline the inquirer to believe that, according to their means, there were many men and women in obscure municipalities all over the world, who were as generous and public-spirited as Pliny.[3] With Pliny, as with those more obscure benefactors, the impelling motive was love for the parent city or the village which was the home of their race, and where the years of youth had been passed. Pliny, the distinguished advocate, the famous man of letters, the darling of Roman society, still remained the loyal son of Como, from which his love never strays.[4] He followed and improved upon the example of his father in munificence to his native place.[5] He had little liking for games and gladiatorial shows, which were the most popular objects of liberality in those days. But he gave a sum of nearly £9000 for the foundation of a town library, with an annual endowment of more than £800 to maintain it.[6] Finding that promising youths of Como had to resort to Milan for their higher education, he offered to

[1] Capitol. *Ant. P.* 8.

[2] Id. *M. Aurel.* 26; cf. Capitol. *Pertin.* 9. He found the interest on Trajan's foundation nine years in arrear. Lamprid. *Alex. Sev.* 57, 7; his charity children were called Mammaeani; Kratz, p. 11.

[3] *Or. Henz.* 6694 to a man who left Tibur his sole heir; 3733 ob munificentiam; 3765, 3766, 3882, 7190, 6993, 7001, 781; cf. Philostr. *Vit. Soph.* ii. 1 sqq. *ἄριστα δὲ ἀνθρώπων πλούτῳ ἐχρήσατο.* Plin. *H. N.* xxix. 4 (8); Friedländer, *Cena Trim. Einl.* 46 sq.

[4] Plin. *Ep.* i. 3, § 1, Comum meae deliciae; v. 11, 2; iv. 13, respublica nostra pro filia vel parente.

[5] *v.* the inscr. in Momms. *Plin.* p. 31.

[6] Plin. *Ep.* i. 8; v. 7; *Or.* 1172.

contribute one-third of the expense of a high school at Como, if the parents would raise the remainder. The letter which records the offer shows Pliny at his best, wise and thoughtful as well as generous.[1] He wishes to keep boys under the protection of home influence, to make them lovers of their mother city; and he limits his benefaction in order to stimulate the interest of the parents in the cause of education, and in the appointment of the teachers. Another sum of between £4000 and £5000 he gave to Como for the support of boys and girls of the poorer class.[2] He also left more than £4000 for public baths, and a sum of nearly £16,000 to his freedmen, and for communal feasts. On two of his estates he built or repaired temples at his own expense.[3] His private benefactions were on a similar scale. It is not necessary to adopt the cynical conclusion that Pliny has told us all his liberality. The kindly delicacy with which Pliny claims the right of a second father to make up the dowry of the daughter of his friend Quintilian, might surely save him from such an imputation.[4] In the same spirit he offers to Romatius Firmus the £2500 which was needed to raise his fortune to the level of equestrian rank.[5] When the philosophers were banished by Domitian, Pliny, who was then praetor, at the most imminent risk visited his friend Artemidorus, and lent him, free of interest, a considerable sum of money.[6] The daughter of one of his friends was left with an embarrassed estate; Pliny took up all the debts and left Calvina with an inheritance free from all burdens.[7] He gave his old nurse a little estate which cost him about £800.[8] But the amount of this good man's gifts, which might shame a modern testator with ten times his fortune, is not so striking as the kindness which prompted them, and the modest delicacy with which they were made.

Yet Pliny, as we have said, is only a shining example of a numerous class of more obscure benefactors. For a thousand who know his Letters, there are few who have read the stone records of similar generosity. Yet these memorials abound for those who care to read them. And any one who will spend a few days, or even a few well-directed hours, in examining the

1 Plin. *Ep.* iv. 13.
2 *Ib.* vii. 18; *Or.* 1172.
3 Plin. *Ep.* iv. 1; cf. ix. 12.
4 *Ib.* vi. 32.
5 *Ib.* i. 19.
6 *Ib.* iii. 11.
7 *Ib.* ii. 4.
8 *Ib.* vi. 3.

inscriptions of the early Empire, will find many a common, self-complacent prejudice melting away. He will discover a profusion of generosity to add to the beauty, dignity, or convenience of the parent city, to lighten the dulness of ordinary life, to bring all ranks together in common scenes of enjoyment, to relieve want and suffering among the indigent. The motives of this extraordinary liberality were indeed often mixed, and it was, from our point of view, often misdirected. The gifts were sometimes made merely to win popularity, or to repay civic honours which had been conferred by the populace. They were too often devoted to gladiatorial shows and other exhibitions which only debased the spectators. Yet the greatest part of them were expended on objects of public utility—baths, theatres, markets, or new roads and aqueducts, or on those public banquets which knitted all ranks together. There was in those days an immense "civic ardour," an almost passionate rivalry, to make the mother city a more pleasant and a more splendid home. The endless foundations for civic feasts to all orders, in which even children and slaves were not forgotten, with a distribution of money at the close, softened the sharp distinctions of rank, and gave an appreciable relief to poverty. Other foundations were more definitely inspired by charity and pity. In remote country towns, there were pious founders who, like Pliny and Trajan, and the Antonines, provided for the nurture of the children of the poor. Bequests were left to cheapen the main necessaries of life.[1] Nor were the aged and the sick forgotten. In Lorium, near the old home of the Antonines, a humble spice dealer provided in his will for a free distribution of medicines to the poor people of the town.[2] The countless gifts and legacies to the colleges, which were the refuge of the poor in that age, in every region of the Roman world, are an irresistible proof of an overflowing charity. Pliny's love of the quiet town where his infancy was passed, and the record of a like patriotism or benevolence in so many others, draw us on to the study of that free and generous municipal life which was the great glory of the Antonine age.

[1] Friedl. *Cena Trim. Einleit.* p. 48. [2] *Or. Henz.* 114.

CHAPTER II

MUNICIPAL LIFE

NEARLY all the intimate friends of Pliny were, like himself, bred in the country, and, as we have seen, he has left us a priceless picture of that rural aristocracy in the calm refinement of their country seats. But of the ordinary life of the provincial town we learn very little from Pliny. Indeed, the silence of Roman literature generally as to social life outside the capital is very remarkable.[1] In the long line of great Latin authors from Ennius to Juvenal, there is hardly one whose native place was Rome. The men who are the glory of Roman letters in epic and lyric poetry, in oratory and history, in comedy and satire, were born in quiet country towns in Italy or the remoter provinces. But the reminiscences of the scenes of their infancy will generally be found to be faint and rare. Horace, indeed, displays a tender piety for that borderland of Apulia, where, in the glades of Mount Vultur as a child, he drank inspiration from the witchery of haunted groves.[2] And Martial, the hardened man about town, never forgot the oak groves and iron foundries of Bilbilis.[3] But for the municipal system and life, the relations of its various social grades, the humdrum routine of the shops and forums, the rustic rites and deities,[4] the lingering echoes of that dim common life with its vices and honest tenderness, its petty ambitions or hopeless griefs, we must generally go to the records in stone, and the remains of buried cities which the spade has given back to the light.

[1] Boissier, *Promenades Archæologiques*, p. 330, ce qui nous échappe c'est la vie de province.

[2] Hor. *Carm.* iii. 4, 9.

[3] Mart. iv. 55, 11; xii. 18, 9; i. 50.

[4] It must, however, be said that Virgil has preserved much of local religious sentiment. Cf. Sellar, *Virgil*, p. 365 sq.

This silence of the literary class is not due to any want of love in the Roman for the calm and freshness and haunting charm of country scenes, still less to callousness towards old associations. Certainly Virgil cannot be charged with any such lack of sensibility. In the Eclogues and the Georgics, the memory of the old farm at Andes breaks through the more conventional sentiment of Alexandrian tradition. In the scenery of these poems, there are "mossy fountains and grass softer than sleep," the hues of violet, poppy, and hyacinth, the shade of ancient ilex, and the yellow wealth of cornfield. We hear the murmur of bees, "the moan of doves in immemorial elms," the rush of the river, the whispering of the wind. The pastoral charm of the midsummer prime is there, from the freshness of fields under the morning star, through the hours alive with the song of the cicala and the lowing of the herds around the pool, through the still, hot, vacant noontide, till the moonbeams are glinting on the dewy grasses of the glades.[1] Nor can any lover of Virgil ever forget the fire of old sentiment in the muster of Italian chivalry in the seventh book of the Aeneid.[2] Tibur and Praeneste, Anagnia, Nomentum, and Amiternum, and many another old Sabine town, which send forth their young warriors to the fray, are each stamped on the imagination by some grace of natural beauty, or some glory of ancient legend. In the Flavian period, as we have seen, the great nobles had their villas on every pleasant site, wherever sea or hill or woodland offered a fair prospect and genial air. To these scenes they hastened, like emancipated schoolboys, when the dog-days set in. They had a genuine love of the unspoilt countryside, with its simple natural pleasures, its husbandry of the olden time, its joyous plenty, above all its careless freedom and repose.[3] The great charm of a rural retreat was its distance from the "noise and smoke and wealth" of Rome. The escape from the penalties of fame, from the boredom of interminable dinners, the intrusive importunity of curious busybodies, the malice of jealous rivals, gives a fresh zest to the long tranquil days under the ilex

[1] Virg. *Ecl.* ii. 48; *Georg.* ii. 466 sqq.; iii. 324–338, et saltus reficit jam roscida luna; cf. Sellar, *Virgil*, pp. 166–167.

[2] *Aen.* vii. 630 sqq.; Sellar, p. 80.

[3] Plin. *Ep.* i. 3; i. 6; i. 9; vii. 30; ix. 36. Mart. iii. 58; i. 56; iv. 66; iv. 90; vi. 43.

shade among the Sabine hills.[1] Horace probably felt more keenly than Juvenal the charm of hill and stream and the scenes of rustic toils and gaiety. Yet the exquisite good sense of Horace would have recoiled from the declamatory extravagance with which Juvenal justifies his friend's retirement from the capital, by a realistic picture of all its sordid troubles and vices and absurdities.[2] "To love Rome at Tibur and Tibur at Rome" was the expression of the educated Roman's feelings in a form which he would have recognised to be as just as it was happy. In spite of the charm of the country, to any real man of letters or affairs, the fascination of Rome was irresistible. Pliny, and no doubt hundreds of his class, from Augustus to Theodosius, grumbled at the wasteful fashion in which their lives were frittered away by monotonous social duties, as imperious as they were generally vain.[3] Yet to Pliny, as to Symmachus, the prospect of never again seeing the city, so seductive and so wearying, would have been absolutely intolerable. Martial, when he retired to Bilbilis, seems to pity his friend Juvenal, wandering restlessly through the noisy Suburra, or climbing the Caelian in hot haste, to hang on the outskirts of a levee.[4] Yet in the preface to this last book, Martial seems to feel his banishment as keenly as Ovid felt his among the frozen rivers of Scythia.[5] He misses in the "provincial solitude" the sympathetic public which was eager for his latest epigram, the fine critical judgment to appreciate, the concourse of elegant idlers to supply the matter for his verses.[6] And worst of all, the most famous wit of Rome is now the mark for the ignorant spite and envy of a provincial clique. Martial evidently feels very much as Dr. Johnson would have felt if he had been compelled to live out his days in Skye. Juvenal may affect to regret the simple ways of those rustic places, where on festal days in the grass-grown theatre the infant in his mother's arms shudders at the awful masks of

[1] Hor. *Carm.* i. 17. [2] Juv. iii.

[3] *v. Rom. Society in the Last Century of the Western Empire*, p. 128 sq. (1st ed.); Sym. i. 101; ii. 26; v. 78. Cf. Auson. *Idyl.* x. 20, 155, 189.

[4] Mart. xii. 18—

Dum per limina te potentiorum
Sudatrix toga ventilat, vagumque
Major Caelius et minor fatigat.

[5] Ov. *Trist.* ii. 196; iii. 2, 21, Roma domusque subit, desideriumque locorum; cf. Hor. *Sat.* ii. 7, 28.

[6] Mart. xii. *Praef.* illam judiciorum subtilitatem, illud materiarum ingenium, bibliothecas, theatra, conventus, quasi destituti desideramus.

the actors, and the aediles take their places in white tunics like the humble crowd.[1] But, in spite of this sentiment, the true Roman had a certain contempt for municipal life,[2] for the narrow range of its interests, the ludicrous assumption of dignity by its petty magistrates, and its provincialisms.[3] It was indeed only natural that the splendour and the vivid energy of life in the capital of the world should throw provincial life into the shade. Yet we can realise now, as a Roman wit or man of fashion could hardly do, that the municipal system, which had overspread the world from the Solway to the edge of the Sahara, was not the least glory of the Antonine age. And in any attempt to estimate the moral condition of the masses in that age, the influence of municipal life should occupy a large place.

It is beyond the scope of this work to trace provincial towns through all their various grades, and their evolution in the hands of Roman statesmanship from the time of Augustus. What we are chiefly concerned with is the spirit and the rapid development of that brilliant civic life, which not only covered the worlds both of East and West with material monuments of Roman energy, but profoundly influenced for good, or sometimes for evil, the popular character. The magical transformation wrought by Roman rule in a century and a half seized the imagination of contemporaries such as the rhetor Aristides. And the mere wreck of that brilliant civilisation which now meets the traveller's eye, in regions that have long returned to waste, will not permit us to treat his eulogy of Rome as only a piece of rhetoric. Regions, once desert solitudes, are thickly dotted with flourishing cities; the Empire is a realm of cities. The world has laid the sword aside, and keeps universal festival, with all pomp and gladness. All other feuds and rivalries are gone, and cities now vie with one another only in their splendour and their pleasures. Every space is crowded with porticoes, gymnasia, temple fronts, with studios and schools.[4]

[1] Juv. iii. 173 sqq.

[2] Illustrations may be found in Plaut. *Mil. Glor.* 653; *Captiv.* 879; *Trinum.* 609; *Bacch.* 24; Cic. *Phil.* iii. 6, 15, videte quam despiciamur omnes qui sumus e municipiis, id est, omnes plane; Tac. *Ann.* iv. 3, seque ac majores et posteros municipali adultero foedabat.

[3] Juv. x. 100; cf. Cic. *post Red. in Sen.* 17; Hor. *S.* i. 5, 34, Insani ridentes praemia scribae, etc.

[4] *Or.* xiv. (223), 391, (Jebb. i. p. 223), *μία δὲ αὕτη κατέχει ἔρις, ὅπως ἔτι καλλίστη καὶ ἡδίστη ἑκάστη φανεῖται· πάντα δὲ μεστὰ γυμνασίων, κρηνῶν, προπυλαίων, νεῶν, δημιουργίων, διδασκάλων.*

Sandy wastes, trackless mountains, and broad rivers present no barriers to the traveller, who finds his home and country everywhere. The earth has become a vast pleasure garden.[1]

This glowing description of the Roman world of the Antonine age is not perhaps strengthened by the appeal to the doubtful statistics of other contemporaries, such as Aelian and Josephus. We may hesitate to accept the statement that Italy had once 1197 cities, or that Gaul possessed 1200.[2] In these estimates, if they have any solid foundation, the term "city" must be taken in a very elastic sense. But there are other more trustworthy reckonings which sufficiently support the glowing description of Aristides. When the Romans conquered Spain and Gaul, they found a system of *pagi* or cantons, with very few considerable towns. The 800 towns which are said to have been taken by Julius Caesar can have been little more than villages. But the Romanisation of both countries meant centralisation. Where the Romans did not find towns they created them.[3] Gradually, but rapidly, the isolated rural life became more social and urban. In the north-eastern province of Spain, out of 293 communities in the time of the elder Pliny, 179 were in some sense urban, 114 were still purely rustic;[4] and we may be sure that this is an immense advance on the condition of the country at the time of the conquest. In the reign of Antoninus Pius, only 27 of these rural districts remained without an organised civic centre.[5] In Gaul, Julius Caesar impressed the stamp of Rome on the province of Narbo, by founding cities of the Roman type, and his policy was continued by Augustus. The loose cantonal system almost disappeared from the province in the south, although it lingered long in the northern regions of Gaul. Yet even in the north, on the borders of Germany, Cologne, from the reign of Claudius, became the envy of the barbarians across the Rhine,[6] and Trèves, from the days of Augustus, already anticipated its glory as a seat of empire from Diocletian to Gratian and Valentinian.[7] In the Agri Decumates, between

[1] Aristid. *Or.* xiv. (225), 393–4, ἡ γῆ πᾶσα οἷον παράδεισος ἐγκεκόσμηται.

[2] Aelian, *V. Hist.* ix. 16, ᾤκησαν καὶ πόλεις τὴν Ἰταλίαν πάλαι ἑπτὰ καὶ ἐνενήκοντα καὶ ἑκατὸν πρὸς ταῖς χιλίαις; Jos. *B. J.* ii. 16.

[3] Arnold, *Rom. Prov. Administration*, p. 203.

[4] *H. N.* iii. 4.

[5] Momms. *Rom. Prov.* i. 73.

[6] *Ib.* p. 168; Tac. *Ann.* i. 36; Marq. *Röm. Staatsverw.* i. 121; Bury, *Rom. Emp.* p. 83.

[7] *C. Theod.* xiii. 3, 11.

the Rhine and Neckar, the remains of baths and aqueducts, the mosaics and bronzes and pottery, which antiquarian industry has collected and explored, attest the existence of at least 160 flourishing and civilised communities.[1] Baden was already a crowded resort for its healing waters when, in A.D. 69, it was given up to fire and sword by Caecina in his advance to meet the army of Otho in the valley of the Po.[2] The Danube was lined with flourishing communities of Roman origin. In the 170 years during which Dacia was included in the Empire, more than 120 towns were organised by the conquering race.[3] Greek cities, like Tomi on the Euxine, record their gratitude to their patrons in the same formal terms as Pompeii or Venusia.[4] If we may believe Philostratus, there were 500 flourishing cities in the province of Asia which more than rivalled the splendour of Ionia before the Lydian and Persian conquests.[5] Many of these were of ancient origin, but many had been founded by Rome.[6] Laodicea, which was treated as an insignificant place in the reign of Tiberius, had risen to great opulence in the days of Strabo.[7] One of its citizens had attained a fortune which enabled him to bequeath it a sum of nearly half a million. The elder Pliny could reckon 40 cities of importance in Egypt, which had in his time a population of over seven millions;[8] and Alexandria, next after Rome herself, was regarded as the most dazzling ornament of the Empire.[9]

Perhaps nowhere, however, had the "Roman peace" worked greater miracles of civic prosperity than in North Africa. That the population of Roman Africa was in the period of the Empire extraordinarily dense, appears from the number of its episcopal sees, which in the fifth century had reached a total of 297.[10] The remains of more than 20 amphitheatres can still be traced. There is indeed no more startling proof of the range and sweep of Roman civilisation than the wreck of

[1] Marq. *Röm. St.* i. 125.

[2] Tac. *Hist.* i. 67; *v.* the dedication of a temple to Isis by a magistrate of Baden and his wife and daughter; *Or.* 457.

[3] Marq. i. 155, in keiner andern Provinz lässt sich die Entwickelung der römischen Städteanlagen so genau verfolgen als in Dacien. Arnold, *R. Prov. Admin.* p. 205.

[4] *Or. Henz.* 5287.

[5] *Vit. Soph.* ii. 3.

[6] Arnold, p. 205; Marq. i. 199.

[7] Tac. *Ann.* iv. 55; Strab. xii. 578.

[8] *H. N.* v. 60; Friedl. *SG.* iii. 110.

[9] Aristid. *Or.* xiv. 223 (392), πόλις ἐγκαλλώπισμα τῆς ὑμετέρας γέγονεν ἡγεμονίας.

[10] Cf. Victor, *Vit.* i. 7; v. 9; Friedl. *SG.* iii. 110; *v.* Migne, *Patrol. Lat.* t. lviii. 270, notitia Africae.

those capitols, forums, aqueducts, and temples in what are now sandy solitudes, not even occupied by a native village. In the province of Numidia, within a few leagues of the Sahara, the Roman colony of Thamugadi (Timgad) was founded, as an inscription tells, by Trajan in the year 100.[1] There, in what is now a scene of utter loneliness and desolation, the remains of a busy and well-organised community have been brought to light by French explorers. The town was built by the third legion, which for generations, almost as a hereditary caste, protected Roman civilisation against the restless tribes of the desert. The chief buildings were probably completed in 117. The preservation of so much, after eighteen centuries, is a proof that the work was well and thoroughly done. The ruts of carriage wheels can still be seen in the main street, which is spanned by a triumphal arch, adorned with marble columns. Porticoes and colonnades gave shelter from the heat to the passers-by, and two fountains played at the further end. Water, which is now invisible on the spot, was then brought in channels from the hills, and distributed at a fixed rate among private houses.[2] The forum was in the usual style, with raised side walks and porticoes, a basilica, a senate-house and rostrum, a shrine of Fortuna Augusta, and a crowd of statues to the emperors from M. Aurelius to Julian.[3] This petty place had its theatre, where the seats can still be seen rising in their due gradation of rank. An imposing capitol, in which, as at home, the Roman Trinity, Jupiter, Juno, and Minerva, were duly worshipped, was restored in the reign of Valentinian I., and dedicated by that Publius Caeonius Albinus who was one of the last of the pagan aristocracy, and who figures in the Letters of Symmachus and the *Saturnalia* of Macrobius.[4] The inscriptions on the site reveal the regular municipal constitution, with the names of seventy decurions, each of whom probably paid his honorarium of £13 or more when he entered on his office.[5] The honours of the duumvirate and the aedileship cost respectively £32 and £24.[6] And here, as elsewhere, the

1 *C.I.L.* viii. 2355; Cagnat, *L'Armée Rom. d'Afrique*, p. 582; Boissier, *L'Afr. Rom.* p. 180.

2 *Or. Henz.* 5326.

3 Boissier, *L'Afr. Rom.* p. 187.

4 *C.I.L.* viii. 2388; Hieron. *Ep.* 107, § 1: Macrob. *Sat.* i. 2, 15.

5 *C.I.L.* viii. 2403; *Suppl.* ii. 17903; *Suppl.* i. 12058. This inscription, from an obscure place, shows how an original honorarium of HS.1600 was finally increased by voluntary generosity to HS.12,000.

6 *Ib.* 2341, 17838.

public monuments and buildings were generally erected by private ambition or munificence. A statue and little shrine of Fortuna Augusta were given by two ladies, at a cost of over £200, in the days of Hadrian.[1]

The greatest glory of the imperial administration for nearly two centuries was the skilful and politic tolerance with which it reconciled a central despotism with a remarkable range of local liberty. It did not attempt to impose a uniform organisation or a bureaucratic control on the vast mass of races and peoples whom the fortune of Rome had brought under her sway. Rather, for ages its guiding principle was, as far as possible, to leave ancient landmarks undisturbed, and to give as much free play to local liberties as was compatible with the safety and efficiency of the imperial guardian of order and peace. Hence those many diversities in the relation between provincial towns and Rome, represented by the names of free, federate, or stipendiary cities, municipium and colonia. Many retained their old laws, constitution, and judicial system.[2] They retained in some cases the names of magistracies, which recalled the days of independence: there were still archons at Athens, suffetes in African towns, demarchs at Naples. The title of medixtuticus still lingered here and there in old Oscan communities.[3] When she had crushed the national spirit, and averted the danger of armed revolt, Rome tolerated, and even fostered, municipal freedom, for more than a hundred years after the last shadowy pretence of popular government had disappeared from her own forum.[4] Central control and uniformity were established in those departments which affected the peace and welfare of the whole vast commonwealth. Although the interference of the provincial governor in local administration was theoretically possible in varying degrees, yet it may well be doubted whether a citizen of Lyons or Marseilles, of Antioch or Alexandria, was often made conscious of any limitation of his freedom by imperial

[1] *C.I.L.* viii.; *Suppl.* ii. 17831.

[2] Marq. *Röm. St.* i. 45; Bury, *Rom. Emp.* p. 77; Arnold, *Rom. Prov. Admin.* p. 210.

[3] *Or. Henz.* 3720, 3800, 3801, 3056, 3057, 3804.

[4] Tac. *Ann.* i. 15; Momms. *Röm. St.* ii. 1002; Duruy, v. pp. 336–346; Gréard, *Plut.* 221, 237; Plut. *Reip. Ger. Pr.* c. 17, 19. The first curatores civitatum are heard of in the reigns of Nerva and Trajan; cf. Marq. i. 510, n. 10

power. While delation and confiscation and massacre were working havoc on the banks of the Tiber, the provinces were generally tranquil and prosperous. The people elected their magistrates, who administered municipal affairs with little interference from government. The provincial administration of a Nero, an Otho, a Vitellius, or a Domitian was often no less prudent and considerate than that of a Vespasian or a Trajan.[1] And the worst of the emperors share with the best in the universal gratitude of the provinces for the blessings of the "Roman peace."[2]

But although for generations there was a settled abstinence from centralisation on the part of the imperial government, the many varieties of civic constitution in the provinces tended by an irresistible drift to a uniform type of organisation. Free and federate communities voluntarily sought the position of a colony or a municipium.[3] Just as the provincial town must have its capitol, with the cult of Jupiter, Juno, and Minerva, or imported the street names Velabrum or Vicus Tuscus, so the little community called itself *respublica*, its commons the *populus*, its curia the senate or the *amplissimus et splendididissimus ordo*; its magistrates sometimes bore the majestic names of praetor, dictator, or censor, in a few cases even of consul.[4] This almost ludicrous imitation of the great city is an example of the magical power which Rome always exercised on her most distant subjects, and even on the outer world of barbarism, down to the last days when her forces were ebbing away. The ease and rapidity of communication along the great routes, the frequent visits of proconsuls and procurators and generals, with the numerous train which attended them, the presence of the ubiquitous Roman merchant and traveller, kept even remote places in touch with the

[1] Suet. *Tib.* 32; Tac. *Ann.* iv. 6; Suet. *Nero*, x.; *Otho*, iii. provinciam administravit moderatione singulari; *Vitell.* v. Vespasian had to increase burdens, Suet. xvi.; Tac. *Hist.* ii. 84; as to Trajan, cf. Plin. *Paneg.* 20; Suet. *Dom.* 8. Nero, it is true, is said to have encouraged plunder (Suet. *Nero*, 32; Plin. *H. N.* 18, 6). Yet the general prosperity was undisturbed, Boissier, *L'Opp.* 170; Arnold, *Rom. Prov. Admin.* 135; Gréard, *Plut.* 199.

[2] See a crowd of inscriptions to Domitian and Commodus in remote places in Africa; cf. *C.I.L.* viii. 1016, 1019; 10570, 8702, in which Commodus is described as indulgentissimus princeps, etc.

[3] Marq. *Röm. St.* i. 517 sq.; Arnold, p. 212.

[4] *Henz.* iii. *Ind.* p. 156; Inscr. 2322, 6980, 4983; Marq. *Röm. St.* i. 477. There were consuls at Tusculum and Beneventum. But the grand style was ridiculed by Cicero, *In Pis.* xi. 24.

capital. The *acta diurna*, with official news and bits of scandal and gossip, regularly arrived in distant provincial towns and frontier camps.[1] The last speech of Pliny, or the freshest epigrams of Martial, were within a short time selling on the bookstalls of Lyons or Vienne.[2] Until the appearance of railways and steamboats, it may be doubted whether there was any age in history in which travelling was easier or more general.

Apart from the immense stimulus which was given to trade and commerce by the pacification of the world, liberal curiosity, or restless ennui, or the passion to preach and propagate ideas, carried immense numbers to the most distant lands.[3] The travelling sophist found his way to towns on the edge of the Scythian steppes, to the home of the Brahmans, or to the depths of the Soudan.[4] The tour up the Nile was part of a liberal culture in the days of Lucian as it was in the days of Herodotus. The romantic charm of travel in Greece was probably heightened for many by the tales of Thessalian brigands and sorceresses which meet us in the novel of Apuleius. The Emperor Hadrian, who visited almost every interesting scene in his dominions, from the Solway to the Euphrates, often trudging for days at the head of his soldiers, is a true representative of the migratory tastes of his time. Seneca, indeed, finds in this rage for change of scene only a symptom of the universal unrest. Epictetus, on the other hand, and Aristides expatiate with rapture on the universal security and wellbeing, due to the disappearance of brigandage, piracy, and war. The seas are alive with merchantmen; deserts have become populous scenes of industry; the great roads are carried over the broadest rivers and the most defiant mountain barriers. The earth has become the common possession of all. Nor is this mere rhetoric. Travelling to all parts of the known world had become expeditious, and even luxurious. From the Second Punic War, traders, couriers, and travellers had moved freely along the great roads.[5] The

[1] Tac. *Ann.* xiii. 31; xvi. 22, diurna per provincias, per exercitus curatius leguntur. Peter, *Gesch. Litt.* i. 212; Macé, *Suétone*, p. 191; Marq. *Priv.* i. 88; cf. *C.I.L.* viii. 11813; Lamprid. *Com.* 15.

[2] Plin. *Ep.* ix. 11, 2; Mart. vii. 88.

[3] Sen. *Ep.* 28, 104; Luc. *Tox.* 27; *De Dips.* 6; *Philops.* 33; *Alex.* 44; Epict. *Dis.* iii. 13.

[4] Philostr. *Apoll. Tyan.* iii. 50, vi.; D. Chrys. *Or.* 36.

[5] Hudemann, *Gesch. des röm. Postwesens*, p. 8 sq. Marq. *Röm. St.* i. 417; Friedl. *SG.* ii. 8.

government post, which was first organised by Augustus on the model of the Persian, provided at regular intervals the means of conveyance for officials, or for those furnished with the requisite diploma. Private enterprise had also organised facilities of travel, and at the gates of country towns such as Pompeii, Praeneste, or Tibur, there were stations of the posting corporations (the *cisiarii* or *jumentarii*) where carriages could be hired, with change of horses at each stage.[1] The speed with which great distances were traversed in those days is at first sight rather startling. Caesar once travelled 100 miles a day in a journey from Rome to the Rhone.[2] The freedman Icelus in seven days carried the news of Nero's death to Galba in Spain,[3] the journey of 332 miles from Tarraco to Clunia having been made at the rate of nearly ten miles an hour. This of course was express speed. The ordinary rate of travelling is probably better represented by the leisurely journey of Horace and Maecenas to Brundisium, or that of Martial's book from Tarraco to Bilbilis.[4] About 130 miles a day was the average distance accomplished by sea. Vessels put out from Ostia or Puteoli for every port in the Mediterranean. From Puteoli to Corinth was a voyage of five days. About the same time was needed to reach Tarraco from Ostia. A ship might arrive at Alexandria from the Palus Maeotis in a fortnight.[5] Many a wandering sophist, like Dion Chrysostom or Apollonius of Tyana, traversed great distances on foot, or with a modest wallet on a mule. The rhetor Aristides once spent a hundred days in a journey at mid-winter from Mysia to Rome.[6] But there was hardly any limit to the luxury and ostentatious splendour with which the great and opulent made their progresses, attended or preceded by troops of footmen and runners, and carrying with them costly plate and myrrhine vases.[7] The thousand carriages which Nero took with him on a progress, the silver-shod mules of Poppaea, the paraphernalia of luxury described by Seneca, if they are not mythical, were probably the exceptional displays of a self-indulgence bordering on lunacy.[8] But practical and sensible comfort in travelling

[1] *Or. Henz.* 4093, 2413, 5163, 6983.
[2] Suet. *Jul. Caes.* 57.
[3] Plut. *Galba*, 7.
[4] Mart. x. 104 ; cf. Hor. *S.* i. 5, 104.
[5] Friedl. *SG.* ii. 12 sqq.
[6] Aristid. *Or.* xxiv. 537 ; cf. Hor. *S.* i. 6, 105.
[7] Sen. *Ep.* 123, § 7.
[8] Cf. Suet. *Nero*, xliv. xxx. ; Sen. *Ep.* 87, § 9 ; 123.

was perhaps then commoner than it was, until quite recently, among ourselves. The carriages in which the two indefatigable Plinies used to ride, enabled them to read at their ease, or dictate to an amanuensis.[1] The inns, from the time of Horace to the time of Sidonius, were as a rule bad, and frequently disreputable, and even dangerous, places of resort.[2] And vehicles were often arranged for sleeping on a journey. We may be sure that many an imperial officer after the time of Julius Caesar passed nights in his carriage, while hurrying to join the forces on the Rhine or the Danube. With all this rapid circulation of officials and travellers, the far-stretching limits of the Roman world must, to the general eye, have contracted, the remotest places were drawn more and more towards the centre, and the inexhaustible vitality of the imperial city diffused itself with a magical power of silent transformation.

The modes in which the fully developed municipalities of the Antonine age had originated and were organised were very various. Wherever, as in the Greek East or Carthaginian Africa, towns already existed, the Romans, of course, used them in their organisation of a province, although they added liberally to the number, as in Syria, Pontus, and Cappadocia.[3] Where a country was still in the cantonal state, the villages or markets were grouped around a civic centre, and a municipal town, such as Nîmes or Lyons, would thus become the metropolis of a considerable tract of territory. The colony of Vienne was the civic centre of the Allobroges.[4] In the settlement of the Alps many of the remote mountain cantons were attached to towns such as Tridentum, Verona, or Brixia.[5] Sometimes, as in Dacia, the civic organisation was created at a stroke.[6] But it is well known that, especially towards the frontiers of the Empire, in Britain, on the Rhine, and in North Africa, the towns of the second century had often grown out of the *castra stativa* of the legions.

The great reorganisation of Augustus had made each legion a permanent corps, with a history and identity of its own. To ensure the tranquillity of the Empire the legions were

[1] Plin. *Ep.* iii. 5, 15; cf. Suet. *Claud.* xxxiii.; Friedl. *SG.* ii. 19.

[2] Apul. *Met.* i. 7; i. 17; Sidon. Apoll. *Ep.* viii. 11. Cf. *Rom. Soc. in the Last Century of the Western Empire*, p. 172 (1st ed.); Friedl. ii. 20.

[3] Marq. *Röm. St.* i. 17, 199, 214, 317; Arnold, *Prov. Adm.* 203.

[4] Arn. 205, 208; Marq. i. 114, 118.

[5] Marq. i. 14.

[6] Id. i. 155.

distributed in permanent camps along the frontier, the only inland cities with a regular military garrison being Lyons and Carthage.[1] Many legions never changed their quarters for generations. The Tertia Augusta, which has left so many memorials of itself in the inscriptions of Lambesi, remained, with only a single break, in the same district from the time of Augustus to that of Diocletian.[2] There, for two generations, it kept sleepless watch against the robber tribes of the Sahara. The legion was also peacefully employed in erecting fortifications and making roads and bridges, when the camp was visited by Hadrian in the year 130.[3] Gradually soldiers were allowed to form family relations, more or less regular, until, under Septimius Severus, the legionary was permitted to live in his household like any other citizen.[4] From the remains at Lambesi, it is now considered certain that, in the third century, the camp had ceased to be the soldier's home. The suttlers and camp-followers had long gathered in the neighbourhood of the camp, in huts which were called *Canabae legionis.* There, for a long time, the soldier, when off duty, sought his pleasures and amusements, and there, after the changes of Septimius Severus, he took up his abode. At first the Canabae of Lambesi was only a *vicus;* it became, under Marcus Aurelius, a *municipium*—the *Respublica Lambaesitanorum*, with the civic constitution which is rendered familiar to us by so many inscriptions.[5] The legionaries seem to have been happy and contented at Lambesi; their sons were trained to arms and followed their fathers in the ranks;[6] the legion became to some extent a hereditary caste. Old veterans remained on the scene of their service, after receiving their discharge with a pension from the chest.[7] The town developed in the regular fashion, and dignified itself by a capitol, an amphitheatre, two forums, a triumphal arch; and the many monuments of public and private life found on the site reveal a highly organised society, moulded out of barbarous and alien

[1] Boissier, *L'Afr. Rom.* p. 104.

[2] See the history of this legion in Cagnat, *L'Armée Rom. d'Afrique*, p. 148 sqq. *C.I.L.* viii., Momms. *Praef.* xix. sq. The legion was first stationed at Thevesta.

[3] *Or. Henz.* 5319; *C.I.L.* viii. 2532, 10048; *v.* Mommsen, p. 21. For the date of this visit, *v.* Cagnat, p. 154. *Vit. Hadr.* 12, 13.

[4] Herodian, iii. 8; cf. Cagnat, p. 451.

[5] *C.I.L.* viii. 2611; *Or. Henz.* 7408.

[6] Cagnat, 365, 453; cf. *C.I.L.* viii. 3015.

[7] Cagnat, 481–87; Marq. ii. 544.

elements, and stamped with the inimitable and enduring impress of Rome. Out of such casual and unpromising materials sprang numbers of urban communities, which reproduced, in their outline and in their social tone, the forms and spirit of the free Republic of Rome. The capitol and the forum are merely the external symbols of a closer bond of parentage. The Roman military discipline did not more completely master and transform the Numidian or Celtic recruit, than the inspiration of her civil polity diffused among races imbruted by servitude, or instinct with the love of a lawless, nomadic freedom, the sober attachment to an ordered civic life which was obedient to a long tradition, yet vividly interested in its own affairs.

On hardly any side of ancient life is the information furnished by the inscriptions so rich as on the spirit and organisation of municipalities. Here one may learn details of communal life which are never alluded to in Roman literature. From this source, also, we must seek the only authentic materials for the reconstruction of a municipality of the first century. The *Album Canusii* and the tablets containing the laws of Malaga and Salpensa have not only settled more than one question as to the municipal organisation of the early Empire, but have enabled us to form almost as clear-cut a conception of it as we have of the corporate organisation of our own great towns.

But, unlike our civic republics, the Roman municipal town was distinctly aristocratic, or rather timocratic, in its constitution. A man's place in the community, as a rule, was fixed by his ancestry, his official grade, or his capacity to spend. The dictum of Trimalchio was too literally true in the municipal life of that age—"a man is what he is worth." Provincial society was already parted and graduated, though less decidedly, by those rigid lines of materialistic demarcation which became gaping fissures in the society of the Theodosian code. The Curia or Senate was open only to the possessor of a certain fortune; at Como, for instance, HS.100,000, elsewhere perhaps even more. On the other hand, the richest freedman could not become a member of the Curia or hold any civic magistracy,[1]

[1] Marq. *Röm. St.* i. 499; Friedl. *Cena Trim. Einl.* 29; Plin. *Ep.* i. 19; Boissier, *L'Afr. Rom.* p. 195.

although he might be decorated with their insignia. His ambition had to be satisfied with admission to the order of the Augustales, which ranked socially after the members of the Curia. In the list of the Curia, which was revised every five years, the order of official and social precedence was most scrupulously observed. In the Album Canusii of the year A.D. 223,[1] the first rank is assigned to thirty-nine patrons, who have held imperial office, or who are senators or knights. Next come the local magnates who have been dignified by election to any of the four great municipal magistracies. Last in order are the *pedani*, that is, the citizens possessing the requisite qualification, who have not yet held any municipal office. At the bottom of the list stand twenty-five *praetextati*, who were probably the sons of the more distinguished citizens, and who, like the sons of senators of the Republic, were silent witnesses of the proceedings in the Curia. From this body, and from all the magistracies, all persons engaged in certain mean or disgraceful occupations were expressly excluded, along with the great mass of the poorer citizens, the *tenuiores*. The taint of servile birth, the possession of *libertinae opes*, was an indelible blot. In countless inscriptions this gradation of rank is sharply accentuated. If a man leaves a bequest for an annual feast, with a distribution of money, the rich patron or the decurio will receive perhaps five times the amount which is doled out to the simple plebeian.[2] The distinction of rank, even in punishment for crime, which meets us everywhere in the Theodosian Code, has already appeared. The *honestior* is not to be degraded by the punishment of crucifixion or by the stroke of the rod.[3] But it is on their tombs that the passion of the Romans for some sort of distinction, however shadowy, shows itself most strikingly. On these slabs every grade of dignity in a long career is enumerated with minute care. The exact value of a man's public benefactions or his official salary will be recorded with pride.[4] Even the dealer in aromatics or in rags will make a boast of some petty office in the college of his trade.[5] But, although rank and office

[1] *Or. Henz.* 3721; Friedl. *Cena Trim. Einl.* 30.

[2] *Or. Henz.* 6989, 7001, 7199, ob duplam sportulam collatam sibi, 4020, 3703.

[3] Hartmann, *De Exilio*, pp. 58 sq.; Duruy, *Hist. Rom.* vi. 643.

[4] *Or. Henz.* 946, 3708.

[5] *Ib.* 7192.

were extravagantly valued in these societies, wealth was after all the great distinction. The cities were in the hands of the rich, and, in return for social deference and official power, the rich were expected to give lavishly to all public objects. The worship of wealth, the monumental flattery of rich patrons and benefactors, was very interested and servile. On the other hand, there probably never was a time when the duties of wealth were so powerfully enforced by opinion, or so cheerfully, and even recklessly, performed.

Yet, although these communities were essentially aristocratic in tone and constitution, the commonalty still retained some power in the Antonine age. On many inscriptions they appear side by side with the Curial "ordo" and the Augustales.[1] They had still in the reign of Domitian the right to elect their magistrates. It was long believed that, with the suppression of popular elections at Rome in the reign of Tiberius, the popular choice of their great magistrates must also have been withdrawn from municipal towns.[2] This has now been disproved by the discovery of the laws of Malaga and Salpensa, in which the most elaborate provisions are made for a free and uncontaminated election by the whole people.[3] And we can still almost hear the noise of election days among the ruins of Pompeii.[4] Many of the inscriptions of Pompeii are election placards, recommending particular candidates. There, in red letters painted on the walls, we can read that "the barbers wish to have Trebius as aedile," or that "the fruit-sellers, with one accord, support the candidature of Holconius Priscus for the duumvirate." The porters, muleteers, and garlic dealers have each their favourite. The master fuller, Vesonius Primus, backs Cn. Helvius as a worthy man. Even ladies took part in the contest and made their separate appeals. "His little sweetheart" records that she is working for Claudius.[5] Personal popularity no doubt then, as always, attracted such electoral support. But the student of the inscriptions may be inclined to think that the free and independent electors had also a keen eye for the man who was likely to build a new colonnade for the forum, or a new *schola* for the guild, or, best

[1] *Or. Henz.* 3703, 3706, 4009, 3937, 3704, 3725, 4020; Plin. *Ep.* x. 111; cf. Ohnesseit, *De Jure Municip.* 41.

[2] Marq. *Röm. St.* i. 472.

[3] *Or. Henz*, 7421; *Lex Mal.* §§ 53, 55.

[4] Mau, 376, 388–89 (Tr.).

[5] Claudium iivir. animula facit, *C.I.L.* iv. 425, 677, 644.

of all, to send down thirty pairs of gladiators into the arena "with plenty of blood."[1]

The laws of Malaga and Salpensa prescribe, in the fullest detail, all the forms to be observed in the election of magistrates. These were generally six in number—two duumvirs,[2] who were the highest officers, two aediles, and two quaestors, for each year. Every fifth year, instead of the duumvirs, two *quinquennales* were elected, with the extraordinary duty of conducting the municipal census.[3] The candidates for all these offices were required to be free born, of the age of twenty-five at least, of irreproachable character, and the possessors of a certain fortune. The qualifications were the same as those prescribed by the *lex Julia* for admission to the municipal Senate, which expressly excluded persons engaged in certain disreputable callings—gladiators, actors, pimps, auctioneers, and undertakers.[4] In the best days the competition for office was undoubtedly keen, and the candidates were numerous. In the year A.D. 4, the year of the death of C. Cæsar, the grandson of Augustus, so hot was the rivalry that the town of Pisa was left without magistrates, owing to serious disturbances at the elections.[5] But it is an ominous fact that the law of Malaga, in the reign of Domitian, makes provision for the contingency of a failure of candidates. In such a case the presiding duumvir was to nominate the required number, they in turn an equal number, and the combined nominees had to designate a third set equal in number to themselves. The choice of the people was then restricted to these involuntary candidates. The city has evidently advanced a stage towards the times of the Lower Empire, when the magistrates were appointed by the Curia from among themselves, with no reference to the people.[6] A man might, indeed, well hesitate before offering himself for an office which imposed a heavy expenditure on the holder of it. The honorarium payable on admission amounted, in an obscure place like Thamugadi, to about £32 for the duumvirate, and £24 for the aedileship.[7] In

[1] Petron. *Sat.* 45, ferrum optimum daturus est, sine fuga, carnarium in medio, etc.

[2] The title of the highest magistracy varied a good deal: cf. Marq. *Röm. St.* i. 475, 89; *Or. Henz.* iii. *Ind.* 154.

[3] Marq. i. 485; *Henz. Ind.* p. 157. Often described as iivir quinquennalis, or iivir censoria potestate quinq. etc., or shortly quinquennalis; cf. *Or. Henz.* 3882, 3721.

[4] Arnold, *Prov. Adm.* pp. 225, 226.

[5] *Or. Henz.* 643.

[6] *Lex Malag.* § 51; *Or.* 7421; Marq. i. 475; *C. Th.* xii. 5, 1.

[7] *C.I.L.* viii. 2341; 17838.

the greater Italian cities it probably would be much more; at Pompeii the newly elected duumvir paid more than £80.[1] But the man chosen by the people often felt bound to outstrip the bare demands of law or custom by a prodigal liberality. He must build or repair some public work, to signalise his year of office, and, at the dedication of it, good taste required him to exhibit costly games, or to give a banquet to the citizens, with a largess to all of every rank small or great.[2]

But in return for its liabilities, the position of a duumvir gave undoubted power and distinction. The office was the image or shadow of the ancient consulship, and occasionally, as the inscriptions attest, a Hadrian or an Antoninus Pius did not disdain to accept it.[3] The duumvirs commanded the local militia, when it was, on emergency, called out.[4] They presided at meetings of the people and the Curia, they proposed questions for their deliberation, and carried the decrees into effect. They had civil jurisdiction up to a certain amount, and their criminal jurisdiction, which, in the third century, had been transferred to imperial functionaries, was, according to the most probable opinion, undiminished at least down to the end of the first century.[5] This judicial power, however, was limited by the *intercessio* of colleagues and the right of appeal. They had extensive responsibilities in finance, for the collection of dues and taxes, and the recovery of all moneys owing to the municipality.[6] After the fall of the free Republic, when so many avenues of ambition were closed, many an able man might well satisfy his desire for power and distinction by the duumvirate of a provincial town.

The Curia, or local senate, is peculiarly interesting to the historical student, because it was to the conversion of the curiales into a hereditary caste, loaded with incalculable liabilities, that the decay of the Western Empire was to a large extent due.[7] But, in the reign of Domitian, the Curia is still erect and dignified. Although the individual decurio seldom or never assumes the title senator in the inscriptions,[8] the Curia as a

[1] Marq. i. 499 n. 13.

[2] *Or. Henz.* 7080, 7082, 3811, 3817, 3882.

[3] *Ib.* 3817; cf. Spart. *Hadr.* c. 19.

[4] *Lex Urson.* § 103.

[5] Friedl. *Cena Trim. Einl.* 28; Duruy, v. 349 sqq.

[6] *Lex Malag.* § 60 sq.

[7] See *Roman Society in the Last Century of the Western Empire*, bk. iii. c. 2.

[8] There is one case in *Or. Henz.* 2279.

whole often bears the august name and titles of the majestic Roman Senate.[1] And assuredly down to the middle of the second century there was no lack of candidates for admission. Every five years the roll of the Curia was revised and drawn up afresh by the quinquennales. The conditions were those for holding a magistracy, including a property qualification, which varied in different places.[2] The number of ordinary members was generally 100.[3] But it was swelled by patrons and other extraordinary members. The quinquennales, in framing the list, took first the members on the roll of the previous term, and then those who had been elected to magistracies since the last census. If any vacancies were still left, they were filled up from the ranks of those who, not having yet held any municipal office, were otherwise qualified by the possession of a sufficient fortune.[4] In the *Album Canusii*, the men who had held official rank constitute at least two-thirds of the Curia. In the composition of such a body there would appear to be ample security for administrative skill and experience. And yet we shall find that it was precisely through want of prudence or skill that the door was opened for that bureaucratic interference which, in the second century, began, with momentous results, to sap the freedom and independence of municipal life.

The honours and powers of the provincial council were long sufficient to compensate the decurio for the heavy demands made upon his generosity. To all but comparatively few the career of imperial office and distinction was closed. His own town became each man's "patria," as Como was even to a man like Pliny, who played so great a part in the life of the capital.[5] There is the ring of a very genuine public spirit and a love for the local commonwealth in a host of the inscriptions of that age.[6] The vastness and overwhelming grandeur of a world-wide Empire, in which the individual citizen was a mere atom, made men crave for any distinction which seemed to raise them above the grey flat level which surrounds a democratic despotism. And even the ordinary

[1] *v. Or. Henz.* vol. iii. *Ind.* p. 152.

[2] Plin. *Ep.* i. 19; at Como the census was HS.100,000; cf. Petron. *Sat.* 44.

[3] The Curia is sometimes designated as Cviri, *Or. Henz.* 764, 3737, 1552. Or., however, interprets CV. as Civium universorum in 764.

[4] Ohnesseit, *De Jure Municip.* p. 55; Marq. *Röm. St.* i. 504.

[5] Plin. *Ep.* iv. 13, 9.

[6] *e.g. Or. Henz.* 3703, 7190.

decurio had some badges to mark him off from the crowd. The pompous honorific titles of the Lower Empire, indeed, had not come into vogue. But the Curial had a place of honour at games and festivals, a claim to a larger share in the distributions of money by private benefactors, exemption, as one of the *honestiores*, from the more degrading forms of punishment, the free supply of water from the public sources,[1] and other perquisites and honours, which varied in different localities. The powers of the Curia were also very considerable. The duumvirs indeed possessed extensive prerogatives which strong men may have sometimes strained.[2] But there was a right of appeal to the Curia from judicial decisions of the duumvirs in certain cases. And their control of games and festivals, and of the finances of the community, was limited by the necessity of consulting the Curia and of carrying out its orders.[3] In the *lex Ursonnitana* we find a long list of matters on which the duumvirs were obliged to take their instructions from the Curia.[4] The quorum needed for a valid decision varied in different places. In the election of a patron a quorum of two-thirds of the decurions was legally required.[5] The names of the duoviri appeared at the head of every curial decree, as those of the consuls in every senatusconsultum.

After the local aristocracy of curial rank came, in order of social precedence, members of the knightly class and the order of the Augustales. In the latter half of the first century equestrian rank had been conferred with perhaps too lavish a hand. And satire was never tired of ridiculing these sham aristocrats, Bithynian knights as they were called, often of the lowest origin, who on public occasions vulgarly asserted their mushroom rank.[6] In particular, the army contributed many new knights to the society of the provincial towns. A veteran, often of humble birth, who had risen to the first place among the sixty centurions of a legion, was, on his discharge with a good pension, sometimes raised to equestrian rank. He frequently returned to his native place, where he became a personage of some mark. Such men, along with old officers of

[1] Friedl. *Cena Trim. Einl.* 31.

[2] Plin. *Ep.* iv. 22. This autocratic act was the abolition of the games at Vienne by a duumvir.

[3] *Lex Urson.* § 129.

[4] *Ib.* § 99; Ohnesseit, *De Jure Municip.* p. 51.

[5] *Ib.* p. 53; *Lex Urson.* §§ 96, 97, 130.

[6] Mart. iii. 29; v. 14; v. 23; Juv. i. 28; iii. 131, 159.

higher grade, frequently appear in the inscriptions invested with priesthoods and high magistracies,[1] and were sometimes chosen as patrons of the community.[2] Many of them were undoubtedly good and public-spirited men, with the peculiar virtues which the life of the Roman camp engendered. But some of their class also displayed that coarse and brutal self-assertion, and that ignorant contempt for the refinement of culture, on which Persius and Juvenal poured their scorn.[3]

The Augustales, ranking next to the curial order, are peculiarly interesting, both as representing the wide diffusion of the cult of the emperors, and as a class composed of men of low, or even servile origin, who had made their fortunes in trade, yet whose ambition society found the means of satisfying, without breaking down the barriers of aristocratic exclusiveness.[4] The origin of the order of the Augustales was long a subject of debate. But it has now been placed beyond doubt that in the provincial towns it was a plebeian institution for the cult of Augustus, and succeeding emperors, modelled on the aristocratic order of the Sodales Augustales, which was established by Tiberius in the capital.[5] The Augustales were elected by vote of the local curia, without regard to social rank, although probably with due respect to wealth, and they included the leaders of the great freedman class, whose emergence is one of the most striking facts in the social history of the time. Figuring on scores of inscriptions, the Augustales are mentioned only once in extant Roman literature, in the novel of Petronius, where the class has been immortalised, and probably caricatured.[6] The inscription, for which Trimalchio gives an order to his brother Augustal, the stone-cutter, is to record his election in absence to the Sevirate, his many virtues and his millions. Actual monuments at Assisi and Brescia show that Trimalchio was not an altogether imaginary person.[7]

[1] *Or. Henz.* 7002, 7018, 3785, 3789, 3798, 3733, 3747.

[2] *Ib.* 2287, 3714, 3851.

[3] Pers. iii. 77; Juv. xvi.

[4] In the Inscr. they are mentioned after the decurions and before the plebs; cf. *Or. Henz.* 4009, 3807, 1167. On the distinction between the Augustales and the Seviri Aug. *v.* Marq. *Röm. St.* i. 514; Ohnesseit, *De Jure Munic.* 46; Nessling, *De Seviris Aug.* *Marq.* says, scheinen die Augustales als lebenslängliche Mitglieder des Collegiums, die Seviri als jährlich wechselnde Beamte desselben zu betrachten zu sein.

[5] Marq. i. 513; Ohnesseit, p. 46; cf. *Or. Henz.* 3959, 7089; Tac. *Ann.* i. 54, 73.

[6] Petron. 65, 71.

[7] *Or.* 2983; *C.I.L.* v. 4482.

Yet the Augustales, in spite of the vulgar ostentation and self-assertion, which have characterised similar classes of the *nouveaux riches* in all ages, were a very important and useful order. They overspread the whole Roman world in the West. Their monuments have been traced, not only in almost every town in Italy, and in great provincial capitals, like Lyons or Tarraco, but in Alpine valleys and lonely outposts of civilisation on the edge of the Sahara.[1] Their special religious duties involved considerable expense, from which no doubt the more aristocratic class were glad to be relieved. They had to bear the cost of sacrifices and festivities on certain days in honour of dead emperors. They had to pay an entrance fee on admission to the college, which the ambitious among them would often lavishly exceed.[2] They were organised on the lines of other colleges, with patrons, quinquennales, and other officials. They had their club-houses where their banquets were regularly held, they possessed landed property, and had their common places of burial.[3] But their expenditure and their interests were by no means limited to their own immediate society. They regarded themselves, and were generally treated as public officials, ranking next to the magistrates of the Curia. They had the right to wear the purple-bordered toga, and to have lictors attending them in the streets.[4] Places of honour were reserved for them at the games and festivals. Although as a class they were not eligible for a seat in the Curia, or for the municipal magistracies, yet the *ornamenta*, the external badges and honours attached to these offices, were sometimes granted even to freedmen who had done service to the community. Thus an Augustal who had paved a road at Cales received the *ornamenta* of a decurio.[5] And another, for his munificence to Pompeii, by a decree of the Curia, was awarded the use of the *bisellium*, a seat of honour which was usually reserved for the highest dignitaries.[6] But the ornaments and dignities of their own particular college became objects of pride and ambition. Thus a man boasts of having been made *primus Augustalis perpetuus*, by a decree of the Curia.[7] A worthy of Brundisium received from the Curia a

[1] *Or. Henz.* 3917, 3924, 1561, 7092, 4077, 3127, 4020, 5655, 2374.
[2] Friedl. *Cena Trim. Einl.* 37.
[3] *Or. Henz.* 3787–8 ; 7103.
[4] Petron. *Sat.* 65.
[5] *Or. Henz.* 6983.
[6] *Ib.* 4044, 7094.
[7] *Ib.* 7112.

public funeral, with the ornaments and insignia of an Augustal.[1] In this way, in a society highly conventional, and dominated by caste feeling, the order of the Augustales provided both a stimulus and a reward for the public spirit of a new class, powerful in its wealth and numbers, but generally encumbered by the heritage of a doubtful origin. It was a great elevation for a man, who, perhaps, had been sold as a boy in some Syrian slave market into the degradation of a minion, and who had emerged, by petty savings or base services, into the comparative freedom of a tainted or despised trade, to find himself at last holding a conspicuous rank in his municipality, and able to purchase honour and deference from those who had trampled on him in his youth.

The Augustales shared with the members of the Curia the heavy burdens which public sentiment then imposed upon the rich. Direct taxation for municipal purposes was in the first century almost unknown. The municipalities often possessed landed property, mines, or quarries. Capua is said to have had distant possessions in the island of Crete.[2] The towns also derived an income from the public baths,[3] from the rent of shops and stalls in the public places, from the supply of water to private houses or estates, and from port dues and tolls. A very considerable item of revenue must have been found in the fee which all decurions, Augustales, and magistrates paid on entering on their office or dignity. Since the reign of Nerva, the towns had the right of receiving legacies and bequests.[4] And, on the occurrence of any desolating calamity, an earthquake or a fire, the emperor was never slow or niggardly in giving relief. In the year 53 A.D. the town of Bologna received an imperial subsidy of about £83,000.[5] The cities of Asia were again and again relieved after desolating earthquakes.[6]

With regard to municipal expenditure, the budget was free from many public charges which burden our modern towns. The higher offices were unpaid, and in fact demanded large generosity from their holders. The lower functions were dis-

[1] *C.I.L.* ix. 58.

[2] Friedl. *Cena Trim. Einl.* 42.

[3] Plin. *Ep.* viii. 8, 6.

[4] Friedl. *Cena Trim. Einl.* 43.

[5] Tac. *Ann.* xii. 58.

[6] Sueton. *Vesp.* 13; Tac. *Ann.* ii. 47; cf. Nipperdey's note referring to the monument erected to Tiberius in A.D. 30, at Puteoli.

charged, to a great extent, by communal slaves. The care or construction of streets, markets, and public buildings, although theoretically devolving on the community through their aediles, was, as a matter of fact, to an enormous extent undertaken by private persons. The city treasury must have often incurred a loss in striving to provide corn and oil for the citizens at a limited price, and the authorities were often reviled, as at Trimalchio's banquet, for not doing more to cheapen the necessaries of life.[1] Although our information as to municipal expenditure on education and medical treatment is scanty, it is pretty clear that the community was, in the Antonine age, beginning to recognise a duty in making provision for both. Vespasian first gave a public endowment to professors of rhetoric in the capital.[2] The case of Como, described in Pliny's Letters, was probably not an isolated one. Finding that the youth of that town were compelled to resort to Milan for higher instruction, Pliny, as we have seen, proposed to the parents to establish by general subscription a public school, and he offered himself to contribute one-third of the sum required for the foundation, the rest to be provided by the townsfolk, who were to have the management and selection of teachers in their hands.[3] The Greek cities had public physicians 500 years before Christ,[4] and Marseilles and some of the Gallic towns in Strabo's day employed both teachers and doctors at the public expense.[5] The regular organisation of public medical attendance in the provinces dates from Antoninus Pius, who required the towns of Asia to have a certain number of physicians among their salaried officers.[6] The title *Archiater,* which in the Theodosian Code designates an official class in the provinces as well as at Rome, is found in inscriptions of Beneventum and Pisaurum belonging to an earlier date.[7] But these departments of municipal expenditure were hardly yet fully organised in the age of the Antonines, and were probably not burdensome. The great field of expenditure lay in the basilicas, temples, amphitheatres, baths, and pavements, whose

[1] Petron. 44.

[2] Suet. *Vesp.* xviii. Latinis Graecisque rhetoribus annua centena constituit.

[3] Plin. *Ep.* iv. 13.

[4] Herodot. iii. 131.

[5] Strab. iv. c. i. 5 (181), σοφιστὰς γοῦν ὑποδέχονται . . . κοινῇ μισθούμενοι καθάπερ καὶ ἰατρούς.

[6] Marq. *Priv.* ii. 777.

[7] *Or. Henz.* 3994, 4017.

vanishing remains give us a glimpse of one of the most brilliant ages in history.

The municipal towns relied largely on the voluntary munificence of their wealthy members for great works of public utility or splendour. But we have many records of such enterprises carried out at the common expense, and the name of a special magistracy (*curator operum publicorum*) to superintend them meets us often in the inscriptions.[1] These undertakings were frequently on a great scale. The famous bridge of Alcantara was erected in the reign of Trajan by the combined efforts of eleven municipalities in Portugal.[2] In Bithynia the finances of some of the great towns had been so seriously disorganised by expensive and ill-managed undertakings that the younger Pliny was in the year 111 A.D. sent as imperial legate by Trajan to repair the misgovernment of the province.[3] Pliny's correspondence throws a flood of light on many points of municipal administration, and foreshadows its coming decay. The cities appear to have ample funds, but they are grossly mismanaged. There is plenty of public money seeking investment, but borrowers cannot be found at the current rate of 12 per cent. Pliny would have been inclined to compel the decurions to become debtors of the state, but Trajan orders the rate of interest to be put low enough to attract voluntary borrowers.[4] Apamea, although it had the ancient privilege of managing its own affairs, requested Pliny to examine the public accounts.[5] He did the same for Prusa, and found many signs of loose and reckless finance, and probable malversation.[6] Nicaea had spent £80,000 on a theatre, which, from some faults either in the materials or the foundation, was settling, with great fissures in the walls.[7] The city had also expended a large sum in rebuilding its gymnasium on a sumptuous scale, but the fabric had been condemned by a new architect for radical defects of structure. Nicomedia has squandered £40,000 on two aqueducts which have either fallen or been abandoned.[8] In authorising the construction of a third the emperor might well emphatically order the responsibility for such blunders to be fastened on the proper

[1] *Or. Henz.* 3716, 6709, 7146.
[2] Friedl. *Sittengesch.* iii. 116; *C.I.L.* ii. pp. 89-96.
[3] Plin. *Ad Traj.* 17.
[4] *Ib.* 54, 55, 23. [5] *Ib.* 47.
[6] *Ib.* 17. [7] *Ib.* 39. [8] *Ib.* 37.

persons.[1] In the same city, when a fire of a most devastating kind had recently occurred, there was no engine, not even a bucket ready, and the inhabitants stood idly by as spectators.[2] Pliny was most assiduous in devising or promoting engineering improvements for the health and convenience of the province, and often called for expert assistance from Rome. Irregularities in the working of the civic constitutions also gave him much trouble. The *ecdicus* or *defensor* has demanded repayment of a largess made to one Julius Piso from the treasury of Amisus, which the decrees of Trajan now forbade.[3] Just as Pliny had suggested that members of a curia should be forced to accept loans from the State, so we can see ominous signs of a wish to compel men to accept the curial dignity beyond the legal number, in order to secure the honorarium of from £35 to £70 on their admission.[4] The *Lex Pompeia*, which forbade a Bithynian municipality to admit to citizenship men from other Bithynian states, had long been ignored, and in numbers of cities there were many sitting in the senate in violation of the law. The Pompeian law also required that a man should be thirty years of age when he was elected to a magistracy or took his place in the Curia, but a law of Augustus had reduced the limit for the minor magistracies to twenty-two. Here was a chance of adding to the strength of the Curia which was seized by the municipal censors. And if a minor magistrate might enter the Curia as a matter of course at twenty-two, why not others equally fit?[5] In another typical case the legate was disturbed by the lavish hospitality of leading citizens. On the assumption of the toga, at a wedding, or an election to civic office, or the dedication of a public work, not only the whole of the Curia, but a large number of the common people, were often invited to a banquet and received from their host one or two denarii apiece.[6] Pliny was probably unnecessarily alarmed. The inscriptions show us the same scenes all over the Empire,[7] and the emperor with calm dignity leaves the question of such entertainments to the prudence of his lieutenant.

[1] Plin. *Ad Traj.* 38.
[2] *Ib.* 33.
[3] *Ib.* 110; cf. Marq. *Röm. St.* i. 522.
[4] Plin. *Ad Traj.* 112, 114, 116.
[5] *Ib.* 79.
[6] *Ib.* 116.
[7] *Or. Henz.* 7001; Friedl. *Cena Trim. Einl.* 53; corruption, however, by means of hospitality is expressly forbidden by the *Lex Urson.* § 132; *C. I. L.* ii. *Suppl.* p. 852.

There are many religious questions submitted to the emperor in these celebrated despatches, especially those relating to the toleration of Christians.[1] But, however profoundly interesting, they lie beyond the scope of this chapter. We are occupied with the secular life of the provincial town. And the Letters of Pliny place some things in a clear light. In the first place, the state has begun in the reign of Trajan to control the municipality, especially in the management of its finances; but the control is rather invited than imposed. At any rate, it has become necessary, owing to malversation or incompetence.[2] Nothing could be more striking than the contrast between the civic bungling exposed by Pliny, and the clear, patient wisdom of the distant emperor. And in another point we can see that the municipalities have entered on that disastrous decline which was to end in the ruin of the fifth century. Wasteful finance is already making its pressure felt on the members of the Curia, and membership is beginning to be thought a burden rather than an honour. From the reign of Trajan we begin to hear of the *Curatores*, who were imperial officers, appointed at first to meet a special emergency, but who became permanent magistrates, with immense powers, especially over finance.[3] The free civic life of the first century is being quietly drawn under the fatal spell of a bureaucratic despotism.

The cities did much for themselves out of the public revenues.[4] But there are many signs that private ambition or munificence did even more. The stone records of Pompeii confirm these indications in a remarkable way. Pompeii, in spite of the prominence given to it by its tragic fate, was only a third-rate town, with a population probably of not more than 20,000.[5] Its remains, indeed, leave the impression that a considerable class were in easy circumstances; but it may be doubted whether Pompeii could boast of any great capitalists among its citizens. Its harbour, at the mouth of the Sarno, was the outlet for the trade of Nola and Nuceria.

[1] Plin. *Ad Traj.* 96.

[2] Friedl. *Cena Trim. Einl.* 33; Gréard, *Plut.* pp. 246-7.

[3] The different classes of Curatores, which must be carefully distinguished, are clearly given by Arnold, *Prov. Admin.* 236. Cf. *Or. Henz.* 3899, 3902, 3989. For a good example of the function of the Curator, cf. *Or.* 3787.

[4] For the sources of these, cf. Marq. *Röm. St.* ii. p. 96.

[5] Mau, *Pompeii* (Eng. Tr.), p. 16.

There were salt works in a suburb near the sea. The fish sauces of Umbricius Scaurus had a great celebrity.[1] The vine and the olive were cultivated on the volcanic offshoot from Vesuvius; but the wine of Pompeii was said by the elder Pliny to leave a lingering headache. Mill-stones were made from the lava of the volcano. The market gardeners drove a flourishing trade, and the cabbage of Pompeii was celebrated. On the high ground towards Vesuvius many wealthy Romans, Cicero, and Drusus, the son of Claudius, built country seats, in that delicious climate where the winters are so short, and the summer heats are tempered by unfailing breezes from the mountains or the western sea. All these things made Pompeii a thriving and attractive place; yet its trade hardly offered the chance of the huge fortunes which could be accumulated in those days at Puteoli or Ostia.[2]

Nevertheless, a large number of the public buildings of Pompeii were the gift of private citizens. The Holconii were a great family of the place in the reign of Augustus. M. Holconius Rufus had been ordinary duumvir five times, and twice quinquennial duumvir; he was priest of Augustus, and finally was elected patron of the town.[3] Such dignities in those days imposed a corresponding burden. And an inscription tells that, on the rebuilding of the great theatre, probably about 3 B.C., Holconius Rufus and Holconius Celer defrayed the expense of the crypt, the tribunals, and the whole space for the spectators. Women did not fall behind men in their public benefactions. On the eastern side of the forum of Pompeii there is a building and enclosure, with the remains of porticoes, colonnades, and fountains, which are supposed to have been a cloth market. In a niche stood a marble statue, dedicated by the fullers of Pompeii to Eumachia, a priestess of the city. And Eumachia herself has left a record that she and her son had erected the building at their own expense.[4] The dedication probably belongs to the reign of Tiberius. The visitor who leaves the forum by the arch, at the north-east corner, and turns into the broadest thoroughfare of the town, soon reaches the small temple of Fortuna Augusta, erected in the reign of Augustus. Both the site and the building were

[1] Mau, *Pompeii* (Eng. Tr.), p. 15.
[2] Petron. *Sat.* 38.
[3] Mau, p. 143.
[4] Id. p. 111.

the gift of one M. Tullius, who had, like M. Holconius, borne all the honours which the city could bestow.[1] The amphitheatre in the south-east corner of the town, the scene of so many gladiatorial combats recorded in the inscriptions, was erected by two men of the highest official rank, C. Quinctius Valgus and M. Porcius, probably the same men who bore at least part of the cost of the smaller theatre of Pompeii.[2] The last instance of this generous public spirit which we shall mention is of interest in many ways. It is well known that in the year 63 A.D. an earthquake overthrew many buildings, and wrought great havoc in Pompeii. Among other edifices, the temple of Isis was thrown down. The temple, of which we can now study the remains, had been built by a boy of six years of age, Numerius Popidius Celsinus, who, in acknowledgment of his own, or rather of his father's liberality, was at that unripe age co-opted a member of "the splendid order."[3] This mode of rewarding a father by advancing his infant son to premature honours is not unknown in other inscriptions.[4]

The literature of the age contains many records of profuse private liberality of the same kind. The circle and family of Pliny were, as we have seen in this, as in other respects, models of the best sentiment of the time. Pliny was not a very rich man, according to the standard of an age of colossal fortunes; yet his benefactions, both to private friends and to the communities in which he was interested, were on the scale of the largest wealth. It has been calculated that he must have altogether given to his early home and fatherland, as he calls it, a sum of more than £80,000; and the gifts were of a thoroughly practical kind—a library, a school endowment, a foundation for the nurture of poor children, a temple of Ceres, with spacious colonnades to shelter the traders who came for the great fair.[5] A great lady, Ummidia Quadratilla, known to us not altogether favourably in Pliny's letters, built a temple and amphitheatre for Casinum.[6] From the elder Pliny we learn that the distinguished court physicians, the two Stertinii, whose professional income is said to have ranged from £2000 to £5000 a year, exhausted their ample fortune in their benefactions to

[1] Mau, p. 124.
[2] Id. pp. 147, 206.
[3] Id. p. 164.
[4] *Or. Henz.* 7008, 7010.
[5] Duruy, v. 396.
[6] *Or.* 781.

the city of Naples.[1] A private citizen bore the cost of an aqueduct for Bordeaux, at an expenditure of £160,000.[2] Another benefactor, one Crinas, spent perhaps £80,000 on the walls of Marseilles.[3] The grandfather of Dion Chrysostom devoted his entire ancestral fortune to public objects.[4] Dion, himself, according to his means, followed the example of his ancestor. The site alone of a colonnade, with shops and booths, which he presented to Prusa, cost about £1800. When Cremona was destroyed by the troops of Vespasian in A.D. 69, its temples and forums were restored by the generous zeal of private citizens, after all the horror and exhaustion of that awful conflict.[5]

But the prince of public benefactors in the Antonine age was the great sophist Herodes Atticus, the tutor of M. Aurelius, who died in the same year as his pupil, 180 A.D. He acted up to his theory of the uses of wealth on a scale of unexampled munificence.[6] His family was of high rank, and claimed descent from the Aeacidae of Aegina. They had also apparently inexhaustible resources. His father spent a sum of nearly £40,000 in supplementing an imperial grant for the supply of water to the Troad. The munificence of the son was extended to cities in Italy, as well as to Corinth, Thessaly, Euboea, Boeotia, Elis, and pre-eminently to Athens. He gave an aqueduct to Canusium and Olympia, a racecourse to Delphi, a roofed theatre to Corinth.[7] He provided sulphur baths at Thermopylae for the visitors from Thessaly and the shores of the Maliac gulf. He aided in the restoration of Oricum in Epirus, and liberally recruited the resources of many another decaying town in Greece. He was certainly benevolent, but he had also a passion for splendid fame, and cherished an ambition to realise the dream of Nero, by cutting a canal across the Corinthian Isthmus.[8] But Attica, where he was born, and where he had a princely house on the Ilissus, was the supreme object of his bounty. In his will he left each Athenian citizen an annual gift of a mina. He would offer to the Virgin Goddess a sacrifice of a hundred oxen on a single day; and, when the great festivals came round, he used to

[1] Plin. *H. N.* xxix. 5.
[2] Duruy, v. 396.
[3] Plin. *l.c.*
[4] D. Chrys. *Or.* 46 (519).
[5] Tac. *Hist.* iii. 34, reposita fora templaque munificentia municipum.
[6] Philostr. *Vit. Soph.* ii. 1; Friedl. *Sittengesch.* ii. p. 120.
[7] Philostr. *Vit. Soph.* ii. 5.
[8] *Ib.* ii. 6.

feast the people by their tribes, as well as the resident strangers, on couches in the Ceramicus. He restored the ancient shrines and stadia with costly marbles. And, in memory of Rhegilla, his wife, he built at the foot of the acropolis a theatre for 6000 spectators, roofed in with cedar wood, which, to the eye of Pausanias, surpassed all similar structures in its splendour.[1]

The liberality of Herodes Atticus, however astonishing it may seem, was only exceptional in its scale. The same spirit prevailed among the leading citizens or the great *patroni* of hundreds of communities, many of them only known to us from a brief inscription or two; and we have great reason to be grateful on this score to the imperial legislation of later days, which did its best to preserve these stone records for the eyes of posterity.[2] But in forming an estimate of the splendid public spirit evoked by municipal life, it is well to remind ourselves that much has necessarily been lost in the wreck of time, and also that what we have left represents the civic life of a comparatively brief period. Yet the remains are so numerous that it is almost impossible to give any adequate idea of their profusion to those who are unacquainted with the inscriptions. The objects of this liberality are as various as the needs of the community—temples, theatres, bridges, markets, a portico or a colonnade, the relaying of a road or pavement from the forum to the port, the repair of an aqueduct, above all the erection of new baths or the restoration of old ones, with perhaps a permanent foundation to provide for the free enjoyment of this greatest luxury of the south. The boon was extended to all citizens of both sexes, and in some cases, even to strangers and to slaves.[3] There is an almost monotonous sameness in the stiff, conventional record of this vast mass of lavish generosity. It all seems a spontaneous growth of the social system. One monument is erected by the senate and people of Tibur to a man who had borne all its honours, and had left the town his sole heir.[4] On another, an Augustal of Cales, who had received the insignia of the duumvirate, tells posterity that he had laid down a broad road through the town.[5] Another bene-

[1] Philostr. *Vit. Soph.* ii. 3.

[2] *C. Theod.* ix. 17, 5; *Nov. Valent.* 5.

[3] *Or. Henz.* 6993, 7013, 7190, 6622, 2287, 6985, 3325.

[4] *Ib.* 6994.

[5] *Ib.* 6983.

factor bore the chief cost of a new meat market at Aesernia, the authorities of the town supplying the pillars and the tiles.[1] A priestess of Calama in Numidia expended a sum of £3400 on a new theatre.[2] Perhaps the commonest object of private liberality was the erection or maintenance of public baths. An old officer of the fourth legion provided free bathing at Suessa Senonum for every one, even down to the slave girls.[3] At Bononia, a sum of £4350 was bequeathed for the same liberal purpose.[4] A magnate of Misenum bequeathed 400 loads of hard wood annually for the furnaces of the baths, but with the stipulation that his son should be made patron of the town, and that his successors should receive all the magistracies.[5]

These are only a few specimens taken at random from the countless records of similar liberality to the parent city. The example of the emperors must have stimulated the creation of splendid public works in the provinces. It has been remarked by M. Boissier that the imperial government at all times displayed the politic or instinctive love of monarchy for splendour and magnificence.[6] The Roman Code, down to the end of the Western Empire, gives evidence of a jealous care for the preservation of the monuments and historic buildings of the past, and denounces with very unconventional energy the "foul and shameful" traffic in the relics of ancient glory which prevailed in the last age of the Empire.[7] After great fires and desolating wars, the first thought of the most frugal or the most lavish prince was to restore in greater grandeur what had been destroyed. After the great conflagration of A.D. 64, which laid in ashes ten out of the fourteen regions of Rome, Nero immediately set to work to rebuild the city in a more orderly fashion, with broader streets and open spaces.[8] Vespasian, on his accession, found the treasury loaded with a debt of £320,000,000. Yet the frugal emperor did not hesitate to begin at once the restoration of the Capitol, and all the other ruins left by the great struggle of A.D. 69 from which his dynasty arose.[9] He even undertook some new

[1] *Or. Henz.* 7013.

[2] *C.I.L.* viii. 5366; she received the honour of five statues in return.

[3] *Or. Henz.* 2287.

[4] *Ib.* 3325.

[5] *Ib.* 3772.

[6] Boissier, *L'Opp.* p. 44.

[7] See *Rom. Soc. in the Last Century of the Western Empire* (1st ed.), p. 202.

[8] Suet. *Nero*, xvi.

[9] Suet. *Vesp.* ix.; D. Cass. lxvi. 10.

works on a great scale, the temple of Peace and the amphitheatre, on the plans projected by Augustus. Titus completed the Colosseum, and erected the famous baths.[1] Domitian once more restored the Capitol, and added many new buildings, temples to his "divine" father and brother, with many shrines of his special patroness Minerva; a stone stadium for 30,000 people, and an Odeum for an audience of 10,000.[2] Trajan was lauded by Pliny for his frugal administration of the treasury, combined with magnificence in his public works.[3] Nor was the encomium undeserved. He made docks and erected warehouses at Ostia; he ran a new road through the Pomptine marshes; he lavished money on aqueducts and baths.[4] His most imposing construction was a new forum between the Capitoline and the Quirinal, with stately memorials of the achievements of his reign. But the prince of imperial builders and engineers was Hadrian. Wherever he went he took with him in his journeys a troop of architects to add something to the splendour or convenience of the cities through which he passed. "In almost every city," says his biographer, "he erected some building."[5] But the capital was not neglected by Hadrian. He restored historic structures such as the Pantheon and the temple of Neptune, the forum of Augustus, and Agrippa's baths, with no ostentatious intrusion of his own name.[6] In his own name he built the temples of Venus and Roma, the bridge across the Tiber, and that stately mausoleum, which, as the castle of S. Angelo, links the memory of the pagan Empire with the mediæval Papacy and the modern world. The example of the imperial masters of the world undoubtedly reinforced the various impulses which inspired the dedication of so much wealth to the public service or enjoyment through all the cities of the Empire.

But the wealthy and public-spirited citizen was also expected to cater for the immediate pleasure or amusement of his neighbours in games and feasts. We have seen that Pliny, during his administration of Bithynia, seems to have regarded the public feasts given to a whole commune on occasions of

[1] Suet. *Tit.* vii. nemine ante se munificentia minor.

[2] Suet. *Domit.* v.

[3] Plin. *Paneg.* 51.

[4] D. Cass. lxviii. 7, 15; Plin. *Paneg.* 29, 51.

[5] Ael. Spart. *Hadr.* c. 29.

[6] *Ib.* c. 19, § 10, eaque omnia propriis auctorum nominibus consecravit.

private rejoicing, as dangerous to the general tranquillity. Yet the usage meets us everywhere in the inscriptions, and even in the literary history of the time. This spacious hospitality was long demanded from the rich and powerful, from the general at his triumph, from the great noble on his birthday or his daughter's marriage, from the rich burgher at the dedication of a temple or a forum which he had given to the city, from the man who had been chosen patron of a town in expectation of such largesses, not to speak of the many private patrons whose morning receptions were thronged by a hungry crowd, eager for an invitation to dinner, or its equivalent in the sportula.[1] Julius Caesar on his triumph in 46 B.C. had feasted the people at 22,000 tables.[2] Great houses, like the sumptuous seat of Caninius Rufus at Como, had enormous banquet halls for such popular repasts.[3] The Trimalchio of Petronius desires himself to be sculptured on his tomb in the character of such a lavish host.[4] There was in that age no more popular and effective way of testifying gratitude for the honours bestowed by the popular voice, or of winning them, than by a great feast to the whole commune, generally accompanied by a distribution of money, according to social or official grade. It was also the most popular means of prolonging one's memory to bequeath a foundation for the perpetual maintenance of such repasts in honour of the dead.[5] One P. Lucilius of Ostia had held all the great offices of his town, and had rewarded his admirers with a munificence apparently more than equivalent to the official honours they had bestowed. He had paved a long road from the forum to the arch, restored a temple of Vulcan, of which he was the curator, and the temples of Venus, Spes, and Fortuna; he had provided standard weights for the meat market, and a tribunal of marble for the forum. But probably his most popular benefaction was a great banquet to the citizens, where 217 couches were arrayed for them.[6] The same munificent person had twice entertained the whole of the citizens at luncheon. Elsewhere a veteran, with a long and varied service, had settled at Auximum where he

[1] On the sportula at this time, cf. Suet. *Nero*, xvi., *Dom.* vii.; Marq. *Pr.* 1, 207 sq.; Momms. *De Coll.* p. 109.

[2] Plut. *Caes.* 55, *ἑστιάσας μὲν ἐν δισμυρίοις καὶ δισχιλίοις τρικλίνοις ὁμοῦ σύμπαντας*: D. Cass. 43, 21, 3.

[3] Plin. *Ep.* i. 3, triclinia illa popularia.

[4] Petron. 71.

[5] *Or. Henz.* 7115, 1368, 4088, 4115.

[6] *Ib.* 3882.

had been elected patron of the community. His old comrades, the centurions of the Second Legion (Traj. Fortis) erected a monument to his virtues, and, at the dedication, he gave a banquet to the townsfolk.[1] One other example, out of the many which crowd the inscriptions, may serve to complete the picture of civic hospitality. Lucius Cornelius of Surrentum received on his death the honour of a public funeral by a vote of the Curia. The inscription on his statue records that, on assuming the garb of manhood, he had provided a meal of pastry and mead for the populace; when he became aedile, he exhibited a contest of gladiators; and, twice reaching the honours of the duumvirate, he repaid the compliment by splendid games and a stately banquet.[2]

At these entertainments a gift of money, always graduated according to the social rank of the guests, decurio, augustal, or plebeian, was generally added to the fare.[3] Sometimes the distribution took the form of a lottery. A high official of Beneventum, who had probably inherited a fortune from his father, a leading physician of the capital, once scattered tickets among the crowd, which gave the finder the right to a present of gold, silver, dress, or other smaller prizes.[4] Women appeared sometimes both as hostesses and guests on these occasions. Caesia Sabina of Veii, on the day on which her husband was entertaining all the citizens, invited the female relatives of the decurions to dinner, with the additional luxury of a gratuitous bath.[5] It is curious to observe that at the festivities in which women are entertained, the sharp demarcation of ranks is maintained as strictly as it is among their male relations. Thus, in a distribution at Volceii, the decurions, augustales, and vicani, receive respectively thirty, twenty, and twelve sesterces apiece; while the proportion observed among the ladies of the three social grades is sixteen, eight, and four. Nor were children, even those of the slave class, forgotten on these festive occasions. One kindly magnate of Ferentinum left a fund of about £750 to give an annual feast of pastry and mead upon his birthday for all the inhabitants with their wives, and at the

1 *Or. Henz.* 3868.
2 *Ib.* 6211.
3 Marq. *Priv.* i. 210; Petron. 45; *Or.* 842; Momms. *Colleg.* p. 110.
4 *Or. Henz.* 3394; cf. Suet. *Calig.* 18.
5 *Or. Henz.* 3738.

same time, 300 pecks of nuts were provided for the children, bond and free.[1]

These provincial societies, as we have already seen, were organised on aristocratic or plutocratic principles. The distinction between *honestior* and *humilior*, which becomes so cruel in the Theodosian Code, was, even in the Antonine age, more sharply drawn and more enduring than is agreeable to our modern notions of social justice. The rich have a monopoly of all official power and social precedence; they have even the largest share in gifts and paltry distributions of money which wealth might be expected to resign and to despise. Their sons have secured to them by social convention, or by popular gratitude and expectancy, a position equal to that of their ancestors. The dim plebeian crowd, save for the right of an annual vote at the elections, which was in a few generations to be withdrawn, seem to be of little more consequence than the slaves; they were of far less consequence than those freedmen who had the luck or the dexterity to build up a rapid fortune, and force their way into the chasm between the privileged and the disinherited. Yet this would hardly be a complete and penetrating view of the inner working and the spirit of that municipal society. The apparent rigidity and harshness of the lines of demarcation were often relieved by a social sentiment which, on the one hand, made heavy demands on rank and wealth, and on the other, drew all classes together by the strong bond of fellowship in a common social life. There has probably seldom been a time when wealth was more generally regarded as a trust, a possession in which the community at large has a right to share. There never was an age in which the wealthy more frankly, and even recklessly, recognised this imperious claim. It would indeed be difficult to resolve into its elements the complicated mass of motives which impelled the rich burgher to undertake such enormous, and often ruinous, expenditure for the common good or pleasure. There was of course much of mere selfish ambition and love of popularity. The passion for prominence was probably never stronger. Direct or even veiled corruption of the electors was, indeed, strictly prohibited by law.[2] But it was a recognised

[1] *C.I.L.* x. 5853; Friedl. *Cena Trim.* p. 55.

[2] *Lex Urson.* § 132.

principle of public life that the city should honour its benefactors, and that those whom she had raised to her highest distinctions should manifest their gratitude by some contribution to the comfort or the enjoyments of the people. But, when we have admitted all vulgar motives of munificence, a man would show himself a very unobservant, or else a very cynical student of the time, if he failed to recognise that, among these countless benefactors, there were many animated, not only by a sense of duty, but by a real ardour of public spirit, men who wished to live in the love and memory of their fellows, and who had a rare perception of the duties of wealth. Philostratus has left us in his own words a record of the principles which inspired Herodes Atticus in his almost fabulous donations to many cities in Asia, Greece, and Italy. Herodes used to say that the true use of money was to succour the needs of others; riches which were guarded with a niggard hand were only a "dead wealth"; the coffers in which they were stowed away were merely a prison; and the worship of money resembled the sacrifice which the fabled Aloidae offered to a god after putting him in chains.[1] The main characteristics of human nature are singularly fixed from age to age, although the objects of its love and devotion may endlessly vary. The higher unselfish impulses must assert themselves in any society which is not plunging into the abyss. The choicer spirits will be always ready to lavish effort or material wealth on objects which are sacred to their own age, although they may seen chimerical or unworthy to the next. And we may well believe that the man who in the second century built a bath or a theatre for fellow townsmen, might possibly, had he lived in the fifth, have dedicated a church to a patron saint, or bequeathed his lands to a monastery.

The Antonine age was on one side perhaps rather coarse in its ideals, passionately fond of splendour and brilliant display, proud of civic dignity, and keenly alive to the ease and comfort and brightness which common effort or individual generosity might add to the enjoyment of life. It was also an intensely sociable age. Men looked for their happiness to their city rather than to the family or the state. If their city could not play a great part as an independent commonwealth,

[1] Philostr. *Vit. Soph.* ii. 1.

it might, by the self-sacrifice of its sons, assert its dignity among its rivals. It could make itself a society which men would proudly or affectionately claim as their "patria" and their parent, and on which they would vie with one another in lavishing their time and their gold. And the buildings and banquets and bright festivals, on which so much was lavished, were enjoyed by all citizens alike, the lowest and the highest, although high and low had sometimes by prescriptive usage an unequal share in the largesses. The free enjoyment of sumptuous baths, of good water from the Atlas, the Apennines, or the Alban Hills, the right to sit at ease with one's fellows when the *Pseudolus* or the *Adelphi* was put upon the boards, the pleasure of strolling in the shady colonnades of the forum or the market, surrounded by brilliant marbles and frescoes, with fountains shedding their coolness around; the good fellowship which, for the time, levelled all ranks, in many a simple communal feast, with a coin or two distributed at the end to recall or heighten the pleasure—all these things tended to make the city a true home, to some extent almost a great family circle. There was much selfishness and grossness, no doubt, in all this civic life. Which later age can cast the first stone? Yet a study of the inscriptions of the Antonine age leaves the impression that, amid all the sharply drawn distinctions of rank, with all the petty ambition and self-assertion, or the fawning and expectant servility, there was also a genuine patriotic benevolence on the one hand, and a grateful recognition of it on the other. The citizens record on many a tablet their gratitude to patron or duumvir or augustal, or to some simple old centurion, returned from far frontier camps, who had paved their promenade, or restored their baths, or given them a shrine of Neptune or Silvanus. They also preserved the memory of many a kindly benefactor who left, as he fondly thought for ever, the funds for an annual feast, with all the graduated shares scrupulously prescribed, to save an obscure tomb from the general oblivion. Thus, although that ancient city life had its sordid side, which is laid bare with such pitiless Rabelaisian realism by Petronius, it had its nobler aspect also. Notwithstanding the aristocratic tone of municipal society in the age of the Antonines, it is possible that the separation of classes in our great centres of population is morally more sharp and decided than it was in the days when the gulf between social ranks was in theory impassable.

There is however another side to this picture of fraternal civic life. If some of its pleasures were innocent and even softening and elevating, there were others which pandered to the most brutal and cruel passions. The love of amusement grew upon the Roman character as civilisation developed in organisation and splendour, and unfortunately the favourite amusements were often obscene and cruel. The calendar of the time is sufficiently ominous. The number of days which were annually given up to games and spectacles at Rome rose from 66 in the reign of Augustus, to 135 in the reign of M. Aurelius, and to 175, or more, in the fourth century. In this reckoning no account is taken of extraordinary festivals on special occasions.[1] The Flavian amphitheatre was inaugurated by Titus with lavish exhibitions extending over 100 days.[2] The Dacian triumphs of Trajan were celebrated by similar rejoicings for 123 days, and 10,000 gladiators were sent down into the arena.[3] The rage of all classes of the Roman populace for these sights of suffering and shame continued unabated to the very end of the Western Empire. The lubricity of pantomime and the slaughter of the arena were never more fiercely and keenly enjoyed than when the Germans were thundering at the gates of Trèves and Carthage.[4]

It is difficult for us now to understand this lust of cruelty among a people otherwise highly civilised, a passion which was felt not merely by the base rabble, but even by the cultivated and humane.[5] There was undoubtedly at all times a coarse insensibility to suffering in the Roman character. The institution of slavery, which involves the denial of ordinary human rights to masses of fellow-creatures, had its usual effect in rendering men contemptuously callous to the fate of all who did not belong to the privileged class. Even a man of high moral tone like Tacitus, while he condemns Drusus for gloating over his gladiatorial shows, has only a word of scorn for the victims of the butchery.[6] And the appetite grew with what it fed on.

[1] Friedl. *Sittengesch.* ii. 142 ; cf. Jul. Capitol. *M. Ant.* c. x.

[2] Suet. *Tit.* vii.

[3] D. Cass. 68. 15, *καὶ θέας ἐν τρισὶ καὶ εἴκοσι καὶ ἑκατὸν ἡμέραις ἐποίησεν . . . καὶ μονομάχοι μύριοι ἠγωνίσαντο.*

[4] Salv. *De Gub. Dei*, vi. § 69.

[5] Aug. *Conf.* vi. 8 ; cf. Sym. *Ep.* ii. 46.

[6] Tac. *Ann.* i. 76, *vili* sanguine nimis gaudens.

From father to son, for nearly seven centuries, the Roman character became more and more indurated under the influence of licensed cruelty. The spectacle was also surrounded by the emperors, even the greatest and best, for politic reasons, with ever growing splendour. The Flavian amphitheatre, which remains as a monument of the glory of the Empire and of its shame, must have been a powerful corruptor. There, tier above tier, was gathered the concentrated excitability and contagious enthusiasm of 87,000 spectators. The imperial circle and the emperor himself, members of high senatorial houses, the great officers of state, the priests, the vestal virgins, gave an impressive national dignity to the inhuman spectacle. And now and then an Eastern prince or ambassador, or the chief of some half-savage tribe in Germany or Numidia,[1] amused the eyes of the rabble who swarmed on the upper benches. Every device of luxurious art was employed to heighten the baser attractions of the scene. The magnificent pile was brightened with gems of artistic skill.[2] The arena was tesselated with rich colouring from the sunlight which streamed through the awnings. The waters of perfumed fountains shot high into the air, spreading their fragrant coolness; and music filled the pauses in the ghastly conflict. From scenes like these was probably drawn the picture in the Apocalypse: *Mulier circumdata purpura et coccino—mater fornicationum—ebria de sanguine sanctorum.*

In the first and second centuries the passion for cruel excitement was as strong in the provincial towns as it was even at Rome. This may have been partly due to the monotony of provincial life. It was also stimulated by the ease with which public sentiment extorted the means for these gratifications from the richer citizens. The opinion of the powerful and enlightened class, with rare exceptions, made no effort to purify and humanise the grossness of the masses. Seneca and Demonax indeed display a modern humanity in their view of the degrading influence of these displays.[3] A humane magistrate of Vienne, one Trebonius Rufinus, in the reign of Trajan, having autocratically abolished them in his city, was called upon to

[1] Suet. *Calig.* xxxv.

[2] Calpurn. *Ecl.* vii. 24 sqq.

Vidimus in caelum trabibus spectacula textis
Surgere, Tarpeium prope despectantia culmen—
. . . . Sic undique fulgor
Percussit: stabam defixus et ore patenti,
Cunctaque mirabar, etc.

[3] Sen. *De Brev. Vit.* xiii.; *Ep.* 95, § 33; Plut. *Reipubl. Ger. Pr.* c. 29; Luc. *Dem.* c. 57.

defend his conduct before the emperor, and Junius Mauricus had the courage to express before the council a wish that they could be abolished also at Rome.[1] Augustus had, by an imperial edict, restrained the cruel exhibitions of the father of Nero.[2] Vespasian, according to Dion Cassius,[3] had little pleasure in the shows of the arena. But the emperors generally, and not least Vespasian's sons, encouraged and pandered to the lust for blood.[4] The imperial gladiators were organised elaborately in four great schools by Domitian,[5] with a regular administration, presided over by officers of high rank. The gentle Pliny, who had personally no liking for such spectacles, applauded his friend Maximus for giving a gladiatorial show to the people of Verona, to do honour to his dead wife, in the true spirit of the old Bruti and Lepidi of the age of the Punic Wars.[6] He found in the shows of Trajan a splendid incentive of contempt for death.

It is little wonder that, with such examples and such approval, the masses gloated unrestrained over these inhuman sports. The rag-dealer at Trimalchio's dinner is certainly drawn to the life.[7] They are going to have a three days' carnival of blood. There is to be no escape; the butcher is to do his work thoroughly in full view of the crowded tiers of the amphitheatre. It was in Etruria, and in Campania, where Trimalchio had his home, that the gladiatorial combats took their rise. Campanian hosts used to entertain their guests at dinner with them in the days before the second Punic War.[8] And it was in Campanian towns that in the first century was displayed most glaringly the not unusual combination of cruelty and voluptuousness. The remains of Pompeii furnish us with the most vivid and authentic materials for a study of the sporting tastes of a provincial town. It is significant that the amphitheatre of Pompeii, which was capable of holding 20,000 people, was built fifty years before the first stone amphitheatre erected by Statilius Taurus at Rome.[9] It is also remarkable that, although Pompeii is mentioned only twice by Tacitus, one of the references is to a bloody riot

[1] Plin. *Ep.* iv. 22.
[2] Suet. *Nero*, iv.
[3] D. Cass. 66. 15; cf. M. Aur. vi. 46.
[4] D. Cass. 68. 10 and 15, 66. 25; Suet. *Nero*, xi.; Suet. *Dom.* iv.
[5] D. Cass. 67. 1; cf. Friedl. ii. 202.
[6] Plin. *Ep.* vi. 34; *Paneg.* 33.
[7] Petron. 45.
[8] Strabo, v. c. 4, 13.
[9] Mau, 206, 207.

arising out of the games of the amphitheatre.[1] In the year 59 A.D. a Roman senator in disgrace, named Livineius Regulus, gave a great gladiatorial show at Pompeii, which attracted many spectators from the neighbouring town of Nuceria. The scenes of the arena were soon reproduced in a fierce street fight between the people of the two towns, in which many Nucerians were left dead or wounded. The catastrophe was brought before the emperor, and referred by him to the Senate, with the result that Pompeii was sternly deprived of its favourite amusement for a period of ten years. But when the interdict was removed, the Pompeians had the enjoyment of their accustomed pleasure for ten years more, till it was finally interrupted by the ashes of Vesuvius.

A building at Pompeii, which was originally a colonnade connected with the theatre,[2] had been converted into barracks for a school of gladiators in the time of the early Empire.[3] Behind the colonnade of more than seventy Doric columns had been built a long row of small cells, with no opening except on the central enclosure. There was a mess room, and the *exedra* on the southern side served as a retiring room for the trainers and the men in the intervals of exercise. The open area was used for practice. These buildings have yielded many specimens of gladiators' arms, helmets, and greaves richly embossed in relief, scores of mail-coats, shields, and horse-trappings. In one room there were found the stocks, and four skeletons with irons on their legs. In another, eighteen persons had taken refuge in the last catastrophe, and, among them, a woman wearing costly jewels. The walls and columns were covered with inscriptions and rude sketches of gladiatorial life. Indeed the graffiti relating to it are perhaps the most interesting in Pompeii. On some of the tombs outside the city we can still read the notices of coming games, painted on the walls by a professional advertiser, one Aemilius Celer, "by the light of the moon."[4] They announce that a duumvir or aedile or flamen will exhibit twenty or thirty pairs of combatants on the calends of May or the ides of April. There will also be a hunt, athletic

[1] Tac. *Ann.* xiv. 17.

[2] Mau, 152.

[3] Friedl. *Sittengesch.* ii. 206.

[4] Mau, 216, 217. The words in one of these, flaminis Neronis Caesaris Aug. fili, fix the date between 50 and 54 A.D.

games, a distribution of gifts, and awnings will be provided. Programmes were for sale in advance, with a list of the events. The contents of one can still be read scratched on a wall, with marginal notes of the results of the competition. In one conflict, Pugnax, in the Thracian arms, had beaten Murranus the Myrmillo, fighting in the arms of Gaul, with the fish upon his helmet; and the fate of Murranus is chronicled in one tragic letter p. (*periit*). Two others fought in chariots in old British fashion. And the Publius Ostorius who won was, as his name may suggest, a freedman, now fighting as a voluntary combatant, according to the inscription, in his fifty-first conflict.[1] The tomb of Umbricius Scaurus, on the highway outside the Herculaneum gate, was adorned in stucco relief with animated scenes from the arena of hunting and battle. Hunters with sword and cloak, like a modern toréador, are engaging lions or tigers. Two gladiators are charging one another on horseback. Here, a vanquished combatant, with upturned hand, is imploring the pity of the spectators, while another is sinking in the agony of death upon the sand. The name, the school, and the fighting history of each combatant are painted beside the figure.[2] The universal enthusiasm for the shows is expressed in many a rude sketch which has been traced by boyish hands upon the walls. The record of the heroes of the arena was evidently then as familiar as that of a champion footballer or cricketer is now to our own sporting youth. In the peristyle of a house in Nola Street, the names of some thirty gladiators can be read, with the character of their arms and the number of their conflicts. Portraits of gladiators are figured on lamps and rings and vases of the period. The charm of their manly strength, according to Juvenal, was fatal to the peace of many a Roman matron of the great world. And the humbler girls of Pompeii have left the memorial of their weakness in more than one frank outburst of rather unmaidenly admiration.[3]

It is a grave deduction from the admiring judgment of the glory of the Antonine age, that its most splendid remains are the stately buildings within whose enclosure, for centuries, the populace were regaled with the sufferings and the blood of

[1] Mau, 217, 218. [2] *Ib.* 411.
[3] *Ib.* 220; Juv. vi. 82 sqq.; cf. Mart. v. 24.

the noblest creatures of the wild animal world and of gallant men. The deserts and forests of Africa and the remotest East contributed their elephants and panthers and lions to these scenes. And every province of the Empire sent its contingent of recruits for the arena, Gaul, Germany, and Thrace, Britain and Dacia, the villages of the Atlas, and the deserts of the Soudan.[1] Just in proportion to the depth of the impress made by Roman civilisation, was the amphitheatre more or less popular in the provinces. In Italy itself the passion was naturally strongest. Quiet little places, buried in the Apennines, or in the mountains of Samnium, had their regular spectacles, and record their gratitude for the pleasure to some magistrate or patron.[2] The little town of Fidenae, in the reign of Tiberius, gained for a moment a sinister fame by the collapse of its amphitheatre, involving the death or mutilation of 50,000 spectators.[3] An augustal of Praeneste endowed his town with a school of gladiators, and received a statue for this contribution to the pleasures of the populace.[4] A. Clodius Flaccus of Pompeii, in his first duumvirate, on the Apollinaria, gave an exhibition in the forum of bull-fighting, pugilism, and pantomime. He signalised his second tenure of the office by a show of thirty-five pairs of gladiators, with a hunting scene of bulls, boars, and bears.[5] At Minturnae, a monument reminds "the excellent citizens" that, in a show lasting for four days, eleven of the foremost of Campanian gladiators had died before their eyes, along with ten ferocious bears.[6] At Compsa in Samnium, a place hardly ever heard of, the common people erected a statue to a priest of Magna Mater, who had given them a splendid show, and he in turn rewarded their gratitude by a feast to both sexes, which lasted over two days.[7] Similar records of misplaced munificence might be produced from Bovianum and Beneventum, from Tibur and Perusia, and many another obscure Italian town. But the brutal insensibility of the age is perhaps nowhere so glaringly paraded as in the days following the short-lived victory of the Vitellian arms at Bedriacum. There, on that ghastly plain, on which his rival had been crushed and had closed a tainted life by a not inglorious death, Vitellius

[1] Friedl. ii. 189.
[2] *Ib.* ii. 92.
[3] Tac. *Ann.* iv. 62.
[4] *Or. Henz.* 2532.
[5] *Ib.* 2530.
[6] *Ib.* 6148; *C.I.L.* x. 1074, 6012. This was given *postulante populo*.
[7] *Or. Henz.* 5963, 5972, 2531; *C.I.L.* x. 228.

gloated over the wreck of the great struggle. The trees were cut down, the crops trampled into mire; the soil was soaked and festering with blood, while mangled forms of men and horses still lay rotting till the vultures should complete their obsequies. Within forty days of the battle, the emperor attended great gladiatorial combats given by his generals at Cremona and Bononia, as if to revive the memory of the carnage by a cruel mimicry.[1] The grim literary avenger of that carnival of blood has pictured the imperial monster's end, within a short space, in colours that will never fade, deserted by his meanest servants, shuddering at the ghastly terrors of the vast, silent solitudes of the palace, dragged forth from his hiding, and flung with insults and execrations down the Gemonian Stairs. The dying gladiator of Cremona was more than avenged.[2]

The western provinces bordering on the Mediterranean, Gaul, Spain, and Africa, drank deepest of the spirit which created the great amphitheatres of Arles, Trèves, and Carthage, Placentia and Verona, of Puteoli, Pompeii, and Capua. But the East caught the infection, and gladiatorial combats were held at Antioch in Pisidia, at Nysa in Caria, and at Laodicea; Alexandria had its amphitheatre from the days of Augustus, and a school of gladiators, presided over by a high imperial officer.[3] The Teutonic regions of the north and Greece were almost the only provinces in which the bloody games were not popular. The one Greek town where the taste for them was fully developed was the mongrel city of Corinth, which was a Roman colony. In the novel of Apuleius we meet a high Corinthian magistrate travelling through Thessaly to collect the most famous gladiators for his shows.[4] Yet even in Greece, even at Athens, which had been the home of kindly pity from the days of Theseus, the cruel passion was spreading in the days of the Antonines. Plutarch urges public men to banish or to restrain these exhibitions in their cities.[5] When the Athenians, from an ambition to rival the splendour of Corinth, were meditating the establishment of a gladiatorial show, the gentle Demonax bade them first to overturn their altar of Pity.[6] The apostles of Hellenism, Dion, Plutarch,

1 Tac. *Hist.* ii. 70-72.

2 *Ib.* iii. 84.

3 *Or. Henz.* 3725, 6156; Strab. xvii. 1, 10; Friedl. ii. 204, 378 sqq.

4 Apul. *Met.* x. 18; cf. iv. 13.

5 Plut. *Reipubl. Ger. Pr.* 30; Philostr. *Apoll. Tyan.* iv. 21.

6 Luc. *Dem.* 57; cf. Mahaffy, *Greek World under Roman Sway*, p. 271.

and Lucian, were unanimous in condemning an institution which sacrificed the bravest men to the brutal passions of the mob.

The games of the arena were sometimes held at the expense of the municipality on great festivals, with a public officer, bearing the title of *curator*,[1] to direct them. But, perhaps more frequently, they were given by great magistrates or priests at their own expense; or some rich *parvenu*, like the cobbler of Bologna or the fuller of Modena, who have been ridiculed by Martial, would try by such a display to force an entrance into the guarded enclosure of Roman rank.[2] There were also frequent bequests to create a permanent agonistic foundation. The most striking example of such a legacy is to be found on an inscription in honour of a munificent duumvir of Pisaurum. He left a capital sum of more than £10,000 to the community. The interest on two-fifths of this bequest, perhaps amounting to £500, was to be spent in giving a general feast on the birthday of the founder's son. The accumulated interest of the remaining three-fifths, amounting, perhaps, to £4000, was to be devoted to a quinquennial exhibition of gladiators.[3] An aedile in Petronius is going to spend between £3000 and £4000 on a three days' show.[4] The cost of these exhibitions, however, must have widely varied. We hear of one in the second century B.C. which cost over £7000.[5] The number of pairs engaged appears from the inscriptions to have ranged from five to thirty. The shows lasted from one to as many as eight days.[6] And the quality of the combatants was also very various. Tiberius once recalled some finished veterans from their retirement at a fee of about £800 each.[7] On the other hand, a grumbler at Trimalchio's dinner sneers at a stingy aedile, whose gladiators were "two-penny men," whom you might knock over with a breath.[8] Besides the great imperial schools at Praeneste, Capua, or Alexandria, and the "families" maintained at all times by some of the great nobles, there

[1] *Or. Henz.* 2373, 7037, 148, 2532.

[2] Mart. iii. 59, 16.

[3] *Or. Henz.* 81.

[4] Petron. 45.

[5] Friedl. *Sittengesch.* ii. 137, Doch diese Summe erscheint gering im Vergleich mit der kolossalen Verschwendung, mit der die Schauspiele in der letzten Zeit der Republik gegeben wurden; cf. *C.I.L.* ii. 6278 (*Suppl.* p. 1032).

[6] *Or. Henz.* 2530, 2533; Friedl. *Cena Trim.* p. 58; Cic. *Ad Att.* 12, 2.

[7] Suet. *Tib.* vii.

[8] Petron. 45.

were vagrant troops, kept up by speculative trainers for hire, such as that gang into which Vitellius sold his troublesome minion Asiaticus.[1]

The profession of gladiator was long regarded as a tainted one, on which social sentiment and law alike placed their ban. It was a calling which included the vilest or the most unfortunate of mankind. Slaves, captives in war, or criminals condemned for serious offences, recruited its ranks.[2] The death in the arena was thus often, really, a deferred punishment for crime. But even from the later days of the Republic, men of free birth were sometimes attracted by the false glory or the solid rewards of the profession. Freedmen sometimes fought at the call of their patrons.[3] And, when Septimius Severus began to recruit the Pretorian guard from the provinces, the youth of Italy, who had long enjoyed the monopoly of that pampered corps, satisfied their combative or predatory instincts by joining the ranks either of the gladiators or of the brigands.[4] The gladiator had, indeed, to submit to fearful perils and a cruel discipline. His oath bound him to endure unflinchingly scourging, burning, or death.[5] His barracks were a closely guarded prison, and, although his fare was necessarily good, his training was entirely directed to the production of a fine fighting animal, who would give good sport in the arena. Yet the profession must have had some powerful attractions. Some of the emperors,[6] Titus and Hadrian, themselves took a pleasure in the gladiatorial exercises. Commodus, as if to confirm the scandal about his parentage, actually descended into the arena,[7] and imperial example was followed by men of high rank, and even, according to the satirist, by matronly viragoes.[8] The splendour of the arms, the ostentatious pomp of the scene of combat, the applause of thousands of spectators on the crowded benches, the fascination of danger, all this invested the cruel craft with a false glory.[9] The mob of all ages are ready to make a hero of the man who can perform rare feats of physical strength or agility. And the

[1] Friedl. *Sittengesch.* ii. 202; Suet. *Vitell.* xii. circumforaneo lanistae vendidit.

[2] Friedl. *Sittengesch.* ii. 192.

[3] Petron. 45; D. Cass. 60. 30.

[4] D. Cass. 74. 2.

[5] Friedl. *Sittengesch.* ii. 196.

[6] D. Cass. 66. 15; Spart. *Hadr.* 14; cf. Suet. *Calig.* xxxiv.

[7] Lamprid. *Com.* xi.; cf. viii.; Friedl. *Sittengesch.* ii. 150.

[8] Suet. *Jul. Caes.* xxxix.; Juv. vi. 252.

[9] Friedl. *Sittengesch.* ii. 198.

skilful gladiator evidently became a hero under the early Empire, like his colleague of the red or green. His professional record was of public interest; the number of his combats and his victories was inscribed upon his tomb.[1] His name and his features were scratched by boys on the street walls. He attracted the unconcealed, and not always discreet, admiration of women,[2] and his praise was sung in classic verse, as his pathetic dignity in death has been immortalised in marble. The memories of a nobler life of freedom sometimes drove the slave of the arena to suicide or mutiny.[3] But he was oftener proud of his skill and courage, and eager to display them. When shows were rare in the reign of Tiberius, a Myrmillo was heard to lament that the years of his glorious prime were running to waste.[4] Epictetus says that the imperial gladiators were often heard praying for the hour of conflict.[5]

Great imperial schools were organised on the strictest military principles, and were under the command of a procurator who had often held high office in the provinces or the army.[6] Each school had attached to it a staff of masseurs, surgeon-dressers, and physicians to attend to the general health of the members. There were various grades according to skill or length of service, and a man might rise in the end to be trainer of a troop. Gladiators, like all other callings in the second century, had their colleges. We have the roll of one of these, in the year 177 A.D., a college of Silvanus.[7] The members are divided into three decuries, evidently according to professional rank, and their names and arms are also given. Their comrades often erected monuments to them with a list of their achievements. Thus a dear companion-in-arms commemorates a young Secutor at Panormus, who died in his thirtieth year, who had fought in thirty-four combats, and in twenty-one came off victorious.[8]

Our authorities do not often permit us to follow the gladiator into retirement. The stern discipline of the *Ludus* no doubt made better men even of those condemned to it for grievous crimes. The inscriptions contain a few brief records

[1] *Or. Henz.* 2571, 2572; *C.I.L.* x. 7364; xii. 5836.
[2] Mau, *Pompeii*, p. 219 sq.
[3] Sen. *Ep.* 70, § 20; Tac. *Ann.* xv. 46; Sym. *Ep.* ii. 46; cf. Friedl. *Sittengesch.* ii. 211.
[4] Sen. *De Prov.* iv.
[5] Epict. *Diss.* i. 29, § 37.
[6] Friedl. *Sittengesch.* ii. 204.
[7] *Or. Henz.* 2566.
[8] *Ib.* 2571.

of their family life, which seems to have been as natural and affectionate as that of any other class; wives and daughters lamenting good husbands and fathers in the usual phrases, and fathers in turn mourning innocent young lives, cut short by the cruelty of the gods.[1] Sometimes the veteran gladiator might be tempted to return to the old scenes for a high fee, or he might become a trainer in one of the schools.[2] His son might rise even to knightly rank;[3] but the career of ambition was closed to himself by the taint of a profession which the people found indispensable to their pleasures, and which they loaded with contempt.

The inscriptions pay all honour to the voluntary, single-minded generosity with which men bore costly charges, and gave time and effort to the business of the city. But there was a tendency to treat public benefactions as the acknowledgment of a debt, a return for civic honours. We can sometimes even see that the gift was extorted by the urgency of the people, in some cases even by menaces and force.[4] The cities took advantage of the general passion for place and social precedence, and, often from sordid motives, crowded their curial lists with *patroni* and persons decorated with other honorary distinctions. On the famous roll of the council of Canusium, out of a total of 164 members, there are 39 *patroni* of senatorial or knightly rank, and 25 *praetextati*, mere boys, who were almost certainly of the same aristocratic class, and were probably destined to be future patrons of the town.[5] In the desire to secure the support of wealth and social prestige, the municipal law as to the age for magisterial office was frequently disregarded, and even mere infants were sometimes raised to the highest civic honours.[6] The position of patron seems to have been greatly prized, as it was heavily paid for. A great man with a liberal soul might be patron of several towns,[7] and sometimes women of rank had the honour conferred on them.[8] The *ornamenta* or external badges of official rank were frequently bestowed on people who were not eligible by law for the magistracy. A resident alien (*incola*),

[1] *Or. Henz.* 2572–9; *C.I.L.* xii. 3329.
[2] *Or. Henz.* 2573–5; D. Cass. 72. 22.
[3] Juv. iii. 158.
[4] *C.I.L.* x. 1074.
[5] *Or. Henz.* 3721.
[6] *Ib.* 7008, 7010; cf. 7082, where a youth of twenty had been iivir quinquennalis, and had given a gladiatorial show. Cf. 3714, quaestor designatus est annorum xxiiii., 3745, 3246, 3768.
[7] *Ib.* 3764.
[8] *Ib.* 3773, 4036, 82, 5134; cf. 3744.

or an augustal, might be co-opted into the "splendid order" of the Curia, or he might be allowed to wear its badges, or those of some office which he could not actually hold.[1] But it is plain that such distinctions had to be purchased or repaid. The city seldom made any other return for generous devotion, unless it were the space for a grave or the pageant of a public funeral. It is true that a generous benefactor or magistrate is frequently honoured with a statue and memorial tablet. Indeed, the honour is so frequently bestowed that it seems to dwindle to an infinitesimal value.[2] And it is to our eyes still further reduced by the agreeable convention which seems to have made it a matter of good taste that the person so distinguished by his fellow-citizens should bear the expense of the record himself![3] Nor did the expectations of the grateful public end even there; for, at the dedication of the monument, it was seemingly imperative to give a feast to the generous community which allowed or required its benefactor to bear the cost of the memorial of his own munificence.[4] It is only fair, however, to say that this civic meanness was not universal, and that there are records to show that even the poorest class sometimes subscribed among themselves to pay for the honour which they proposed to confer.[5]

The Antonine age was an age of splendid public spirit and great material achievement. But truth compels us to recognise that even in the age of the Antonines, there were ominous signs of moral and administrative decay. Municipal benefactors were rewarded with local fame and lavish flattery; but the demands of the populace, together with the force of example and emulation, contributed to make the load which the rich had to bear more and more heavy. Many must have ruined themselves in their effort to hold their place, and to satisfy an exacting public sentiment. Men actually went into debt to do so;[6] and as municipal life became less attractive or more burdensome, the career of imperial office opened out and offered far higher distinction. The reorganisation of the

[1] *Or. Henz.* 3709, 3750; *C.I.L.* xii. 3203, 3219.

[2] Plut. *Reipubl. Ger. Pr.* c. 27.

[3] *Or. Henz.* 6992.

[4] *Ib.* 3811, 3722, 6999, 7007, 7004 (honore usus inpensam remisit), 7011, 7190, 4100.

[5] *Ib.* 3865, ex aere collato; 6996.

[6] This seems clear from Plut. *Reip. Ger. Pr.* c. 31, *καὶ μὴ δανειζόμενον οἰκτρὸν ἅμα καὶ καταγέλαστον εἶναι περὶ τὰς λειτουργίας.*

imperial service by Hadrian had immense effects in diverting ambition from old channels. It created a great hierarchy of office, which absorbed the best ability from the provinces. Provincials of means and position were constantly visiting the capital for purposes of private business or pleasure, or to represent their city as envoys to the emperor. They often made powerful friends during their stay, and their sons, if not they themselves, were easily tempted to abandon a municipal career for the prospect of a high place in the imperial army or the civil service.[1] It is true that the local tie often remained unbroken. The country town, of course, was proud of the distinction to which its sons rose in the great world; and many a one who had gained a knighthood or some military rank, returned to his birthplace in later years, and was enrolled among its patrons. We may be sure that many a successful man, like the Stertinii of Naples, paid "nurture fees" in the most generous way. But already in the reign of Domitian, as we have seen, legal provision had to be made for the contingency of an insufficient number of candidates for the municipal magistracies. Already, in the reign of Trajan, the cities of Bithynia are compelling men to become members of the Curia, and lowering the age of admission to official rank.[2] Plutarch laments that many provincials are turning their backs on their native cities and suing for lucrative offices at the doors of great Roman patrons.[3] Apollonius of Tyana was indignant to find citizens of Ionia, at one of their great festivals, masquerading in Roman names.[4] The illustrious son of Chaeronea, with a wistful backward glance at the freedom and the glories of the Periclean age, frankly recognises that, under the shadow of the Roman power, the civic horizon has drawn in.[5] It is a very different thing to hold even the highest magistracy at Thebes or Athens from what it was in the great days of Salamis or Leuctra. But Plutarch accepts the Empire as inevitable. He appreciates its blessings as much as Aristides or Dion Chrysostom. He has none of the revolutionary rage which led Apollonius to cast reproaches at Vespasian, or to boast of his complicity

[1] Plut. *Reip. Ger. Pr.* c. 18; cf. c. 10.
[2] Plin. *Ep.* x. 113; 79.
[3] Plut. *Reip. Ger. Pr.* c. 18.
[4] Philostr. *Apoll. T.* iv. 5.
[5] Plut. *Reip. Ger. Pr.* c. 32; cf. Gréard, *Morale de Plut.* p. 230.

in the overthrow of Nero.[1] He has little sympathy with philosophers like Epictetus, who would sink the interests of everyday politics in the larger life of the universal commonwealth of humanity. The Empire has extinguished much of civic glory and freedom, but let us recognise its compensating blessings of an ordered peace. *Spartam nactus es, hanc exorna*, might be the motto of Plutarch's political counsels. He himself, with a range of gifts and culture, which has made his name immortal, did not disdain to hold a humble office in the poor little place which was his home. And he appeals to the example of Epameinondas, who gave dignity to the magistracy which was concerned with the duty of the cleansing of the sewers and streets of Thebes.[2] He tells his young pupil that, although we have now no wars to wage, no alliances to conclude, we may wage war on some evil custom, revive some charitable institution, repair an aqueduct, or preside at a sacrifice. Yet Plutarch has a keen insight into the municipal vices of his age, the passion for place and office, the hot unscrupulous rivalry which will stoop to any demagogic arts, the venality of the crowd, and the readiness of the rich to pamper them with largesses and shows, the insane passion for pompous decrees of thanks and memorial statues; above all, the eager servility which abandoned even the poor remnant of municipal liberty, and was always inviting the interference of the prince on the most trivial occasions.[3] Such appeals paralyse civic energy and hasten the inevitable drift of despotism. He exhorts men to strive by every means to raise the tone of their own community, instead of forsaking it in fastidious scorn, or ambition for a more spacious and splendid life.

The growing distaste for municipal honours was to some extent caused by bureaucratic encroachments on the independence of the Curia. As early as the reign of Trajan there are unmistakable signs, as we have seen, of financial mismanagement and decay. The case of Bithynia, in Trajan's reign, is sometimes treated as an exceptional one. It may be doubted whether it is not a conspicuous example of general disorganisation. The Bithynian towns were probably not alone in their ill-considered expenditure on faultily planned aqueducts

[1] Philostr. *Apoll. T.* v. 41, 10; cf. Gréard, p. 227.

[2] Plut. *Reip. Ger. Pr.* c. 15.

[3] *Ib.* c. 27, 29, 30, 20.

and theatres. Apamea was certainly not the only city which called for an imperial auditor of its accounts. Inscriptions of the reign of Trajan show that many towns in Italy, Como, Canusium, Praeneste, Pisa, Bergamum, and Caere, had curators of their administration appointed, some as early as the reigns of Hadrian or Trajan.[1] These officers, who were always unconnected with the municipality, took over the financial control, which had previously belonged to the duumvirs and quaestors. They were often senators or equites of high rank, and a single curator sometimes had the supervision of several municipalities. The case of Caere is peculiarly instructive and interesting.[2] There, an imperial freedman, named Vesbinus, proposed to erect at his own cost a club-house (*phretrium*), for the augustales, and asked the municipal authorities for a site close to the basilica. At a formal meeting of the Curia, the ground was granted to him, subject to the approval of Curiatius Cosanus, the curator, with a vote of thanks for his liberality. A letter to that official was drawn up, stating the whole case, and asking for his sanction. The curator, writing from Ameria, granted it in the most cordial terms. It is noteworthy that at the very time when Caere was consulting its curator about the proposal of Vesbinus,[3] the Bithynian cities were laying bare their financial and engineering difficulties to Pliny and Trajan. The glory of free civic life is already on the wane. The municipality has invited or submitted to imperial control. The burdens of office have begun to outweigh its glory and distinction. In a generation or two the people will have lost their elective power, and the Curia will appoint the municipal officers from its own ranks. It will end by becoming a mere administrative machine for levying the imperial taxes; men will fly from its crushing obligations to any refuge; and the flight of the curiales will be as momentous as the coming of the Goths.[4]

The judgment on that externally splendid city life of the

[1] *Or. Henz.* 4007 (Canusium), 2391 (Praeneste), 4491 (Pisa), 3898 (Bergamum), 3787 (Caere). For places out of Italy, cf. *C.I.L.* xii. 3212 (datus a Trajano); viii. 2403, 2660 (Timgad and Lambesi; iii. 3485 (Aquincum); ii. 484 (Emerita); 4112 (Tarraco); cf. x.; ii. p. 1158; Capitol. *M. Ant.* c. 11.

[2] *Or. Henz.* 3787, placuit tibi scribi an in hoc quoque et tu consensurus esses.

[3] A.D. 113, as the names of the consuls show.

[4] See *Roman Society in the Last Century of the Western Empire*, p. 208 sqq. (1st ed.).

Antonine age will be determined by the ideals of the inquirer. There was a genuine love of the common home, a general pride in its splendour and distinction. And the duty, firmly imposed by public sentiment on the well-endowed to contribute out of their abundance to its material comfort and its glory, was freely accepted and lavishly performed. Nor was this expenditure all devoted to mere selfish gratification. The helplessness of orphanhood and age, the penury and monotonous dulness of the lives of great sunken classes, the education of the young, were drawing forth the pity of the charitable. Munificence was often indeed, in obedience to the sentiment of the time, wasted on objects which were unworthy, or even to our minds base and corrupting. Men seemed to think too much of feasting and the cruel amusement of an hour. Yet when a whole commune was regaled at the dedication of a bath or a temple, there was a healthy social sympathy diffused for the moment through all ranks, which softened the hard lines by which that ancient society was parted.

Yet, in looking back, we cannot help feeling that over all this scene of kindliness and generosity and social goodwill, there broods a shadow. It is not merely the doom of free civic life, which is so clearly written on the walls of every curial hall of assembly from the days of Trajan, to be fulfilled in the long-drawn tragedy of the fourth and fifth centuries; three hundred years have still to run before the inevitable catastrophe. It is rather the feeling which seems to lurk under many a sentence, half pitiful, half contemptuous, of M. Aurelius, penned, perhaps, as he looked down on some gorgeous show in the amphitheatre, when the Numidian lion was laid low by a deft stroke of the hunting-spear, or a gallant Myrmillo from the Thames or the Danube sank upon the sand in his last conflict.[1] It is the feeling of Dion, when he watched the Alexandrians palpitating with excitement over a race in the circus, or the cities of Bithynia convulsed by some question of shadowy precedence or the claim to a line of sandhills. It is the swiftly stealing shadow of that mysterious eclipse which was to rest on intellect and literature till the end of the Western Empire. It is the burden of all religious philosophy from Seneca to Epictetus,

[1] M. Aurel. vi. 46; vii. 3; ix. 30.

which was one long warning against the perils ot a materialised civilisation. The warning of the pagan preacher was little heeded; the lesson was not learnt in time. Is it possible that a loftier spiritual force may find itself equally helpless to arrest a strangely similar decline?

CHAPTER III

THE COLLEGES AND PLEBEIAN LIFE

THE *Populus* or *Plebs* of a municipal town of the early Empire is often mentioned in the inscriptions along with the *Ordo* and the Augustales, generally in demanding some benefaction, or in doing honour to some benevolent patron.[1] They also appear as recipients of a smaller share at public feasts and distributions. They occasionally engage in a fierce conflict with the higher orders, as at Puteoli in the reign of Nero, when the discord was so menacing as to call for the presence of a praetorian cohort.[2] The election placards of Pompeii also disclose a keen popular interest in the municipal elections.[3] But the common people are now as a rule chiefly known to us from the inscriptions on their tombs. Fortunately there is an immense profusion, in all the provinces as well as in Italy, of these brief memorials of obscure lives. And although Roman literature, which was the product of the aristocratic class or of their dependents, generally pays but little attention to the despised mass engaged in menial services or petty trades, we have seen that the novel of Petronius flashes a brilliant light upon it in the reign of Nero.

The immense development of the free proletariat, in the time of the early Empire, is one of the most striking social phenomena which the study of the inscriptions has brought to light. It has sometimes been the custom to speak of that society as depending for the supply of its wants entirely on slave labour. And undoubtedly at one time slave labour occupied the largest part of the field of industry. A household in the

[1] *Or. Henz. Ind.* 151; *C.I.L.* xii. p. 940; *Or. Henz.* 3763, 7170 (consensus plebis); *C.I.L.* xii. 3185 (ex postulatione populi); x. 5067, 1030, 8215, 3704.

[2] Tac. *Ann.* xiii. 48; Hi (*i.e.* plebs) magistratuum et primi cujusque avaritiam increpantes.

[3] *C.I.L.* iv. 202, 710, 787.

time of the Republic, of even moderate wealth, might have 400 slaves, while a Crassus would have as many as 20,000, whom he hired out in various industries.[1] But several causes conspired gradually to work a great industrial revolution. From the days of Augustus, the wars beyond the frontier, which added fresh territory and yielded crowds of captives to the slave-markets, had become less frequent. And it is probable that births among the slave class hardly sufficed to maintain its numbers against the depletion caused by mortality and manumission. The practice of emancipating slaves of the more intelligent class went on so rapidly that it had even to be restrained by law.[2] Masters found it economically profitable to give skilful slaves an interest in the profits of their industry, and the *peculium*, which was thus accumulated, soon provided the means of purchasing emancipation. At the same time, the dispersion of colossal fortunes, gained in the age of rapine and conquest, and squandered in luxury and excess, together with the exploitation of the resources of favoured regions, which were now enjoying the blessings of unimpeded commerce, rapid intercommunication, and perfect security, must have given an immense stimulus to free industry. A very casual glance at the inscriptions, under the heading *Artes et Opificia*,[3] will show the enormous and flourishing development of skilled handicrafts, with all the minutest specialisation of the arts that wait on a highly-organised and luxurious society. The epitaphs of these obscure toilers have been brought to light in every part of the Roman world, in remote towns in Spain, Gaul, Noricum, Dacia, and North Africa, as well as in the ancient centres of refinement in Italy or the Greek East. On a single page or two you can read the simple record of the bridle-maker or flask-maker of Narbonne, the cabriolet-driver of Senegallia, the cooper of Trèves, the stone-cutter of Nîmes, the purple-dealer of Augsburg, beside those of the wool-comber of Brescia, the oculist of Bologna, the plumber of Naples, or the vendors of unguents in the Via Sacra, and the humble fruiterer of the Circus Maximus.[4] Many of these people had risen from

[1] Marq. *Priv.* i. 159, 160; Duruy, *Hist. des Rom.* v. 631; Athen. vi. 272 D.
[2] Suet. *Octav.* 40; D. Cass. 55. 13.
[3] *Or. Henz.* iii. *Ind.* p. 180.
[4] *Or. Henz.* 4148, 4143, 4268, 4154. For the provinces cf. *C.I.L.* ii. Suppl. p. 1171; viii. p. 1102; x. 1163; xii. p. 943.

slavery into the freedman class. Most of them are evidently humble folk, although, like a certain female pearl-dealer of the Via Sacra, they may have freedmen and freedwomen of their own, for whom they provide a last resting-place beside themselves.[1] The barber, or auctioneer, or leather-seller, who had become the owner of lands and houses, and who could even give gladiatorial shows, excited the contempt of Juvenal and Martial.[2] But these insignificant people, although despised by the old world of aristocratic tradition, were proud of their crafts. They tell posterity who and what they were, without any vulgar concealment; nay, they have left expensive tombs, with the emblems or instruments of their petty trades proudly blazoned upon them like the armorial devices of our families of gentle birth. In the museum of S. Germain may be seen the effigy of the apple-seller commending his fruit to the attention of the ladies of the quarter; the cooper, with a cask upon his shoulder; the smith, hammer in hand, at the forge; the fuller, treading out and dressing the cloth.[3] This pride in honest industry is a new and healthy sign, as a reaction from the contempt for it which was engrained in old Roman society, and which is always congenial to an aristocratic caste supported by slave labour. In spite of the grossness and base vulgarity of sudden wealth, portrayed by Petronius and Juvenal, the new class of free artisans and traders had often, so far as we can judge by stone records, a sound and healthy life, sobered and dignified by honest toil, and the pride of skill and independence. Individually weak and despised, they were finding the means of developing an organisation, which at once cultivated social feeling, heightened their self-respect, and guarded their collective interests. While the old aristocracy were being rapidly thinned by vice and extravagance, or by confiscation, the leaders of the new industrial movement probably founded many a senatorial house, which, in the fourth and fifth centuries, in an ever-recurring fashion, came to regard manual industry with sublime contempt, and traced themselves to Aemilius Paullus or Scipio, or even to Aeneas or Agamemnon.[4]

The organisation of industry through the colleges attained

[1] *Or. Henz.* 4148, Marcia margitaria de Via Sacra legavit . . . libertis libertabusque suis . . .

[2] Juv. i. 24; x. 224; Mart. iii. 16, 59.

[3] Duruy, v. 637.

[4] S. Hieron. *Ep.* 108, § 3.

an immense development in the Antonine age, and still more in the third century, after the definite sanction and encouragement given to these societies by Alexander Severus. The records of the movement are numerous, and we can, after the scholarly sifting of recent years, now form a tolerably complete and vivid conception of these corporations which, springing up at first spontaneously, in defiance of government, or with its reluctant connivance, were destined, under imperial control, to petrify into an intolerable system of caste servitude in the last century of the Empire of the West.[1]

The sodalitia and collegia were of immemorial antiquity. Certain industrial colleges and sacred sodalities were traced back to Numa, and even to the foundation of Rome.[2] In the flourishing days of the Republic they multiplied without restraint or suspicion, the only associations at which the law looked askance being those which met secretly or by night. It was only in the last century of the Republic that the colleges came to be regarded as dangerous to the public peace, and they were, with some necessary exceptions, suppressed by a decree of the Senate in 64 B.C. They were revived again for factious or revolutionary purposes in 58 B.C. by Clodius.[3] The emperors Julius and Augustus abolished the free right of association, except in the case of a few consecrated by their antiquity or their religious character.[4] And it was enacted that new colleges could not be created without special authorisation. In the middle of the second century, the jurist Gaius lays it down that the formation of new colleges was restrained by laws, decrees of the Senate, and imperial constitutions, although a certain number of societies, both in Rome and the provinces, such as those of the miners, salt workers, bakers, and boatmen, were authorised.[5] And down to the time of Justinian, the right of free association was jealously watched as a possible menace to the public peace. The refusal of Trajan to sanction the formation of a company of firemen in Nicomedia, with the reasons which he gave to Pliny for his decision, furnishes the best concrete illustration

[1] *Roman Society in the Last Century of the Western Empire* (1st. ed.), p. 193.

[2] Momms. *De Coll.* (Morel) p. 28 sq.; Boissier, *Rel. Rom.* ii. 278; Plut. *Numa*, c. 17, ἦν δὲ διανομὴ κατὰ τὰς τέχνας αὐλητῶν, χρυσοχόων, κτλ.

[3] Momms. *De Coll.* p. 76.

[4] Suet. *Caes.* 42; *Octav.* 32.

[5] Momms. *De Coll.* p. 84.

of the imperial policy towards the colleges.[1] That the danger from the colleges to the public order was not an imaginary one, is clear from the passage in Tacitus describing the bloody riots between the people of Nuceria and Pompeii in the reign of Nero, which had evidently been fomented by "illicit" clubs.[2] It is seen even more strikingly in the serious troubles of the reign of Aurelian, when 7000 people were killed in the organised outbreak of the workmen of the mint.[3] Yet it is pretty clear that, in spite of legislation, and imperial distrust, the colleges were multiplying, not only in Rome, but in remote, insignificant places, and even in the camps, from which the legislator was specially determined to avert their temptations. In the blank wilderness, created by a universal despotism, the craving for sympathy and mutual succour inspired a great social movement, which legislation was powerless to check. Just as in the reigns of Theodosius and Honorius, imperial edicts and rescripts were paralysed by the impalpable, quietly irresistible force of a universal social need or sentiment. One simple means of evasion was provided by the government itself, probably as early as the first century. In an inscription of Lanuvium, of the year 136 A.D., there is a recital of a decree of the Senate according the right of association to those who wish to form a funerary college, provided the members did not meet more than once a month to make their contributions.[4] It appears from Marcian's reference to this law that other meetings for purposes of religious observance might be held, the provisions of the *senatusconsultum* against illicit colleges being carefully observed.[5] Mommsen has shown that many other pious and charitable purposes could be easily brought within the scope of the funerary association. And it was not difficult for a society which desired to make a monthly contribution for any purpose to take the particular form recognised by the law. In the reign of M. Aurelius, although membership of two colleges is still prohibited, the colleges obtained the legal right to receive bequests, and to emancipate

[1] Plin. *Ep.* x. 34.

[2] Tac. *Ann.* xiv. 17, re ad patres relata . . . collegia quae contra leges instituerant dissoluta.

[3] Vop. *Aurel.* c. 38.

[4] *Or. Henz.* 6086; cf. Momms. *De Coll.* p. 98; Boissier, *Rel. Rom.* ii. 313; Duruy, v. 408.

[5] Momms. *De Coll.* p. 87.

their slaves. And finally, Alexander Severus organised all the industrial colleges and assigned them *defensores*.[1]

The law against illicit associations, with all its serious penalties, remained in the imperial armoury. But the Empire, which had striven to prevent combination, really furnished the greatest incentive to combine. In the face of that world-wide and all-powerful system, the individual subject felt, ever more and more, his loneliness and helplessness. The imperial power might be well-meaning and beneficent, but it was so terrible and levelling in the immense sweep of its forces, that the isolated man seemed, in its presence, reduced to the insignificance of an insect or a grain of sand. Moreover, the aristocratic constitution of municipal society became steadily more and more exclusive. If the rich decurions catered for the pleasures of the people, it was on the condition that they retained their monopoly of political power and social precedence. The plebeian crowd, recruited from the ranks of slavery, and ever growing in numbers and, in their higher ranks, in wealth, did not indeed dream of breaking down these barriers of exclusiveness; but they claimed, and quietly asserted, the right to organise a society of their own, for protection against oppression, for mutual sympathy and support, for relief from the deadly dulness of an obscure and sordid life. Individually weak and despised, they might, by union, gain a sense of collective dignity and strength. To our eyes, as perhaps to the eyes of the Roman aristocrat, the dignity might seem far from imposing. But these things are greatly a matter of imagination, and depend on the breadth of the mental horizon. When the brotherhood, many of them of servile grade, met in full conclave, in the temple of their patron deity, to pass a formal decree of thanks to a benefactor, and regale themselves with a modest repast, or when they passed through the streets and the forum with banners flying, and all the emblems of their guild, the meanest member felt himself lifted for the moment above the dim, hopeless obscurity of plebeian life.

No small part of old Roman piety consisted in a scrupulous reverence for the dead, and a care to prolong their memory by solid memorial and solemn ritual, it might be to maintain some faint tie of sympathy with the shade which had passed

[1] Lamprid. *Alex. Sev.* c. 33; cf. Duruy, v. 408.

into a dim and rather cheerless world. The conception of that other state was always vague, often purely negative. It is not often that a spirit is sped on its way to join a loved one in the Elysian fields, and we may fear that such phrases, when they do occur, are rather literary and conventional.[1] The hope of blessed reunion after death seldom meets us till we come to some monument of a Christian freedman.[2] But two of the deepest feelings in the Roman mind did duty for a clear faith in the life beyond the tomb: one was family piety, the other the passionate desire of the parting spirit to escape neglect and oblivion. Whoever will cast his eyes over some pages of the sepulchral inscriptions will be struck with the intensity and warmth of affection, the bitterness of loss and grief, which have been committed to the stone. The expressions, of course, are often conventional, like obituary memorials in every age. The model wife appears again and again, loving, chaste, pious, a woman of the antique model, a keeper at home, who spun among her maids and suckled her own children, who never gave her husband a moment's vexation, except when she died.[3] Good husbands seem to have been not less common. And the wife's grief sometimes far outruns the regular forms of eulogy or regret. In one pathetic memorial of a union formed in earliest youth, the lonely wife begs the unseen Powers to let her have the vision of her spouse in the hours of night, and bring her quickly to his side.[4] There is just the same pure affection in the less regular, but often as stable, unions of the slaves and soldiers, and the *contubernalis* is lamented with the same honourable affection as the great lady, although the faulty Latin sometimes betrays the class to which the author belongs. The slave world must always have its shame and tragedy; yet many an inscription shows, by a welcome gleam of light, that even there human love and ties of family were not always desecrated.[5] The slave nurse erects a monument to her little foster child; or a master and mistress raise an affectionate memorial to two young *vernae*

[1] *Or. Henz.* 4841, Elysiis campis floreat umbra tibi; but cf. 4793, manus levo contra deum qui me innocentem sustulit; 4796, Dii irati aeterno somno dederunt.

[2] *Ib.* 4662, Qutia Silvana Uxor virum expecto meum.

[3] *Ib.* 2677, 2655, 4626, 4639, 4848, Domum servavit, lanam fecit. Dixi, abei.

[4] *Ib.* 4775.

[5] *Ib.* 2669, 4653, 2413, 2414.

who died on one day. A freedman bewails, with warm sincerity, a friendship begun in the slave market, and never interrupted till the last fatal hour.[1] The common tragedies of affection meet us on these slabs, as they are reproduced from age to age with little variation. The prevalent note is, *Vale vale in aeternum,* with thoughts of the ghostly ferryman and the infernal stream and hopeless separation. Now and then, but seldom, a soul passes cheerfully from the light which it has loved, happy to escape the burden of old age.[2] And sometimes, too, but seldom, we meet with a cold, hard grossness, which looks back with perfect content upon a full life of the flesh and takes the prospect of nothingness with a cheerful acquiescence.[3]

The true Roman had a horror of the loneliness of death, of the day when no kindly eye would read his name and style upon the slab, when no hand for evermore would bring the annual offering of wine and flowers. It is pathetic to see how universal is the craving to be remembered felt even by slaves, by men plying the most despised or unsavoury crafts. The infant Julius Diadumenus, who has only drawn breath for four hours, receives an enduring memorial. A wife consoles her grief with the thought that her husband's name and fame will be forever prolonged by the slab which she dedicates.[4] On another monument the traveller along the Flaminian Way is begged to stop and read again the epitaph on a boy of nine.[5] Many are tortured by the fear of the desertion or the violation of their "eternal home." An old veteran bequeaths from his savings a sum of about £80, to provide a supply of oil for the lamp above his tomb.[6] An unguent seller of Montferrat leaves a fine garden to afford to the guardians of his grave an annual feast upon his birthday, and the roses which are to be laid upon it for ever.[7] Many a prayer, by the gods of the upper and the lower worlds, appeals to the passing wayfarer not to disturb the eternal rest.[8] The alienation or desecration of a tomb is forbidden with curses or the threat of heavy

[1] *Or. Henz.* 2815, 2817, 4687, 4777, 4653.

[2] *Ib.* 4852, effugi crimen longa senecta tuum.

[3] *Ib.* 4816, balnea, vina, Venus corrumpunt corpora nostra, sed vitam faciunt. Vixi; quod comedi et ebibi tantum meum est. Non fui, fui; non sum, non curo; 4807, 7407, 7387.

[4] *Ib.* 4795, 7406.

[5] *Ib.* 4836.

[6] *Ib.* 4416.

[7] *Ib.* 4417.

[8] *Ib.* 4781, 4783, 4.

penalties.[1] A place of burial was a coveted possession, which was not easily attainable by the poor and friendless, and practical persons guarded their repose against lawless intrusion by requiring the delinquent to pay a heavy fine to the municipal or to the imperial treasury, or to the pontifical college. It was the most effectual way of securing the peace of the dead. For the public authorities had a direct pecuniary interest in enforcing the penalty for the desecration. But it would be interesting to know how long these provisions to protect for ever the peace of the departed fulfilled the hopes of the testator.

The primary object of a multitude of colleges, like that of the worshippers of Diana and Antinous at Lanuvium, was undoubtedly, after the reign of Nerva, the care of the memory of their members after death. In the remarkable inscription of Lanuvium, as we have seen, the formal permission by decree of the Senate, to meet once a month for the purpose of a funerary contribution is recorded.[2] It was a momentous concession, and carried consequences which the legislator may or may not have intended.[3] The jurist Marcian, who gives an imperfect citation of this part of the decree, goes on to add, that meetings for a religious purpose were not prohibited, provided that the previous legislation against illicit societies was observed.[4] And the law of the Lanuvian College shows how often such meetings might take place. It did not need much ingenuity to multiply occasions for reunion. The anniversary of the foundation, the birthday of founders or benefactors, the feast of the patron deity, the birthday of the emperor, these and the like occasions furnished legal pretexts for meetings of the society, when the members might have a meal together, and when the conversation would not always be confined to the funerary business of the college. At a time when, according to juristic theory, a special permission was needed for each new foundation, and when the authority was grudgingly accorded, the whole vast plebeian mass of petty traders, artisans, freedmen, and slaves were at one stroke

[1] *Or. Henz.* 4386, 4357, 4360, 4362, 4388, 4396, 4423, 4425, 4427.

[2] *Ib.* 6086. Ex S.C.P.R. quibus coire convenire collegiumque habere liceat qui stipem menstruam conferre volent in funera, in id collegium coeant neque sub specie ejus collegii nisi semel in mense coeant, etc.

[3] Boissier, *Rel. Rom.* ii. 313.

[4] Momms. *De Coll.* p. 87.

allowed to organise their societies for burial. We may fairly assume that, liberally interpreted, the new law was allowed to cover with its sanction many a college of which funeral rites were not the sole, or even the primary object. And this would be made all the easier because many of the industrial colleges, and perhaps still more of the strictly religious colleges, had a common burial-place, and often received bequests for funerary purposes. This is the case, for example, with a college of worshippers of Hercules at Interamna, and a similar college at Reate.[1] A young Belgian, belonging to the guild of armourers of the 20th legion, was buried by his college at Bath.[2] One C. Valgius Fuscus gave a burial-ground at Forum Sempronii, in Umbria, to a college of muleteers of the Porta Gallica, for their wives or concubines, and their posterity.[3] There is even a burial-place, duly defined by exact measurement, for those "who are in the habit of dining together," a description which, as time went on, would have applied as accurately as any other to many of these clubs.[4]

We are, by a rare piece of good fortune, admitted to the interior of one of the purely funerary colleges. In the reign of Hadrian there was at Lanuvium a college which, by a curious fancy, combined the worship of the pure Diana with that of the deified minion of the emperor. It was founded in A.D. 133, three years after the tragic death of the young favourite. And in 136, the patron of the society, who was also a magnate of the town, caused it to be convened in the temple of Antinous. There he announced the gift of a sum of money, the interest of which was to be spent at the festivals of the patron deities; and he directed that the deed of foundation should be inscribed on the inner walls of the portico of the temple, so that newly admitted members might be informed of their rights and their obligations. This document, discovered among the ruins of the ancient Lanuvium in 1816, reveals many important facts in the constitution and working of funerary colleges.[5] It recites, as we have seen, a part of the *senatusconsultum*, which

[1] *Or. Henz.* 2399, 2400.

[2] *Ib.* 4079.

[3] *Ib.* 4093.

[4] *Ib.* 4073, Loc. sep. convictor. qui una epulo vesci solent.

[5] *Ib.* 6086; Momms. *De Coll.* p. 98; Boissier, *Rel. Rom.* ii. p. 309 sqq.; Duruy, v. 412.

authorised the existence of such colleges, and after loyal wishes for the prosperity of the emperor and his house, it prays for an honest energy in contributing to the due interment of the dead, that by regular payments the society may prolong its existence.

The entrance fee of the college is to be 100 sesterces (16s. 8d.), together with a flagon of good wine. A monthly subscription of five asses is appointed. It is evident that the members are of the humblest class, and one clause shows that they have even a sprinkling of slaves among them, who, with the permission of their masters, might connect themselves with these burial clubs.[1] The brethren could not aspire to the erection even of a *columbarium*, still less to the possession of a common burial-ground. They confined themselves to making a funeral grant of HS.300 to the appointed heir of each member who had not intermitted his payments to the common fund.[2] Out of this sum, HS.50 are to be paid to members present at the funeral. The member dying intestate will be buried by the society, and no claim upon his remaining interest in it will be recognised. The slave, whose body was retained by his master after death, was to have a *funus imaginarium*, and probably a cenotaph. In the case of a member dying within a radius of twenty miles from Lanuvium, three members, on timely notice, were deputed to arrange for the funeral, and required to render an account of the expenses so incurred. A fee of HS.20 was granted to each. But if any fraud were discovered in their accounts, a fine of quadruple the amount was imposed. Lastly, when a member died beyond the prescribed limit, the person who had arranged his funeral, on due attestation by seven Roman citizens, and security given against any further claims, received the burial grant, with certain deductions.[3] In such precise and orderly fashion, with all the cautious forms of Roman law, did this poor little society order its performance of duty to the dead.

Our knowledge of the funerary colleges is still further amplified by an inscription of a date twenty years later than

[1] *Or. Henz.* 6086; Col. ii., placuit ut quisquis servus ex hoc collegio liber factus fuerit etc.

[2] Momms. *De Coll.* p. 99; Boissier, *Rel. Rom.* ii. p. 309.

[3] Momms. *De Coll.* p. 104.

that of Lanuvium.[1] In the reign of Antoninus Pius a lady named Salvia Marcellina resolved to commemorate her husband by a gift to the college of Aesculapius and Hygia. She presented to it the site for a shrine close to the Appian Way, a marble statue of Aesculapius, and a hall opening on a terrace, where the banquets of the brotherhood should be held. To this benefaction Marcellina, along with one P. Aelius Zeno, who apparently was her brother, added two donations of HS.15,000 and HS.10,000 respectively, the interest of which was to be distributed in money, or food and wine, at six different festivals. The proportions assignable to each rank in the college were determined at a full meeting, held in the shrine of the "Divine Titus." Marcellina attaches certain conditions to her gift. The society is to be limited to sixty members, and the place of each member, on his decease, is to be filled by the co-optation of his son. If any member chooses to bequeath his place and interest, his choice is confined to his son, his brother, or his freedman, and he is required to pay for this limited freedom of selection by refunding one-half of his burial grant to the chest of the college.[2] The college of Aesculapius is nominally a religious and funerary corporation, yet there is only a single reference, in a long document, to the subject of burial. No information is given as to the amount of the *funeraticium* or burial grant, the sources from which it is derived, or the conditions on which it is to be paid. The chief object of Marcellina seems to have been to connect the memory of her husband with a number of festivals, for the perpetuity of which she makes provision, to promote social intercourse, and to prevent the intrusion of strangers by making membership practically hereditary.

The colleges, of whose inner working we have tried to give a picture, are classed as religious corporations in the collections of the inscriptions. They bear the name of a god, and they provide a solemn interment for their members. But in these respects they do not differ from many other colleges which are regarded as purely secular. The truth is, that any attempt to make a sharp division of these societies on such lines seems futile. Sepulture and religion being admitted by the

[1] *Or. Henz.* 2417; Junio Rufino Cos. *i.e.* A.D. 153; Momms. p. 73.
[2] Momms. *De Coll.* p. 93.

government as legitimate objects for association, any college, however secular in its tone, might, and probably would, screen itself under sacred names. Nor would this be merely a hypocritical pretence. It is clear that many of the purely industrial colleges, composed as they were of poor people who found it impossible to purchase a separate burial-place, and not easy, unaided, to bear the expense of the last rites, at once consulted their convenience, and gratified the sentiment of fraternity, by arranging for a common place of interment. And with regard to religion, it is a commonplace to point out that all Graeco-Roman societies, great or small, rested on religion. The state, the clan, the family, found their ideal and firmest bond in reverence for divine or heroic ancestors, a reverent piety towards the spirits who had passed into the unseen world. The colleges, as we shall see presently, were formed on the lines of the city which they almost slavishly imitated.[1] It would be strange and anomalous if they should desert their model in that which was its most original and striking characteristic. And just as Cleisthenes found divine and heroic patrons for his new tribes and demes,[2] so would a Roman college naturally place itself under the protection of one of the great names of the Roman pantheon. Sometimes, no doubt, there may not have been much sincerity in this conformity to ancient pieties. But do we need to remind ourselves how long a life the form of ancient pieties may have, even when the faith which gave birth to them has become dim and faint?

The usual fashion of writing Roman history has concentrated attention on the doings of the emperor, the life of the noble class in the capital, or on the stations of the legions and the political organisation of the provinces. It is a stately and magnificent panorama. But it is apt to throw the life of the masses into even deeper shadow than that in which time has generally enwrapped them. We are prone to forget that, behind all this stately life, there was a quiet yet extraordinarily busy industrial activity which was its necessary basis and which catered for all its caprices. In the most cursory way Tacitus tells us that a great part of Italy

[1] They have their ordo, plebs, decuriones, quinquennales, curatores, honorati, patroni, quaestores, etc.; *v. Henz. Ind.* p. 176 sqq.

[2] Herodot. v. 66.

was gathered for the great fair at Cremona, on the fateful days when the town was stormed by the army of Vespasian.[1] Yet what a gathering it must have been! There were laid out in the booths the fine woollens of Parma and Mutina, the mantles of Canusium, the purples of Tarentum, the carpets of Patavium. Traders from Ilva brought their iron wares, Pompeii sent its fish sauces, and Lucania its famous sausages. Nor would there be missing in the display the oil of Venafrum, and the famous Setine and Falernian vintages.[2] The improvement of the great roads in the reign of Trajan must have given a vast stimulus to inland commerce. And we may be sure that many a petty merchant with his pack was to be seen along the Aemilian or Flaminian ways, like the travelling vendor of honey and cheese, whom Lucius, in the tale of Apuleius, meets hurrying to Hypata.[3] The great roads of Spain, since the days of Augustus, carried an immense traffic, which made even the distant Gades a magnificent emporium and one of the richest places in the Roman world.[4]

The wandering traders in Germany, Spain, or Syria, by a natural instinct drew together in their exile. In the revolt of Julius Civilis, they are found settled among the Batavians, and a *collegium peregrinorum* has left its memorial on the lower Rhine.[5] The *sodalicium urbanum* at Bracara Augusta is a similar society.[6] Another mercantile college meets us at Apulum in Dacia.[7] The Syrians of Berytus had a club at Puteoli, and there were at least two clubs of Syrian traders at Malaga.[8] The graves of Syrian traders have been found at Sirmium in Pannonia, and, on the other hand, there are memorials of Roman merchants at Apamea and Tralles, at Salamis and Mitylene.[9] Immense stimulus to this transmarine trade must have been given by the Emperor Claudius, who provided insurance against loss by storms, and a liberal system of bounties and rewards for shipping enterprise.[10] Apollonius of Tyana once expostulated with a young Spartan, who claimed descent from Callicratidas, for having forsaken the true career

[1] Tac. *Hist.* iii. 32, tempus quoque mercatus ditem alioqui coloniam majore opum specie complebat.
[2] Friedl. *Cena Trim. Einl.* p. 63.
[3] Apul. *Met.* i. 5.
[4] Momms. *Rom. Prov.* i. 74.
[5] *Or. Henz.* 178; Tac. *Hist.* iv. 5.
[6] *C.I.L.* ii. 2423.
[7] *Ib.* iii. 1500.
[8] *Ib.* x. 1634, 1579.
[9] *Ib.* iii. 365, 444, 455, 6051.
[10] Suet. *Claud.* xviii.; cf. Merivale, vi. 126 sq.

of a man of his race, to soil himself with the trade of Carthage and Sicily. It is the sentiment of Juvenal who treats as a lunatic the man who will venture his life with a cargo on the wintry Aegean.[1] But the antiquarian rhetoric attributed to Apollonius embalms the fact that at the opening of a springtime in the reign of Domitian, a great merchant fleet was lying at Malea, ready to sail to the western seas.[2] These wandering merchants, wherever they went, banded themselves in colleges for mutual protection and for society. In the same way, old soldiers, on their return from long service on the frontiers, gathered in military brotherhoods at such places as Ostia or Misenum.[3] The veterans of Augustus seem to have become a distinct and recognised class, like the Augustales.[4] Colleges of youth sprang up everywhere from the days of Nero, at Beneventum, Cremona, and Ameria, or at Moguntiacum, Lauriacum, and Paetovio.[5] They were formed, like our own sporting clubs, for exercise and healthy rivalry, often under the patronage of the divine hero who, to all the moralists of that age, had become the mythic type of the continent vigour of early manhood. There is one sodality at least devoted to the preservation of chastity.[6] But it is balanced by the clubs of the "late sleepers" and "late drinkers" of Pompeii.[7]

The colleges in which the artisans and traders of the Antonine age grouped themselves are almost innumerable, even in the records which time has spared. They represent almost every conceivable branch of industry or special skill or social service, from the men who laid the fine sand in the arena, to the rich wine merchants of Lyons or Ostia.[8] The mere catalogue of these associations in an index will give an enlarged conception of the immense range and minute specialisation of Roman industry. It may be doubted whether a similar enumeration of our English crafts would be longer or more varied. The great trades, which minister to the first necessities of human life, occupy of course the largest space, the bakers, the cloth-makers, the smiths, carpenters, and wood-

[1] Juv. xiv. 276.

[2] Philostr. *Apoll. Tyan.* iv. 34.

[3] *Or. Henz.* 6111, 6835.

[4] *Ib.* 4109.

[5] *Ib.* 6414, 2211, 4095, 4100, 4096; *C.I.L.* x. 5928, 1493; iii. 4045, 5678.

[6] *Or. Henz.* 2401.

[7] *C.I.L.* iv. 575, 581.

[8] *Or. Henz.* 4063, 4072, 4087, 7007.

merchants, trades often grouped together, the shoemakers and fullers and carders of wool. The mechanics, who made the arms and engines for the legions, naturally hold a prominent place. Nor less prominent are the boatmen of Ostia, and of the Rhone and the Saône.[1] The sailors of these great rivers had several powerful corporations at Lyons, and, on many an inscription,[2] claim the wealthiest citizens, men who have gained the whole series of municipal honours, as their chiefs and patrons. Arles, which was then a great sea-port, had its five corporations of sailor-folk, and Ostia an equal number, charged with the momentous task of taking up the cargoes of the African corn-ships for the bakeries of Rome.[3] Transport by land is represented by colleges of muleteers and ass drivers in the Alps and Apennines.[4] All the many trades and services which ministered to the wants or pleasures of the capital were similarly banded together, the actors and horn-blowers, the porters and paviors, down to the humble dealers in pastils and salt fish.[5] We have seen that even the gladiators, in their barrack-prisons, were allowed to form their clubs. Although traces of these combinations are found in remote and obscure places all over the Roman world, it is at great commercial centres, at Ostia, Puteoli, Lyons, and Rome itself, that they have left the most numerous remains. They had probably for one of their objects the protection of their members against encroachments or fiscal oppression. Strabo once came across a deputation of fishermen on their way to plead with the Emperor for a reduction of their dues.[6] Yet it would be a mistake to suppose that these trades unions were always organised for trade objects, or that the separate colleges were composed of people engaged in the same occupation. They had many honorary members from among the richer classes, and, even in the lower ranks, in defiance of the law,[7] a dealer in salt might be enrolled among the boatmen of the Rhone, and member of a college of builders.[8] In truth, the great object of association among these humble people appears to have been not so much the protection of their trade, as the cheer-

[1] *Or. Henz.* 4243, 7205, 6950.
[2] *Ib.* 7007, 7254, 4110, 6950.
[3] *Ib.* 3655, 6029, 3178.
[4] *Ib.* 4093, 7206.
[5] *Ib.* 4105, 2619, 4113, 4112, 2625.
[6] Boissier, *Rel. Rom.* ii. p. 286.
[7] *Dig.* L. 7.
[8] Boissier, *Rel. Rom.* ii. 287.

fulness of intercourse, the promotion of fellowship and good-will, the relief of the dulness of humdrum lives.

Probably no age, not even our own, ever felt a greater craving for some form of social life, wider than the family, and narrower than the State. It was a movement at which, as we have seen, even the greatest and strongest of the emperors had to connive. It penetrated society down to its lowest layers. Even the slaves and freedmen of great houses organised themselves in colleges. There were colleges in the imperial household.[1] T. Aelius Primitivus, chief of the imperial kitchen, being a man of great posthumous ambition, left the care of his own and his wife's monument to the college of the palatine cooks.[2] In the inscriptions of Moesia there is the album of a Bacchic club of household slaves containing 80 names, with apparently different grades among them, designated by such titles as *archimysta*, *bouleuta*, *frater* and *filius*.[3] A similar club of the servile class, devoted to the worship of Isis, existed at Tarraco.[4] The officers of another bear the pompous titles of tribune, quaestor, and triumvir, and the slab records the thanks of one Hilara, that her ashes have been allowed to mingle in the same urn with those of Mida the chamberlain.[5] A provincial treasurer at Ephesus, who was a *verna Augusti*, commits the custody of his wife's monument to five colleges of slaves and freedmen in the emperor's household. One of the colleges bears the name of Faustina. Another college is devoted to the cult of the Lares and images of Antoninus Pius.[6] Private masters seem to have encouraged the formation of such associations among their dependents, and sometimes to have endowed them with a perpetual foundation.[7] It was probably politic, as well as kind, to provide for slaves social pleasures within the circle of the household, and thus to forestall the attractions of the numerous clubs outside, which freely offered their hospitality.[8] We may be sure that the college "which was in the house of Sergia Paulina" was not encouraged by the mistress without good reason.

[1] *Or. Henz.* 6302.
[2] *Ib.*
[3] *C.I.L.* iii. 2, 6150.
[4] *Ib.* ii. 6004.
[5] *Or. Henz.* 2863, Hilara viva rogavit ut ossa sua in olla Midaes coicerentur cum mort. esset.
[6] *C.I.L.* iii. 6077, *v.* note.
[7] *Or. Henz.* 2386, 4938, 4123.
[8] Such as that in *Or. Henz.* 6086.

Thus it appears that in every part of the Roman world, in the decaying little country town, and in the great trading centres, the same great movement of association is going on apace. It swept into its current almost every social grade, and every trade, handicraft or profession, the pastil-makers, the green-grocers and unguent sellers of Rome, the muleteers of the Alps, the fullers of Pompeii, the doctors at Beneventum, the boatmen of the Seine, the wine merchants of Lyons. Men formed themselves into these groups for the most trivial or whimsical reasons, or for no reason at all, except that they lived in the same quarter, and often met.[1] From the view which the inscriptions give us of the interior of some of these clubs, it is clear that their main purpose was social pleasure. And this is especially true of the clubs of the humblest class. M. Boissier has well remarked that the poor workman, the poor freedman, with the brand of recent slavery upon him, who was often engaged in some mean or disgusting occupation, amidst a society which from tradition regarded any industry soiled by servile touch with distant scorn, must have felt themselves solitary exiles in the desert of a great town, the most awful desert in the world. The remote splendour of the court and aristocratic life must have deepened the gloom of isolation and helplessness. Shut out for ever from that brilliant world of fashion and pleasure and power, whose social life seemed so charming and gay and friendly, the despised and lonely toiler sought a refuge in little gatherings of people as lonely as himself. At some chance meeting, some one, more energetic than the rest, would throw out the suggestion to form a club, on the model of some of the old trade societies which had always been authorised by the State from the days of Numa, or of those newer associations which were now tacitly permitted under the guise of religion. A small entrance fee would meet, for the time, their modest expenses. In that age of generous or ambitious profusion, it was not hard to find some influential patron, a kindly gracious noble, or an aspiring or generous *parvenu*, to give the infant society his countenance, along with a substantial donation for the building of a club-house, and for simple convivial pleasures on his birthday, and other festivals which could easily be multiplied. Then the

[1] *Or. Henz.* 6010, Colleg. Capitolinorum, etc.; cf. Cic. *Ad Quint. Fratr.* ii. 5.

brethren met in solemn form to frame their constitution and commemorate their benefactor, on one of those many monuments which illuminate a social life on which the literature of the age is generally silent.

The continuity and repetition of proved political organisation is a notable characteristic of the great races which have left, or are destined to leave, their mark on history. The British settlers on the prairies of Oregon or Manitoba immediately order themselves into communities, which are modelled on a social system as old as the Heptarchy. The Latin race had perhaps an even more stubborn conservatism than the English. Under the most various circumstances, the Roman instinctively clung to forms and institutions of tested strength and elasticity, and consecrated by the immemorial usage of his race. The most distant and most humble municipality was fashioned after the pattern of the great "city which had become a world."[1] It had its senate, the *ordo splendidissimus et amplissimus,* and the popular assembly which elected the magistrates. The municipal magistrates, if they do not always bear the ancient names, reproduce in shadowy form the dictators, the praetors, the aediles, quaestors, and censors of the old republic.[2] The same continuity of form is seen in the colleges. As the municipal town was modelled on the constitution of the State, so we may say that the college was modelled on the municipal town. The college, indeed, became a city for the brotherhood, at once a city and a home. They apply to it such terms as *respublica collegii.*[3] The meetings often took place in a temple, whether of a patron deity or of an emperor, as those of the Roman Senate were held in the temple of Concord or of Bellona. There they elected their administrative officers, generally for a period of one year; in some cases, by way of special distinction, for life. The heads of these little societies bear various names, *magistri, curatores, quinquennales, praefecti,* or *praesides.*[4] They have also quaestors,[5] who managed their financial affairs, which, although perhaps on no great scale, still involved the investment of trust moneys to yield the prescribed amounts which had to be distributed either as burial

[1] Rutil. Namat. i. 63.

[2] *Or. Henz. Ind.* p. 154 sqq.

[3] *Ib.* 4068, 4107.

[4] *Ib.* 6127, 7181, 7182, 3217, 4138 (*v.* Orelli's note to this Inscription), 4071; *C.I.L.* x. p. 1163; iii. (2) p. 1180.

[5] *Or. Henz.* 2863, 7183, 5372.

payments, or in food and money on the high festivals. The number of the members was generally limited, either by the government in the interests of public order, or by the will of a benefactor, to prevent the progressive diminution in the value of the divisible shares of the income.[1] A periodical revision of the roll of members was therefore conducted every five years, as it was in the municipality, by the chief officers, exercising for the time censorial powers in miniature. Fortunately the albums of three or four colleges have been preserved. The lists throw a vivid light on their constitution and social tone. We have drawn attention in a former chapter to the strict gradation of social rank in the city polity. The same characteristic is repeated in the collegiate organisation. In these humble plebeian coteries, composed of "men without a grandfather," of men, perhaps, whose father was a slave, or of men who were slaves themselves, there emerges, to our astonishment, a punctilious observance of shadowy social distinctions, which is an inheritance from the exclusive aristocratic pride of the old republic. This characteristic has excited in some French critics and historians a certain admiration,[2] in which it is not altogether easy to join. Gradation of rank to ensure devotion and order in public service is a precious and admirable thing. But artificial and unreal distinctions, invented and conferred to flatter wealth, to stimulate or reward the largesses of the rich patron, to gratify the vulgar self-complacency of the *parvenu*, are only a degrading form of mendicancy. Some indulgence is no doubt due to men who were still under the yoke of slavery, or only just released from it; the iron had entered into their souls. But both the college and the municipality of the Antonine age cannot be relieved of the charge of purchased or expectant deference to mere wealth. Hence we cannot altogether share the pleasure of M. Boissier in these pale and vulgar reproductions of the hierarchy of a real aristocracy. But the image of the hierarchy is there, and it is very instructive. In a college of smiths in Tarraconensis, there were fifteen patrons at the head of the roll, followed by twelve decurions, including two doctors and a soothsayer, one

[1] *Or.* 2417, ut ne plures adlegantur quam numerus s. s. etc.; *C.I.L.* ii. 1167, collegio hominum centum dumtaxet constituto. Cf. Plin. x. 33, where the coll. fabrorum is to be limited to 150.

[2] Boissier, *Rel. Rom.* ii. 295.

man isolated by the honours of the *bisellium*, two honorary members, twenty-eight plain plebeians. There were also several "mothers" and "daughters" of the society.[1] The album of another club at Ostia shows a list of nine patrons, two holders of quinquennial rank, and one hundred and twenty-three plebeians.[2] The plebs of many colleges included slaves, and in more than one inscription the men of ingenuous and those of servile birth are carefully distinguished, the slaves being sometimes placed at the bottom of the roll.[3] Yet it was surely a great advance when slaves and freemen could meet together for the time, on a certain footing of equality, for business or convivial intercourse. The rigid lines of old pagan society are indeed still marked on the face of these clubs. And yet many an inscription leaves the impression that these little societies of the old pagan world are nurseries, in an imperfect way, of the gentle charities and brotherliness which, in shy retirement, the young Church was cultivating in her disciples to be the ideal of the world.

These colleges became homes for the homeless, a little fatherland, or *patria*, for those without a country. Sometimes they may have met in low taverns, which were on that account jealously watched by some of the emperors.[4] But they generally attained to the possession of a club-room or *schola*, a name which had been previously given to the lounging-room of the public baths. Sometimes the *schola* was erected at their own cost, the site being perhaps granted by some rich patron, or by the town council, on a vacant spot close to the basilica or the theatre.[5] But frequently a hall was built for them by some generous friend. A like generosity often provided for them a little chapel of their patron deity, with a shaded court, or a balcony open to the air and sun, where the brethren took their common meals.[6] Or a rich patron, anxious to secure some care and religious observance of his last resting-place, would bequeath to a college a pleasant garden adjoining the tomb, with a house in which to hold their meetings.[7] And, as a further security

[1] *Or. Henz.* 4055.

[2] *Ib.* 4054, 2417, 4056.

[3] The ranks are mingled, however, in *Or.* 2394; *C.I.L.* iii. 633.

[4] D. Cass. 60. 6, *τά τε καπηλεῖα ἐς ἃ συνιόντες ἔπινον κατέλυσε, κτλ.*

[5] *Or. Henz.* 4088, 3298, 2279, 3787, 4085.

[6] *Ib.* 2417, solarium tectum junctum in quo populus collegi s. s. epuletur.

[7] *Ib.* 4070.

against neglect and oblivion, a sum of 10,000 or 15,000 sesterces would be invested to provide a dinner for the college on their benefactor's birthday.[1] As years went on, the scene of many a pleasant gathering became a centre round which clustered a great deal of sentiment, and even pride. We may imagine that, allowing for differences of time and faith, the little school or shrine would, in the course of years, attract something of the feeling which consecrates an ancient village church in England, or a little Bethel which was built in the year of the visit of John Wesley. It became a point of honour to make gifts to the schola, to add to its comfort or beauty. One benefactor would redeem a right of ancient lights, or build a boundary wall.[2] Another would make a present of bronze candelabra on a marble stand, with the device of a Cupid holding baskets in his hands.[3] Or a college would receive from its curator a gift of some silver statues of the gods, on the dedication of the *schola*, with a brass tablet, no doubt recording the event.[4] The gift of a place where the brethren of the club might be buried beside their wives or concubines, was probably, to these poor people, not the least valued benefaction.[5] Many a humble donation was probably made, which was too slight for a memorial. But it happens that we have one record of gifts evidently offered by poor, insignificant people. It is contained in a very interesting inscription found upon a rock near the theatre at Philippi in Macedonia.[6] It records that P. Hostilius Philadelphus, in recognition of the aedileship of the college, which had been conferred upon him, bore the expense of polishing the rock, and inscribing upon it the names of the members of a college of Silvanus, sixty-nine in number, together with a list of those who had presented gifts to their temple. The college was a religious one, with a priest who is named in the first place. It is also a funerary society, and seems to be composed of freedmen and of slaves, either belonging to the colony or private masters. They had just erected a temple of their patron god, to which some had given subscriptions in money, while others made various offerings for its adornment. One

[1] *Or. Henz.* 65,900, 4088; cf. 4107, 4366.

[2] *Ib.* 2416, 4057.

[3] *Ib.* 4068.

[4] *Ib.* 2502.

[5] *Ib.* 2400, 4093.

[6] *C.I.L.* iii. 1, 633.

brother presents an image of the god in a little shrine, another statuettes of Hercules and Mercury. There is another donation of some stone-work in front of the temple, and Hostilius, at his own expense, cut away the rock to smooth the approach to the shrine. Most of the gifts are of trifling value, a poor little picture worth 15 *denarii*, a marble image of Bacchus costing not much more. But they were the offerings of an enthusiastic brotherhood, and the good Hostilius has given them an immortality of which they never dreamed.

The contributions of the members would generally have been but a sorry provision for the social and religious life of a college. Reproducing, as it did, the constitution and the tone of the city in so many traits, the college in nothing follows its model so closely as in its reliance on the generosity of patronage. At the head of the album of the society there is a list, sometimes disproportionately long, of its *patroni*. Countless inscriptions leave us in no doubt as to the reason why the patron was elected. His *raison d'être* in the club is the same as in the city; it is to provide luxuries or amusements for the society, which the society could not generally obtain for itself. The relation of patron and client is, of all the features of ancient life, the one which, being so remote from the spirit of our democratic society, is perhaps most difficult for us to understand. The mutual obligations, enforced by a powerful traditional sentiment, were of the most binding, and sometimes burdensome character. And in that form of relation, between former master and freedman, which became so common in the first age of the Empire, the old master was bound to continue his support and protection to the emancipated slave.[1] Although there was much that was sordid and repulsive in the position of the client in Juvenal's and Martial's days, we must still recognise the fact that the fortune of the rich patron had to pay a heavy price for social deference. Not less heavy was the demand made on the patrons of municipalities and colleges.

There must have been wide distinctions of dignity and importance among the industrial colleges of the Empire. The *centonarii*, the *fabri*, and *dendrophori* of the more important centres, such as Aquileia, Lyons and Milan, the

[1] Marq. *Priv.* i. 203.

boatmen of Arles or Ostia, would probably have looked down with scorn on the flute-players of the Via Sacra, the hunters of Corfinium, or the muleteers of the Porta Gallica.[1] And there was a corresponding variety in the rank of the patrons. Some are high officials of the Empire, procurators of provinces, curators of great public works, or distinguished officers of the legions. Or they are men evidently of high position and commanding influence in their province, priests of the altar of Augustus, augurs of the colony, magistrates or decurions of two or three cities.[2] Sometimes the patron is a great merchant, with warehouses of oil or wine at Lyons or Tarragona or Ostia.[3] Yet in spite of his wealth, the patron's social position in those days might be rather uncertain, and we may without difficulty, from modern analogies, believe that a new man might find his vanity soothed, or his position made less obscure, by being known as the titular head of an ancient corporation of the cloth-workers, or *dendrophori*, or of the boatmen on the Saône. Probably in obscure country towns, remote from the seat of Empire, these bourgeois dignities were even more valued.[4] The humbler colleges would have to be content with one of the new freedmen, such as the vulgar friends of Trimalchio, who, after a youth of shameful servitude, had leapt into fortune by some happy chance or stroke of shrewdness, and who sought a compensation for the contempt of the great world in the deference and adulation of those who waited for their largesses.

The election of a patron was an event of great moment, especially to a poor college. And it was conducted with a formal preciseness, and an assumption of dignity, which, at this distance of time, are sometimes rather ludicrous. In a little town of Cisalpine Gaul in the year 190, the college of smiths and clothworkers met in solemn session in their temple. Their quaestors, who may have had the financial condition of the college in view, made a formal proposal that the college should set an example of the judicious reward of merit, by electing one Tutilius Julianus, a man distinguished by his modesty and liberality, as the patron of their society The meeting

[1] *Or. Henz.* 4082, 4118.

[2] *Ib.* 4082, 194, 73, 4077, 6654, 4109, 4069; *C.I.L.* iii. 1, 1209, 1497, 1051; x. 228; 1696; 3910.

[3] *Or. Henz.* 7007, 4109.

[4] *C.I.L.* iii. 1968; *Or. Henz.* 3927, 3321, 6275.

commended the sage proposal of the quaestors, and formally resolved that the honourable Julianus should be requested to accept the distinction, with an apology for so tardy a recognition of his merits, and that a brass plate, containing a copy of this decree, should be placed above his door.[1]

It is significant that the patrons were, in very many cases, Seviri and Augustales, a body which in the provinces, as we have seen, was generally composed of new men of the freedman class. Although they were steadily rising in importance and in strength of organisation, the provincial Augustales always ranked after the decurions of a town. They often displayed boundless liberality to their city and to their own order.[2] But the leading Augustales seem to have been quite as generous to the other corporations who placed themselves under their patronage. And they were not unfrequently patrons of several colleges.[3] It is no long task to find men who were the titular protectors of two or three, of eight, or even of as many as twelve or fifteen colleges. One inscription to Cn. Sentius of Ostia would seem to include among his dependents almost every industrial college in that busy port.[4] Sentius must have been a very wealthy and a very generous man to accept the patronage of so many societies, which in those days expected or demanded that their honours should be paid for in solid cash. The crowning distinction of a statue, or a durable inscription, was often solemnly decreed with all seemly forms of deference or unstinted flattery in a full meeting of the society. But in a great majority of cases we are amused or disgusted to read that, after all his other liberalities, the benefactor or his heir is permitted to pay for the record of popular gratitude.[5] This fact may explain the extraordinary abundance of these honours, if it somewhat lowers their value in the eyes of posterity.

But, besides the benefactions which sprang either from ambition or real generosity, a vast number were inspired by the Roman passion for long remembrance, and for the continuity of funerary ritual. The very position of so many tombs by the side of the great roads beyond the city gates, was a silent

1 *Or. Henz.* 4133.

2 *Ib.* 7116, 3914, 3923, 4080, qui facultates suas coll. reliq.

3 *Ib.* 4109; 194, 4069, 4071, 4094, 7194.

4 *Ib.* 4109.

5 *Ib.* 3724, honore usus impensam remisit; cf. 7011, 6992, 7190, so *passim*.

appeal to the passing traveller not to forget the departed. The appeal is also often expressly made on the stone by those who had no other means of prolonging their own memory or that of some one they loved. It is impossible to read without some emotion the prayer of an old Spanish soldier, that his brethren of the college may never suffer grief like his, if they will only keep the lamp burning for ever over the tomb of his child.[1] The more opulent took more elaborate measures to provide for the guardianship of their "last home."[2] They often attached to the tomb a field or gardens of considerable extent, to be cultivated for profit, or to bear the roses for the annual offering. The whole area, the dimensions of which, in many inscriptions, are defined with mathematical precision, would be surrounded by a wall. Within the enclosure there would be a little shrine containing statues of the dead, an arbour and a well, and a hall in which the kindred of coming generations might hold their annual banquet, till the tie was dissolved by the cruel oblivion of time.[3] There will be a cottage (*taberna*) in which a freedman or dependent of the house may be lodged, to watch over the repose of the dead.[4] But all these precautions, as the testator feels, were likely to be defeated in the end by the vicissitudes of human fortunes.[5] He had, indeed, before his eyes the fate of many a forsaken and forgotten tomb of old worthies of the Republic. Families die out; faithful freedmen and their children cannot keep their watch for ever. The garden will grow wild, a time may come when no kindly hand will pour the libation or scatter the roses on the natal day. Families will die out, but a college may go on for ever by the perpetual renewal of its members. Inspired with this idea, a worthy of Nîmes created a funerary college to dine regularly in his honour.[6] It was to consist of thirty persons, and the number was to be maintained by co-optation into the places of deceased members. Members of the college who were obliged to be absent might send one of their friends to join in the repast. Thus the dead man, who had taken such care to prolong his

[1] *C.I.L.* ii. 2102.

[2] *Or. Henz.* 4371, 4070, 4400, 7365; cf. Marq. *Pr.* i. 370.

[3] *Or. Henz.* 4456 aediculae in quibus simulacra, etc., 4510, 4400 area quae ante se est maceria cincta long. p. xliix., lat. p. xxxix., 7365, 4337, 4070, 4085.

[4] *Ib.* 4366 ejusque mausolei claves duae penes aliquem libertorum meorum . . . sint, 4637, 4352.

[5] *Ib.* 6206.

[6] *Ib.* 4366.

memory, would at no distant date be festively celebrated by people who barely knew his name. Many another left a bequest to a college to be spent in a feast on the testator's memorial day.[1] A freedman of Mevania leaves a tiny legacy of HS.1000 to the guild of clothworkers, of whom he is patron, with the condition that not less than twelve of their number shall feast once a year in memory of him.[2] A more liberal provision for convivial enjoyment was left to a college of Silvanus in honour of Domitian. It consisted of the rents of four estates, with their appurtenances, which were to be spent on the birthdays of the emperor and his wife, "for all time to come," with the sacrifices proper to such a holy season.[3] Due provision is often made for the seemly and impressive performance of a rite which was at once a religious duty and a convivial pleasure. There is a curious letter of the time of Antoninus Pius containing a deed of gift to the college of the *fabri* at Narbo, in return for their constant favours to the donor. One Sextus Fadius presents them with the sum of 16,000 sesterces, the interest of which is to be divided every year at the end of April for ever, at a banquet on his birthday; the guests on this festive occasion are to be habited in their handsomest attire.[4]

But the fullest and minutest arrangements for these modest meals are to be found in the document relating to the foundation of the poor college of Diana and Antinous, to which reference has already been made. The master of the feast was taken in regular order from the roll of the society. Each brother had to accept this office in his turn, or pay a fine of five shillings of our money. The regular festivals of the club were six in the year, on the natal days of Diana and Antinous, and those of the founder and some of his relatives. There is some obscurity in the regulations for these common feasts, and at first sight they are a ludicrous contrast to the pontiff's famous banquet in the days of Julius Caesar, described by Macrobius.[5] M. Boissier naturally refuses to imagine that even the poor brethren of the club of Diana and Antinous would be contented with bread, four sardines, a bottle of good wine, with hot water and the

1 *Or. Henz.* 3999, 4076, 4107, 4088.
2 *Ib.* 3999.
3 *Ib.* 6085.
4 *Ib.* 7215 (A.D. 149).
5 Macrob. *Sat.* iii. 13, 11–13.

proper table service. The slave steward of Horace probably found much better fare in his *popina*.[1] Dr. Mommsen has resolved the mystery. It is evident, from several inscriptions, that *sportulae* were sharply distinguished from distributions of bread and wine.[2] The *sportula* was a gift of richer food or dainties, which in public distributions might be carried home; it was sometimes an equivalent in money. If those who received the *sportula* preferred to enjoy it at a common table, an appointed member of the college would have the food prepared, or convert the money into dishes for the feast. The bread and wine he might add from his own pocket, if they were not provided by the foundation. How much for these meals came from the club funds, and how much out of the pocket of the *magister coenae*, is not always clearly stated. But we may be sure, from the tone of the times, that additions to a modest *menu* were often made by the generosity of patrons and officers of the club.

It would be futile and uninteresting to pursue into all its minute details throughout the inscriptions, the system of *sportulae* founded by so many patrons and benefactors. Any one who wishes can temperately regale himself for hours at these shadowy club-feasts of the second century. Perhaps the clearest example of such distributions is the donation of Marcellina and Aelius Zeno to the little college of Aesculapius, to which reference has been made for another purpose.[3] On seven different anniversaries and festivals, sums of money, with bread and wine, were distributed to the brethren of the college in due proportions, according to their official dignity and social rank. Thus, in the division on the 4th of November, the fête-day of the society, the shares in money, according to the various grades, from the father of the college downwards, are six, four, and two. The division of the wine, according to social rank, follows the proportion of nine, six, and three. A slightly different scale is followed on the birthday of the Emperor Antoninus Pius in September, and on the day for New Year's gifts in January. But in these benefactions the difference of grade is always observed, the patron and the chief magistrates and

[1] Boissier, *Rel. Rom.* ii. 319; Marq. *Pr.* i. 208; Hor. *Ep.* i. 14, 21.

[2] Momms. *De Colleg.* p. 109; cf. *Or.* 2385 (panem vinum et sportulas dedit), 3949.

[3] *Or. Henz.* 2417.

magnates of the society always receiving a larger share than the obscure brethren at the bottom of the list. In the college of Aesculapius, Marcellina herself, and Aelius Zeno, the two great benefactors of the society, along with the highest of its dignitaries, are allotted three times as much as the plebeian brother. The excellent Marcellina, who, in the fourth century might perhaps have followed S. Jerome and Paula to Bethlehem, was the widow of a good and tender husband, who had been curator of the imperial picture galleries.[1] Had she been drawn into the ranks of that hidden society, who were beginning to lay their dead in the winding vaults beneath the Appian Way, she would certainly have dealt out her bounty on a different scale and on different principles. Her bequest to the college of Aesculapius reveals how deep in the soul of a charitable pagan woman, who was probably sprung from servile stock, lay that aristocratic instinct of the Roman world which survived the advent of the Divine Peasant and the preaching of the fishermen of Galilee, for far more than four hundred years.

The most curious and interesting among the regulations for these club entertainments are those relating to order and decorum. The club of Diana and Antinous was not very select, being probably composed of poor freedmen and slaves.[2] The manners of this class, if we may judge by the picture given by Petronius, were, to say the least, wanting in reserve and self-restraint. The great object of such reunions was, as the founder tells us, that the brethren might dine together cheerfully and quietly.[3] Hence he most wisely orders that all serious proposals and complaints shall be reserved for business meetings. If any member quits his place or makes a disturbance, he is to pay a fine of four sesterces. Twelve sesterces is the penalty for insulting a fellow-guest. The man who, under the influence of good wine, so far forgot himself as to insult the chief officer of the society, was to be punished by a forfeit of twenty sesterces, which would probably be a powerful discouragement of bad manners to most of the brotherhood of Antinous.

Many another gift or bequest, of the same character as

[1] Fl. Apolloni Proc. Aug. qui fuit a pinathecis . . . Optimi piissimi, etc.

[2] *Or. Henz.* 6086, quisquis ex hoc collegio servus defunctus fuerit, etc.; cf. the composition of the club in *Or.* 2394.

[3] *Ib.* ut quieti et hilares diebus solemnibus epulemur, etc.

Marcellina's, meets the eye of the student of the inscriptions. The motives are singularly uniform—to repay the honours conferred by a college, to celebrate the dedication of a statue, to save from forgetfulness a name which to us is only a bit of the wreckage of time. Everything is conventional about these bequests. The money is nearly always left for the same purpose, an anniversary repast in honour of the humble dead, of the emperor, or of the patron gods. Sometimes the burial fee is refunded to the college, with the prayer that on the natal day the poor pittance derived from the gift be spent on pious rites, with roses strewn upon the grave.[1] Another will beg only that the lamp in the humble vault may be kept for ever burning. These pieties and longings, which have their roots in a rude pagan past before the dawn of history, were destined to prolong their existence far into Christian times. The lamp will be kept burning over many a tomb of saint or martyr in the fourth or fifth century. And the simple feasts which the clothworkers of Brescia, or the boatmen of Ostia or Lyons, observed to do honour to some departed patron, will be celebrated, often in riotous fashion, over the Christian dead in the days of S. Augustine and S. Paulinus of Nola.[2]

Dr. Mommsen believes that the collegiate life which blossomed forth so luxuriantly in the early Empire, was modelled on the sacred union of the Roman family.[3] And the instinct of the Roman nature for continuity in institutions prepossesses us in favour of the theory. In the college endowed by Marcellina and Zeno, there are a father and a mother, and elsewhere we read of daughters of a college. The members sometimes call themselves brethren and sisters.[4] One of the feasts of the brotherhood is on the day sacred to "dear kinship," when relations gathered round a common table, to forget in kindly intercourse any disturbance of affection.[5] They also met in the early days of January, when presents were exchanged. Above all, like the primal society, they gathered on the birthdays of the revered dead to whom they owed duty and remembrance. And in many cases the members of the society reposed beside

[1] *Or. Henz.* 4107.

[2] S. Paul. Nol. *Carm.* xxvii. 547-585; S. Aug. *Ep.* 32; *Serm.* v.

[3] *De Coll.* p. 3.

[4] *Or. Henz.* 2417, 4055, 2392, 3774, 3815, 1485, 4134.

[5] *Ib.* 2417, Item viii K. Mart. die Karae cognationis eodem loco dividerent sportulas, etc.

one another in death.[1] The college was a home of fraternal equality in one sense. As M. Boissier has pointed out, the members had equal rights in the full assembly of the club. A quorum was needed to pass decrees and to elect the officers. And, in the full conclave, the slave member had an equal voice with the freeman, and might, perchance, himself even be elected to a place of dignity.[2] He might thus, in a very humble realm, wield authority for the time over those who were accustomed to despise him. It is true that he needed his master's leave to join a college, and his master had the legal power to deny to him the last boon of burial by the hands of his collegiate brethren.[3] Yet it was undoubtedly a great stride in advance when a slave could sit at table or in council on equal terms with free-born men, and might receive pious Roman burial, instead of being tossed like a piece of carrion into a nameless grave. The society of one of these humble colleges must have often for the moment relieved the weariness and misery of the servile life, and awakened, or kept alive, some sense of self-respect and dignity. The slave may have now and then felt himself even on the edge of political influence, as when his college placarded its sympathies in an election contest on the walls of Pompeii. Yet we must not allow ourselves to be deceived by words and appearances. In spite of legislative reform, in spite of a growing humane sentiment, whether in the Porch or the Christian Church, the lot of the slave and of the poor plebeian will be in many respects as hopeless and degraded in the reign of Honorius as it was in the reign of Trajan.[4] Even in the reign of Trajan, it is true, perhaps even in the reign of Nero, there were great houses like the younger Pliny's, where the slaves were treated as humble friends, where their weddings were honoured by the presence of the master, where, in spite of legal disabilities, they were allowed to dispose of their savings by will.[5] And the inscriptions record the gratitude

[1] *Or. Henz.* 2399, 4073, 4093.

[2] *C.I.L.* i. 1406 ; ii. 5927.

[3] Momms. *De Coll.* p. 102 ; Plin. *Ep.* viii. 16.

[4] For the contempt for slaves in the fourth and fifth centuries, *v.* S. Hieron. *Ep.* 54, § 5 ; Salv. *De Gub. Dei*, iv. 26. For humaner sentiment, cf. Macrob. *Sat.* i. 11, 12 sqq. ; *C. Theod.* ix. 6, 2, 3 ; vii. 13, 8 ; ix. 7, 4 ; ix. 9, 1 ; ix. 12, 1.

[5] Plin. *Ep.* viii. 16, § 1 ; on the more humane feeling to slaves, cf. Sen. *Ep.* 47 ; *De Ira*, iii. 24, 32 ; *De Clem.* i. 18 ; *De Ben.* iii. 18, 19, 20 ; Juv. xiv. 16 ; Spart. *Hadr.* c. 18 ; Wallon, *L'Esclav.* i. c. 11 ; Marq. *Pr.* i. 177.

and affection to their masters and mistresses of many who were in actual slavery, or who had but just emerged from it. But these instances cannot make us forget the cruel contempt and barbarity of which the slave was still the victim, and which was to be his lot for many generations yet to run. And therefore the improvement in the condition of the slave or of his poor plebeian brother by the theoretical equality in the colleges, may be easily exaggerated. In the humblest of these clubs, the distribution of good fare and money is not according to the needs of the members, but regulated by their social and official rank. We cannot feel confident that in social intercourse the same distinction may not have been coldly observed. In modern times we often see a readiness to accord an equality of material enjoyment, along with a stiff guardianship of social distinctions which are often microscopic to the detached observer. And it would not be surprising to discover that the "master" or the "mother" of the college of Antinous protected their dignity by an icy reserve at its festive meetings.

The question has been raised whether the ordinary colleges were in any sense charitable institutions for mutual help. And certainly the inscriptions are singularly wanting in records of bequests made directly for the relief of poverty, for widows and orphans or the sick. The donations or bequests of rich patrons seem to have had chiefly two objects in view, the commemoration of the dead and the provision for social and convivial enjoyment. It is true that, just as in municipal feasts, there is often a distribution of money among the members of colleges. But this appears to be deprived of an eleemosynary character by the fact that by far the largest shares are assigned to those who were presumably the least in need of them. Yet it is to be recollected that we probably have left to us the memorial of only a small proportion of these gifts, and that, if we had a full list of all the benefactions bequeathed to some of the colleges, the total amount received by each member in the year might be very considerable, if judged by the standard of ordinary plebeian incomes. To the ambitious slave any addition, however small, to his growing *peculium*, which might enable him to buy his freedom, would certainly be grateful.

There is one class of colleges, however, which were undoubtedly formed to meet various exigencies in the course of life, as well as to make a provision for decent burial. These are the military clubs, on the objects and constitution of which a flood of light has been thrown by the study of the inscriptions in the great legionary camps of North Africa.[1] A passage of Vegetius shows us the provident arrangement made by government for the future of the ordinary legionary.[2] It is well known that, on the accession of each new emperor, or on the occurrence of some interesting event in the history of the prince's family, or of some great military success, and often without any particular justification, a donative was distributed throughout the army. It sometimes reached a considerable amount, ranging from the 25 *denarii* granted by Vespasian, to the 5000 of M. Aurelius.[3] One half of this largess was by orders set aside, and retained under the custody of the standard-bearers, to provide a pension on the soldier's retirement from the service. Another fund, entirely different, was formed by the soldiers' own contributions, to furnish a decent burial for those who died on service. But the law against the formation of colleges fell with peculiar severity on the soldier.[4] Not even for a religious purpose was he permitted to join such a society. This prohibition, however, seems to have been relaxed in the case of the officers, and some of the more highly skilled corps.[5] And we have among the inscriptions of Lambesi a few instructive records of these military colleges.[6]

Lambesi, as we have seen, was one of those camps which developed into a regular municipality, after the recognition of soldiers' marriages by Septimius Severus. Henceforth the camp became only a place of drill and exercise, and ceased to be the soldier's home. And on the ground where the soldiers' huts used to stand, there are left the remains of a number of buildings of the basilica shape, erected probably in the third century, which were the club-houses of the officers of the Tertia Augusta. The interior was adorned with statues of imperial personages, and on the wall was inscribed the law of the college,

[1] Cagnat, *L'Armée Rom.* pp. 457 sqq.
[2] Veget. ii. 20.
[3] D. Cass. 65. 22; Capitol. *M. Ant.* c. 7; D. Cass. 73. 8; Cagnat, p. 459; Marq. *Röm. St.* ii. pp. 136, 543.
[4] Cf. Marcian ap. Momms. *De Coll.* p. 87, neve milites collegia in castris habeant.
[5] Cagnat, p. 463.
[6] *C.I.L.* viii. 2552-7.

commencing with an expression of gratitude for the very liberal pay which enabled the college to make provision for the future of its members.[1] The provision was made in various ways. An ambitious young officer was allowed a liberal viaticum for a journey across the sea to seek promotion. If promotion came, he received another grant to equip him. One half the amount granted in these cases was mercifully paid to him in the unpleasant contingency of his losing his grade. If he died on active service, his heir received a payment on the larger scale. And, when a man, in due course, retired from the army, he received the same sum under the name of *anularium*, which has puzzled the antiquary.[2]

It has been maintained that these military clubs were really and primarily funerary societies.[3] And provision for burial was certainly one of their objects. Yet, on a reading of the law of the society of the *Cornicines*, it may be doubted whether the subject of burial is more prominent than the other contingencies of the officer's life, and in some of the inscriptions, burial is not even alluded to. The grant on retirement or promotion, and the grant to his heir on the death of a member, are the same. But probably the majority of officers had the good fortune to carry the money with them into peaceful retirement, if not into higher rank in another corps. In this case they would probably join another college, whether of soldiers or veterans, and secure once more the all-important object of a decent and pious interment. The military clubs seem rather intended to furnish an insurance against the principal risks and occasions of expenditure in a soldier's career. A calculation shows that, after providing for all these liabilities, the military college must have had a considerable surplus.[4] How it was spent, it is not hazardous to conjecture. If the poor freedmen and slaves at Ostia or Lanuvium could afford their modest meals, with a fair allowance of good wine, drunk to the memory of a generous

[1] Cagnat, pp. 467, 540; cf. Boissier *L'Afr. Rom.* p. 111. *C.I.L.* viii. 2554, optiones scholam suam cum statuis et imaginibus domus div. ex largissimis stipendiis . . . fecerunt, etc.

[2] *C.I.L.* viii. 2552, 3, 4; 2557, iii. 3524; *Henz.* 6790; Cagnat, p. 472; Marq. *Röm. St.* ii. 544.

[3] Cagnat, p. 474.

[4] The Cornicines of the 3rd Legion at Lambesi paid an entrance fee of 750 denarii (*Scamnari nomine*). The anularium on retirement, and the funeraticium, were each 500 *denarii*. It would seem that there must have been a considerable surplus. *C.I.L.* viii. 2557.

benefactor, we may be sure that the college of the *Cornicines* at Lambesi would relieve the tedium of the camp by many a pleasant mess dinner, and that they would have been astonished and amused on such occasions to hear themselves described merely as a burial society.

The foundation law of the college of Diana and Antinous betrays some anxiety lest the continuity of the society should be broken. And in many a bequest, the greatest care is taken to prevent malversation or the diversion of the funds from their original purpose.[1] We feel a certain pathetic curiosity, in reading these records of a futile effort to prolong the memory of obscure lives, to know how long the brotherhoods continued their meetings, or when the stated offerings of wine and flowers ceased to be made. In one case the curiosity is satisfied and we have before our eyes the formal record of the extinction of a college. It is contained in a pair of wooden tablets found in some quarry pits near Alburnus, a remote village of Dacia. The document was drawn up, as the names of the consuls show, in the year 167, the year following the fierce irruption of the Quadi and Marcomanni into Dacia, Pannonia, and Noricum, in which Alburnus was given to the flames.[2] Artemidorus the slave of Apollonius, and Master of the college of Jupiter Cernenius, along with the two quaestors, places it on record, with the attestation of seven witnesses, that the college has ceased to exist. Out of a membership of fifty-four, only seventeen remain. The colleague of Artemidorus in the mastership has never set foot in Alburnus since his election. The accounts have been wound up, and no balance is left in the chest. For a long time no member has attended on the days fixed for meetings, and, as a matter of course, no subscriptions have been paid. All this is expressed in the rudest, most ungrammatical Latin, and Artemidorus quaintly concludes by saying, that, if a member has just died, he must not imagine that he has any longer a college or any claim to funeral payments! The humble brothers of the society, whom

[1] *Or. Henz.* 6086, universi consentire debemus ut longo tempore inveterescere possimus; cf. 4357, 4360, 4366, 4386, 4395.

[2] The diptych, which has been singularly preserved, was found in a deserted mine or quarry about 1780, along with some other private documents of a commercial character; *v. C.I.L.* iii. p. 213, and 921. The dates range from 131 to 167 A.D. Cf. *Or. Henz.* 6087; Schiller, *Gesch. der röm. Kaiserzeit*, i. 2, p. 643.

Artemidorus reproaches for their faithless negligence, may probably have fled to some refuge when their masters' lands were devastated by the Marcomanni, or been swept on in the fierce torrent of invaders which finally broke upon the walls of Aquileia.

BOOK III.

NEC PHILOSOPHIA SINE VIRTUTE EST NEC SINE PHILOSOPHIA VIRTUS

CHAPTER I

THE PHILOSOPHIC DIRECTOR

PHILOSOPHY in the time of Seneca was a very different thing from the great cosmic systems of Ionia and Magna Graecia, or even from the system of the older Stoicism. Speculative interest had long before his time given way to the study of moral problems with a definite practical aim. If the stimulus of the searching method of Socrates gave an impetus for a century to abstract speculation, it had an even more decided and long-lived influence in diverting thought to moral questions from the old ambitious paths. His disciples Antisthenes and Aristippus prepared the way for the Stoic and Epicurean schools which dominated the Roman world in the last century of the Republic and the first of the Empire. And even Plato and Aristotle indirectly helped forward the movement. It is not merely that, for both these great spirits, the cultivation of character and the reform of society have a profound interest. But even in their metaphysics, they were paving the way for the more introspective and practical turn which was taken by post-Aristotelian philosophy, by giving to what were mere conceptions of the mind a more real existence than to the things of sense.[1] The "ideas" or "forms" which they contrast with the world of concrete things, are really creations of the individual mind of which the reality must be sought in the

[1] See Zeller, *Phil. der Griech.* iii. 1, 13, 14, Jener dualistische Idealismus, welchen Plato begründet, und auch Aristoteles nicht grundsätzlich überwunden hatte, fuhrt in letzter Beziehung auf nichts anderes zurück, als auf den Gegensatz des Inneren und Aeusseren des Denkens und der gegenständlichen Welt. . . . Es war nur ein Schritt weiter in dieser Richtung, wenn die nacharistotelische Philosophie den Menschen in grundsätzlicher Abkehr von der Aussenwelt auf sich selbst wies, um in seinem Innern die Befriedigung zu suchen, etc.

depths of consciousness, however they may be divinised and elevated to some transcendental region beyond the limits of sense and time. With Aristotle, as with Plato, in the last resort, the higher reason is the true essence of man, coming into the body from a diviner world, and capable of lifting itself to the ideal from the cramping limitations of sensuous life. The philosopher in the *Phaedo* who turns his gaze persistently from the confusing phantasmagoria of the senses to that realm of real existence, eternal and immutable, of which he has once had a vision, is really the distant progenitor of the sage of Stoicism, who cuts himself off from the external objects of desire, to find within a higher law, and the peace which springs from a life in harmony with the Reason of the world.

The ancient schools, if they maintained a formal individuality even to the days of Justinian,[1] had worked themselves out. A host of scholarchs, from all the cities of the Greek East, failed to break fresh ground, and were content to guard the most precious or the least vulnerable parts of an ancient tradition. Moreover, the scrutiny of the long course of speculation, issuing in such various conclusions, with no criterion to decide between their claims, gave birth to a scepticism which sheltered itself even under the great name of the Academy. And as the faith in the truth of systems dwindled, the marks of demarcation between them faded; men were less inclined to dogmatise, and began to select and combine elements from long discordant schools. In this movement the eclectic and the sceptic had very much the same object in view —the support and culture of the individual moral life.[2] The sceptic sought his ideal in restrained suspense of judgment and in moral calm. The eclectic, without regard to speculative consistency, and with only a secondary interest in speculation, sought for doctrines from any quarter which provided a basis for the moral life, and, in the conflict of systems on the deeper questions, would fall back, like Cicero, on intuition and the consent of consciousness.[3] Creative power in philosophy was no more. Speculative curiosity, as pictured in the *Phaedo* or

[1] See Luc. *Eun.* c. 3, συντέτακται ἐκ βασιλέως μισθοφορά τις οὐ φαύλη κατὰ γένη τοῖς φιλοσόφοις, Στωϊκοῖς λέγω, κτλ. Cf. Capitol. *M. Ant.* c. 3; Philostr. *Apoll. T.* i. 7, § 8.

[2] Zeller, iii. 1, 16.

[3] *Ib.* 493-5; Überweg, *Hist. of Phil.* i. 220; Cic. *De Nat. Deor.* i. c. 17; *De Fin.* i. c. 9.

the *Theaetetus*, had lost its keenness. The imperious craving was for some guide of life, some medicine for the deeply-felt maladies of the soul.

The extinction of the free civic life of Greece, the conquests of Macedon, the foundation of the world-wide empire of Rome, had wrought a momentous moral change. In the old city-state, religion, morals, and political duty were linked in a gracious unity and harmony. The citizen drew moral support and inspiration from ancestral laws and institutions clothed with almost divine authority. Even Plato does not break away from the old trammels, but requires the elders of his Utopia as a duty, after they have seen the vision of God, to descend again to the ordinary tasks of government. But when the corporate life which supplied such vivid interests and moral support was wrecked, the individual was thrown back upon himself. Morals were finally separated from politics. Henceforth the great problem of philosophy was how to make character self-sufficing and independent; how to find the beatitude of man in the autonomous will, fenced against all assaults of chance and change.[1] At the same time, the foundation of great monarchies, Macedonian or Roman, embracing many tribes and races and submerging old civic or national barriers, brought into clearer light the idea of a universal commonwealth, and placed morals on the broad foundation of a common human nature and universal brotherhood. The mundane city of old days, which absorbed, perhaps too completely, the moral life and conscience of her sons, has vanished for ever. And in its place and over its ruins has risen an all-embracing power which seems to have all the sweep of an impersonal force of nature, though it is sometimes impelled by one wild, lawless will. If, in return for the loss of civic freedom, ambitious and patriotic energy, or pride of civic life, it has given to its subjects a marvellous peace and order and culture, have not the mass of men become grosser and more materialised? If there is greater material well-being and better administration, have not the moral tone and ideal, in the lack of stimulus, been lowered? Has not vice become more shameless, and the greed for all things pleasant grown harder and more cruel? Are not the mass of men

[1] Bussell, *School of Plato*, p. 264; Zeller, iii. 1; p. 8, 9.

hopelessly and wearily wandering in a tangled maze without a clue?[1]

With such questionings ringing in his inner ear, the man with some lingering instinct of goodness might well crave, beyond anything else, for an inner law of life which should bring order into the chaos of his conduct and desires.[2] And philosophy, having in magnificent effort failed to scale the virgin heights, fell back on conduct, which seemed then, even more than to a lost teacher of our youth, "three-fourths of life." The great science which, in the glory and fresh vigour of the Hellenic prime, aspired to embrace all existence and all knowledge, to penetrate the secret of the universe and God, by general consent narrowed its efforts to relieve the struggles of this transient life set "between two eternities." The human spirit, weary of the fruitless quest of an ever-vanishing ideal of knowledge, took up the humbler task of solving the ever-recurring problem of human happiness and conduct. Henceforth, in spite of traditional dialectic discordance, all the schools, Stoic or Epicurean, Sceptic or Eclectic, are seeking for the secret of inner peace, and are singularly unanimous in their report of the discovery.[3] The inner life of the spirit becomes all in all. Speculation and political activity are equally unimportant to the true life of the soul. Calm equipoise of the inner nature, undisturbed by the changes of fortunes or the solicitations of desire, is the ideal of all, under whatever difference of phrase. What has he to do with any single state who realises his citizenship in the great commonwealth of man? If the secret of peace cannot be won by launching in adventurous thought into the Infinite, perchance it may be found in discipline of the rebellious will. Philosophy, then, must become the guide of life, the healer of spiritual maladies.[4] It must teach the whole duty of man, to the gods, to the state, to parents and elders, to women and to slaves. It must attempt the harder task of bringing some principle of order into the turmoil of

[1] On pessimism in the reign of Augustus, *v.* Boissier, *Rel. Rom.* i. p. 241. Cf. Sen. *De Ira*, ii. 8; *De Ben.* i. 10; *Ad Marc.* 20, 22; Tac. *Hist.* ii. 37; Petron. 88.

[2] Cf. Epict. iii. 13, §§ 9, 10, where the contrast between the "pax Romana" and moral unrest is drawn.

[3] Zeller, iii. 1, pp. 12, 14; cf. Baur, *Ch. Hist.* i. p. 14 (Tr.).

[4] Cic. *Tusc.* iii. 3, est profecto animi medicina philosophia; Sen. *Ep.* 22, vena tangenda est; *Ep.* 53; Epict. iii. 23, § 30, *ἰατρεῖόν ἐστι τὸ τοῦ φιλοσόφου σχολεῖον.*

emotion and passion: it must teach us, amid the keen claims of competing objects of desire, to distinguish the true from the false, the permanent from the fleeting.

The moral reformer cannot indeed dispense with theory and a ground of general principles,[1] but he will not forget that his main business is to impart the *ars vivendi;* he will be more occupied with rules which may be immediately applied in practice, than with the theory of morals. A profound acquaintance with the pathology of the soul, minute study of the weaknesses of character, long experience of the devices for counteracting them, will be worth far more than an encyclopædic knowledge of centuries of speculation.[2] He will not undervalue the moral discourse, with the practical object of turning souls from their evil ways; but he has only contempt for the rhetoric of the class-room which desecrates solemn themes by the vanities of phrase-making.[3] The best and most fruitful work of practical philosophy is done by private counsel, adapted to the special needs of the spiritual patient. He must be encouraged to make a full confession of the diseases of his soul.[4] He must be trained in daily self-examination, to observe any signs of moral growth or of backsliding. He must be checked when over confident, and cheered in discouragement. He must have his enthusiasm kindled by appropriate examples of those who have trodden the same path and reached the heights.[5]

This serious aim of philosophy commended itself to the intensely practical and strenuous spirit of the Romans. And although there were plenty of showy lecturers or preachers in the first century who could draw fashionable audiences, the private philosophic director was a far more real power. The triumph of Aemilius Paulus brought numbers of Greek exiles to Italy, many of whom found a home as teachers in Roman families.[6] Panaetius, who revolutionised Stoicism, and made it a working system, profoundly influenced the circle of Scipio Aemilianus, in whose house he lived. Great generals and leaders of the last age of the Republic, a Lucullus or a Pompey, often carried philosophers in their train. From Augustus to

[1] Sen. *Ep.* 94, § 5, § 22.

[2] *Ep.* 64, § 8.

[3] Plut. *De Rect. Rat. Aud.* c. 8; Epict. iii. 23, § 23.

[4] Plut. *De Rect. Rat. Aud.* c. 12.

[5] Plut. (?) *De Lib. Ed.* c. 14.

[6] Zeller, *Phil. der Griech.* iii. 1, 487; Plut. *Aemil. P.* c. vi.; Plin. *H. N.* xxxv. 135; Polyb. xxxii. 10. But cf. Mahaffy on Zeller's view, in *Greek World under Roman Sway*, p. 67.

Elagabalus we hear of their presence at the imperial court. The wife of Augustus sought consolation on the death of Drusus from Areus, her husband's philosophic director.[1] Many of these men indeed did not take their profession very seriously, and in too many cases they were mere flatterers and parasites whom the rich patron hired from ostentation and treated with contumely.[2] Both Nero and Hadrian used to amuse themselves with the quarrels and vanity of their philosophers.[3] But in the terror of the Claudian Caesars, the Stoic director is often seen performing his proper part. Julius Canus, when ordered to execution by Caligula, had his philosopher by his side, with whom he discussed till the last fatal moment the future of the soul.[4] The officer who brought the sentence of death to Thrasea found him absorbed in conversation with the Cynic Demetrius on the mystery which the lancet was in a few moments to resolve.[5]

Of this great movement to cultivate a moral life in paganism L. Annaeus Seneca was not the least illustrious representative. Musonius, his younger contemporary, and Epictetus, the pupil of Musonius, were engaged in the same cure of souls, and taught practically the same philosophic gospel. They equally paid but slight attention to the logic and physics of the older schools.[6] Virtue, to all of them, is the one great end of philosophic effort. They were all deeply impressed by the spiritual wants of the time,[7] and they all felt that men needed not subtleties of disquisition or rhetorical display, but direct, personal teaching which appealed to the conscience. To all of them the philosopher is a physician of souls. Musonius and Epictetus were probably loftier and more blameless characters than Seneca. Epictetus especially, from the range and simple attractiveness of his teaching, might seem to many a better representative of the philosophic director than Seneca. Seneca, as the wealthy minister of Nero, excites a repugnance in some minds, which prevents them doing justice to his unquestionable power and fascination. His apparent inconsistency has

[1] Sen. *Ad Marc.* 4.

[2] Luc. *De Merc. Cond.* 2, 4, 25.

[3] Tac. *Ann.* xiv. 16, etiam sapientiae doctoribus tempus impertiebat post epulas, utque contraria adseverantium discordia frueretur ; Spart. *Hadr.* 15.

[4] Sen. *De Tranq.* xiv. § 7.

[5] Tac. *Ann.* xvi. 34.

[6] Zeller, iii. 1, 656, 663.

[7] Epict. iii. 23, §§ 24–34 ; i. 4, § 9, οὗτος, φησίν, ἤδη δι' αὑτοῦ δύναται Χρύσιππον ἀναγιγνώσκειν. Εὖ, νὴ τοὺς θεούς, προκόπτεις ἄνθρωπε. Ποίαν προκοπήν ;

condemned him in the eyes of an age which professes to believe in the teaching of the Mount, and idolises grandiose wealth and power. His rhetoric offends a taste that can tolerate and applaud verbose banalities, with little trace of redeeming art. He cannot always win the hearing accorded to the repentant sinner, whose dark experience may make his message more real and pungent. The historian, however, must put aside these rather pharisaic prejudices, and give Seneca the position as a moral teacher which his writings have won in ages not less earnest than ours. Nor need we fear to recognise a power which led the early Fathers to trace the spiritual vision of Seneca to an intercourse with S. Paul,[1] supported by a feigned correspondence which imposed on S. Augustine and S. Jerome.[2] The man who approaches Seneca thinking only of scandals gleaned from Tacitus and Dion Cassius,[3] and frozen by a criticism which cannot feel the power of genius, spiritual imagination, and a profound moral experience, behind a rhetoric sometimes forced and extravagant, had better leave him alone. The Christianity of the twentieth century might well hail with delight the advent of such a preacher, and would certainly forget all the accusations of prurient gossip in the accession of an immense and fascinating spiritual force. The man with any historical imagination must be struck with amazement that such spiritual detachment, such lofty moral ideals, so pure an enthusiasm for the salvation of souls, should emerge from a palace reeking with all the crimes of the haunted races of Greek legend. That the courtier of the reigns of Caligula and Claudius, the tutor and minister of Nero, should not have escaped some stains may be probable: that such a man should have composed the Letters and the *De Ira* of Seneca is almost a miracle. Yet the glow of earnestness and conviction, the intimate knowledge of the last secrets of guilty souls, may well have been the reward of such an ordeal.

Seneca's career, given a latent fund of moral enthusiasm, was really a splendid preparation for his mission, as an analyst of a corrupt society and a guide to moral reform. He lived

[1] Tertull. *De An.* c. 20, Seneca saepe noster; S. Hieron. *Adv. Jovin.* i. 49.

[2] S. Hieron. *Adv. Jovin.* i. 29; *De Scrip. Eccl.* 12; S. Aug. *Ep.* 153, cujus etiam ad Paulum apostolum leguntur epistolae.

[3] The worst about Seneca is collected in D. Cass. 61. 10. But cf. the attack of P. Suillius, Tac. *Ann.* xiii. 42 and xiv. 52.

through the gloomiest years of the imperial tyranny; he had been in the thick of its intrigues, and privy to its darkest secrets; he had enjoyed its favour, and knew the perils of its jealousy and suspicion. He came as an infant from Cordova to Rome in the last years of Augustus.[1] In spite of weak health, he was an ardent student of all the science and philosophy of the time, and he fell under the influence of Sotion, a member of the Sextian School, which combined a rigorous Stoicism with Pythagorean rules of life.[2] As a young advocate and prosperous official, he passed unharmed through the terror and ghastly rumours of the closing years of Tiberius.[3] His eloquence in the Senate excited the jealousy of Caligula, and he narrowly escaped the penalty.[4] In the reign of Claudius he must have been one of the inner circle of the court, for his banishment, at the instance of Messalina, for eight years to Corsica was the penalty of a supposed intrigue with Julia, the niece of the emperor.[5] Seneca knew how to bend to the storm, and, by the influence of Agrippina, he was recalled to be the tutor of the young Nero, and on his accession four years afterwards, became his first minister by the side of Burrus.[6] The famous *quinquennium*, an oasis in the desert of despotism, was probably the happiest period of Seneca's life. In spite of some misgivings, the dream of an earthly Providence, as merciful as it was strong, seemed to be realised.[7] But it was, after all, a giddy and anxious elevation, and the influence of Seneca was only maintained by politic concessions, and was constantly threatened by the daemonic ambition of Agrippina.[8] And Seneca had enemies like P. Suillius, jealous of his power and his millions, and eagerly pointing to the hypocrisy of the Stoic preacher, whom gossip branded as an adulterer and a usurer.[9] The death of Burrus gave the last shock to his power.[10] His enemies poured in to the assault. The emperor had long wished to shake off the incubus of a superior spirit; and the

[1] Sen. *Ad Helv.* xix. § 2.

[2] Sen. *Ep.* 108, §§ 13–17.

[3] *Ep.* 108, § 22. He abandoned Pythagorean abstinence, as suspicious, during the persecution of eastern cults; cf. Suet. *Tib.* 36.

[4] D. Cass. 59. 19.

[5] *Ib.* 60. 8; 61. 10; Tac. *Ann.* xiii. 42, schol. Juv. v. 109.

[6] D. Cass. 61. 4; Tac. *Ann.* xiii. 2. Dion suggests an intrigue with Agrippina, 61. 10.

[7] Sen. *De Clem.* i. 5, 8.

[8] Tac. *Ann.* xiii. 2, quo facilius . . . voluptatibus concessis retinerent, etc.

[9] *Ib.* xiii. 42; D. Cass. 61. 10.

[10] Tac. *Ann.* xiv. 52, mors Burri infregit Senecae potentiam, etc.

riches, the pointed eloquence, and more pointed sarcasms, the gardens and villas and lordly state of the great minister, suggested a possible aspirant to the principate. Seneca acted on his principles and offered to give up everything.[1] But his torture was to be prolonged, and his doom deferred for about two years. His release came in the fierce vengeance for the Pisonian conspiracy.[2]

Seneca was an ideal director for the upper class of such an age. He had risen to the highest office in a world-wide monarchy, and he had spent years in hourly fear of death. He had enjoyed the society of the most brilliant circles, and exchanged epigrams and repartees with the best; he had also seen them steeped in debauchery and treachery, and terror-stricken in base compliance. He had witnessed their fantastic efforts of luxury and self-indulgence, and heard the tale of wearied sensualism and disordered ambition and ineffectual lives.[3] His disciples were drawn, if not from the noblest class, at any rate from the class which had felt the disillusionment of wealth and fashion and power. And the vicissitudes in his own fate and character made him a powerful and sympathetic adviser. He had long to endure the torturing contrast of splendid rank and wealth, with the brooding terror of a doom which might sweep down at any moment. He was also tortured by other contrasts, some drawn by the fierceness of envious hatred, others perhaps acknowledged by conscience. Steeped in the doctrines of Chrysippus and Pythagoras, he had subdued the ebullient passions of youth by a more than monastic asceticism.[4] He had passionately adopted an ethical creed which aimed at a radical reform of human nature, at the triumph of cultivated and moralised reason and social sympathy over the brutal materialism and selfishness of the age. He had pondered on its doctrines of the higher life, of the nothingness of the things of sense, on death, and the indwelling God assisting the struggling soul, on the final happy release from all the sordid misery and terror, until every earthly pleasure and ambition faded away in the presence of a glorious moral ideal.[5] And yet this pagan monk, this idealist, who would have been at home with S. Jerome or Thomas à Kempis, had accumulated

[1] Tac. *Ann.* xiv. 54.
[2] *Ib.* xv. 56 sqq.
[3] Sen. *Ep.* 55; *De Tranq.* 1 and 2.
[4] Sen. *Ep.* 108, §§ 17-22.
[5] Cf. Baur, *Ch. Hist.* i. p. 16 (Tr.).

a vast fortune, and lived in a palace which excited the envy of a Nero. He was suspected of having been the lover of two princesses of the imperial house.[1] He was charged with having connived at, or encouraged the excesses of Nero, and even of having been an accomplice in the murder of Agrippina, or its apologist.[2] Some of these rumours are probably false, the work of prurient imaginations in the most abandoned age in history. Yet there are traces in Seneca's writings that he had not passed unscathed through the terrible ordeal to which character was exposed in that age. There are pictures of voluptuous ease and jaded satiety which may be the work of a keen sympathetic observation, but which may also be the expression of repentant memory.[3] In any case, he had sounded the very depths of the moral abysses of his time. He had no illusions about the actual condition of human nature. The mass of men, all but a few naturally saintly souls, were abandoned to lust or greed or selfish ambition. Human life was an obscene and cruel struggle of wild beasts for the doles flung by fortune into the arena.[4] The peace and happiness of the early Eden have departed for ever, leaving men to the restlessness of exhausted appetite, or to the half-repentant sense of impotent lives, spent in pursuing the phantoms of imaginary pleasure, with broken glimpses now and then of a world for ever lost.[5] With such a scene about him in his declining years, whatever his own practice may have been, Seneca came to feel an evangelistic passion, almost approaching S. Paul's, to open to these sick perishing souls the vision of a higher life through the practical discipline of philosophy.

The tendency to regard the true function of philosophy as purely ethical, reforming, guiding and sustaining character and conduct, finds its most emphatic expression in Seneca. He is far more a preacher, a spiritual director, than a thinker, and he would have proudly owned it. His highest, nay, one may almost say his only aim, is, in our modern phrase, to which his own sometimes approaches, to save souls. Philosophy

[1] D. Cass. 61. 10.

[2] Tac. *Ann.* xiii. 13; xiv. 7; and 11, sed Seneca adverso rumore erat, quod oratione tali confessionem scripsisset.

[3] Sen. *Ep.* 77, § 6, 16, ecquid habes propter quod expectes? Voluptates ipsas quae te morantur consumpsisti. . . . Nihil tibi luxuria tua in futuros annos reservavit intactum: cf. *Ep.* 89, § 21; 90, § 42.

[4] *De Ira*, ii. 8.

[5] *Ep.* 90, §§ 38–41.

in its highest and best sense is not the pursuit of knowledge for its own sake, nor the disinterested play of intellect, regardless of intellectual consequences, as in a Platonic dialogue.[1] It is pre-eminently the science or the art of right living, that is of a life conformed to right reason.[2] Its great end is the production of the *sapiens*, the man who sees, in the light of Eternal Reason, the true proportions of things, whose affections have been trained to obey the higher law, whose will has hardened into an unswerving conformity to it, in all the difficulties of conduct.[3] And the true philosopher is no longer the cold, detached student of intellectual problems, far removed from the struggles and the miseries of human life. He has become the *generis humani paedagogus*,[4] the schoolmaster to bring men to the Ideal Man. In comparison with that mission, all the sublimity or subtlety of the great masters of dialectic becomes mere contemptible trifling, as if a man should lose himself in some game, or in the rapture of sweet music, with a great conflagration raging before his eyes. In the universal moral shipwreck, how can one toy with these old world trifles, while the perishing are stretching out their hands for help?[5] Not that Seneca despises the inheritance of ancient wisdom, so far as it has any gospel for humanity.[6] He will accept good moral teaching from any quarter, from Plato or Epicurus, as readily as from Chrysippus or Panaetius.[7] He is ready to give almost divine honours to the great teachers of the human race. But he also feels that no moral teaching can be final. After a thousand ages, there will still be room for making some addition to the message of the past. There will always be a need for fresh adjustments and applications of the remedies which past wisdom has handed down.[8]

It is almost needless to say that Seneca has almost a contempt for the so-called liberal studies of his day.[9] There is only one truly liberal study, that which aims at liberating the will from the bondage of desire. Granted that it is necessary as a

[1] *Ep.* 49, § 5, non vaco ad istas ineptias: ingens negotium in manibus est; *Ep.* 75, § 5, non delectent, verba nostra, sed prosint . . . non quaerit aeger medicum eloquentem; *Ep.* 88, § 36, plus scire quam sit satis, intemperantiae genus est. Cf. *Ep.* 71, § 6.

[2] *Ep.* 89, § 8, nec philosophia sine virtute est, nec sine philosophia virtus.

[3] *Ep.* 66, § 12.

[4] *Ep.* 89, § 13; 117, §§ 30, 31.

[5] *Ep.* 48, § 8; 75, § 6.

[6] *Ep.* 64, § 3; 58, § 26.

[7] *De Vita B.* xiii, where he defends Epicurus.

[8] *Ep.* 64, § 8.

[9] *Ep.* 88, § 37, § 20.

mental discipline to submit to the grammarian in youth; yet experience shows that this training does nothing to form the virtuous character.[1] Who can respect a man who wastes his mature years, like Didymus, in inquiries as to the relative ages of Hecuba or Helen, or the name of the mother of Æneas, or the character of Anacreon or Sappho?[2] The man of serious purpose will rather try to forget these trifles than continue the study of them. And Seneca treats in the same fashion the hair-splitting and verbal subtleties of some of the older Stoics. He acquiesces indeed, in their threefold division of Philosophy into Logic, Physics, and Ethics; but for the first department he seems to have but scant respect, though once or twice he amuses his pupil Lucilius by a disquisition on Genus and Species, or the Platonic and Aristotelian "Causes," in the style of the Stoic scholasticism.[3] Seneca was writing for posterity; he has his intellectual vanity; and he probably wished to show that, while he set but little store by such studies, this was not due to an imperfect knowledge of them. It is because life is too short, and its great problems are too urgent, to permit a serious man to spend his precious years in fruitless intellectual play. He calls on Lucilius to leave such barren subtleties, which bring the greatest of all themes down to the level of intellectual jugglery.[4]

For the department of Physics Seneca has much more respect, and he evidently devoted much attention to it. We have traces of some lost works of his on scientific subjects, and there is still extant a treatise in seven books on *Natural Questions*, which became a handbook of science in the Middle Ages.[5] It deals with such subjects as we meet with in the poem of Lucretius, thunder and lightning, winds and earthquakes, and rising and failing springs. But it has perhaps less of the scientific spirit than Lucretius, according to our modern standards. We have abundant reference to old physical authorities, to Thales, Anaximenes, Anaximander, Diogenes of Apollonia, to Caecina and Attalus. But the conception of any scientific method beyond more or

[1] *Ep.* 88, § 2, unum studium vere liberale est quod liberum facit, etc.

[2] *Ib.* § 39; cf. *Ep.* 88.

[3] *Ep.* 89; 66, § 33; 58, § 8.

[4] *Ib.* 71, § 6, erige te et relinque istum ludum literarium philosophorum qui rem magnificam ad syllabas vocant, etc.

[5] Teuffel, ii. § 284, n. 6; cf. Zeller, *Phil. der Griech.* iii. 1, p. 623.

less ingenious hypothesis, or of any scientific verification of hypothesis, is utterly absent. This is of course a general characteristic of most of the scientific effort of antiquity. The truth is that, although Seneca probably had some interest in natural phenomena, he had a far more profound interest in human nature and human destiny. The older Stoics, with some variations, subordinated Physics to Ethics, as of inferior and only subsidiary importance.[1] Seneca carries this subordination almost to extremes, although he also is sometimes inconsistent.[2] He thinks it significant that while the World-Spirit has hidden gold, the great tempter and corruptor, far beneath our feet, it has displayed, in mysterious yet pompous splendour, in the azure canopy above us, the heavenly orbs which are popularly believed to control our destiny in the material sense, and which may really govern it, by raising our minds to the contemplation of an infinite mystery and a marvellous order.[3] To Seneca, as to Kant, there seems a mystic tie between the starry heavens above and the moral law within. In the prologue to the *Natural Questions*, indeed, carried away for the moment by the grandeur of his theme, Seneca seems to exalt the contemplation of the infinite distances and mysterious depths and majestic order of the stellar world far above the moral struggles of our mundane life. The earth shrinks to a mere point in infinitude, an ant-hill where the human insects mark out their Lilliputian territories and make their wars and voyages for their lifetime of an hour.[4] This, however, is rather a piece of rhetoric than a careful statement of Seneca's real view. In the Letters, again and again, we are told that virtue is the one important thing, that the conquest of passion raises man to be equal to God,[5] and that in the release of the rational or divine part of us from bondage to the flesh, man recovers a lost liberty, a primeval dignity. But in this struggle the spirit may refresh and elevate itself by looking up to the divine world from which it draws its origin, and to which it may, perchance, return. To Seneca's mind the so-called physics really involve

[1] Zeller, iii. 1, p. 56.

[2] *Ep.* 117, § 19; *Nat. Quaest. Prol.*; *Ep.* 65, § 15; cf. Zeller, iii. 1, 622.

[3] *Nat. Quaest.* v. 15; cf. *Ep.* 88, § 15

[4] *Nat. Quaest. Prol.* § 11, formicarum iste discursus est in angusto laborantium. . . . Punctum est istud in quo navigatis, in quo bellatis; Sursum ingentia spatia sunt, etc.; cf. Macrob. *Som. Scip.* i. 16, § 6.

[5] Sen. *Ep.* 73, § 13, sic deus non vincit sapientem felicitate etiamsi vincit aetate.

theology and metaphysics. In the contemplation of the vastness of the material universe, the mind may be aroused to the urgency and interest of the great questions touching God, His relation to fate, to the world, and man.[1] The scientific interest in Seneca is evidently not the strongest. There are still indeed the echoes of the old philosophies which sought man's true greatness and final beatitude in the clear vision of abstract truth. But Seneca is travelling rapidly on the way which leads to another vision of the celestial city, in which emotion, the passionate yearning for holiness as well as truth, blends with and tends to overpower the ideal of a passionless eternity of intellectual intuition. In Seneca's rapturous outburst on the gate of deliverance opened by death, making allowance for difference of associations and beliefs, there is surely a strange note of kindred sympathy, across the gulf of thirteen centuries, with Thomas à Kempis.[2]

The *Natural Questions* were, as he tells us, the work of his old age.[3] He has a lofty conception of his task, of the importance of the subject to the right culture of the spirit, and he summons up all his remaining energy to do it justice. But the work falls far short, in interest and executive skill, of a treatise like the *De Beneficiis*, and the principle of edification—*omnibus sermonibus aliquid salutare miscendum*[4]—is too obtrusive, and sometimes leads to incongruous and almost ludicrous effects. A reference to the mullet launches him on a discourse on luxury.[5] A discourse on mirrors would hardly seem to lend itself to moralising. Yet the invention furnishes to Seneca impressive lessons on self-knowledge, and a chance of glorifying the simple age when the unkempt daughter of a Scipio, who received her scanty dowry in uncoined metal, had never had her vanity aroused by the reflected image of her charms.[6] The subject of lightning

[1] Cf. Pl. *Phaed.* 79 D; Arist. *Eth.* ix. 8, § 7.

[2] *Ep.* 102, § 26, dies iste, quem tanquam extremum reformidas, aeterni natalis est . . . discutietur ista caligo et lux undique clara percutiet . . . nulla serenum umbra turbabit. Cf. *De Imit.* iii. 48, § 1, O supernae civitatis mansio beatissima! O dies aeternitatis clarissima, quam nox non obscurat, sed summa Veritas semper irradiat! Lucet quidem Sanctis perpetua claritate splendida, sed non nisi a longe et per speculum peregrinantibus in terra.

[3] *Nat. Quaest.* iii. Praef., non praeterit me quam magnarum rerum fundamenta ponam senex.

[4] *Ib.* ii. 59, § 2.

[5] *Ib.* iii., § 18.

[6] *Ib.* i. 17, § 8, An tu existimas auro inditum habuisse Scipionis filias speculum cum illis dos fuisset aes grave?

naturally gives occasion to a homily against the fear of death.[1] A prologue, on the conflict to be waged with passion and luxury and chance and change, winds up abruptly with the invitation—*quaeramus ergo de aquis . . . qua ratione fiant.*[2] The investigation closes with an imaginative description of the great cataclysm which is destined to overwhelm in ruin the present order. The earthquakes in Campania in 66 A.D. naturally furnish many moral lessons.[3] The closing passage of the *Natural Questions* is perhaps the best, and the most worthy of Seneca. In all these inquiries, he says, into the secrets of nature, we should proceed with reverent caution and self-distrust, as men veil their faces and bend in humbleness before a sacrifice.[4] How many an orb, moving in the depths of space, has never yet risen upon the eyes of man.[5] The Great Author Himself is only dimly visible to the inner eye, and there are vast regions of His universe which are still beyond our ken, which dazzle us by their effulgence, or elude our gross senses by their subtle secrecy. We are halting on the threshold of the great mysteries. There are many things destined to be revealed to far-distant ages, when our memory shall have passed away,[6] of which our time does not deserve the revelation. Our energies are spent in discovering fresh ingenuities of luxury and monstrous vice. No one gives a thought to philosophy; the schools of ancient wisdom are deserted and left without a head.[7] It is in this spirit that Seneca undertook his mission as a saviour of souls.

Seneca, in the epilogue to the *Natural Questions*, remarks sarcastically that, as all human progress is slow, so, even with all our efforts of self-indulgence, we have not yet reached the finished perfection of depravity; we are still making discoveries in vice. In another passage he maintains that his own age is no worse than others.[8] But this is only because at all times the mass of men are bad. Such pessimism in the first and second centuries was a prevalent tone We meet it alike in Persius, Petronius, Martial, and Juvenal, and in Seneca, Tacitus, Pliny, Epictetus,

[1] *Nat. Quaest.* ii. 59, § 3.

[2] *Ib.* iii. 1, § 1.

[3] *Ib.* vi. 32.

[4] *Ib.* vii. 30, § 1.

[5] *Ib.* vii. 30, § 3, quam multa praeter hos per secretum eunt nunquam humanis oculis orientia?

[6] *Ib.* § 5, multa venientis aevi populus ignota nobis sciet, multa saeculis tunc futuris, cum memoria nostra exoleverit, reservantur.

[7] *Ib.* vii. 31.

[8] *De Benef.* i. 10.

and Marcus Aurelius.[1] The rage for wealth and luxury, the frenzy of vice which perverted natural healthy instincts and violated the last retreats of modesty, the combination of ostentation and meanness in social life, the cowardice and the cruelty which are twin offspring of pampered self-indulgence, the vanity of culture and the vanishing of ideals, the vague restless ennui, hovering between satiety and passion, between faint glimpses of goodness and ignominious failure, between fits of ambition and self-abandoned languor, all these and more had come under the eye of Seneca as an observer or a director of souls.[2] It is a lost world that he has before him, trying fruitless anodynes for its misery, holding out its hands for help from any quarter.[3] The consuming earnestness of Seneca, about which, in spite of his rhetoric, there can be no mistake, and his endless iteration are the measure of his feeling as to the gravity of the case. Seneca is the earliest and most powerful apostle of a great moral revival. His studied phrase, his epigrammatic point seem often out of place; his occasionally tinsel rhetoric sometimes offends a modern taste. We often miss the austere and simple seriousness of Epictetus, the cultivated serenity and the calm clear-sighted resignation of Marcus Aurelius. Still let us admit that here is a man, with all his moral faults which he freely confesses, with all his rhetoric which was a part of his very nature, who felt he had a mission, and meant to fulfil it with all the resources of his mind. He is one of the few heathen moralists who warm moral teaching with the emotion of modern religion, and touch it with the sadness and the yearning which spring from a consciousness of man's infinite capacities and his actual degradation; one in whose eyes can be seen the *amor ulterioris ripae*, in whose teaching there are searching precepts which go to the roots of conduct, and are true for all ages of our race. He adheres formally to the lines of the old Stoic system in his moments of calm logical consistency. But when the enthusiasm of humanity, the passion to win souls to goodness and moral truth is upon him, all the old philosophical differences fade, the new wine bursts the old bottles; the Platonic dualism, the eternal conflict of

[1] Sen. *De Ira*, ii. 8, 9; *Ad Marc.* ii. 11, 17, 20; Tac. *Hist.* ii. 37; Petron. *Sat.* 88; M. Aurel. v. 33; v. 10.

[2] Sen. *Ep.* 77, § 6; 24, § 25; 89, § 21; 95, § 16; *De Tranq.* c. i.

[3] *Ep.* 48, § 8.

flesh and spirit,[1] the Platonic vision of God, nay, a higher vision of the Creator, the pitiful and loving Guardian, the Giver of all good, the Power which draws us to Himself, who receives us at death, and in whom is our eternal beatitude, these ideas, so alien to the older Stoicism, transfigure its hardness, and its cold, repellent moral idealism becomes a religion.[2] Seneca's system is really a religion; it is morality inspired by belief in a spiritual world and "touched by emotion." In a remarkable letter, he discusses the question whether, for the conduct of life, precept is sufficient without dogma, whether a man can govern his life by empirical rules, without a foundation of general principles. Can a religion dispense with dogma?[3] Seneca, as a casuist and spiritual director, was not likely to undervalue the importance of definite precept, adapted to the circumstances of the case. The philosopher, who was a regular official in great families, probably dealt chiefly in precept, on a basis of authority concealed and rarely scrutinised. But Seneca is not an ordinary professional director. He has a serious purpose; he feels that he is dealing with the most momentous of all problems—how to form or reform a life, with a view to its true end, how the final good of man is to be realised only in virtuous action. But action will not be right and virtuous unless the will be also right, and rightness of will depends on ordered habit of the soul,[4] and that again springs from right general principles or dogmas. In other words, a true theory of conduct is necessary to virtue in the highest sense. Mere imperative precept and rule cannot give steadiness and continuity to conduct. The motive, the clear perception of the guiding principle, can alone dignify an act with a peculiar moral distinction. In order to possess that character, the external act must be rooted in a faith in the rational law of conduct. Particular precepts may produce an external obedience to

[1] *Ep.* 71, § 27; 94, § 50; *Ad Marc.* 24, § 5; *Ep.* 79, § 12, tunc animus noster habebit quod gratuletur sibi, cum emissus his tenebris, in quibus volutatur, non tenui visu clara perspexerit . . . et caelo redditus suo fuerit; Zeller, iii. i. 637.

[2] *Ep.* 79, § 12; 102, § 22, per has mortalis aevi moras illi meliori vitae longiorique proluditur, §§ 26, 28; *Ep.* 73, § 15, Deus ad homines venit, etc. But cf. Zeller, iii. 1, 650; and, for a different view, Burgmann. *Seneca's Theologie in ihrem Verhältn. zum Stoicismus*, etc., pp. 20–32. That Burgmann's is the truer view appears from Sen. *Ep.* 95, § 49; 65, § 9; *De Clem.* i. 5, § 7; *De Benef.* ii. 29, § 4; *De Prov.* v. 10; *De Ira*, ii. 28, § 1; *Ep.* 41, § 2

[3] *Ep.* 95, § 10.

[4] *Ib.* § 57, rursus voluntas non erit recta nisi habitus animi rectus fuerit, etc.

that law, but they cannot give the uniformity and certainty of the inner light and the regulated will.

Seneca is not a sectarian dogmatist, although he lays so much stress on the necessity of dogma to virtuous conduct. He boldly declares that he does not follow absolutely any of the Stoic doctors. He defends Epicurus against the vulgar misunderstanding of his theory of pleasure, and the more vulgar practical deductions from it. He often quotes his maxims with admiration to Lucilius.[1] In his views of the nature of God and His relation to the external world and to the human soul, Seneca often seems to follow the old Stoic tradition. There are other passages where he seems to waver between different conceptions of God, the Creator of the universe, the incorporeal Reason, the divine breath diffused through all things, great and small, Fate, or the immutable chain of interlinked causation.[2] It is also clear that, from the tone of his mind, and the fact that the centre of philosophical interest for him is the moral life of man, he tends towards a more ethical conception of the Deity, as the Being who loves and cares for man. All this may be admitted and will be further noticed on a later page. Yet Seneca, in strict theory, probably never became a dissenter from the physical or ontological creed of his school. He adhered, in the last resort, to the Stoic pantheism, which represented God and the universe, force and formless matter, as ultimately issuing from the one substratum of the ethereal fire of Heraclitus, and in the great cataclysm, returning again to their source.[3] He also held theoretically the Stoic materialism, and the Stoic principle, that only corporeal natures can act on one another.[4] The force which moulds indeterminate matter into concrete form is spirit, breath, in the literal sense, interfused in rude matter, and by its tension, outward and again inward upon itself, producing form and quality and energy. Mere matter could never mould itself, or develop from within a power of movement and action. But

[1] *De Vit. Beat.* xii. § 4, nec aestimant, voluptas illa Epicuri quam sobria et sicca sit, sed ad nomen ipsum advolant quaerentes libidinibus suis patrocinium aliquod ac velamentum. Cf. *Ep.* 18, § 14; 16, § 7; 22, § 13; 28, § 9.

[2] *Ad Helv.* viii. § 3, quisquis formator universi fuit, sive ille deus est potens omnium, sive incorporalis ratio ingentium operum artifex, sive divinus spiritus per omnia aequali intentione diffusus, sive fatum et immutabilis causarum inter se cohaerentium series. Cf. *N. Quaest.* ii. 45, § 2.

[3] *Ep.* 71, § 14.

[4] *Ep.* 57, § 8; 66, § 12; 117, § 2.

this material force which shapes the universe from within is also rational, and the universe is a rational being, guided by the indwelling reason to predestined ends, and obedient to a universal law. The God of the Stoics is thus a very elastic or comprehensive conception. He may be viewed as the ubiquitous, impalpable force, which may, in the lack of more accurate expression, be called air, ether, fire. He is the soul, the breath, the Anima Mundi. He is also the universal law, the rational principle, underlying all the apparently casual and fitful phenomena of physical nature and human life. God may also surely be regarded as the eternal Fate, the power in the ruthless, yet merciful sequence of inevitable causation.[1] And, in milder and more optimistic moods, we may view Him as a watchful Providence, caring for men more than they seem to care for themselves, saving them from the consequences of their own errors and misdeeds. In Seneca, He develops into a moral and spiritual Being, the source of all spiritual intuition and virtuous emotion, the secret power within us making for righteousness, as He is the secret force in all nature making for order.[2]

It seems a little crude and superficial to contrast the materialist and idealist conceptions of God in the later Stoic creed. What human conception of Him is free from similar contradictions? How can any conception of Him, expressed in human language, avoid them? And in Seneca's conception of soul, even as material, there is something so thin, so subtle, and elusive, that the bounds of matter and spirit seem to melt away and disappear.[3] However loyal he may be in form to Stoic materialism, Seneca in the end regards God as no mere material force, however refined and etherealised, but a spiritual power; not perhaps limited by the bounds of personality, but instinct with moral tendencies, nay, a moral impetus, which no mere physical force could ever develop.[4] The growing dualism in Seneca's metaphysics is the result of the growing dualism of his psychology. In accord with the old Stoic doctors, he sometimes formulates the material nature of the soul, and its essential unity. It is, like the Anima Mundi,

[1] Zeller, *Phil. der Griech.* iii. 1, 122; cf. *Nat. Quaest.* ii. 45, § 2.

[2] *De Prov.* i. ii. § 6; *De Ira*, ii. 27; *De Benef.* ii. 29; *Ep.* 73, § 16.

[3] *Ep.* 57, § 8, animus qui ex tenuissimo constat, deprehendi non potest, etc.

[4] Burgmann, *Seneca's Theologie*, p. 41.

warm breath or subtle fire, penetrating all parts of the body, discharging currents from the central heart to the several organs. It is primarily rational, and all the lower powers of passion are derived from the controlling and unifying reason. It is a spark of the universal Spirit, holding the same place in the human organism as the Divine Spirit does in the universe.[1] But experience and reflection drove Seneca more and more into an acceptance of the Platonic opposition of reason and passion, an unceasing struggle of the flesh and spirit, in which the old Stoic theory of the oneness of the rational soul tended to disappear.[2] This is only one, but it is the most important, modification of ancient theory forced on Seneca by a closer application of theory to the facts of human life, and a completer analysis of them. The individual consciousness, and the spectacle of human life, alike witness to the inevitable tendency of human nature to corruption. Even after the great cataclysm, when a new earth shall arise from the waters of the deluge, and a new man, in perfect innocence, shall enter on this fair inheritance, the clouds will soon gather again, and darken the fair deceitful dawn.[3] The weary struggle of flesh and spirit will begin once more, in which the flesh is so often the victor. For to Seneca, as to the Orphic mystics and to Plato, the body is a prison, and life one long punishment.[4] Such is the misery of this mortal life, such the danger of hopeless corruption, that no one would accept the gift of existence if he could foresee the evil in store for him.[5] And death, the object of dread to the blind masses, is really the one compensation for the calamity of birth, either as a happy return to antenatal tranquillity, or as the gateway to a glorious freedom and vision of the Divine.[6] Seneca, indeed, does not always express himself in this strain. He is often the consistent, orthodox Stoic, who glories in the rounded perfection of the

[1] *Ep.* 65, § 24, quem in hoc mundo deus obtinet, hunc in homine animus.

[2] Pl. *Phaed.* 83 C, D; 79 B; D; cf. Zeller, *Phil. der Griech.* iii. 183; iii. 2, p. 634; Sen. *Ep.* 71, § 27.

[3] *Nat. Quaest.* iii. 30, § 8, sed illis quoque innocentia non durabit—cito nequitia subrepit.

[4] *Ep.* 120, § 14; 65, § 16, nam corpus hoc animi pondus ac poena est; premente illo urgetur, in vinculis est, etc. *Ad Polyb.* ix. § 6, omnis vita supplicium est; *Ad Marc.* xx. § 2.

[5] *Ib.* 22, § 3.

[6] *Ep.* 24, § 18, mors nos aut consumit aut eximit; *Ep.* 36, § 10; 102, § 23; *De Prov.* vi. § 6; *Ad Marc.* 25, § 1; *ib.* 19, § 5; 20, § 2, quae efficit ut nasci non sit supplicium; cf. Epict. ii. 1; iii. 10; iii. 13; iv. 1; M. Aurel. viii. 18; vi. 28; iii. 3; ix. 3.

sapiens, triumphing, even in this life, over all the seductions of sense and the fallacies of perverted reason, and, in virtue of the divine strength within him, making himself, even here below, equal with God in moral purity and freedom.[1] In such moods, he will adhere to the Stoic psychology: reason will be all in all; virtue will be uniform, complete, attained by one supreme victorious effort. But the vision is constantly crossed and darkened by doubts which are raised by the terrible facts of life. The moral problem becomes more difficult and complicated; the vision of perfection recedes to an infinite distance, and the glorious deliverance is reserved for an immortal life of which the older Stoics did not often dream.

Still, we can find in Seneca all the Stoic gospel, and moral idealism. "Nil bonum nisi verum" is the fundamental principle. The failures, aberrations, and sins of men arise from a false conception of what is good, produced by the warping effect of external things upon the higher principle. The avaricious, the ambitious, the sensual, live in a vain show. They are pursuing unreal objects of desire, which cheat and befool the reason, and turn to ashes when they are won. The "kingdom of Heaven is within." It is the freedom, the peace, the tranquil sense of power over all that is fortuitous and external and fleeting, which alone can realise the highest good of man.[2] It is attained only by virtue, that is, by living in obedience to the law of reason, which has its voice and representative in each human soul. The summons to yield ourselves to the law of nature and reason simply calls us to obey our highest part (τὸ ἡγεμονικόν), which is a steadfast witness to the eternal truth of things, and, if unbribed and unperverted, will discern infallibly the right line of conduct amid all the clamorous or seductive temptations of the flesh or of the world. Nothing is a real good which has not the stamp and hall-mark of reason, which is not within the soul itself, that is within our own power. Everything worth having or wishing for is within. External things, wealth, power, high place, the pleasures of sense, are transitory, deceptive, unstable, the gifts of Fortune, and equally at her

[1] *Ep.* 53, § 11, est aliquid quo sapiens antecedat deum; cf. *Ep.* 59, § 16, talis est sapientis animus, qualis mundus super lunam; semper illic serenum est; 72, § 8.

[2] *Ep.* 74, § 1; 62, § 3, brevissima ad divitias per contemptum divitiarum via est; 59, § 14.

mercy. In the mad struggle for these ephemeral pleasures, the wise man retires unobserved from the scene of cruel and sordid rapacity, having secretly within him the greatest prize of all, which Fortune cannot give or take away.[1] If these things were really good, then God would be less happy than the slave of lust and ambition, than the sensualist who is fascinated by a mistress or a minion, the trader who may be ruined by a storm, the wealthy minister who may at any moment be ordered to death by a Nero.[2] The only real liberty and human dignity are to be found in renunciation. If we jealously guard and reverence the divine reason within us, and obey its monitions, which are in truth the voice of God, the Universal Reason, then we have an impregnable fortress which cannot be stormed by any adverse fortune. The peace and freedom so won may be called, although Seneca does not so call it, the "peace of God." For it is in fact the restored harmony between the human spirit and the Reason of the world, and the cessation of the weary conflict between the "law in the members" and "the law of the mind," which ends so often in that other peace of a "mare mortuum," a stillness of moral death.[3]

The gospel of Seneca, with all its searching power, seems wanting in some of the essentials of an effective religion which can work on character. Where, it may be asked, is the force to come from which shall nerve the repentant one to essay the steep ascent to the calm of indefectible virtue? And what is the reward which can more than compensate for the great renunciation? With regard to the first question, the Stoic answer is clear. The reforming force is the divine reason, indwelling in every human soul,[4] which, if it is able, or is permitted, to emancipate itself from bondage to the things of sense, will inevitably gravitate to the divine world, from which it sprang. The question of necessity and freedom of the will has not much interest for Seneca, as a practical moralist. He believes theoretically in the old Stoic dogmas on the subject.

[1] *Ep.* 74, §§ 6–12; cf. M. Aurel. v. 15, *νῦν δὲ ὅσῳ περ πλείω τις ἀφαιρῶν ἑαυτοῦ τούτων ἢ καὶ ἀφαιρούμενός τι τούτων ἀνέχηται, τοσῷδε μᾶλλον ἀγαθός ἐστι*: Epict. ii. 16, § 18; iii. 3, § 14.

[2] Sen. *Ep.* 31, § 10; 74, § 14 aut ista bona non sunt, quae vocantur, aut homo felicior deo est, etc.

[3] *Ep.* 67, § 14.

[4] *Ep.* 66, § 12, ratio autem nihil aliud est quam in corpus humanum pars divini spiritus mersa.

From one point of view, God may be regarded as the eternal Fate, the inevitable law of causation. And as the Universal Reason, He cannot act otherwise than He does, without violating His very nature. But His action is self-determined and therefore free and spontaneous.[1] This freedom man only attains by breaking away from the cruel servitude to passion and external circumstance. As a practical moral teacher, Seneca is bound to say that we can take the higher road if we will. The first step towards freedom is to grasp firmly the fundamental law of the moral life—that the only good lies in conformity to reason, to the higher part of our being. If we yield to its bidding, we can at once cut ourselves off from the deceitful life of the senses, and the vision of the true beatitude in virtue at once opens on the inner eye. When that vision has been seen, we must then seek to form a habit of the soul which shall steadily conform to the universal law, and finally give birth to a settled purpose, issuing inevitably in virtuous act.[2] It is this fixed and stable resolution which is the Stoic ideal, although experience showed that it was rarely attained. The great renunciation is thus the entrance on a state of true freedom, which is realised only by submitting ourselves to the law of reason, that is of God. By obedience to rational law man is raised to a level far transcending the transient and shadowy dignities of the world. His rational and divine part is reunited to the Divine Spirit which "makes for righteousness"; he places himself in the sweep and freedom of a movement which finds its image and counterpart in the majestic and ordered movements of the heavenly spheres. If we ask, how can poor humanity, so abject, so brutalised, so deadened by the downward pressure of the flesh and the world, ever release itself and rise to those empyrean heights, the answer is, through the original strength of the rational, which is the divine element in the human soul. It may be, and actually is, in the mass of men, drugged and silenced by the seductions of sense and the deceptions of the world. But if, in some moment of detachment and elation, when its captors and jailors relax their guard, it can escape their clutches, it will at

[1] *Nat. Quaest.* ii. 36; *De Prov.* 5, § 8, eadem necessitate et deos adligat . . . ille ipse omnium conditor scripsit quidem fata, sed sequitur; semper paret, semel jussit.

[2] *Ep.* 95, § 57; cf. 116, § 7, satis natura dedit roboris si illo utamur.

once seek the region of its birth, and its true home. It is in the kindred of the human reason with the Divine, the Reason of the world, that we must seek the reconciliation of two apparently opposite points of view. At one time the Stoic doctor tells us that we must trust to our own strength in the moral struggle. And again Seneca, in almost Christian phrase, comforts his disciple with the vision of God holding out a succouring hand to struggling virtue, just as he warns the backslider of an eye "that seeth in secret." Woe to him who despises that Witness.[1]

With such a conception of the relation of the human reason to the Divine, Seneca was bound to believe that human nature, as it is, had fallen away from original and spontaneous innocence. In the equal enjoyment of the unforced gifts of nature, in the absence of the avarice and luxury which the development of the arts, the exploitation of the earth's hidden wealth, and the competitive struggle, born of a social life growing more and more complicated, have generated, the primeval man was unsolicited by the passions which have made life a hell.[2] Yet this blissful state was one of innocence rather than of virtue; it was the result of ignorance of evil rather than determined choice of good.[3] And the man who, in the midst of a corrupt society, fights his way to virtue, will take far higher moral rank than our simple ancestors, who wandered in the unravaged garden of the Golden Age. For the man born in a time when the nobler instincts have been deadened by the lust of gold and power and sensual excess, the virtuous will can only be won by a hard struggle.

Confronted with the facts of life, and fired with a passion to win men to a higher law, the later Stoicism had in some points to soften the rigid lines of earlier theory. The severe idealism of the great doctors was a mere dream of an impossible detachment, the inexorable demand of a pitiless logic. Virtue, being conformity to the immutable law of reason, was conceived as a rounded, flawless whole, to which nothing could be added, and to which nothing must be wanting. It presupposes, or is

[1] *Ep.* 73, § 15, non sunt di fastidiodosi: adscendentibus manum porrigunt; *Ep.* 83, § 1, nihil deo clusum est; *Ep.* 43, § 5, O te miserum si contemnis hunc testem.

[2] *Ep.* 90, § 38 sqq. avaritia omnia fecit aliena et in angustum ex immenso redacta paupertatem intulit, et multa concupiscendo omnia amisit.

[3] *Ib.* § 46, non fuere sapientes; . . . ignorantia rerum innocentes erant.

identical with, a settled intellectual clearness, an unclouded knowledge of the truly good, which must inevitably issue in perfect act. It is a single, uniform mental state from which all the separate virtues spring as from a single root.[1] The moral value of an act depends entirely on will, intention, that is, on the intellectual perception. And as there are no gradations in the mental state, so there are no gradations in moral conduct which issues from it. There are no distinctions between things morally good, between "divine" things; and so, just as in the older Calvinistic system, there is no class intermediate between the wise and the foolish, the saved and the lost. And conversion, "transfiguration," the change from folly to wisdom, is regarded as instantaneous and complete.[2] Even those who are struggling upward, but have not yet reached the top, are still to be reckoned among the foolish, just as the man a few inches below the waves will be drowned as certainly as if he were sunk fathoms deep. And, as there is no mean state in morals, so the extremes are necessarily finished and perfect types of virtue and reprobacy. The ideal *sapiens*, who combines in himself all the moral and intellectual attributes that go to make up the ideal of serene, flawless virtue, has been the mark for ridicule from the days of Horace.[3] Such an ideal, soaring into the pure cold regions of virgin snow, left the great mass of men grovelling in filth and darkness. And it was in this light that the severe Stoic regarded the condition of the multitude. They are all equally bad, and they will always be bad, from age to age. Every generation mourns over its degeneracy, but it is no worse than its ancestors, and its posterity will be no better. The only variation is in the various fashion of the vices.[4] In any crowded scene, says Seneca, in the forum or the circus, you have a mere gathering of savage beasts, a spectacle of vice incarnate.[5] In the garb of peace, they are engaged in a truceless war, hating the fortunate, trampling on the fallen.

[1] Sen. *Ep.* 66, § 13 sqq.; 113, § 14; Cic. *Tusc.* iv. 15, 34; Plut. *Virt. Mor.* c. 2; Zeller, iii. 1, p. 224.

[2] Zeller, *Phil. der Griech.* iii. 1, p. 235; Plut. *De Prof. in Virt.* i. ὥστε τὸν πρωῒ κάκιστον ἑσπέρας γεγονέναι κράτιστον κτλ.; *Adv. St.* c. x.; cf. Sen. *Ep.* 76, § 19.

[3] Hor. *Sat.* i. 3, 124; Sen. *Ep.* i. 1, 106; cf. *Ep.* 73, § 13; Aelian, *Var. Hist.* iv. 13; Luc. *Vit. Auct.* c. 20, μόνος οὗτος σοφός, μόνος καλός, μόνος ἀνδρεῖος βασιλεὺς ῥήτωρ, κτλ.

[4] Sen. *De Benef.* i. 10, § 1, hoc majores nostri questi sunt, hoc nos querimur, hoc posteri nostri querentur, eversos mores, regnare nequitiam, in deterius res humanas labi. Cf. *Ad Polyb.* c. iv.

[5] *De Ira*, ii. 8, § 1, istic tantumdem esse vitiorum quantum hominum.

Viewing this scene of shameless lust and cupidity where every tie of duty or friendship is violated, if the wise man were to measure his indignation by the atrocity of the offenders, his anger must end in madness. But we are all bad men living among the bad, and we should be gentle to one another.

The idealism and the pessimism of the earlier Stoics were alike fatal to any effort of moral reform. The cold, flawless perfection of the man of triumphant reason was an impossible model which could only discourage and repel aspirants to the higher life. The ghastly moral wreck of ordinary human nature, in which not a single germ of virtuous impulse seemed to have survived the ruin, left apparently no hope of rescue or escape. If morals were to be anything but an abstract theory, if they were to have any bearing on the actual character and destiny of man, their demand must be modified. And so in many essential points it was, even before Seneca.[1] The ideal contempt for all external things had to give way to an Aristotelian recognition of the value of some of them for a virtuous life. And Seneca is sometimes a follower of Aristotle, as in the admission, so convenient to the millionaire, that wealth may be used by the wise man for higher moral ends.[2] He will not be the slave of money; he will be its master. He will admit it to his home, but not to his heart, as a thing which may take to itself wings at any moment, but which may meanwhile be used to cheer and warm him in his struggles, and may be dispensed in beneficent help to dependents. In the same way, beside the ideal of perfect conformity to the law of reason, there appeared a class of conditional duties. To conform absolutely to the law of reason, to realise the highest good through virtue, remains the highest Stoic ideal. But if, beside the highest good, it is permitted to attach a certain value to some among the external objects of desire, manifestly a whole class of varying duties arises in the field of choice and avoidance.[3] And again the ideal of imperturbable calm, which approached the apathy of the Cynics, was softened by the admission of rational dispositions of feeling.[4] These concessions to im-

[1] Zeller, *Phil. der Griech.* iii. 1, p. 637; cf. p. 249. Cf. Martha, *Mor. sous l'Emp.* p. 62. On Seneca's relation to the old Stoic theology, *v.* Burgmann, *Seneca's Theologie*, p. 42 sq.

[2] Sen. *De Vit. Beat.* c. 22.

[3] *Ep.* 74, § 17; 87, § 29 sq.: *De Ben.* v. 13, § 1 sq.; Zeller, iii. 1, p. 638.

[4] εὐπάθειαι, cf. *De Brev. Vit.* xiv. § 2; *De Ira*, ii. 2-4; Zeller, iii. 1, p. 216.

perious facts of human life, of course, modified the awful moral antithesis of wise and foolish, good and reprobate. Where is the perfectly wise man, with his single moral purpose, his unruffled serenity, his full assurance of his own impregnable strength, actually to be found?[1] He is not to be discovered among the most devoted adherents of the true philosophic creed. Even a Socrates falls short of the sublime standard. If we seek for the wise man in the fabulous past, we shall find only heroic force, or a blissful, untempted ignorance, which are alike wanting in the first essential of virtue.[2] As the perfect ideal of moral wisdom, imperturbable, assured, and indefectible, receded to remote ideal distances, so the condemnation of all moral states below an impossible perfection to indiscriminate reprobacy[3] had to be revoked. Seneca maintains that men are all bad, but he is forced to admit that they are not all equally bad, nay, that there are men who, although not quite emancipated from the snares of the world and the flesh, have reached various stages on the upward way. He even distinguishes three classes of *proficientes*, of persons on the path of moral progress.[4] There is the man who has conquered many serious vices, but is still captive to others. Again, there is the man who has got rid of the worst faults and passions, but who is not secure against a relapse. There is a third class who have almost reached the goal. They have achieved the great moral victory; they have embraced the one true object of desire; they are safe from any chance of falling away; but they want the final gift of full assurance reserved for the truly wise.[5] They have not attained to the crowning glory of conscious strength. Seneca is still in bondage to the hard Stoic tradition, in spite of his aberrations from it. The great Catholic virtue of humility is to him still, theoretically at least, a disqualification for the highest spiritual rank.

And yet Seneca is far from wanting in humility. In giving counsels of perfection, he candidly confesses that he is himself far from the ideal.[6] Indeed, his *Letters* reveal a character

[1] *De Tranq.* vii. § 4, ubi enim istum invenies quem tot seculis quaerimus? Pro optimo est minime malus. *Ep.* 42, § 1.

[2] *Ep.* 90, § 44 sqq.

[3] *Ep.* 72, §§ 6–11.

[4] *Ep.* 75, § 8 sqq.

[5] *Ep.* 72, § 8 sapiens laetitia fruitur maxima, continua, sua.

[6] *Ep.* 57, § 3, non de me loquor, qui multum ab homine tolerabili, nedum a perfecto absum: cf. *Ep.* 89, § 2.

which, with lofty ideals, and energetic aspiration, is very far removed from the serene joy and peace of the true Stoic sage. He has not got the invulnerable panoply from which all the shafts of fortune glance aside. He shows again and again how deep a shadow the terror of his capricious master could cast over his life, how he can be disturbed even by the smaller troubles of existence, by the slights of great society, by the miseries of a sea voyage, or the noises of a bath.[1] In the counsels addressed to Lucilius, Seneca is probably quite as often preaching to himself. The ennui, the unsteadiness of moral purpose, the clinging to wealth and power, the haunting fears or timid anticipations of coming evil, for which he is constantly suggesting spiritual remedies, are diagnosed with such searching skill and vividness that we can hardly doubt that the physician has first practised his art upon himself.[2] Nor has he entire faith in his own insight or in the potency of the remedies which ancient wisdom has accumulated. The great difficulty is, that the moral patient, in proportion to the inveteracy of his disease, is unconscious of it.[3] Society, with its manifold temptations of wealth and luxury and irresponsible ease, can so overwhelm the congenital tendency to virtue,[4] that the inner monitor may be silenced, and a man may come to love his depravity.[5] If men are not getting better, they are inevitably getting worse. There is such a state, in the end, as hopeless, irreclaimable reprobacy. Yet even for the hoary sinner Seneca will not altogether despair, so long as there lingers in him some divine discontent, however faint, some lingering regret for a lost purity. He will not lose hope of converting even a mocker like Marcellinus, who amuses himself with jeers at the vices and inconsistencies of professing philosophers, and does not spare himself. Seneca may, perchance, give him a pause in his downward course.[6]

Seneca's gospel, as he preaches it, is for a limited class. With all his professed belief in the equality and brotherhood of men, Seneca addresses himself, through the aristocratic Epicurean Lucilius, to the slaves of wealth and the vices

[1] *Ad Polyb.* ii. § 1; *Ep.* 53, § 4; 56 §§ 1-3.
[2] *Ep.* 24; esp. § 14.
[3] *Ep.* 53, § 7, quo quis pejus se habet, minus sentit.
[4] *Ep.* 94, §§ 55, 56.
[5] *Ep* 112, vitia sua et amat simul et odit.
[6] *Ep.* 29.

which it breeds. The men whom he wishes to save are masters of great households, living in stately palaces, and striving to escape from the weariness of satiety by visits to Baiae or Praeneste.[1] They are men who have awful secrets, and whose apparent tranquillity is constantly disturbed by vague terrors,[2] whose intellects are wasted on the vanities of a conventional culture or the logomachies of a barren dialectic.[3] They are people whose lives are a record of weak purpose and conflicting aims, and who are surprised by old age while they are still barely on the threshold of real moral life.[4] With no religious or philosophic faith, death is to such men the great terror, as closing for ever that life of the flesh which has been at once so pleasant and so tormenting.[5] In dealing with such people, Seneca recognises the need both of the great principles of right living and of particular precepts, adapted to varieties of character and circumstance. The true and solid foundation of conduct must always be the clear perception of moral truth, giving birth to rightly-directed purpose and supplying the right motive. For example, without a true conception of God as a spirit, worship will be gross and anthropomorphic.[6] The doctrine of the brotherhood of all men in the universal commonwealth is the only solid ground of the social charities and of humanity to slaves. Yet dogma is not enough; discipline must be added. The moral director has to deal with very imperfect moral states, some of quite rudimentary growth, and his disciples may have to be treated as boys learning to write, whose fingers the master must guide mechanically across the tablet.[7] The latent goodness of humanity must be disencumbered of the load which, through untold ages, corrupt society has heaped upon it. The delusions of the world and the senses must be exposed, the judgment, confused and dazzled by their glamour, must be cleared and steadied, the weak must be encouraged, the slothful and backsliding must be aroused to continuous effort in habitual converse with some good man who has trodden the same paths before.[8]

[1] *Ep.* 28, § 1.
[2] *Ep.* 13, § 4 sq.; *Ep.* 24, § 11.
[3] *Ep.* 117, § 31; 75, § 6.
[4] *Ep.* 13, § 17, quid est turpius quam senex vivere incipiens?
[5] *Ep.* 24.
[6] *Ep.* 95, § 49.
[7] *Ep.* 94, § 5, digiti puerorum teneutur et aliena manu per literarum simulacra ducuntur.
[8] *Ep.* 11, § 8; Plut. *De Pr. Virt.* xv.

Thus the great "Ars Vitae," founded on a few simple principles of reason, developed into a most complicated system of casuistry and spiritual direction. How far it was successful we cannot pretend to say. But the thoughtful reader of Seneca's *Letters* cannot help coming to the conclusion that, even in the reign of Nero, there must have been many of the *proficientes,* of candidates for the full Stoic faith. If Seneca reveals the depths of depravity in his age, we are equally bound to believe that he represents, and is trying to stimulate, a great moral movement, a deep seated discontent with the hard, gross materialism, thinly veiled under dilettantism and spurious artistic sensibility, of which Nero was the type. Everything that we have of Seneca's, except the *Tragedies,* deals with the problems or troubles of this moral life, and the demand for advice or consolation appears to have been urgent. Lucilius, the young Epicurean procurator, who has been immortalised by the *Letters,* is only one of a large class of spiritual inquirers. He not only lays his own moral difficulties before the master, but he brings other spiritual patients for advice.[1] There were evidently many trying to withdraw from the tyranny or temptations of high life, with a more or less stable resolution to devote themselves to reflection and amendment. It is a curious pagan counterpart to the Christian ascetic movement of the fourth and fifth centuries.[2] And, just as in the days of S. Jerome and S. Paulinus, the deserter from the ranks of fashion and pleasure in Nero's time had to encounter a storm of ridicule and misrepresentation. Philosophic retreat was derided as mere languid self-indulgence, an unmanly shrinking from social duty, nay, even a mere mask for the secret vices which were, too often with truth, charged against the *soi-disant* philosopher.[3] Sometimes the wish to lead a higher life was openly assailed by a cynical Epicureanism. Virtue and philosophy were mere idle babble. The only happiness is to make the most of the senses while the senses still keep their fresh lust for pleasure. The days are fleeting away never to return in which we can drink with keen zest

[1] *Ep.* 25, § 1.

[2] S. Hieron. *Ep.* 127, §§ 5–7; *Ep.* 118, § 5; Sulp. *Sev.* ii. 13, § 7.

[3] Sen. *Ep.* 36, § 1, illum objurgant quod umbram et otium petierit; *Ep.* 123, § 15, illos quoque nocere nobis existimo, qui nos sub specie Stoicae sectae hortantur ad vitia: hoc enim jactant solum sapientem et doctum esse amatorem.

the joys of the flesh. What folly to spare a patrimony for a thankless heir![1] Seneca had to deal with many souls wavering between the two ideals. One of his treatises is addressed to a kinsman, Annaeus Serenus, who had made a full confession of a vague unrest, an impotence of will, the conflict of moral torpor with high resolve.[2] In his better moments, Annaeus inclines to simplicity of life and self-restraint. Yet a visit to a great house dazzles him and disturbs his balance, with the sight of its troops of elegant slaves, its costly furniture and luxurious feasting. He is at one time drawn to philosophic quietude; at another he becomes the strenuous ambitious Roman of the old days, eager for the conflicts of the forum. He is always wavering between a conviction of the vanity of literary trifling and the passion for literary fame.[3] Cannot Seneca, to whom he owes his ideal, furnish some remedy for this constant tendency to relapse and indecision?

It is in the sympathetic handling of such cases, not in broad philosophic theory, that the peculiar strength of Seneca lies. His counsels were adapted to the particular difficulties presented to him. But many of them have a universal validity. He encourages the wish to retire into meditative quietude, but only as a means to moral cure.[4] Retreat should not be an ostentatious defiance of the opinion of the world.[5] Nor is it to be a mere cloak for timid or lazy shrinking from the burdens of life. You should withdraw from the strife and temptations of the mundane city, only to devote yourself to the business of the spiritual city, to cultivate self-knowledge and self-government, to inspire the soul with the contemplation of the Eternal and the Divine. Solitude may be a danger, unless a man lives in the presence of "One who seeth in secret,"[6] from whom no evil thought is hidden, to whom no prayer for evil things must be addressed.[7] And, lest the thought of God's presence may not come home with sufficient

[1] Sen. *Ep.* 123, § 10. Cf. *Inscr. Or. Henz.* 480[illegible], 4807, 4816.

[2] *De Tranq.* i.

[3] *Ib.* i. §§ 13–15, nec aegroto nec valeo; . . . In omnibus rebus haec me sequitur bonae mentis infirmitas. *Ib.* § 17, rogo, si quod habes remedium quo hanc fluctuationem meam sistam, dignum me putes qui tibi tranquillitatem debeam.

[4] *Ep.* 7, § 8; 19, § 2.

[5] *Ep.* 68, ipsum otium absconde; jactandi autem genus est nimis latere.

[6] *Ep.* 43, § 4; cf. 83, § 1; 10, § 2, mecum loquor . . . cave ne cum homine malo loquaris.

[7] *Ep.* 10, § 5, turpissima vota dis insusurrant; cf. Pers. *Sat.* ii. 7–18; Sen. *Ep.* 41, § 1.

urgency, Seneca recommends his disciples to call up the image of some good man or ancient sage, and live as if under his eye.[1] The first step in moral progress is self-knowledge and confession of one's faults.[2] Ignorance of our spiritual disease, the doom of the indurated conscience, is the great danger, and may be the mark of a hopeless moral state. Hence the necessity for constant daily self-examination. In the quiet of each night we should review our conduct and feeling during the day, marking carefully where we have fallen short of the higher law, and strengthening ourselves with any signs of self-conquest. Seneca tells us that this was his own constant practice.[3] For progress is only slow and difficult. It requires watchful and unremitting effort to reach that assured and settled purpose which issues spontaneously in purity of thought and deed, and which raises man to the level of the Divine freedom. There must be no pauses of self-complacency until the work is done. There is no mediocrity in morals. There must be no halting and unsteadiness of purpose, no looking back to the deceitful things of the world. Inconstancy of the wavering will only shortens the span of this short life. How many there are who, even when treading the last stage to death, are only beginning to live, in the true sense, and who miss the beatitude of the man who, having mastered the great secret, can have no addition to his happiness from lengthened years. In the long tract of time any life is but a moment, and of that the least part by most men is really lived.[4] And this unsettled aim is liable to constant temptation from without. We are continually within sight and earshot of the isles of the Sirens, and only the resolution of a Ulysses will carry us past in safety.[5] In fact no isle of the Sirens can have been more dangerous than the life of a great household in the Neronian age, when the dainties and the vices of every land assailed the senses with multiplied seductions, and men craved in vain for a heightened and keener sensibility. Perpetual change of scene to the shores of Baiae,

[1] *Ep.* 11, § 8; 104, § 21, vive cum Chrysippo, cum Posidonio.

[2] *Ep.* 6, § 1; *Ep.* 28; *Ep.* 50, § 4; Plut. *De Prof. in Virt.* c. xi. τὸ πάθος λέγειν καὶ τὴν μοχθηρίαν ἀποκαλύπτειν οὐ φαῦλον ἂν εἴη προκοπῆς σημεῖον.

[3] *De Ira*, iii. 36, § 3.

[4] *Ep.* 32, § 2, in tanta brevitate vitae quam breviorem inconstantia facimus, etc.; *Ep.* 99, § 11, intelliges etiam in longissima vita minimum esse quod vivitur.

[5] *Ep.* 56, § 15; 51, § 5.

to Apulia, to some glen in the Apennines, or to the northern lakes, or even further, to the Rhone, the Nile, the Atlas, was sought by the jaded man of pleasure or the man struggling in vain to reform. But Seneca warns his disciple that wherever he may go he will take his vices and his weakness with him.[1] Let him try to work out his salvation within his great palace on the Esquiline. Surrounded by splendour and luxury, let him, for a time, isolate himself from them; let him lie on a hard bed, and live on scanty fare, and fancy himself reduced to that poverty which he dreads so much and so foolishly.[2] The change will be good for body and soul; and the temporary ascetic may return to his old life, at least released from one of his bugbears, and refreshed with a new sense of freedom.

Such were some of the precepts by which Seneca strove to fortify the struggling virtue of his disciples. But he never concealed from them that it is only by struggle that the remote ideal can be attained. "Vivere militare est." And almost in the words of S. Paul, he uses the example of the gladiator or the athlete, to arouse the energy of the aspirant after moral perfection.[3] "They do it for a corruptible crown."[4] The reward of the Stoic disciple is vain and poor to the gross materialist. But, from the serene heights, where ideal Reason watches the struggle, the only victor is the man who has adopted the watchwords—self-knowledge, renunciation, resignation. Only by following that steep path can any one ever reach the goal of assured peace within, and be delivered from the turmoil of chance and change. The misery of the sensual, the worldly, and the ambitious lies in the fact that they have staked their happiness on things which are beyond their own power, which are the casual gifts of fortune, and may be as capriciously withdrawn. This state is one of slavery to external things, and the pleasure, after all, which can be drawn from them is fleeting. Hence it is that the sensualist is equally miserable when his pleasures are denied, and when they are exhausted.[5] He places his happiness in one brief

[1] *Ep.* 51, § 4; 104, § 20, si vis peregrinationes habere jucundas, tuum comitem sana.

[2] *Ep.* 17, § 5; 18, § 8; *Ep.* 87, § 1; cf. Martha, p. 42.

[3] *Ep.* 96, § 5.

[4] *Ep.* 78, § 16, 4, nos quoque evincamus omnia, quorum praemium non corona nec palma est, etc.

[5] *De Vit. Beat.* vii. § 4; *Ep.* 83, § 27.

moment, with the danger or the certainty either of privation or satiety. The wise man of the Stoics, on the other hand, has built his house upon the rock. He shuns, according to the Pythagorean maxim, the ways of the multitude, and trusting to the illumination of divine Reason, he takes the narrow path.[1] His guiding light is the principle that the "kingdom of heaven is within," that man's supreme good depends only on himself, that is, on the unfettered choice of reason. To such a man "all things are his," for all worth having is within him. His mind creates its own world, or rather it rediscovers a lost world which was once his. He can, if he will, annihilate the seductions of the flesh and the world, which cease to disturb when they are contemned. He may equally extinguish the griefs and external pains of life, for each man is miserable just as he thinks himself.[2] Human nature, even unfortified by philosophic teaching, has been found capable of bearing the extremity of torture with a smile. The man who has mastered the great secret that mind may, by its latent forces, create its own environment, should be able to show the endurance of a Scaevola or a Regulus.[3] All he needs to do is to unmask the objects of his dread.[4] For just as men are deluded by the show of material pleasure, so are they unmanned by visionary fears. Even the last event of life should have no terror for the wise man, on any rational theory of the future of the soul. The old mythical hell, the stone of Sisyphus, the wheel of Ixion, Cerberus, and the ghostly ferryman, may be dismissed to the limbo of fable.[5] For the man who has followed the inner light, death must either be a return to that antenatal calm of nothingness which has left no memory, or the entrance to a blissful vision of the Divine.[6] Even in this luxurious and effeminate time, men and women of all ranks and ages have shown themselves ready to escape from calamity or danger by a voluntary death.[7] And what after all is death? It is not the terminus of life, a single catastrophe of a moment. In the very hour of birth we enter on the first stage in the journey to the grave. We are dying daily, and our last day

[1] *Ep.* 37.
[2] *Ep.* 96; 98, §§ 2, 7.
[3] *De Prov.* iii. § 4.
[4] *Ep.* 24, § 13, rebus persona demenda est.
[5] *Ib.* § 18; cf. *Ep.* 36, § 10; *Ep.* 30, § 17; *Ep.* 58, § 27; cf. Epict. ii. 1.
[6] *De Prov.* vi. § 6; *Ad Marc.* 25; *Ep.* 102, §§ 23–26, Per has mortalis aevi moras illi meliori vitae longiorique proluditur.
[7] *Ep.* 24, § 11.

only completes the process of a life-long death.[1] And as to the shortness of our days, no life is short if it has been full.[2] The mass of men are only living in an ambiguous sense; they linger or vegetate in life, they do not really live. Nay, many are long since dead when the hour of so-called death arrives. And the men who mourn over the shortness of their days are the greatest prodigals of the one thing that can never be replaced.[3] In the longest life, on a rational estimate, how small a fraction is ever really lived! The whole past, which might be a sure and precious possession, is flung away by the eager, worldly man.[4] The fleeting present is lost in unrest or reckless procrastination, or in projecting ourselves into a future that may never come. Thus old age surprises us while we are mere children in moral growth.[5]

At certain moments, the Stoic ideal might seem to be in danger of merging itself in the self-centred isolation of the Cynic, asserting the defiant independence of individual virtue, the nothingness of all external goods, the omnipotence of the solitary will. And undoubtedly, in the last resort, Seneca has pictured the wise man thus driven to bay, and calmly defying the rage of the tyrant, the caprices of fortune, the loss of health and wealth, nay the last extremity of torture and ignominious death. His own perilous position, and the prospect of society in the reign of Nero, might well lead a man of meditative turn so to prepare himself for a fate which was always imminent. But the Stoic doctor could never acquiesce in a mere negative ideal, the self-centred independence of the individual soul. He was too cultivated, he had drunk too deep of the science and philosophy of the past, he had too wide an outlook over the facts of human life and society, to relegate himself to a moral isolation which was apt to become a state of brutal disregard of the claims of social duty, and even of personal self-respect.[6] Such a position was absolutely impossible to a man like Seneca. Whatever his practice may have been, it is clear that in temperament he was almost too soft and emotional. He was a man with an

[1] *Ep.* 24, § 20; *Ep.* 36.

[2] *Ep.* 93, § 2, longa est vita si plena est; cf. 101, § 10, singulos dies singulas vitas puta.

[3] *De Brev. Vit.* viii. § 1.

[4] *Ib.* x.

[5] *Ib.* ix. § 4, pueriles adhuc animos senectus opprimit.

[6] Zeller, *Phil. der Griech.* iii. 1, p. 329, der Stoiker ist zu gebildet . . . um den Werth der wissenschaftlichen Weltbetrachtung zu verkennen.

intense craving for sympathy, and lavish of it to others; he was the last man in the world who could enjoy a solitary paradise of self-satisfied perfection. It is true the Roman world to the eyes of Seneca lay in the shadow of death, crushed under a treacherous despotism, and enervated by gross indulgence. Yet, although he sees men in this lurid light, he does not scorn or hate them. It was not for nothing that Seneca had been for five years the first minister of the Roman Empire. To have stood so near the master of the world, and felt the pulse of humanity from Britain to the Euphrates, to have listened to their complaints and tried to minister to their needs, was a rare education in social sympathy. It had a profound effect on M. Aurelius, and it had left its mark on Seneca.[1]

Two competing tendencies may be traced in Stoicism, and in Seneca's exposition of it. On the one hand, man must seek the harmony of his nature by submitting his passions and emotions to his own higher nature, and shaking himself free from all bondage to the flesh or the world. On the other hand, man is regarded as the subject of the universal Reason, a member of the universal commonwealth, whose maker and ruler is God.[2] The one view might make a man aim merely at isolated perfection; it might produce the philosophic monk. The other and broader conception of humanity would make man seek his perfection, not only in personal virtue, but in active sympathy with the movement of the world. The one impulse would end in a kind of spiritual selfishness. The other would seek for the full development of spiritual strength in the mutual aid and sympathy of struggling humanity, in friendship,[3] in the sense of a universal brotherhood and the fatherhood of God. There are two cities, says Seneca, in which a man may be enrolled—the great society of gods and men, wide as the courses of the sun; the other, the Athens or the Carthage to which we are assigned by the accident of birth.[4] A man may give himself to the service of both societies, or he may serve the one and neglect the other. The wise man alone realises to the full his citizenship in the spiritual commonwealth, in pondering on the problems of

[1] Cf. Zeller, *Phil. der Griech.* iii. 1, p. 277, die Philosophie immer nur die geschichtlich vorhandenen Zustände abspiegele.

[2] Burgmann, *Seneca's Theologie*, p. 26.

[3] *Ep.* 109, § 10; 9, § 15.

[4] *De Otio*, iv.; *Ep.* 68, § 2; cf. S. Aug. *De Civ. Dei*, xi. 1.

human conduct, the nature of the soul, of the universe and God, and conforming his moral being to the eternal law of Nature. The sage, a Zeno or a Chrysippus, may rightly devote himself exclusively to contemplation and moral self-culture.[1] He may not, by wealth and station, have access to the arena of active life. And, although a seeming recluse, he may really be a far greater benefactor of his kind than if he led the Senate, or commanded armies. There may be cases in which a man may be right in turning his back on public life, in order to concentrate all his energies on self-improvement. And Seneca does not hesitate to counsel Lucilius to withdraw himself from the thraldom of office.[2] Yet Zeno's precept was that the wise man will serve the State unless there be some grave impediment in his way.[3] For, on Stoic principles, we are all members one of another, and bound to charity and mutual help. And all speculation and contemplation are vain and frivolous unless they issue in right action. Yet the practical difficulty for the *sapiens* was great, if not insuperable. What earthly commonwealth could he serve with consistency; is it an Athens, which condemned a Socrates to death, and drove an Aristotle into exile?[4] How please the vulgar sensual crowd without displeasing God and conscience? It might seem that the true disciple of Stoicism could not take a part in public life save under some ideal polity, such as Plato or Chrysippus dreamed of.[5] Here, as elsewhere, the problem was solved with varying degrees of consistency. The problem is stated by Seneca—"Se contentus est sapiens ad beate vivendum, non ad vivendum."[6] It is the ever-recurring conflict between lofty idealism and the facts of human life, which is softened, if not solved, from age to age by casuistry. The wise and good man should have the springs of his happiness in himself. Yet a wise friend may call forth his powers, and furnish an object of self-sacrifice.[7] The wise man will not entangle himself in the cares of family life.[8] Yet wife and child are

[1] Zeller, *Phil. der Griech.* iii. 1, p. 274; Stob. *Flor.* 45, 29; Sen. *Ep.* 29, § 11.

[2] *Ep.* 19, § 6, subduc cervicem jugo tritam.

[3] *De Otio*, iii. § 2, accedet ad rempublicam nisi si quid impedierit.

[4] *Ib.* viii. § 1, interrogo ad quam rempublicam sapiens sit accessurus, ad Athenas in qua Socrates damnatur, etc.; cf. Diog. *Laert.* v. 1.

[5] *Ib.* vii. § 131.

[6] Sen. *Ep.* 9, § 13.

[7] *Ep.* 109, § 3 sqq.

[8] Epict. *Diss.* iii. 22, § 69.

needed to give completeness to the life of the citizen. Since man exists for the general order, how can he avoid lending his services to the State, unless there be some insuperable bar? The controversy between the dream of solitary perfection and altruism was variously solved, and the particular solution could always be defended in the light of the great law of life. Epictetus, cut off from the great world by servile birth and poverty, could make light of marriage, of the begetting of future citizens, and the duties of political life.[1] On the other hand, M. Aurelius, by nature as detached as Epictetus, might refuse to follow the transcendental counsels of Chrysippus and Seneca. He might strive painfully to reconcile devotion to an irksome political charge with a dream of that unseen commonwealth "in which the cities of men are as it were houses."[2]

Yet in spite of these difficulties about public duty, no one outside the pale of Christianity has perhaps ever insisted so powerfully on the obligation to live for others, on the duty of love and forgiveness, as Seneca has done. We are all, bond or free, ruler or subject, members one of another, citizens of a universal commonwealth.[3] We have all within us a portion of the Divine spirit. No man can live entirely to himself.[4] If we are not doing good to others we are doing harm. The nature of man and the constitution of the universe make it a positive obligation to seek the welfare of our fellows.[5] The social instinct is innate and original in us. As man is flung upon the world at birth, or in the natural state, with all his immense possibilities as yet undeveloped, no creature is so helpless.[6] It was only by combination and mutual good offices that men were able to repel the dangers which surrounded the infancy of the race, and to conquer the forces of nature. Man is born for social union, which is cemented by concord, kindness, and love,[7] and he who shows anger, selfishness, perfidy, or cruelty to his fellows strikes at the

[1] Epict. *Diss.* i. 9, § 1 sqq. ἢ τὸ τοῦ Σωκράτους, μηδέποτε πρὸς τὸν πυθόμενον, ποδαπός ἐστιν, εἰπεῖν ὅτι Ἀθηναῖος ἢ Κορίνθιος, ἀλλ' ὅτι Κόσμιος.

[2] M. Aurel. iii. 11; vi. 44, πόλις καὶ πατρὶς ὡς μὲν Ἀντωνίνῳ μοι ἡ Ῥώμη, ὡς δὲ ἀνθρώπῳ ὁ Κόσμος.

[3] Sen. *Ep.* 95, § 52; cf. M. Aurel. iv. 4, ὁ κόσμος ὡσανεὶ πόλις ἐστί: Epict. *Diss.* i. 13, § 3; Cic. *De Leg.* i. 7, 23, ut jam universus hic mundus una civitas sit communis deorum atque hominum existimanda.

[4] Sen. *Ep.* 47, § 2, alteri vivas oportet, si vis tibi vivere; *Ep.* 55, non sibi vivit qui nemini.

[5] *De Otio*, iii. § 5.

[6] *De Benef.* iv. 18, § 2, nudum et infirmum societas munit.

[7] *De Ira*, i. 5, § 2.

roots of social life. Nor should the spectacle of universal depravity cause us to hate or despise our kind.[1] It is quite true that the mass of men are bad, and always will be bad, with only rare exceptions. If society is the source of many blessings, it is also a great corruptor, and the conquest of nature and the development of the arts have aroused insatiable passions which have darkened the eye of reason.[2] Yet this crowd of sinners are our brothers, with the germs of virtue in their grain. They have taken the broad way almost necessarily, because it is broad. A general may punish individual soldiers, but you must pardon an army when it deserts the standards. The truly wise, not knowing whether to laugh or weep, will look kindly on the erring masses, as sick men who need a physician.[3] And beside the few truly wise, who can cast the first stone? We are all more or less bad, we have all gone astray.[4] And yet we constantly show the utmost severity to the faults of others, while we forget or ignore our own.[5] Even as God is long-suffering to transgressors, and sends His rain upon the evil and good alike, so should we be merciful in judgment and lavish in beneficence.[6] The spectacle of universal greed and selfishness and ingratitude should not harden us against our fellows, but rather make us turn our eyes to our own faults.[7] Sometimes, indeed, the note of humility is absent, and Seneca is the serene *sapiens contra mundum*, or the proud Roman gentleman who will not demean himself to resent or even notice the insults or injuries of the spiteful crowd.[8] They will pass him by as the licensed jests of the slaves on the Saturnalia. He reminds himself that it is the lower air which is turbid with storm and thunder; the ether which spreads around the stars is never vexed and darkened by the tempest.[9] This is one of the recurring contrasts in Seneca between the moral tone of the old world and that of the great movement which was setting in. But the new prevails in the end. The conception of God as cold reason or impersonal law

[1] *De Ira*, ii. 10, § 5 sqq.
[2] *Ib.* ii. 8 and 9; *Ep.* 90, § 9 sqq.; *N. Quaest.* v. 15.
[3] *Ib.* ii. 10, §§ 6–8.
[4] *De Clem.* i. 6, § 3, peccavimus omnes.
[5] *De Ira*, ii. 28, § 8, aliena vitia in oculis habemus, a tergo nostra sunt.
[6] *De Ben.* iv. 4 and 5; iv. 28; *De Ira*, iii. 26.
[7] *De Ira*, ii. 28.
[8] *Ib.* iii. 5, ingens animus et verus aestimator sui non vindicat injuriam quia non sentit . . . Ultio doloris confessio est.
[9] *Ib.* iii. 6.

or fate gives way to the thought of a God who guides by His providence, who embraces all by His love, whose goodness is as boundless as His power, who is best worshipped by the imitation of His goodness.[1] As the vision grows, the pride of the invulnerable *sapiens*, who might make himself the equal or more than the equal of God,[2] shrinks and is abased. We are all more or less bad, and we should be gentle to one another.[3] Do we complain of coldness and ingratitude? Let us think how many a kindness done to us in early days, the tenderness of a nurse, a friend's wise counsel or help in critical times, we have carelessly let slip from memory.[4] The faults which irritate us in another are often lurking in ourselves. Forgive if you wish for forgiveness; conquer evil with good; do good even to those who have wrought you evil.[5] Let us copy the serene example of those Eternal Powers who constantly load with their benefits even those who doubt of their existence, and bear with unruffled kindness the errors of frail souls that stumble by the way.

And as we shall not be harsh to those of our own external rank, so shall we soften the lot of those whom fortune has condemned to slavery. Even the slave is admitted to that great city of gods and men, which has no frontiers, which embraces all races and ranks, where all ranks should be levelled by the consciousness of a common Divine descent and a universal brotherhood of men.[6] The conquests of Macedon and Rome, overthrowing all old-world national barriers, had prepared the way for the greatest and most fruitful triumph of ancient philosophy. And the Stoic school has the glory of anticipating the diviner dream, yet far from realised, of a human brotherhood under the light from the Cross. Seneca has never risen higher, or swept farther into the future than in his treatment of slavery. He is far in advance of many a bishop or abbot or Christian baron of the middle age. Can a slave confer a benefit? he asks.[7] Is his service, however lavish, not merely a duty to his lord, which, as it springs

[1] *Ep.* 65, § 24; *Ad Helv.* viii. § 3; *Ep.* 41, § 2; *De Ben.* iv. 4 and 7; *Ep.* 10, § 5, sic vive tamquam deus videat; Siedler, *De Sen. Phil. Mor.* p. 14; Burgmann, *Seneca's Theologie*, p. 32.

[2] *De Prov.* vi. § 6, hoc est quo deum antecedatis.

[3] *De Ira*, iii. 26; *De Ben.* i. 10.

[4] *De Ben.* vii. 28, § 2.

[5] *De Ira*, iii. 26; ii. 28; ii. 31.

[6] *De Ben.* iii. 28, unus omnium parens mundus est. Cf. *Ep.* 47; *De Ira*, iii. 24; iii. 35; *De Clem.* i. 18.

[7] *De Ben.* iii. 18.

from constraint, is undeserving of gratitude? Seneca repudiates the base suggestion with genuine warmth. On the same principle a subject cannot confer a benefit on his monarch, a simple soldier on his general. There is a limit beyond which power cannot command obedience. There is a line between cringing compliance and generous self-sacrifice. And the slave has often passed that limit. He has often borne wounds and death to save his master's life in battle. He has often, in the years of the terror, endured the last extremity of torture, rather than betray his secrets.[1] The body of the slave is his master's; his mind is his own.[2] It cannot be bought and sold. And in his inner soul, the slave is his master's equal. He is capable of equal virtue and equal culture; nay, in both he may be his master's superior. He can confer a benefit if he can suffer injury in the outrages which cruelty and lust inflict upon him. When he confers a benefit, he confers it as man upon man, as an equal in the great family whose Father is God.

Seneca gives a lurid picture of the corruption of women in the general licence of his age.[3] Yet he has a lofty ideal of what women might become. Like other Stoic preachers, it was his good fortune to be surrounded by good women from his infancy. He remembers the tenderness of his aunt, in whose arms he first entered Rome as a child, who nursed him through long sickness, and broke through her reserve to help him in his early career of ambition. Her blameless character escaped even the petulance of Alexandrian gossip.[4] His letters to his mother, Helvia, reveal a matron of the best Roman type—strong, self-denying, proud of her motherhood, and despising the extravagance and ostentation of her class. In spite of her father's limited idea of female culture, she had educated herself in liberal studies, and found them a refuge in affliction.[5] Marcia was of a softer type, and gave way to excessive grief for a lost child. Yet it is to her that Seneca unfolds most fully his ideal of feminine character. He will not admit the inferior aptitude of women for virtue and culture.[6]

[1] *De Ben.* iii. 19 and 26; cf. Macrob. *Sat.* i. 11, § 16.

[2] *De Ben.* iii. 20, interior illa pars mancipio dari non potest.

[3] *Ad Helv.* xvi. § 3; *Ep.* 95, § 21, libidine vero ne maribus quidem cedunt.

[4] *Ad Helv.* xix. § 2, § 6; Marcia's husband, probably Vitrasius Pollio, was governor of Egypt.—Teuffel, *R. Lit.* § 282, 1.

[5] *Ad Helv.* xv.-xvii. § 3.

[6] *Ad Marc.* xvi. par illis, mihi crede, vigor, etc.

Women have the same inner force, the same capacity for nobleness as men. The husband of Paulina who surrounded him with affectionate sympathy, and was prepared to die along with him, the man who had witnessed the stern courage and loving devotion of the wives of the Stoic martyrs, might well have a lofty ideal of woman's character.[1] But to any true disciple of the Porch that ideal had a surer ground than any personal experience, however happy. The creed which Seneca held was at once a levelling and an elevating creed. It found the only nobility or claim to rank in higher capacity for virtue.[2] It embraced in the arms of its equal charity all human souls, bond or free, male or female, however they might be graded by convention or accident, who have a divine parentage, and may, if they will, have a lofty, perhaps an eternal future.

And now, in taking leave of Seneca, let us forget the fawning exile in Corsica, the possible lover of Julia or Agrippina, the millionaire minister of Nero, who was surrounded by a luxury and state which moved the envy of the tyrant.[3] Rather let us think of the ascetic from his early youth, who, raised by his talents to the highest place, had to reconcile an impossible ideal with the sordid or terrible realities of that rank which was at once a "pinnacle and a precipice."[4] He was continually torn by the contrast between the ideal of a lofty Stoic creed and the facts of human life around him, between his own spiritual cravings and the temptations or the necessities of the opportunist statesman. He was imbued with principles of life which could be fully realised only in some Platonic Utopia; he had to deal with men as they were in the reign of Nero, as they are painted by Tacitus and Petronius. If he failed in the impossible task of such a reconciliation, let us do him the justice of recognising that he kept his vision clear, and that he has expounded a gospel of the higher life, which, with all its limitations from temperament or tradition, will be true for our remotest posterity, that he had a vision of the City of God.[5] He was not personally perhaps so pure and clear a soul as Plutarch or Aristides or Dion Chrysostom. But he

[1] Tac. *Ann.* xv. 63, 64; Sen. *Ep.* 104, §§ 1-6.

[2] *De Ben.* iii. 28; iii. 20.

[3] *Ad Polyb.* xii. xiii. § 4; D. Cass. lxi. 10; Tac. *Ann.* xiii. 42.

[4] *Ep.* 94, § 73, quae aliis excelsa videntur, ipsis praerupta sunt.

[5] *De Otio,* iv. duas respublicas animo complectamur, etc.

had utterly cast off that heathen anthropomorphism which crossed and disturbed their highest visions of the Divine.[1] Seneca is far more modern and advanced than even the greatest of the Neo-Platonic school, just because he saw that the old theology was hopelessly effete. He could never have joined in the last struggle of philosophic paganism with the Church. And so the Church almost claimed him as her son, while it never dreamt of an affinity with Plutarch or Plotinus.

Indeed, there needed only the change of some phrases to reconcile the teaching of Seneca with that of the great ascetic Christian doctors. Many of the headings of the *Imitation* might be attached to paragraphs of Seneca—"of bearing with the faults of others"; "of inordinate affections"; "of the love of solitude and silence"; "of meditation on death"; "of humble submission"; "that to despise the world and serve God is sweet"; "of the acknowledgment of our own infirmities, and the remembrance of God's benefits"; "of the contempt of temporal honour and vain secular knowledge"; "of the day of eternity and this life's straitness." In truth, the great spirits of all ages who have had a genius for religion, after due allowance for difference of association and difference of phrase, are strangely akin and harmonious. And Seneca had one great superiority over other equally religious souls of his time, which enables him to approach mediaeval and modern religious thought —he had broken absolutely with paganism. He started with belief in the God of the Stoic creed; he never mentions the Stoic theology which attempted to reconcile Him with the gods of the Pantheon. In spite of all his rhetoric, he tries to see the facts of human life and the relation of the human spirit to the Divine in the light of reason, with no intervening veil of legend. God is to Seneca the great Reality, however halting human speech may describe Him, as Fate, or Law, or Eternal Reason, or watchful loving Providence. God is within us, in whatever mysterious way, inspiring good resolves, giving strength in temptation, with all-seeing eye watching the issue of the struggle. God is without us, loading us with kindness

[1] Sen. *Frag.* ap. Aug. *De Civ. Dei*, vi. 10; *Ep.* 41, § 1, non sunt ad caelum elevandae manus, nec exorandus aedituus, ut nos ad aurem simulacri quasi magis exaudiri possimus admittat.

even when we offend, chastising us in mercy, the goal of all speculation, He from whom we proceed, to whom we go at death. The true worship of Him is not in formal prayer and sacrifice, but in striving to know and imitate His infinite goodness. We mortal men in our brief life on earth may be citizens of two commonwealths, one the Rome or Corinth of our birth, the other that great city of gods and men, in which all are equally united, male and female bond and free, as children of a common Father. In this ideal citizenship, in obedience to the law of the spiritual city, the eternal law which makes for righteousness, man attains his true freedom and final beatitude in communion with kindred souls.

Yet, as in mediaeval and puritan religious theory, there is in Seneca a strange conflict between pessimism and idealism. To the doomed philosophic statesman of the reign of Nero, the days of man's life are few and evil. Life is but a moment in the tract of infinite age, and so darkened by manifold sins and sorrows that it seems, as it did to Sophocles, a sinister gift.[1] On the other hand, its shortness is a matter of no importance; the shortest life may be full and glad if it be dignified by effort and resignation and conformity to the great law of the universe. The wise and pious man, ever conscious of his brief time of probation, may brighten each passing day into a festival and lengthen it into a life. The shortness of a life is only an illusion, for long or short have no meaning when measured by the days of eternity. And the philosopher may unite many lives in one brief span. He may join himself to a company of sages who add their years to his, who counsel without bitterness and praise without flattery; he may be adopted into a family whose wealth increases the more it is divided; in him all the ages may be combined in a single life.[2] To such a spirit death loses all its terrors. The eternal mystery indeed can be pierced only by imaginative hope. Death, we may be sure, however, can only be a change. It may be a passage into calm unconsciousness, as before our birth, which will release us from all the griefs and tumults of the life here below. It may, on the other hand, prove to be the morning of an eternal day, the entrance to a radiant and untroubled world of infinite possibilities. In any case, the spirit which

[1] Sen. *Ad Polyb.* iv. [2] *De Brev. Vit.* xv. § 3 sq.

has trained itself in obedience to eternal law, will not tremble at a fate which is surely reserved for the universe, by fire or flood or other cataclysmal change. The future in store for the soul is either to dwell for ever among things divine, or to sink back again into the general soul, and God shall be all in all.

CHAPTER II

THE PHILOSOPHIC MISSIONARY

THE gospel of philosophy expounded by Seneca was rather an esoteric or aristocratic creed. With all his liberal sentiment, his cosmopolitanism, his clear conception of human equality and brotherhood, Seneca always remains the director of souls like his own, enervated by wealth, tortured with the ennui of jaded sensibility, haunted by the terror of the Caesars.[1] Indeed Stoicism was always rather a creed for the cultivated upper class than for the crowd. In its prime, its apparatus of logical formulae, its elaborate physics and metaphysics, its essentially intellectual solution of the problems both of the universe and human life, necessarily disabled it from ever developing into a popular system. And in the later days of the Republic, theory became more important than practice, and logic passed into casuistry.[2] But in the first century, Stoicism came to be much more a religion than a philosophy, or even a theology. Its main business, as conceived by men like Seneca, is to save souls from the universal shipwreck of character[3] caused by the capricious excesses of luxury, the idolatry of the world and the flesh, which sprang from a riotous pride in the material advantages of imperial power, without a sobering sense of duty or a moral ideal. But, in the nature of things, this wreck of character was most glaringly seen among the men who were in close contact with the half insane masters of the world in the first century, and who possessed the resources to exhaust the possi-

[1] Sen. *Ep.* 77, § 6, cogita quamdiu jam idem facias: cibus, somnus, libido; per hunc circulum curritur; *Ep.* 24, § 25, quosdam subit eadem faciendi videndique satietas; *Ep.* 89, § 21; 95, § 20; 13, § 4; 24, §§ 11–14; 91, § 5, 6; *De Tranq.* ii. § 13; x. § 5, 6.

[2] Zeller, *Phil. der Griech.* iii. 1, pp. 46, 47; cf. Sen. *Ep.* 88, § 20; 117, § 20.

[3] Sen. *Ep.* 48, § 8, omnes undique ad te manus tendunt, etc.

bilities of pleasure or the capacities of the senses to enjoy. It is to people of this class, who still retained some lingering instincts of goodness, weary with indulgence, bewildered and tortured by the conflict of the lower nature with the weak, but still disturbing, protests of the higher, that Seneca addresses his counsels.

But what of the great masses lying outside the circle of cultivated and exhausted self-indulgence, that plebeian world of which we have seen the picture in their municipalities and colleges? It is clear from the records of their daily life, their ambitions, their tasks and amusements, that, although perhaps not generally tainted with such deep corruption as the nobles of the Neronian age, their moral tone and aspirations hardly correspond to the material splendour of the Empire. Even apart from the glimpses of low life in Petronius, Martial, and Apuleius, apart from the revelations of Pompeii, and the ghastly traditions which haunt the ruins of countless theatres and amphitheatres, the warnings of preachers of that age, such as Dion Chrysostom, and the reflections of the infinitely charitable M. Aurelius, leave no very favourable impression of the moral condition of the masses.[1] How could it be otherwise? The old paganism of Rome did indeed foster certain ancestral pieties which were the salt of the Roman character. But it unfortunately also gave its sanction to scenes of lust and cruelty which went far to counteract in later times any good it did. Nor had the old religion any means for edification and the culture of character. It had no organisation for the care and direction of souls in moral doubt and peril. If its oracles might, from a few old-world examples, seem to supply such a spiritual want, the appearance is delusive even according to pagan testimony. Poets and moralists alike thundered against the shameless impiety which often begged the sanction of a prophetic shrine for some meditated sin,[2] and the charge has been confirmed by the resurrection of these old profanities from the ruins of Dodona.[3] But even without

[1] M. Aurel. ix. 29, 34; v. 33, *γυμνὰ νόμιζε βλέπειν τὰ ψυχάρια αὐτῶν. ὅτε δοκοῦσι βλάπτειν ψέγοντες ἢ ὠφελεῖν ἐξυμνοῦντες, ὅση οἴησις; . . . καὶ κυνίδια διακναιόμενα καὶ παιδία φιλόνεικα, γελῶντα, εἶτα εὐθὺς κλαίοντα. Πίστις δὲ καὶ αἰδὼς καὶ δίκη καὶ ἀλήθεια πρὸς Ὄλυμπον ἀπὸ χθονὸς εὐρυοδείης.* Petron. *Sat.* 88; Sen. *De Ira*, ii. 8; D. Chrys. xiii. § 13, 33; vii. 133.

[2] Pers. ii. 4 sqq.; cf. Herod. vi. 86; Luc. *Icaromen.* 25.

[3] Bernays, *Lucian und die Kyniker*, p. 34.

direct testimony, we might fairly conclude that the Antonine Age was, by reason of its material development, in special need of spiritual teaching and evangelism. The whole stress of public and private effort was towards the provision of comfort or splendour or amusement for the masses. And, within the range of its ambition, it succeeded marvellously. Nor should an impartial inquirer refuse to admit that such an immense energy has its good moral side. The rich were rigorously taught their duty to society, and they improved upon the lesson. The masses responded to their generous public spirit with gratitude and affection; and the universal kindliness and fraternity diffused through all ranks on days of high religious festival or civic interest, afforded a very wholesome and gratifying spectacle.[1] There was an undoubted softening of the Roman character. And the labours of the great Stoic lawyers were giving expression to cultivated moral feeling, in a more liberal recognition of the natural rights of the weak and oppressed, of women and of slaves. Yet a society may be humane and kindly while it is also worldly and materialised. To us at least, the forces of the Antonine age seem to have expended themselves chiefly on the popular pleasures and external adornments of life, or a revival, often in the grossest and most absurd forms, as we shall see in a later chapter, of the superstitions of the past. With all its humanitarian sentiment and all its material glories, the Roman world had entered on that fatal incline, which, by an unperceived yet irresistible movement, led on to the sterilisation of the higher intellect, and the petrifaction of Roman society which ended in the catastrophe of the fifth century.

The triumphs and splendour of corporate life in the age of the Antonines are certainly a dazzling spectacle. Yet to the student who is more occupied with the painful moral education of the race, the interest lies in a different direction. It was a worldly age, but it was also an age ennobled by a powerful protest against worldliness. And in this chapter we shall study a great movement, which, under the name of philosophy or culture, called the masses of men to a higher standard of life. This movement, like all others of the same kind, had its

[1] *v.* p. 231 of this work. Yet cf. Luc. *Somn. seu Gallus*, 22, οἱ δὲ πλούσιοι φρίττουσι καὶ διανομαῖς ἱλάσκονταί σε κτλ.

impostors who disgraced it. Yet the man who has pursued them with such mordant ridicule and pitiless scorn, the man who was utterly sceptical as to the value of all philosophic effort, in the last resort approaches very near to the view of human life which was preached by the men whom he derides.[1] Lucian belonged to no philosophic school; he would himself have repudiated adhesion to any system. The advice of Teiresias to Menippus, when he sought him in the shades, would certainly have been Lucian's to any young disciple who consulted him. Have done with all these verbal subtleties and chimeras; swear allegiance to no sect; make the best of the present; and take things generally with a smile.[2] Yet who can read the *Dialogues of the Dead* without feeling that there is a deeper and more serious vein in Lucian than he would confess? Although he poured his contempt upon the Cynic street preachers, although in the *Auction of Lives* the Cynic's sells for the most paltry price, the Cynic alone is allowed to carry with him across the river of death his characteristic qualities, his boldness and freedom of speech, his bitter laughter at the follies and illusions of mankind.[3] There are many indications in these dialogues that, if Lucian had turned Cynic preacher, he would have waged the same war on the pleasures and illusory ambitions of man, he would have outdone the Cynics in brutal frankness of exposure and denunciation, as he would have surpassed them in rhetorical and imaginative charm of style.[4] He has a vivid and awful conception of Death, the great leveller, and sees all earthly wealth and glory in the grey light of the land where all things are forgotten. Rank and riches, beauty and strength, the lust of the eye and the pride of life, are all left behind on the borders of the realm of "sapless heads."[5] If Lucian has any gospel it is that the kingdom of heaven belongs to the poor. He is as ready as some of the Christian Fathers to condemn the rich eternally.[6] And therefore we are not surprised that Lucian has little eye for the splendour of his age, unless indeed in

[1] Croiset, *Lucien*, p. 164, il a subi fortement leur influence en écrivant les *Dialogues des morts*.

[2] Luc. *Menip.* c. 21.

[3] Luc. *Vit. Auct.* 11; *Traj.* 24; *Dial. Mort.* x. 9.

[4] Cf. Luc. *Char.* 15, 20; *Dial. Mort.* i. 3; *Somn.* 21.

[5] Luc. *Traj.* 15; *Necyom.* 12.

[6] *Traj.* 19; *Cyn.* 7; *Menip.* 11, χωρὶς δὲ οἵ τε πλούσιοι προσῄεσαν ὠχροί κτλ. Cf. *Somn.* 14, 15, οἱ δὲ (πλούσιοι) εὖ ἴσθι πολὺ ὑμῶν ἀθλιώτερον τὸν βίον βιοῦσι, cf. 22.

the phrase, "Great cities die as well as men."[1] He seems to have little appreciation for its real services to humanity. Its vain, pretentious philosophy, its selfishness of wealth, its vices hidden under the guise of virtue, drew down his hatred and scorn. Yet one cannot help feeling, in reading some of Lucian's pieces, that, man of genius as he was, a man of no age, or a man of all ages, he is looking at human life from far above, with no limitations of time, and passing a judgment which may be repeated in the thirtieth century.[2]

This lofty or airy detachment in regarding the toils and ambitions of men is perhaps best seen in the *Charon*. In this piece Lucian shows us the ideal spectator taking an outlook over the scene of human life. The ferryman of the dead, who has heard so many laments from his passengers for the joys they have lost, wishes to have a glance at this upper world which it seems so hard to leave behind. He joins the company of Hermes, and, by an old-world miracle, they gain an observatory on high-piled Thessalian mountains from which to watch for a while the comedy or the tragedy of human life.[3] A magic verse of Homer gives the spectral visitor the power to observe the scene so far below. And what a sight it is! It is a confused spectacle of various effort and passion—men sailing, fighting, ploughing, lending at usury, suing in the law-courts. It is also a human swarm stinging and being stung. And over all the scene flits a confused cloud of hopes and fears and follies and hatreds, the love of pleasure and the love of gold. Higher still, you may see the eternal Fates spinning for each one of the motley crowd his several thread. One man, raised high for the moment, has a resounding fall; another, mounting but a little way, sinks unperceived. And amidst all the tumult and excitement of their hopes and alarms, death kindly snatches them away by one of his many messengers. Yet they weep and lament, forgetting that they have been mere sojourners for a brief space upon earth and are only losing the pleasures of a dream.[4] To Charon the bubbles in a fountain are the truest image of their phantom

[1] *Char.* 23, ἀποθνήσκουσι γάρ, ὦ πορθμεῦ, καὶ πόλεις ὥσπερ ἄνθρωποι.

[2] As in *Icaromen.* 15; *Char.* 17.

[3] *Char.* 3; cf. a saying of Plato, quoted in M. Aurel. vii. 48, καὶ δὴ περὶ ἀνθρώπων τοὺς λόγους ποιούμενον ἐπισκοπεῖν δεῖ καὶ τά ἐπίγεια, ὥσπερ ποθὲν ἄνωθεν, κατὰ ἀγέλας . . . γάμους, γενέσεις, θανάτους, σικαστηρίων θόρυβον, ἑορτάς, θρήνους, κτλ.

[4] Luc. *Char.* 17, ἀπίασιν ὥσπερ ἐξ ὀνείρατος πάντα ὑπὲρ γῆς ἀφέντες.

life—some forming and bursting speedily, others swelling out for a little longer and more showy life, but all bursting at the last. Charon is so moved by the pathos of it all, that, from his mountain peaks, he would fain preach a sermon to the silly crowd and warn them of the doom which is in store for all. But the wiser or more cynical Hermes tells him that all except a few have their ears more closely stopped than the crew of Odysseus when they passed the Siren isles.

This view of human life, half-contemptuous, half-pathetic, which the great iconoclast of all the dreams of religion or philosophy in his time has sketched with his own graphic power, was the view of the very philosophy which he derided. Philosophy had a second time turned from heaven to earth. The effort to solve the riddle of the universe by a single formula, or by the fine-drawn subtleties of dialectic, has been abandoned. In Lucian's *Auction of Lives*, in which the merits of the various schools are balanced and estimated in terms of cash, it is significant that only a slight and perfunctory reference is made to the great cosmic or metaphysical theories of Elea or Ionia, to the Pythagorean doctrine of numbers, to the Ephesian doctrine of the eternal flow, or the ideal system of Plato.[1] We have seen that, although Seneca has a certain interest in the logic and physics of the older Stoicism, he makes all purely speculative inquiry ancillary to moral progress. The same diversion of interest from the field of speculation to that of conduct is seen even more decidedly in Epictetus and M. Aurelius.[2] The philosophic Emperor had, of course, studied the great cosmic systems of Heraclitus and Epicurus, Plato and Aristotle.[3] They furnish a scenery or background, sometimes, especially that of Heraclitus, a dimly-seen foundation, for his theory of conduct. But, in spite of his sad, weary view of the pettiness and sameness of the brief space of consciousness between "the two eternities," the whole thought of M. Aurelius is concentrated on the manner in which that brief moment may be worthily spent. So, Epictetus asks, What do I care whether all things are composed of atoms or similar parts or of fire or earth? Is it not enough to know the

[1] Luc. *Vit. Auct.* 3, 13, 16.

[2] Epict. *Diss.* iv. i. 138, Ἆρον ἐκεῖνα τὰ τῶν σχολαστικῶν καὶ τῶν μωρῶν κτλ. M. Aurel. vii. 67; cf. Zeller, *Phil. der Griech.* iii. 2, p. 203; Hatch, *Hibbert Lec.* p. 142.

[3] M. Aurel. vi. 15; vii. 19; vi. 24, 42, 47; viii. 6; xi. 20; viii. 3; vii. 67.

nature of good and evil?[1] Just as in the days of Socrates the whole stress of philosophy is directed towards the discovery of a rule of life, a source of moral clearness and guidance, with a view to the formation or reformation of character.

Seneca and Epictetus and Lucian and M. Aurelius all alike give a gloomy picture of the moral condition of the masses. And we may well believe that, in spite of the splendour of that age, in spite of a great moral movement which was stirring among the leaders of society, the mass of men, as in every age, had little taste for idealist views of life. Yet Seneca, notwithstanding his pessimism, speaks of the multitudes who were stretching out their hands for moral help. There must have been some demand for that popular moral teaching which is a striking feature of the time. Men might jeer at the philosophic missionary, but they seem to have crowded to listen to him—on the temple steps of Rome or Ephesus, in the great squares of Alexandria,[2] or in the colonnades at Olympia, or under the half-ruined walls of an old Milesian colony on the Euxine.[3] The rush of the porters and smiths and carpenters to join the ranks of the Cynic friars, which moved the scorn of Lucian,[4] must have corresponded to some general demand, even if the motive of the vagrant missionary was not of the purest kind. There must have been many an example of moral earnestness like that of Hermotimus, who had laboured hard for twenty years to find the true way of life, and had only obtained a distant glimpse of the celestial city.[5] After Dion's conversion, as we may fairly call it, he deems it a sacred duty to call men to the way of wisdom by persuasion or reproach, and to appeal even to the turbulent masses.[6] We shall see how well he fulfilled the duty. For nearly a century at Athens, the gentle Demonax embodied the ideal which his friend Epictetus had formed of the Cynic father of all men in God; and his immense ascendency testifies at least to a widespread respect and admiration for such teaching and example.[7] It is not necessary

[1] Epict. *Fr.* 175; cf. *Diss.* iii. 21, § 23, *ἀλλά, εἴ σε ψυχαγωγεῖ τὰ θεωρήματα, καθήμενος αὐτὰ στρέφε αὐτὸς ἐπὶ σεαυτοῦ· φιλόσοφον δὲ μηδέποτ' εἴπῃς σεαυτόν*: cf. M. Aurel. ii. 17, *τοῦ ἀνθρωπίνου βίου ὁ μὲν χρόνος στιγμή . . . τί οὖν τὸ παραπέμψαι δυνάμενον; ἓν καὶ μόνον, φιλοσοφία.*

[2] Philostr. *Apoll. Tyan.* v. 26; D. Chrys. *Or.* xxxii.

[3] Philostr. *Apoll. Tyan.* iv. 41; iv. 24; D. Chrys. xxxvi. § 17.

[4] Luc. *Fug.* c. 12.

[5] *Hermot.* c. 2, 25.

[6] D. Chrys. *Or.* lxxviii.; Martha, *Mor. sous l'Emp. rom.* p. 300.

[7] Luc. (?) *Dem.* c. 7, 8.

to suppose that the people who thought it an honour if Demonax invited himself to their tables, the magistrates who rose up to do him reverence as he passed, or the riotous assembly which was awed into stillness by his mere presence, were people generally who had caught his moral enthusiasm.[1] They were at the very time eager to have gladiatorial shows established under the shadow of the Acropolis. But it is something when men begin to revere a character inspired by moral forces of which they have only a dim conjecture. And amid all the material splendour and apparent content of the Antonine age, there were signs that men were becoming conscious of a great spiritual need, which they often tried to satisfy by accumulated superstitions. The ancient routine was broken up; the forms of ancestral piety no longer satisfied even the vulgar; the forms of ancient scholastic speculation had become stale and frigid to the cultivated; the old philosophies had left men bewildered. Henceforth, philosophy must make itself a religion; the philosopher must become an "ambassador of God."

"There is no philosophy without virtue; there is no virtue without philosophy," said Seneca,[2] and herein he expressed truly the most earnest thought of his own age and the next. Lucian, in the dialogue which is perhaps his most powerful exposure of the failure of philosophy, bears testimony to the boundless expectations which it aroused in its votaries. Hermotimus, the elderly enthusiast, whom the mocker meets hurrying with his books to the philosophic school, has been an ardent student for twenty years; he has grown pale and withered with eager thought. Yet he admits that he has only taken a single step on the steep upward road. Few and faint and weary are they who ever reach the summit.[3] Yet Hermotimus is content if, at the close of the efforts of a lifetime, he should, if but for a moment, breathe the air of the far-off heights and look down on the human ant-hill below. Such spirits dream of an apotheosis like that which crowned the hero on Mount Oeta, when the soul shall be purged of its earthly passions as by fire, and hardly a memory of the illusions of the past will remain.[4] Lycinus, his friend, has once himself had a vision of a celestial city, from

[1] Luc. (?) *Dem.* c. 63.

[2] Sen. *Ep.* 89, § 6; cf. A. Gell. xvii. 19, 4.

[3] Luc. *Hermot.* c. 5.

[4] *Ib.* c. 7, καὶ οὗτοι δὴ ὑπὸ φιλοσοφίας ὥσπερ ὑπό τινος πυρὸς ἅπαντα ταῦτα περιαιρεθέντες κτλ.

which ambition and the greed of gold are banished, where there is no discord or strife, but the citizens live in a deep peace of sober virtue. He had once heard from an aged man how any one might share its citizenship, rich or poor, bond or free, Greek or barbarian, if only he had the passion for nobleness and were not overcome by the hardness of the journey. And the sceptic avows that long since he would have enrolled himself among its citizens, but the city is far off, and only dimly visible. The paths which are said to lead to it run in the most various directions, through soft meadows and cool shaded slopes, or mounting over bare rough crags under a pitiless blaze. And at the entrance to each avenue there is a clamorous crowd of guides, each vaunting his peculiar skill, abusing his rivals, and pointing to the one sure access of which he alone has the secret key. A similar scene, equally illustrative of the moral ferment of the time, is sketched in another charming piece.[1] It is that in which the rustic Pan, with his memories of the shepherd's pipe and the peace of Arcadian pastures, describes the strange turmoil of contending sects which rings around his cave on the edge of the Acropolis. There, in the Agora below, rival teachers, with dripping brow and distended veins, are shouting one another down before an admiring crowd. And the simple old deity, to whom the language of their dialectic is strange, seems to think that the victory rests with the loudest voice and the most blatant self-assertion.

The sly ridicule of Lucian, so often crossed by a touch of pathos, is perhaps the best testimony to the overpowering interest which his age felt in the philosophy of conduct. And it was no longer the pursuit merely of an intellectual aristocracy. Common, ignorant folk have caught the passion for apostleship. Everywhere might be met the familiar figure, with long cloak and staff and scrip, haranguing in the squares or lanes to unlettered crowds.[2] And the preacher is often as unlearned as they, having left the forge or the carpenter's bench or the slave prison,[3] to proclaim his simple gospel of renunciation, with more or less sincerity. Lucian makes sport of the quarrels and contradictions of the schools. And it is true that the old

[1] Luc. *Bis Acc.* c. 11.

[2] *Ib.* c. 6, *ἀπανταχοῦ πώγων βαθὺς καὶ βιβλίον ἐν τῃ ἀριστερᾳ καὶ πάντες ὑπὲρ σοῦ φιλοσοφοῦσι κτλ.*

[3] *Fug.* c. 12; *Vit. Auct.* c. 10; D. Chrys. xxxii. 9; xxxiv. 3.

names still marked men off in different camps, or rather churches. But their quarrels in Lucian and in Philostratus[1] seem to be personal, the offspring of very unphilosophic ambition and jealousy, or greed or petty vanity, rather than the wholesome and stimulating collision of earnest minds contending for what they think a great system of truth. The rival Sophists under the Acropolis were quarrelling for an audience and not for a dogma. Scientific interest in philosophy was to a great extent dead. For centuries no great original thinker had arisen to rekindle it. And in the purely moral sphere to which philosophy was now confined, the natural tendency of the different schools, not even excluding the Epicurean, was to assimilation and eclecticism.[2] They were all impartially endowed at the university of Athens, and a youth of enthusiasm would attend the professors of all the schools. Apollonius, although he finally adopted the Pythagorean discipline, pursued his studies at Aegae under Platonists and Stoics,[3] and even under Epicureans. Seneca came under Pythagorean influences in his youth, and he constantly rounds off a letter to Lucilius with a quotation from Epicurus. Among the tutors of M. Aurelius were the Peripatetic Claudius Severus, and Sextus the Platonist of Chaeronea.[4] Hence, although a man in the second century might be labelled Platonist or Stoic, Cynic or Pythagorean, it would often be difficult from his moral teaching to discover his philosophic ancestry and affinities. And, just as in modern Christendom, although sectarian landmarks and designations are kept up, the popular preaching of nearly all the sects tends to a certain uniformity of emphasis on a limited number of momentous moral truths, so the preaching of pagan philosophy dwells, almost to weariness, on the same eternal principles of true gain and loss, of the illusions of passion, of freedom through renunciation.

The moral teaching or preaching of the Antonine age naturally adapted its tone to the tastes of its audience; there was the discourse of the lecture-room, and the ruder and more boisterous appeal to the crowd. Both passed under the name of philosophy, and both often degraded that great name by an affectation and insincerity which cast discredit on a

[1] Philostr. *Apoll. Tyan.* v. 37.

[2] Zeller, *Phil. der Griech.* iii. 1, p. 483. Renan, *Les Év.* p. 384, les différences des écoles étaient à peu près effacées. Un éclecticisme superficie était à la mode.

[3] Philostr. *Apoll. Tyan.* i. 7.

[4] Capitol. *M. Ant.* c. 3.

great and beneficent movement of reform. The philosophic lecturer who has a serious moral purpose is in theory distinguished from the rhetorical sophist, who trades in startling effects, who rejoices in displaying his skill on any subject however trivial or grotesque, who will expatiate on the gnat or the parrot, or debate the propriety of a Vestal's marriage.[1] The exercises of the rhetorical school had gone on for five hundred years, and, with momentous effects on Roman culture, they were destined to continue with little change till the Goths were masters of Rome.[2] The greed, the frivolity, and the overweening vanity of these intellectual acrobats are a commonplace of literary history.[3] The sophist and the lecturing philosopher were theoretically distinct. But unfortunately a mass of evidence goes to show that in many cases the lecturing philosopher became a mere showy rhetorician. A similar desecration of a serious mission is not unknown in modern times. The fault is often not with the preacher, but with his audience. If people come not to be made better, but to be amused, to have their ears soothed by flowing declamation, to have a shallow intellectual curiosity titillated by cheap displays of verbal subtlety or novelty, the unfortunate preacher will often descend to the level of his audience. And in that ancient world, according to the testimony of Seneca, Musonius, Plutarch, and Epictetus, the philosophic preacher too often was tempted to win a vulgar applause by vulgar rhetorical arts.[4] He was sometimes a man of no very serious purpose, with little real science or originality. He had been trained in the school of rhetoric, which abhorred all serious thought, and deified the master of luscious periods and ingenious turns of phrase. He was, besides, too often a mere vain and mercenary adventurer, trading on an attenuated stock of philosophic tradition, and a boundless command of a versatile rhetoric, cultivating intellectual insolence as a fine art, yet with a servile craving for the applause of his audience.[5] Many a scene in the now faded history of their failures or futile triumphs comes down to us

[1] Martha, *Moralistes sous l'Emp.* p. 275; Capes, *Univ. Life*, p. 58 sqq.

[2] *Roman Society in the Last Century of the Western Empire* (1st ed.), p. 355.

[3] Capes, *Univ. Life*, p. 69.

[4] Epict. ii. 19; iii. 23; Plut. *De Recta Rat. Aud.* vii. viii.; A. Gell. v. i.; Zeller, iii. 1, p. 657.

[5] Philostr. *Vit. Soph.* i. 3.

from Plutarch and Epictetus and Philostratus.[1] Sometimes the gaps upon the benches, the listless, inattentive air, the slow feeble applause, sent the vain preacher home with gloomy fears for his popularity. On other days, he was lifted to the seventh heaven by an enthusiastic genteel mob, who followed every deft turn of expression with shouts and gestures of delight, and far-fetched preciosities of approbation. At the close, the philosophic performer goes about among his admirers to receive their renewed tribute. "Well, what did you think of me?"—"Quite marvellous, I swear by all that is dear to me."—"But how did you like the passage about Pan and the nymphs?"—"Oh, superlative!" It is thus that a real winner of souls describes the impostor.[2] Even estimable teachers did not disdain to add to the effect of their lectures by carefully polished eloquence, an exquisite toilet, and a cultivated dignity. Such a courtly philosopher was Euphrates, the Syrian Stoic, whose acquaintance Pliny had made during his term of service in the East. Euphrates was stately and handsome, with flowing hair and beard, and a demeanour which excited reverence without overawing the hearer.[3] Irreproachable in his own life, he condemned sin, but was merciful to the sinner. Pliny, the amiable man of the world, who had no serious vices to reform, found Euphrates a charming lecturer, with a subtle and ornate style which was entirely to his taste. He treats Euphrates as a rhetorician rather than as a philosopher with a solemn message to deliver. To serious moralists like Seneca, Musonius, Plutarch, and Epictetus the showy professor of the art of arts was an offence. With their lofty conception of the task of practical philosophy, they could only feel contempt or indignation for the polished exquisite who trimmed or inflated his periods to please the ears of fashionable audiences. They all condemn such performances in almost identical terms. The mission of true philosophy is to make men examine themselves, to excite shame and pain and penitence, to reveal a law of life and moral freedom which may lead to amendment and peace.[4]

[1] Philostr. *Vit. Soph.* i. iv. ἔθελγε τῇ τε ἠχῇ τοῦ φθέγματος καὶ τῷ ῥυθμῷ τῆς γλώττης. A. Gell. v. 1, 3; Sen. *Ep.* 108, § 6, non id agunt ut aliqua illo vitia deponant sed ut oblectamento aurium perfruantur. Cf. Philostr. *Vit. Soph.* i. 7.

[2] Epict. iii. 23, ἀλλ' ἐπαίνεσόν με· εἰπέ μοι Οὐᾶ καὶ Θαυμαστῶς. Plut. *De Recta Rat. Aud.* c. viii.; cf. Hatch, *Hibbert Lec.* p. 95.

[3] Plin. *Ep.* i. 10.

[4] Epict. iii. 21; ii. 1; ii. 23; Sen. *Ep.* 108, § 6.

"There is no good in a bath or in a discourse which does not cleanse." The true disciple and the true teacher will be too much absorbed in the gravity of the business to think of the pleasure of mere style. To make aesthetic effect the object of such discourses, when the fate of character is at stake, is to turn the school into a theatre or a music-hall, the philosopher into a flute-player.[1]

The volume and unanimity of these criticisms of the rhetorical philosopher show that such men abounded; but they also show that there must have been a great mass of serious teachers whom they travestied. It has perhaps been too little recognised that in the first and second centuries there was a great propaganda of pagan morality running parallel to the evangelism of the Church.[2] The preaching was of very different kinds, according to the character of the audiences. The preachers, as we have said, belonged to all the different schools, Stoic or Platonist, Cynic or Pythagorean; sometimes, like Dion, they owed little academic allegiance at all. Sometimes the preaching approached to modern conceptions of its office;[3] at others, it dealt with subjects and used a style unknown to our pulpits.[4] The life of Apollonius of Tyana may be a romance; it certainly contains many narratives of miracles and wonders which cast a suspicion upon its historical value. Yet even a romance must have real facts behind to give it probability, and the preaching, at least, of Apollonius seems to belong to the world of reality. Apollonius was probably much nearer to the true ecclesiastic and priest of modern times than any ancient preacher. He had been trained in all the philosophies; he had drunk inspiration from the fountain of all spiritual religion, the East. He was both a mystic and a ritualist. He rejoiced in converse with the Brahmans, and he occupied himself with the revival or reform of the ritual in countless Greek and Italian temples.[5] He had an immense and curious faith in ancient legend.[6] The man who could busy himself

[1] A. Gell. v. 1, 2, tum scias neque illi philosophum loqui sed tibicinem canere. Philostr. *Vit. Soph.* iii. 3, *ῥυθμούς τε ποικιλωτέρους αὐλοῦ καὶ λύρου ἐσηγάγετο ἐς τὸν λόγον.* D. Chrys. *Or.* xxxv. §§ 7, 8.

[2] For a comparative estimate see Capes, *Univ. Life in Ancient Athens*, p. 90; Hatch, *Hibbert Lec.* p. 105.

[3] Philostr. *Apoll. Tyan.* iv. 3; iv. 42; D. Chrys. xxxiii. § 28; xxxiv. § 4; xl. § 31.

[4] Cf. A. Gell. xii. 1, nihil, inquit, dubito quin filium lacte suo nutritura sit.

[5] Philostr. *Apoll. Tyan.* iii. 41 sqq.; iv. 24; iv. 18, 20; i. 11; i. 31.

[6] *Ib.* iv. 13, 16, 19, 20, 33; vi. 40.

with the restoration of the true antique form of an obsolete rite at Eleusis or Athens or Dodona, also held conceptions of prayer and sacrifice and mystic communion with God, which might seem irreconcilable with any rigidly formal worship.[1] The ritualist was also the preacher of a higher morality. From the steps of the temples he used to address great audiences on their conspicuous faults, as Dion did after him. In the parable of the sparrow who by his twitter called his brethren to a heap of spilt grain, he taught the people of Ephesus the duty of brotherly helpfulness.[2] He found Smyrna torn by factious strife, and he preached a rivalry of public spirit.[3] Even at Olympia, before a crowd intent on the strife of racers and boxers and athletes, he discoursed on wisdom and courage and temperance.[4] At Rome, under the tyranny of Nero, he moved from temple to temple exciting a religious revival by his preaching.[5] One text, perhaps, contains a truth for all generations—"My prayer before the altars is—Grant me, ye Gods, what is my due."[6] What effect on the masses such preaching had we cannot tell—who can tell at any time? But there are well-attested cases of individual conversion under pagan preaching. Polemon, the son of a rich Athenian, was a very dissolute youth who squandered his wealth on low pleasure. Once, coming from some revel, he burst with his companions into the lecture room of Xenocrates, who happened to be discoursing on temperance. Xenocrates calmly continued his remarks. The tipsy youth listened for a while, then flung away his garland, and with it also his evil ways;[7] he became the head of the Academy. A similar change was wrought by the teaching of Apollonius on a debauched youth of Corcyra, which we need not doubt although it was accompanied by a miracle.[8]

Musonius, another preacher, was a younger contemporary of Apollonius. His fame as an apostle of the philosophic life aroused the suspicions of Nero, and he was exiled to Gyarus.[9]

[1] Philostr. *Apoll. Tyan.* v. 25, *τὸ δὲ τῶν ταύρων αἷμα καὶ ὁπόσα ἐθύετο, οὐκ ἐπῄνει τὰ τοιάδε, κτλ.*

[2] *Ib.* iv. 3.

[3] *Ib.* iv. 8.

[4] *Ib.* iv. 31.

[5] *Ib.* iv. 41.

[6] *Ib.* i. 11; iv. 40, *ὧδε εὔχομαι, ὦ θεοὶ δοίητέ μοι τὰ ὀφειλόμενα.*

[7] Diog. Laert. iv. 3, 1, *καί ποτε . . . μεθύων καὶ ἐστεφανωμένος εἰς τὴν Ξενοκράτους ἧξε σχολὴν κτλ.*: Epict. iii. 1, § 14; Hor. *Sat.* ii. 3, 253, quaero, faciasne, quod olim Mutatus Polemon? Cf. the conversion of Isaeus, Philostr. *Vit. Soph.* i. 217.

[8] Philostr. *Apoll. Tyan.* iv. 20; cf. i. 13.

[9] *Ib.* vii. 16; cf. Tac. *Ann.* xv. 71; D. Cass. lxii. 27.

The suspicion may have been confirmed by his intimacy with Rubellius Plautus and great Stoics like Thrasea.[1] He met with gentler treatment under the Flavians,[2] and he probably saw the reign of Trajan. He is not known to have written anything. The fragments of his teaching in Stobaeus are probably drawn from notes of his lectures, as the teaching of Epictetus has been preserved by Arrian. Musonius is not a speculative philosopher but a physician of souls. Philosophy is the way to goodness: goodness is the goal of philosophy. And philosophy is not the monopoly of an intellectual caste; it is a matter of precept and practice, not of theory. The true moral teacher, working on the germ of virtue which there is in each human soul, thinking only of reforming his disciples, and nothing of applause, may win them to his ideal. Musonius fortified the austere Stoic and Cynic precepts by the ascetic discipline of the Pythagorean school. He taught the forgiveness of injuries and gentleness to wrongdoers. He is one of the few in the ancient world who have a glimpse of a remote ideal of sexual virtue. While his ascetic principles do not lead him to look askance at honourable marriage, he denounces all unchastity, and demands equal virtue in man and woman.[3] He was, according to Epictetus, a searching preacher. He spoke to the conscience, so that each hearer felt as if his own faults were set before his eyes. His name will go down for ever in the pages of Tacitus. When the troops of Vespasian and Vitellius were fighting in the lanes and gardens under the walls of Rome, Musonius joined the envoys of the Senate, and at the risk of his life harangued the infuriated soldiery on the blessings of peace and the horrors of civil war.[4] Many of the moral treatises of Plutarch are probably redacted from notes of lectures delivered in Rome. As we shall see in a later chapter, Plutarch is rather a moral director and theologian than a preacher. But his wide knowledge of human nature, his keen analysis of character and motive and human weakness, his spiritual discernment in discovering remedies and sources of strength, above all his lofty moral ideal, would have made him a powerful preacher in any age of the world. But it is in

[1] Tac. *Ann.* xv. 71; xiv. 59; Epict. i. 1, 27. The Rufus is Musonius Rufus.

[2] D. Cass. lxvi. 13, *πάντας τοὺς φιλοσόφους ὁ Οὐεσπασιανὸς πλὴν τοῦ Μουσωνίου ἐκ τῆς Ῥώμης ἐξέβαλε.*

[3] Zeller, *Phil. der Greich.* iii. 1, pp. 651-658.

[4] Tac. *Hist.* iii. 81.

the discourses of Maximus of Tyre that we have perhaps the nearest approach in antiquity to our conception of the sermon. Probably if any of us were asked to explain that conception, he might say that a sermon was founded on some definite idea of the relation of man to the Infinite Spirit, that its object was, on the one hand, to bring man into communion with God, and, on the other, to teach him his duty to his fellowmen and to himself. The discourses of Maximus have all these characteristics. Maximus of Tyre is little known now, and although to the historian of thought and moral life he is attractive, he has not the strength of a great personality. Yet, along with Plutarch, he shows us paganism at its best, striving to reform itself, groping after new sources of spiritual strength, trying to wed new and purer spiritual ideals to the worn-out mythology of the past. Maximus is very much in the position of one of our divines who finds himself bound in duty to edify the spiritual life of his flock, without disowning the religious traditions of the past, and without refusing to accept the ever-broadening revelation of God. Some of his discourses may seem to us frigid and scholastic, with a literary rather than a religious interest. But in others, there is a combination of a systematic theology with a mystic fervour and a moral purpose, which seems hardly to belong to the ancient world.[1]

In his oration to the Alexandrians,[2] Dion Chrysostom speaks with unwonted asperity of the Cynics, haranguing with coarse buffoonery a gaping crowd in the squares and alleys or in the porches of the temples. He thinks that these men are doing no good, but rather bringing the name of philosophy into contempt. It is hardly necessary to remind the reader that this view of the Cynic profession was very general in that age. The vulgar Cynic, with his unkempt beard, his mantle, wallet, and staff, his filth and rudeness and obscenity, insulting every passer-by with insolent questions, exchanging coarse jests and jeers with the vagabond mob which gathers at his approach, is the commonest figure in Greek and Roman literature of the time. The "mendicant monks" of paganism have been painted with all the vices of the dog and ape by Martial and Petronius

[1] Max. Tyr. v. viii. §§ 3, 10; xi.; xiv. § 8; xvii. For the little known of him, *v.* Zeller, *Phil. der Griech.* iii. 2, p. 182, n. 3.

[2] D. Chrys. *Or.* xxxii. § 9, *οὗτοι δὲ (οἱ Κυνικοὶ) ἔν τε τριόδοις καὶ στενωποῖς καὶ πυλῶσιν ἱερῶν ἀγείρουσι καὶ ἀπατῶσι παιδάρια καὶ ναύτας, κτλ.*

and Seneca, by Dion and Athenaeus and Alciphron and Epictetus, above all by Lucian.[1] The great foe of all extravagance or enthusiasm in religion and philosophy fastened on the later followers of Diogenes with peculiar bitterness. His hostility, we may surmise, is directed not against their tenets, but their want of decent culture. In the *Banquet*, the Cynic Alcidamas is drawn with a coarse vigour of touch which is intended to match the coarseness of the subject. He bursts into the dinner-party of Aristaenetus uninvited, to the terror of the company, ranges about the room, snatching tit-bits from the dishes as they pass him, and finally sinks down upon the floor beside a mighty flagon of strong wine. He drinks to the bride in no elegant fashion, challenges the jester to fight, and, when the lamp is extinguished in the obscene tumult, is finally found trying to embrace the dancing girl.[2] But Lucian's bitterest attack on the class is perhaps delivered in the dialogue entitled the *Fugitives*. Philosophy, in the form of a woman bathed in tears, appears before the Father of the gods. That kindly potentate is affected by her grief, and inquires the cause of it. Philosophy, who had been commissioned by Zeus to bring healing and peace to human life in all its confusion and ignorance and violence, then unfolds the tale of her wrongs.[3] It is a picture of vulgar pretence, by which her fair name has been besmirched and disgraced. Observing the love and reverence which her true servants may win from men, a base crew of ignorant fellows, trained in the lowest handicrafts, have forsaken them, to assume the garb and name of her real followers.[4] It is a pleasant change from a life of toil and danger and hardship, to an easy vagabond existence, nor is the transformation difficult. A cloak and a club, a loud voice and a brazen face and a copious vocabulary of scurrilous abuse, these are all the necessary equipment. Impudent assurance has its usual success with the crowd, who are unable to see through the disguise. If any one attempts to challenge the

[1] Sen. *Ep.* 5, § 1 ; 29, § 1 ; Mart. iv. 53, cum baculo peraque senem . . . cui dat latratos obvia turba cibos ; Epict. iii. 22 ; D. Chrys. *Or.* xxxiv. § 2 ; Athen. iii. 113 ; Petron. 14 ; Alciphr. iii. 55 ; Caspari, *De Cynicis*, p. 10.

[2] Luc. *Conviv.* c. 16, 35, etc.

[3] *Fug.* c. 5, 15.

[4] *Ib.* c. 12, κατεῖδον τὴν αἰδῶ ὅση παρὰ τῶν πολλῶν ἐστι τοῖς ἑταίροις τοῖς ἐμοῖς, . . . ταῦτα πάντα τυραννίδα οὐ μικρὰν ἡγοῦντο εἶναι.

claims of the impostors, he is answered with a blow or a taunt. And thus by terrorism or deceit, they usurp the respect which is due to the real philosopher, and manage to live in plenty and even in luxury. Nor is this the worst. For these pretended ascetics, who profess to scorn delights, and to endure all manner of hardness, are really coarse common sensualists, who go about corrupting and seducing. Many of them heap up a fortune in their wanderings, and then bid farewell to scrip and cloak and the tub of Diogenes. And so plain unlearned men come to regard the very name of philosophy with hatred and contempt, and all her work is undone, like another Penelope's web.[1]

Even the stoutest defender of the Cynic movement, as a whole, feels constrained to admit that the charges against the Cynics were, perhaps, in many cases, true.[2] It was a movement peculiarly attractive to the lawless, restless hangers-on of society, who found in an open defiance of social restraints and a wandering existence, a field of licence and a chance of gain. Some of the great Cynics, indeed, were interested in physical speculation, and were widely cultivated men.[3] But the Cynic movement, as a whole, rested on no scientific tradition, and the most serious and effective preacher of its doctrine needed only a firm hold of a few simple truths, with a command of seizing and incisive phrase.[4] There was no professional barrier to exclude the ignorant and corrupt pretender. For the Cynics, from the very nature of their mission and their aims, never formed an organised school or society. Each went his own way in complete detachment. To the superficial observer, the only common bond and characteristic were the purely external marks of dress and rough bearing and ostentatious contempt for the most ordinary comforts and decencies of life, which could easily be assumed by the knave and the libertine. Hence, as time went on, although good Cynics, like Demonax or Demetrius, acquired a deserved influence, yet the greed, licentiousness, and brutal

[1] Luc. *Fug.* c. 17–21, οἱ ἰδιῶται δὲ ταῦτα ὁρῶντες καταπτύουσιν ἤδη φιλοσοφίας, κτλ.

[2] Bernays, *Die Kyniker*, p. 39. Roheit und arbeitsscheues Vagabundenthum . . . mussten die Kynische Lebensweise sehr bequem finden.

[3] Plut. (?) *De Plac. Phil.* ii. 8 ; iv. 5 ; Luc. (?) *Demon.* 4, ποιηταῖς σύντροφος ἐγένετο . . . καὶ τὰς ἐν φιλοσοφίᾳ προαιρέσεις . . . ἠπίστατο : cf. Caspari, *De Cyn.* p. 6 ; Zeller, iii. 1, p. 685.

[4] Cf. Luc. (?) *Dem.* 14 sqq. ; Caspari, p. 6.

violence of others brought great discredit on the name. Epictetus, who had a lofty ideal of the Cynic preacher as an ambassador of God, lays bare the coarse vices of the pretender to that high service with an unsparing hand.[1] It is evident, however, that certain of the gravest imputations, which had been developed by prurient imaginations, were, by an unwholesome tradition, levelled at even the greatest and best of the Cynics.[2] And S. Augustine, in referring to these foul charges, affirms, with an honourable candour, that they could not be truly made against the Cynics of his own day.[3] Moreover, the Roman nature never took very kindly, even in some of the cultivated circles, to anything under the name of philosophy.[4] Even M. Aurelius could not altogether disarm the suspicion with which it was regarded. And the revolt of Avidius Cassius was to some extent an outburst of impatience with the doctrinaire spirit of the *philosopha anicula*, as Cassius dared to call him.[5] And there were many things in the Cynic movement which specially tended to provoke the ordinary man. It threw down the gauntlet to a materialised age. It preached absolute renunciation of all social ties and duties, and of all the pleasures and refinements with which that society had surrounded itself. In an age which, even on its tombstones, bears the stamp of a starched conventionality and adherence to use and wont, the Cynic was a defiant rebel against all social restraints. In an age which was becoming ever more superstitious, he did not shrink from attacking the faith in the gods, the efficacy of the mysteries, the credit of the most ancient oracles.[6] And, finally, while philosophy in general after Domitian found support and patronage at the imperial court, no emperor gave his countenance to the Cynics till the Syrian dynasty of the third century.[7] We have here surely a sufficient accumulation of reasons for hesitating to

[1] Epict. iii. 22, § 80, *εἰς τοὺς νῦν ἀποβλέπομεν τοὺς τραπεζῆας πυλαωροὺς κτλ.*, Luc. *Fug.* 14, *καὶ οὐ πολλῆς πραγματείας δεῖ τριβώνιον περιβαλέσθαι.*

[2] Luc. *Ver. Hist.* ii. 18; Athen. iv. 158; xiii. 588.

[3] S. Aug. *Civ. D.* xiv. 20, nemo tamen eorum audet hoc facere.

[4] D. Chrys. *Or.* lxxii. 2; Pers. v. 189; Petron. *Sat.* 71; Tac. *Agr.* 4; *Hist.* iv. 5; Plin. *Ep.* i. 22; Quintil. xi. 1, 35; xii. 2, 6.

[5] Capitol. *Avid. Cass.* 1, § 8, in a letter of Verus, te philosopham aniculam, me luxuriosum morionem vocat: cf. c. 14.

[6] Bernays, *Die Kyniker*, p. 31, sie sind die am reinsten deistische Sect, welche das hellenisch-römische Alterthum hervorgebracht hat.

[7] *Ib.* p. 30; cf. D. Cass. lxxvii. 19, for the favours showered on the Cynic Antiochus by Severus.

accept the wholesale condemnation of a class of men who, instead of disarming opposition, rather plumed themselves on provoking it.

A good example of the merciless, and not altogether scrupulous fashion in which the Cynics were handled by contemporaries is to be found in Lucian's piece on the death of Peregrinus.[1] Peregrinus was a native of Parium on the Propontis, and a man of fortune. He loved to call himself Proteus, and, indeed, the strange vicissitudes of his career justified his assumption of the name.[2] On reaching manhood, he wandered from land to land, and in Palestine he joined a Christian brotherhood, in which he rose to a commanding influence, which drew down the suspicion of the government, and he was thrown for a time into prison.[3] His persecution called forth, as Lucian ungrudgingly admits, all the fearless love and charity of the worshippers of "the crucified Sophist." Released by a philosophic governor of the type of Gallio, he gave up the remnant of his paternal property, amounting to fifteen talents, to his native city.[4] Peregrinus had already assumed the peculiar dress of the Cynic, and set out on fresh wanderings, having, from some difference on a point of ritual, severed his connection with the Christian brotherhood. He then came under the influence of an Egyptian ascetic and of the mysticism of the East. In a visit to Italy he acquired celebrity by his fierce invectives, which did not spare even the blameless and gentle Antoninus Pius.[5] The Emperor himself paid little heed to him, but the prefect of the city thought that Rome could well spare such a philosopher, and Peregrinus was obliged to return to the East. Henceforth Greece, and especially Elis, was the scene of his labours. He abated none of his energy, dealing out his denunciations impartially, and not sparing even the philosophic millionaire Herodes Atticus for providing the visitors to Olympia with the luxury of pure water.[6] He even tried to stir up Greece to armed revolt. His fame and power among the Cynic brotherhood were at their height, or perhaps beginning to wane, when

[1] On Lucian's *Peregrinus*, *v.* Caspari, *De Cyn.* p. 24 sq.; Bernays, p. 42 sqq.
[2] Luc. *De Morte Peregr.* c. 5, 10 sq.
[3] *Ib.* c. 11, 12.
[4] *Ib.* c. 14.
[5] *Ib.* c. 17, 18; cf. the rudeness of Demetrius to Vespasian, Suet. *Vesp.* xiii.; D. Cass. lxvi. 13.
[6] Luc. *De Morte Peregr.* c. 19, κακῶς ἠγόρευεν ὡς καταθηλύναντα τοὺς Ἕλληνας.

he conceived the idea of electrifying the world and giving a demonstration of the triumph of philosophy even over death by a self-immolation at Olympia. There, before the eyes of men gathered from all quarters, like Heracles, the great Cynic exemplar, on Mount Oeta, he resolved to depart in the blaze and glory of the funeral pyre kindled by his own hand. And perhaps some rare lettered Cynic brother set afloat a Sibylline verse, such as abounded in those days, bidding men prepare to revere another hero, soon to be enthroned along with Heracles in the broad Olympus.

Such a career, ambiguous, perhaps, on the most charitable construction, attracted the eye of the man who sincerely believed, under all his persiflage, that both the religion and the philosophy of the past were worn out, and were now being merely exploited by coarse adventurers for gain or ambition. Moreover, the Philoctetes of the Cynic Heracles, his pupil Theagenes, was attracting great audiences in the Gymnasium of Trajan at Rome.[1] The self-martyrdom of their chief had given a fresh inspiration to the Cynic brotherhood. Who knows but a legend may gather round his name, altars may be raised to him, and the ancient glamour of the "flashing Olympus" will lend itself to glorify the uncultivated crew who profane the name of philosophy, and are an offence to culture?

There is no mistaking the cold merciless spirit in which Lucian, by his own avowal, addressed himself to the task of exposing what he genuinely believed to be a feigned enthusiasm. Even the lover of Lucian receives a kind of shock from the occasional tone of almost cruel hardness in his treatment of the Cynic apostle. When Lucian's narrative of the youthful enormities of Peregrinus is analysed, it is perceived that the accuser is anonymous, and that other names and particulars are carefully suppressed.[2] For the gravest charges of youthful depravity no proof or authority is given; they seem to be the offspring of that prurient gossip which can assail any character. They are the charges which were freely bandied about in the age of Pericles and M. Aurelius, in the age of Erasmus and the age of Milton. There must have been something at least

[1] Caspari, *De Cyn.* p. 16; Bernays, *Luc. u. die Kyniker*, p. 16.
[2] *Ib.* p. 54.

remarkable and fascinating, although marred by extravagance,[1] about the man who became a great leader and prophet among the Christians of Palestine, and who was almost worshipped as a god. When he was thrown into jail, their widows and orphans watched by the gates; his jailers were bribed to admit some of the brethren to console his solitude; large sums were collected from the cities of Asia for his support and defence.[2] The surrender of his paternal property to his native city, an act of generosity which had many parallels in that age, is attributed to no higher motive than the wish to hush up a rumour that Peregrinus had murdered his father. The charge apparently rested on nothing more substantial than malignant gossip.[3] The migration of Peregrinus from the Christian to the Cynic brotherhood was not so startling in that age as it may appear to us. Transitions to and fro were not uncommon between societies which had the common bond of asceticism and contempt for the world.[4] Moreover, Lucian, with all his delicate genius, had little power of understanding the force of religious enthusiasm. It is pretty clear that Peregrinus was not an ordinary Cynic; he had felt the spell of Oriental and Pythagorean mysticism. His Cynicism was probably tinctured with a religion of the same type as that of Apollonius of Tyana.[5] And it is his failure to appreciate the fervour of this mystical elation in Peregrinus and his disciples which misled Lucian, and makes his narrative misleading.

Lucian suggests that, when he visited Olympia for the fourth time, he found that the influence of Peregrinus was on the wane.[6] Yet even from Lucian's own narrative it is clear that Peregrinus and his doings were attracting almost as much attention as the games. On Lucian's arrival, the first thing he heard was a rumour that the great Cynic had resolved to die upon a flaming pyre, like the hero who was the mythic patron of the school. Peregrinus professed that by his self-

[1] This offended Demonax, cf. Luc. (?) *Dem.* c. 21, Περεγρῖνε οὐκ ἀνθρωπίζεις.

[2] Luc. *De Morte Peregr.* c. 13.

[3] *Ib.* 10, 14, 37; Bernays, p. 54.

[4] Cf. Aristid. *Or.* xlvi. (Dind. vol. ii. p. 402), τοῖς ἐν τῇ Παλαιστίνῃ δυσσεβέσι παραπλήσιοι τοὺς τρόπους. Bernays, p. 36, Übertritte aus dem einen in das andere Lager vorkamen; Hatch, *Hib. Lec.* p. 166; cf. Caspari, *De Cyn.* p. 25; Jul. *Or.* vii. 224. C. τὰ δὲ ἄλλα γε πάντα ἐστὶν ὑμῖν τε κἀκείνοις (*i.e.* Χριστιανοῖς) παραπλήσια. καταλελοίπατε τὴν πατρίδα ὥσπερ ἐκεῖνοι.

[5] Luc. *De Morte Peregr.* c. 36, ἐς τὴν μεσημβρίαν ἀποβλέπων: c. 25, ὅπως τὴν καρτερίαν ἐπιδείξηται ὥσπερ οἱ Βραχμᾶνες, ἐκείνοις γὰρ αὐτὸν ἠξίου Θεαγένης εἰκάζειν.

[6] *Ib.* c. 2.

immolation he was going to teach men, in the most impressive way, to make light of death. And many a Cynic sermon was evidently delivered on the subject, the greatest preacher being Theagenes, for whom Lucian displays a particular aversion. There were, of course, many sceptics like Lucian himself. And it is in the mouth of one of these enemies of the sect, in reply to Theagenes, that Lucian has put the defamatory version of the life of Peregrinus,[1] to which we have referred.

Lucian assumes from the first that the self-martyrdom of Peregrinus was prompted by mere vulgar love of notoriety.[2] Yet it is quite possible that this is an unfair judgment. The Stoic school, with which the Cynics had such a close affinity, allowed that, in certain circumstances, suicide might be not only a permissible, but a meritorious, nay, even a glorious act of self-liberation.[3] Seneca had often looked gladly to it as the ever open door of escape from ignominy or torture. The brilliant Stoic Euphrates, the darling of Roman society, weary of age and disease, sought and obtained the permission of Hadrian to drink the hemlock.[4] And that emperor himself, in his last sickness, begged the drug from his physician who killed himself to escape compliance.[5] Diogenes had handed the dagger to his favourite pupil, Antisthenes, when tortured by disease.[6] The burden of the Cynic preaching was the nothingness of the things of sense and contempt for death. Is it not possible that what Lucian heard from the lips of Peregrinus himself was true, and that he wished, it may be with mingled motives, by his own act to show men how to treat with indifference the last terror of humanity?

That the end of Peregrinus was surrounded by superstition and magnified by grandiose effects is more than probable. Such things belonged to the spirit of the age. And the calm, critical good sense of Lucian, which had no sympathy with these weaknesses, saw nothing in the scene but calculating imposture. Already oracles were circulating in which Pere-

[1] Luc. *De Morte Peregr.* c. 7 sqq.

[2] *Ib.* c. 4, εἰς κενοδοξίαν τινὲς τοῦτο ἀναφέρουσι.

[3] Sen. *Ep.* 58, § 36; 70, § 8; *De Prov.* ii. 10; vi. § 7; *De Ira*, iii. 15; *De V. Beat.* 19; Epict. i. 24. Cf. Plin. *Ep.* i. 12; i. 22; iii. 7; iii. 9; vi. 24; Boissier, *L'Opp.* p. 212 sqq.

[4] D. Cass. lxix. 8, καὶ ὁ Εὐφράτης ὁ φιλόσοφος ἀπέθανεν ἐθελοντής, ἐπιτρέψαντος αὐτῷ καὶ τοῦ Ἀδριανοῦ κωνεῖον διὰ τὸ γῆρας καὶ διὰ τὴν νόσον πιεῖν.

[5] Ael. Spart. *Hadr.* c. 24.

[6] Diog. Laert. vi. 18; cf. vi. 77, for the death of Diogenes himself.

grinus appears as the phœnix, rising unscathed and rejuvenescent from the pyre, predicting that he is to be a guardian spirit of the night, that altars will rise in his honour, and that he will perform miracles of healing. Theagenes blazed abroad a Sibylline verse which bade men, "when the greatest of the Cynics has come to lofty Olympus, to honour the night-roaming hero who is enthroned beside Hephaestus and the princely Hector."[1] Lucian found himself wedged in a dense crowd who came to hear the last apology of the Cynic apostle. Some were applauding, and some denouncing him as an impostor. Lucian could hear little in the melée. But now and then, above the roar, he could hear the pale, tremulous old man tell the surging crowd that, having lived liked Heracles, he must die like Heracles, and mingle with the ether, "bringing a golden life to a golden close."[2] Lucian thought his paleness was due to terror at the nearness of his self-imposed death. It was more probably the result of ascetic fervour and overstrained excitement. The spectacle sent Lucian away in a fit of rather cruel laughter.[3]

The closing scene, which took place two or three miles from Olympia, was ordered with solemn religious effect. It evidently impressed even the sceptic's imagination. A high pyre had been prepared, with torches and faggots ready. As the moon rose, the voluntary victim appeared in the garb of his sect, surrounded by his leading disciples. He then disrobed himself, flung incense on the flame, and, turning to the south, cried aloud—"Daemons of my father and my mother graciously receive me." After these words, he leapt into the blaze which at once enveloped him, and he was seen no more.[4] The Cynic brothers stood long gazing into the pyre in silent grief, until Lucian aroused their anger by some jeers, not, perhaps, in the best taste. On his way back to Olympia, he pondered on the follies of men, and the craving for empty fame.[5] To Lucian there was nothing more in the tragic scene than that. And he amused himself by the way with the creation of a myth, and watching how it would grow. To some who met

[1] Luc. *De Morte Peregr.* c. 29.
[2] *Ib.* c. 33.
[3] *Ib.* c. 34, ἐγὼ δέ, εἰκάζεις, οἶμαι, πῶς ἐγέλων. *v.* Baur's view of this piece (*Ch. Hist.* ii. 170). He thinks the self-immolation of Peregrinus pure fiction, and that Lucian's object throughout was to discredit Christianity.
[4] Luc. *De Morte Peregr.* c. 36.
[5] *Ib.* c. 38.

him on the road, too late for the spectacle, he told how, as the pyre burst into flame, there was a great earthquake accompanied by subterranean thunder, and a vulture rose from the fire, proclaiming in a high human voice, as it winged its way heavenwards, "I have left earth behind, and I go to Olympus."[1] The poor fools, on whose credulity Lucian was rather heartlessly playing, with a shudder of awe fell to questioning him whether the bird flew to the east or the west. And, on his return to Olympia, he was rewarded in the way he liked best, by finding the tale which he had cradled already full grown. A venerable man, whom he encountered, related that with his own eyes he had seen the vulture rising from the pyre, and added that he had just met Peregrinus himself walking in the "seven-voiced cloister," clothed in white raiment, and with a chaplet of olive on his head.[2]

Lucian's picture of the death of Peregrinus, whatever we may think of its fairness and discernment, is immensely valuable for many things besides the light which it casts on Lucian's attitude to all forms of extravagance and superstition. In spite of his contempt for them, he himself reveals that the Cynics were a great popular force. We see also that Cynicism was, in spite of its generally deistic spirit, sometimes leagued with real or affected religious sentiment. As to the real character of Peregrinus, there is reason to believe that Lucian did not read it aright. The impression which the Cynic made on Aulus Gellius was very different. When Gellius was at Athens in his student days, he used often to visit Peregrinus, who was then living in a little hut in the suburbs, and he found the Cynic's discourses profitable and high-toned. In particular, Peregrinus used to tell his hearers that the chance of apparent evasion or concealment would never tempt the wise man to sin. Concealment was really impossible, for, in the words of Sophocles, "Time, the all-seeing, the all-hearing, lays bare all secrets." Evidently Peregrinus had other admirers besides the Cynic brethren who hailed his apotheosis at Olympia.[3] Who can draw the line, in such an age, between the fanatic and the impostor?

The bitterness with which Lucian assails the Cynics

[1] Luc. *De Morte Peregr.* c. 39.
[2] *Ib.* c. 40.
[3] A. Gell. xii. 11, virum gravem atque constantem vidimus . . . deversantem in quodam tugurio extra urbem.

of his day, while it was justified by the scandalous morals of a certain number, is also a testimony to the world-wide influence of the sect. The ranks of these rude field-preachers would not have attracted so many impostors if the profession had not commanded great power and influence over the masses. The older Cynicism, which sprang from the simpler and more popular aspect of the Socratic teaching, had long disappeared. Its place was taken by the Stoic system, which gave a broad and highly elaborated scientific basis to the doctrine of the freedom and independence of the virtuous will. The rules of conduct were deduced from a well-articulated theory of the universe and human nature, and they were expounded with all the dexterity of a finished dialectic. The later Stoicism, as we have seen, like the other schools, tended to neglect theory, in the effort to form the virtuous character—a tendency which is seen at its height in Musonius and Epictetus. But, as Stoicism became less scientific, it inclined to return more and more to the spirit and method of the older Cynicism. The true, earnest Cynic seems to be almost the philosophic ideal of Epictetus. Thus it was that, in the first century after Christ, Cynicism emerged from its long obscurity to take up the part of a rather one-sided popular Stoicism. It was really pointed or sensational preaching of a few great moral truths, common to all the schools, which the condition of society urgently called for.[1]

The ideal of the Cynic life has been painted with gentle enthusiasm by Epictetus.[2] The true Cynic is a messenger from Zeus, to tell men that they have wandered far from the right way, that they are seeking happiness in regions where happiness is not to be found. It is not to be found in the glory of consulships, or in the Golden House of Nero.[3] It lies close to us, yet in the last place where we ever seek it, in ourselves, in the clear vision of the ruling faculty, in freedom from the bondage to imagined good, to the things of sense.[4] This preaching was also to be preaching by example.

[1] Zeller, *Phil der. Griech.* iii. 1, p. 685 ; Bernays, *Luc. u. die Kyniker*, p. 27 sq.

[2] Epict. *Diss.* iii. 22, § 23, ἀλλ' εἰδέναι δεῖ ὅτι ἄγγελος ἀπὸ Διὸς ἀπέσταλται πρὸς τοὺς ἀνθρώπους, περὶ ἀγαθῶν καὶ κακῶν ὑποδείξων αὐτοῖς ὅτι πεπλάνηνται καὶ ἀλλαχοῦ ζητοῦσι τὴν οὐσίαν τοῦ ἀγαθοῦ ὅπου οὐκ ἔστιν, ὅπου δ' ἔστιν οὐκ ἐνθυμοῦνται κτλ.

[3] *Ib.* iii. 22, §§ 28–30.

[4] *Ib.* § 38, ὅπου οὐ δοκεῖτε οὐδὲ θέλετε ζητῆσαι αὐτό. εἰ γὰρ ἠθέλετε, εὕρετε ἂν ἐν ὑμῖν ὃν κτλ.

The gospel of renunciation has been discredited from age to age when it has come from the lips of a man lapped in downy comfort, who never gave up anything in his life, and who indolently points his flock to the steep road which he never means to tread with his own feet. But the Cynic of Epictetus, with a true vocation, could point to himself, without home or wife or children, without a city, without possessions, having forsaken all for moral freedom.[1] He has done it at the call of God, not from mere caprice, or a fancy to wander lawlessly on the outskirts of society.[2] He has done it because the condition of the world demands such stern self-restraint in the chief who would save the discipline of an army engaged in desperate battle. It is a combat like the Olympian strife which he has to face, and woe to him who enters the lists untrained and unprepared.[3] The care of wife and children is not for one who has laid upon him the care of the family of man, who has to console and admonish, and guide them into the right way.[4] All worldly loves and entanglements must be put aside by one who claims to be the "spy and herald of God." The Cynic is the father of all men; the men are his sons, the women his daughters.[5] When he rebukes them, it is as a father in God, a minister of Zeus. Nor may he take a part in the government of any earthly state, which is a petty affair in comparison with the ministry with which he is charged. How should he meddle with the administration of Athens or Corinth, who has to deal with the moral fortunes of the whole commonwealth of man.[6] Possessing in himself the secret of happiness and woe, he never descends into the vulgar contest, where he may be overcome by the vilest and poorest spirits, for objects which he has trained himself to regard as absolutely indifferent or worthless. And so, he is proof against the spitefulness of fortune and the baseness or violence of man. He will calmly suffer blows or insults as sent by Zeus, just as Heracles bore cheerfully and triumphantly the toils which were laid on him by Eurystheus. The true Cynic will even love those who buffet and insult him.[7] He will also resemble his patron hero

[1] Epict. *Diss.* iii. 22, § 47, ἴδετέ με, ὅτι ἄπολίς εἰμι, ἄοικος, ἀκτήμων, ἄδουλος.

[2] *Ib.* § 56, Κυνικῷ δὲ Καῖσαρ τίς ἐστιν ἢ ὁ καταπεπομφὼς αὐτὸν καὶ ᾧ λατρεύει, ὁ Ζεύς.

[3] *Ib.* § 52.

[4] *Ib.* § 67.

[5] *Ib.* § 81, πάντας ἀνθρώπους πεπαιδοποίηται, τοὺς ἄνδρας υἱοὺς ἔχει, τὰς γυναῖκας θυγατέρας.

[6] *Ib.* § 84.

[7] *Ib.* § 100.

in the fresh comely strength of his body, which is the gift of temperance and long days passed under the open sky.[1] Above all, he will have a conscience clearer than the sun, so that, at peace with himself and having assurance of the friendship of the gods, he may be able to speak with all boldness to his brothers and his children.[2] This was the kind of moral ministry which was needed by the age, and, in spite of both undeserved calumny, and the real shame of many corrupt impostors in its ranks, the missionary movement of Cynicism was one of undoubted power and range. The resemblance, in many points, of the Cynics to the early Christian monks and ascetics has been often noticed, and men sometimes passed from the one camp to the other without any violent wrench.[3] The rhetor Aristides, in a fierce attack on the Cynic sect, makes it a reproach that they have much in common with "the impious in Palestine." Tatian, and others of the Gnostic ascetics, were in close connection with leading Cynics.[4] How easily they were absorbed into the bosom of the Church we can see from the tale of Maximus, an Egyptian Cynic of the fourth century, who continued to wear the distinctive marks of the philosophic brotherhood, till he was installed as bishop of Constantinople.[5] And the contemporary eulogies of Cynic virtue by John Chrysostom and Themistius testify at once to the importance of a movement the strength of which was not spent till after the fall of the Western Empire, and to its affinities for the kindred movement of Christian asceticism.

These "ambassadors of God," as they claimed to be, cared little, like S. Paul, for "the wisdom of the world," or for the figments of the poets, and those great cosmic theories which enabled Seneca to sustain or rekindle his moral faith. With rare exceptions, such as Oenomaus of Gadara, they seldom committed their ideas to writing.[6] For the serried dialectic of the Stoics they substituted the sharp biting epigram and lively repartee, in which even the gentle Demonax indulged.[7] Demetrius, who saw the reigns of both Caligula and Domitian,[8] was a man of real power and distinction. He was revered by

[1] Epict. iii. 22, §§ 86, 87.

[2] *Ib.* § 93, *πρὸ πάντων δὲ τὸ ἡγεμονικὸν αὐτοῦ δεῖ καθαρώτερον εἶναι τοῦ ἡλίου.*

[3] Bernays, *Luc. u. die Kyniker*, pp. 36–38.

[4] *Ib.* p. 99.

[5] *Ib.* p. 37; Caspari, *De Cyn.* p. 25.

[6] *Ib.* p. 5.

[7] Luc. (?) *Dem.* c. 16–21.

[8] Sen. *Ben.* vii. 11; Philostr. *Apoll. T.* vii. 42.

Seneca as a moral teacher of remarkable influence, "a great man even if compared with the greatest,"[1] who lived up to the severest counsels which he addressed to others. He would bear cold and nakedness and hard lodging with cheerful fortitude; he was a man whom not even the age of Nero could corrupt. His poverty was genuine, and he would never beg.[2] He set little store by philosophical theory, in comparison with diligent application of a few tried and well-conned precepts.[3] Yet he had the brand of culture, and once, when his taste was offended by a bad, tactless reader, who was ruining a passage in the *Bacchae*, he snatched the book from his hands and tore it in pieces.[4] Although he disdained the trimmed, artificial eloquence of the schools, he had the fire and impetus of the true orator.[5] With little taste for abstract musings, he consoled the last hours of Thrasea in prison with a discourse on the nature of the soul and the mystery of its severance from the body at death.[6] He formed a close alliance for a time with that roaming hierophant of philosophy, Apollonius of Tyana, the bond between them being probably a common asceticism and a common hatred of the imperial tyranny.[7] For Demetrius, if not a revolutionary, was a leader of the philosophic opposition, which assailed the emperors, not so much in their political capacity, as because they too often represented and stimulated the moral lawlessness and materialism of the age. Our sympathies must be with Demetrius when he boldly faced the dangerous scowl of Nero with the *mot*, "You threaten me with death, but nature threatens you."[8] But our sympathies will be rather with Vespasian, the plain old soldier, who, when Demetrius openly insulted him, treated the "Cynic bark" with quiet contempt.[9] In truth, the Flavian emperors, till the expulsion of the philosophers by Domitian, seem to have been on the whole indulgent to the outspoken freedom of the Cynics.[10] Occasionally, however, the daring censor had, in the interests of

[1] Sen. *Ben.* vii. i. 3, vir meo judicio magnus etiamsi maximis comparetur; vii. 8, 2.

[2] Id. *Ep.* 20, 9; *Vit. B.* xviii. 3.

[3] Id. *De Ben.* vii. 1, § 3, egregia hoc dicere solet, Plus prodesse, si pauca praecepta sapientiae teneas, sed illa in promptu tibi sint, etc.

[4] Luc. *Adv. Indoct.* 19.

[5] Sen. *De Ben.* vii. 8, 2.

[6] Tac. *Ann.* xvi. 34.

[7] Philostr. *Apoll. Tyan.* iv. 25, 42; vi. 13; viii. 10; vii. 42.

[8] Epict. *Diss.* i. 25, § 22, ἀπειλεῖς μοι θάνατον σοὶ δ' ἡ φύσις.

[9] Suet. *Vesp.* xiii. philosophorum contumaciam lenissime tulit; *Dom.* x.; D. Cass. lxvi. 13.

[10] Bernays, *Luc. u. die Kyniker*, p. 29.

authority, to be restrained. Once, when Titus was in the theatre, with the Jewess Berenice by his side, a Cynic, bearing the name of the founder of the sect, gave voice in a long bitter oration to popular feeling against what was regarded as a shameful union. This Cynic John the Baptist, got off with a scourging.[1] A comrade named Heros, however, repeated the offensive expostulation, and lost his head. Peregrinus, for a similar attack on Antoninus Pius, was quietly warned by the prefect to leave the precincts of Rome. In the third century there was a great change in the political fortunes and attitude of the sect; Cynics are even found basking in imperial favour, and lending their support to the imperial power.[2]

The Cynics, from the days of Antisthenes, had poured contempt on the popular religion and the worship of material images of the Divine. They were probably the purest monotheists that classical antiquity produced.[3] Demetrius is almost Epicurean in his belief in eternal Fate, and his contempt for the wavering wills and caprices which mythological fancy ascribed to the Olympian gods.[4] Demonax, the mildest and most humane member of the school in imperial times, refused to offer sacrifices or even to seek initiation in the Mysteries of Eleusis.[5] When he was impeached for impiety before the Athenian courts, he replied that, as for sacrifices, the Deity had no need of them, and that touching the Mysteries, he was in this dilemma : if they contained a revelation of what was good for men, he must in duty publish it; if they were bad and worthless, he would feel equally bound to warn the people against the deception. But the most fearless and trenchant assailant of the popular theology among the Cynics was Oenomaus of Gadara, in the reign of Hadrian.[6] Oenomaus rejected, with the frankest scorn, the anthropomorphic fables of heathenism. In particular, he directed his fiercest attacks against the revival of that faith in oracles and divination which was a marked characteristic of the Antonine age. Plutarch, in a charming walk

[1] D. Cass. lxvi. 15.

[2] Luc. *De Morte Peregr.* c. 19; the attempt of Peregrinus in Greece is probably referred to in Jul. Capitol. *Ant. P.* 5, § 5; cf. Bernays, p. 30; Caspari, *De Cyn.* p. 15.

[3] Bernays, p. 31.

[4] Sen. *De Prov.* 5, §§ 5–7.

[5] Luc. *Dem.* c. 11; Oenom. *Fr.* 13, οὐκ ἀθάνατοι, ἀλλὰ λίθινοι καὶ ξύλινοι δεσπόται ἀνθρώπων, 14; cf. Julian, *Or.* vii. 204, *a.*

[6] Caspari, *De Cyn.* p. 12; Bernays, p. 35; Zeller, *Phil. der Griech.* iii. 1, p. 690.

round the sights of Delphi, in which he acts as cicerone, describes a Cynic named Didymus as assailing the influence of oracles on human character.[1] But Oenomaus, as we know him from Eusebius, was a far more formidable and more pitiless iconoclast than Didymus. He constructed an elaborate historical demonstration to show that the oracles were inspired neither by the gods nor by daemons, but were a very human contrivance to dupe the credulous. And in connection with the subject of oracles, he dealt with the question of free-will, and asserted man's inalienable liberty, and the responsibility for all his actions which is the necessary concomitant of freedom. Oenomaus treated Dodona and Delphi with such jaunty disrespect that, at the distance of a century and a half, his memory aroused the anger of Julian to such a degree, that the imperial champion of paganism could hardly find words strong enough to express his feelings.[2] Oenomaus is a wretch who is cutting at the roots, not only of all reverence for divine things, but of all those moral instincts implanted in our souls by God, which are the foundation of all right conduct and justice. For such fellows no punishment could be too severe; they are worse than brigands and wreckers.[3]

The resolute rejection of the forms of popular worship, and of the claims of divination, is hardly less marked in the mild and tolerant Demonax.[4] Demonax, whose life extended probably from 50 to 150 A.D.,[5] sprang from a family in Cyprus of some wealth and distinction, and had a finished literary culture.[6] But he had conceived from childhood a passion for the philosophic life, according to the ideal of that age. His teachers were Cynics or Stoics, but in speculative opinion he was broadly Eclectic. In his long life he had associated with Demetrius and Epictetus, Apollonius and Herodes Atticus.[7] When asked once who was his favourite philosopher, he replied that he reverenced Socrates, admired Diogenes, and loved Aristippus.[8] His tone had perhaps the greatest affinity for the simplicity of

[1] Plut. *De Def. Or.* vii.

[2] Julian, *Or.* vii. 209.

[3] Jul. vii. 209, 210, *διαφέρουσι γὰρ οὗτοί τι τῶν ἐπ' ἐρημίας ληστευόντων καὶ κατειληφότων τὰς ἀκτὰς ἐπὶ τῷ λυμαίνεσθαι τοῖς καταπλέουσι.*

[4] Bernays, *Luc. u. die Kyniker*, p. 104, agrees with Bekker that the *Demonax* can hardly be a genuine work of Lucian. But its author was a contemporary and friend of Demonax (c. i. *ἐπὶ μήκιστον συνεγενόμην*).

[5] Zeller, *Phil. der Griech.* iii. 1, p. 691, n. 6.

[6] Luc. *Dem.* c. 3 sqq.

[7] *Ib.* c. 3, 24, 31.

[8] *Ib.* c. 62.

the Socratic teaching. But he did not adopt the irony of the master, which, if it was a potent arm of dialectic, often left the subject of it in an irritated and humiliated mood. Demonax was a true Cynic in his contempt for ordinary objects of greed and ambition,[1] in the simple, austere fashion of his daily life, and in the keen epigrammatic point, often, to our taste, verging on rudeness, with which he would expose pretence and rebuke any kind of extravagance.[2] But although he cultivated a severe bodily discipline, so as to limit to the utmost his external wants, he carefully avoided any ostentatious singularity of manner to win a vulgar notoriety. He had an infinite charity for all sorts of men, excepting only those who seemed beyond the hope of amendment.[3] His counsels were given with an Attic grace and brightness which sent people away from his company cheered and improved, and hopeful for the future. Treating error as a disease incident to human nature, he attacked the sin, but was gentle to the sinner.[4] He made it his task to compose the feuds of cities and to stimulate unselfish patriotism; he reconciled the quarrels of kinsmen; he would, on occasion, chasten the prosperous, and comfort the failing and unfortunate, by reminding both alike of the brief span allotted to either joy or sorrow, and the long repose of oblivion which would soon set a term to all the agitations of sorrow or of joy.[5]

But there was another side to his teaching. Demonax was no supple, easy-going conformist to usages which his reason rejected. Early in his career, as has been said, he had to face a prosecution before the tribunals of Athens, because he was never seen to sacrifice to the gods, and declined initiation at Eleusis. In each case, he defended his nonconformity in the boldest tone.[6] To a prophet whom he saw plying his trade for hire, he put the dilemma: "If you can alter the course of destiny, why do you not demand higher fees? If everything happens by the decree of God, where is the value of your art?"[7] When asked if he believed the soul to be immortal, he answered, "It is as immortal as everything else."[8] He derided, in almost brutal style, the effeminacy of the sophist Favorinus, and the extravagant grief of Herodes Atticus for his son.[9] He ruth-

[1] Luc. (?) *Dem.* c. 5, 6.
[2] *Ib.* c. 14.
[3] *Ib.* c. 7.
[4] *Ib.* 6.
[5] *Ib.* 9, 10.
[6] *Ib.* c. 11, τραχύτερον ἢ κατὰ τὴν ἑαυτοῦ προαίρεσιν ἀπελογήσατο.
[7] *Ib.* c. 37.
[8] *Ib.* 32.
[9] *Ib.* c. 12, 24.

lessly exposed the pretences of sham philosophy wherever he met it. When a youthful Eclectic professed his readiness to obey any philosophic call, from the Academy, the Porch, or the Pythagorean discipline of silence, Demonax cried out, "Pythagoras calls you."[1] He rebuked the pedantic archaism of his day by telling an affected stylist that he spoke in the fashion of Agamemnon's time.[2] When Epictetus advised him to marry and become the father of a line of philosophers, he asked the celibate preacher to give him one of his daughters.[3] The Athenians, from a vulgar jealousy of Corinth, proposed to defile their ancient memories by establishing gladiatorial shows under the shadow of the Acropolis. Demonax, in the true spirit of Athens from the time of Theseus, advised them first to sweep away the altar of Pity.[4]

Demonax lived to nearly a hundred years. He is said never to have had an enemy. He was the object of universal deference whenever he appeared in public. In his old age he might enter any Athenian house uninvited, and they welcomed him as their good genius. The children brought him their little presents of fruit and called him father, and as he passed through the market, the baker-women contended for the honour of giving him their loaves. He died a voluntary death, and wished for no tomb save what nature would give him. But the Athenians were aware that they had seen in him a rare apparition of goodness; they honoured him with a splendid and imposing burial and mourned long for him. And the bench on which he used to sit when he was weary they deemed a sacred stone, and decked it with garlands long after his death.[5]

Demonax, by a strange personal charm, attained to an extraordinary popularity and reverence. But the great mass of philosophic preachers had to face a great deal of obloquy and vulgar contempt. Apart from the coarseness, arrogance, and inconsistency of many of them, which gave just offence, their very profession was an irritating challenge to a pleasure-loving and worldly age. Men who gloried in the splendour of their civic life, and were completely absorbed in it, who

[1] Luc. (?) *Dem.* c. 14, *οὗτος, ἔφη, προσειπὼν τὸ ὄνομα, καλεῖ σε Πυθαγόρας.*

[2] *Ib.* c. 26, *σὺ δέ μοι ὡς ἐπ' Ἀγαμέμνονος ἀποκρίνῃ.*

[3] *Ib.* c. 55.

[4] *Ib.* c. 57.

[5] *Ib.* c. 63 sqq.

were flattered and cajoled by their magistrates and popular leaders, could hardly like to be told by the vagrant, homeless teacher, in beggar's garb, that they were ignorant and perverted and lost in a maze of deception. They would hardly be pleased to hear that their civilisation was an empty show, without a solid core of character, that their hopes of happiness from a round of games and festivals, from the splendour of art in temples and statues, were the merest mirage. The message *Beati pauperes spiritu—Beati qui lugent*, will never be a popular one. That was the message to his age of the itinerant Cynic preacher, and his unkempt beard and ragged cloak and the fashion of his life made him the mark of cheap and abundant ridicule. Sometimes the contempt was deserved; no great movement for the elevation of humanity has been free from impostors. Yet the severe judgment of the Cynic missionaries on their age is that of the polished orator, who had as great a scorn as Lucian for the sensual or mercenary Cynic, and yet took up the scrip and staff himself, to propagate the same gospel as the Cynics.[1]

Dion Chrysostom was certainly not a Cynic in the academic sense, but he belonged to the same great movement. He sprang from a good family at Prusa in Bithynia.[2] He was trained in all the arts of rhetoric, and taught and practised them in the early part of his life. A suspected friendship led to his banishment in the reign of Domitian, and in his exile, with the *Phaedo* and the *De Falsa Legatione* as his companions, he wandered over many lands, supporting himself often by menial service.[3] He at last found himself in his wanderings in regions where wild tribes of the Getae for a century and a half had been harrying the distant outposts of Hellenic civilisation on the northern shores of the Euxine.[4] The news of the death of Domitian reached a camp on the Danube when Dion was there. The soldiery, faithful to their emperor, were excited and indignant, but, under the spell of Dion's eloquence, they were brought to acquiesce in the accession of the blameless Nerva. Dion at length returned to Rome, and rose to high favour at court. Trajan often

[1] D. Chrys. *Or.* xxxiv. § 2; lxxii. § 2.

[2] Cf. Philostr. *Vit. Soph.* i. 7. For other authorities *v.* Zeller, *Phil. der Griech.* iii. 1, p. 729, n. 1. Martha, *Moralistes sous l'Emp. rom.* 294, gives a good sketch of Dion's career.

[3] D. Chrys. *Or.* xiii. § 1.

[4] Philostr. *Vit. Soph.* i. 7.

invited him to his table, and used to take him as companion in his state carriage, although the honest soldier did not pretend to appreciate Dion's rhetoric.[1]

During his exile, as he tells us, Dion had been converted to more serious views of life. The triumphs of conventional declamation before fashionable audiences lost their glamour. Dion became conscious of a loftier mission to the dim masses of that far-spreading empire through whose cities and wildernesses he was wandering.[2] As to the eyes of Seneca, men seemed to Dion, amid all their fair, cheerful life, to be holding out their hands for help. Wherever he went, he found that, in his beggar's dress, he was surrounded by crowds of people eager to hear any word of comfort or counsel in the doubts and troubles of their lives. They assumed that the poor wanderer was a philosopher. They plied him with questions on the great problem, How to live; and the elegant sophist was thus compelled to find an answer for them and for himself.[3]

Dion never quite shook off the traditions and tone of the rhetorical school. The ambition to say things in the most elegant and attractive style, the love of amplifying, in leisurely and elaborate development, a commonplace and hackneyed theme still clings to him. His eighty orations are many of them rather essays than popular harangues. They range over all sorts of subjects, literary, mythological, and artistic, political and social, as well as purely ethical or religious. But, after all, Dion is unmistakably the preacher of a great moral revival and reform. He cannot be classed definitely with any particular school of philosophy. He is the apostle of Greek culture, yet he admires Diogenes, the founder of the Cynics.[4] If he had any philosophic ancestry, he would probably have traced himself to the Xenophontic Socrates.[5] But he is really the rhetorical apostle

[1] Philostr. *Vit. Soph.* i. 2; ἔλεγε θαμὰ ἐπιστρεφόμενος ἐς τὸν Δίωνα "τί μὲν λέγεις, οὐκ οἶδα, φιλῶ δέ σε ὡς ἐμαυτόν."

[2] D. Chrys. *Or.* xiii. § 6, 9, 10, στολήν τε ταπεινὴν ἀναλαβὼν καὶ τἄλλα κολάσας ἐμαυτὸν ἠλώμην πανταχοῦ.

[3] *Ib.* § 12, πολλοὶ γὰρ ἠρώτων προσιόντες, ὅ τι μοι φαίνοιτο ἀγαθὸν ἢ κακόν. ὥστε ἠναγκαζόμην φροντίζειν ὑπὲρ τούτων ἵνα ἔχοιμι ἀποκρίνεσθαι τοῖς ἐρωτῶσιν. With the conversion of Dion cf. that of Isaeus and Polemon, etc., Philostr. *Vit. Soph.* i. p. 218; *Apoll. Tyan.* i. 13; iv. 20; Epict. iii. 1; Diog. Laert. iv. 3, § 1.

[4] D. Chrys. *Or.* xxxvii. § 25; iv. § 1; vi.

[5] *Or.* liv.; xiii. § 13, 14, ἐνίοτε ὑπὸ ἀπορίας ᾖα ἐπί τινα λόγον ἀρχαῖον λεγόμενον ὑπό τινος Σωκράτους κτλ.: cf. xviii. § 14, πάντων ἄριστος ἐμοὶ καὶ λυσιτελέστατος πρὸς ταῦτα πάντα Ξενοφῶν.

of the few great moral principles which were in the air, the common stock of Platonist, Stoic, Cynic, even the Epicurean. Philosophy to him is really a religion, the science of right living in conformity to the will of the Heavenly Power. But it is also the practice of right living. No Christian preacher has probably ever insisted more strongly on the gulf which separates the commonplace life of the senses from the life devoted to a moral ideal.[1] The only philosophy worth the name is the earnest quest of the path to true nobility and virtue, in obedience to the good genius, the unerring monitor within the breast of each of us, in whose counsels lies the secret of happiness properly so called.[2] Hence Dion speaks with the utmost scorn alike of the coarse Cynic impostor, who disgraces his calling by buffoonery and debauchery,[3] and the philosophic exquisite who tickles the ears of a fashionable audience with delicacies of phrase, but never thinks of trying to make them better men. He feels a sincere indignation at this dilettante trifling, in view of a world which is in urgent need of practical guidance.[4] For Dion, after all his wanderings through the Roman world, has no illusions as to its moral condition. He is almost as great a pessimist as Seneca or Juvenal. In spite of all its splendour and outward prosperity, society in the reign of Trajan seemed to Dion to be in a perilous state. Along with his own conversion came the revelation of the hopeless bewilderment of men in the search for happiness. Dimly conscious of their evil plight, they are yet utterly ignorant of the way to escape from it. They are swept hither and thither in a vortex of confused passions and longings for material pleasures.[5] Material civilisation, without any accompanying moral discipline, has produced the familiar and inevitable result, in an ever-increasing appetite for wealth and enjoyment and showy distinction, which ends in perpetual disillusionment. Dion warns the people of Tarsus that they are all

[1] D. Chrys. *Or.* lxx. § 1, 7; *καθόλου βίος ἄλλος μὲν τοῦ φιλοσοφοῦντος, ἄλλος δὲ τῶν πολλῶν ἀνθρώπων*; cf. xiii. § 33.

[2] *Ib.* xiii. § 28; xxiii. § 7, *οὐκοῦν τὸν τυχόντα ἀγαθοῦ δαίμονος ἡγῇ δικαίως ζῆν καὶ φρονίμως καὶ σωφρόνως*; cf. Epict. i. § 14, *ἐπίτροπον ἑκάστῳ παρέστησε, τὸν ἑκάστου δαίμονα κτλ.* M. Aurel. v. 27.

[3] D. Chrys. *Or.* xxxii. § 9; xxxv. § 2, 3; xxxiv. § 2.

[4] *Or.* xvi. § 2, 3; xxxv. § 8; cf. xiii. § 11, *οἱ μὲν γὰρ πολλοὶ τῶν καλουμένων φιλοσόφων αὑτοὺς ἀνακηρύττουσιν κτλ.*

[5] *Or.* xiii. § 13, 34, *ἐδόκουν δέ μοι πάντες ἄφρονες, φερόμενοι τάντες ἐν ταὐτῷ καὶ περὶ τὰ αὐτά, περί τε χρήματα καὶ δόξας καὶ σωμάτων τινὰς ἡδονάς κτλ.*

sunk in a deep sensual slumber, and living in a world of mere dreams, in which the reality of things is absolutely inverted. Their famous river, their stately buildings, their wealth, even their religious festivals, on which they plume themselves, are the merest show of happiness.[1] Its real secret, which lies in temperance, justice, and true piety, is quite hidden from their eyes. When that secret is learnt, their buildings may be less stately, gold and silver will perhaps not be so abundant, there will be less soft and delicate living, there may be even fewer costly sacrifices as piety increases; but there will be a clearer perception of the true values of things, and a chastened temperance of spirit, which are the only security for the permanence of society. And the moralist points his audience to the splendid civilisations of the past that have perished because they were without a soul. Assyria and Lydia, the great cities of Magna Graecia which lived in a dream of luxury, what are they now? And, latest example of all, Macedon, who pushed her conquests to the gates of India, and came into possession of the hoarded treasures of the great Eastern Empires, is gone, and royal Pella, the home of the race, is now a heap of bricks.[2]

It needed a courage springing from enthusiasm and conviction to preach such unpalatable truths to an age which gloried in its material splendour. Dion is often conscious of the difficulty of his task; and he exerts all his trained dexterity to appease opposition, and gain a hearing for his message.[3] As regards the reform of character, Dion has no new message to deliver. His is the old gospel of renunciation for the sake of freedom, the doctrine of a right estimate of competing objects of desire and of the true ends of life. Dion, like nearly all Greek moralists from Socrates downwards, treats moral error and reform as rather a matter of the intellect than of emotional impulse. Vice is the condition of a besotted mind, which has lost the power of seeing things as they really are;[4]

[1] *Or.* xxxiii. § 17, 23, 32; cf. the ghastly exposure in *Or.* vii. § 133.

[2] *Or.* xxxiii. §§ 24–28, *εἴ τις διέρχοιτο Πέλλαν οὐδὲ σημεῖον ὄψεται πόλεως, οὐδὲν δίχα τοῦ πολὺν κέραμον εἶναι συντετριμμένον ἐν τῷ τόπῳ.* Cf. xiii. §§ 33, 34.

[3] A good example is the opening of *Or.* xxxii.

[4] *Or.* xiv. § 2; xiii. § 13, *ἐδόκουν δέ μοι πάντες ἄφρονες, κτλ.*: cf. Zeller, *Phil. der Gr.* iii. 1, p. 730, er zeigt mit den Stoikern, dass die wahre Freiheit mit der Vernünftigkeit, die Sklaverei mit der Unvernunft zusammenfalle; cf. *Or.* xvi. § 4.

conversion must be effected, not by appeals to the feelings, but by clarifying the mental vision. There is but little reference to religion as a means of reform, although Dion speaks of the love of God as a support of the virtuous character. As an experienced moral director, Dion knew well the necessity of constant iteration of the old truths. Just as the sick man will violate his doctor's orders, well knowing that he does so to his hurt, so the moral patient may long refuse to follow a principle of life which his reason has accepted.[1] And so the preacher, instead of apologising for repeating himself, will regard it as a duty and a necessity to do so.

But Dion did not aim at the formation of any cloistered virtue, concentrated on personal salvation. He has a fine passage in which he shows that retreat, (ἀναχώρησις) detachment of spirit, is quite possible without withdrawing from the noises of the world.[2] And he felt himself charged with a mission to bring the higher principles of conduct into the civic life of the time. We know from Pliny's correspondence with Trajan, that the great cities of Bithynia, and not least Dion's birthplace,[3] were then suffering from unskilful administration and wasteful finance. Dion completes the picture by showing us their miserable bickerings and jealousies about the most trivial things. He denounces the unscrupulous flattery of the masses by men whose only object was the transient distinction of municipal office, the passion for place and power, without any sober wish to serve or elevate the community. He also exposes the caprice, the lazy selfishness, and the petulant ingratitude of the crowd.[4] Dion, it is true, is an idealist, and his ideals of society are perhaps not much nearer realisation in some of our great cities than they were then. He often delivered his message to the most unpromising audiences. Some of his finest conceptions of social reorganisation were expounded before rude gatherings on the very verge of civilisation.[5] Once, in his wanderings, he found himself under the walls of a half-ruined Greek town, which had been attacked, the day before, by a horde of Scythian barbarians. There, on the steps of the temple of Zeus, he

[1] *Or.* xvii. 2, 3.

[2] *Or.* xx. § 8, μὴ οὖν βελτίστη καὶ λυσιτελεστάτη πασῶν ἡ εἰς αὑτὸν ἀναχώρησις κτλ. Hatch, *Hib. Lec.* p. 150.

[3] Plin. *Ep.* x. 17, 23, 24, 58; Bury, *Rom. Emp.* p. 439.

[4] D. Chrys. *Or.* xxxiv. § 10, 14, 48; xxxviii. § 11; xxxiv. § 16, 19, 29, 31.

[5] *Ib.* xxxvi.

expounded to an eager throng of mean Greek traders, with all the worst vices, and only some faded traces of the culture of their race, the true meaning of city life.[1] It is a society of men under the kingship of law, from which all greed, intemperance, and violence have been banished; a little world which, in its peaceful order and linked harmonies, should be modelled on the more majestic order of the great city of the universe, the city of gods and men.

How far from their ideal were the cities of his native land, Dion saw only too well. The urban life of Asia, as the result of the Greek conquests, has perhaps never been surpassed in external splendour and prosperity, and even in a diffusion of intellectual culture. The palmy days of the glorious springtime of Hellenic vigour and genius in Miletus, Phocaea, and Rhodes, seemed to be reproduced even in inland places, which for 1500 years have returned to waste.[2] Agriculture and trade combined to produce an extraordinary and prosperous activity. Education was endowed and organised, and literary culture became almost universal.[3] Nowhere did the wandering sophist find more eager audiences, and no part of the Roman world in that age contributed so great a number of teachers, physicians, and philosophers. The single province of Bithynia, within half a century, could boast of such names as Arrian, Dion Cassius, and Dion Chrysostom himself. But moral and political improvement did not keep pace with an immense material and intellectual progress. The life of the cities indeed was very intense; but, in the absence of the wider interests of the great days of freedom, they wasted their energies in futile contests for visionary distinctions and advantages. A continual struggle was going on for the "primacy" of the province, and the name of metropolis. Ephesus, the real capital, was challenged by Smyrna, which on its coins describes itself as "first in greatness and beauty."[4] The feuds between Nicomedia and its near neighbour Nicaea caused Dion particular anxiety, and his speech

[1] D. Chrys. *Or.* xxxvi. § 15, 8, 9, πάντες οἱ Βορυσθενῖται περὶ τὸν ποιητὴν ἐσπουδάκασιν κτλ. Cf. § 20, 23.

[2] Momms. *Rom. Prov.* i. pp. 326, 354; cf. Aristid. *Or.* xiv. xv. 223–230 (Dind.).

[3] Momms. *Rom. Prov.* i. p. 362; cf. Philostr. *Apoll. Tyan.* i. 7; *Vit. Soph.* i. p. 220, καὶ προβήσεσθαι ἐπὶ μέγα τὰς Κλαζομενὰς ἡγουμένων εἰ τοιοῦτος δὴ ἀνὴρ ἐμπαιδεύσοι σφισὶν κτλ.

[4] Momms. *Rom. Prov.* i. pp. 329, 330; cf. Aristid. *Or.* xv.; Philostr. *Apoll. Tyan.* iv. 7, φρονεῖν ἐκέλευεν ἐφ' ἑαυτοῖς μᾶλλον ἢ τῷ τῆς πόλεως εἴδει. D. Chrys. *Or.* xxxiv. 48; Friedl. *Sitteng.* iii. p. 111.

to the people of Nicomedia is the best picture of the evils which we are describing.[1]

The two cities have much in common. Their families have intermarried; they are constantly meeting in their markets and great religious festivals. They are bound together by innumerable ties of private friendship.[2] The primacy for which they contend is the merest figment; there are no material advantages at stake. Rather, these dissensions give a corrupt Roman governor, who trades upon them, the power to injure both the rival claimants.[3] The same is true of other cities. Tarsus is engaged in bitter contention with Mallus for a mere line of sandhills on their frontiers.[4] Dion's native Prusa has an exasperated quarrel with Apamea for no solid reason whatever, although the two towns are closely linked by nature to one another, and mutually dependent through their trade and manufactures. All this miserable and foolish jealousy Dion exposes with excellent skill and sense; and he employs an abundant wealth of illustration in painting the happiness which attends harmony and good-will. It is the law of the universe, from the tiny gregarious insect whose life is but for a day, to the eternal procession of the starry spheres. The ant, in the common industry of the Lilliputian commonwealth, yields to his brother toiler, or helps him on his way.[5] The primal elements of the Cosmos are tempered to a due observance of their several bounds and laws. The sun himself hides his splendour each night to give place to the lesser radiance of the stars. This is rhetoric, of course, but it is rhetoric with a moral burden. And it is impossible not to admire the lofty tone of this heathen sophist, preaching the duty of forgiveness, of mutual love and deference, the blessing of the quiet spirit "which seeketh not her own, is not easily provoked, thinketh no evil."[6] There is a certain pathos in remembering that, within the very walls where these elevated orations were delivered, there were shy companies of men and women meeting in the early dawn to sing hymns to One who, three generations before in Galilee, had taught a similar gospel of love

[1] D. Chrys. *Or.* xxxviii. § 7, 31, 36.

[2] *Ib.* xl. § 27, ἡ δὲ τῶν ἐγγὺς οὕτως καὶ ὁμόρων διαφορὰ καὶ τὸ μῖσος οὐδὲν ἄλλο ἔοικεν ἢ στάσει μιᾶς πόλεως ὅπου καὶ γάμων κοινωνία, κτλ.

[3] *Ib.* xxxviii. §§ 26–31.

[4] *Ib.* xxxiv. §§ 44–48, αἱ μὲν οὖν θῖνες καὶ τὸ πρὸς τῇ λίμνῃ χωρίον οὐδενὸς ἄξια.

[5] *Ib.* xl. § 35.

[6] *Ib.* xxxviii. §§ 42–46.

and self-suppression, but with a strange mystic charm, denied to the pagan eloquence, and that Dion seems never to have known those with whom he had so close a kindred.[1]

In many another oration Dion strove to raise the moral tone of his age. His speech to the Alexandrians is probably his most gallant protest against the besetting sins of a great population. Alexandria was a congeries of many races, in which probably the Hellenic type of the Ptolemies had succumbed to the enduring Egyptian *morale*.[2] It was a populace at once sensual and superstitious, passionately devoted to all excitement, whether of games or orgiastic religious festival, with a jeering irreverent vein, which did not spare even the greatest Emperors. It was a curious medley—the seat of the most renowned university of the ancient world, the gathering-place and seed-ground of ideas which united the immemorial mysticism of the East with the clear, cold reason of Hellas—and yet a seething hot-bed of obscenity, which infected the Roman world, a mob who gave way to lunatic excitement over the triumph of an actor, or a singer, or the victor in a chariot-race.[3] It required no ordinary courage to address such a crowd, and to charge them with their glaring faults. The people of Alexandria are literally intoxicated with a song. The music which, according to old Greek theory, should regulate the passions, here only maddens them.[4] And in the races all human dignity seems to be utterly lost in the futile excitement of the spectators over some low fellow contending for a prize in solid cash.[5] Such a mob earns only the contempt of its rulers, and men say that the Alexandrians care for nothing but the "big loaf" and the sight of a race.[6] All the dignity which should surround a great people is forgotten in the theatre. It is useless to boast of the majestic and bounteous river, the harbours and markets crowded with the merchandise of Western or Indian seas, of the visitors from every land, from Italy, Greece, and Syria, from the Borysthenes, the Oxus, and the Ganges.[7] They come to witness the shame of the second

[1] Plin. *Ep.* x. 96, § 7.

[2] Mahaffy, *Greek World under Roman Sway*, p. 242; Merivale, viii. p. 239; Momms. *Rom. Prov.* ii. p. 264.

[3] Momms. ii. p. 263; D. Chrys. xxxii.; Tac. *Hist.* iv. 81; Ael. Spart. *Hadr.* c. 12, 14; D. Cass. lxix. 11; Petron. 31, 68.

[4] D. Chrys. *Or.* xxxii. § 57, 41, 51, 55; Pl. *Rep.* iii. 399; Arist. *Pol.* viii. 5.

[5] D. Chrys. *Or.* xxxii. § 75.

[6] *Ib.* § 31, *οἷς μόνον δεῖ παραβάλλειν τὸν πολὺν ἄρτον.*

[7] *Ib.* § 40.

city in the world, which, in the wantonness of prosperity, has lost the temperate dignity and orderly calm that are the real glory of a great people.

As a foil to the feverish life of luxury, quarrelsome rivalry, and vulgar excitement which prevailed in the great towns, Dion has left a prose idyll to idealise the simple pleasures and virtues of the country.[1] It is also a dirge over the decay of Greece, when crops were being reaped in the agora of historic cities, and the tall grasses grew around the statues of gods and heroes of the olden time.[2] A traveller, cast ashore in the wreck of his vessel on the dreaded Hollows of Euboea, was sheltered, in a rude, warm-hearted fashion, by some peasants. Their fathers had been turned adrift in the confiscation of the estate of a great noble in some trouble with the emperor, and they had made themselves a lonely home on a pastoral slope, close to a stream, with the neighbouring shade of trees. They had taken into tillage a few fields around their huts; they drove their cattle to the high mountain pastures in summer time, and in the winter they turned to hunting the game along the snowy tracks. Of city life they know hardly anything. One of them, indeed, had been twice in the neighbouring town, and he tells what he saw there in a lively way. It is all a mere shadow or caricature of the old civic life of Greece. There are the rival orators, patriot or demagogue, the frivolous and capricious crowd, the vote of the privilege of dining in the town-hall. The serious purpose of the piece, however, is to idealise the simple virtue and happiness of the country folk, and to discuss the disheartening problem of the poor in great cities.[3] It is in the main the problem of our modern urban life, and Dion had evidently thought deeply about it, and was an acute observer of the social misery which is the same from age to age. Fortified by the divine Homer and ordinary experience, he points out that the poor are more generous and helpful to the needy than are the rich out of their ample store. Too often the seeming bounty of the wealthy benefactor is of the nature of a loan, which is to be returned with due interest.[4] The struggles and temptations of the poor in great cities suggest a

[1] See an excellent analysis of this piece (vii.) in Mahaffy's *Greek World under Roman Sway*, pp. 277-288.

[2] D. Chrys. *Or.* vii. § 34 sqq.

[3] *Ib.* §§ 105-108.

[4] *Ib.* §§ 82-89, αἱ γὰρ δὴ φιλοφρονήσεις καὶ χάριτες, ἐὰν σκοπῇ τις ὀρθῶς, οὐδὲν διαφέρουσιν ἐράνων καὶ δανείων.

discussion of the perpetual problem of prostitution, which probably no ancient writer ever faced so boldly. The double degradation of humanity, which it involved in the ancient world, is powerfully painted;[1] and the plea that the indulgence in venal immorality is the only alternative to insidious attacks on family virtue is discussed with singular firmness and yet delicacy of touch.[2] The same detachment from contemporary prejudice is shown in Dion's treatment of slavery. He sees its fell effects on the masters, in producing sensuality, languor, and helpless dependence on others for the slightest services. He points out that there is no criterion afforded by nature to distinguish slave and free. The so-called free man of the highest rank may be the offspring of a servile amour, and the so-called slave may be ingenuous in every sense, condemned to bondage by an accident of fortune.[3] Just as external freedom does not imply moral worth, so legal enslavement does not imply moral degradation.[4] If moral justice always fixed the position of men in society by their deserts, master and slave would often have to change places.[5] In Dion's judgment as to the enervating effects of slavery on the slave-owning class, and the absence of any moral or mental distinction to justify the institution, he is in singular harmony with Seneca.

The similarity of tone between Seneca and Dion is perhaps even more marked in their treatment of monarchy. Inherited, like so much else, from the great Greek thinkers of the fifth and fourth centuries B.C., the ideal of a beneficent and unselfish prince, the true "shepherd of the people," the antithesis of the lawless and sensual tyrant, had become, partly, no doubt, through the influence of the schools of rhetoric, a common possession of cultivated minds. Vespasian gave it a certain reality, if his son Domitian showed how easily the king might pass into the tyrant. The dream of an earthly providence, presiding over the Roman world, dawned in more durable splendour with the accession of Trajan, and Pliny, his panegyrist, has left us a sketch of the patriot prince,

[1] D. Chrys. *Or.* vii. § 133; Musonius, Stob. *Flor.* vi. 61; cf. on this subject Denis, *Idées Morales*, etc. ii. p. 134.

[2] D. Chrys. *Or.* vii. § 139.

[3] *Ib.* x. § 13; xv. § 5; 6, 31; cf. Juv. xiv. 16; Sen. *Ben.* iii. 21; *Ep.* 47; cf. Denis, ii. 152; Boissier, *Rel. Rom.* ii. p. 354.

[4] Cf. Newman's *Politics of Aristotle*, Introd. p. 144.

[5] D. Chrys. *Or.* xv. § 31.

which is almost identical with the lines of Dion's ideal.[1] Both Dion and Pliny were favourites of Trajan, and some of Dion's orations were delivered before his court. As a court preacher, he justly boasts that he is no mere flatterer, although we may suspect that his picture of the ideal monarch might have been interpreted as drawn from the character of Trajan, just as his picture of the tyrant was probably suggested by Domitian.[2] Still, we may well believe the orator when he says that the man who had bearded the one at the cost of long exile and penury, was not likely to flatter the other for the gold or honours which he despised. And in these discourses, Dion seems full of the sense of a divine mission. Once, on his wanderings, he lost his way somewhere on the boundaries of Arcadia, and, ascending a knoll to recover the track, he found himself before a rude, ruined shrine of Heracles, hung with votive offerings of the chase.[3] An aged woman sat by them who told him that she had a spirit of divination from the gods. The shepherds and peasants used to come to her with questions about the fate of their flocks and crops. And she now entrusted Dion with a message to the great ruler of many men whom she prophesied Dion was soon to meet.[4] It was a tale of Heracles, the great benefactor of men from the rising to the setting sun, who, by his simple strength, crushed all lawless monsters and gave the world an ordered peace. His father inspired him with noble impulse for his task by oracle and omen, and sent Hermes once, when Heracles was still a boy at Thebes, to show him the vision of the Two Peaks, and strengthen him in his virtue.[5] They rose from the same rocky roots, amid precipitous crags and deep ravines, and the noise of many waters. At first they seemed to be one mountain mass, but they soon parted wide asunder, the one being sacred to Zeus, the other to the lawless Typhon. On the one crest, rising into the cloudless ether, Kingship sits enthroned, in the likeness of a fair, stately woman, clad in robes of glistening white, and wielding a sceptre of brighter and purer metal than any silver or gold. Under her steady gaze of radiant dignity, the good felt a

[1] D. Chrys. *Or.* i. § 13 ; ii. §§ 75–77 ; iii. § 39, 62, 107 ; iv. § 63 ; cf. Plin. *Paneg.* 72, 80, 67 ; Sen. *De Clem.* i. 13, § 4 ; i. 19, § 2.

[2] D. Chrys. *Or.* i. § 79 ; cf. iii. §§ 5, 6.

[3] *Ib.* i. § 52.

[4] *Ib.* § 56.

[5] *Ib.* § 66.

cheerful confidence, the bad quailed and shrank away. She was surrounded by handmaidens of a beauty like her own, Justice and Peace and Order. The paths to the other peak were many and secret, and skirted an abyss, streaming with blood or choked with corpses. Its top was wrapped in mist and cloud, and there sat Tyranny on a far higher and more pompous throne, adorned with gold and ivory and many a gorgeous colour, but a throne rocking and unstable. She strove to make herself like to Kingship, but it was all mere hollow pretence. Instead of the gracious smile, there was a servile, hypocritical leer; instead of the glance of dignity, there was a savage scowl. And around her sat a throng bearing ill-omened names, Cruelty and Lust, Lawlessness and Flattery and Sedition. On a question from Hermes, the youthful Heracles made his choice, and his father gave him his commission to be the saviour of men.

In this fashion Dion, like Aeschylus, recasts old myth to make it the vehicle of moral instruction, just as he finds in Homer the true teacher of kings.[1] The theory of ideal monarchy is developed at such length as may have somewhat wearied the emperor. But it really is based on a few great principles. True kings, in Homer's phrase, are sons of Zeus, and they are shepherds of the people. All genuine political power rests on virtue, and ultimately on the favour of Heaven. A king is appointed by God to work the good of his subjects. And, as his authority is divine, an image on earth of the sovereignty of Zeus, the monarch will be a scrupulously religious man in the highest sense,[2] not merely by offering costly sacrifices, but by righteousness, diligence, and self-sacrifice in performing the duties of his solemn charge. The many titles addressed to Father Zeus represent so many aspects of royal activity and virtue. The true prince will be the father of his people, surrounded and guarded by a loving reverence, which never degenerates into fear. His only aim will be their good. He will keep sleepless watch over the weak, the careless, those who are heedless for themselves. Commanding infinite resources, he will know less of mere pleasure than any man within his realm. With such immense responsibilities, he will be the most laborious of all. His only advantage over the private citizen is in his boundless

[1] *Or.* iv. § 39. [2] *Ib.* iii. §§ 51, 62, *τὸ ἄρχειν οὐδαμῶς ῥᾴθυμον ἀλλ' ἐπίπονον κτλ.*

command of friendship; for all men must be well-wishers to one wielding such a beneficent power, with whom, from his conception of his mission, they must feel an absolute identity of interest. And the king's greatest need is friendship, to provide him with myriads of hands and eyes in the vast work of government.[1] Herein lies the sharpest contrast between the true king and the tyrant, a contrast which was a commonplace in antiquity, but which was stamped afresh by the juxtaposition of the reign of Domitian and the reign of Trajan. The universal hatred which pursued a bad Caesar even beyond the grave, which erased his name from monuments and closed its eyes even to intervals of serious purpose for the general weal, was a terrible illustration of the lonely friendlessness of selfish power.[2] Instead of loyal and grateful friendship, the despot was mocked by a venal flattery which was only its mimicry. The good monarch will treat flatterers as false coiners who cause the genuine currency to be suspected. This counsel and others of Dion were often little regarded by succeeding emperors. Yet even the last shadowy princes of the fifth century professed themselves the guardians of the human race, and are oppressed by an ideal of universal beneficence which they are impotent to realise.[3]

Hitherto we have been occupied with the preaching of Dion on personal conduct, the reform of civic life, or the duties of imperial power. It cannot be said that he discusses these subjects without reference to religious beliefs and aspirations.[4] But religion is rather in the background; the reverence for the Heavenly Powers is rather assumed as a necessary basis for human life rightly ordered. There is one oration, however, of supreme interest to the modern mind, in which Dion goes to the root of all religion, and examines the sources of belief in God and the justification of anthropomorphic imagery in representing Him. This utterance was called forth by a visit to Olympia when Dion was advanced in years.[5] The games of Olympia were a dazzling and

[1] D. Chrys. *Or.* iii. §§ 38, 88, 107.

[2] Sueton. *Dom.* xxxiii.; *Calig.* lx. abolendam Caesarum memoriam ac diruenda templa censuerunt; cf. *Or. Henz.* 698, 699, 767, where the names of Caligula and Domitian have been erased.

[3] *Nov. Valent.* tit. viii.; *Leg. Anthem.* tit. i.; *Nov. Mart.* ii.

[4] D. Chrys. *Or.* vii. § 135, where the gods of pure wedlock are appealed to against vagrant vice.

[5] *Ib.* xii. § 20.

inspiring spectacle, and the multitude which gathered there from all parts of the world was a splendid audience. But, with the sound of the sacred trumpet, and the herald's voice, proclaiming the victor, in his ears, Dion turns away from all the glory of youthful strength and grace, even from the legendary splendour of the great festival,[1] to the majestic figure of the Olympian Zeus, which had been graved by the hand of Pheidias more than 500 years before, and to the thoughts of the divine world which it suggested. That greatest triumph of idealism in plastic art, inspired by famous lines in the *Iliad,* was, by the consent of all antiquity, the masterpiece of Pheidias. Ancient writers of many ages are lost in admiration of the mingled majesty and benignity which the divine effigy expressed. To the eyes of Lucian it seemed "the very son of Kronos brought down to earth, and set to watch over the lonely plain of Elis."[2] There it sat watching for more than 800 years, till it was swept away in the fierce, final effort to dethrone the religion of the past. Yet the majestic image, which attracted the fury of the iconoclasts of the reign of Theodosius, inspired Dion with thoughts of the Divine nature which travelled far beyond the paganism either of poetry or of the crowd. It was not merely the masterpiece of artistic and constructive skill which had fascinated the gaze, and borne the vicissitudes, of so many centuries, that moved his admiration; it was also, and more, the moral effect of that miracle of art on the spectator. The wildest and fiercest of the brute creation might be calmed and softened by the air of majestic peace and kindness which floated around the gold and ivory. "Whosoever among mortal men is most utterly toil-worn in spirit, having drunk the cup of many sorrows and calamities, when he stands before this image, methinks, must utterly forget all the terrors and woes of this mortal life."[3]

But the thoughts of Dion, in presence of the majestic figure at Olympia, take a wider range. His theme is nothing

[1] D. Chrys. *Or.* xii. § 26.

[2] Luc. *De Sacrif.* 11, *οἴονται ὁρᾶν . . . αὐτὸν τὸν Κρόνου καὶ Ῥέας εἰς τὴν γῆν ὑπὸ Φειδίου μετῳκισμένον καὶ τὴν Πισαίων ἐρημίαν ἐπισκοπεῖν κεκελευσμένον.*

[3] *Or.* xii. § 51, *ἀνθρώπων δέ, ὃς ἂν ᾖ παντελῶς ἐπίπονας τὴν ψυχήν, πολλὰς ἀπαντλήσας ξυμφορὰς καὶ λύπας ἐν τῷ βίῳ . . καὶ ὃς δοκεῖ μοι κατεναντίον στὰς τῆσδε τῆς εἰκόνος ἐκλαθέσθαι πάντων ὅσα ἐν ἀνθρωπίνῳ βίῳ δεινὰ καὶ χαλεπὰ γίγνεται παθεῖν.*

less than the sources of our idea of God, and the place of art in religion. He pours his scorn upon hedonistic atheism. Our conception of God is innate, original, universal among all the races of men.[1] It is the product of the higher reason, contemplating the majestic order, minute adaptation, and beneficent provision for human wants in the natural world. In that great temple, with its alternations of gloom and splendour, its many voices of joy or of terror, man is being perpetually initiated in the Great Mysteries, on a grander scale than at Eleusis, with God Himself to preside over the rites. The belief in God depends in the first instance on no human teaching, any more than does the love of child to parent. But this original intuition and belief in divine powers finds expression through the genius of inspired poets; it is reinforced by the imperative prescriptions of the founders and lawgivers of states; it takes external form in bronze or gold and ivory or marble, under the cunning hand of the great artist; it is developed and expounded by philosophy.[2] Like all the deepest thinkers of his time, Dion is persuaded of the certainty of God's existence, but he is equally conscious of the remoteness of the Infinite Spirit, and of the weakness of all human effort to approach, or to picture it to the mind of man. We are to Dion like "children crying in the night, and with no language but a cry."[3] Yet the child will strive to image forth the face of the Father, although it is hidden behind a veil which will never be withdrawn in this world. The genius of poetry, commanding the most versatile power of giving utterance to the religious imagination, is first in order and in power. Law and institution follow in its wake. The plastic arts, under cramping limitations, come later still to body forth the divine dreams of the elder bards. Dion had thought much on the relative power of poetry and the sculptor's art to give expression to the thoughts and feelings of man about the Divine nature. The boundless power or licence of language to find a symbol for every thought or image on the phantasy is seen at its height in Homer, who

[1] *Or.* xii. §§ 27, 28, 33, 42; cf. Sen. *Ep.* 117, § 6, omnibus insita de dis opinio est.

[2] D. Chrys. *Or.* xii. §§ 42, 43.

[3] *Ib.* § 61, *ὥσπερ νήπιοι παῖδες πατρὸς ἢ μητρὸς ἀπεσπασμένοι . . ὀρέγουσι χεῖρας οὐ παροῦσι πολλάκις ὀνειρώττοντες κτλ.*

riots in an almost lawless exercise of his gifts.[1] But the chief importance of the discussion lies in an arraignment of Pheidias for attempting to image in visible form the great Soul and Ruler of the universe, Whom mortal eye has never seen and can never see. His defence is very interesting, both as a clear statement of the limitations of the plastic arts, and as a justification of material images of the Divine.

Pheidias pleads in his defence that the artist could not, if he would, desert the ancient religious tradition, which was consecrated in popular imagination by the romance of poetry;[2] that is fixed for ever. Granted that the Divine nature is far removed from us, and far beyond our ken; yet, as little children separated from their parents, feel a strong yearning for them and stretch out their hands vainly in their dreams, so the race of man, from love and kindred, longs ever to draw nigh to the unseen God by prayer and sacrifice and visible symbol. The ruder races will image their god in trees or shapeless stones, or may seek a strange symbol in some of the lower forms of animal life.[3] The higher may find sublime expression of His essence in the sun and starry spheres. For the pure and infinite mind which has engendered and which sustains the universe of life, no sculptor or painter of Hellas has ever found, or can ever find, full and adequate expression.[4] Hence men take refuge in the vehicle and receptacle of the noblest spirit known to them, the form of man. And the Infinite Spirit, of which the human is an effluence, may perhaps best be embodied in the form of His child.[5] But no effort or ecstasy of artistic fancy, in form or colour, can ever follow the track of the Homeric imagination in its majesty and infinite variety of expression. The sculptor and painter have fixed limits set to their skill, beyond which they cannot pass. They can appeal only to the eye; their material has not the infinite ductility and elasticity of the poetic dialect of many tribes and many generations. They can seize only a single moment of action or passion, and fix it for ever in bronze or stone. Yet Pheidias, with a certain

[1] D. Chrys. *Or.* xii. § 62.

[2] *Ib.* § 56.

[3] *Ib.* § 61; cf. Plut. *De Is. et Osir.* lxxi., lxxii., lxxvi.; Philostr. *Apoll. Tyan.* vi. 19; Max. Tyr. *Diss.* viii. § 5.

[4] D. Chrys. *Or.* xii. § 59, νοῦν γὰρ καὶ φρόνησιν αὐτὴν καθ' αὑτὴν οὔτε τις πλάστης οὔτε τις γραφεὺς εἰκάσαι δυνατὸς ἔσται: Plut. *De Is.* lxxix.

[5] Cf. Max. Tyr. *Diss.* viii. § 3, τὸ μὲν Ἑλληνικὸν τιμᾶν τοὺς θεοὺς ἐνομίσε τῶν ἐν γῇ τοῖς καλλίστοις, ὕλῃ μὲν καθαρᾷ μορφῇ δὲ ἀνθρωπίνῃ τέχνῃ δὲ ἀκριβεῖ.

modest self-assertion, pleads that his conception of the Olympian Zeus, although less various and seductive than Homer's, although he cannot present to the gazer the crashing thunderbolt or the baleful star, or the heaving of Olympus, is perhaps more elevating and inspiring.[1] The Zeus of Pheidias is the peace-loving and gentle providence of an undisturbed and harmonious Greece, the august giver of all good gifts, the father and saviour and guardian of men. The many names by which men call him may each find some answering trait in the laborious work of the chisel. In the lines of that majestic and benign image are shadowed forth the mild king and father, the hearer of prayer, the guardian of civic order and family love, the protector of the stranger, and the power who gives fertile increase to flock and field. The Zeus of Pheidias and of Dion is a God of mercy and peace, with no memory of the wars of the Giants.[2]

Dion is a popular teacher of morality, not a thinker or theologian. But this excursion into the field of theology shows him at his best. And it prepares us for the study of some more formal efforts to find a theology in the poetry of legend.

[1] D. Chrys. *Or.* xii. § 78. [2] *Ib.* §§ 74, 75.

CHAPTER III

THE PHILOSOPHIC THEOLOGIAN

THE times were ripe for a theodicy. Religion of every mood and tone, of every age and clime, was in the air, and philosophy had abandoned speculation and turned to the direction of conduct and spiritual life. The mission of philosophy is to find the one in the many, and never did the religious life of men offer a more bewildering multiplicity and variety, not to say chaos, to the ordering power of philosophy. The scepticism of the Neronian age had almost disappeared. The only rationalists of any distinction in the second century were Lucian and Galen.[1] It was an age of imperious spiritual cravings, alike among the cultivated and the vulgar. But the thin abstractions of the old Latin faith and the brilliant anthropomorphism of Greece had ceased to satisfy even the crowd. It was an age with a longing for a religious system less formal and coldly external, for a religion more satisfying to the deeper emotions, a religion which should offer divine help to human need and misery, divine guidance amid the darkness of time; above all, a divine light in the mystery of death. The glory of classic art had mysteriously closed. It was an age rather of material splendour, and, at first sight, an age of bourgeois ideals of parochial fame and mere enjoyment of the hour. Yet the Antonine age has some claim to spiritual distinction. In the dim, sub-conscious feelings of the masses, as well as in the definite spiritual effort of the higher minds, there was really a great movement towards a ruling principle of conduct and a spiritual vision. Men often, indeed, followed

[1] Friedl. *Sittengesch.* iii. pp. 430, 435; cf. Thiersch, *Politik u. Phil. in ihrem Verhältn. zur Religion*, p. 9.

the marsh-light through strange devious paths into wildernesses peopled with the spectres of old-world superstition. But the light of the Holy Grail had at last flashed on the eyes of some loftier minds. From the early years of the second century we can trace that great combined movement of the new Platonism and the revived paganism,[1] which so long retarded the triumph of the Church, and yet, in the Divinely-guided evolution, was destined to prepare men for it.

The old religion had not lost all hold on men's minds, as it is sometimes said to have done, in rather too sweeping language. The punctilious ritual with which, in the stately narrative of Tacitus, the Capitol was restored by Vespasian, the pious care with which the young Aurelius recited the Salian litany in words no longer understood, the countless victims which he offered to the guardian gods of Rome in evil days of pestilence and doubtful war, these things reveal the strength of the religion of Numa. Two centuries after M. Aurelius was in his grave, the deities which had cradled the Roman state, and watched over its career, were still objects of reverence to the conservative circle of Symmachus. A religion which was intertwined with the whole fabric of government and society, which gave its sanction or benediction to every act and incident in the individual life, which was omnipresent in game and festival, in temple and votive monument, was placed far beyond the influence of changing fashions of devotion. It was a powerful stay of patriotism, a powerful bond of civic and family life; it threw a charm of awe and old-world sanctity around everything it touched. But for the deeper spiritual wants and emotions it furnished little nutriment. To find relief and cleansing from the sense of guilt, cheer and glad exaltation of pious emotion, consolation in the common miseries of life, and hope in the shadow of death, men had to betake themselves to other systems. The oriental religions were pouring in like a flood, and spreading over all the West. One Antonine built a shrine of Mithra,[2] another took the tonsure of Isis.[3] The priests and acolytes of the Egyptian goddess were everywhere, chanting their litanies in solemn processions

[1] Thiersch, *Politik und Philosophie in ihrem Verhältniss zur Religion*, pp. 14, 15.

[2] Réville, *Rel. unter den Sev.* p. 81.

[3] Lamprid. *Commodus*, c. 9.

along the streets, instructing and baptizing their catechumens, and, in the alternating gloom and splendour of their mysteries, bearing the entranced soul to the boundaries of life and death.[1] Mithra, "the Unconquered," was justifying his name. In every district from the Euxine to the Solway he brought a new message to heathendom. Pure from all grossness of myth, the Persian god of light came as the mediator and comforter, to soothe the poor and broken-hearted, and give the cleansing of the mystic blood. His hierarchy of the initiated, his soothing symbolic sacraments, his gorgeous ritual, and his promise of immortality to those who drank the mystic Haoma, gratified and stimulated religious longings which were to find their full satisfaction in the ministry of the Church.

But the religious imagination was not satisfied with historic and accredited systems. Travel and conquest were adding to the spiritual wealth or burden of the Roman race. In lonely Alpine passes, in the deserts of Africa, or the Yorkshire dales, in every ancient wood or secret spring which he passed in his wanderings or campaigns, the Roman found hosts of new divinities, possible helpers or possible enemies, whose favour it was expedient to win.[2] And, where he knew not their strange outlandish names, he would try to propitiate them all together under no name, or any name that pleased them.[3] And, as if this vague multitude of ghostly powers were not large enough for devotion, the fecundity of imagination created a host of genii, of haunting or guarding spirits, attached to every place or scene, to every group or corporation of men which had a place in Roman life. There were genii of the secret spring or grove, of the camp, the legion, the cohort, of the Roman people, above all, there was the genius of the emperor.[4] Apotheosis went on apace—apotheosis not merely of the emperors, but of a theurgic philosopher like Apollonius, of a minion like Antinous, of a mere impostor like Alexander of Abonoteichos.[5] Old oracles, which had been suppressed or decadent in the reign of Nero, sprang into fresh life and popularity in the reign of Trajan. New sources of oracular

[1] Apul. *Met.* xi. c. 11, 22.

[2] *Or. Henz.* 186, 193, 228 sqq., 275, 1637, 1580, 5873, 5879, 5887, 1993.

[3] *C.I.L.* vi. 110, 111.

[4] *Or. Henz.* 6628 (fontis), 4922 (castrorum), 1704 (legionis), 1812 (Neronis), 3953 (Hadriani).

[5] Lamprid. *Alex. Sev.* c. 29; Spart. *Hadr.* 14, § 5; Luc. *Peregr.* c. 29; Friedl. *Sittengesch.* iii. pp. 454–456. Thiersch, *Pol. u. Phil. in Verhältn. zur Rel.* p. 10.

inspiration were opened, some of them challenging for the time the ancient fame of Delphi or Dodona.[1] According to Lucian, oracles were pealing from every rock and every altar.[2] Every form of revelation or divination, every avenue of access to the Divine, was eagerly sought for, or welcomed with pious credulity. The study of omens and dreams was reduced to the form of a pseudo-science by a host of writers like Artemidorus. The sacred art of healing through visions of the night found a home in those charming temples of Asclepius, which rose beside so many hallowed springs, with fair prospect and genial air, where the god revealed his remedy in dreams, and a lore half hieratic, half medical, was applied to relieve the sufferer.[3] Miracles and special providences, the most marvellous or the most grotesque, were chronicled with unquestioning faith, not only by fanatics like Aelian, but by learned historians like Tacitus and Suetonius. Tales of witchcraft and weird sorcery are as eagerly believed at Trimalchio's dinner-table[4] as in lonely villages of Thessaly. On the higher level of the new Pythagorean faith, everything is possible to the pure spirit. To such a soul God will reveal Himself by many voices to which gross human clay is deaf; the future lays bare its secrets; nature yields up her hidden powers. Spiritual detachment triumphs over matter and time; and the Pythagorean apostle predicts a plague at Ephesus, casts out demons, raises the dead, vanishes like a phantom from the clutches of Domitian.[5]

At a superficial glance, a state of religion such as has been sketched might seem to be a mere bewildering chaos of infinitely divided spiritual interest. Men seem to have adopted the mythologies of every race, and to have superadded a new mythology of positively boundless fecundity. A single votive tablet will contain the names of the great gods of Latium and Greece, of Persia, Commagene, and Egypt, and beside them, strange names of British or Swiss, Celtic, Spanish, or Moorish gods, and the vaguely-designated spirits who now seemed to float in myriads around the scenes of human life.[6] Yet,

[1] Luc. *Alex.* 19; Friedl. *Sitteng.* iii. p. 470; Thiersch, p. 19.

[2] Luc. *Deor. Conc.* 12, ἀλλὰ ἤδη πᾶς λίθος καὶ πᾶς βωμὸς . . . χρησμῳδεῖ.

[3] Friedl. *Sitteng.* iii. pp. 474-478; Wolff, *De Nov. Orac. Aetate*, p. 29 sq.

[4] Petron. *Sat.* 61, 62.

[5] Philostr. *Apoll. Tyan.* v. 12; iv. 5; iv. 10; vii. 5.

[6] *C.I.L.* xii. 3070, 4316; viii. 9195; viii. 4578, Jovi, Junoni, Minervae, Soli Mithrae, Herculi, Marti, Genio loci, Diis, Deabusque omnibus; cf. viii. 4578; vi. 504.

unperceived by the ordinary devotee, amid all this confused ferment, a certain principle of unity or comprehension was asserting its power. Although the old gods in Lucian's piece might comically complain that they were being crowded out of Olympus by Mithra and Anubis and their barbarous company,[1] there was really little jealousy or repulsion among the pagan cults. Ancient ritual was losing its precision of outline; the venerable deities of classical myth were putting off the decided individuality which had so long distinguished them in the popular imagination.[2] The provinces and attributes of kindred deities melted into one another and were finally identified; syncretism was in the air. Without the unifying aid of philosophy, ordinary piety was effecting unconsciously a vast process of simplification which tended to ideal unity. In the Sacred Orations of Aristides, Poseidon, Athene, Serapis, Asclepius, are dropping the peculiar powers by which they were so long known, and rising, without any danger of collision, to all-embracing sway. So, the Isis of Apuleius, the "goddess of myriad names," in her vision to Lucius, boldly claims to be "Queen of the world of shades, first of the inhabitants of Heaven, in whom all gods find their unchanging type."[3] Of course, to the very end, the common superstitious devotion of the masses was probably little influenced by the great spiritual movement which, in the higher strata, was moulding heathen faith into an approach to monotheism. The simple peasant still clung to his favourite deity, as his Catholic descendant has to-day his favourite saint. But it is in the higher minds that the onward sweep of great spiritual movements can really be discerned. The initiation of Apuleius in all the mysteries, the reverent visits of Apollonius to every temple and oracle from the Ganges to the Guadalquivir, the matins of Alexander Severus in a chapel which enshrined the images of Abraham and Orpheus, of Apollonius and Christ;[4] these, and many other instances of all-embracing devotion, point forward to the goal of that Platonist théodicée which it is the purpose of this chapter to expound.

The spectacle of an immense efflorescence of pure paganism,

[1] Luc. *Jup. Trag.* 8, 9; *Deor. Conc.* 8 sqq.

[2] Philostr. *Apoll. T.* vi. 40; Baumgart, *Aristides als Repräsentant der Soph. Rhet.* pp. 62, 84; cf. Apul. *Met.* xi. c. 5; Macrob. *Sat.* i. 17.

[3] Apul. *Met.* xi. cc. 3–6.

[4] Lamprid. *Alex. Sev.* c. 29.

most of it born of very mundane fears and hopes and desires, to men like Lucian was a sight which might, according to the mood, move to tears or laughter. But the same great impulse which drove the multitude into such wild curiosity of superstition, was awaking loftier conceptions of the Divine, and feelings of purer devotion in the educated. And sometimes the very highest and the very lowest developments of the protean religious instinct may be seen in a single mind. Was there ever such a combination of the sensualist imagination with the ideal of ascetic purity, of the terrors and dark arts of anile superstition with the mystic vision of God, as in the soul of Apuleius? The painter of the foulest scenes in ancient literature seems to have cherished the faith in a heavenly King, First Cause of all nature, Father of all living things,[1] Saviour of spirits, beyond the range of time and change, remote, ineffable. The prayer of thanksgiving to Isis might, *mutatis mutandis,* be almost offered in a Christian church. The conception of the unity and purity of the Divine One was the priceless conquest of Greek philosophy, and pre-eminently of Plato. It had been brought home to the Roman world by the teaching of Stoicism. But there is a new note in the monotheism of the first and second centuries of the Empire. God is no longer a mere intellectual postulate, the necessary crown and lord of a great cosmic system. He has become a moral necessity. His existence is demanded by the heart as well as by the intellect. Men craved no longer for a God to explain the universe, but to resolve the enigma of their own lives; not a blind force, moving on majestically and mercilessly to "some far-off event," but an Infinite Father guiding in wisdom, cherishing in mercy, and finally receiving His children to Himself. This is the conception of God which, from Seneca to M. Aurelius, is mastering the best minds, both Stoic and Platonist.[2] Seneca, as we have seen in a former chapter, often speaks in the hard tones of the older Stoicism. Sometimes

[1] Apul. *Apol.* c. 64 (536), totius naturae causa et ratio, summus animi genitor, aeternus animantum sospitator . . . neque tempore neque loco neque vice ulla comprehensus, nemini effabilis; cf. *Met.* xi. c. 25; Denis, *Hist. des Idées Morales,* ii. p. 264.

[2] Thiersch, *Pol. u. Phil. in ihrem Verhältn. zur Rel.* p. 21, man nennt den Marcus einen Stoiker. . . . Aber seine Dogmatik und seine ganze Seelenbestimmung gehört schon weit mehr dem Neoplatonismus an. Cf. Bussell, *School of Plato,* pp. 278–290.

God, Nature, Fate, Jupiter, are identical terms.[1] But the cold, materialistic conception of God is irreconcilable with many passages in his writings. Like Epictetus and M. Aurelius, Seneca is often far more emotional, we may say, far more modern, than his professed creed. The materialistic *Anima Mundi*, interfused with the universe and the nature of man, becomes the infinitely benign Creator, Providence, and Guardian, the Father, and almost the Friend of men. He is the Author of all good, never of evil: He is gentle and pitiful, and to attribute to Him storm or pestilence or earthquake or the various plagues of human life is an impiety. These things are the result of physical law. To such a God boundless gratitude is due for His goodness, resignation in the wise chastenings of His hand. He chastises whom he loves. In bereavement, He takes only what He has given. He is our ready helper in every moral effort; no goodness is possible without His succour. In return for all His benefits, He asks for no costly material offerings, no blood of victims, no steaming incense, no adulation in prayer. Faith in God is the true worship of Him. If you wish to propitiate Him, imitate His goodness. And for the elect soul the day of death is a birthday of eternity, when the load of corporeal things is shaken off, and the infinite splendour of the immortal life spreads out with no troubling shadow.[2]

Hardly less striking is the warmth of devout feeling which suffuses the moral teaching of Epictetus and M. Aurelius. They have not indeed abandoned the old Stoic principle that man's final good depends on the rectitude of the will. But the Stoic sage is no longer a solitary athlete, conquering by his proud unaided strength, and in his victory rising almost superior to Zeus. Growing moral experience had taught humility, and inspired the sense of dependence on a Higher Power in sympathy with man.[3] No true Stoic, of course, could ever forget the Divine element within each human soul which linked it with the cosmic soul, and through which man might bring himself into harmony with the great polity of

[1] Sen. *De Ben.* iv. 7.

[2] Zeller, *Phil. der Griech.* iii. 1, p. 649. Cf. Sen. *Ep.* 10, § 5; *Ep.* 73, § 16; *Ep.* 41, § 2; *Ep.* 63, § 7; *Ep.* 83, § 1; *Ep.* 95, § 50; *Ep.* 102, § 28, nulla serenum umbra turbabit; *De Prov.* iv. 7; *De Ira*, ii. 27; *De Clem.* i. 7; *De Ben.* 1. 29.

[3] Epict. i. 9, § 7, *τὸ δὲ τὸν θεὸν ποιητὴν ἔχειν καὶ πατέρα καὶ κηδεμόνα, οὐκέτι ἡμᾶς ἐξαιρήσεται λυπῶν καὶ φόβων*: cf. i. 3, § 3; Denis, *Hist. des Idées Morales*, ii. p. 241.

gods and men. But, somehow, the Divine Power immanent in the world, from a dim, cold, impalpable law or fate or impersonal force, slowly rounds itself off into a Being, if not apart from man, at any rate his superior, his Creator and Guardian, nay, in the end, his Father, from whom he comes, to whom he returns at death. Some may think this a decline from the lofty plane of the older school. The answer is that the earlier effort to find salvation through pure reason in obedience to the law of the whole, although it may have been magnificent, was not a working religion for man as he is constituted. The eternal involution of spirit and matter in the old Stoic creed, the cold, impersonal, unknowable power, which, under whatever name, Law, Reason, Fate, Necessity, permeates the universe, necessarily exclude the idea of design, of providence, of moral care for humanity. The unknown Power which claims an absolute obedience, has no aid or recognition for his worshipper. The monism of the old Stoics breaks down. The human spirit, in striving to realise its unity with the Universal Spirit, realises with more and more intensity the perpetual opposition of matter and spirit, while it receives no aid in the conflict from the power which ordains it; it "finds itself alone in an alien world." The true Stoic has no real object of worship. If he addresses the impassive centre and soul of his universe, sometimes in the rapturous tones of loving devotion, it is only a pathetic illusion born of the faiths of the past, or inspired by a dim forecast of the faiths of the coming time. How could the complex of blind forces arouse any devotion? It demanded implicit submission and self-sacrifice, but it gave no help, save the name of a Divine element in the human soul; it furnished no inspiring example to the sage in the conflicts of passion, under obloquy, obstruction, and persecution. Meanwhile, in this forlorn struggle, the human character was through stress and storm developing new powers and virtues, lofty courage in the face of lawless power, pious resignation to the blows of fortune, gentle consideration and mercy even for slaves and the outcasts of society, ideals of purity unknown to the ancient world in its prime. The sage might, according to orthodox theory, rest in a placid content of rounded perfection. But human nature is not so constituted. In proportion to spiritual progress is the force of spiritual longings; *beati mundo corde, ipsi Deum videbunt.* The fruitful part of Stoicism as a religion was the doctrine that the human reason is a part of the soul of the world, a spark of the Divine mind. At first this was only conceived in the fashion of a materialistic pantheism.[1] The kindred between the individual and the general soul was little more than a physical doctrine. But it developed in minds like Epictetus and Seneca a profound spiritual meaning; it tapped the source of all real religion. Pure reason can never solve the religious problem. The history of religions shows that a conception of God which is to act effectually on composite human nature is never reached by the speculative intellect. What reason cannot do is effected by the "sub-conscious self,"[2] which is the dim seat of the deeper intuitions, haunted by vague memories, hereditary pieties, and emotional associations, the spring of strange genius, of heroic sacrifice, of infinite aspiration. There throbs the tide "which drew from out the boundless deep." Thus the Stoic of the later time became a mystic, in the sense that "by love and emotion he solved the dualism of the world."[3] God is no longer a mere physical law or force, however subtilised, sweeping on in pitiless impetus or monotony of cyclic change. God is within the human soul, not as a spark of empyreal fire, but as the voice of conscience, the spiritual monitor and comforter, the "Holy Spirit,"[4] prompting, guarding, consoling in life and death. God is no longer found so much in the ordered movement of the spheres and the recurring processes or the cataclysms of the material universe. He is heard in the still small voice. It is thus that the later Stoicism melts into the revived Platonism.

Probably Seneca and Epictetus, had they been interrogated, would have loyally resolved their most rapturous and devout language into the cold terms of Stoic orthodoxy. But the emotional tone is a really new element in their teaching, and the language of spiritual abandonment, joyful resignation to a Higher Will, free and cheerful obedience to it in the confidence of love, would be absurdly incongruous if addressed to an

[1] Zeller, *Phil. der Griech.* iii. 1, pp. 179, 184.

[2] James, *Varieties of Religious Belief*, pp. 511, 512.

[3] Bussell, *School of Plato*, p. 296.

[4] Sen. *Ep.* 41, § 2, sacer intra nos spiritus sedet.

abstract law or physical necessity.[1] The fatherhood of God and the kinship of all men as His sons is the fundamental principle of the new creed, binding us to do nothing unworthy of such an ancestry.[2] At other times we are soldiers of God in a war with evil, bound to military obedience, awaiting calmly the last signal to retreat from the scene of struggle.[3] The infinite benevolence of God is asserted in the face of all appearances to the contrary. This of course is all the easier to one trained in the doctrine that the external fortune of life has nothing to do with man's real happiness. The fear of God is banished by the sense of His perfect love. The all-seeing eye, the all-embracing providence, leave no room for care or foreboding. The Stoic optimism is now grounded on a personal trust in a loving and righteous will: "I am Thine, do with me what Thou wilt." "For all things work together for good to them who love Him." The external sufferings and apparent wrongs of the obedient sons of God are no stumbling-blocks to faith.[4] The great heroic example, Heracles, the son of Zeus, was sorely tried by superhuman tasks, and won his crown of immortality through toil and battle. "Whom He loves He chastens." Even apparent injustice is only an education through suffering. These things are "only light afflictions" to him who sees the due proportions of things and knows Zeus as his father. Even to the poor, the lame, the blind, if they have the divine love, the universe is a great temple, full of mystery and joy, and each passing day a festival. In the common things of life, in ploughing, digging, eating, we should sing hymns to God. "What else can I do," says Epictetus, "a lame old man, than sing His praise, and exhort all men to join in the same song?"[5] Who shall say what depth of religious emotion, veiled under old-world phrase, there was in that outburst of M. Aurelius: "All harmonises with me which is in harmony with thee, O Universe. Nothing for me is too early nor too late which is in due season for thee. . . . For thee are all things, in thee are all things,

[1] Yet cf. Zeller, iii. 1, p. 649, der göttliche Beistand, welchen er verlangt, ist kein übernatürlicher. Seneca had broken away unconsciously from the old Stoic idea of God, more than Zeller will admit, or his words have no meaning.

[2] Sen. *Ep.* 95, §§ 51, 52.

[3] *Ib.* 107, § 9; Epict. *Diss.* iii. 24.

[4] Epict. *Diss.* iii. 20, § 11, *κακὸς γείτων; Αὐτῷ· ἀλλ' ἐμοὶ ἀγαθός· γυμνάζει μου τὸ εὔγνωμον, τὸ ἐπιεικές*: iv. 1, § 89; M. Aurel. vi. 44.

[5] Epict. i. 16, § 20, *τί γὰρ ἄλλο δύναμαι γέρων χωλὸς εἰ μὴ ὑμνεῖν τὸν θεόν; κτλ.*

to thee all things return. The poet says, Dear City of Cecrops; and wilt not thou say, Dear City of Zeus?"[1]

The attitude of such souls to external worship in every age may be easily divined without the evidence of their words. If God is good and wishes only the good of His creatures, then to seek to appease His wrath and avert His capricious judgments becomes an impiety. If men's final good lies in the moral sphere, in justice, gentleness, temperance, obedience to the higher order, then prayer for external goods, for mere indulgences of sense or ambition, shows a hopeless misconception as to the nature of God and the supreme destiny of man.[2] On the other hand, without giving up the doctrine that the highest good depends on the virtuous will, the later Stoics and Platonists have begun to feel that man needs support and inspiration in his moral struggles from a higher Power, a Power without him and beyond him, yet who is allied to him in nature and sympathy. Prayer is no longer a means of winning temporal good things "for which the worthy need not pray, and which the unworthy will not obtain." It is a fortifying communion with the Highest, an act of thanksgiving for blessings already received, an inspiration for a fuller and diviner life.[3] It is an effort of gratitude and adoration to draw from the Divine source of all moral strength.

It must always remain to moderns an enigma how souls living in such a spiritual world refused to break with heathen idolatry. Seneca, indeed, poured contempt on the grossness of myth in a lost treatise on superstition;[4] and he had no liking for the external rites of worship. But in some strange way M. Aurelius reconciled punctilious devotion to the popular gods with an austere pantheism or monotheism. It is in Platonists such as Dion or Maximus of Tyre that we meet with an attempted apology for anthropomorphic symbolism of the Divine.[5] The justification lies in the vast gulf which separates the remote, ineffable, and inconceivable purity of God from the feebleness and grossness of man. Few

[1] M. Aurel. iv. 23.

[2] *Ib.* ix. 40; Sen. *Ep.* 10, § 5.

[3] Philostr. *Apoll. Tyan.* iv. 40, *ὧδε εὔχομαι, ὦ θεοί, δοίητέ μοι τὰ ὀφειλόμενα.* Max. Tyr. *Diss.* xi. 8, *ἀλλὰ σὺ μὲν ἡγεῖ τὴν τοῦ φιλοσόφου εὐχὴν αἴτησιν εἶναι τῶν οὐ παρόντων· ἐγὼ δὲ ὁμιλίαν καὶ διάλεκτον πρὸς τοὺς θεοὺς περὶ τῶν παρόντων καὶ ἐπίδειξιν τῆς ἀρετῆς.*

[4] *Frag.* preserved in S. Aug. *De Civ. Dei*, vi. 10.

[5] D. Chrys. *Or.* xii. § 24 (412 R); Max. Tyr. *Diss.* viii. 10.

are they who can gaze in unaided thought on the Divine splendour unveiled. Images, rites, and sacred myth have been invented by the wisdom of the past, to aid the memory and the imagination of weak ordinary souls. The symbols have varied with the endless variety of races. Animals or trees, mountain or river, rude unhewn stones, or the miracles of Pheidias in gold and ivory, are simply the sign or picture by which the soul is pointed to the Infinite Essence which has never been seen by mortal eye or imaged in human phantasy. The symbol which appeals to one race may be poor and contemptible in the eyes of another. The animal worship of Egypt gave a shock to minds which were lifted heavenwards by the winning majesty of the Virgin Goddess or of the Zeus of Olympia. The human form, as the chosen tabernacle of an effluence of the Divine Spirit, might well seem to Dion and Maximus the noblest and most fitting symbol of religious worship. Yet, in the end, they are all ready to tolerate any aberration of religious fancy which is justified by its use.[1] The most perfect symbol is only a faint adumbration of "the Father and Creator of all, Who is older than the sun and heavens, stronger than time and the ages and the fleeting world of change, unnamed by any lawgiver, Whom tongue cannot express nor eye see. Helpless to grasp His real essence, we seek a stay in names or images, in beast or plant, in river or mountain, in lustrous forms of gold and silver and ivory. Whatever we have of fairest we call by His name. And for love of Him, we cling, as lovers are wont, to anything which recalls Him. I quarrel not with divers imagery, if we seek to know, to love, to remember Him."[2] This is the outburst of a tolerant and eclectic Platonism, ready to condone everything in the crudest religious imagery. But a more conscientious scrutiny even of Grecian legend demanded, as we shall see, a deeper solution to account for dark rites and legends which cast a shadow on the Infinite Purity.

The Stoic theology, which resolved the gods of legend into thin abstractions, various potencies of the Infinite Spirit interfused with the universe,[3] was in some respects congenial

[1] Max. Tyr. *Diss.* viii. §§ 5–10; Philostr. *Apoll. Tyan.* vi. 19.

[2] Max. Tyr. viii. 10, *οὐ νεμεσῶ τῆς διαφωνίας, ἴστωσαν μόνον, ἐράτωσαν μόνον, μνημονευέτωσαν μόνον.*

[3] Zeller, *Phil. der Griech.* iii. 1, p. 299 sqq.; S. Aug. *De Civ. Dei*, vi. 5.

to the Roman mind, and reflected the spirit of old Roman religion. That religion of arid abstractions, to which no myth, no haunting charm of poetic imagination attached,[1] easily lent itself to a system which explained the gods by allegory or physical rationalism. That was not an eirenicon for the second century, at least among thoughtful, pious men. The philosophic effort of so many centuries had ended in an eclecticism for purely moral culture, and a profound scepticism as to the attainment of higher truth by unaided reason.[2] Mere intellectual curiosity, the desire of knowledge for its own sake, and the hope of attaining it, are strangely absent from the loftiest minds, from Seneca, Epictetus, and M. Aurelius.[3] Men like Lucian, sometimes in half melancholy, half scornful derision, amused themselves with ridiculing the chaotic results of the intellectual ambition of the past.[4] They equally recognised the immense force of that spiritual movement which was trying every avenue of accredited religious system or novel superstition, that might perchance lead the devotee to some glimpse of the divine world. And side by side with the recrudescence of old-world superstitions, there were spreading, from whatever source, loftier and more ethical conceptions of God, a dim sense of sin and human weakness, a need of cleansing and support from a Divine hand. Stoicism, with all its austere grandeur, had failed in its interpretation both of man and of God. Popular theology, however soothing to old associations and unregenerate feelings, often gave a shock to the quickened moral sense and the higher spiritual intuitions. Yet the venerable charm of time-honoured ritual, glad or stately, the emotional effects and dim promise of revelation in the mysteries of many shrines, the seductive allurements of new cults, with a strange blending of the sensuous and the mystic, all wove around the human soul such an enchanted maze of spiritual fascination that escape was impossible, even if it were desired. But it was no longer desired even by the highest intellects. The efforts of pure reason to solve the mystery of God and of man's destiny had failed. Yet men were ever "feeling after God, if haply they might find Him." And the

[1] Mommsen, *Hist. of Rome*, i. p. 183 (Tr.); Preller, *Rom. Myth.* p. 2.

[2] Zeller, *Phil. der Griech.* iii. 1, pp. 18–20.

[3] Sen. *Ep.* 117, §§ 19–30; Epict. *Diss.* i. 17; M. Aurel. vii. 67. But cf. viii. 13; xii. 14; viii. 3.

[4] Luc. *Hermot.* c. 25, 34, 37 sqq.

God whom they sought for was one on whom they might hang, in whom they might have rest. Where was the revelation to come from? Where was the mediator to be sought to reconcile the ancient faiths or fables with a purified conception of the Deity and the aspiration for a higher moral life?

The revived Pythagorean and Platonist philosophy which girded itself to attempt the solution was really part of a great spiritual movement, with its focus at Alexandria.[1] In that meeting-point of the East and West, of all systems of thought and worship, syncretism blended all faiths. Hadrian, in his letter to Servianus, cynically observes that the same men were ready to worship impartially Serapis or Christ.[2] Philosophy became more and more a religion; its first and highest aim is a right knowledge of God. And philosophy, having failed to find help in the life according to nature, or the divine element in individual consciousness, had now to seek support in a God transcending nature and consciousness, a God such as the mysticism of the East or the systems of Pythagoras and Plato had foreshadowed. But such a God, transcending nature and consciousness, remote, ineffable, only, in some rare moment of supreme exaltation, dimly apprehensible by the human spirit,[3] could not call forth fully the loving trust and fervent reverence which men longed to offer. Heaven being so far from earth, and earth so darkened by the mists of sense, any gleam of revelation must be welcomed from whatever quarter it might break. And thus an all-embracing syncretism, while it gratified ancestral piety, and the natural instinct of all religion to root itself in the past, offered the hope of illumination from converging lights. Or rather, any religion which has won the reverence of men may transmit a ray from the central Sun. The believer in God, who longs for communion with Him, for help at His hands, might by reverent selection win from all religions something to satisfy his needs. A revelation was the imperious demand. Where should men be so likely to find it as in the reverent study of great historic efforts of humanity to pierce the veil?

[1] Überweg, *Hist. Phil.* i. p. 232; Zeller, *Phil. der Griech.* iii. 2, p. 83; Thiersch, *Politik u. Phil.* etc., pp. 15, 16.

[2] Flav. Vop. *Vit. Saturn*, c. 8, § 2, illic qui Serapem colunt Christiani sunt, et devoti sunt Serapi, qui se Christi episcopos dicunt, etc.

[3] Max. Tyr. *Diss.* xiv. 8, *ᾗ γὰρ ἂν τῷ διὰ μέσου πολλῷ τὸ θνητὸν πρὸς τὸ ἀθάνατον διετειχίσθη τῆς οὐρανίου ἐπόψεώς τε καὶ ὁμιλίας ὅτι μὴ τῆς δαιμονίου ταύτης φύσεως, κτλ.* Cf. xvi. 9.

The philosophy which was to attempt the revival of paganism in the second century, and which was to fight its last battles in the fourth and fifth, traced itself to Pythagoras and Plato. Plato's affinity with the older mystic is well known. And the reader of the *Phaedo* or the *Republic* will not be surprised to find the followers of the two masters of Greek thought who believed most in a spiritual vision and in an ordered moral life, united in an effort which extended to the close of the Western Empire,[1] to combine a lofty mysticism with ancestral faith. The two systems had much in common, and yet each contributed a peculiar element to the great movement. Pythagoreanism, although its origin is veiled in mystery, was always full of the mysticism of the East. Platonism was essentially the philosophy of Greek culture. The movement in which their forces were combined was one in which the new Hellenism of Hadrian's reign reinforced itself for the reconstruction of western paganism with those purer and loftier ideas of God of which the East is the original home. The effort of paganism to rehabilitate itself in the second century drew no small part of its inspiration from the regions which were the cradle of the Christian faith.[2]

Seneca seems to regard Pythagoreanism as extinct.[3] Yet one of his own teachers, Sotion, practised its asceticism,[4] and in the first century B.C., the traces of at least ninety treatises by members of the school have been recovered by antiquarian care, many of them forgeries foisted on ancient names.[5] As a didactic system, indeed, the school had long disappeared, but the Pythagorean *askesis* seems never to have lost its continuity. It drew down the ridicule of the New Comedy. It may have had a share in forming the Essene and Therapeutic discipline.[6] In the first century B.C. it had a distinguished adherent in P. Nigidius Figulus, and a learned expositor in Alexander Polyhistor. Its enduring power as a spiritual creed congenial to paganism is shown by the fact that Iamblichus, one of the latest Neo-Platonists, and one of the ardent devotees of superstition, expounded the Pythagorean system in many treatises and composed an imaginative bio-

[1] Macrob. *Som. Scip.* i. 8; ii. 17.

[2] Zeller, *Phil. der Griech.* iii. 2, pp. 57-62.

[3] Sen. *Nat. Q.* vii. 32, 2, Pythagorica illa invidiosa turbae schola praeceptorem non invenit.

[4] Sen. *Ep.* 49, § 2; 108, § 17.

[5] Zeller, iii. 2, p. 85.

[6] Überweg, *Hist. Phil.* i. p. 228; cf. Hatch, *Hibbert Lec.* p. 148.

graphy of the great founder.[1] To the modern it is best known through the romantic life of Apollonius of Tyana, by Philostratus, which was composed at the instance of Julia Domna, the wife of Septimius Severus, who combined with a doubtful virtue a love for the mysticism of her native East.[2] Apollonius is surrounded by his biographer with an atmosphere of mystery and miracle. But although the critical historian must reject much of the narrative, the faith of the Pythagorean missionary of the reign of Domitian stands out in clear outline. Apollonius is a true representative of the new spiritual movement. His mother had a vision before his birth. His early training at Aegae was eclectic, like the spirit of the age, and he heard the teaching of doctors of all the schools, not even excluding the Epicurean.[3] But he early devoted himself to the severe asceticism of the Pythagorean sect, wore pure linen, abstained from wine and flesh, observed the five years of silence, and made the temple his home. The worship of Asclepius, which was then gaining an extraordinary vogue, had a special attraction for him, with its atmosphere of serenity and ritual purity and its dream oracles of beneficent healing. Apollonius combines in a strange fashion, like Plutarch and the eclectic Platonists, a decided monotheism with a conservative devotion to the ancient gods. He looks to the East, to the sages of the Ganges, for the highest inspiration. He worships the sun every day.[4] Yet he has a profound interest in the popular religion of the many lands through which he travelled. He frequented the temples of all the gods, discoursed with the priests on the ancient lore of their shrines, and corrected or restored, with an authority which seems to have never been challenged, their ritual where it had been forgotten or mutilated in the lapse of ages.[5] He sought initiation in all the mysteries. He wrote a book on Sacrifices which dealt with the most minute details of worship.[6] He had a profound interest in ancient legend, and the fame of the great Hellenic heroes, and, having spent a weird night with the shade of Achilles in the Troad, he constrained the Thessalians

[1] Überweg, *Hist. Phil.* i. p. 252; cf. Eunapius, *Vit. Iambl.*

[2] Philostr. *Apoll. Tyan.* i. 3, 1; cf. Ael. Spart. *Vit. Sev.* 18.

[3] Philostr. *Apoll. Tyan.* i. 7.

[4] *Ib.* ii. 38.

[5] *Ib.* i. 11, § 16; i. 31; iv. 19, 20; iv. 41.

[6] *Ib.* iii. 41.

to restore his fallen honours.[1] The temples recognised in him at once a champion and a reformer. The oracular seats of Ionia showed an unenvious admiration of his gift of prophecy, and hailed him as a true son of Apollo.[2] His visit to Rome in the darkest hour of the Neronian terror seems to have aroused a strange religious fervour; the temples were thronged with worshippers; it was a heathen revival.[3]

Yet this strange missionary held principles which ought to have been fatal to heathen worship. He drew his central principle from Eastern pantheism, which might seem irreconcilable with the anthropomorphism of the West. It is true that under the Infinite Spirit, as in the Platonist théodicée, the gods of heathen devotion find a place as His ministers and viceroys.[4] But the eternal antithesis of spirit and matter, and the contempt for the body as a degrading prison of the divine element in man,[5] the ascetic theory that by crucifying the flesh and attenuating its powers, the spirit might lay itself open to heavenly influences, these are doctrines which might appear utterly hostile to a gross materialist ritual. And as a matter of fact, Apollonius to some extent obeyed his principles. He scorned the popular conception of divination and magic.[6] The only legitimate power of foreseeing the future or influencing the material world is given to the soul which is pure from all fleshly taint and therefore near to God. He feels profoundly that the myths propagated by the poets have lowered the ideal of God and the character of man, and he greatly prefers the fables of Aesop, which use the falsehoods of the fancy for a definite moral end.[7] The mutilation of a father, the storming of Olympus by the Giants, incest and adultery among the gods, must be reprobated, however they have been glorified by poetry. Apollonius poured contempt on the animal worship of Egypt, even when defended by the dialectic subtlety of Greece.[8] He was repelled by the grossness of bloody sacrifices, however consecrated by immemorial use. For the nobler symbolism of

[1] Philostr. *Apoll. Tyan.* iv. 13; iv. 16.

[2] *Ib.* iv. 1, *λόγοι τε περὶ αὐτοῦ ἐφοίτων οἱ μὲν ἐκ τοῦ Κολοφῶνι μαντείου κοινωνὸν τῆς ἑαυτοῦ σοφίας καὶ ἀτεχνῶς σοφὸν τὸν ἄνδρα ᾄδοντες, οἱ δὲ ἐκ Διδύμων.*

[3] *Ib.* iv. 41.

[4] *Ib.* iii. 35, *τὴν δὲ* (*ἕδραν ἀποδοτέον*) *ἐπ' ἐκείνῃ θεοῖς, οἳ τὰ μέρη αὐτοῦ κυβερνῶσι*: cf. Max. Tyr. *Diss.* xiv. § 6 sqq.

[5] Philostr. *Apoll. Tyan.* ii. 37; vi. 11; vii. 26; Max. Tyr. *Diss.* xiii. § 5.

[6] Philostr. *Apoll. Tyan.* vi. 10; iv. 40; v. 12; iv. 18; iv. 44.

[7] *Ib.* iv. 13; iii. 25.

[8] *Ib.* vi. 19.

Hellenic art he had a certain sympathy, like Dion, but only as symbolism. Any sensible image of the Supreme, which does not carry the soul beyond the bounds of sense, defeats its purpose and is degrading to pure religion. Pictured or sculptured forms are only aids to that mystic imagination through which alone we can see God. Finally, his idea of prayer is intensely spiritual or ethical. "Grant me, ye gods, what is my due" is the highest prayer of Apollonius.[1] Yet, as we have already seen, the religion of Apollonius is thoroughly practical. He was a great preacher. He addressed vast crowds from the temple steps at Ephesus or Olympia, rebuking their luxury and effeminacy, their feuds and mean civic ambition, their love of frivolous sports or the bloody strife of the arena.[2] Next to the knowledge of God, he preached the importance of self-knowledge, and of lending an attentive ear to the voice of conscience. He crowned his life by asserting fearlessly the cause of righteousness in the awful presence-chamber of Domitian.

About the very time when Apollonius was bearding the last of the Flavians, and preaching a pagan revival in the porticoes of the Roman temples, it is probable that Plutarch, in some respects a kindred spirit, was making his appearance as a lecturer at Rome.[3] The greatest of biographers has had no authentic biography himself.[4] The few certain facts about his life must be gleaned from his own writings. He was the descendant of an ancient family of Chaeronea, famous as the scene of three historic battles, "the War-God's dancing-place," and his great-grandfather had tales of the great conflict at Actium.[5] In the year 66 A.D., when Nero was distinguishing or disgracing himself as a competitor at the Greek festivals, Plutarch was a young student at the university of Athens, under Ammonius,[6] who, if he inspired him with admiration for Plato, also taught him to draw freely from all the treasures of Greek thought. Plutarch, before he finally settled down at Chaeronea, saw something of the great Roman world. He had visited Alex-

[1] Philostr. *Apoll. Tyan.* iv. 40.

[2] *Ib.* iv. 22; iv. 41; v. 26.

[3] Gréard, *De la Morale de Plutarch*, p. 32; Volkmann, *Leben*, etc. p. 37.

[4] For the apocryphal accounts, *v.* Gréard, p. 3 sqq.

[5] *Vit. Anton.* c. 68, ὁ γοῦν πρόπαππος ἡμῶν Νίκαρχος διηγεῖτο κτλ.: Volkmann, p. 21.

[6] Plut. *De* EI *ap. Delph.* c. 1; cf. 17; *Vit. Themist.* c. 32; *Sympos.* iii. 1, § 1; ix. 14, § 2; ix. 14, § 7; i. 9; Eunap. *Vit. Soph. Prooem.* 5, ἐν οἷς Ἀμμώνιός τε ἦν Πλουτάρχου τοῦ θειοτάτου γεγονὼς διδάσκαλος.

andria and some part of Asia Minor.[1] He was at an early age employed to represent his native town on public business,[2] and he had thus visited Rome, probably in the reign of Vespasian, and again, in the reign of Domitian.[3] It was a time when original genius in Roman literature was showing signs of failure, but when minute antiquarian learning was becoming a passion.[4] It was also the age of the new sophist. Hellenism was in the air, and the lecture theatres were thronged to hear the philosophic orator or the professional artist in words.[5] Although Plutarch is never mentioned beside men like Euphrates, in Pliny's letters, he found an audience at Rome, and the famous Arulenus Rusticus was once among his hearers.[6] While he was ransacking the imperial libraries, he also formed the acquaintance, at pleasant social parties, of many men of academic and official fame, some of whom belonged to the circle of Pliny and Tacitus.[7]

But his native Greece, with its great memories, and his native Chaeronea, to which he was linked by ancestral piety, had for a man like Plutarch far stronger charms than the capital of the world. With our love of excitement and personal prominence, it is hard to conceive how a man of immense culture and brilliant literary power could endure the monotony of bourgeois society in depopulated and decaying Greece.[8] Yet Plutarch seems to have found it easy, and even pleasant. He was too great to allow his own scheme of life to be crossed and disturbed by vulgar opinion or ephemeral ambition. His family relations were sweet and happy. His married life realised the highest ideals of happy wedlock.[9] He had the respectful affection of his brothers and older kinsmen. The petty magistracies, in which he made it a duty to serve

[1] *Sympos.* v. 5, § 1; *Vit. Agesil.* c. 19; Volkmann, pp. 34, 63.

[2] *Praec. Ger. Reipub.* c. 20.

[3] *Sympos.* viii. 7, § 1; *Vit. Dem.* c. 2. In this passage he says, *οὐ σχολῆς οὔσης γυμνάζεσθαι περὶ τὴν Ῥωμαικὴν διάλεκτον ὑπὸ χρειῶν πολιτικῶν . . . ὀψέ ποτε καὶ πόρρω τῆς ἡλικίας ἠρξάμεθα Ῥωμαικοῖς γράμμασιν ἐντυγχάνειν.* Cf. *Frat. Am.* 4.

[4] Suet. *Dom.* c. xx.; Spart. *Vit. Hadr.* c. 16, § 5; Aul. Gell. xii. 2; Luc. *Lexiph.* c. 20; Friedl. *Sittengesch.* iii. p. 278; Macé, *Suétone*, p. 96; Gréard, *Morale de Plut.* p. 33; cf. Sen. *Ep.* 114, § 13, multi ex alieno seculo petunt verba: duodecim tabulas loquuntur.

[5] Friedl. *Sittengesch.* iii. p. 360.

[6] Plut. *De Curios.* c. 15, *ἐμοῦ ποτε ἐν Ῥώμῃ διαλεγομένου Ῥούστικος ἐκεῖνος ὃν ἀπέκτεινε Δομιτιανὸς . . . ἠκροᾶτο κτλ.*

[7] Plut. *De Tranq.* c. 1; *Sympos.* i. 9; v. 7, § 10; viii. 1; *De Cohib. Ira*, c. i.; *Sympos.* ii. 3; i. 5; cf. Plin. *Ep.* i. 9; iv. 5; *Ep.* i. 13; iv. 4; Tac. *Agr.* c. 2; cf. Suet. *Vesp.* c. xxii.

[8] For a description of this society, see Mahaffy's *Greek World under Rom. Sway*, c. xliv.

[9] Plut. *Consol. ad Ux.* c. iv. x.; *Conj. Praec.* c. xliv.

his native town, were dignified in his eyes by the thought that Epameinondas had once been charged with the cleansing of the streets of Thebes.[1] His priesthood of Apollo at Delphi was probably far more attractive than the imperial honours which, according to legend, were offered to him by Trajan and Hadrian.[2] To his historic and religious imagination the ancient shrine which looked down on the gulf from the foot of the "Shining Rocks," was sacred as no other spot on earth. Although in Plutarch's day Delphi had declined in splendour and fame,[3] it was still surrounded with the glamour of immemorial sanctity and power. It was still the spot from which divine voices of warning or counsel had issued to the kings of Lydia, to chiefs of wild hordes upon the Strymon, to the envoys of the Roman Tarquins, to every city of Hellenic name from the Euxine to the Atlantic. We can still almost make the round of its antiquarian treasures under his genial guidance. Probably Plutarch's happiest hours were spent in accompanying a party of visitors,—a professor on his way home from Britain to Tarsus, a Spartan traveller just returned from far Indian seas,—around those sacred scenes; we can hear the debate on the doubtful quality of Delphic verse or the sources of its inspiration: we can watch them pause to recall the story of mouldering bronze or marble, and wake the echoes of a thousand years.[4]

Plutarch must have been a swift and indefatigable worker, for his production is almost on the scale of Varro, Cicero, or the elder Pliny. Yet he found time for pleasant visits to every part of Greece which had tales or treasures for the antiquary. He enjoyed the friendship of the brightest intellects of the day, of Herodes Atticus, the millionaire rhetorician,[5] of Favorinus, the great sophist of Gaul, the intimate friend of Herodes and the counsellor of the Emperor Hadrian, of Ammonius, who was Plutarch's tutor; of many others, noted in their time, but who are mere shadows to us. They met in a convivial way in many places, at Chaeronea, at Hyampolis, at Eleusis after the Mysteries, at Patrae, at Corinth during

[1] Plut. *Praec. Ger. Reipub.* c. 15; cf. *Sympos.* vi. 8, § 1.

[2] Plut. *An Seni Sit Ger. Resp.* c. 17, οἶσθά με τῷ Πυθίῳ λειτουργοῦντα πολλὰς πυθιάδας. Suidas, Πλούταρχος: cf. Volkmann, p. 91.

[3] *De Def. Orac.* c. v. viii.

[4] *Ib.* c. ii.

[5] Trench, *Plutarch*, p. 22; Volkmann, p. 58.

the Isthmian games, at Thermopylae, and Athens in the house of Ammonius, or at Aedepsus, the Baden of Euboea, where in the springtime people found pleasant lodgings and brisk intercourse to relieve the monotony of attendance at the baths.[1] Plutarch had a large circle of relatives,—his grandfather Lamprias, who had tales from an actual witness of the revels of Antony at Alexandria;[2] Lamprias his elder brother, a true Boeotian in his love of good fare, a war-dance, and a jest;[3] his younger brother Timon, to whom Plutarch was devotedly attached.[4] His ordinary society, not very distinguished socially, was composed of grammarians, rhetoricians, country doctors, the best that the district could afford.[5] The talk is often on the most trivial or absurd subjects, though not more absurdly trivial than those on which the polished sophist displayed his graces in the lecture-hall.[6] Yet graver and more serious themes are not excluded,[7] and the table-talk of Greece in the end of the first century is invaluable to the student of society. In such scenes Plutarch not only cultivated friendship, the great art of life, not only watched the play of intellect and character; he also found relief from the austere labours which have made his fame. It is surely not the least of his titles to greatness that, in an environment which to most men of talent would have been infinitely depressing, with the irrepressible vitality of genius he contrived to idealise the society of decaying Greece by linking it with the past.

And, with such a power of reviving the past, even the dulness of the little Boeotian town was easily tolerable. We can imagine Plutarch looking down the quiet street in the still vacant noontide, as he sat trying to revive the ancient glories of his race, and to match them with their conquerors, while he reminded the lords of the world, who, in Plutarch's

[1] Plut. *Sympos.* ii. 2, § 1 (Eleusis); v. 8, § 1 (Athens); i. 10, § 1; ii. 1, § 1 (Patrae); iii. 1, § 1; iv. 4, § 1 (Aedepsus), *χωρίον κατεσκευασμένον οἰκήσεσι . . . μάλιστα δ' ἀνθεῖ τὸ χωρίον ἀκμάζοντος ἔαρος. πολλοὶ γὰρ ἀφικνοῦνται τὴν ὥραν αὐτόθι, καὶ συνουσίας ποιοῦνται μετ' ἀλλήλων ἐν ἀφθόνοις πᾶσι, καὶ πλείστας περὶ λόγους ὑπὸ σχολῆς διατριβὰς ἔχουσι*: cf. Volkmann, p. 57.

[2] *Vit. Anton.* c. 28, *διηγεῖτο γοῦν ἡμῶν τῷ πάππῳ Λαμπρίᾳ Φιλώτας ὁ Ἀμφισσεὺς ἰατρὸς εἶναι μὲν ἐν Ἀλεξανδρείᾳ τότε μανθάνων τὴν τέχνην, κτλ.*

[3] *Sympos.* ii. 2, § 1; ix. 15, § 1; viii. 6, § 5.

[4] *De Fr. Am.* c. 16.

[5] *Sympos.* iv. 1, 1; iv. 4, 1; v. 10, 1; v. 5, 1.

[6] *Ib.* ix. 4, § 1; Mahaffy, *Greek World, etc.* p. 338.

[7] Plut. *Sympos.* viii. 2; viii. 7.

early youth, seemed to be wildly squandering their heritage, of the stern, simple virtue by which it had been won. For in the Lives of great Greeks and Romans, the moral interest is the most prominent. It is biography, not history, which Plutarch is writing.[1] Setting and scenery of course there must be; but Plutarch's chief object is to paint the character of the great actors on the stage. Hence he may slur over or omit historic facts of wider interest, while he records apparently trivial incidents or sayings which light up a character. But Plutarch has a fine eye both for lively social scenes and the great crises of history. The description of the feverish activity of swarming industry in the great days of Pheidias at Athens, once read, can never be forgotten.[2] Equally indelible are the pictures of the younger Cato's last morning, as he finished the *Phaedo*, and the birds began to twitter,[3] of the flight and murder of Pompey, of the suicide of Otho on the ghastly field of Bedriacum, which seemed to atone for an evil life. Nor can we forget his description of one of the saddest of all scenes in Greek history, which moved even Thucydides to a restrained pathos, —the retreat of the Athenians from the walls of Syracuse.

Plutarch was before all else a moralist, with a genius for religion. His ethical treatises deserve to be thoroughly explored, and as sympathetically expounded, for the light which they throw on the moral aspirations of the age, as Dr. Mahaffy has skilfully used them for pictures of its social life. He must be a very unimaginative person who cannot feel the charm of their revelation. But the man of purely speculative interest will probably be disappointed. Plutarch is not an original thinker in morals or religion. He has no new gospel to expound. He does not go to the roots of conduct or faith. Possessing a very wide knowledge of past speculation, he might have written an invaluable history of ancient philosophy. But he has not done it. And, as a man of genius, with a strong practical purpose to do moral good to his fellows, his choice of his vocation must be accepted without cavil. He was the greatest Hellenist of his day, when Hellenism was capturing

[1] *Vit. Alex.* c. 1, οὔτε γὰρ ἱστορίας γράφομεν ἀλλὰ βίους οὔτε ταῖς ἐπιφανεστάταις πράξεσι πάντως ἔνεστι δήλωσις ἀρετῆς ἢ κακίας. So *Vit. Nic.* c. 1, οὐ τὴν ἄχρηστον ἀθροίζων ἱστορίαν ἀλλὰ τὴν πρὸς κατανόησιν ἤθους καὶ τρόπου παραδιδούς

[2] *Vit. Pericl.* c. 12.

[3] *Vit. Cat. Min.* c. 70.

the Roman world. He was also a man of high moral ideals, sincere piety, and absorbing interest in the fate of human character. With all that wealth of learning, philosophic or historical, with all that knowledge of human nature, what nobler task could a man set himself than to attempt to give some practical guidance to a generation conscious of moral weakness, and distracted between new spiritual ideals and the mythologies of the past? The urgent need for moral culture and reform of character, for a guiding force in conduct, was profoundly felt by all the great serious minds of the Flavian age, by Pliny and Tacitus, by Juvenal and Quintilian. But Plutarch probably felt it more acutely than any, and took endless pains to satisfy it. It was an age when the philosophic director and the philosophic preacher were, as we have seen, to be met with everywhere. And Plutarch took his full share in the movement, and influenced a wide circle.[1] If he did not elaborate an original ethical system, he had studied closely the art of moral reform, and Christian homilists, from Basil to Jeremy Taylor, have drawn freely from the storehouse of his precept and observation. In many tracts he has analysed prevailing vices and faults of his time,—flattery, vain curiosity, irritable temper, or false modesty,—and given rules for curing or avoiding them. In these homilies, the fundamental principle is that of Musonius, perhaps adapted from an oracle to the people of Cirrha "to wage war with vice day and night, and never to relax your guard."[2] The call to reform sounded all the louder in Plutarch's ears because of the high ideal which he had conceived of what life might be made if, no longer left to the play of passion and random influences, character were moulded from early youth to a temperate harmony. To such a soul each passing day might be a glad festival, the universe an august temple full of its Maker's glories, and life an initiation into the joy of its holy mysteries.[3]

In the work of moral and religious reconstruction Plutarch and his contemporaries could only rely on philosophy as their guide. Philosophy to Plutarch, Apollonius, or M. Aurelius, had a very different meaning from what it bore to the great

[1] Gréard, *Morale de Plut.* pp. 36, 52, 67.

[2] Cf. A. Gell. xviii. 2.

[3] Plut. *De Tranq.* c. xx. ἀνὴρ δὲ ἀγαθὸς οὐ πᾶσαν ἡμέραν ἑορτὴν ἡγεῖται; κτλ.

thinkers of Ionia and Magna Graecia. Not only had it deserted the field of metaphysical speculation; it had lost interest even in the mere theory of morals. It had become the art rather than the science of life. The teacher of an art cannot indeed entirely divorce it from all scientific theory. The relative importance of practical precept and ethical theory was often debated in that age. But the tendency was undoubtedly to subordinate dogma to edification.[1] And where dogma was needed for practical effect, it might be drawn from the most opposite quarters. Seneca delights in rounding off a letter by a quotation from Epicurus. M. Aurelius appeals both to the example of Epicurus and the teaching of Plato.[2] Man might toy with cosmic speculation; the Timaeus had many commentators in the first and second centuries.[3] But, for Plutarch and his contemporaries, the great task of philosophy was to bring some sort of order into the moral and religious chaos. It was not original thought or discovery which was needed, but the application of reason, cultivated by the study of the past, to the moral and religious problems of the present. The philosopher sometimes, to our eyes, seems to trifle with the smallest details of exterior deportment or idiom or dress; he gives precepts about the rearing of children; he occupies himself with curious questions of ritual and antiquarian interest.[4] These seeming degradations of a great mission, after all, only emphasise the fact that philosophy was now concerned with human life rather than with the problems of speculation. It had in fact become an all-embracing religion. It supplied the medicine for moral disease; it furnished the rational criterion by which all myth and ritual must be judged or explained.[5]

Plutarch was an eclectic in the sense that, knowing all the moral systems of the past, he was ready to borrow from any of these principles which might give support to character. Whether, if he had been born four or five hundred years earlier, he might have created or developed an original theory himself, is a question which may be variously answered. One may reasonably hesitate to assent to the common opinion that

[1] Sen. *Ep.* 88, ad virtutem nihil conferunt liberalia studia; cf. *Ep.* 94, 95, § 41.

[2] M. Aurel. vii. 35; ix. 41; Epict. *Frag.* lii.

[3] Zeller, *Phil. der Gr.* iii. 1, p. 720 n.

[4] A. Gell. i. 10; ii. 26; vii. 13; xii. 1; Philostr. *Apoll. Tyan.* iv. 20; v. 16.

[5] Oakesmith, *Rel. of Plutarch*, p. 64.

Plutarch had no genius for original speculation. Had he come under the influence of Socrates, it is not so certain that he might not have composed dialogues with a certain charm of fresh dialectic and picturesque dramatic power. It is a little unhistorical to decry a man of genius as wanting in speculative originality, who was born into an age when speculation had run dry, and thought was only subsidiary to conduct. When the dissonant schools forsook the heights of metaphysic and cosmology to devote themselves to moral culture, an inevitable tendency to eclecticism, to a harmony of moral theory, set in. The practical interest prevailed over the infinitely divisive forces of the speculative reason. Antiochus, the teacher of Cicero,[1] while he strove to re-establish Platonism, maintained the essential agreement of the great schools on the all-important questions, and freely adopted the doctrines of Zeno and Aristotle.[2] Panaetius, the chief representative of Roman Stoicism in the second century B.C., had a warm admiration for Plato and Aristotle, and in some essential points forsook the older teaching of the Porch.[3] Seneca, as we have seen, often seems to cling to the most hard and repellent tenets of the ancient creed. Yet a sense of practical difficulties has led him to soften and modify many of them—the identity of reason and passion, the indifference of so-called "goods," the necessity of instantaneous conversion, the unapproachable and unassailable perfection of the wise man. Plutarch's own ethical system, so far as he has a system, is a compound of Platonic and Aristotelian ideas, with a certain tincture of Stoicism.[4] Platonism, which had shaken off its sceptical tendencies in the first century B.C., had few adherents at Rome in the first century of the Empire.[5] The Stoic and Epicurean systems divided the allegiance of thinking people till the energetic revival of Hellenism set in. Epictetus indeed speaks of women who were attracted by the supposed freedom of sexual relations in Plato's Utopia.[6] Seneca often refers to Plato, and was undoubtedly influenced by his spirit.

[1] Plut. *Cic.* c. 4.

[2] Zeller, *Phil. der Gr.* iii. 1, p. 534, in der Hauptsache die bedeutendsten Philosophenschulen übereinstimmen, etc.

[3] *Ib.* p. 503.

[4] *Ib.* iii. 2, pp. 144, 145.

[5] Sen. *Nat. Qu.* vii. 32, 2; Academici et veteres et minores nullum antistitem reliquerunt.

[6] Epict. *Fr.* liii.

But in the second century, the sympathetic union of Platonic and Pythagorean ideas with a vigorous religious revival became a real power, with momentous effects on the future of philosophy and religion for three centuries. Plutarch's reverence for the founder of the Academy, even in little things, was unbounded.[1] It became with him almost a kind of cult. And he paid the most sincere reverence to his idol by imitating, in some of his treatises, the mythical colouring by which the author of the *Phaedo* and the *Republic* had sought to give body and reality to the unseen world.[2] Plutarch condemned in very strong language the coarse and sophistical modes of controversy with which the rival schools assailed one another's tenets.[3] Yet he can hardly be acquitted of some harshness in his polemic against the Stoics and Epicureans. Archbishop Trench, in his fascinating and sympathetic treatment of Plutarch, laments that he did not give a more generous recognition to that noblest and most truly Roman school which was the last refuge and citadel of freedom.[4] We may join the archbishop in wishing that Plutarch, without compromising principle, had been more tolerant to a system with which he had so much in common, and which, in his day, had put off much of its old hardness. But he was essentially a practical man, with a definite moral aim. He took from any quarter principles which seemed to him to be true to human nature, and which furnished a hopeful basis for the efforts of the moral teacher. But he felt equally bound to reject a system which absorbed and annihilated the emotional nature in the reason,[5] which cut at the roots of moral freedom, which recognised no degrees in virtue or in vice, which discouraged and contemned the first faint struggles of weak humanity after a higher life, and froze it into hopeless impotence by the remote ideal of a cold, flawless perfection, suddenly and miraculously raised to a divine independence of all the minor blessings and helps to virtue.[6]

[1] *Sympos.* vii. 1; *Consol. ad Apoll.* xxxvi.

[2] *e.g. De Gen. Socr.* xxii. sqq.; *De Ser. Num. Vind.* xxii.

[3] *Non posse Suav. vivi sec. Epic.* c. ii. τὰ γὰρ αἴσχιστα ῥήματα, βωμολοχίας, ληκυθισμούς, ἀλαζονείας, ἑταιρήσεις, ἀνδροφονίας . . . συνάγοντες Ἀριστοτέλους καὶ Σωκράτους καὶ Πυθαγόρου καὶ τίνος γὰρ οὐχὶ τῶν ἐπιφανῶν, κατεσκέδασαν: *Adv. Col.* c. ii.

[4] Trench, *Plut.* p. 93.

[5] Plut. *De Virt. Mor.* c. vii. sqq.

[6] *Adv. Stoicos*, c. x. ἀλλὰ ὥσπερ ὁ πηχὺν ἀπέχων ἐν θαλάσσῃ τῆς ἐπιφανείας οὐδὲν ἧττον πνίγεται τοῦ καταδεδυκότος ὀργυιὰς πεντακοσίας, κτλ. Cf. Sen. *Ep.* 66, § 10; Zeller, *Phil. der Griech.* iii. 1, p. 230.

Such an ideal may be magnificent, but it is not life. For man, constituted as he is, and placed in such an environment, it is a dangerous mental habit to train the soul to regard all things as a fleeting and monotonous show, to cultivate the *taedium vitae,* or a calm resignation to the littleness of man placed for a brief space between the two eternities.[1] The philosophic sufferer may brace himself to endure the round of human duties, and to live for the commonwealth of man; he may be generous to the ungrateful and tolerant to the vulgar and the frivolous; he may make his life a perpetual sacrifice to duty and the higher law, but it is all the while really a pathetic protest against the pitiless Power which has made man so little and so great, doomed to the life of the leaves and the insects, yet tortured with the longing for an infinite future.

On some great central truths, such as the inwardness of happiness and the brotherhood of man, Plutarch and the Stoics were at one. And the general tone of his moral teaching bears many marks of Stoic influence.[2] But the Stoic psychology, the Stoic fatalism and pantheism aroused all the controversial vehemence of Plutarch.[3] The Stoic held the essential unity of the soul, that reason and passion are not two distinct principles, but that passion is reason depraved and diverted to wrong objects. It is the same simple, indivisible power which shifts and changes and submits itself to opposing influences. Passion, in fact, is an impetuous and erring motion of the reason, and vice, in the old Socratic phrase, is an error of judgment, a fit of ignorance of the true ends of action. But as, according to Stoic theory, the human reason is a portion of the Divine, depravity becomes thus a corruption of the Divine element, and the guarantee for any hope of reform is lost. For himself, Plutarch adopts the Platonic division of the soul into the rational, spirited, and concupiscent elements, with some Aristotelian modifications.[4] The great fact of man's moral nature is the natural opposition between the passions and the rational element of the soul; it corresponds to a similar division in the mundane soul.[5] All experience attests a con-

[1] M. Aurel. ix. 32; xii. 32; ix. 14; xi. 1; vii. 1; vi. 46; ix. 14.

[2] *De Tranq.* c. iii., iv., xiv., xvii.; *De Cup. Div.* iii., iv.; *De Exil.* v.; *De Alex. Virt.* c. vi.; ad init.; Zeller, iii. 1. p. 281.

[3] Zeller, *Phil. der Gr.* iii. 1, p. 208; cf. iii. 2, p. 163; Plut. *De Virt. Mor.* c. vii.

[4] *De Virt. Mor.* l. c.

[5] Zeller. iii. 2, p. 154.

stant, natural, and sustained rebellion of the lower against the higher. Principles so alien and disparate cannot be identified, any more than you can identify the hunter and his quarry.[1] But, although in the unregulated character, they are in violent opposition, they may, by proper culture, be brought at last into a harmony. The function of the higher element is not to extinguish the lower, but to guide and control and elevate it.[2] Passion is a force which may be wasted in vagrant, wild excess, but which may also be used to give force and energy to virtue. To avoid drunkenness, a man need not spill the wine; he may temper its strength. A controlled anger is the spur of courage. Passion in effect is the raw material which is moulded by reason into the forms of practical virtue, and the guiding principle in the process is the law of the mean between excess and defect of passion.[3] This is, of course, borrowed from Aristotle, and along with it the theory of education by habit, which to Plato had seemed a popular and inferior conception of the formation of the virtuous character.[4] By the strong pressure of an enlightened will, the wild insurgent forces of the lower nature are brought into conformity to a higher law. It is a slow, laborious process, demanding infinite patience, daily and hourly watchfulness, self-examination, frank confession of faults to some friend or wise director of souls.[5] It needs the minutest attention to the details of conduct and circumstance, and a steady front against discouragement from the backsliding of the wavering will.[6] In such a system the hope of reform lies not in any sudden revolution. Plutarch has no faith in instant conversion, reversing in a moment the ingrained tendencies of years, and setting a man on a lofty height of perfection, with no fear of falling away. That vain dream of the older Stoicism, which recognised no degrees in virtuous progress, made virtue an unapproachable ideal, and paralysed struggling effort. It was not for an age stricken or blest with a growing sense of moral weakness, and clutching eagerly at any spiritual stay. Plutarch loves rather to think of character under the image of a holy and royal building whose founda-

[1] *De Virt. Mor.* vii.

[2] *Ib.* iv. sq.; *De Cur.* i.

[3] *De Virt. Mor.* vi.; Gréard, p. 78.

[4] Pl. *Phaed.* 82 B; cf. Archer-Hind, App. i. to *Phaed.*

[5] Plut. *De Cohib. Ira*, i. ii.; *De Prof. in Virt.* xiii. xi. iii.

[6] *De Prof.* iv.; *De Cohib. Ira*, ii.

tions are laid in gold, and each stone has to be chosen and carefully fitted to the line of reason.[1]

Plutarch also accepted from the Peripatetic school the principle, which Seneca was in the end compelled to admit, that the finest paragon of wisdom and virtue is not quite self-sufficing, that virtuous activity needs material to work upon,[2] and that the good things of the world, in their proper place, are as necessary to the moral musician as the flute to the flute-player. Above all, Plutarch, with such a theory of character, was bound to assert the cardinal doctrine of human freedom. He had a profound faith in a threefold Providence, exercised by the remote Supreme Deity, by the inferior heavenly powers, and by the daemons.[3] But Providence is a beneficent influence, not a crushing force of necessity. To Plutarch fatalism is the blight of moral effort. Foreknowledge and Fate are not conterminous and coextensive. Although everything is foreseen by heavenly powers, not everything is foreordained.[4] The law of Fate, like the laws of earthly jurisprudence, deals with the universal, and only consequentially with the particular case. Certain consequences follow necessarily from certain acts, but the acts are not inevitably determined.[5] Man, by nature the most helpless and defenceless of animals, becomes lord of creation by his superior reason, and appropriates all its forces and its wealth by his laborious arts.[6] And the art of arts, the art of life, neither trusting to chance nor cowed by any fancied omnipotence of destiny, uses the will and reason to master the materials out of which happiness is forged. Thus the hope of a noble life is securely fenced in the fortress of the autonomous will. To the Stoic the vicious man was a fool, whose reason was hopelessly besotted. The Platonist cherished the better hope, that reason, though darkened for a time and vanquished by the forces of sense, could never assent to sin, that there still remained in every human soul a witness to the eternal law of conduct.

[1] *De Prof.* xvii. ἀλλ' οἵ γε προκόπτοντες, οἷς ἤδη καθάπερ ἱεροῦ τινος οἰκοδομήματος καὶ βασιλικοῦ τοῦ βίου κεκρότηται χρυσέα κρηπὶς οὐδὲν εἰκῇ προσίενται τῶν γινομένων, κτλ.

[2] *Adv. St.* iv. vii.

[3] *De Fato*, c. ix. (572). (Plut. ?)

[4] *Ib.* c. iv. v. οὐ πάντα καθαρῶς οὐδὲ διαρρήδην ἡ εἱμαρμένη περιέχει, ἀλλ' ὅσα καθόλου.

[5] *Ib.* c. iv. οὕτω καὶ ὁ τῆς φύσεως νόμος τὰ μὲν καθόλου συμπεριλαμβάνει προηγουμένως, τὰ δὲ καθ' ἕκαστα ἑπομένως.

[6] *De Fort.* c. iii. iv.

With such a faith as this, an earnest man like Plutarch was bound to become a preacher of righteousness and a spiritual director. Many of his moral treatises are the expanded record of private counsel or the more formal instruction of the lecture-hall. He had disciples all over the Roman world, at Rome, Chaeronea, Ephesus, and Athens.[1] His conception of the philosophic gathering, in which these serious things were discussed, is perhaps the nearest approach which a heathen ever made to the conception of the Christian church.[2] In theory, the philosopher's discourse on high moral themes was a more solemn affair than the showy declamation of the sophist, whose chief object was to dazzle and astonish his audience by a display of rhetorical legerdemain on the most trivial or out-worn themes. But the moral preacher in those days, it is to be feared, often forgot the seriousness of his mission, and degraded it by personal vanity and a tinsel rhetoric to win a cheap applause.[3] The sophist and the philosopher were in fact too often undistinguishable, and the philosophic class-room often resounded with new-fangled expressions of admiration. For all this Plutarch has an indignant contempt. It is the prostitution of a noble mission. It is turning the school into a theatre, and the reformer of souls into a flatterer of the ear. To ask rhetoric from the true philosopher is as if one should require a medicine to be served in the finest Attic ware.[4] The profession of philosophy becomes in Plutarch's eyes a real priesthood for the salvation of souls. He disapproves of the habit, which prevailed in the sophist's lecture theatre, of proposing subtle or frivolous questions to the lecturer in order to make a display of cleverness. But he would have those in moral difficulty to remain after the sermon, for such it was, and lay bare their faults and spiritual troubles.[5] He watched the moral progress of his disciples, as when Fundanus is congratulated on his growing mildness of temper.[6] The philosopher was in those

[1] Gréard, p. 68 sq.

[2] Plut. *De Rect. Rat. Aud.* c. vi. *διὸ δεῖ ἀκροᾶσθαι τοῦ λέγοντος ἵλεων καὶ πρᾷον ὥσπερ ἐφ' ἑστίασιν ἱερὰν καὶ θυσίας ἀπαρχὴν παρειλημμένον κτλ.*: cf. viii. *ἀλλ' εἰς διδασκαλεῖον ἀφῖκται τῷ λόγῳ τὸν βίον ἐπανορθωσόμενος*: c. xii.

[3] *Ib.* c. vii. viii.; cf. Sen. *Ep.* 108, § 6, magnam hanc auditorum partem videbis cui philosophi schola diversorium otii sit, etc.; Epict. *Diss.* ii. 23.

[4] *De Rect. Rat. Aud.* c. ix. *ὅμοιός ἐστι μὴ βουλομένῳ πιεῖν ἀντίδοτον ἂν μὴ τὸ ἀγγεῖον ἐκ τῆς Ἀττικῆς κωλιάδος ᾖ κεκεραμευμένον.*

[5] *Ib.* c. xii.

[6] *De Cohib. Ira*, c. i. *τὸ δὲ σφοδρὸν ἐκεῖνο καὶ διάπυρον πρὸς ὀργὴν ὁρῶντί μοι*

days, and often too truly, charged with gross inconsistency in his private conduct. Plutarch believed emphatically in teaching by example. The preacher of the higher life should inspire such respect that his frown or smile shall at once affect the disciple.[1] Plutarch evidently practised his remedies on himself. His great gallery of the heroes of the past was primarily intended to profit others. But he found, as the work went on, that he was himself "much profited by looking into these histories, as if he looked into a glass, to frame and fashion his life to the mould and pattern of these virtuous noblemen." [2]

Plutarch, as we have seen, waged determined war with the older Stoic and Epicurean systems; yet his practical teaching is coloured by the spirit of both. This is perhaps best seen in the tract on Tranquillity, which might almost have been written by Seneca. Although Plutarch elsewhere holds the Peripatetic doctrine that the full life of virtue cannot dispense with the external gifts of fortune, he asserts as powerfully as any Stoic that life takes its predominant colour from the character, that "the kingdom of Heaven is within," that no change of external fortune can calm the tumults of the soul. You seem to be listening to a Stoic doctor when you hear that most calamities draw their weight and bitterness from imagination, that excessive desire for a thing engenders the fear of losing it, and makes enjoyment feeble and uncertain, that men, by forgetting the past in the vanishing present, lose the continuity of their lives.[3] Is it Plutarch himself, or some Christian preacher, who tells us that seeming calamity may be the greatest blessing, that the greatest folly is unthankfulness and discontent with the daily lot, that no wealth or rank can give such enchanted calm of spirit as a conscience unstained by evil deed or thought, and the power of facing fortune with steady open eye? [4] It is surely the greatest literary genius of his age, buried in a dull Boeotian town, who bids us think of the good things we have, instead of envying a life whose inner griefs we know not, who ever looks on the brighter side of things and dignifies an obscure

πρᾷον οὕτω καὶ χειρόηθες τῷ λογισμῷ γεγενημένον ἐπέρχεται πρὸς τὸν θυμὸν εἰπεῖν κτλ.

[1] *De Rect. Rat. Aud.* c. xii.; cf. *De Prof.* c. xv. τίθεσθαι πρὸ ὀφθαλμῶν τοὺς ὄντας ἀγαθοὺς ἢ γεγενημένους καὶ διανοεῖσθαι τί δ' ἂν ἔπραξεν ἐν τούτῳ Πλάτων κτλ.

[2] Trench, *Plut.* p. 33.

[3] *De Tranq.* c. xvi. xvii. xiv. xv.

[4] *Ib.* c. xix. ἀγνοοῦντες ὅσον ἐστὶ πρὸς ἀλυπίαν ἀγαθὸν τὸ μελετᾶν καὶ δύνασθαι πρὸς τὴν τύχην ἀνεῳγόσι τοῖς ὄμμασιν ἀντιβλέπειν.

lot by grateful content, who is not vexed by another's splendid fortune, because he knows that seeming success is often a miserable failure, and that each one has within him the springs of happiness or misery.[1]

The discipline by which this wise mood, which contains the wisdom of all the ages, is to be attained is expounded by Plutarch in many tracts, which are the record of much spiritual counsel. The great secret is a lover's passion for the ideal and a scorn for the vulgar objects of desire.[2] Yet moral growth must be slow, though steady and unpausing, not the rush of feverish excitement, which may be soon spent and exhausted.[3] The true aspirant to moral perfection will not allow himself to be cast down by the obstacles that meet him at the entrance to the narrow way, nor will he be beguiled by pomp of style or subtlety of rhetoric to forget the true inwardness of philosophy. He will not ask for any witness of his good deeds or his growth in virtue; he will shrink from the arrogance of the mere pretender. Rather will he be humble and modest, harsh to his own faults, gentle to those of others. Like the neophyte in the mysteries, he will be awed into reverent silence, when the light bursts from the inner shrine.[4] This humility will be cultivated by daily self-scrutiny, and in this self-examination no sins will seem little, and no addition to the growing moral wealth, however slight, will be despised.[5] To stimulate effort, we must set the great historic examples of achievement or self-conquest before our eyes, and in doubt or difficulty, we must ask what would Plato or Socrates have done in such a case?[6] Where they have suffered, we shall love and honour them all the more. Their memory will work as a sacred spell.

Plutarch expounded the gospel of a cheerful and contented life, and he evidently practised what he preached. Yet, like all finely strung spirits, he had his hours when the pathos of

[1] Plut. *De Tranq.* c. xi. xiii. xiv. *ὅτι ἕκαστος ἐν ἑαυτῷ τὰ τῆς εὐθυμίας καὶ τῆς δυσθυμίας ἔχει ταμεῖα.*

[2] *De Prof.* c. xiv. *δήλωμα δὲ αὐτοῦ πρῶτα μὲν ὁ πρὸς τὰ ἐπαινούμενα ζῆλος καὶ τὸ ποιεῖν εἶναι προθύμους, ἃ θαυμάζομεν, κτλ.*

[3] *Ib.* c. i.–iv.

[4] *Ib.* c. x. *ὁ δὲ ἐντὸς γενόμενος καὶ φῶς μέγα ἰδὼν οἷον ἀνακτόρων ἀνοιγομένων, ὥσπερ θεῷ τῷ λόγῳ ταπεινὸς συνέπεται κτλ.*

[5] *Ib.* c. xvii.

[6] *Ib.* c. xv; cf. Sen. *Ep.* 11, § 8; aliquis vir bonus nobis eligendus est . . . ut sic tanquam illo spectante vivamus, et omnia tanquam illo vidente faciamus.

life was heavy upon him, and death seemed the sovereign remedy for it all. Any one who shares the vulgar notion that the Greeks, even of the great age, were a race living in perpetual sunshine and careless enjoyment of the hour, should read the Consolation to Apollonius on the death of his son. He will there find all the great poets, from Homer downwards, cited in support of the most pessimist view of human life.[1] In the field of philosophy, it finds the most withering expression in the doctrine of Heraclitus, which did so much to mould the thought of Plutarch's great master, and which coloured so many of the meditations of M. Aurelius.[2] Our life is but in miniature a counterpart of the universal flux, and each moment is the meeting place of life and death. Years, many or few, are but a point, a moment in the tract of infinite age.[3] The noble fulness of a life must be sought not in a sum of years, but in a rounded completeness of virtue. When we look at the chance and change and sorrow of life, death seems really the great deliverer, and in certain moments, it may be hailed as Heaven's last, best gift.[4] Whether it be an unawaking sleep or the entrance to another scene of being, it cannot be an evil; it may perchance be a blessing. If there is nothing after it, we only return to our calm antenatal unconsciousness.[5] Or if there be another life, then for the good and noble there is a place assuredly prepared in some happy island of the West, or other mystic region, which we may picture to ourselves, if we please, in the Orphic visions glorified by Pindar.[6]

We are now on the threshold of another world, from which many voices were coming to the age of Plutarch. After philosophy has done its utmost to mould the life of sixty or seventy years into a moral harmony, with its music in itself,[7] the effort ends in a melancholy doubt. The precept of Seneca and Plutarch, that you should live under the tutelary eye of some patron sage of the past, revealed a need of exterior help

[1] Plut. (?) *Consol. ad Apoll.* c. vi. vii. sqq.

[2] M. Aurel. vii. 1; vii. 19; vi. 15; *ἐν δὴ τούτῳ τῷ ποταμῷ τί ἄν τις τούτων παραθεόντων ἐκτιμήσειεν ἐφ' οὗ στῆναι οὐκ ἔξεστιν*: ix. 32; cf. *Consol. ad Apoll.* c. x. *καὶ ᾗ φησιν Ἡράκλειτος, ταὐτό τ' ἔνι ζῶν καὶ τεθνηκός.*

[3] *Consol. ad Apoll.* c. xvii. *τό τε πολὺ δήπουθεν ἢ μικρὸν οὐδὲν διαφέρειν δοκεῖ πρὸς τὸν ἄπειρον ἀφορῶσιν αἰῶνα.*

[4] *Ib.* c. xiv.

[5] *Ib.* c. xv.; cf. Sen. *Ep.* 99, § 30; *Ep.* 36; *Ep.* 24.

[6] *Consol. ad Apoll.* c. xxxiv. xxxv. *καὶ χῶρός τις ἀποτεταγμένος ἐν ᾧ διατρίβουσιν αἱ τούτων ψυχαί*: Pind. *Ol.* ii. 106 sqq.

[7] Plut. *De Virt. Mor.* c. vi.

for the virtuous will. The passion for continued existence was sobered by the sense of continued moral responsibility and the shadow of a judgment to come. Vistas of a supernatural world opened above the struggling human life on earth and in far mysterious distances beyond. When philosophy had done its utmost to heal the diseases of humanity, it was confronted with another task, to give man a true knowledge of God and assurance of His help in this world and the next. Philosophy had for ages held before the eyes of men a dim vision of Him, sublime, remote, ineffable. But it was a vision for the few, not for the many. It was rather metaphysical than moral and spiritual. It paid little heed to the myths and mysteries by which humanity had been seeking to solve its spiritual enigmas. This long travail of humanity could not be ignored by a true religious philosophy. Some means must be found to reconcile ancient religious imagination with the best conception of the Divine.

The problem indeed was not a new one, except in the sense that an intense revival of religious faith or superstition demanded a fresh théodicée. As early as the sixth century B.C., the simple faith in legend had been shaken among the higher minds in a great philosophic movement which extended over many ages. Some had rejected the myths with scorn. Others had proceeded by the method of more or less critical selection. Others, again, strove to find in them a historical kernel, or an esoteric meaning veiled in allegory. The same methods reappeared in the age of Varro and Scaevola,[1] and, five centuries later, in the theology of Macrobius.[2] The effort, however, of the Platonists of the second century has a peculiar interest, because some fresh elements have been added to the great problem since the days of Xenophanes and Euhemerus and Varro.

To Plutarch, theology is the crown of all philosophy.[3] To form true and worthy conceptions of the Divine Being is not less important than to pay Him pious worship. Plutarch's lofty conception of the Infinite and Supreme, like that of Maximus of Tyre, dominates all his system. In a curious

[1] S. Aug. *De Civ. Dei*, iv. 27; vi. 2.

[2] Macrob. *Sat.* i. c. 17; cf. *Roman Society in the Last Century of the W. Empire*, p. 77 (1st ed.).

[3] *De Def. Or.* c. 2.

treatise on Isis and Osiris, he reviews many a device of scholastic subtlety, many a crude guess of embryonic science, many a dream of Pythagorean mysticism, to find an inner meaning in the Egyptian myth. Yet it embalms, in all this frigid scholasticism, the highest and purest expression of Plutarch's idea of the Supreme. In the end he breaks away from all lower mundane conceptions of the Divine, and reveals a glimpse of the beatific vision. "While we are here below," he says, "encumbered by bodily affections, we can have no intercourse with God, save as in philosophic thought we may faintly touch Him, as in a dream. But when our souls are released, and have passed into the region of the pure, invisible, and changeless, this God will be their guide and king who depend on Him and gaze with insatiable longing on the beauty which may not be spoken of by the lips of man."[1] To Plutarch God is the One, Supreme, Eternal Being, removed to an infinite distance from the mutable and mortal—the Being of whom we can only predicate that "He is," who lives in an everlasting "now," of whom it would be irrational and impious to speak in the terms of the future or the past.[2] He is the One, the Absolute of Eleatic or Pythagorean philosophy, the Demiurgus of Plato, the primal motive power of Aristotle, the World-Soul of the Stoics. Yet Plutarch is as far removed from the Epicureanism which banishes God from the universe as he is from the pantheism of east or west, which interfuses the world and God.[3] Plutarch never abandons the Divine personality, in whatever sense he may hold it. God is the highest perfection of goodness and intelligence, the Creator, the watchful and benevolent Providence of the world, the Author of all good. His power, indeed, is not unlimited. There is a power of evil in the world which must be recognised. And, as good cannot be the author of evil, the origin of evil must be sought in a separate and original principle, distinct from, but not co-equal with, God: a principle recognised in many a theology and philosophy of east and west, and called by many

[1] *De Is. et Osir.* c. lxxix.

[2] *De* EI *ap. Delph.* c. xix. ὅθεν οὐδ' ὅσιόν ἐστιν οὐδὲν τοῦ ὄντος λέγειν ὡς ἦν ἢ ἔσται.

[3] *De Is. et Osir.* c. 54, 78; *De* EI *ap. Delph.* c. 20; *Def. Or.* c. 9, *ad fin.*; Oakesmith, *Rel. of Plut.* p. 88; Zeller, *Phil. der Griech.* iii. 2, p. 148; *De Is. et Osir.* c. 40, 66; *non p. Suav.* c. 22, βοηθεῖν πέφυκεν, ὀργίζεσθαι δὲ καὶ κακῶς ποιεῖν οὐ πέφυκεν: *De Ser. Num. Vind.* c. iv. v. xviii.; Nitsch, *De Plut. Theologo*, p. 8; Gréard, *Morale de Plut.* p. 263; cf. Burgmann, *Seneca's Theologie*, pp. 14–20.

names—Ahriman or Hades, the "dyad" of Pythagoras, the "strife" of Empedocles, the "other" of Plato.[1] Its seat is the World-Soul, which has a place alongside of God and Matter, causing all that is deadly in nature, all moral disorder in the soul of man. Matter is the seat both of evil and good.[2] In its lower regions it may seem to be wholly mastered by the evil principle; yet in its essence it is really struggling towards the good, and, as a female principle, susceptible to the formative influence of the Divine, as well as exposed to the incursions of evil. Plutarch's theory of creation is, in the main, that of the Timaeus, with mingled elements of Stoic cosmogony. Through number and harmony the Divine Mind introduces order into the mass of lawless chaos. But while God stands outside the cosmos as its creator, He is not merely the divine craftsman, but a penetrating power. For from Him proceeds the soul which is interfused with the world and which sustains it. Through the World-Soul, God is in touch with all powers and provinces of the universe. Yet throughout the universe, as in the human soul, there are always present the two elements side by side, the principles of reason and unreason, of evil and of good.[3]

The vision of the one eternal, passionless Spirit, far removed from the world of chance and change and earthly soilure, was the conquest of Greek philosophy, travailing for 800 years. But it was a vision far withdrawn; it was separated by an apparently impassable gulf alike from the dreams of Hellenic legend and from the struggling life of humanity. The poets, and even the poet of divinest inspiration, had bequeathed a mass of legend, often shocking to the later moral sense, yet always seductive by its imaginative charm. How to reconcile the fictions of poetry, which had so long enthralled all imaginations, with higher spiritual intuitions, that was the problem. It was not indeed a new problem. It had driven Xenophanes into open revolt, it had exercised the mind of the reverent Pindar and the sceptical Euripides. It had suggested to Plato the necessity of recasting myth in the light of the Divine purity.[4] But the

[1] Zeller, iii. 2, p. 152; *De Is.* c. 45–49; *De St. Rep.* c. 33.

[2] Plut. *De An. Procr.* c. 6.

[3] Zeller, *Phil. der Griech.* iii. 2, p. 155; Plat. *Tim.* 29, 30.

[4] Diog. Laert. ix. § 18, *γέγραφε δὲ καὶ* [*Ξενοφάνης*] *ἰάμβους καθ' Ἡσιόδου καὶ Ὁμήρου ἐπισκώπτων αὐτῶν τὰ περὶ θεῶν εἰρημένα*: *v.* extracts in Ritter and Preller, *Hist. Phil.* p. 82; Plat. *Rep.* ii. pp. 378–380.

new Hellenism of the second century was a great literary, even more than a theological or philosophic, movement; and the glory of Greek literature was inseparably linked with the glory and the shame of Greek mythology. To discard and repudiate the myths was to give the lie to the divine poets. To explain them away by physical allegory, in the fashion of the Stoic theology, or to lower the "blessed ones" of Olympus to the stature of earthly kings and warriors, after the manner of Euhemerus, was to break the charm of poetic legend, and violate the instincts of ancestral piety.[1] And there were many other claimants for devotion beside the ancient gods of Rome and Greece. Persia and Phrygia, Commagene and Egypt, every region from the Sahara to Cumberland, were adding to the pantheon. Soldiers and travellers were bringing their tales of genii and daemons from islands in the British seas and the shores of the Indian Ocean.[2] How could a man trained in the mystic monotheism of 800 years reconcile himself to this immense accretion of alien superstition?

On the other hand, from whatever quarter, a new spiritual vision had opened, strange to the ancient world. It is not merely that the conception of God has become more pure and lofty; the whole attitude of the higher minds to the Eternal had altered. A great spiritual revolution had concurred with a great political revolution. The vision of the divine world which satisfied men in the age of Pericles or in the Punic wars, when religion, politics, and morality were linked in unbroken harmony, when, if spiritual vision was bounded, spiritual needs were less clamorous, and the moral life less troubled and self-conscious, could no longer appease the yearnings of the higher minds. Both morality and religion had become less formal and external, more penetrating and exigent. Prayer was no longer a formal litany for worldly blessings or sinful indulgence, but a colloquy with God, in a moment of spiritual exaltation.[3] The true sacrifice was no longer "the blood of bulls," but a quiet spirit. Along with a sense of frailty and bewilderment, men felt the need of

[1] Plut. *De Is.* c. xxiii. ὃς (Εὐήμερος) . . . πᾶσαν ἀθεότητα κατασκεδάννυσι τῆς οἰκουμένης.

[2] Plut. *De Def. Or.* c. 18, 21.

[3] Sen. *Ep.* 10, § 5; *Ep.* 41, § 1; Pers. ii. 73; Max. Tyr. *Diss.* xi. § 8, σὺ μὲν ἡγεῖ τὴν τοῦ φιλοσόφου εὐχὴν αἴτησιν τῶν οὐ παρόντων· ἐγὼ δὲ ὁμιλίαν καὶ διάλεκτον πρὸς τοὺς θεοὺς περὶ τῶν παρόντων, κτλ.: Martha, *Moralistes sous l'Emp.* p. 163; Denis, *Idées Morales*, ii. p. 245 sqq.

purification and spiritual support. The old mysteries and the new cults from the East had fostered a longing for sacramental peace and assurance of another life, in which the crooked should be made straight and the perverted be restored.

In Maximus of Tyre,[1] although he has no claim to the reputation of a strong and original thinker, we see this new religious spirit of the second century perhaps in its purest form. Man is an enigma, a contradiction, a being placed on the confines of two worlds. A beast in his fleshly nature, he is akin to God in his higher part, nay, the son of God.[2] Even the noblest spirits here below live in a sort of twilight, or in a heady excitement, an intoxication of the senses. Yet, cramped as it is in the prison of the flesh, the soul may raise itself above the misty region of perpetual change towards the light of the Eternal. For, in the slumber of this mortal life, the pure spirit is sometimes visited by visions coming through the gate of horn,[3] visions of another world seen in some former time. And, following them, the moral hero, like Heracles, the model of strenuous virtue, through toil and tribulation may gain the crown. On this stormy sea of time, philosophy gives us the veil of Leucothea to charm the troubled waters. It is true that only when release comes at death, does the soul attain to the full vision of God. For the Highest is separated from us by a great gulf. Yet the analysis of the soul which Maximus partly borrows from Aristotle, discovers His seat in us, the highest reason, that power of intuitive, all-embracing, instantaneous vision, which is distinct from the slower and tentative operations of the understanding. It is by this higher faculty that God is seen, so far as He may be, in this mixed and imperfect state.[4] For the vision of God can only in any degree be won by abstraction from sense and passion and everything earthly, in a struggle ever upwards, beyond the paths of the heavenly orbs, to the region of eternal calm "where falls not rain or hail or any snow, but a white cloudless radiance spreads over all."[5] And when may we see God? "Thou shalt see Him fully," Maximus says, "only when

[1] Of the life of Maximus of Tyre little is known. He began his career as a teacher probably about 155 A.D. Like other philosophers of his time, he had travelled widely. See the references to Arabia and Phrygia in *Diss.* viii., *e.g.* § 8, Ἀράβιοι μὲν σέβουσι μὲν ὅντινα δὲ οὐκ οἶδα· τὸ δὲ ἄγαλμα εἶδον, λίθος ἦν τετράγωνος. Cf. Zeller, iii. 2, p. 183 n.

[2] Max. Tyr. *Diss.* iv. § 7.

[3] *Ib.* xvi. § 1, § 8.

[4] *Ib.* xvii. § 8.

[5] *Ib.* § 10.

He calls thee, in age or death, but meantime glimpses of the Beauty which eye hath not seen nor can tongue speak of, may be won, if the veils and wrappings which hide His splendour be torn away.[1] But do not thou profane Him by offering vain prayers for earthly things which belong to the world of chance or which may be obtained by human effort, things for which the worthy need not pray, and which the unworthy will not obtain. The only prayer which is answered, is the prayer for goodness, peace, and hope in death."[2]

How could a Platonist of the second century, we may ask, holding such a spiritual creed, reconcile himself to Greek mythology, nay, to all the mythologies, with all the selfish grossness of their ritual? Plutarch and Maximus of Tyre answer the question by a piously ingenious interpretation of ancient legend, and partly by a system of daemons, of mediating and ministering spirits, who fill the interval between the changeless Infinite and the region of sin and change.

In religion, they say, in effect, we must take human nature as we find it. We are not legislating for a young race, just springing from the earth, but for races with conceptions of the Divine which run back through countless ages. There may be, here and there, an elect few who can raise their minds, in rare moments, to the pure vision of the Eternal. But heaven is so far from earth, and earth is so darkened by the mists of sense, that temple and image and sacred litany, and the myths created by the genius of poets, or imposed by lawgivers, are needed to sustain and give expression to the vague impotent yearnings of the mass of men.[3] The higher intuitions of religion must be translated into material symbolism; "here we see, as through a glass darkly." And the symbols of sacred truth are as various as the many tribes of men. Some, like the Egyptian worship of animals, are of a degraded type. The Greek anthropomorphism, although falling far short of the grandeur and purity of the Infinite, yet furnishes its noblest image, because it has glorified by artistic genius the human body, which has been chosen as the earthly home of the rational soul.[4] And the cause of myth and plastic art are really one; nay, there is no opposition or con-

[1] Max. Tyr. *Diss.* xvii. § 11.

[2] *Ib.* xi. § 2, § 7.

[3] *Ib.* viii. § 2, ἀλλ' ἀσθενὲς ὂν κομιδῇ τὸ ἀνθρωπεῖον καὶ διεστὸς τοῦ θείου ὅσον οὐρανοῦ γῆ, σημεῖα ταῦτα ἐμηχανήσατο.

[4] D. Chrys. *Or.* xii. § 59 (404 R).

trast, in fact, between poetic mythology and religious philosophy. They are different methods of teaching religious truth, adapted to different stages of intellectual development. Myth is the poetic philosophy of a simple age, for whose ears the mystic truth must be sweetened by music, an age whose eyes cannot bear to gaze on the Divine splendour unveiled.[1] Philosophic theology is for an age of rationalism and inquiry; it would have been unintelligible to the simple imaginative childhood of the race. Maximus has the same faith as Plutarch that the mythopoeic age possessed, along with an enthralling artistic skill, all the speculative depth and subtlety of later ages. It is almost a profanity to imagine that Homer or Hesiod or Pindar were less of philosophers than Aristotle or Chrysippus.[2] It was assumed that the early myth-makers and lawgivers possessed a sacred lore of immense value and undoubted truth, which they dimly shadowed forth in symbolism of fanciful tale or allegory.[3] The myth at once hides and reveals the mystery of the Divine. If a man comes to its interpretation with the proper discipline and acumen, the kernel of spiritual or physical meaning which is reverently veiled from the profane eye will disclose itself. And thus the later philosophic theologian is not reading his own higher thoughts of God into the grotesque fancies of a remote antiquity; he is evolving and interpreting a wisdom more original than his own. In this process of rediscovering a lost tradition, he pushes aside the mass of erroneous interpretations which have perverted the original doctrine, by literal acceptance of what is really figurative, by abuse of names and neglect of realities, by stopping at the symbol instead of rising to the divine fact.[4]

The treatise of Plutarch on Isis and Osiris is the best illustration of this attitude to myth. Plutarch's theology, though primarily Hellenic, does not confine its gaze to the Greek Olympus; it is intended to be the science of human religion in general. It gives formal expression to the growing tendency to syncretism. The central truth of it is, that as the sun and moon, under many different names, shed their

[1] Max. Tyr. *Diss.* x. § 3, ἡ ψυχὴ . . . ἐδεῖτο φιλοσοφίας μουσικῆς τινος κτλ. Cf. § 5, πάντα μεστὰ αἰνιγμάτων καὶ παρὰ ποιηταῖς καὶ παρὰ φιλοσόφοις.

[2] *Ib.* x. § 3.

[3] Plut. *De Is.* lxviii.; xx.; Max. Tyr. x. §§ 5–7; cf. Macrob. *Som. Scip.* i. 2, 7–19; Hatch, *Hibbert Lec.* p. 55 sq.

[4] Plut. *De Is.* lxvi. *ad fin.*

light on all, so the gods are variously invoked and honoured by various tribes of men.[1] But there is one supreme Ruler and Providence common to all. And the lower deities of different countries may often be identified by the theologian, under all varieties of title and attribute. So, to Plutarch as to Herodotus, the immemorial worships of Egypt were the prototypes or the counterparts of the cults of Greece.[2] There was a temple of Osiris at Delphi, and Clea, to whom Plutarch's treatise is addressed, was not only a hereditary priestess of the Egyptian god, but held a leading place among the female ministers of Dionysus.[3] It was fitting that a person so catholic in her sympathies should have dedicated to her the treatise in which Plutarch expounds his all-embracing theology.

In this treatise we see the new theology wrestling in a hopeless struggle to unite the thought of Pythagoras and Plato with the grossness of Egyptian myth. It is a striking, but not a solitary, example of the misapplication of dialectic skill and learning, to find the thoughts of the present in the fancies of the past, and from a mistaken piety, to ignore the onward march of humanity. Arbitrary interpretations of myth, alike unhistorical and unscientific, make us wonder how they could ever have occurred to men of intellect and learning. Yet the explanation is not far to seek. More elevated conceptions of God, the purged and clarified religious intuition, do not readily find a substitute for the old symbolism to express their visions. Religion, beyond any other institution, depends for its power on antiquity, on the charm of ancestral pieties. A religious symbol is doubly sacred when it has ministered to the devotion of many generations.

In interpreting the powerful cult of Isis, which was spreading rapidly over the western world, Plutarch had two objects in view. By reverent explanation of its legends and ritual, he desired to counteract its immoral and superstitious tendencies;[4] he also wished, in discussing a worship so multiform as that of Isis, to develop his attitude to myth in general. We

[1] Plut. *De Is.* c. lxvii. *ὥσπερ ἥλιος καὶ σελήνη καὶ οὐρανὸς καὶ γῆ κοινὰ πᾶσιν, ὀνομάζεται δ' ἄλλως ὑπ' ἄλλων, οὕτως ἑνὸς λόγου τοῦ ταῦτα κοσμοῦντος καὶ μιᾶς προνοίας ἐπιτροπευούσης, καὶ δυνάμεων ὑπουργῶν ἐπὶ πάντας τεταγμένων, ἕτεραι παρ' ἑτέροις κατὰ νόμους γεγόνασι τιμαὶ καὶ προσηγορίαι, κτλ.*

[2] *Ib.* c. lxi. ; xxxv. ; cf. Herodot. ii. c. 50.

[3] Plut. *De Is.* c. xxxv.

[4] *Ib.* c. xx.

cannot follow him minutely in his survey of the various attempts of philosophy to find the basis of truth in Egyptian legend. Some of these explanations, such as the Euhemerist, he would dismiss at once as atheistic.[1] On others, which founded themselves on physical allegory, he would not be so dogmatic, although he might reject as impious any tendency to identify the gods with natural powers and products.[2] As a positive contribution to religious philosophy, the treatise is chiefly valuable for its theory of Evil and of daemonic powers, and above all for the doctrine of the unity of God, the central truth of all religions.

The daemonology of the Platonists of the second century had its roots deep in the Hellenic past, as it was destined to have a long future. But it was specially evoked by the needs of the pagan revival of the Antonine age. The doctrine had assumed many forms in previous Greek thought from the days of Hesiod, and it has various aspects, and serves various purposes, in the hands of Plutarch, Apuleius, and Maximus of Tyre. It was in the first place an apologetic for heathenism in an age distracted between a lofty conception of one infinite Father and legends of many lands and many ages, which were consecrated by long tradition, yet often shocking to the spiritual sense. As the conception of God became purer and seemed to withdraw into remoter distances, souls like Apuleius, wedded to the ancient rites, found in the daemons, ranging between earth and ether, the means of conveying answers to prayer, of inspiring dreams and prophecy, of ordering all the machinery of divination.[3] To others, such as Maximus of Tyre, the doctrine seemed to discover a spiritual support for human frailty, guardians in temptation and the crises of life, mediators between the human spirit, immured for a time in the prison of the flesh, and the remote purity of the Supreme.[4] To other minds the daemon is no external power, but dwelling within each soul, as its divine part, a kind of ideal personality,[5] in following whose ghostly promptings lies the secret of happiness.

[1] Plut. *De Is.* c. xxiii. πᾶσαν ἀθεότητα κατασκεδάννυσι τῆς οἰκουμένης.

[2] *Ib.* c. lxvi.

[3] Apul. *De Deo Socr.* c. vi. (133).

[4] Max. Tyr. *Diss.* xiv. §§ 7, 8.

[5] Cf. Rohde, *Psyche*, ii. 361, 1. M. Aurel. v. 10, 27, ὅτι ἔξεστί μοι μηδὲν πράττειν παρὰ τὸν ἐμὸν θεὸν καὶ δαίμονα: vii. 17; Epict. i. 14, § 12, καὶ (ὁ θεὸς) ἐπίτροπον ἑκάστῳ παρέστησε, τὸν ἑκάστου δαίμονα, καὶ παρέδωκε φυλάσσειν αὐτὸν αὐτῷ, κτλ.

Finally, the doctrine created an eschatology by which vistas of moral perfection were opened before purer spirits in worlds to come, and the infinite responsibilities of this life were terribly enforced by threats of endless degradation.[1]

The daemons who came to the aid of mythology in the Antonine age, were composite beings, with a double nature corresponding to the two worlds of the Divine and human which they linked together. They are at once divine in power and knowledge, and akin to humanity in feeling and passion.[2] They are even liable to mortality, as was proved by the famous tale of the voice which floated to the Egyptian pilot from the Echinad isles, announcing that the great Pan was dead.[3] Their sphere is the middle space between the lofty ether and the mists of earth. This spiritual mediation, as Maximus points out, is not an exceptional principle. There is a chain of being in the universe, as it had been developed in the cosmic theory of Aristotle, by which the remote extremes are linked in successive stages, and may be blended or reconciled, in a mean or compound, as in a musical harmony. The principle is seen operating in the relation of the great physical elements. Thus, for example, fire and water are at opposite poles: they cannot pass immediately into one another, but air furnishes a medium between the two, and reconciles their opposition by participating in the warmth of the one element and in the moisture of the other.[4] The suggestions of cosmic theory seemed to receive support from many tales which, in that age of luxuriant superstition, were accepted even in educated circles. Travellers, returning from Britain, told weird stories of desolate islands in the northern seas which were the haunts of genii.[5] A Spartan visitor to Delphi related how, on the shores of the Indian Ocean, he had met with a hermit of a beautiful countenance and proof against all disease, who spoke with many tongues, and derived his mystic powers from intercourse with the spirits which haunted those distant solitudes.[6]

Plutarch also justifies his theory of daemons by an appeal to the authority of Hesiod, of Pythagoras and Plato, Xenocrates

[1] Plut. *De Sera Num. Vind.* c. xxii.

[2] Apul. *De Deo Socr.* c. xiii.; Max. Tyr. xv. § 4; Plut. *De Def. Or.* c. x.

[3] Plut. *De Def. Or.* c. xvii.

[4] Max. Tyr. xv. § 3.

[5] Plut. *De Def. Or.* c. xviii.

[6] *Ib.* c. xxi.

and Chrysippus.[1] He might have added others to the list. For, indeed, the conception of these mediators between the ethereal world and the world of sense has a long history—too long to be developed within our present limits. Its earliest appearance in Greece was in the *Works and Days* of Hesiod, who first definitely sketched a great scale of being—gods, heroes, daemons, and mortal men. Hesiod's daemons are the men of the golden age, translated to a blissful and immortal life, yet linked in sympathy with those still on earth—"Ministers of good and guardians of men."[2] The conception was introduced at a time when new moral and spiritual forces were at work, which were destined to have a profound and lasting influence on paganism for a thousand years. The glamour of the radiant Olympus and the glory of heroic battle were fading. Men were settling down to humdrum toil, and becoming acutely conscious of the troubles and sadness of life. With a craving for support and comfort which the religion of Homer could not give, the pessimist view of life, which colours Hesiod's poetry, sought consolation in a mysticism altogether strange to Homer, and even to Hesiod. The feeling that humanity had declined from a glorious prime and, in its weakness and terror at death, needed some new consolations, was met by a system which, although Orpheus may never have existed, will always be called by his name.[3] The Chthonian deities, Dionysus and Demeter, sprang into a prominence which they had not in Homer. The immortal life began to overshadow the present, and in the mysteries men found some assurance of immortality, and preparation for it by cleansing from the stains of time. That idea, which was to have such profound influence upon later thought, that there is a divine element in man, which is emancipated from the prison of the flesh at death, became an accepted doctrine. At the same time, the faith in helpers and mediators, half human, half divine, lent itself to the support of human weakness. The heroic soul who passed victoriously through the ordeal of this life, might in another world become the guardian and exemplar of those who were still on earth.

In the Ionian and Eleatic schools the doctrine was held

[1] Plut. *De Is.* c. xxv.; *De Def. Or.* c. x.

[2] Hes. *Op. et D.* 125; cf. Rohde, *Psyche*, i. p. 96.

[3] For the spiritual influences at work *v.* Lobeck, *Aglaoph.* p. 312; Grote, i. p. 23; Bury, *Hist. of Greece*, p. 312; Hardie, *Lectures*, p. 57.

in some sense by all the great thinkers, by Thales, Anaximander, Heraclitus, Xenophanes. To Thales the world was full of daemons.[1] In the mystic teaching of Heraclitus the universe teems with such spirits, for in the perpetual flux and change, the divine is constantly passing into the death of mortal life and the mortal into the divine.[2] Empedocles, in conformity with his cosmic dualism, first made the distinction between good and bad daemons, and followed Pythagoras in connecting daemonic theory with the doctrine of a fall from divine estate, and long exile and incarnation in animal forms.[3] It was in the dim system of Pythagoras that the doctrine became a really religious tenet, as it was to the Platonists of the Antonine age. Pythagoras was more priest and mystic than philosopher. He had far more in common with the Orphici, with Abaris and Epimenides, than with Thales or Anaximander. His school, for we can hardly speak of himself, connected the doctrine of daemons with the doctrines of metempsychosis and purification and atonement in another world. Souls released from the prison-house of the flesh are submitted to a purgatorial cleansing of a thousand years. Some pass the ordeal victoriously, and ascend to higher spheres. · Others are kept in chains by the Erinnyes. The beatified souls become daemons or good spirits, ranging over the universe, and manifesting themselves in dreams and omens and ghostly monitions, sometimes becoming even visible to the eye.[4] But their highest function is to guide men in the path of virtue during life, and after death to purify the disembodied spirit, which may become a daemon in its turn. This is the theory, which, with some modifications, was adopted by the later Platonists. It was popularised by Pindar, "the Homer of the Pythagorean school." He was captivated by its doctrine of the migrations of the soul, of its ordeal in a future life, and its chastisement or elevation to lofty spiritual rank as daemon or hero. In the second Olympian ode, the punishment of the

[1] Diog. Laert. i. 27, *ἀρχὴν δὲ τῶν πάντων ὕδωρ ὑπεστήσατο, καὶ τὸν κόσμον ἔμψυχον καὶ δαιμόνων πλήρη.*

[2] *Heracl. Reliq.* p. 26 Bywater, *Ἀθάνατοι θνητοί, θνητοὶ ἀθάνατοι ζῶντες τὸν ἐκείνων θάνατον, τὸν δὲ ἐκείνων βίον τεθνεῶτες. ὁ δὲ Ἡράκλειτός φησιν ὅτι καὶ τὸ ζῆν καὶ τὸ ἀποθανεῖν καὶ ἐν τῷ ζῆν ἡμᾶς ἐστι καὶ ἐν τῷ τεθνάναι, κτλ.* Cf. *ἀνὴρ νήπιος ἤκουσε πρὸς δαίμονος ὅπωσπερ παῖς πρὸς ἀνδρός.* Ritter and Preller, *Hist. Phil.* p. 23; Diog. Laert. ix. 1, § 7.

[3] Ritter and Preller, *Hist. Phil.* pp. 126, 7; Hild, *Étude sur les Démons*, p. 228.

[4] Diog. Laert. viii. 1, § 30 sqq.

wicked and the beatitude of noble spirits, in the company of Peleus and Achilles in the happy isles, are painted in all the glowing imagery of the Apocalypse.[1]

The daemonology of Pythagoras, along with the doctrine of metempsychosis in its moral aspect, was adopted by Plato, whether as a serious theory or as a philosophic myth. The chief passages in Plato where the daemons are mentioned are suffused with such mythic colour that it would perhaps be rash to extract from them any sharp dogmatic theory.[2] But Plato, holding firmly the remote purity of God, strove to fill the interval between the mortal and the Infinite by a graded scheme of superhuman beings. The daemon is a compound of the mortal and the divine, spanning the chasm between them. This is the power which conveys to God the prayers and sacrifices of men, and brings to men the commands and rewards of the gods, which operates in prophecy, sacrifice, and mystery. And again the daemon is a power which is assigned to each soul at birth, and which at death conducts it to the eternal world, to receive judgment for its deeds, and perhaps to be condemned to return once more to earth. The reason in man, his truly divine part, is also called his daemon, his good genius. It is the power whose kindred is with the world of the unseen, which is immortal, and capable of a lofty destiny.

Like his master Plato, Maximus of Tyre seems to know nothing of the evil daemons, who, as we shall presently see, were used by Plutarch to account for the immorality of myth. To Maximus the daemons are rather angelic ministers, sent forth to advise and succour weak mortal men.[3] They are the necessary mediators between the one Supreme and our frail mortal life. Dwelling in a region between earth and ether, they are of mingled mortal and divine nature, weaker than the gods, stronger than men, servants of God and overseers of men, by kinship with either linking the weakness of the mortal with the Divine. Great is the multitude of this heavenly host, interpreters between God and man: "thrice ten thousand are they upon the fruitful earth, immortal, ministers of Zeus," healers of the sick, revealers of what is dark, aiding the

[1] Pind. *Ol.* ii. 105 sqq. *ἔνθα μακάρων νᾶσος ὠκεανίδες αὖραι περιπνέοισιν· ἄνθεμα δὲ χρυσοῦ φλέγει τὰ μὲν χερσόθεν ἀπ' ἀγλαῶν δενδρέων, ὕδωρ δ' ἄλλα φέρβει.*

[2] *Sympos.* 202 E; *Polit.* 271 D; *Phaed.* 107 D, 108 B; *Tim.* 90 A.

[3] Max. Tyr. *Diss.* xiv. § 8.

craftsman, companions of the wayfarer. On land and sea, in the city and the field, they are ever with us. They inspired a Socrates, a Pythagoras, a Diogenes, or a Zeno; they are present in all human spirits. Only the lost and hopeless soul is without the guardianship of such an unearthly friend.

The earlier Platonist or Pythagorean daemonology was not employed to explain or rehabilitate polytheism. Although Plato would not banish myth from his Utopia, he placed his ban on the mythopoeic poets who had lent their authority to tales and crimes and passions of the gods. Myth could only be tolerated in the education of the young if it conformed to the standard of Divine perfection.[1] God cannot be the author of evil, evil is the offspring of matter; it is a limitation or an incident of the fleeting world of sense. It is only relative and transitory, and can never penetrate the realm of the ideal. But to Plutarch evil was an ultimate principle in the universe, ever present along with the good, although not perhaps of equal range and power.[2] And Plutarch would not banish and disown the poets for attributing to the gods passions and crimes which would have been dishonouring to humanity. He would not abandon the ancient ritual because it contained elements of gloom and impurity which shocked a refined moral sense. Mythology and ritual, as they had been moulded by poets or imposed by lawgivers, were intertwined with the whole life of the people and formed an essential element in the glory of Hellenic genius. The piety and aesthetic feeling of the priest of Delphi still clung to ancient ritual and legend, even when the lofty morality of the Platonist was offended by the grossness which mingled with their artistic charm. Might it not be possible to moralise the pagan system without discrediting its authors, to reconcile the claims of reason and conservative religious feeling? Might it not be possible to save at once the purity and majesty of God and the inspiration of the poets?

To Plutarch the doctrine of daemons seemed to furnish an answer to this question; it also satisfied other spiritual cravings which were equally urgent. The need of some mixed nature

[1] Plat. *Rep.* ii. 377–380.

[2] Plut. *De Is.* c. xlv. αἰτίαν δὲ κακοῦ τἀγαθὸν οὐκ ἂν παράσχοι, δεῖ γένεσιν ἰδίαν καὶ ἀρχήν, ὥσπερ ἀγαθοῦ καὶ κακοῦ, τὴν φύσιν ἔχειν: cf. Hatch, *Hibbert Lec.* p. 218.

to mediate between the ethereal world and the region of sense became all the more imperious as the philosophic conception of God receded into a more remote and majestic purity. The gradation of spiritual powers, which had been accepted by so many great minds from the time of Hesiod, at once guarded the aloofness of the Supreme and satisfied the craving of the religious instinct for some means of contact with it, for divine help in the trials of time. These mediating spirits were also made in Plutarch's theology to furnish an explanation of oracles and all forms of prophecy, of the inspired enthusiasm of artist, sage, and poet. Finally, the theory, with the aid of mythic fancy, cast a light on the fate of souls beyond the grave, and vindicated the Divine justice by a vision of a judgment to come.

Plutarch's daemonology, as he admits himself, is an inheritance from the past. The daemons are beings half divine, half human; they are godlike in power and intelligence, they are human in liability to the passions engendered by the flesh. This host of spirits dwell in the borderland below the moon, between the pure changeless region of the celestial powers and the region of the mutable and the mortal. Linking the two worlds together by their composite nature, the daemons differ in degrees of virtue; some are more akin to the Divine perfection, others more tainted by the evil of the lower world.[1] The good spirits, as they are described by Maximus of Tyre, are true servants of God and faithful guardians of human virtue. But the bad daemons assume a special prominence in the theology of Plutarch. Nor was the development unnatural. His conception of immortality, and the necessity of purification in another world, raised the question as to the destiny of souls whose stains were indelible. If purified souls are charged as daemons with offices of mercy, may not the impure prolong their guilt in plaguing and corrupting mankind? May not the existence of such sombre spirits account for the evil in the world, the existence of which cannot be blinked? Although there are traces of this moral dualism long before Plutarch's time, both in Greek poetry and speculation, it was Xenocrates who first formulated the doctrine of evil daemons in relation to mythology.[2] "It can-

[1] *De Is.* c. xxvi. ὡς τῶν δαιμόνων μικτὴν καὶ ἀνώμαλον φύσιν ἐχόντων καὶ προαίρεσιν: *De Def. Or.* c. x., c. xvi.

[2] *De Is.* c. xxv.

not be," he taught, "that unlucky days and festivals, conducted with scourgings and fasts, lamentations and lacerations and impure words and deeds, are celebrated in honour of the blessed gods or good daemons. They are rather offered to those powerful and terrible spirits of evil in the air whose sombre character is propitiated by such gloomy rites." These sinister spirits assert their vast power, and display their malevolence, not only in plague, pestilence, and dearth, and all the desolating convulsions of the physical world, but in the moral perversion and deception of the human race. They are accountable for all that shocks the moral sense in the impure or ghastly tales which the poets have told of the gods, and in the gloomy or obscene rites which are celebrated in their honour. The poets and early myth-makers have not invented the evil in myth and rite; they have been deceived as to the authors of the evil. Each of the blessed gods has attached to him a daemon who is in some respects his counterpart, wielding his power, but who may perpetrate every kind of moral enormity in his name, and who demands to be honoured and propitiated after his own evil nature. The bad daemons, in fact, masquerade as gods and bring disgrace upon them. It was not the Blessed Ones who mutilated a father, who raised rebellion in Olympus and were driven into exile, who stooped to be the lovers of mortal women. These are the works of spirits of evil, using their fiendish cunning to deceive a simple age. Its poetry was seduced to cast a magical charm over their lusts and crimes; its superstition was terrified into appeasing the fiends by shameful orgies or dark bloody rites. Poets and founders of ritual have been faithful to supernatural fact, but they did not see that in the supernatural order there are evil powers as well as good. They are sound in their record but wrong in their interpretation. In this fashion Plutarch and his school strove to reconcile a rational faith with the grossness of superstition, to save the holiness of God and the glory of Homer.

But the bad daemons who were called in to save the ancient cults proved dangerous allies in the end. Few who really know him will be inclined to question the sincere monotheistic piety of Plutarch. And a sympathetic critic will even not withhold from him a certain respect for his old-world attachment to the forms of his ancestral worship. He knew no other avenue of approaching the Divine. Yet only the imperious religious cravings and the spiritual contradictions of that age could excuse or account for a system which was disastrous both to paganism and philosophy. The union of gross superstition with ingenious theology, the licence of subtlety applied to the ancient legends, demanded too much credulity from the cultivated and too much subtlety from the vulgar. It undermined the already crumbling polytheism; it made philosophy the apostle of a belief in a baleful daemonic agency. If a malign genius was seated beside every god to account for the evil in nature or myth, might not a day come when both friends and enemies would confound the daemon and the god?[1] Might not philosophy be led on in a disastrous decline to the justification of magic, incantations, and all theurgic extravagance? That day did come in the fourth century when Platonism and polytheism in close league were making a last stand against the victorious Church. Even then indeed a purer Platonism still survived, as well as a purer paganism sustained by the mysteries of Mithra or Demeter. But the paganism which the Christian empire found it hardest to conquer, and which propagated itself far into the Christian ages, was the belief in magic and occult powers founded on the doctrine of daemons. And the Christian controversialist, with as firm a faith in daemons as the pagan, turned that doctrine against the faith which it was invented to support. The distinction of good and bad daemons, first drawn by Xenocrates and Chrysippus, and developed by Plutarch, was eagerly seized upon by Tatian and S. Clement of Alexandria, by Minucius Felix and S. Cyprian.[2] But the good became the heavenly host of Christ and His angels; the bad were identified with the pagan gods. What would have been the anguish of Plutarch could he have foreseen that his theology, elaborated

[1] Mr. Oakesmith thinks that Plutarch tended to identify them, *Rel. of Plut.* p. 127.

[2] Tatian, *Adv. Gr.* 20; Clem. Alex. *Ad Gent.* 26; Cypr. *Ep.* 75, 10; Min. Felix, c. 26, 27, isti igitur impuri spiritus daemones, . . . sub statuis et imaginibus delitescunt, et adflatu suo auctoritatem quasi praesentis numinis consequuntur, dum inspirant interim vates, dum fanis immorantur . . . sortes regunt, oracula efficiunt, falsis pluribus involuta, etc. Cf. Tertull. *Apol.* c. xxii. operatio eorum est hominis eversio . . . Itaque corporibus quidem et valitudines infligunt et aliquos casus acerbos, etc. Cf. *De Idol.* c. ix; Maury, *La Magie*, p. 99 sqq.

with such pious subtlety and care, would one day be used against the gracious powers of Olympus, and that the spirits he had conjured up to defend them would be exorcised as maleficent fiends by the triumphant dialectic of S. Augustine.[1]

The daemonology of Plutarch also furnished a theory of prophetic powers, and especially of the inspiration of Delphi. It was in the porticoes of the shrine of Apollo, or among the monuments of ancient glory and devotion, that the most interesting of Plutarch's religious essays were inspired. He probably bore the honours of the Delphic priesthood down to the last days of his long life. But in the years when Plutarch was ordering a sacrifice or a procession, or discussing antiquarian and philosophic questions with travellers from Britain or the eastern seas, Delphi had lost much of its ancient power and renown. Great political and great economic changes had reduced the functions of the oracle to a comparatively humble sphere. It was no longer consulted on affairs of state by great potentates of the East and West. The farmers of Boeotia or the Arcadian shepherds now came to seek the causes of failure in their crops or of a murrain among their herds, to ask advice about the purchase of a piece of land or the marriage of a child. So far back as the days of Cicero the faith in oracles had been greatly shaken,[2] and even the most venerable shrines were no longer resorted to as of old. Powerful philosophic schools, the Cynic and the Epicurean, poured contempt on all the arts of divination. Many of the ancient oracles had long been silent. In Boeotia, where, in the days of Herodotus, the air was full of inspiration,[3] the ancient magic only lingered around Lebadea. Sheep grazed around the fanes of Tegyra and the Ptoan Apollo. While in old days at Delphi, the services of two, and even three, Pythian priestesses were demanded by the concourse of votaries, in Plutarch's time one priestess sufficed.[4] But the second century brought, along with a general religious revival, a restoration of the ancient faith in oracles. The voice of Delphi had been silenced for a time by Nero, and the sacred chasm had been choked with corpses because the

[1] Aug. *De Civ. Dei*, viii. 14-22.

[2] Cic. *De Div.* ii. 57, 117, cur isto modo jam oracula Delphis non eduntur . . . ut nihil possit esse contemptius? Strab. vii. 7, 9, ἐκλέλοιπε δέ πως καὶ τὸ μαντεῖον τὸ ἐν Δωδώνῃ καθάπερ τἆλλα.

[3] Herodot. viii. 134.

[4] Plut. *De Def. Or.* c. v. viii.

priestess had branded the emperor as another Orestes.[1] But the oracle, although shorn of much of its glory, recovered some of its popularity in the second century. It received offerings once more from wealthy votaries. The emperor Hadrian characteristically tested its omniscience by a question as to the birthplace of Homer. Curious travellers from distant lands, even philosophers of the Cynic and Epicurean schools, came to visit the ancient shrine, to make the round of its antiquarian treasures, and to discuss the secret of its inspiration.[2] A new town sprang up at the gates of the sanctuary; sumptuous temples, baths, and halls of assembly replaced the solitude and ruins of many generations. The god himself seemed to the pious Plutarch to have returned in power to his ancient seat.[3]

The revival of Delphi gladdened the heart of Plutarch as a sign of reviving religion and Hellenism. And although the oracle no longer wielded an oecumenical primacy, its antiquities and its claims to inspiration evidently attracted many curious inquirers. We are admitted to their conversations in the Delphic treatises of Plutarch. His characters bear the names of the old-world schools, but there is a strangely modern tone in their discussions. Sometimes we might fancy ourselves listening to a debate on the inspiration of Scripture between an agnostic, a Catholic, and an accommodating broad Churchman. Plutarch himself, or his representative, generally holds the balance between the extreme views, and tries to reconcile the claims of reason and of faith. It is clear that even in that age of religious revival there was no lack of a scepticism like that of Lucian. Even in the sacred courts of Delphi the Epicurean might be heard suggesting that, because, among a thousand random prophecies of natural events, one here and there may seem to tally with the fact, it does not follow that the prediction was sure and true at the moment of deliverance;[4] the wandering word may sometimes hit the mark. The fulfilment is a mere coincidence, a happy chance. Boethus, the sceptic, is easily refuted by the orthodox Serapion, who makes an

[1] D. Cass. lxiii. 14, *καὶ τὸ μαντεῖον κατέλυσεν, ἀνθρώπους ἐς τὸ στόμιον, ἐξ οὗ τὸ ἱερὸν πνεῦμα ἀνῄει, σφάξας.*

[2] Plut. *De Def. Or.* c. ii.

[3] *De Pyth. Or.* c. xxix.; *v.* Gréard, p. 252.

[4] *De Pyth. Or.* c. x. *τοῦτό γε μᾶλλον ῥίψαι καὶ διασπεῖραι λόγους . . . οἷς πλανωμένοις ἀπήντησε πολλάκις ἡ τύχη, κτλ.*

appeal to well-known oracles which have been actually fulfilled, not merely in a loose, apparent fashion, but down to the minutest details of time, place, and manner.[1] In these discussions, although the caviller is heard with a tolerant courtesy, it is clear that faith is always in the ascendant. Yet even faith has to face and account for an apparent degeneracy which might well cause some uneasiness. For instance, is it not startling that, in the name of the god of music, many oracles should be delivered in trivial, badly-fashioned verses?[2] Can it be that Apollo is a meaner artist than Hesiod or Homer? On the other side, it may be said that the god is too lofty to care to deck his utterances in the graces of literary form, or, by a more probable theory, he inspires the vision but not the verse. But what of the oracles of later days, which are delivered in the baldest prose? Is this not a disturbing sign of degeneracy? Can this be worthy of the god? The defender of the faith has no difficulty in quieting the suspicion. Even in the great ages we know that oracles were sometimes delivered in prose,[3] and in ancient times excited feeling ran naturally into verse.[4] The stately hexameter was the appropriate form of utterance when the oracle had to deal with great events affecting the fate of cities and of nations. Inspiration is not independent of surrounding circumstances, and the functions of the oracle have changed since the days of Croesus and Themistocles. The whole style of human life and the taste of men are less imposing and stately. The change in the style of the oracle is only part of a general movement.[5] For ages simple prose has taken the place of artistic rhythm in other departments besides the sphere of prophecy. We do not despise the philosophy of Socrates and Plato, because it does not come to us clothed in verse, like the speculations of Thales, Parmenides, and Empedocles. And who can expect the simple peasant girl, who now occupies the tripod, to speak in the tones of Homer?[6] The dim grandeur of the old poetic oracles had indeed some advantages, in aiding the memory by the use of measured and musical expression, and in veiling the full meaning of the God from irreverent or hostile eyes. But

[1] *De Pyth. Or.* c. xi.
[2] *Ib.* c. v. xvii.
[3] *Ib.* c. xix.
[4] *Ib.* c. xxiii.
[5] *Ib.* c. xxiv.
[6] *Ib.* xxii. τραφεῖσα ἐν οἰκίᾳ γεωργῶν πενήτων κτλ.

their pompous ambiguity, providing apparently so many loopholes for evasion, brought discredit on the sacred art, and encouraged the imitative ingenuity of a host of venal impostors who, around the great temples, cheated the ears of slaves and silly women with a mockery of the mysterious solemnity of the Pythian verse.[1]

The more serious question as to the cause of the extinction of oracles brings the discussion nearer to the great problem of the sources of inspiration. It is true that the fact may be accounted for to some extent by natural causes. Oracles have never ceased, but the number has been diminished. God measures His help to men by their needs, and as they grow more enlightened they feel less need for supernatural guidance. This, however, is evidently dangerous ground. But surely the poverty and depopulation of Greece are enough to account for the disappearance of oracles. A country which can hardly put three thousand hoplites in the field—as many as Megara alone sent forth to fight at Plataea—cannot need the many shrines which flourished when Greece was in its glory.[2] But it may be admitted that oracles can and do disappear. And this is in no way derogatory to the power of God. For it is not the great God Himself who utters the warning or the prophecy by the voice of the priestess. Such a doctrine is lowering to His greatness and majesty. In prophecy and divination, as in other fields, God operates, through instruments and agents, on a given matter, and in concurrence with physical causes. The matter in this case is the human soul, which, in greater or less degrees, can be acted on by supernatural influences.[3] The exciting cause of the "enthusiasm" or inspiration, applying a sudden stimulus to the soul, may be some vapour or exhalation from the earth, such as that which rose from the cleft beneath the Delphic tripod.[4] Lastly, there is the daemon, a supernatural being, who, by his composite nature, as we have seen, is the channel of sympathy between the human and the Divine.[5] But among the causes of afflatus or inspiration,

[1] *De Pyth. Or.* c. xxv. πλείστης μέντοι ποιητικὴν ἐνέπλησεν ἀδοξίας τὸ ἀγυρτικὸν καὶ ἀγοραῖον καὶ περὶ τὰ μητρῷα καὶ σεράπεια βωμολόχον καὶ πλανώμενον γένος κτλ.

[2] *De Def. Or.* c. viii.

[3] *Ib.* c. ix. εὐηθὲς γὰρ κομιδῇ τὸ οἴεσθαι τὸν θεὸν αὐτὸν . . . ἐνδυόμενον εἰς τὰ σώματα τῶν προφητῶν ὑποφθέγγεσθαι; c. xlviii.; *De Pyth. Or.* c. xxi.

[4] *De Def. Or.* xlii. ψυχῆς τὸ μαντικὸν ὥσπερ ὄμμα δεῖται τοῦ συνεξάπτοντος οἰκείου καὶ συνεπιθήγοντος.

[5] *Ib.* c. x. xii. φύσεις εἰσί τινες ἐν μεθορίῳ θεῶν καὶ ἀνθρώπων, δεχόμεναι

some may, in cases, disappear and cease to operate. The intoxicating fume or vapour is a force of varying intensity, and may exhaust itself and be spent, as a spring may fail, or a mine may be worked out.[1] The daemon may migrate from one place to another, and with its disappearance, the oracle will become silent, as that of Teiresias at Orchomenus has long been, just as the lyre becomes silent when the musician ceases to strike the strings.[2]

In all this theory Plutarch is careful to guard himself against a purely materialistic theory of the facts of inspiration.[3] Physical causes may assist and predispose, but physical causes alone will not account for the facts of inspiration. The daemon is a necessary mediator between the human soul and God, a messenger of the divine purpose. But the real problem of inspiration is in the soul of man himself, in the possibility of contact between the soul and a supernatural power. This question is illuminated in Apuleius and Plutarch and Maximus of Tyre by a discussion of the daemon of Socrates. It was by a natural instinct that the Antonine Platonists went back to the great teacher of Plato for support of the system which was to link religion with philosophy by the daemonic theory. In Plutarch's dialogue on the Genius of Socrates, the various theories of that mysterious influence current in antiquity are discussed at length. The language in which Socrates or his disciples spoke of its monitions lent itself to different interpretations. Was his daemon an external sign, as in augury, an audible voice, or an inner, perhaps supernatural light, a voice of reason, speaking to the soul's highest faculty, through no uttered word or symbol?[4] The grosser conceptions of it may be dismissed at once. The daemon of Socrates does not belong to the crude materialism of divination, although the philosopher could forecast the disaster of Syracuse.[5] Nor was it any ordinary faculty of keen intellectual shrewdness, strengthened and sharpened by the cultivation of experience. Still less was it any hallucination,

πάθη θνητά, οὓς δαίμονας ὀρθῶς ἔχει κατὰ νόμον πατέρων σέβεσθαι: cf. Plat. *Sympos.* 202 E; Apul. *De Deo Socr.* c. vi.; Max. Tyr. *Diss* xiv. §§ 2–8.

[1] *De Def. Or.* c. xliii. *τῶν δὲ περὶ αὐτὴν (τὴν γῆν) δυνάμεων πῇ μὲν ἐκλείψεις πῇ δὲ γενέσεις . . . εἰκός ἐστι συμβαίνειν, κτλ.*

[2] *Ib.* c. xxxviii.; Maury, p. 149.

[3] Plut. *De Def. Or.* c. xlvi.

[4] *De Gen. Socr.* c. xi. xx.; cf. Hild, *Étude sur les Démons*, p. 263 sqq.

[5] *De Gen. Socr.* c. xi. *ἀκούω δὲ καὶ τὴν ἐν Σικελίᾳ τῆς Ἀθηναίων δυνάμεως φθορὰν προειπεῖν αὐτόν κτλ.*

bordering on insanity, which is merely a perversion of the senses and reason. It was rather a spiritual intuition, an immediate vision, not darkened or weakened by passing through any symbolic medium of the senses, a flash of sudden insight such as is vouchsafed only to the select order of pure and lofty spirits, in whom from the beginning the higher portion of the soul has always risen high above the turbid and darkening influence of the senses.[1] That such a faculty exists is certain to the Platonist and the Pythagorean. But in the mass of men it is struggling against fleshly powers, sometimes defeated, sometimes victorious, inspiring ideals, or stinging with remorse, until perchance, late and slowly, after chastisement and struggle, it emerges into a certain calm. Pythagoreans, such as Apollonius, taught that the diviner, the mantic, faculty in man was more open to higher influences when emancipated from the body in sleep, and that it could be set free in waking hours by abstinence and ascetic discipline.[2] Plutarch laid stress on the latter part of this theory, but ridiculed the notion that the soul could be most clear and receptive when its powers were relaxed. But the capacity of the higher reason in the loftier souls is almost without limit. The reason, which is the daemon in each, when unimpeded by bodily obstruction, is open to the lightest, most ethereal touch. Spirit can act directly by immediate influence upon spirit, without any sensuous aid of word or sign.[3] The influence is a "wind blowing where it listeth," or a strange sudden illumination, revealing truth as by a flash. The disembodied spirit, cleansed and freed from the servitude of the body, and now a real daemon, possesses all these powers and receptivities in the fullest measure. But it gains no new power when it quits the body, although its spiritual faculties may have been dulled and obstructed by the flesh. The sun does not lose its native radiance when for a moment it is obscured by clouds.[4] And thus a Socrates may even here below have a spiritual vision denied to us; a Pythia may be inspired by the daemon of the shrine to read the future of a campaign. Nor is there anything more

[1] Plut. *De Gen. Socr.* c. xx.

[2] Philostr. *Apoll. T.* vi. 11.

[3] *De Gen. Socr.* c. xx. αἱ δὲ τῶν δαιμόνων φέγγος ἔχουσαι τοῖς δυναμένοις ἐλλάμπουσιν, οὐ δεόμεναι ῥημάτων οὐδ' ὀνομάτων κτλ. οὕτως οἱ τῶν δαιμόνων λόγοι διὰ πάντων φερόμενοι μόνοις ἐνηχοῦσι τοῖς ἀθόρυβον ἦθος καὶ νήνεμον ἔχουσι τὴν ψυχήν· οὓς δὴ καὶ ἱεροὺς καὶ δαιμονίους ἀνθρώπους καλοῦμεν; cf. *De Def. Or.* c. xxxviii.

[4] *De Def. Or.* c. xxxix.

wonderful in prediction than in memory.[1] In this unresting flux of existence, the present of brief sensation is a mere moment between the past which has ceased to be and the future which is to be born. If we can still grasp the one, may we not anticipate the other?

It is thus that, by a far-reaching theory of inspiration, Plutarch strove to rehabilitate the faith in oracular lore. The loftier philosophic conception of the Supreme is saved from contamination with anything earthly by the doctrine of daemons, themselves released from the body, yet, through the higher faculty in all souls, able to act directly upon those still in the flesh. The influence is direct and immediate, yet not independent of purely physical causes or temperament. "The treasure is in earthen vessels." But the full vision is only reserved for the spirit unpolluted and untroubled by sense and passion. Plutarch is preparing the way for the "ecstasy" of later Neo-Platonism. All this speculation of course lent itself to a revival of heathen superstition. Yet it is interesting to see how, in many a flash of insight, Plutarch reveals a truth for all generations. We, in our time, are perhaps too much inclined to limit the powers of the human spirit to the field of sense and observation. The slackening hold on faith in a spiritual world and a higher intuition may well be visited by the proper Nemesis, in the darkening of the divine vision, whether as religious faith or artistic inspiration. The dream of an earthly paradise enriched with every sensuous gratification by a science working in bondage to mere utility may have serious results for the spiritual future of humanity. It may need a bitter experience to dispel the gross illusion; yet men may once more come to believe with Plutarch that, as it were, at the back of every soul there is an opening to the divine world from which yet may come, as of old, the touch of an unseen hand.

[1] *De Def. Or.* c. xxxix.

BOOK IV.

ADSCENDENTIBUS DI MANUM PORRIGUNT

CHAPTER I

SUPERSTITION

SUPERSTITION in all ages is a term of unstable meaning. Men even of the same time will apply it or deny its application to the same belief. The devout beliefs of one period may become mere superstitions to the next. And, conversely, what for a time may be regarded as alien superstition, may in course of time become an accepted portion of the native creed. This was the history of those Eastern cults which will be described in coming chapters. At first, they fell under Cicero's definition of superstition, viz. any religious belief or practice going beyond the prescription of ancestral usage.[1] But a day came when they were the most popular worships of the Roman world, when great nobles, and even the prince himself, were enthusiastic votaries of them.[2] The religion of Mithra, when it was confined to an obscure circle of slaves or freedmen at Ostia, was a superstition to the pontifical college. It took its place with the cult of the Roman Trinity when Aurelian built his temple to the Sun and endowed his priesthood.[3]

Plutarch devoted a treatise to the subject of superstition. And his conception of it is more like our own, less formal and external, than that of Cicero. He develops his view of the degradation of the religious sense by contrasting it with atheism. Atheism is a great calamity, a blindness of the reason to the goodness and love which govern the universe. It is the extinction of a faculty rather than the perversion of one.[4]

[1] Cic. *De Nat. Deor.* i. 17, 42, § 117; ii. 28, § 70; *De Div.* ii. 72; Sen. *Ep.* 123; Boissier, *Rel. Rom.* i. 23.

[2] Lamprid. *Com.* c. 9.

[3] Vop. *Aurelian.* c. 35, § 3.

[4] Plut. *De Superst.* c. 5, 6, *ἡ μὲν ἀθεότης ἀπάθεια πρὸς τὸ θεῖόν ἐστι . . . ἡ δὲ δεισιδαιμονία πολυπάθεια κακὸν τὸ ἀγαθὸν ὑπονοοῦσα.*

But superstition both believes and trembles. It acknowledges the existence of supernatural powers, but they are to it powers of evil who are ready to afflict and injure, to be approached only in terror and with servile prostration. This craven fear of God fills the whole universe with spectres. It leaves no refuge whither the devil-worshipper can escape from the horrors which haunt him night and day. Whither can he flee from that awful presence? Sleep, which should give a respite from the cares of life, to his fevered mind, swarms with ghostly terrors.[1] And death, the last sleep, which should put a term to the ills of life, only unrolls before the superstitious votary an awful scene of rivers of fire and blackness of darkness, and sounds of punishment and unutterable woe.[2] To such a soul the festivals of ancestral religion lose all their solemn gladness and cheering comfort. The shrines which should offer a refuge to the troubled heart, even to the hunted criminal, become to him places of torture. And the believer in a God of malignant cruelty betakes himself in despair to dark rites from foreign lands, and spends his substance on impostors who trade upon his fears. Better, says the pious Plutarch, not believe in God at all, than cringe before a God worse than the worst of men. Unbelief, calamity though it be, at least does not dishonour a Deity whose existence it denies. The true impiety is to believe that God can be wantonly faithless and revengeful, fickle and cruel.[3]

The earnestness, and even bitterness, with which Plutarch assails the degrading fear of the supernal Powers have caused some rather shallow critics to imagine that he had a sympathy with scepticism.[4] How such an idea could arise in the mind of any one who had read his treatise on the Genius of Socrates or on Isis and Osiris, or on the Delays of Divine Justice, it is difficult to imagine. Plutarch's hatred of superstition is that of a genuinely pious man, with a lofty conception of the Divine love and pity, who is revolted by the travesty of pure religion,

[1] *De Superst.* c. 3, *μόνη γὰρ οὐ σπένδεται πρὸς τὸν ὕπνον . . . εἴδωλα φρικώδη καὶ τεράστια φάσματα καὶ ποινάς τινας ἐγείρουσα καὶ στροβοῦσα τὴν ἀθλίαν ψυχήν.*

[2] *Ib.* c. 4, *συνάπτουσα τῷ θανάτῳ κακῶν ἐπίνοιαν ἀθανάτων.*

[3] *Ib.* c. 6, *φοβοῦνται τοὺς θεοὺς καὶ καταφεύγουσιν ἐπὶ τοὺς θεούς, κολακεύουσι καὶ λοιδοροῦσιν.* Cf. Bacon's *Essays*, *Of Superstition*, "It were better to have no opinion of God at all, than such an opinion as is unworthy of Him."

[4] Gréard, p. 269.

which is repeated from age to age. It is the feeling of a man to whom religion is one of the most elevating joys of life, when he sees it turned into an instrument of torture. But the force of the protest shows how rampant was the evil in that age. Lucretius felt with the intensity of genius all the misery which perverted conceptions of the Divine nature had inflicted on human life.[1] But the force of Roman superstition had endlessly multiplied since the days of Lucretius. It was no longer the exaggeration of Roman awe at the lightning, the flight of birds, the entrails of a sacrificial victim, or anxious observance of the solemn words of ancestral formulae, every syllable of which had to be guarded from mutilation or omission. All the lands which had fallen to her sword were, in Plutarch's day, adding to the spiritual burden of Rome. If in some cases they enriched her rather slender spiritual heritage, they also multiplied the sources of supernatural terror. If in the mysteries of Isis and Mithra they exalted the soul in spiritual reverie and gave a promise of a coming life,[2] they sent the Roman matron to bathe in the freezing Tiber at early dawn and crawl on bleeding knees over the Campus Martius, or purchase the interpretation of a dream from some diviner of Palestine or a horoscope from some trader in astral lore.[3] The Platonist, nourished on the pure theism of the *Phaedo* and the *Republic*, and the priest of that cheerful shrine, which the young Ion had each bright morning swept with myrtle boughs and sprinkled with the water of the Castalian spring,[4] whose holy ministry gladdened even the years of boyhood—a man with such experience had a natural horror of the dark terrors which threatened to obscure the radiant visions of Delphi and Olympus.

Livy complained of the neglect in his day of signs and omens which formerly were deemed worthy of historical record.[5] The contempt for augury in the time of Cicero was hardly concealed among the cultivated.[6] The details of parts of the ancient bird-lore eluded the researches of the elder Pliny. The emperor Claudius, lamenting the neglect of the ancient science, demanded a decree of the Senate to restore it

[1] Luc. i. 65; iii. 991; cf. Cic. *De Div.* ii. 72.
[2] Apul. *Met.* xi. c. 24.
[3] Juv. vi. 523, 547; Mart. vii. 54; Luc. *Philops.* c. 7–13.
[4] Eurip. *Ion*, 104.
[5] Liv. xliii. 13.
[6] Cic. *De Div.* ii. 24.

to its former efficiency.[1] These are some signs of that general decay of old Roman religion in the last century of the Republic, which was partly due to philosophic enlightenment, partly to the confusion and demoralisation of civil strife, but perhaps even more to the dangerous seductions of foreign superstitions.[2] Among the counsels of Maecenas to Augustus, none is more earnest and weighty than the warning against these occult arts.[3] Augustus is advised to observe, and enforce the observance of the time-honoured ancestral forms, but he must banish sorcerers and diviners, who may sow the seeds of conspiracy against the prince. The advice was acted on. While the emperor rebuilt the fallen temples and revived the ancient Latin rites, 2000 books of unlicensed divination were in one day given to the flames.[4] The old religion, which had absorbed so much from the augural lore of Etruria,[5] was itself certainly not free from superstition. The wrath of the Lemures,[6] the darkness of the inner forest, the flash of lightning, the flight of birds, the entrails of a sacrifice, excited many a fear, and might cause a man to suspend a journey, or break up an assembly of the people. But the Romans had, in the early ages, after their orderly legal fashion, reduced the force of these terrors by an elaborate art which provided a convenient resource of statecraft, and a means of soothing the alarms of the crowd.

But foreign and unregulated superstitions, from the second century B.C., were pouring in from the East to put a fresh load on the human spirit or to replace the waning faith in Italian augury. In 139 B.C. Cornelius Scipio Hispalus vainly strove by an edict to stop the inroads of the star readers.[7] But treatises on this pretended science were in vogue in Varro's time, and are quoted by the great savant with approval.[8] These impostors were swarming in Rome at the time of Catiline's conspiracy,[9] inflating the hopes of the plotters.

[1] Tac. *Ann.* xi. 15, rettulit deinde ad senatum super collegio haruspicum, ne vetustissima Italiae disciplina per desidiam exolesceret.

[2] Warde Fowler, *Rom. Festivals*, p. 343.

[3] D. Cass. lii. 36, *τοὺς δὲ δὴ ξενίζοντάς τι περὶ τὸ θεῖον καὶ μίσει καὶ κόλαζε.*

[4] Suet. *Octav.* xxxi.

[5] Cic. *De Leg.* ii. 9; Fowler, *Rom. Fest.* p. 233.

[6] Ov. *Fast.* iii. 285; Lucr. i. 131; Liv. i. 20.

[7] Val. Max. i. 3, 3; cf. Cic. *De Div.* ii. 43.

[8] Aul. Gell. iii. 10.

[9] Cic. *In Catil.* iii. 4; cf. Plut. *Vit. Cic.* c. 17.

Suetonius has surpassed himself in the collection, from many sources, of the signs and wonders which foreshadowed the great destiny, and also the death of Augustus. And it is noteworthy that, among these predictions, are some founded on astrology.[1] On the day of the emperor's birth, P. Nigidius, a learned astrologer, found that the position of the stars foretold a coming master of the world. Augustus himself received a similar forecast from Theagenes, a star-reader of Apollonia. He had his horoscope drawn out, and a silver coin was struck with the stamp of Capricorn.

This fatalist superstition infected nearly all the successors of Augustus in the first and second centuries. Astrology is essentially a fatalist creed, and the heir to the great prize of the principate, with the absolute control of the civilised world, was generally designated by that blind impersonal power whose decrees might be read in the positions of the eternal spheres, or by signs and omens upon earth. Suetonius, Tacitus, Dion Cassius, have chronicled, with apparent faith, the predictions of future power which gathered round the popular candidate for the succession, or the dark warnings of coming disaster which excited the prince's fears and gave courage to enemies and rivals. It is not hard to see why the emperors at once believed in these black arts and profoundly distrusted their professors. They wished to keep a monopoly of that awful lore, lest it might excite dangerous hopes in possible pretenders.[2] To consult a Chaldaean seer on the fate of the prince, or to possess his horoscope, was always suspicious, and might often be fatal.[3] The astonishing thing is, that men had such implicit faith in the skill of these Eastern impostors, along with such distrust of their honesty. They were banished again and again in the first century, but persecution only increased their power, and they always returned to exercise greater influence than ever.[4] Never was there a clearer proof of the impotence of government in the face of a deep-seated popular belief.

Tiberius, who had probably no real religious faith, was,

[1] Suet. *Octav.* xciv. xcvii.

[2] Cf. D. Cass. lxvi. 9, τούς τε ἀστρολόγους ἐκ τῆς Ῥώμης ἐξώρισεν (Οὐεσπασιανὸς) καίτοι πᾶσι τοῖς ἀρίστοις χρώμενος.

[3] Suet. *Dom.* x. interemit Met. Pompeianum quod habere imperatoriam genesin vulgo ferebatur.

[4] Tac. *Ann.* xii. 52; ii. 32, 75; D. Cass. xlix. 43; Suet. *Vitell.* xiv.

from his youth, the slave of astrology.[1] An adept had, at his birth, predicted his lofty destiny.[2] He had in his train one Thrasyllus, a noted professor of the science, who had often to read the stars in the face of death, and he was surrounded in his gloomy retirement at Capreae by a "Chaldaean herd."[3] Claudius was pedantic and antiquarian in his religious tastes, and, while he tried to revive old Roman augury, he banished the astrologers.[4] A great noble who had the temerity to consult them as to the time of the emperor's death shared the same fate. Nero, who despised all regular religion, except that of the Syrian goddess, was the prey of superstitious terror. The Furies of the murdered Agrippina, as in Aeschylean tragedy, haunted him in dreams, and he used the aid of magic to evoke and propitiate the awful shade.[5] When, towards the end of his reign, his prospects grew more threatening, the appearance of a comet drove him to consult Balbillus, his astrologer, who advised that the portended danger should be diverted from the emperor by the destruction of the great nobles. Some of the craft had predicted that Nero should one day be deserted and betrayed, while others consoled him with the promise of a great monarchy of the East with its seat at Jerusalem.[6] The terrible year which followed Nero's death was crowded with portents, and all the rivals for the succession were equally slaves of the adepts, who exploited their ambitions or their fears. The end of Galba was foreshadowed, from the opening of his reign, by ominous dreams and signs.[7] The hopes of Otho had long been inflamed by the diviner Seleucus,[8] and by Ptolemaeus, who was his companion during his command in Spain.[9] When he had won the dangerous prize, Otho was tortured by nightly visions of the spirit of Galba, which he used every art to lay. Yet this same man set out for the conflict on the Po in defiant disregard of omens warranted by the ancient religion.[10] His end, which, by a certain calm

[1] Suet. *Tib.* lxix., circa deos neglilgentior quippe addictus mathematicae, etc.

[2] *Ib.* xiv. Yet cf. his love of mythical *nugae, ib.* lxx.

[3] Juv. x. 94. See the remarkable chapters in Tac. *Ann.* vi. 21–22.

[4] Tac. *Ann.* xii. 52.

[5] Suet. *Ner.* lx.; xxxiv., facto per magos sacro ovocare manes et exorare tentavit.

[6] *Ib.* xl.

[7] Suet. *Galb.* xviii.

[8] Suet. *Otho,* iv.

[9] Tac. *Hist.* i. 22.

[10] Suet. *Otho,* vii. viii.

nobility, seemed to redeem his life, was portended by a sign which Tacitus records as a fact. At the very hour when Otho was falling on his dagger, a bird of strange form settled in a much frequented grove, and sat there undisturbed by the passers-by, or by the flocks of other fowls around.[1] The horoscope of Otho's rival Vitellius had been cast by the astrologers, and their reading of his fate gave his parents acute anxiety. He used to follow the monitions of a German sorceress. Yet, like so many of his class in that age, he had but scant respect for accredited beliefs. It was noted with alarm that he entered on his pontificate on the black day of the Allia.[2] The astrologers he probably found more dangerous than helpful, and he ordered them to be expelled from Italy.[3] But it is a curious sign of their conscious power and their audacity, that a mocking counter edict to that of Vitellius was immediately published by unknown hands, ordaining the death of the persecutor within a certain day.[4]

The emperors of the Flavian dynasty, although their power was stable and the world was settling down, were not less devoted to Eastern superstitions than any of their predecessors. Vespasian indeed once more exiled the astrologers, but he still kept the best of them in his train.[5] He had consulted the oracle on Mount Carmel, and obeyed the vision vouchsafed in the temple of Serapis.[6] His son Titus, who may have had romantic dreams of an Eastern monarchy, consulted foreign oracles, worshipped in Egyptian temples, and was a firm believer in the science of the stars.[7] Domitian was perhaps the most superstitious of all his race. The rebuilder of Roman temples and the restorer of Roman orthodoxy had also a firm faith in planetary lore. He lived in perpetual fear of his sudden end, the precise hour and manner of which the Chaldaeans had foretold in his early youth.[8] Among the many reasons for his savage proscription of the leading nobles, one of the most deadly was the possession of an imperial horoscope. On his side too, the haunted tyrant diligently studied the birth-hour of suspected or possible

[1] Tac. *Hist.* ii. 50.
[2] Suet. *Vitell.* iii. xi. xiv.
[3] Tac. *Hist.* ii. 62.
[4] D. Cass. lxv. 1, ἀντιπαρήγγειλαν ἀπαλλαγῆναι ἐκ τοῦ βίου ἐντὸς τῆς ἡμέρας κτλ.
[5] *Ib.* lxvi. 9, 10.
[6] Tac. *Hist.* ii. 78.
[7] Suet. *Titus,* v. viii. ix.
[8] Id. *Dom.* xiv. xv.

pretenders to the throne. In the last months of his reign, his terror became more and more and more intense; never in the same space of time had the lightning been so busy. The Capitol, the temple of the Flavians, the palace, even Domitian's own sleeping chamber, were all struck from heaven. In a dream, the haunted emperor beheld Minerva, the goddess whom he specially adored, quitting her chapel, with a warning that she could no longer save him from his doom. On the day before his death, the emperor predicted that, on the next, the moon would appear blood red in the sign of Aquarius. On his last morning, a seer, who had been summoned from Germany to interpret the menacing omens, and who had foretold a coming change, was condemned to death.[1]

Hadrian, that lover of the exotic and the curious, was particularly fascinated by the East. He had probably no settled faith of any kind, but he dabbled in astrology, as he dabbled in all other arts.[2] It was a study which had been cultivated in his family. His great-uncle, Aelius Hadrianus, was an adept in the science of the stars, and had read the prediction of his nephew's future greatness.[3] When the future emperor was a young military tribune in lower Moesia, he found the forecast confirmed by a local astrologer. He consulted the *sortes Virgilianae* about his prospects, with not less hopeful results. He practised with intense curiosity other dark magical arts, and the mysterious death of Antinous on the Nile was by many believed to have been an immolation for the Emperor's safety.[4] Hadrian was glad to think that the spirit of his minion had passed into a new star which had then for the first time appeared. On every 1st of January, Hadrian predicted, with perfect assurance, the events of the year, down to his own last hour.[5] Even the last great imperial figure in our period is not free from the suspicion of having tampered with the dark arts. Julius Capitolinus reports a rumour that M. Aurelius consulted the Chaldaeans about the infatuated passion of Faustina for a gladiator.[6] In his

[1] Suet. *Dom.* x. xiv. xv. xvi.; D. Cass. lxvii. 15, *πάντως γὰρ καὶ ὁ Δομιτιανὸς τῶν πρώτων τάς τε ἡμέρας καὶ τὰς ὥρας ἐν αἷς ἐγεγένηντο διασκοπῶν . . . προανήλισκε.*

[2] Spart. *Hadr.* c. 16; cf. Renan, *L'Égl. Chrét.* c. 2.

[3] Spart. *Hadr.* c. 2, § 4.

[4] D. Cass. lxix. 11, *μαντείαις μαγγανείαις τε παντοδαπαῖς ἐχρῆτο κτλ.*

[5] Spart. *Hadr.* c. 16, § 7.

[6] Id. *M. Anton.* c. 19.

account of the famous rainfall that miraculously refreshed the Roman troops in the Marcomannic war, D. Cassius ascribes the miracle to the magic arts of an Egyptian sorcerer whom M. Aurelius kept in his train.[1] Xiphilinus, however, who attributes the marvel to the prayers of the Thundering Legion, expressly denies that the emperor gave his countenance to these impostors. Another suspicious incident comes to us on the authority of Lucian. When the war on the Danube was at its height, the new oracle of Alexander of Abonoteichos had, by mingled audacity and skill, rapidly gained an extraordinary influence even among the greatest nobles in Italy. Rutilianus, one of the foremost among them, was its special patron and devotee, and actually married the daughter of Alexander by an amour with Selene! Probably through his influence, an oracle, in verse of the old Delphic pattern, was despatched to the headquarters of the emperor, ordering that a pair of lions should be flung into the Danube, with costly sacrifices and all the fragrant odours of the East.[2] The oracle was obeyed, but the rite was followed by an appalling disaster to the Roman arms. The impostor was equal to the occasion, and defended himself by the example of the ambiguity of the Delphic oracle to Croesus, before the victory of Cyrus. What part M. Aurelius had in this scene we cannot pretend to tell, but the ceremony could hardly have been performed without, at least, his connivance. Nor does his philosophic attitude exclude the possibility of a certain faith in oracular foresight and divination. He believed that everything in our earthly lot was ordained from eternity, and, with the Stoic fatalism, he may have held the almost universal Stoic faith in the power to discover the decrees of fate.[3]

Nearly all the writers from whom we derive our impressions of that age were more or less tinged with its superstitions. Even the elder Pliny, who rejected almost with scorn the popular religion, was led by a dream to undertake his history of the wars in Germany.[4] His nephew, although he rejoiced at being raised to the augurate, and restored a temple of Ceres on his lands, seems to have clung to the old religion rather

[1] D. Cass. lxxi. 8.

[2] Luc. *Alex.* c. 35, 47.

[3] M. Aurel. x. 5; ix. 27: on the Stoic belief in divination, *v.* Cic. *De Div.* i. 38 (82); Zeller, *Phil. der Griechen*, iii. 1, p. 313 sqq.

[4] Plin. *Ep.* iii. 5, § 4.

as a matter of sentiment than from any real faith. But he had a genuine belief in dreams and apparitions, and he sends his friend Sura an elaborate account of the romance of a haunted house at Athens.[1] His friend Suetonius had been disturbed by a dream as to the success of a cause in which he was to appear. Pliny consoled him with the hackneyed interpretation of dreams by contraries.[2] The biographer of the Caesars may contend with Dion Cassius for the honour of being probably the most superstitious chronicler who ever dealt with great events. Suetonius is shocked by the arrogance of Julius Caesar when he treated with disdain the warning of a diviner from the inspection of a victim's entrails.[3] He glorifies the pious Augustus by a long catalogue of signs and celestial omens which foretold the events of his career.[4] Suetonius must have been as keen in collecting these old wives' tales as the more sober facts of history,[5] and, if we may believe him, the palace of the Caesars for a hundred years was as full of supernatural wonders and the terrors of magic and dark prophecy as the Thessalian villages of Apuleius.[6] The superstitions of the Claudian and Flavian Caesars could nowhere have found a more sympathetic chronicler.

Immensely superior in genius as Tacitus is to Suetonius, even he is not emancipated from the superstition of the age. But he wavers in his superstition, just as he wavers in his conception of the Divine government of the world.[7] Although he occasionally mentions, and briefly discusses, the tenets of the Epicurean and the Stoic schools, it does not seem probable that Tacitus had much taste for philosophy. Full of the old senatorial ideals, he considered such a study, if carried to any depth, or pursued with absorbing earnestness, to be unbecoming the gravity and dignity of a man of rank and affairs.[8] Moreover, his views of human destiny and the Divine government were coloured and saddened by the Terror. Having lived himself through the reign of Domitian, and seen all the horrors of its

[1] Plin. *Ep.* vii. 27.
[2] *Ib.* i. 18, v. 5, 5; cf. Mayor's learned note on iii. 5, 4; Gregorovius, *Hadrian*, p. 229 sqq.
[3] Suet. *Jul. Caes.* lxxvii.
[4] Id. *Octav.* xciii.
[5] Cf. Macé, *Suétone*, p. 59 sqq.
[6] Apul. *Met.* iv. 27; i. 8; cf. Petron. *Sat.* 62, 63.
[7] *v.* Fabian, *Quid Tac. de num. div. judicaverit*, pp. 7, 13, 16, 21, 24, 29; Nipperdey, *Einleitung*, xiv. xxvi.; Tac. *Hist.* v. 5; ii. 38; *Ann.* iii. 18; vi. 22; xiv. 12; cf. Peter, *Die Gesch. Litt.* ii. p. 221.
[8] Tac. *Agric.* c. 2, 4; *Hist.* iv. 5; *Ann.* xiv. 12.

close, having witnessed, in humiliating silence, the excesses of frenzied power and the servility of cringing compliance, Tacitus had little faith either in Divine benevolence or in tempted human virtue.[1] Even the quiet and security of Trajan's reign seemed to him but a precarious interval, not to be too eagerly or confidently enjoyed, between the terror of the past and the probable dangers of a coming age.[2] The corruption of Roman virtue has justly earned the anger of gods, who no longer visit to protect, but only to avenge.[3] And, in the chaos of human affairs, the Divine justice is confused; the good suffer equally with the guilty.[4] Amid obscure and guarded utterances, we can divine that, to Tacitus, the ruling force in human fortunes is a destiny which is blind to the deserts of those who are its sport.[5] He probably held the widespread belief that the fate of each man was fixed for him at his birth, and, although he has a profound scorn for the venality and falsehood of the Chaldaean tribe, he probably had a wavering faith in the efficacy of their lore.[6] Nor did he reject miracle and supernatural portent on any ground of a scientific conception of the universe.[7] His language on such subjects is often perhaps studiously ambiguous. Sometimes he appears to report the tale of a portent, as a mere piece of vulgar superstition. But at other times, he records the marvel with no expression of scepticism.[8] And in his narrative of Otho's death and the miracles of Vespasian, the threats of heaven which ushered in Galba's brief reign in darkness broken by lurid lightnings, the neglected signs of the coming doom of Jerusalem, the glare of arms from contending armies in the sky, the ghostly voices, as of gods departing from the Holy of Holies, as in the tale of many another omen, dream, or oracle, the historian gives an awe and grandeur to a superstition which he does not explicitly reject.[9]

Nor need we be superciliously surprised that the greatest

[1] *Agric.* c. 45; *Hist.* i. 2; iii. 37; *Ann.* i. 7.

[2] *Ann.* i. 1.

[3] *Hist.* i. 3 *ad fin.*

[4] *Ann.* xvi. 33, aequitate deum erga bona malaque documenta.

[5] *Ib.* vi. 22; cf. Mackail, *Rom. Lit.* p. 210.

[6] *Hist.* i. 22, genus hominum potentibus infidum sperantibus fallax, quod in civitate nostra et vetabitur et retinebitur; cf. *Hist.* v. 4; *Ann.* vi. 28; iv. 58; cf. Fabian, p. 19.

[7] *Hist.* ii. 50.

[8] *Ib.* iv. 81; cf. Nipperdey, *Einl.* xxvi.

[9] *Hist.* ii. 50; iv. 81; i. 6; i. 18; v. 13; *Ann.* i. 65; ii. 14; *Hist.* iii. 56; iv. 83; cf. Fabian, *Quid Tac. de num. div. judicaverit*, p. 19.

master of historic tragedy, born into such an age, should have had the balance of his faith disturbed. His infancy and boyhood coincided with the last years of Nero.[1] His youthful imagination must have been disordered and inflamed by the tales, circulating in grave old Senatorial houses, of wild excess or mysterious crime on the Palatine, the daring caprice of imperial harlots, the regal power and fabulous wealth and luxury of the imperial freedmen, the lunacy of the great line which had founded the Empire, and which seemed destined to end it in shame and universal ruin. That the destinies of the world should be at the mercy of a Pallas, a Caligula, or an Agrippina was a cruel trial to any faith. The carnival of lust and carnage in which the dynasty disappeared,[2] the shock of the fierce struggle on the Po, in which the legions of the East and the West fought with demoniac force for the great prize, deepened the horrors of the tragedy and the gloomy doubts of its future historian. The dawn of a timorous hope, which broke under the calm, strong rule of Vespasian, was overcast, during the early manhood of Tacitus, by the old insanity of power which seemed to revive in the last of the Flavians. Such an experience and such an atmosphere were enough to disorder any imagination. The wild Titanic ambition in the Claudian Caesars, a strange mixture of vicious, hereditary insanity,[3] with a fevered imagination which, intoxicated with almost superhuman power, dreamt of unheard of conquests over nature, made the Julio-Claudian emperors, in the eyes of men, a race half-fiend, half-god. Men hated and loathed them, yet were ready to deify them. It did not seem unnatural that Caligula should throw a gigantic arch over the Forum, to link the imperial palace with the temple of Jupiter on the Capitol.[4] Men long refused to believe in the death of Nero, and his reappearance was expected for generations.[5] In spite of the Augustan revival, the calm, if rather formal, sanity of old Roman religion had lost its power over cultivated minds. The East, with its fatalist superstitions, its apotheosis of lofty earthly sovereignty, its enthronement of an evil power beside the good, was completing the overthrow of the national faith. The air was

[1] Peter, *Gesch. Litt.* ii. p. 42.

[2] Tac. *Hist.* iii. 83, simul cruor et strues corporum, juxta scorta et scortis similes, etc.

[3] Suet. *Nero*, c. iv. vi.

[4] Id. *Calig.* xxi. xxii. xxix. xxxiv. xxxvii.; cf. Mackail, *Rom. Lit.* p. 213.

[5] Suet. *Nero*, lvii.

full of the lawless and the supernatural. Science, in the modern sense, was yet unborn; it was a mere rudimentary mass of random guesses, with as little right to command the reason as the legends which sprang from the same lawless imagination. Philosophic speculation in any high sense had almost disappeared. The most powerful system which still lingered, resolved the gods into mere names for the various potencies of that dim and awful Power which thrills through the universe, which fixes from the beginning the destinies of men and nations, and which deigns to shadow forth its decrees in omen or oracle. Awestruck and helpless in the face of a cruel and omnipresent despotism, with little light from accredited systems of philosophy or religion, what wonder that even the highest and most cultivated minds were darkened and bewildered, and were even ready to lend an ear to the sorcery of the mysterious East? The hesitating acceptance of the popular belief in clairvoyance hardly surprises us in a man like Tacitus, bewildered by the chaos of the Empire, and possessing few reasoned convictions in religion or philosophy. It is more surprising to find so detached a mind as Epictetus recognising in some sort the power of divination. He admits that men are driven to practise it by cowardice or selfish greed.[1] He agrees that the diviner can only predict the external changes of fortune, and that on their moral bearing, on the question whether they are really good or evil, he can throw no light. Yet even this preacher of a universal Providence, of the doctrine that our true good and happiness are in our own hands, will not altogether deny that the augur can forecast the future. We should, indeed, Epictetus says, come to consult him, without any selfish passion, as a wayfarer asks of a man whom he meets which of two roads leads to his journey's end.[2] But the field for such guidance is limited. Where the light of reason or conscience is a sufficient guide, the diviner's art is either useless or corrupting. Nor should any ominous signs deter a man from sharing a friend's peril, even though the diviner may give warning of exile or death.

Next to Aristides, there is probably no writer who reveals

[1] Epict. *Diss.* ii. 7, § 10, *τί οὖν ἡμᾶς ἐπὶ τὸ συνεχῶς μαντεύεσθαι ἄγει; Ἡ δειλία, τὸ φοβεῖσθαι τὰς ἐκβάσεις.*

[2] *Ib.* *ὡς ὁ ὁδοιπόρος πυνθάνεται . . . ποτέρα τῶν ὁδῶν φέρει . . . οὕτως ἔδει καὶ ἐπὶ τὸν θεὸν ἔρχεσθαι, ὡς ὁδηγόν.* Cf. *Ench.* 32.

so strikingly the mingled pietism and superstition of the time as Aelian. Although he preferred to compose his works in Greek, he was a native of the Latian Praeneste, that cool retreat of the wearied Roman, and the seat of the famous shrine of Fortuna Primigenia.[1] It is a disputed point whether Aelian belongs to the second century or the third. But the more probable conclusion, favoured by the authority of Suidas, is that he lived shortly after the time of Hadrian.[2] His historical Miscellanies are a good example of that uncritical treatment of history and love of the sensational which were held up to scorn by Lucian.[3] But it is in the fragments of his work on Providence, that we have the best illustration of his religious attitude. The immediate interference of the Heavenly Powers, to reward the pious believer, or to punish the defiant sceptic, is triumphantly proclaimed. Miracles, oracles, presages, and warning dreams startle the reader on every page. Aelian wages war *à outrance* with the effeminate and profane crew of the Epicureans, whom he would certainly have handed over pitilessly to the secular arm, if he had had the power.[4] He records with delight the physical maladies which are said to have afflicted Epicurus and his brothers, and the persecution of their sect at Messene and in Crete.[5] After the tale of some specially impressive interference of Providence, he launches ferocious anathemas at the most famous sceptics, Xenophanes, Diagoras, and Epicurus.[6] He pursues Epicurus even to the tomb, and pours all his scorn on the unbelieving voluptuary's arrangements for biennial banquets to his shade.[7] He exults in the fate of one who, without initiation, tried to get a sight of the holy spectacle at Eleusis, and perished by falling from his secret point of observation.[8] It is needless to say that miraculous cures by Asclepius are related with the most exuberant faith. Aristarchus the tragic poet, and Theopompus the comedian, were restored from wasting and hopeless sickness by the god.[9] Another patient of the shrine had the vision, which

[1] Warde Fowler, *Roman Festivals*, p. 72; Preller, *Rom. Myth.* (Tr.), p. 381.

[2] Philostr. *Vit. Soph.* ii. p. 273, *ἐθαύμαζε δὲ τὸν Ἡρώδην ὡς ποικιλώτατον ῥητόρων*: cf. *Praef. Jac. Perizonii ed. Aeliani*, Gronov.; Suid. *καὶ ἐσοφίστευσεν ἐν Ῥώμῃ αὐτῇ ἐπὶ τῶν μετὰ Ἀδριανὸν χρόνων*.

[3] Ael. *Var. Hist.* xi. 13.

[4] *v. Fragm. Ael. ap. Gronov.* p. 1014.

[5] *Ib.* p. 1022.

[6] *Ib.* p. 1024.

[7] *Ib.* p. 1023.

[8] *Ib.* p. 1011.

[9] *Ib.* p. 1030.

was probably often a real fact, of a priest standing beside his bed in the night, bringing counsels of healing.[1] But the climax of ludicrous credulity is reached in the tale of the pious cock of Tanagra.[2] This favoured bird, being maimed in one leg, appeared before the shrine of Asclepius, holding out the injured limb, and, taking his place in the choir that sung the morning paean, begged the god for relief and healing. It came before the evening, and the grateful bird, with crest erect, with stately tread, and flapping wings, gave voice to his deliverance in his own peculiar notes of praise! The Divine vengeance is also displayed asserting itself in dreams. A traveller, stopping for the night at Megara, had been murdered for his purse of gold by the keeper of his inn, and his corpse, hidden in a dung-cart, was carried through the gates before dawn. At that very hour his wraith appeared to a citizen of the place, and told him the tale of the tragedy. The treacherous assassin was caught at the very point indicated by the ghost.[3] The last dream of Philemon is of a more pleasing kind.[4] The poet, being then in his full vigour, and in possession of all his powers, once had a vision in his home at Peiraeus. He thought he saw nine maidens leaving the house, and heard them bidding him adieu. When he awoke, he told the tale to his boy, and finished the play on which he was at work; then, wrapping himself in his cloak, he lay down to sleep, and when they came to wake him, he was dead. Aelian challenges Epicurus to deny that the maidens of the vision were the nine Muses, quitting an abode which was soon to be polluted by death.

Publius Aelius Aristides is one of the best representatives of the union of high culture with the forces of the religious revival. He saw the beginning and the end of the Antonine age. He was born in 117 A.D. at Adriani, in Mysia, where his family held a high position, his father being priest of Zeus. He received the most complete rhetorical training, and had been a pupil of Herodes Atticus. Travelling through Greece, Italy, and Egypt, and giving exhibitions of his skill in the fashion of the day,[5] Aristides won a splendid reputation, which swelled

[1] *Fragm. Ael.* pp. 1009, 1034.
[2] *Ib.* p. 1013.
[3] *Ib.* p. 1049.
[4] *Ib.* 1051.
[5] *v.* Jebb's *Aristides, Collect. Hist.* § vi.

his vanity to proportions rare even in a class whose vanity was proverbial. He won the restoration of the ruined Smyrna from M. Aurelius, by an oration which moved the Emperor to tears.[1] With a naturally feeble constitution and epileptic tendencies, the excitement of the sophist's life brought on an illness which lasted thirteen years. During that long ordeal, he developed a mystic superstition which, along with an ever-growing self-consciousness, inspired the *Sacred Orations,* which appeared in 177, long after his health had been restored. He visited many seats of sacred healing—Smyrna, Pergamum, Cyzicus, Epidaurus—and, often in a cataleptic state, between sleep and waking, he had visitations of the Higher Powers in dreams. They gave him prescriptions of the strangest remedies, along with eulogies on his unrivalled talent, which he was solemnly enjoined to devote to the celebration of his deliverance by the Divine favour.[2]

Aristides zealously obeyed the Divine command. But whether his sole inspiration was simple gratitude and unsophisticated piety, crossed by superstition, as has generally been assumed, may well be doubted.[3] The truth is, that in Aristides met all the complex influences of his age, both intellectual and spiritual. He was the most elaborate product of the rhetorical school, with its cultivated mastery of phrase, its exuberant pride in the power of words, its indifference to truth, in comparison with rhetorical effect. The whole force of revived Hellenism was concentrated in this declamatory skill.[4] At the same time, the religious revival was very far from being a return to the old religion, in its clear firm outlines and simple wholeness.[5] The Zeus and Athene and Poseidon of the age of Aristides were not the divinities of the great age. Many influences had been at work to blur the clean-cut outlines of Hellenic imagination, and to sophisticate the ancestral faith both of Greece and Rome. Men wished to believe in the ancient gods, but they were no longer the gods of Homer or of Aeschylus, the gods worshipped by the men who fought

[1] Philostr. *Vit. Soph.* ii. p. 253.

[2] Friedl. *Sittengesch.* iii. p. 440 sqq.; Baumgart, *Ael. Aristides als Repräsentant der Soph. Rhet.* pp. 68, 96.

[3] Baumgart rejects Welcker's view of the essentially religious character of Aristides, pp. 112, 113.

[4] Baumgart, pp. 62, 102, Bald ist in der ganzen Heilungsgeschichte dies die Hauptsache, dass nun sein Rhetorentum die höchste Weihe erhalten habe.

[5] Id. p. 62.

in the Samnite or the Punic wars. Greek philosophy for eight centuries had been teaching a doctrine of one Divine force or essence, transcending the powers and limitations of sense, or immanent in the fleeting world of chance and change. Pagan theology had elaborated a celestial hierarchy, in which the Deity, removed to an infinite distance, was remotely linked to humanity by a graduated scale of inferior spiritual beings, daemons, and heroes.[1] Then came the religions of the East, with their doctrines of expiation for sin and ascetic preparation for communion, and visions of immortality. And, alongside of all these developments, there was a portentous growth of vulgar superstition, belief in dreams, omens, and oracles, in any avenue to the "Great Mystery." Sophistic rhetoric, from its very nature and function, was bound to reflect the religious spirit of the age, in all its confusion. The ancient myths, indeed, were revived and decked out with rich poetic colouring. Yet it is not the simple, naïve, old pagan faith which inspires the rhetorical artist. The pantheistic or theosophist doctrines, which were in the air, disturbed the antique character of the piece[2] But the sophist, if he occasionally catches the tone of new mysticism, or even of rationalist interpretation, is nothing if not orthodox on the whole, and he anathematises the impiety of free-thinking philosophy, with the same energy as Aelian. Above all, Aristides is in harmony with the infinite faith in miracle and heavenly vision which was rife.

From whatever cause, the worship of Asclepius had attained an extraordinary popularity in the age of the Antonines.[3] The conditions of health and disease are so obscure, the influences of will and imagination on our bodily states are so marked, that, in all ages, the boundaries between the natural and the unknowable are blurred and may be easily crossed. The science of medicine, even down to the age of Hippocrates, or the age of Galen, had not abandoned all faith in the magical and mysterious.[4] Incantations long held their ground beside more scientific remedies. Health being the most precious and the most precarious of earthly blessings, it is not strange that, in an age of revived belief in the super-

[1] Baumgart, pp. 60, 61.
[2] Id. p. 64.
[3] *v.* c. iii. of Pater's *Marius the Epicurean.*
[4] Philostr. *Apoll. Tyan.* iii. 44; D. Cass. lxix. 22, Ἁδριανὸς δὲ μαγγανείαις μέν τισι καὶ γοητείαις ἐκενοῦτό ποτε τοῦ ὑγροῦ.

natural, the god of health should attain a rank even on a level with the great Olympian gods. His temples rose in every land where Greek or Roman culture prevailed. They were generally built with an eye to beauty of scenery, or the virtues of some clear, cold, ancient spring, or other health-giving powers in the site, which might reinforce the more mysterious influences of religion. And in every temple there was a hierarchy of sacred servants, who guarded a tradition of hieratic ceremonial and of medical science.[1] There was the chief priest, who may or may not have been a trained physician. There were the *daduchi* and *pyrophori*, who attended to the punctual service of the altars. There were the *neocori*, who were probably physicians, and who waited on the patients, interpreting their visions, and often supplementing them by other visions of their own.[2] There were also, in a lower rank, nurses, male and female, who, if we may judge from Aristides, performed the sympathetic part of our own hospital-nurses.[3] The patients came from all parts of the Graeco-Roman world. After certain offerings and rites, the sufferer took his place in the long dormitory, which often contained beds for 200 or 300, with windows open all night long to the winds of the south. The sick man brought his bed-coverings, and made his gift on the altar. The lamps were lighted in the long gallery, a priest recited the vesper prayers. At a later hour, the lights were extinguished, strict silence was enjoined, and a hope for some soothing vision from above was left as a parting gift or salutation by the minister as he retired.[4]

Divination by dreams was one of the most ancient and universal of superstitions in the pagan world.[5] It was also one of the most persistent to the last days of paganism in the West. The god of Epidaurus was still visiting his votaries by night, when S. Jerome was composing his commentary on Isaiah.[6] Nor is the superstition unnatural. Sleep, the most mysterious of physical phenomena, gives birth to mental states which are a constant surprise. Thoughts and powers which are latent in the waking hours, then start into life with a strange vivid-

[1] Caton, *Temples and Ritual of Asklepios*, p. 27.

[2] Baumgart, p. 97 ; cf. Aristid. *Or.* p. 574 (Jebb's Ed.), 531.

[3] Aristid. *Or.* p. 530 (Jebb).

[4] Caton, p. 29.

[5] Maury, *La Magie*, p. 231.

[6] S. Hieron. in *Is.* c. lv. p. 482.

ness and energy. Memory and imagination operate with a force which may well, in an age of faith, be taken for inspiration. The illusion of a double personality, which results from the helplessness of the mind to react on the impressions of sense, also easily passes into the illusion of messages and promptings from powers beyond ourselves. Religious hopes and cravings may thus easily and honestly seem to be fulfilled.

But external causes also reinforced in the ancient world the deceptions of the inner spirit. The dream-oracle was generally on a site where nature might touch the awe and imagination of the votary. Few could have descended into the gloom of the cave of Trophonius without having their fancy prepared for visions.[1] Exhalations from secret chasms, as at Delphi and Lebadea, aided by the weird spells of the Nymphs who haunted such scenes, often produced a physical excitement akin to madness. Opiates and potions administered by the priests, with the effect of solemn religious rites, prepared the votary for voices from another world.[2] Soul and body were still further prepared for the touch of a Divine hand by rigorous fasting, which was enjoined as a preparatory discipline in so many mysteries of the renascent paganism.[3] The heavenly vision could only come to the clear spirit, purged as far as might be from the grossness of the flesh.[4] Ἐγκοίμησις for the sake of healing became a great, and probably in the main, a beneficent institution in the temples of many deities,[5] pre-eminently in those of Isis, Serapis, and Asclepius. The temple of Serapis at Canopus in Strabo's time was thronged by patients of the noblest rank, and was famous for its miraculous cures.[6] Among the many attributes of Queen Isis, none made a deeper impression than her benignant power of healing even the most desperate cases.[7] Her temples rose everywhere. Her dream interpreters were famous from the days of Cicero.[8] In her shrine at Smyrna Aristides had many of his most startling experiences. According to Diodorus, her priests could point to numberless proofs of the power of the great goddess to cure

[1] Pausan. ix. 39, § 4; Max. Tyr. *Diss.* xiv. 2.

[2] Plut. *De Def. Or.* c. 41–46; Philostr. *Apoll. Tyan.* i. 8; cf. Maury, *La Magie*, p. 237.

[3] Apul. *Met.* xi. c. 22.

[4] Max. Tyr. xvi. i.; Philostr. *Apoll. Tyan.* ii. 37; vi. 11.

[5] See a list in Tertullian, *De Anima*, c. 46.

[6] Strab. xvii. 17 (1052).

[7] Diod. Sic. i. 25.

[8] Cic. *De Div.* i. 58.

the most inveterate disease. But the great healer was, of course, Asclepius. The remains of his splendid shrine at Epidaurus are a revelation at once of his fame and power, and of the scenes and occupations in which the devout health-seekers passed their days and nights. In his temple on the island in the Tiber, dreams of healing were still sought in the time of Iamblichus. His shrine at Pergamum, which was the scene of so many of the strange visions of Aristides, in his many years of struggle with disease, was one of the most famous, and its inspired dreams were sought long afterwards by the emperor Caracalla.[1]

It would be idle to speculate on the relative effects of sound medical treatment and of superstition, stimulated by more or less pious arts, upon the constitution of the sufferer. The virtues of herb or mineral drug, of regulated food and abstinence, of bathing in naturally medicated waters, above all of a continual freshness in the air, must have become a tradition in these sacred homes of the god of health. Physical disease is often rooted in moral disorder, and for such troubled, tainted souls, with hereditary poison in vein and nerve, the bright cheerfulness, the orderly calm and confidence of the ritual, which had such a charm for the soul of Plutarch, may have exorcised, for the time, many an evil spirit, and wiped out the memory of old sins. Soothed and relieved in mind and body, the sufferer lay in the dimly lighted corridor, sinking to sleep, with a confidence that the god would somehow make his power felt in visions of the night.[2] Through a sliding panel, hidden in the wall, a dim figure of gracious aspect might glide to the side of his couch, and whisper strange sweet words of comfort. But in many cases, there is no need to assume the existence of sanctified imposture.[3] A debilitated frame, nerves shattered by prolonged suffering, an imagination excited by sacred litany, ghostly counsels and tales of miracle, the all-pervading atmosphere of an immemorial faith, may easily have engendered visions which seemed to come from another world.[4]

[1] Wolff, *De Nov. Orac. Aet.* p. 29.

[2] Caton, p. 28.

[3] Diod. Sic. i. 25.

[4] Wolff, *De Nov. Orac. Aet.* p. 31, Ejus sacerdotes fraudibus famosi opportune Isidis templo Pompeiano culpae convicti sunt; ubi ipse scalinam vidi secretam, etc. Maury, *La Magie*, pp. 237-8.

But from whatever source the visions came, they had a powerful effect on the imagination, and, through that, on the bodily health. Some of the prescriptions indeed given by these voices of the night may seem to us ludicrous or positively dangerous.[1] But the tone and surroundings of these shrines, and the sense of being encompassed by Divine as well as human sympathy, probably counteracted any ill effects of quackery. The calm, serene order, which the hieratic spirit cultivates at its best, the cheerful routine of the sacred service, blending indistinguishably with the ministry to suffering, and consecrating and ennobling it, the confidence inspired by the sedate cheerfulness of the priests and attendants, reinforced by the countless cases of miraculous cures recorded on the walls,[2]—all this must have had a powerful and beneficent influence. And the visitors were not all invalids. The games and festivals drew together many merely for society and amusement. The theatre at Epidaurus must have provided constant entertainment for a far larger concourse than the patients of the temple.[3] A healthy regimen, which is abundantly attested,[4] with the charms of art and surrounding beauties of hill and woodland, tended of themselves to restore peace and balance to disordered nerves. And the social life, especially to Greeks, was probably the most potent influence of all. We can see from Aristides that troublesome cases were watched by a circle of curious sympathisers.[5] In those marble seats, which can still be seen on the site, many a group, through many generations, must have sat listening to music or recitation, or discussing high themes of life and death, or amused with the more trivial gossip of all gatherings of men.

Amid such scenes Aristides spent thirteen years of the prime of his manhood. With all the egotism of the self-pitying invalid, he has recorded the minutest details of his ailments. He seems to have been disordered in every organ, dropsical, asthmatic, dyspeptic, with a tumour of portentous size, and agonising pains which reduced him to the extremity of weakness.[6] But the extraordinary toughness and vitality

[1] Cf. Maury, p. 240.
[2] See a list in Caton, p. 36 sq.
[3] Caton, p. 28; Pausan. ii. 27, § 5; cf. Strab. viii. 6, § 15.
[4] Caton, pp. 40, 38.
[5] Baumgart, p. 101.
[6] Cf. Aristid. *Or.* 536–538 (Jebb, t. i.).

of the man is even more striking than his sufferings. Aristides regarded health as the greatest of all blessings, the condition on which the value of all other blessings depends. And he acted on the belief. His hundred days journey to Rome is a miracle of endurance.[1] Racked with fever and asthma, unable to take any food except milk, he struggled along, alternately through plains turned into lakes, or across the frozen Hebrus, amid storm or rain or freezing cold.

The effects of this journey in aggravated suffering from asthma, dropsy, nervous agony, are described with painful vividness. They were dealt with by the Roman surgeons in a fashion which makes one wonder how the patient survived such laceration.[2] The invalid hastened home to Asia by sea. The voyage was long and weary, a very Odyssey of storm and wandering. Aristides reached Smyrna in mid-winter, and all the physicians were puzzled to find any alleviation for his troubles.[3] Henceforth he passed, for thirteen years, from one temple to another, at the bidding of the gods—from Smyrna to Pergamum, or Chios, or Cyzicus, or Epidaurus—enduring often frightful hardships by land or sea. The description of his sufferings sometimes excites the suspicion that a warm imagination and the vanity of the literary artist have heightened the effect. A tumour of monstrous size,[4] agonies of palpitation and breathlessness, the torture of dyspepsia, vertigo, and neuralgia which doubled up his limbs, and seemed to bend the spine outward like a bow[5]—these are only a few of the morbid horrors which afflicted him.

The divine prescriptions were often as astounding as the malady was severe. Fresh air, exercise, bathing in the sacred wells, fasting and abstinence, indeed, may often have been sound treatment. But to these were added astonishing prescriptions of food or drugs, purgings and blood-letting which drained the body of its slight remaining strength, and which horrified the attendant physicians.[6] But these were

[1] Aristid. *Or.* 537, Ἕβρος πᾶς ἠπείρωτο ὑπὸ κρυστάλλου, πεδία δὲ λιμνάζοντα.

[2] *Ib.* 538, καὶ τέλος, οἱ ἰατροὶ κατέτεμνον ἐκ τοῦ στήθους ἀρξάμενοι πάντα ἑξῆς ἄχρι πρὸς τὴν κύστιν κατω. κτλ.

[3] *Ib.* 541, οὔτε βοηθεῖν εἶχον οὔτε ἐγνώριζον τὴν ποικιλίαν τῆς νόσου. τοσοῦτον δ' οὖν συνέδοξεν εἰς τὰς πηγὰς τὰς θερμὰς κομίσαι. Cf. 514, κτλ, and *Collect. Hist. ad an.* 160, in Jebb's Ed.

[4] *Ib.* 504.

[5] *Ib.* 554, τὸ δὲ στῆθος ἔξω παρεωθεῖτο καὶ τὸ νῶτον εἰς τοὔπισθεν ἀντεσπᾶτο ἠρέμει δὲ οὐδὲν τοῦ σώματος, κτλ.

[6] Arist. *Or.* 501–3, 506, 531, 532.

not the worst. Again and again, Aristides was enjoined, when in a high fever, to bathe two or three times in an ice-cold river running in full flood, and then race a mile at full speed in the face of a northerly gale. He obeyed in spite of all remonstrance, and the doctors and his anxious friends could only follow him to await the result of such extraordinary remedies. Strange to relate, their fears and forebodings proved groundless. Religious excitement, combined with immense vanity and a strange vitality, carried Aristides victoriously through these ordeals,[1] and his friends received him at their close, with an indescribable genial warmth spreading through his whole body, and a lightness and cheerfulness of spirit which more than rewarded him for these strange hardships of superstition.

The faith of Aristides must have been very robust. His tortures lasted for nearly thirteen years, during which the divine prescriptions only seemed to add to their poignancy. But he was upheld by the belief that he was a special object of the Divine favour, and he persistently followed Divine recipes, which ordinary human skill and prudence would have rejected. No doubts, such as troubled his attendants, ever crossed his mind. How far his illness was prolonged by this obstinate adherence to the illusions of sleep and superstition,[2] in the face of expert advice, is a matter on which it would be useless to speculate. It is probable that the imagination and exuberant vanity of Aristides made him a more difficult patient than the ordinary people who frequented these shrines of healing. It is also evident that there was a body of more or less skilled medical opinion connected with the cult of Asclepius. Practical physicians came to the temples,[3] with the benevolence and the curiosity of their craft in all ages, to observe and study, or to advise a cautious interpretation of the revelations of the night. Aristides has preserved the names of some—Theodotus, Asclepiacus, and Satyrus. Long observation of the freaks of individual temperament and constitution must have suggested to thoughtful minds, with some instincts of scientific method, that the supernatural vision should be interpreted in the light of experience. An awful dream of Aristides that all his bones

[1] Aristid. *Or.* 521.
[2] *Ib.* 504-5, 541-2.
[3] Baumgart, p. 101; Aristid. *Or.* p. 550 (Jebb, t. i.).

and sinews must be excised, turned, in the hands of a faithful attendant, into a prediction of renewed vitality.[1] And although some of the nurses, to whom he is so grateful, confirmed his visions by precisely similar revelations of their own,[2] others, of the more skilled physicians, openly blamed his too confident reliance on his dreams, and his unwillingness to try the effect of more scientific treatment.[3] Their proposals, however, were sometimes so severe and heroic that we may excuse him for preferring on the whole the more patient and gentle methods of the god. The sufferer was sometimes favoured with epiphanies of Athene, Apollo, Serapis, and other great divinities, exalting him far above the rank of common votaries.[4] And Asclepius himself, to whom his special devotion was given, not only lightened his physical tortures, although after long years, but endowed him with hitherto unknown powers of rhetorical skill and readiness. The god became the patron of his whole professional life.[5] And Aristides regarded him as the source of fresh inspiration, in the exercise of that word-craft of which he was the greatest master in his time. It is not hard to discern the meaning of this self-deception. Before Aristides began to visit the temples of the god, he was already a finished rhetor, possessed of all the skill which the Greek schools could impart.[6] Prostrated by bodily suffering for years, cut off from that life of brilliant display, which was so lavishly rewarded by applauding crowds, the vain and ambitious declaimer had lost not only his bodily health, but all the joy and excitement of rhetorical triumph. Suddenly he found his balance restored; the tide of energy returned to its old channels. He could once more draw music from the almost forgotten instrument. He had once more the full lecture-hall under his spell. What wonder that he should feel his powers redoubled when they were recovered, and that he should regard the god who had healed his bodily ailments as the author of a fresh literary inspiration?

[1] Aristid. *Or.* 553; Baumgart, p. 99.

[2] Aristid. *Or.* 506, 515; cf. Baumgart, p. 122.

[3] Aristid. *Or.* 505, *οἱ δὲ ἐνεκάλουν ὡς λίαν ἅπαντα ἐπὶ τοῖς ὀνείρασι ποιουμένῳ, κτλ.*

[4] *Ib.* 529.

[5] Baumgart, p. 64, und dabei entwickelte sich der Glaube, dass er dem Asklepios alles verdanke, Leib, Leben, und speciell die Gabe der Rede, etc.; cf. p. 68, erhebt er ihn auch als den eigentlichen Verleiher und Spender seiner rednerischen Gaben, etc., p. 69, er dem Gotte einen stärkeren und bleibenden Einfluss auch auf die Gestaltung seines inneren Lebens zuschreibt.

[6] Id. p. 69.

The debt was repaid in these Sacred Orations.[1] Some treat them as the expression of a genuine mystical piety, others are inclined to think that the incorrigible rhetorician is quite as evident as the pious votary.[2] It would be an excess of scepticism to doubt that Aristides believed in his visions, and in the beneficent power of the god, for which he was full of pious gratitude. Yet the rhetorical spirit of that age was an influence of singular intensity. It mastered not only the faculty of utterance, but the whole mind and life of the rhetorician. The passion to produce a startling or seductive effect on the audience had become a second nature. Truth was a secondary matter, not from any moral obliquity, but from the influence of prolonged training. And so, we may retain a belief in the genuine piety or superstition of Aristides, while we may distrust his narrative. The piety or the mystic superstition may not have been less sincere, although it was mingled with egregious vanity, and expressed itself in the carefully moulded and highly coloured phrases of the schools. Nor should we doubt the piety of Aristides because he deemed himself the special object of Divine favour. On such a principle all prayer for personal benefits would become profane egotism. And although Aristides was profoundly conscious that he was the first of Greek orators,[3] he was also profoundly grateful for the Divine grace which had renewed his powers for the glory of God and the delight and profit of mankind. Whether he would have been content to enjoy his mystic raptures without publishing them to the world, is a question which will be variously answered according to the charity and spiritual experience of the inquirer.

Many another less famous shrine than that of Epidaurus offered this kind of revelation. The gods were liberal in their prophetic gifts in that age, and dreams were as freely sent as they were generally expected. There is no more striking example of the superstition of the age than the treatise of Artemidorus on the interpretation of dreams. Artemidorus lived towards the end of the second century. He was a native of Ephesus, but he called himself Daldianus, in order to share his distinction with an obscure little town in Lydia,

[1] Aristid. *Or.* 512, *εὐθὺς ἐξ ἀρχῆς προεῖπεν ὁ θεὸς ἀπογράφειν τὰ ὀνείρατα.*

[2] Baumgart, pp. 112, 123.

[3] On his vanity *v.* Baumgart, p. 110. The most glaring example is in *Or. Sac* 4, 591–2, *ἐξεβόησα, εἶς, λέγων τὸν θεόν, καὶ ὅς ἔφη, σὺ εἶ.*

which was the birthplace of his mother.[1] The treatise is in five books, three of which are dedicated to Cassius Maximus, a Roman of rank, who was an adept in this pretended science; the others are inscribed to the son of the author. In spite of absurd credulity, wild and perverted ingenuity, and a cold, quasi-scientific tolerance of some of the worst moral enormities of antiquity, Artemidorus seems to have been an earnest and industrious man, who wrote with the mistaken object of doing a service both to his own age and to posterity.[2] Like other pious men of the time, he was afflicted by the profane attitude of the sceptics,[3] and determined to refute them by the solid proofs of a sifted experience. He also wished to furnish guidance to the crowd, who believed in their visions, but were bewildered from the want of clear canons of interpretation. There was evidently afloat a voluminous oneirocritic literature. But it was, according to Artemidorus, frequently wanting in depth and system,[4] and random guesses had too often been the substitute for minute, exhaustive observation and a clear scientific method. Artemidorus was inspired to supply the want by a vision from Apollo, his ancestral patron.[5] He procured every known treatise on dreams.[6] He travelled all over Asia, Greece, and Italy, and the larger islands, visiting the great festivals and centres of population, and consulting with all the seers and diviners, even those of the lowest repute. He took the greatest pains to ascertain the facts of the reported fulfilment of dreams, and to compare and sift the facts of his own observation. No austere scientific student of nature in our day ever took himself more seriously than this collector of the wildest and foulest hallucinations of pagan imagination. Artemidorus really believed that he was founding an enduring science for the guidance of all coming generations.

Yet the foundation of it all is essentially unscientific. To Artemidorus dreams are not the result of natural causes, of physical states, or of the suggestions of memory and

[1] Artemid. *Oneirocrit.* iii. 66.

[2] *Ib.* i. 1, *διὰ τὴν εὐχρηστίαν οὐ μόνον τὴν ἡμῶν αὐτῶν ἀλλὰ καὶ τῶν μετέπειτα ἐσομένων ἀνθρώπων.*

[3] *Ib.* Cf. Tertullian, *De An.* 46, 47.

[4] Artemid. *Oneirocrit.* *οὐ γὰρ ἀπὸ πείρας ἀλλ' αὐτοσχεδιάζοντες . . . οὕτως ἔγραφον.*

[5] *Ib.* ii. 70, *ad fin.*

[6] *Ib.* i. Praef., *οὐκ ἔστιν ὅ τι βιβλίον οὐκ ἐκτησάμην ὀνειροκριτικόν.*

association. They are sent directly by some god, as a promise or warning of the future. Nor should any apparent failure of the prediction tempt us to impeach the truthfulness of the Divine author. Artemidorus affirms as emphatically as Plato, that the gods can never lie.[1] But although they sometimes express themselves plainly, they also frequently veil their meaning in shadowy, enigmatic form, in order to test men's faith and patience.[2] Hence there is need of skilled interpretation, which demands the widest observation, acute criticism combined with reverent faith, and deference to ancient custom and traditional lore. It is curious to see how this apostle of what, to our minds, is a pestilent superstition, pours his scorn on the newer or lower forms of divination.[3] The Pythagorean dream-readers, the interpreters from hand and face and form, the interpreters of sieve and dish and dice, are all deceivers and charlatans. The old formulated and accredited lore of birds and sacrificial entrails, of dreams and stars and heavenly portents, should alone be accepted by an orthodox faith. It is needless to say that Artemidorus believed in astrology as he believed in oneiromancy. Both beliefs go back to the infancy of the race, and both extended their dominion far into the Middle Ages.[4]

It would be impossible, in our space, to give any detailed conception of the treatment of dreams by Artemidorus. Nor would the attempt reward the pains; the curious specialist must read the treatise for himself. He will find in it one of the most astonishing efforts of besotted credulity to disguise itself under the forms of scientific inquiry. He will find an apparently genuine piety united with an unprotesting record of the most revolting prurience of the lawless fancy. He will find a subtlety and formalism of system and distinction worthy of a finished schoolman of the fourteenth century, and all employed to give order and meaning to the wildest vagaries of vulgar fancy. The classification of dreams by Artemidorus is a great effort, and is followed out in an exhaustive order. Every possible subject, and many that seem to a modern almost inconceivable, are catalogued, each in its proper place, with the appropriate principles of explanation. The hierarchy

[1] Artemid. *Oneirocrit.* iv. 71.

[2] *Ib.* ἀλλὰ ποτὲ μὲν ἁπλῶς λέγουσι, ποτὲ δὲ αἰνίσσονται . . . ἐπειδὴ καὶ σοφώτεροι ὄντες ἡμῶν αὐτῶν οὐδὲν ἡμᾶς ἀβασανίστως βούλονται λαμβάνειν.

[3] *Ib.* ii. 69.

[4] Maury, p. 241.

of gods and heroes in their various grades, the orbs of the sky, the various parts of the bodily frame, from the hair of the head to the toes and nails, the various occupations and multiform incidents in the life of man from the cradle to the grave,[1] the whole list of animals, plants, and drugs which serve his uses,—all these things, and many others which might conceivably, or inconceivably, enter into the fabric of a dream, are painfully collected and arranged for the guidance of the future inquirer. And this demands not only an effort of logical classification, but also an immense knowledge of the customs and peculiarities of different races,[2] the special attributes of each of the gods, and a minute acquaintance with the natural history of the time. For, special circumstances and details cannot be safely neglected in the interpretation of dreams. It may make the greatest difference whether the same dream comes to a rich man or a poor man,[3] to a man or a woman, to a married woman or a virgin, to old or young, to king or subject. To one it may mean the greatest of blessings, to another calamity or death. For instance, for a priest of Isis to dream of a shaven head is of good omen; to any other person it is ominous of evil.[4] To dream that you have the head of a lion or elephant is a prediction of a rise above your natural estate; but to dream that you have the horns of an ox portends violent death.[5] To dream of shoemaking and carpentry foretells happy marriage and friendship, but the vision of a tanner's yard, from its connection with foul odours and death, may foreshadow disgrace and disaster.[6] To dream of drinking cold water is a wholesome sign; but a fancied draught of hot fluid, as being unnatural, may forbode disease or failure.[7] A man dreamt that his mother was bearing him a second time; the issue was that he returned from exile to his motherland, found his mother ill, and inherited her property. Another had a vision of an olive shooting from his head; he developed a vigour and clearness of thought and language worthy of the goddess to whom the olive is sacred.[8] It would be wearisome, and even disgusting, to give other examples of this futile and almost

[1] Artemid. *Oneiroerit.* iv. Praef.
[2] *Ib.* ii. 4.
[3] *Ib.* i. 13, 17.
[4] *Ib.* i. 22.
[5] *Ib.* i. 37, 39.
[6] *Ib.* i. 51.
[7] *Ib.* i. 66.
[8] *Ib.* v. 18.

idiotic superstition, masquerading as a science. A painstaking student might easily classify the modes of interpretation. They are tolerably uniform, and rest on fanciful but obvious conceits, superficial analogies, mere play upon words and impossible etymologies. The interpretations are as dull and monotonous as the dreams are various and fantastic. Many of these visions seem like the wildest hallucinations of prurient lunacy. It is difficult to conceive what was the ordinary state of mind and the habits of a people whose sleep was haunted by visions so lawless. It is perhaps even harder to imagine a father, with the infinite industry of which he is so proud, compiling such a catalogue for the study of his son.[1]

Lucian, through the mouth of Momus, pours his scorn on the new oracles which were chanting from every rock, vending their lies at two obols apiece, and overshadowing the ancient glories of the more ancient shrines.[2] In the last century of the Republic, and in the first century of the Empire, the faith in oracles had suffered a portentous decay. The exultation of the Christian Fathers at the desertion of the ancient seats of prophecy seems to find an echo in the record of heathen authors. Cicero speaks as if Delphi were almost silent.[3] Strabo tells us that Delphi, Dodona, and Ammon had shared in the general contempt which had fallen on oracular divination.[4] From Plutarch we have seen that in Boeotia, the most famous home of the art, all the oracular shrines were silent and deserted, except that of Trophonius at Lebadea.[5] And curious inquirers gave various explanations of this waning faith. Strabo thought that, with the spread of Roman power, the Sibylline prophecies and the Etruscan augury eclipsed the Greek and Eastern oracles. The explanation in Plutarch, as we have seen, is involved in an interesting discussion of the various sources of inspiration, and, in particular, of the office of daemons. One theorist of the positive type attributes the failure of the Greek oracles to the growing depopulation of Greece. It is a question of demand and supply. Others find

[1] Artemid. *Oneirocrit.* v. Praef.

[2] Luc. *Concil. Deor.* c. 12, ἀλλ' ἤδη πᾶς λίθος καὶ πᾶς βωμὸς χρησμῳδεῖ, κτλ. Cf. Philostr. *Apoll. Tyan.* iv. 14.

[3] Cic. *De Div.* ii. 57, cur isto modo jam oracula Delphis non eduntur non modo nostra aetate, sed jamdiu, jam ut nihil possit esse contemptius?

[4] Strab. ix. 3, 4, (419), ὠλιγώρηται δ' ἱκανῶς καὶ τὸ ἱερόν, κτλ.: vii. 7, 9, (328) (Dodona); xvii. 1, 43 (Ammon).

[5] Plut. *De Def. Or.* c. 5.

the explanation in physical changes, which have extinguished or diverted the exhalation that used to excite the prophetic powers of the Pythia. Another falls back on the theory of daemonic inspiration, which, mysteriously vouchsafed, may be as mysteriously withdrawn.[1]

The eclipse of the oracles was really a phase of that pagan unbelief or indifference which tended to disappear towards the end of the first century A.D. And the eclipse perhaps was not so complete as it is represented. Cicero himself consulted the Pythia about his future fame, and received an answer which revealed insight into his character.[2] Germanicus in the reign of Tiberius visited the shrine of the Clarian Apollo, and that of Apis at Memphis;[3] Tiberius tried the sacred lottery at Padua,[4] Caligula that of Fortune at Antium.[5] Nero, although he is said to have choked the sacred chasm at Delphi with corpses, had previously sought light from the god on his perilous future.[6] Before the altar of the unseen God on Mount Carmel, Vespasian received an impressive prophecy of his coming greatness.[7] Titus had his hopes confirmed in the shrine of the Paphian Venus.[8] When these lords of the world, some of whom were notorious sceptics, thus paid deference to the ancient homes of prophecy, it may be doubted whether their prestige had been seriously shaken.

Although Delphi had not for many ages wielded the enormous political, and even international, power which it enjoyed before the Persian wars, still, even in the days of its greatest obscurity, it was the resort of many who came to consult it in the ordinary cares of life. Apollonius of Tyana, in the reign of Nero, visited the old oracular centres, Delphi, Dodona, Abae, and the shrines of Amphiaraus and Trophonius.[9] They seem to be still active, although the sage had, in fulfilment of his mission, to correct their ritual. The newer foundations, like that at Abonoteichos, found it politic to defer to the authority of oracles, such as those of Clarus and Didyma, with a great past.[10] If the conquests of Rome for a time obscured their fame, the ease and rapidity of com-

[1] Plut. *De Def. Or.* c. 8, 38.
[2] Id. *Cic.* c. 5.
[3] Tac. *Ann.* ii. 54.
[4] Suet. *Tib.* c. xiv.
[5] Id. *Calig.* c. lvii.
[6] Id. *Nero*, xl.
[7] Tac. *Hist.* ii. 78.
[8] Suet. *Tit.* c. v.
[9] Philostr. *Apoll. Tyan.* iv. 24.
[10] Luc. *Alex.* c. 29.

munication along the Roman roads, and the safety of the seas, must have swelled the number of their votaries from all parts of the world. It is a revelation to find a Tungrian cohort at a remote station in Britain setting up a votive inscription in obedience to the voice of the Clarian Apollo.[1] If new oracles were springing up in the Antonine age, the old were certainly not quite neglected. In the reign of Trajan the shrine of Delphi recovered from its degradation by the violence of Nero.[2] And Hadrian, as we have seen, tested the inspiration of the Pythia by a question as to the birthplace of Homer, which was answered by a verse tracing his ancestry to Pylos and Ithaca.[3] The ancient oracles were in full vigour under the emperors of the third century. Some of the greatest and most venerable —Delphi, Didyma, Mallus, and Dodona—were not reduced to silence till the reign of Constantine.[4]

But the old oracles could not satisfy the omnivorous superstition of the time. The outburst of new oracles may be compared, perhaps, to the fissiparous tendencies of Protestantism in some countries, at each fresh revival of religious excitement. Any fresh avenue to the "Great Mystery" was at once eagerly crowded. And the most recent claimant to inspiration sometimes threatened to overshadow the tradition of a thousand years, and to assert an oecumenical power.

One such case has been recorded and exposed with the graphic skill and penetrating observation of the greatest genius of the age. Lucian's description of the foundation of the new oracle of Asclepius at Abonoteichos in Paphlagonia, if it is wanting in the sympathetic handling which modern criticism has attained or can affect, is an unrivalled revelation of the superstition of the time. And a brief narrative of the imposture will probably give a more vivid idea of it than any abstract dissertation.

Alexander, the founder, was a man of mean parentage, but of remarkable natural gifts. Tall and handsome in no ordinary degree, he had eyes with a searching keenness, a look of inspiration, and a voice most clear and sweet.[5] His mental gifts were equal to his physical charm. In memory, quick

[1] Friedl. *Sittengesch.* iv. p. 469.
[2] D. Cass. lxiii. 14.
[3] *v.* Wolff. *De Nov. Orac. Aet.* p. 5.
[4] *Ib.* pp. 6, 52.
[5] Luc. *Alex.* c. 3, ὀφθαλμοὶ πολὺ τὸ γοργὸν καὶ ἔνθεον διεμφαίνοντες, κτλ.

perception, shrewdness, and subtlety, he had few equals. But from his early youth, with the affectation of Pythagorean asceticism, he had all the vices which go to make the finished reprobate.[1] After a youth of abandoned sensuality, in concert with a confederate of no better character, he determined to found an oracle. The times were favourable for such a venture. Never had selfish desire and terror, twin roots of superstition, such a hold on mankind.[2] The problem was, where to establish the new shrine. It must be founded among a crassly stupid population, ready to accept any tale of the marvellous with the most abandoned credulity.[3] Paphlagonia seemed to the shrewd observers the readiest prey. Tablets were dug up, which predicted an epiphany of Asclepius at Abonoteichos. A Sibylline oracle, in enigmatic verse, heralded the coming of the god. Alexander, magnificently attired, appeared upon the scene, with all the signs of mysterious insanity, and the Paphlagonians were thrown into hysterical excitement.[4] Their last new god was fished up from a lake in the form of a young serpent, which had been artfully sealed up in a goose's egg. When the broken shell revealed the nascent deity, the multitude were in an ecstasy of excitement at the honour vouchsafed to their city. The infant reptile was soon replaced by one full grown, to which a very elementary art had attached a human head. It was displayed to the crowds who trooped through the reception-room of the impostor, and they went away to spread throughout all Asia the tidings of the unheard-of miracle.[5] Alexander had carefully studied the system of the older oracles, and he proceeded to imitate it. He received inquiries on sealed tablets, and, with all ancient pomp and ceremony of attendance, returned them, apparently untouched, with the proper answer. But Lucian minutely explains the art with which the seal of the missive was dexterously broken and restored.[6] A hot needle and a delicate hand could easily reveal the secret of the question, and hide the trick. The oracle was primarily medical. Prescriptions were given in more or less ambiguous phrases. The charge for each consultation was, in our money, the

[1] Luc. *Alex.* c. 4, 5.

[2] *Ib.* c. 8, *ῥᾳδίως κατενόησαν τὸν τῶν ἀνθρώπων βίον ὑπὸ δυοῖν τούτοιν μεγίστοιν τυραννούμενον.*

[3] *Ib.* c. 9.

[4] *Ib.* c. 12.

[5] *Ib.* c. 15–18.

[6] *Ib.* c. 20.

small fee of a shilling.[1] Alexander was evidently a shrewd business man, and his moderate charges attracting a crowd of inquirers, the income of the oracle rose, according to Lucian, to the then enormous sum of nearly £7000 a year.[2] But the manager was liberal to his numerous staff of secretaries, interpreters, and versifiers.[3] He had, moreover, missionaries who spread his fame in foreign lands, and who offered the service of the oracle in recovering runaway slaves, discovering buried treasure, healing sickness, and raising the dead.[4] Even the barbarians on the outskirts of civilisation were attracted by his fame, and, after an interval required to find a translator among the motley crowd who thronged from all lands, an answer would be returned even in the Celtic or Syrian tongue.[5] The fame of the oracle, of course, soon spread to Italy, where the highest nobles, eager for any novelty in religion, were carried away by the pretensions of Alexander. None among them stood higher than Rutilianus, either in character or official rank. But he was the slave of every kind of extravagant superstition.[6] He would fall down and grovel along the way before any stone which was shining with oil or decked with garlands. He sent one emissary after another to Abonoteichos to consult the new god. They returned, some full of genuine enthusiasm, some hiding their doubts by interested exaggeration of what they had seen. Soon society and the court circle felt all the delight of a new religious sensation. Great nobles hurried away to Paphlagonia, and fell an easy prey to the gracious charm and the ingenious charlatanry of Alexander.[7] Some, who had consulted the oracle by questions which might have a sinister meaning, and suggest dangerous ambitions, he knew how to terrify into his service by the hint of possible disclosure.[8] All came back to swell the fame of the Paphlagonian oracle and to make it fashionable in Italy. But none were so besotted as Rutilianus. This great Roman noble, who had been proved in a long career of office,[9]

[1] Luc. *Alex.* c. 23, ἐτέτακτο δὲ καὶ μισθὸς ἐφ' ἑκάστῳ χρησμῷ δραχμὴ καὶ δύ' ὀβολώ.

[2] If I am right in interpreting Lucian's statement, ἀλλ' εἰς ἑπτὰ ἢ ὀκτὼ μυριάδας ἑκάστου ἔτους ἤθροιζεν.

[3] Luc. *Alex.* c. 23 ἅπασιν ἔνεμεν ἑκάστῳ τὸ κατ' ἀξίαν.

[4] *Ib.* c. 24.

[5] *Ib.* c. 51, ἀλλὰ καὶ βαρβάροις πολλάκις ἔχρησεν . . . Συριστὶ ἢ Κελτιστί.

[6] *Ib.* c. 30, ἀλλόκοτα περὶ τῶν θεῶν πεπιστευκώς, κτλ.

[7] *Ib.* c. 31.

[8] *Ib.* c. 32.

[9] *Ib.* c. 30, ἐν πολλαῖς τάξεσι ἐξητασμένος.

at the mature age of sixty, stooped to wed the supposed daughter of the vulgar charlatan by Selene, who had honoured him with the love which she gave of old to Endymion![1] And Rutilianus henceforth became the stoutest champion of Alexander against all assaults of scepticism. For, in spite of the credulity of the crowd and of the visitors from Rome, there was evidently a strong body of sturdy dissent. There were, in those days, followers of Epicurus even in Paphlagonia, and, by a strange freak of fortune, the followers of Christ found themselves making common cause against a new outbreak of heathenism with the atheistic philosophy of the Garden.[2] An honest Epicurean once convicted Alexander of a flagrant deception, and narrowly escaped being stoned to death by the fanatics of Paphlagonia.[3] One of the books of Epicurus was publicly burnt in the agora by order of Alexander, and the ashes cast into the sea. Lucian himself, with his sly, amused scepticism, tested and exposed the skill of the oracle at the most imminent risk to his life.[4]

But in spite of all exposure and opposition, the oracle, managed with such art and supported with such blind enthusiasm, conquered for a time the Roman world. It was a period of calamity and gloom. Plague and earthquake added their horrors to the brooding uncertainty of the dim conflict on the Danube.[5] The emissaries of Alexander went everywhere, exploiting the general terror. Prediction of coming evil was safe at such a time; any shred of comfort or hope was eagerly sought for. A hexameter verse, promising the help of Apollo, was inscribed over every doorway as an amulet against the awful pestilence of 166 A.D. Another ordered two lion's cubs to be flung into the Danube, to check the advance of the Marcomanni.[6] Both proved dismal failures, but without shaking the authority of the impostor, who found an easy apology in the darkness of old Delphic utterances. He established mysteries after the model of Eleusis, from which Christians and Epicureans were excluded under a solemn ban. Scenes of old and new mythologies were presented with brilliant effects—the labour of

[1] Luc. *Alex.* c. 35.

[2] *Ib.* c. 38, εἴ τις ἄθεος ἢ Χριστιανὸς ἢ Ἐπικούρειος ἥκει κατάσκοπος τῶν ὀργίων, κτλ. : cf. 25, λέγων ἀθέων ἐμπεπλῆσθαι καὶ Χριστιανῶν τὸν Πόντον, κτλ.

[3] *Ib.* c. 46.

[4] *Ib.* cc. 53 sqq.

[5] Jul. Capitol. *M. Ant.* cc. 22, 17.

[6] Luc. *Alex.* cc. 36–48.

Leto, the birth of Apollo, the birth of Asclepius, the epiphany of Glycon, the new wondrous serpent-deity of Abonoteichos, the loves of Alexander and Selene. The second Endymion lay sleeping, as on Latmus in the ancient story, and the moon goddess, in the person of a great Roman dame, descended from above to woo a too real earthly lover.[1]

Lucian's history of the rise of the new oracle in Paphlagonia is not, perhaps, free from some suspicion of personal antipathy to the founder of it. He attributes to Alexander not only the most daring deceit and calculating quackery, but also the foulest vices known to the ancient world. These latter charges may or may not be true. Theological or anti-theological hatred has in all ages too often used the poisoned arrow. And the moral character of Alexander has less interest for us than the spiritual condition of his many admirers and votaries. He can hardly be acquitted of some form of more or less pious imposture. How far it was accompanied by real religious enthusiasm is a problem which will be variously solved, and which is hardly worth the trouble of investigation, even if the materials existed for a certain answer. But the eager readiness of a whole population to hail the appearance of a new god, and the acceptance of his claims by men the most cultivated and highly placed in the Roman Empire, are facts on which Lucian's testimony, addressed to contemporaries, cannot be rejected. Nor is there anything in our knowledge of the period from other sources which renders the thing doubtful. Creative mythology had revived its activity. Not long before the epiphany of Glycon, in a neighbouring part of Asia Minor the Apostles Paul and Barnabas, after the miraculous cure of the impotent man, had difficulty in escaping divine honours. The Carpocratians, a Gnostic sect, about the same time built a temple in honour of the youthful son of their founder.[2] The corn-goddess Annona first appears in the first century, and inscriptions, both in Italy and Africa, were set up in honour of the power who presided over the commissariat of the Roman mob.[3] The youthful favourite of Hadrian, after his mysterious death in the waters of the Nile, was glorified by instant apotheosis.

[1] Luc. *Alex.* c. 38.

[2] Friedl. *Sittengesch.* iv. 456.

[3] *Or. Henz.* 1810, 5320; cf. Preller, *Rom. Myth.* (Tr.), p. 415.

His statues rose in every market-place and temple court; his soul was supposed to have found a home in a new star in the region of the milky way; temples were built in his honour, and the strange cult was maintained for at least a hundred years after any motive could be found for adulation.[1] The Cynic brothers, and the gaping crowd who stood around the pyre of Peregrinus at Olympia were eager, as we have seen, to hail the flight of a great soul to join the heroes and demigods in Olympus.[2] The cult of M. Aurelius was maintained by an enthusiasm very different from the conventional apotheosis of the head of the Roman State. We are told that he was adored, by every age and sex and class, long after his death. His sacred image found a place among the *penates* of every household, and the home where it was not honoured was of more than suspected piety. Down to the time of Diocletian, the saintly and philosophic emperor, who had preached an imperturbable indifference to the chances and changes of life, was believed to visit his anxious votaries with dreams of promise or warning.[3]

Maximus of Tyre may have been guilty of no exaggeration when he reckoned the heavenly host as thrice ten thousand.[4] The cynical voluptuary of Nero's reign, who said that a town of Magna Graecia was inhabited by more gods than men, only used a comic hyperbole to enforce a striking fact.[5] The anthropomorphic conceptions of Deity, which were prevalent, easily overleapt the interval between the human and Divine. The crowds of the Antonine age were as ready to recognise the god in human form as the Athenians of the days of Pisistratus, who believed that they saw in the gigantic Phye an epiphany of the great goddess of their Acropolis, leading the tyrant home.[6] In the minds of a philosophic minority, nurtured on the theology of Plato, there might be the dim conception of one awful and remote Power, far removed from the grossness of earth, far above the dreams of mythologic poetry and the materialist imagination of the masses. Yet

[1] D. Cass. lxix. 11; cf. Gregorov. *Hadrian*, p. 128.

[2] Luc. *De Morte Peregr.* c. 29.

[3] Jul. Capitol. *M. Ant.* c. 18, hodieque in multis domibus M. Antonini statuae consistunt inter deos penates . . . sacrilegus judicatus est qui ejus imaginem in sua domo non habuit.

[4] Max. Tyr. *Diss.* xiv. 8.

[5] Petron. *Sat.* 17.

[6] Herod. i. 60.

even philosophy, as we have already seen, had succumbed to the craving for immediate contact, or for some means of communication, with the Infinite Spirit. The daemons of Plutarch and Maximus of Tyre were really a new philosophic mythology, created to give meaning and morality to the old gods. These hosts of baleful or ministering spirits, with which the Platonist surrounded the life of man, divine in the sweep of their power, human in their passions or sympathies, belong really to the same order as the Poseidon who pursued Odysseus with tempest, or the Moon goddess who descended on Latmus to kiss the sleeping Endymion. Anthropomorphic paganism was far from dead; it was destined to live openly for more than three hundred years, and to prolong a secret life of subtle influence under altered forms, the term of which who shall venture to fix?

The daemons of the Platonic philosophers find their counterpart in the popular cult of *genii*. If there was a visible tendency to syncretism and monotheistic faith in the second century, there was a no less manifest drift to the endless multiplication of spiritual powers. The tendency, indeed, to create divine representatives of physical forces and dim abstract qualities was from early ages congenial to the Roman mind. All the phenomena of nature—every act, pursuit, or vicissitude in human life—found a spiritual patron in the Roman imagination.[1] But the tendency received an immense impulse in the age with which we are dealing, and the inscriptions of the imperial period reveal an almost inexhaustible fertility of religious fancy. Every locality, every society and occupation of men, has its patron genius, to whom divine honours are paid or recorded,—the canton, the municipality, the curia; the spring or grove; the legion or cohort or troop; the college of the paviors or smiths or actors; the emperors, or even the great gods themselves.[2]

The old gods of Latium still retained a firm hold on the devotion of the simple masses, as crowds of inscriptions record. But ancient religion, in its cruder forms, divided and localised the Divine power by endless demarcations of place and function. Although the Roman centurion or merchant might

[1] Preller, *Myth. Rom.* p. 65, 66, 387.

[2] Cf. *Or. Henz.* Ind. pp. 27, 28; *v.* especially 1730 (genius Jovis), 1812 (Neronis), 193 (Arvernorum), 2204 (Col. Ostiensis), 689 (municipii), 1704 (legionis), 4113 (pavimentariorum), 6628 (fontis).

believe in the power of his familiar gods to follow him with their protection, and never forgot them, still each region, to which his wanderings carried him, had its peculiar spirits, who wielded a special potency within their own domain, and whom it was necessary to propitiate. On hundreds of provincial inscriptions we can read the catholic superstition of the Roman legionary. The mystery of desert or forest, the dangers of march and bivouack, stimulated his devotion. If he does not know the names of the strange deities, he will invoke them collectively side by side with the gods whom he has been taught to venerate. He will adore the "genius loci,"[1] or all the gods of Mauritania or of Britain. And so the deities of Alsace and Dacia and Lusitania, of the Sahara and Cumberland, easily took their place in his growing pantheon.[2] They were constantly identified with the great figures of Greek or Roman mythology. Many an inscription is dedicated to Apollo Grannus of Alsace, whom Caracalla invoked for the recovery of his health, along with Serapis and Aesculapius.[3] Apollo Belenus, a favourite deity in Southern Gaul, was the special patron of Aquileia.[4] Batucardus and Cocideus received vows and dedications in Cumberland and Westmorland, Arardus and Agho in the Pyrenees, Abnoba in the Black Forest;[5] and many another deity with strange, outlandish name, like their provincial votaries, were honoured with sacred Roman citizenship, and took their places, although in a lower grade, with Serapis of Alexandria or Aesclepius of Epidaurus. The local heroes were also adored at wayside shrines or altars, which met the traveller in lonely passes. In the heart of the Nubian desert, inscriptions, scratched on obelisk or temple porch, attest the all-embracing faith of the Roman legionary.[6] At Carlsbourg in Transylvania, a legate of the 5th Legion records his own gratitude to Aesculapius and all the gods and goddesses of the place, and that of his wife and daughter, for the recovery of his sight.[7] A praetorian prefect, visiting the hot springs of Vif, left a graceful inscription to

1 *Or. Henz.* 2135, Sei Deo Sei Deivae Sac. etc.; 1580, Aesculapio et Hygiae caeterisque diis deabusque hujus loci Salutaribus; 5902, Hospitibus diis Mauricis et genio loci, etc.

2 Cf. Tertull. *Apol.* c. 24.

3 *Or. Henz.* 1997–2001; cf. D. Cass. lxxvii. 15.

4 *Or. Henz.* 823, 1967.

5 *ib.* 1959, 1986, 1954; cf. *C.I.L.* xii. 1556, 3097; viii. 9195, 4578, 8834.

6 Friedl. *Sittengesch.* iv. pp. 482–4.

7 *Or. Henz.* 1580.

the gods of the eternal fire.[1] A legate of the 5th Legion returns pious thanks to Hercules and the *genius loci*, at the baths in Dacia sacred to the hero.[2] Many a slab pays honour to the nymphs who guarded the secret spring, especially where a source, long since forgotten, had resumed its flow.[3] A chief magistrate of Lambesi is specially grateful that the town has been refreshed by a new fountain during his year of office.[4] The heroes of poetic legend were still believed to haunt the scene of their struggles. Apollonius once spent a night in ghostly converse with the shade of Achilles beside his tomb in the Troad, and was charged by the divine warrior to convey his reproaches for the neglect of his worship in the old Thessalian home of the Myrmidons.[5] The Troad had a hero of much later date, the proconsul Neryllinus, who was believed to deliver oracles and to heal the sick.[6]

In a time of such vivid belief in the universal presence of divine beings, faith in miracle was a matter of course. Christian and pagan were here at least on common ground. Nay, the Christian apologists did not dispute the possibility of pagan miracles, or even of pagan oracular inspiration. It is curious to see that Origen and Celsus, as regards the probability of recurring miracle, are on very much the same plane of spiritual belief, and that the Christian apologist is fighting with one arm tied. He is disabled from delivering his assaults at the heart of the enemy's position. The gods of heathenism are still to him living and potent spirits, although they are spirits of evil.[7] The pagan daemonology, on its worse side, had been accepted by the champion of the Church. Yet it is hard to see how, on such principles, he could deal with the daemon of the Apolline shrine at Delphi, when he denounced the Spartan Glaucus for the mere thought of a breach of faith to his friend,[8] or the daemon who lurked under the pure stately form of Athene Polissouchos, when she threw

[1] *Or. Henz.* 5689.

[2] *Ib.* 1560.

[3] *Ib.* 1632, 4, 7; Nymphis ob reditum aquarum, etc.

[4] *Ib.* 5758.

[5] Philostr. *Apoll. Tyan.* iv. 16, Θετταλοὶ γὰρ τὰ ἐναγίσματα χρόνον ἤδη πολὺν ἐκλελοίπασί μοι.

[6] Friedl. *Sittengesch.* iii. p. 479.

[7] Orig. *C. Celsum*, lib. iii. p. 124, ed. Spencer; lib. vii. p. 334, Friedl. iv. p. 458; S. Aug. *De Civ. D.* xix. 23, quis ita stultus est qui non intelligat . . . consilio simili ab impuris daemonibus ita fuisse responsa, etc.; cf. viii. 22, mirabilibus et fallacibus signis sive factorum sive praedictorum deos se esse persuaserunt.

[8] Herodot. vi. 86.

a maiden goddess's protection around the Antigones of Athens. In the field of miracle in the second century the heathen could easily match the Christian. With gods in every grove and fountain, and on every mountain summit; with gods breathing in the winds and flashing in the lightning, or the ray of sun and star, heaving in the earthquake or the November storm in the Aegean, watching over every society of men congregated for any purpose, guarding the solitary hunter or traveller in the Alps or the Sahara, what is called miracle became as natural to the heathen as the rising of the sun. In fact, if the gods had not displayed their power in some startling way, their worshippers would have been shocked and forlorn. But the gods did not fail their votaries. Unquestioning and imperious faith in this kind is always rewarded, or can always explain its disappointments. The Epicurean, the Cynic, or the Aristotelian, might pour their cold scorn on tales of wonder. An *illuminé* like Lucian, attached to no school, and living merely in the light of clear cultivated sense, might shake his sides with laughter at the tales which were vouched for by a spiritualist philosophy. But the drift of the time was against all such protests. The Divine power was everywhere, and miracle was in the air.

Enough has been said of the dreams and signs and omens which in the first and second century heralded every accession to the throne and every death of a prince, and which even Tacitus records with more or less vacillating faith. Enough, too, has been said of the miracles of healing which were wrought by the sons of Asclepius in his many shrines from Pergamum to the island in the Tiber. The miracles wrought by Vespasian at Alexandria are the most hackneyed example of belief in miracle, because the tale is told by the greatest master of vivid narrative in a book which every educated man has read. The sensible Vespasian was not confident of his power to give energy to the impotent, even on the strength of a dream sent by Serapis, just as he jested on his deathbed about his approaching apotheosis. But the efficiency of the imperial touch was vouched for by eye-witnesses, to whom Tacitus would not refuse his credence. The chronicler of the age of Diocletian has surrounded the death-bed of Hadrian with similar wonders. A blind man from Pannonia came and touched the fever-wracked emperor, and immediately regained his sight. The legend of the Thundering Legion was long the battle-ground of opposing faiths equally credulous, and equally bent on securing the credit of supernatural powers. The timely rainfall was attributed with equal assurance to the incantations of an Egyptian sorcerer, to the prayers of the believers in Jupiter, or the prayers of the believers in Christ. Apuleius, who was himself prosecuted for practising the black art, has filled his Thessalian romance with the most astounding tales of fantastic sorcery. He may have copied other lawless romances, but he would hardly have given such space to these weird arts if his public had not had an uneasy belief in them. The home of Medea in the days of M. Aurelius was a veritable witch's cave: the air is tremulous with superstitious fear: everything seems possible in the field of miraculous metamorphosis or monstrous vice. If Apuleius had meant to discredit superstition by wedding it to disgusting sensuality, he could hardly have succeeded better. But he was more probably bent, with perverted skill, on producing a work which might allure imaginations haunted by the ghosts of hereditary sensuality and a spiritual terror revived in redoubled force. An Egyptian priest with tonsure and linen robes raises a dead man to life who has been "floating on the Stygian streams." Or you are admitted to a witch's laboratory, open to all the winds and stored with all the wreckage of human life—timbers of ships splintered on cruel rocks, the curdled blood and mangled flesh of murdered men, toothless skulls gnawed by beasts of prey. You see the transformation going on before your eyes under the magic of mysterious unguents, the feathers springing from the flesh, or the human sinking into the ass's form. Tales like these, which to us are old wives' tales, may have had a strange charm for an age when human life was regarded as the slave of fate, or the sport of the inscrutable powers of the unseen universe.

CHAPTER II

BELIEF IN IMMORTALITY

A GREAT part of the charm of those oriental religions, on the study of which we are about to enter, lay in the assurance which they seemed to give of an immortal life. It would, therefore, appear a necessary preface to such a review to examine some of the conceptions of the state of the departed which the missionaries of Isis and Mithra found prevalent in the minds of their future votaries. Immortality, in any worthy sense, is inseparable from the idea of God. And the conception of continued life must always be shaped by the character of a people's beliefs as to the powers of the unseen world. A pantheon of dim phantasms or abstractions will not promise more than a numb spectral future to the human shade. The nectar and ambrosia of Olympian feasts may have their human counterpart in an "eternal debauch." The Platonist will find his eternal hope in emancipation from the prison of the flesh, and in the immediate vision of that Unity of all beauty, truth, and goodness, which is his highest conception of God. But not only does religion necessarily colour the conception of the eternal state: it may also furnish the warrant for a belief in it. And a religion which can give men a firm ground for that faith will have an immense advantage over others which are less clear and confident as to another world. It is generally admitted that the long array of philosophic arguments for immortality have by themselves little convincing power. They are not stronger, nor perhaps so strong as the argument from the wish for continued life, inveterate in the human spirit, on which Plutarch laid so much stress.[1] Even amid the

[1] Plut. *Non posse suav. vivi*, etc. c. 26 sq.; *De Ser. Num. Vind.* c. 18.

triumphant dialectic of the *Phaedo*, an undertone of doubt in any human proof of immortality is sometimes heard, along with the call for some "divine doctrine" as a bark of safety on perilous seas.[1] The inextinguishable instinct of humanity craves for a voice of revelation to solve the mystery of life and death.

The Roman spirit, down to the Antonine age, had been the subject of many influences which had inspired widely various ideas of the future state. And the literary and funerary remains from Nero to M. Aurelius are full of contradictions on the subject. Nor, in the absence of authoritative revelation on a field so dark to reason, is this surprising. Even Christian teaching, while it offers a sure promise of a life to come, has not lifted the veil of the great mystery, and the material imagery of the Apocalypse, or the shadowed hints of Jesus or S. Paul, have left the believer of the twentieth century with no clearer vision of the life beyond the tomb than that which was vouchsafed to Plato, Cicero, Virgil, or Plutarch. "We know not what we shall be," is the answer of every seer of every age. Something will always "seal the lips of the Evangelist," as the key of the Eumolpidae closed the lips of those who had seen the vision of Eleusis.[2] The pagans of the early Empire were thus, in the absence of dogma and ecclesiastical teaching, free to express, with perfect frankness, their unbelief or their varying conceptions of immortality, according to the many influences that had moulded them. Nor could these influences be kept apart even in the same mind. Even the poet seer, who was to be the guide of Dante in the shades, has failed to blend the immemorial faith of the Latin race with the dreams of future beatitude or anguish which came to him from Pythagorean or Platonic teaching.[3] In the sixth book of the *Aeneid* the eschatologies of old Rome and Greece are combined, but not blended, with the doctrines of transmigration and purgatorial expiation descending from Pythagoras or the Orphic mystics. Virgil, in fact, mirrors the confusion of beliefs which prevailed in his own age, and which pre-eminently characterised the age of the Antonines.

[1] Plat. *Phaed.* 85 D, *εἰ μή τις δύναιτο ἀσφαλέστερον ἐπὶ βεβαιοτέρου ὀχήματος [ἢ] λόγου θείου τινὸς διαπορευθῆναι.*

[2] Soph. *O.C.* 1055.

[3] Sellar's *Virgil*, p. 367; cf. Boissier, *Rel. Rom.* i. 367.

Along with other archaic elements of the Latin faith, the cult of the Manes held its ground, especially in secluded homes of old Italian piety. The most ancient Indo-European conception of the state after death was that of a continuance or faint, shadowy reproduction of the life on earth; it was not that of a vast and mysterious change to a supernatural order. The departed spirit was believed to linger in a dim existence in the vault or grave near the familiar homestead.[1] The tomb is not a temporary prison, but an everlasting home,[2] and often provides a chamber where the living members of the family or clan may gather on solemn days around the ashes of the dead.[3] Provision is made for the sustenance of this spectral life. Vessels for food and drink, the warrior's arms, the workman's tools, the cosmetics of the lady, the child's playthings, are buried with them.[4] Or they are figured on their tombs cheerfully engaged in their familiar crafts,[5] not with folded hands, and calm, expectant faces, like the marble forms which lie in our cathedral aisles awaiting the Resurrection.

With such views of the tomb, the perpetual guardianship of it became to the Roman a matter of supreme moment. It is a chapel or an altar, as well as a last home.[6] It is the meeting-place, in faint ghostly communion, of the society which embraced, by its solemn rites, the members of the household church in the light or in the shades. All the cautious forms of Roman law are invoked to keep the sepulchre, with its garden and enclosure, from passing into alien hands. Its site is exactly described, with the minutest measurements, and the intruder or the alienator is threatened with curses or with fines, to be paid into the public treasury.[7] Here, among his children and remotest descendants, among his freedmen and freedwomen, the Roman dreamed of resting for ever undisturbed.[8] And many an appeal comes to us from the original slab not to violate the eternal peace.[9] What that dim

[1] Cic. *Tusc.* i. 16, sub terra censebant reliquam vitam agi mortuorum; cf. F. de Coulanges, *La Cité Ant.* p. 8.

[2] *Or. Henz.* 4525.

[3] *Ib.* 4433, posticum cum apparitorio, et compitum a solo pecun. sua fecerunt, etc.; cf. 4353; Petron. c. 71.

[4] Marq. *Priv.* i. 367.

[5] Cf. Duruy, *Hist. Rom.* v. 637.

[6] Aesch. *Choeph.* 92, 488; F. de Coulanges, *La Cité Ant.* p. 16.

[7] *Or. Henz.* 7364, 7338, 4076, 4417, 4422.

[8] *Ib.* 4428, somno aeterno sacr. . . fecerunt sibi et suis libertis libertabusque, etc., 4631, 4435.

[9] *Ib.* 4781, 3, 5, 6, 4790, quisquis hoc sustulerit aut laeserit ultimus suorum moriatur.

life beneath the marble or the sod, at least in the later times, was conceived to be, how far it involved a more or less vivid consciousness of what was passing in the world above, how far it was a numb repose, almost passing into "the eternal sleep," seems to be uncertain. The phrases on the tomb in all ages are apt to pass into conventional forms, and personal temperament and imagination must always give varying colour to the picture. Such phrases as "eternal sleep," however, did not probably at any time imply complete unconsciousness. The old Latin faith that the Manes had a real life and some link of sympathy with the living was still strong and vivid in an age which was eager to receive or answer voices from the world beyond the senses. The wish to maintain, in spite of the severance and shock of death, a bond of communion between the living and the departed was one of the most imperious instincts of the Latin race. It was not a mere imagination, projected on far distant years, which craved for the yearly offering of violets and roses, or the pious *ave* of the passing traveller.[1] The dwellers in the vault still remained members of the family, to which they are linked for ever by a dim sympathy expressed in ritual communion. Every year, on the *dies parentales* in February, there was a general holiday, cheerfully kept in honour of all those whose spirits were at peace.[2] On the eighth day, the festival of *cara cognatio*, there was a family love-feast, in which quarrels were forgotten, and the members in the spirit-world joined in the sacred meal. But besides this public and national commemoration, the birthday of each departed member was observed with offerings of wine and oil and milk. The tomb was visited in solemn procession; dead and living shared the sacred fare; flowers were scattered, and with an *ave* or a prayer for help and good fortune, the shade was left to its renewed repose.[3] Many a slab makes anxious provision for these communions, and the offering of violets and roses in their season.[4]

But the Roman in his tomb longed to be near the sound of

[1] *Or. Henz.* 4775, 4419, 4420, 4415, 4737; T. Lollius positus propter viam ut dicant praeterientes, Lolli ave, cf. 4745.

[2] Fowler, *Rom. Festivals*, p. 307.

[3] *Or. Henz.* 4414, 4417, nam curatores substituam qui vescantur ex horum hortorum reditu natali meo et praebeant rosam in aeternum. Hos neque dividi neque alienari volo.

[4] *Ib.* 4084, 4100, 4420.

busy human life, and to feel the tread of pious feet, which might turn aside for a moment to salute even a stranger's memory. This feeling is expressed in the long rows of vaults which line so many of the great roads, the Via Appia, or the way from Pompeii to Nola.[1] There were many like that Titus Lollius who had himself laid close to the road into Aquae Sextiae, that the passers might for ever greet his spirit with an *ave.*[2] Others leave a prayer for all good things to those who will stop an instant and read the legend; "may the earth lie light upon them when they too depart."[3] The horror of the lonely soul, cut off from the kindly fellowship of the living, and lingering on in a forgotten grave, to which no loving hand should ever more bring the libation or the violets in spring, which should one day awake no memory or sympathy in any human heart, was to the old Roman the worst terror in death. This passion for continued memory, especially in great benefactors of their kind, is used by Cicero as an argument for immortality,[4] and the passion for enduring life blends indistinguishably with the wish to be long remembered. Even Epicurus, the apostle of annihilation, made provision in his last testament for yearly offerings in honour of himself and Metrodorus his disciple—a curious instance of agnostic conformity.[5] The passion for remembrance was responded to by the dutiful devotion of many generations. The cult of the dead long survived in the cult of martyrs, and the pagan feasting at their tombs disturbed and perplexed S. Augustine and S. Paulinus of Nola.[6]

The old Roman thought of his departed friends as a company of good and kindly spirits, who watched over the family on earth. But there was another conception of spirits in the other world, whether derived from the gloomy superstition of Etruria, or descending from days anterior to orderly devotion to the dead.[7] The Lemures were a name of fear. They

[1] Marq. *Priv.* i. 362; Mau, *Pompeii*, p. 421 sqq.; cf. Cic. *Tusc.* i. 16.

[2] *Or. Henz.* 4737.

[3] *Ib.* 7396, 7402, vivite felices qui legitis.

[4] Cic. *Tusc.* i. 12, 27, quas (caeremonias sepulcrorum) ingeniis praediti nec tanta cura coluissent, nec violatas tam inexpiabili religione sanxissent, nisi haereret in eorum mentibus mortem non interitum esse omnia tollentem, etc.

[5] Aelian, *Fr.* p. 1023 (Gronov.).

[6] S. Paulin. Nol. *Carm.* 27; S. Aug. *Ep.* 22, *Serm.* v. xvii.; cf. Sidon. Apoll. v. 17; Bingham, *Antiq. of Chr. Church*, ii. p. 1165.

[7] Fowler, *Rom. Festivals*, p. 108.

were dark, malevolent spirits who craved for blood, as they had departed this life by a violent end. Their festival, the Lemuria in May, was quite distinct from the festival of the Manes, and the household ritual for laying the ghosts by the spitting of black beans and a ninefold form of exorcism savours of a far-gone age. These maleficent powers were propitiated by blood—especially by the blood of men in the combats of the arena.

The visitations of these beings, whether as guardian, ministering spirits or as evil powers, were expected and believed in for many ages by all classes of Roman minds. The ancient Latin faith as to the state of the dead was, according to Cicero, confirmed by many tales of spiritual apparition. There are pathetic memorials which end with an appeal in which the lonely wife entreats the lost one sometimes to return in dream or vision.[1] One vivacious inscription challenges the sceptic to lay his wager and make the experiment of a summons from the unseen world.[2] The spread of cremation instead of burial gradually led to a new conception of the spirit as having a separate existence from the body, now reduced to a handful of grey ashes.[3] And spirits no longer clung to the body in the family vault, but were gathered in a dim region near the centre of the earth, where, according to gloomy Etrurian fancy, they were under the cruel care of the conductor of the dead, a brutal figure, with wings and long, matted beard, and armed with a hammer, who for ages appeared in human form to close the last ghastly scene in the gladiatorial combats.[4] From this limbo of the departed a sort of gateway was provided in every Latin town in the *Mundus*, a deep trench intended to represent an inverted heaven, which was dug before the *pomoerium* was traced. Its lower aperture was closed by the stone of the Manes, which on three solemn days, in August, October, and November, was lifted to permit the spirits from the deep to pass for a time into the upper world. Thus a public sanction was given to the belief in the commerce between this life and the next.[5]

[1] *Or. Henz.* 4775, horis nocturnis ut eum videam, et possim dulcius et celerius aput eum pervenire.

[2] *Ib.* 7346.

[3] Marq. *Priv.* i. pp. 438–9 ; Preller, *Rom. Myth.* (Tr.), p. 331.

[4] Momms. *Rom. Hist.* i. p. 189 ; Tertull. *Apol.* xv. vidimus et Jovis fratrem gladiatorum cadavera cum malleo deducentem.

[5] Fowler, *Rom. Festivals*, p. 211.

Cicero had said that the faith in immortality was sustained by the fact of spirits returning to the world of sense. In the first and second centuries there was no lack of such aids to faith. Apparitions became the commonest facts of life, and only the hardiest minds remained incredulous about them. Philosophers of all schools, except the Epicurean, were swept into the current. The *Philopseudes* of Lucian is a brilliant effort to ridicule the superstition of the age, but the attack would have been discredited if it had not had a foundation of fact. There, around the sick-bed of Eucrates, himself saturated with philosophy, are gathered a Stoic, a Peripatetic, a Pythagorean, a Platonist, and a trained physician.[1] And they regale one another with the most weird and exciting tales of the marvellous. Ion, the Platonic student, has seen the exorcism of a black and smoky daemon.[2] Eucrates has seen such spirits a thousand times, and, from long habit, has lost all fear of them. At vintage time, he once saw a gigantic Gorgon figure in the woods in broad daylight, and by the turning of a magic ring had revealed to him the gulf of Tartarus, the infernal rivers, and been even able to recognise some of the ghosts below.[3] On another day, as he lay upon his bed reading the *Phaedo*, his "sainted wife," who had recently died, appeared and reproached him because, among all the finery which had been burnt upon her pyre, a single gold-spangled shoe, which slipped under the wardrobe, had been forgotten.[4] Plutarch reports, apparently with perfect faith, the appearance of such spectral visitors at Chaeronea.[5] The younger Pliny consulted his friend Sura as to the reality of such apparitions, and reveals his faith in the gruesome tale of a haunted house at Corinth, where a restless ghost, who had often disturbed the quiet of night with the clank of chains, was tracked to the mystery of a hidden grave.[6] Suetonius, of course, welcomes tales of this kind from every quarter. Before Caligula's half-burnt remains were borne stealthily to a dishonoured burial, the keepers of the Lamian Gardens had been disturbed each night by ghostly terrors.[7] The pages of Dion Cassius abound in similar wonders.

[1] Luc. *Philops.* c. 6.

[2] *Ib.* c. 16.

[3] *Ib.* cc. 22–24.

[4] *Ib.* c. 27.

[5] Plut. *Cim.* c. 1, ἐπὶ πολὺν χρόνον εἰδώλων τινῶν ἐν τῷ τόπῳ προφαινομένων, ὡς οἱ πατέρες ἡμῶν λέγουσι, κτλ.

[6] Plin. *Ep.* vii. 27.

[7] Suet. *Calig.* c. 59.

When Nero attempted to cut through the Isthmus of Corinth, the dead arose in numbers from their graves.[1] In such an age the baleful art of "evocation" acquired a weird attraction and importance. By spells and incantations Hecate was invoked to send up spirits, often for evil ends.[2] And there were dark rumours of the spell being fortified by the blood of children. Many of the emperors from Tiberius to Caracalla had dabbled in this witchcraft.[3] When Nero was haunted by the Furies of his murdered mother, he is said to have offered a magic sacrifice to evoke and appease her spirit.[4] The early Neo-Platonists were, of course, eager to admit the reality of such visits from the unseen world. In anxious quest of any link of sympathy between this world and the next, Maximus tries to fortify his doctrine of daemons by stories of apparitions.[5] Hector has been often seen darting across the Troad in shining armour. At the mouth of the Borysthenes, Achilles has been espied by mariners, who were sailing past his isle, careering along with his yellow locks and arms of gold, and singing his paean of battle.

In enlarging its rather blank and poor conception of the future state, the Latin race, as in other fields, was content to borrow rather than invent. The Sixth Book of the Aeneid was an effort not only to glorify the legendary heroes of Rome, but to appease a new or revived longing for the hope of immortality, after the desolating nihilism of the Epicurean philosophy had run its course.[6] Virgil has some touches of old Roman faith about the dead, but the scenery of his Inferno is mainly derived from Greek poetry inspired by Orphism, and the vision is moralised, and also confused, by elements drawn from Pythagoras or Plato.[7] The scene of Aeneas's descent to the underworld is laid by the lake of Avernus, where, buried amid gloomy woods, was the cave of the Cumaean Sibyl. Cumae was the oldest Greek colony in the West. Its foundation was placed long before the days of Romulus. Rich, prosperous, and cultivated, at a time when the Romans were a band of rude warriors, it must have early transmitted Greek

[1] D. Cass. lxii. 17.
[2] Lobeck, *Aglaoph.* i. p. 221.
[3] D. Cass. lvii. 15.
[4] Suet. *Nero*, c. xxxiv.
[5] Max. Tyr. xv. 7.
[6] Boissier, *Rel. Rom.* i. p. 316.
[7] *Ib.* p. 279; cf. Conington, *Introd. Aen.* vi. p. 419; Rohde, *Psyche*, ii. p. 165.

ideas of religion to the rising power on the Tiber.[1] The Etrurians also, who affected so profoundly the tone of Roman religion, had come under Greek influences. The spectral ferryman of the dead was a familiar figure in Etruscan art. Thus, both on the south and north, Latium had points of contact with the world of Hellenic legend. And from the early days of the Republic, the worship of Greek gods—Apollo, Asclepius, or the Dioscuri—became naturalised at Rome. Probably of even earlier date was the influence of the oracular lore of Greece through Delphi and the oracle of Cumae.[2]

On the threshold of the underworld Aeneas and the Sibyl are confronted by the monstrous forms of Hellenic legend—Centaurs and Scyllas, Harpies and Gorgons, the fire-armed Chimaera, and the hissing hydra of Lerna.[3] They have to pass the ninefold barrier of the Styx in Charon's steel-grey bark. The grisly ferryman of the infernal stream, foul and unkempt, with fixed eyes of flame, is surrounded by a motley crowd, thick as autumnal leaves, all straining and eager for the further shore. Landed on a waste expanse of mud and sedge,[4] they pass the kennel of triple-headed Cerberus, and on to the judgment seat, where Minos assigns to each soul its several doom, according to the deeds done in the body. Thence they traverse the "mourning fields,"[5] where are those sad queens of Grecian tragedy whose wild loves have been their undoing, and among them Phoenician Dido, who, with stony silence and averted gaze, plunges into the darkness of the wood.[6] As the dawn is breaking, they find themselves before the prison-house of the damned, rising amid the folds of the river of fire, with walls of iron and adamant, its portals watched by a sleepless Fury in blood-red robe.[7] From within are heard the cries of anguish and the clank of chains, as the great rebels and malefactors of old-world story—Ixion, Salmoneus, and the Titans—are tortured by lash and wheel and vulture.[8] And with them, sharing the same agony, are those who have violated the great laws on which the Roman character was built.[9] Through other dusky ways and Cyclopean portals they at last reach the home of the blessed, as it was

[1] Grote, ii. p. 518 (ed. 1862).
[2] Mommsen, *R. Hist.* i. p. 187; Preller, *Rom. Myth.* pp. 197, 407, 438.
[3] *Aen.* vi. 289.
[4] *Ib.* 313, 416.
[5] *Ib.* 441.
[6] *Ib.* 472.
[7] *Ib.* 555.
[8] *Ib.* 600.
[9] *Ib.* 608.

pictured long before in the apocalypse of Pindar—the meads and happy groves of Elysium, under another sun and other stars than ours, and bathed in the splendour of an ampler air.[1] Here is the eternal home of the heroic souls of a nobler age, men who have died for fatherland, holy priests and bards and founders of the arts which soften and embellish the life of men. But though their home is radiant with a splendour not of earth, they are, in old Roman and Greek fashion, occupied with the toils or pleasures of their earthly life. Youthful forms are straining their sinews in the wrestling-ground as of old. The ancient warriors of Troy have their shadowy chariots beside them, their lances planted in the sward, their chargers grazing in the meadow. Others are singing old lays or dancing, and the bard of Thrace himself is sweeping the lyre, as in the days when he sped the Argo through the "Clashing Rocks" in the quest of the fleece of gold.[2]

The vision closes with a scene which criticism has long recognised as irreconcilable with the eschatology of Greek legend hitherto followed by the poet, but which is drawn from a philosophy destined to govern men's thoughts of immortality for many ages. In a wooded vale, far withdrawn, through which Lethe glided peacefully, countless multitudes are gathered drinking the "water of carelessness and oblivion." These are they, as Anchises expounds to his son, who, having passed the thousand purgatorial years, to cleanse away the stains of flesh in a former life, and, having effaced the memory of it, now await the call of Destiny to a new life on earth.[3] This theory of life and death, coming down from Pythagoras, and popularised by Platonism, with some Stoic elements, had gained immense vogue among educated men of the last period of the Republic. Varro had adopted it as a fundamental tenet of his theology, and Cicero had embalmed it in his dream of Scipio, which furnished a text for Neo-Platonist homilies in the last days of the Western Empire.[4]

[1] *Aen.* 640; cf. Pind. *Ol.* ii. 130.

[2] *Aen.* vi. 645.

[3] *Ib.* 748; cf. Conington's *Virg. Introd. Aen.* vi. p. 419; Lobeck, *Aglaoph.* ii. 798.

[4] Diog. Laert. *Vit. Pythag.* viii. 1, § 14; *πρῶτόν τέ φασι τοῦτον ἀποφῆναι τὴν ψυχὴν κύκλον ἀνάγκης ἀμείβουσαν ἄλλοτ' ἄλλοις ἐνδεῖσθαι ζῴοις*: S. Aug. *De Civ. D.* vii. 6; cf. Liebaldt, *Theolog. Varr.* i. p. 14; Cic. *Rep.* vi. 15–25; Macrob. *Som. Scip.* i. 14.

A fiery spirit animates the material universe, from the farthest star in ether down to the lowest form of animal life. The souls of men are sparks or emanations from this general soul which have descended into the prison of the body, and during the period of their bondage have suffered contamination.[1] And the prison walls hide from their eyes for a time the heaven from which they come. Nor when death releases them do they shake off the engrained corruption. For a thousand years they must suffer cleansing by punishment till the stains are washed away, the deeply festering taint burnt out as by fire. Then only may the pure residue of ethereal spirit seek to enter on another life on earth.

Virgil, in his Nekuia, mirrored the confusion of beliefs as to the future state prevailing in his time. For his poetic sensibility, the old Roman faith of the Manes, the Greek legends of Tartarus and Elysium, the Pythagorean or Orphic doctrine of successive lives and purgatorial atonement, had each their charm, and a certain truth. On a subject so dim and uncertain as the future life, the keenest minds may have wavering conceptions, and in different moods may clothe them in various guise. This is the field of the protean poetic imagination inspired by religious intuition, not of the rigorous dogmatist. But a great poet like Virgil not only expresses an age to itself: he elevates and glorifies what he expresses. He gives clear-cut form to what is vague, he spreads the warmth and richness of colour over what is dim and blank, and he imparts to the abstract teaching of philosophy a glow and penetrating power which may touch even the unthinking mass of men. The vision of the Sixth Book, moreover, like the Aeneid as a whole, has a high note of patriotism. Beside the water of Lethe are gathered, waiting for their call to earthly life, all the great souls from the Alban Silvius to the great Julius, all the Scipios, Gracchi, Decii, and Fabricii, who were destined through storm and stress to give the world the calm of the Roman peace.[2] The poet of Roman destiny had a marvellous fame among his countrymen. Men rose up to do him honour when he entered the theatre; the

[1] Rohde, *Psyche*, ii. 161, n. 1, 34, 312; Cic. *De N. D.* i. 11, 27; Pythagoras qui censuit animum esse per naturam rerum omnem intentum et commeantem, ex quo nostri animi carperentur, etc.

[2] *Aen.* vi. 756 sqq.

street boys of Pompeii scratched his verses on the walls.[1] Can we doubt that the grandest part of his great poem, which lifts for a moment the veil of the unseen world, had a profound effect on the religious imagination of the future?

The opinion long prevailed that the period of the early Empire was one of unbelief or scepticism as to the future life. The opinion was founded on literary evidence accepted without much critical care. Cicero and Seneca, Juvenal and Plutarch,[2] had spoken of the Inferno of Greek legend, its Cerberus and Chimaera, its gloom of Tartarus, as mere old wives' fables, in which even children had ceased to believe. But such testimony should always be taken with a good deal of reserve. The member of a comparatively small literary and thoughtful circle is apt to imagine that its ideas are more widely diffused than they really are. It may well have been that thoughtful men, steeped in Platonic or Pythagorean faith as to the coming life, rejected as anthropomorphic dreams the infernal scenery of Greek legend, just as a thoughtful Christian of our day will hardly picture his coming beatitude in the gorgeous colouring of the Book of Revelation. Yet the mass of men will always seek for concrete imagery to body forth their dim spiritual cravings. They always live in that uncertain twilight in which the boundaries of pictured symbolism and spiritual reality are blurred and effaced. Lucian was a pessimist as to spiritual progress, and he may have exaggerated the materialistic superstition of his time; he had ample excuse for doing so. Yet, artist as he was, his art would have been futile and discredited in his own time, if it had not had a solid background in widely accepted beliefs. And we cannot refuse to admit his testimony that the visions of the grim ferryman over the waters of Styx, the awful judge, the tortures of Tartarus, the asphodel meads, and the water of Lethe, the pale neutral shades who wandered expectant of the libation on the grave, filled a large space in the imagination of the crowd.[3] Plutarch, who sometimes agrees with Juvenal and Seneca as to the general incredulity, at others holds that a large class of remorseful sinners have a wholesome fear of the

[1] *C.I.L.* iv. 2361, 1982; Mau, *Pompeii*, 486–8; Friedl. iii. p. 300.

[2] Sen. *Ad Marc.* xix. 4; Cic. *Tusc.* i. 21, 48; Juv. xiii. 48; Plut. *De Superst.* c. 4.

[3] Luc. *De Luctu*, cc. 1–10.

legendary tortures of lost souls, and that they are eager to purge their guilt before the awful ordeal of the Eternal Judgment.[1] And, however pure and etherealised his own views may have been as to the life to come, no one has left a more lurid picture of the flames, the gloom, the sounds of excruciating anguish from the prison-house of the damned, which oppressed the imagination of the multitude in his time. One part of that vision had a peculiarly tenacious hold.[2] The belief in the gruff ferryman of the dead, who sternly exacted his fare, and drove from the banks of Styx those who had no right to cross the awful stream, was widely diffused and survived far into the medieval times. For many centuries, long before and long after the coming of Christ, the coin which was to secure the passage of the shade into the world below was placed in the mouth of the corpse.[3]

The inscriptions might be supposed to give authoritative evidence as to the belief of ordinary men about the future state. The funerary monuments from every part of the Roman world are almost countless for the period of the early Empire. Yet such records, however abundant, are not so clear and satisfactory as they are by some taken to be. The words of a tombstone are sometimes a sincere utterance of real affection and faith. They are also not unfrequently purely conventional, representing a respectable, historic creed, which may not be that of the man who erects the slab. Just as a Frenchman, who has never from infancy entered a church, may have his wife interred with all the solemn forms with which the Catholic Church makes the peace of the passing soul, so the Roman pagan may have often inscribed on his family tomb words which expressed the ancient creed of his race rather than his personal belief. Heredity in religion is a potent influence, and may be misleading to the inquirer of a later age. An epitaph should not be construed as a confession of faith.

The great mass of these inscriptions are couched in the same phrases, with only slight variations. The dedication Dis Manibus, representing the old Roman faith, is the heading of

1 Plut. *Non p. Suav.* c. 27.

2 Id. *De Ser. Num. Vind.* iv. 44; *De Gen. Socr.* c. 22.

3 Luc. *De Luctu*, c. 10; Friedl. iii. p. 632; Rohde, *Psyche*, i. p. 306, n. 3; Maury, *La Magie*, p. 158.

the majority of them. The vault is an "eternal home," whose peace is guarded by prayers or threats and entreaties. There is a rare dedication to the "ashes" of the dead. There are many to their "eternal repose."[1] But it is surely rather absurd to find in expressions which occur almost in the same form in the niches of the Catacombs a tinge of Epicureanism. The poor grammarian of Como, who left all his substance to his town, may be permitted to enjoy "the calm peace" he claims after all the troubles of his life, without a suspicion that he meant the peace of nothingness.[2] A pious Christian may rejoice at escaping the miseries of old age, and even hail death as the last cure of all mortal ills.[3] Death and sleep have always seemed near akin, and when the Roman spoke of the sleep of death, he probably did not often mean that it had no awaking. The morning indeed, as we have seen, to old imaginations was not very bright. "The day of eternity" was not irradiated with the golden splendour of Pindar's Happy Isles; it was grey and sad and calm. But that it was felt to be a real existence is shown by the insistent demand on scores of monuments for the regular service of the living. Every possible precaution is taken by the testator that his family or his club shall maintain this sympathetic observance for ever.[4] With the idea of prolonged existence, of course, is blended the imaginative hope of having a continued memory among men. And probably the majority of the funerary inscriptions express this feeling chiefly. But the same is true of the monuments of every age, and warrants no conclusion as to the opinions about immortality held by those who raised them. There is abundance of the purest affection expressed on these memorials, and sometimes, although not very often, there is the hope of reunion after death. The wife of a *philologus* at Narbonne confidently expects to meet him, or a mother prays her son to take her to himself.[5] Such expressions of a natural feeling, the same from age to age, have really little value as indications of religious belief. But there are not wanting in the inscriptions references to Tartarus and the Elysian fields, to Pluto and Proserpine, to Orcus who has snatched away some one in his bloom. "One little soul has been

[1] *Or. Henz.* 4443. [2] *Ib.* 1197. [3] *Ib.* 2982.
[4] *Ib.* 4433, 4416, 4417. [5] *Ib.* 4662, 4755.

received among the number of the gods."[1] There are others, impregnated with the prevalent philosophy, which speak of the soul returning to its source, or of being dissolved into the infinite ether, or of passing to a distant home in the stars.[2] This, however, as M. Boissier says,[3] must have been the dream of a small minority. The funerary inscriptions leave the impression that, down to the final triumph of the Church, the feeling of the Romans about death was still in the main the feeling of their remote ancestors of the Samnite and Punic wars. It was a social feeling, in the prospect of a dim life dependent on the memory of the living, a horror of loneliness and desertion, the longing for a passing prayer even from a stranger. Blessings are heaped on him who will not forget the pious duty to the shade. On him who refuses it is invoked the bitterest curse to Roman imagination—"May he die the last of his race."

But no dogmatic ecclesiastical system deterred the Roman from expressing frankly his unbelief in any future state. And the rejection of all hope for the future, sometimes coupled with a coarse satisfaction with a sensual past, is the note of not a few epitaphs of this period. Matrinia, the wife of one C. Matrinius Valentius, an Epicurean philosopher, dedicates a tablet to his "eternal sleep," which in this case is no conventional phrase.[4] And others, in even more decided language, parade their withering faith that this brief life is only a moment of consciousness between the blank of the past and the blank of the future, and record their indifference at passing again into the nothingness from which they came. The formula is frequent—"Non fueram, non sum, nescio"; or "Non fui, fui; non sum, non curo." Another adds "non mihi dolet."[5] The subjects of some of these epitaphs seem to have obeyed literally the counsel of their master Lucretius, though in a sense different from his, and to have risen up sated with the banquet of life. They express, with cynical grossness, their only faith in the joys of the flesh, and their perfect content at having made the most of them.

[1] *Or. Henz.* 4581, 4841, 4849, 4701, 7352.

[2] *Ib.* 7392.

[3] *Rel. Rom.* i. 342.

[4] *Or. Henz.* 1192.

[5] *Ib.* 7387, 4809, 4810, 4811, 4807, 4813, vixi dum vixi bene; jam mea peracta mox vestra agetur fabula; valete et plaudite, 7411.

"Balnea, Vina, Venus," sums up the tale.[1] "What I have eaten, what I have drunk, is my own. I have had my life."[2] And the departing voluptuary exhorts his friends to follow his example: "My friends, while we live, let us live"; "Eat, drink, disport thyself, and then join us."[3] A veteran of the fifth legion records, probably with much truth, that "while he lived he drank with a good will,"[4] and he exhorts his surviving friends to drink while they live. Under the confessional of St. Peter's at Rome, in the year 1626, was found a monument of one Agricola of Tibur and his wife. There was a figure holding a wine-cup, and an inscription so frankly sensual that the whole was destroyed by order of the Pope. From the copy which was kept, it appears that Agricola was perfectly satisfied with his life, and recommended his example to others, "since it all ends in the grave or the funeral fire."[5] But inscriptions such as these are the exception. The funerary records, as a whole, give a picture of a society very like our own, with warm affections of kindred or friendship, clinging to ancestral pieties, ready to hope, if sometimes not clear and confident in faith.

There was probably a much more settled faith in immortality among the ordinary masses than among the highly educated. The philosophy of Greece came to the cultivated Roman world with many different voices on the greatest problem of human destiny. And the greatest minds, from Cicero to M. Aurelius, reflect the discordance of philosophy. Nay, some of those who, in more exalted moods, have left glowing pictures of the future beatitude, have also at times revealed a mood of melancholy doubt as to any conscious future life. The prevailing philosophy in the last generation of the Republic, demoralised by an internecine strife, was that of Epicurus.[6] It harmonised with the decay of old Roman religion, and with the more disastrous moral deterioration in the upper cultivated class. The cultivated patrician, enervated by vice and luxury, or intoxicated with the

[1] *Or. Henz.* 4806, 7; 4; 4816, hic secum habet omnia. Balnea, vina, venus corrumpunt corpora nostra, set vitam faciunt.

[2] *Ib.* 7407.

[3] *C.I.L.* ii. 1877.

[4] *Or. Henz.* 6674, dum vixi bi(bi) libenter; bibite vos qui vivitis.

[5] *Ib.* 7410—miscete Lyaeum, etc., caetera post obitum tellus consumit et ignis.

[6] Boissier, *Rel. Rom.* i. 312–316; Thiersch, *Politik und Phil. in ihrem Verhältn. zur Rel.* p. 13.

excitement of civil war and the dreams of disordered ambition, flung off all spiritual idealism, and accepted frankly a lawless universe and a life of pleasure or power, to be ended by death. The great poem of Lucretius, the greatest *tour de force* in Latin, if not in any literature, braving not only the deepest beliefs of the Latin race, but the instinctive longings of humanity, was a herculean attempt to relieve men from the horrors of Graeco-Etruscan superstition. Even the gay frivolity of the comic stage reveals the terror which the path to Acheron inspired in the thoughtless crowd[1]—the terror from which, with all the fervid zeal of an evangelist, Lucretius sought to relieve his countrymen.[2] The pictures of Tartarus had burnt themselves into the popular imagination. And no message of Epicurus seems to his Roman interpreter so full of peace and blessing as the gospel of nothingness after death, the "morningless and unawakening sleep" which ends the fretful fever of life. As we felt no trouble when the storm of Punic invasion burst on Italy, we shall be equally unconscious when the partnership of soul and body is dissolved, even in the clash and fusion of all the elements in some great cosmic change.[3] The older Stoicism permitted the hope of a limited immortality until the next great cataclysm, in which, after many ages, all things will be swallowed up.[4] But Chrysippus admitted this prolonged existence only for the greater souls. And Panaetius, in the second century B.C., among other aberrations from the old creed of his school, abandoned even this not very satisfactory hope of immortality.[5] Aristotle, while he held the permanence of the pure thinking principle after death, had given little countenance to the hope of a separate conscious personality. And the later Peripatetics, like Alexander Aphrodisias, had gone farther even than their master in dogmatic denial of immortality.[6] Whatever support the instinctive craving of humanity for prolonged existence could obtain from philosophy was offered by the

[1] Boissier, *Rel. Rom.* i. 310.

[2] Lucret. iii. 952, 991.

[3] *Ib.* 844 sqq.

[4] Plut. (?) *De Plac. Phil.* iv. 7, οἱ Στωικοὶ ἐξιοῦσαν ἐκ τῶν σωμάτων ὑποφέρεσθαι, τὴν μὲν ἀσθενεστέραν ἅμα τοῖς συγκρίμασι γενέσθαι· τὴν δὲ ἰσχυροτέραν, οἷα ἐστὶ περὶ τοὺς σοφούς, καὶ μέχρι τῆς ἐκπυρώσεως.

[5] Zeller, *Phil. der Griech.* iii. 1, p. 185; Cic. *Tusc.* i. 32, 79.

[6] Zeller, iii. 1, p. 711, keine Seelenthätigkeit ist ohne körperliche Bewegung möglich; Renan, *Averroès*, pp. 128 sq., 418; Rohde, *Psyche*, ii. p. 309.

Platonic and Neo-Pythagorean schools. And their influence grew with the growing tendency to a revival of faith in the supernatural. For Plato, with his intense belief in the divine affinity of the human spirit, must always be the great leader of those who seek in philosophy an interpreter and a champion of religious intuition. The Phaedo was the last consolation of many a victim of conscription or imperial tyranny. Its fine-spun arguments may not have been altogether convincing, as they hardly seem to be even to the Platonic Socrates. But Plato was not merely a dialectician, he was also a seer and a poet. And, on a subject so dim as immortality, where mere intellectual proof, it is generally recognised, can be no more than tentative and precarious, men with a deep spiritual instinct have always felt the magnetism of the poet who could clothe his intuitions in the forms of imagination, who, from a keener sensibility and a larger vision, could give authority and clearness to the spiritual intuitions of the race.[1] The philosophy of the Porch gave to the Antonine age some of its loftiest characters. But it was not the philosophy of the future. It was too cold, and too self-centred. It had too little warmth of sympathy with religious instincts which were becoming more and more imperious. Although, as we have seen in Seneca, it was softened by elements borrowed from Platonic sources, in Epictetus and M. Aurelius, in spite of a rare spiritual elevation, it displays the old aloofness from the mass of men, and a cold temperance of reserve on the great question of the future of the soul.

There can be little doubt that in the last age of the Republic a negative philosophy conspired with a decaying religious sense to stifle the hope of immortality among the cultivated class. Lucretius was certainly not a solitary member of his order. His great poem, by its combination of dialectic subtlety, poetic charm, and lofty moral earnestness, may have made many converts to its withering creed. In the debate on the fate of the Catilinarian conspirators, Julius Caesar could assert, without fear of contradiction or disapproval, that death was the final term alike of joy and sorrow in human life.[2] This philosophy,

[1] Cf. Graham, *Creed of Science* (2nd ed.), p. 183, "The poets must count for much in the argument, since they possess in higher degree than others the great creative faculty of imagination which outlives the province of the possible"; Jowett, *Plato*, i. pp. 389 sqq., etc.

[2] Sall. *Catil.* c. 51.

indeed, was waning in force in the time of Augustus, and its forces were spent before the close of the first century. Yet the elder Pliny, who saw the reign of Vespasian, inveighs almost fiercely against the vanity or madness which dreams of a phantom life beyond the tomb, and robs of its great charm the last kindly boon of nature.[1] Seneca on this, as on many other questions of high moment, is not steady and consistent. In moments of spiritual exaltation he is filled with apocalyptic rapture at the vision of an eternal world. At other times he speaks with a cold resignation, which seems to have been the fashion with men of his class and time, at the possibility of extinction in death. To the toil-worn spirit, weary of the travail and disappointments of life, death will be a quiet haven of rest.[2] The old terrors of Charon and Cerberus, of the awful Judge and the tortures of Tartarus, are no longer believed in even by children.[3] And stripped of its mythic horrors, death, being the loss of consciousness, must be the negation of pain and desire and fear. It is, in fact, a return to the nothingness from which we come, which has left no memory. *Non miser potest esse qui nullus est.*[4] The literary men and men of the world in the age of the Flavians, like their successors ever since, probably occupied themselves little with a problem so long debated and so variously solved. Quintilian treats the question of the existence of the disembodied spirit as an open one for dialectical debate.[5] Tacitus, at once credulous and sceptical, is no clearer on the subject of immortality than he is on the subject of miracles, or omens, or Providence. In his eulogy on Agricola he expresses a faint, pious hope of eternal peace for his hero, if there is a place in some other world for pious shades, and the sages are right in thinking that great souls do not perish with the body.[6] This is a very guarded and hypothetical hope; and, probably, the only immortality for his friend in which Tacitus had much confidence was the undying fame with which the pen of genius can invest its subject. Tacitus, like so many of his

[1] Plin. *H. N.* vii. 55, 188.

[2] Cf. Plut. (?) *Cons. ad Apoll.* c. xii. xiii.

[3] Sen. *Ad Marc.* c. xix.

[4] Sen. *Ep.* 54, 99, § 30; *De Prov.* vi. § 6; *Ad Marc.* 25.

[5] Quint. *Inst.* v. 14, 13, cum, soluta corpore anima an sit immortalis vel ad tempus certe maneat, sit in dubio.

[6] Tac. *Agric.* c. 46; cf. Rohde, *Psyche*, ii. p. 318, n. 3.

class, had the old Roman distrust of philosophy, and the philosophies of which men of his generation had a tincture had no very confident or comforting message about the soul's eternal destiny.

Hadrian, the most interesting of the emperors, was probably a sceptic on this as on all kindred subjects. The greatest practical genius in the imperial line had, in the field of religion and speculation, an infinite passion for all that was curious and exotic.[1] Tramping at the head of his legions through his world-wide domains, he relieved the tedium of practical administration by visiting the scenes of historic fame or the homes of ancient religion both in the East and West. The East particularly attracted him by its infinite fecundity of superstition. He came to see whether there was anything in these revelations of the unseen world; he went away to mock at them. His insatiable curiosity had an endless variety of moods, and offered an open door to all the influences from many creeds. The restorer of ancient shrines, the admirer of Epictetus, the dabbler in astrology, the votary of Eleusis[2] and all the mysteries of the East, the munificent patron of all professors of philosophy and the arts, the man who delighted also to puzzle and ridicule them,[3] had probably few settled convictions of his own. His last words to his soul, in their mingled lightness and pathos, seem to express rather regret for the sunlight left behind than any hope in entering on a dim journey into the unknown.

The Antonine age was for the masses an age of growing faith, and yet three or four of its greatest minds, men who had drunk deep of philosophy, or who had a rare spiritual vision, either denied or doubted the last hope of humanity. Epictetus came from Phrygia as the slave of a freedman of Nero.[4] Even in his days of slavery, he had absorbed the teaching of Musonius.[5] He received his freedom, but lived in poverty and physical infirmity till, in the persecution of Domitian's reign he was, with the whole tribe of philosophic preachers, driven from Rome,[6] and he settled at Nicopolis in Epirus, where Arrian heard his discourses on the higher life.

[1] Spart. *Hadr.* c. 13, § 3; 14, § 3; 17, § 9; cf. Gregorovius, p. 303.

[2] Spart. *Hadr.* 13, § 1.

[3] *Ib.* c. 15, § 12; 16, § 8.

[4] Zeller, *Phil. der Griech.* iii. 1, p. 660 n.

[5] Epict. *Diss.* iii. 6, § 10.

[6] A. Gell. xv. 11.

According to Hadrian's biographer, he lived in the greatest intimacy with that emperor.[1] He refers more than once to the reign of Trajan,[2] but it is hardly possible that the tradition is true which carries his life into the reign of M. Aurelius, although the great philosophic emperor owed much to his teaching.[3]

Epictetus is an example of a profoundly religious mind, to whom personal immortality is not a necessity of his religion. The great law of life is glad submission to the will of God, to the universal order. Death, as an event which is bound to come soon or late, should be regarded without fear. The tremors it excites are like the shuddering of children at a tragic mask of Gorgon or Fury. Turn the mask, and the terror is gone.[4] For what is death? A separation of soul and body, a dissolution of our frame into the kindred elements.[5] The door is opened, God calls you to come, and to no terrible future. Hades, Acheron, and Cocytus are mere childish fancies.[6] You will pass into the wind or earth or fire from which you come. You will not exist, but you will be something else of which the world now has need, just as you came into your present existence when the world had need of you. God sent you here subject to death, to live on earth a little while in the flesh, to do His will and serve His purpose, and join in the spectacle and festival. But the spectacle for you is ended; go hence whither He leads, with adoration and gratitude for all that you have seen and heard. Make room for others who have yet to be born in accordance with His will.[7] Language like this seems to give slight hope of any personal, conscious life beyond the grave. Epictetus, like the pious Hebrew of many of the Psalms, seems to be satisfied with the present vision of God, whether or not there be any fuller vision beyond the veil. Yet he elsewhere uses almost Platonic language, which seems to imply that the soul has a separate life, that it is a prisoner for a time in the bonds of the flesh, and that it passes at death to the kindred source from which

[1] Ael. Spart. *Hadr.* c. 16.

[2] Epict. *Diss.* iv. 5, § 17.

[3] M. Aurel. i. 7, *καὶ τὸ ἐντυχεῖν τοῖς Ἐπικτητείοις ὑπομνήμασιν ὧν οἴκοθεν μετέδωκε.*

[4] Epict. *Diss.* ii. 1, § 17.

[5] *Ib.* iii. 24, § 93; cf. M. Aurel. iv. 14, 21, and Rohde, *Psyche*, ii. 330.

[6] Epict. *Diss.* iii. 13, § 15.

[7] *Ib.* § 14, *ὅταν δὲ μὴ παρέχῃ τἀναγκαῖα, τὸ ἀνακλητικὸν σημαίνει, τὴν θύραν ἤνοιξε, καὶ λέγει σοι, Ἔρχου, Ποῦ; Εἰς οὐδὲν δεινόν· ἀλλ᾽ ὅθεν, ἐγένου, εἰς τὰ φίλα καὶ συγγενῆ, εἰς τὰ στοιχεῖα.*

it sprang.[1] Yet even here the hope of an individual immortality, of any future reproduction on a higher scale of the life on earth, need not be implied; it is indeed probably absent. It is enough for the profoundly religious spirit of Epictetus that God calls us; whither He calls us must be left to His will.

Galen the physician shows a similar detachment from the ordinary hopes of humanity as to a future life, although it springs from a very different environment and training from those of Epictetus. Born in the reign of Hadrian, and dying in the reign of Septimius Severus, Galen represents the religious spirit of the Antonine age in his firm belief in a spiritual Power and Providence.[2] But in philosophy he was an eclectic of the eclectics. His medical studies began at the age of seventeen. The influence of the Platonist, Albinus of Smyrna, above all his stay at Alexandria, while they gave him a wide range of sympathy, account for the mingled and heterogeneous character of his philosophic creed, which contains elements from every system except that of Epicurus.[3] The result is a curious hesitation and equipoise between conflicting opinions on the greatest questions. He is particularly uncertain as to the nature of the soul and its relation to the body. The Platonic doctrine that the soul is an immaterial essence, independent of corporeal support, seems to Galen very disputable. How can immaterial essences have any separate individuality? How can they diffuse themselves over a corporeal frame and alter and excite it, as in lunacy or drunkenness? And again, if the Peripatetic doctrine be true, that the soul is the "form" of the body, we are soon landed in the Stoic materialism from which Galen shrank. The soul will become, as in the well-known theory refuted in the Phaedo,[4] a "temperament" of bodily states, and its superior endurance, its immortality, will become a baseless dream. On these great questions the cautious man of science will not venture to come to any dogmatic conclusion.[5]

Galen came to Rome in the year 164, at the beginning of the reign of M. Aurelius. He soon rose to great fame in his profession, and when, in 168, he had returned to his native

[1] *Diss.* i. 9, § 14, ἄφες ἡμᾶς ἀπελθεῖν ὅθεν ἐληλύθαμεν κτλ.
[2] Überweg, *Hist. Phil.* i. p. 237.
[3] Zeller, iii. 1, p. 735.
[4] *Phaedo*, 86 B.
[5] Zeller, iii. 1, p. 740; Überweg, *Hist. Phil.* i. p. 237.

Pergamum, he was recalled by the emperors to meet them at Aquileia. It was an anxious time. It was the second year of the campaign against the Marcomanni, and the legions, returning with Verus from the East, had brought with them the taint of a pestilence which spread a desolation throughout Italy from which it did not recover for ages. The slaves were called to arms as in the Punic invasion, along with the gladiators, and even the brigands of Dalmatia, and the massing of the forces on the Adriatic only concentrated the malignity of the plague.[1] Galen remained with the army for some time, lending his skill to mitigate the horrors of the disease. He returned to Rome in 170, and was left there in charge of the youthful Commodus. The philosophic Emperor and his philosophic physician must have often met in those dreadful years. And we may be sure, from the detachment of M. Aurelius, that their conversations would take a wider range than the sanitary arrangements of the camp. With death in the air, how could two such men, trained under such masters, fail to question one another as to the sequel of death? At any rate the fact remains that M. Aurelius on this question is as submissive as Epictetus, as hesitating as Galen.

M. Aurelius is commonly spoken of as realising Plato's dream of the philosopher on the throne. And yet the description is, without some additions and explanations, somewhat misleading. Philosopher, in the large speculative sense, he certainly is not in his Meditations. For the infinite curiosity of intellect, the passion to pierce the veil of the unknown, to build a great cosmic system, he seems to have had but little sympathy.[2] His is the crowning instance of philosophy leaving the heights and concentrating itself on conduct, which becomes not merely "three-fourths of life," but the whole, and his philosophy is really a religion. It is a religion because it is founded on the great principle of unquestioning, uncomplaining submission to the will of God, the law of the whole universe. It is a religion because the repellent and rigorous teaching of the older Stoicism is, as it is in Epictetus, suffused with a glow of emotion.[3] And yet this religion, which

[1] Jul. Capit. *M. Ant.* c. 13; c. 21; cf. Merivale, *Rom. Hist.* viii. pp. 335–6.

[2] M. Aurel. vii. 67; Zeller, iii. 1, p. 677.

[3] M. Arnold, *Essays in Criticism*, p. 427.

makes such immense demands on human nature, cuts itself off from any support in the hope of a future life.

On the subject of immortality, indeed, M. Aurelius sometimes seems to waver. He puts the question hypothetically, or he suggests immortality as an alternative to extinction at death. "If thou goest indeed to another life, there is no want of gods, not even there. But if to a state without sensation, thou wilt cease to be held by pains and pleasures, and to be a slave to the vessel."[1] In one doubtful passage he speaks of "the time when the soul shall fall out of this envelop, like the child from the womb."[2] He does not dogmatise on a subject so dark. But his favourite conception of death is that of change, of transformation, of dissolution into the original elements. An Infinite Spirit, of which the individual soul is an emanation, pervades the universe, and at death the finite spirit is reabsorbed by the Infinite.[3] With this is coupled the doctrine of the dark Ephesian philosophy, which through Platonism had a profound influence on later thought. Life is but a moment of consciousness in the unresting flow of infinite mutation;[4] it is a dream, a mere vapour, the sojourn of a passing stranger. And the last thought of Aurelius probably was that there was no place for a hope of separate conscious existence after the last mortal change. Soul and body alike are swept along the stream of perpetual transformation, and this particular "ego," with all its dreams and memories, will never re-emerge in a separate personality.

M. Aurelius, from the frequency with which he returns to the subject, seems fully conscious of the instinctive passion for continued life. But he refuses to recognise it as original and legitimate, and therefore demanding some account to be given of it.[5] Still less would he ever dream of erecting it, as Cicero and Plutarch did, into a powerful argument for some corresponding satisfaction in another world. It is simply one

[1] M. Aurel. iii. 3, *εἰ δὲ ἐν ἀναισθησίᾳ, παύσῃ πόνων καὶ ἡδονῶν ἀνεχόμενος, καὶ λατρεύων τοσούτῳ χείρονι τῷ ἀγγείῳ ἢ περίεστι τὸ ὑπηρετοῦν*: Rohde, *Psyche*, ii. pp. 327–28.

[2] ix. 3, *οὕτως ἐκδέχεσθαι τὴν ὥραν ἐν ᾗ τὸ ψυχάριόν σου τοῦ ἐλύτρου τούτου ἐκπεσεῖται.*

[3] xii. 30–32.

[4] vi. 42, 47; ix. 29, 32; vi. 15; vii. 19; vi. 36, *πᾶν τὸ ἐνεστὼς τοῦ χρόνου, στιγμὴ τοῦ αἰῶνος*: Rohde, *Psyche*, ii. p. 147.

[5] M. Aurel. vi. 49, *μήτι δυσχεραίνεις ὅτι τοσῶνδέ τινων λιτρῶν εἶ καὶ οὐ τριακοσίων; οὕτω δὲ καὶ ὅτι μέχρι τοσῶνδε ἐτῶν βιωτέον σοι καὶ οὐ μέχρι πλείονος.*

of the irrational appetites, a form of rebellion against the universal order, which must be crushed and brought into submission to inexorable law. Neither do we find in M. Aurelius any feeling of the need for a rectification of the injustices of time, for any sphere for the completion of ineffectual lives, where the crooked may be made straight and the perverted be restored. He has, apparently, no sympathy with the sadness so often felt by the noblest minds, at having to go hence with so little done, so little known. The philosopher seems to have no wish to explore in some coming life the secrets of the universe, to prolong under happier conditions the endless quest of the ideal in art and knowledge and thought, which seems so cruelly baffled by the shortness of the life here below. The affectionate father and husband and friend seems to have no dream of any reunion with kindred souls. Above all, this intensely religious and devout spirit seems to have no conception, such as sometimes flashes on the mind of Seneca and of Plutarch, of a future beatitude in the full vision of God. This austere renunciation, if it was deliberate, of feelings and hopes so dear to humanity, excites a certain admiration, as the result of a stern self-discipline. It is the resignation of what are thought to be mere fond, self-flattering fancies in the cold light of truth, and, as such, it must ever command a reverent respect. Yet how completely the renunciation cuts off M. Aurelius from the spiritual movement of his time, from the great onward sweep of humanity to a spiritual reconstruction!

The attitude of M. Aurelius to the instinctive longing for immortality is partly dictated by logical loyalty to the fundamental principles of his theory of life, partly by personal temperament and sad experience. The cosmic theory of Heraclitus, the infinite flux of cyclic change, left little ground for faith in the permanence of consciousness. The Stoic principle of submission to the law of the whole made it a duty to acquiesce calmly, or even cheerfully, in what has been ordained for us. The whole duty, the sole blessedness of man, lie in bringing his will into conformity with the Eternal Reason, and in moulding this brief mundane life into a slight counterpart of the order of the mighty world. From one point of view the single human life is infinitely small, a mere point in infinite age,[1] agitated by hopes and fears which are mere flitting dreams of a momentary consciousness. Nay, the grandest features of its earthly home shrink to mean proportions before the eye of reason. Asia is a mere corner, the sea a drop, Athos a tiny clod in the universe.[2] Life is so little a thing that death is no evil.[3] Yet, looked at on another side, the daemon, the divine spark within each of us, may, by its irresistible power, create a moral whole in each human spirit which, during its short space of separate being, may have the rounded harmony and perfectness of the whole vast order—it may become a perfect miniature of the universe of God.[4] This consummate result, attainable, though so rarely attained, is the ideal which alone gives dignity to human life. The ideal of humanity lies not in any future life or coming age; it may be, were the will properly aroused to its divine strength, realised here and now in our short span of forty years of maturity.[5] Get rid of gross fears and hopes, aim only at the moral ends which the will, aided by the daemon within, can surely reach, dismiss the fear of censure from the ephemeral crowd around us, the craving for fame among ephemeral generations whom we shall not see,[6] let the divine impulse within us gravitate to its proper orbit, and this poor human life is swept into the eternal movement of the great whole, and, from a moment of troubled consciousness, becomes a true life in God. Such a life, having fulfilled the true law of its being, is in itself rounded and complete: it needs no dreams of future beatitude to rectify its failures or reward its eager effort. Death to such a soul becomes an unimportant incident, fixed, like all other changes, in the general order. And the length or shortness of life is not worth reckoning. The longest life is hardly a moment in eternity: the shortest is long enough if it be lived well. This life, as fixed by eternal law, is a whole, a thing by itself, a thing with innumerable counterparts in the infinite past, destined to be endlessly reproduced in the years of the limitless future.[7] To repine at

[1] M. Aurel. ix. 32, *ἀχανὲς δὲ τὸ πρὸ τῆς γενέσεως ὡς καὶ τὸ μετὰ τὴν διάλυσιν ὁμοίως ἄπειρον.*

[2] *Ib.* vi. 36, *ἡ 'Ασία, ἡ Εὐρώπη, γωνίαι τοῦ κόσμου . . . Αθως βωλάριον τοῦ κόσμου.*

[3] *Ib.* vii. 35.

[4] *Ib.* x. 33; v. 11; v. 27.

[5] *Ib.* xi. 1.

[6] *Ib.* vi. 16; vi. 2; vi. 51; vii. 21, *ἐγγὺς μὲν ἡ σὴ περὶ πάντων λήθη· ἐγγὺς δὲ ἡ πάντων περὶ σοῦ λήθη.*

[7] *Ib.* xi. 1; vii. 1.

its shortness is no more rational than to mourn the swift passing of a springtime, whose glorious promise, yet ever-withering charm, have come and gone in the self-same way through myriads of forgotten years.

This is the ideal view of an austere creed, with a grandeur of its own which all generations of the West have agreed to venerate. But the temperament and the history of M. Aurelius had also their share in shaping his views of life and death. With infinite charity, indulgence, and even love for his fellows, he was a pessimist about human life.[1] He had good excuse for being so. In the words of one who knew that age as only genius combined with learning can, *le monde s'attristait;* and with good cause. The horizon was darkened with ominous thunder-clouds. The internal forces of the Empire were becoming paralysed by a mysterious weakness. The dim hordes beyond the Danube had descended with a force only to be repelled in many weary campaigns. Famine and pestilence were inflicting worse horrors than the Marcomanni. It was the beginning of the end, although the end was long deferred. The world was growing sad; but there was no sadder man than the saintly Stoic on the throne, who had not only to face the Germans on the Danube, and bear the anxieties of solitary power, but who had to endure the keener anguish of a soul which saw the spiritual possibilities of human nature, but also all its littleness and baseness. The Emperor needed all the lessons of self-discipline and close-lipped resignation which he had painfully learnt for himself, and which he has taught to so many generations. There have been few nobler souls, yet few more hopeless. Like the arch mocker of the time, although from a very different point of view, he sees this ephemeral life, with its transient pleasures and triumphs, ending in dust and oblivion.[2] And its fragility is only matched by its weary sameness from age to age. The wintry torrent of endless mutation sweeps all round in an eternal vortex.[3] This restless change is a movement of cyclic monotony.[4] Go back to Vespasian or

[1] M. Aurel. vi. 46, 47; vii. 3; ix. 30.

[2] *Ib.* vi. 47; cf. Luc. *Icaromenippus*, c. 18; *Traj. sive Tyr.* c. 8; *Charon*, c. 17; *Menip.* c. 15, ἀλλ' ὅμοια τὰ ὀστᾶ ἦν, ἄδηλα καὶ ἀνεπίγραφα κτλ.

[3] M. Aurel. vii. 19, διὰ τῆς τῶν ὅλων οὐσίας, ὡς διὰ χειμάρρου, διεκπορεύεται πάντα τὰ σώματα. Cf. ix. 29, χειμάρρους ἡ τῶν πάντων αἰτία· πάντα φέρει.

[4] *Ib.* vii. 49; vii. 1; ix. 14; x. 23; xi. 1.

Trajan: you will find the same recurring spectacle, men plotting and fighting, marrying and dying.[1] The daughter who watches by her mother's death-bed soon passes away under other eyes. The soul can in vision travel far, and survey the infinity of ages.[2] It can stretch forward into the endless ages to come, as it can go back in historic imagination through the limitless past. Yet it finds nothing strange in the experience of the past, as there will be nothing new in the experience of our remotest posterity. The man whose course has run for forty years, if he has any powers of perception, has concentrated in his brief span the image of all that has been, all that ever will be in human thought or fate. The future is not gilded by any dream of progress: it is not to be imaged in any magic light of a Platonic Utopia, or City of God descending from heaven like a bride.[3] From this "terrene filth," from these poor frivolous souls, what celestial commonwealth could ever emerge?[4] The moral is, both on the ground of high philosophy and sad experience—"be content, thou hast made thy voyage, thou hast come to shore, quit the ship."

But even in heathendom, long before M. Aurelius was born, the drift of thought towards the goal of a personal immortality was strong and intense. And this was only one consequence of a movement which had profoundly affected human thought, and had compelled Stoicism to recast itself, as in the teaching of Seneca. Pure reason could not explain the relation of man to the universe, it could not satisfy the deepest human instincts. The maxim, "live according to Nature," was interpreted by the Stoic to mean a life in accordance with our own higher nature, the Divine element within us. Yet this interpretation only brought out the irreconcilable discordance between the two conceptions of Nature in the physical universe and in the human spirit. There are depths and mysteries in the one which have no answering correspondence in the other. Something more than reason is needed to solve the problems of human destiny, the mysterious range of human aspiration. Nature, as a system of cold impersonal processes, has no sympathy with man, she may be icily indifferent or actively hostile. To conform one's

[1] M. Aurel. iv. 32.

[2] *Ib.* xi. 1.

[3] *Ib.* ix. 29, μηδὲ τὴν Πλάτωνος πολιτείαν ἔλπιζε, ἀλλ' ἀρκοῦ εἰ τὸ βραχύτατον πρόεισι.

[4] *Ib.* vii. 47; ix. 34.

life to the supposed dictates of an abstract Reason, asserting itself in physical laws, which seem often to make a mockery of the noblest effort and aspiration of man, demanded a servility of submission in human nature, and called upon it to disown a large part of its native powers and instincts. Man, a mere ghost of himself, attenuated to a bloodless shade, finds himself in presence of a power cold, relentless, unmoral, according to human standards, a power which makes holocausts of individual lives to serve some abstract and visionary ideal of the whole. The older Stoicism provided no object of worship. For worship cannot be paid to an impersonal law without moral attributes. You may in abject quietism submit to it, but you cannot revere or adore it. It is little wonder that the Stoic sage, who could triumph over all material obstructions by moral enthusiasm, was sometimes exalted above the Zeus who represented mere passionless physical law. Such an idea—for it cannot be called a Being—has no moral import, it supplies no example, succour, or inspiration. The sage may for a moment have a superhuman triumph, in his defiance of the temptations or calamities with which Nature has surrounded him, but it is a lonely triumph of inhuman pride.[1] It may be the divine element within him which has given him the victory, but this is conceived as the mere effluence of that subtle material force which moves under all the phenomena of physical Nature. In surrendering yourself to the impulse of such a power you are merely putting yourself in line with the other irrational subjects of impersonal law. There is here, it need not be said, no stimulus to moral life, there is the absolute negation of it. The affinity of the human soul with the soul of the world is a mere physical doctrine, however refined and subtle be the "fiery breath" which is the common element of both. But prolonged ethical study and analysis combined with the infiltration of Platonism by degrees to modify profoundly the Stoic conception of the nature of God, and of the relation of man to Him. God tended to become more and more a person, a moral power, a father. And the indwelling God became the voice of conscience, consoling, prompting, supporting, inspiring an ideal of fuller communion in another sphere. Was the longing for continued life, in communion with kindred souls,

[1] Sen. *Ep.* 109, § 9.

with a Divine Spirit, which has made us what we are, to be relegated to the limbo of anthropomorphic dreams?

Seneca, as we have seen in a former chapter, still retains some of the hard orthodoxy of the older Stoicism. In his letters to Lucilius he occasionally uses the language of the old Stoic materialism.[1] But there can be little doubt that Seneca had assimilated other conceptions antagonistic to it. God becomes more a Person, distinct from the world, which He has created, which He governs, which He directs to moral ends.[2] He is not merely the highest reason, He is also the perfect wisdom, holiness, and love. He is no longer a mere blind force or fate; He is the loving, watchful Father, and good men are His sons. The apparent calamities which they have to suffer are only a necessary discipline, for, "whom He loves He tries and hardens by chastisement."[3] God can never really injure, for His nature is love, and we are continually loaded with His benefits.[4] In his view of the constitution of man, Seneca has deviated even further from the creed of his school. He appears indeed to assert sometimes that the soul is material, but it is matter so fine and subtle as to be indistinguishable from what we call spirit. And the ethical studies of Seneca compelled him to abandon the Stoic doctrine of the simple unity of the soul for the Platonic dualism, with the opposition of reason and animal impulse. The latter has its seat in the body, or the flesh, as he often calls it. And of the flesh he speaks with all the contempt of the *Phaedo*. It is a mere shell, a fetter, a prison; or a humble hostelry which the soul occupies only for a brief space.[5] With the flesh the spirit must wage perpetual war, as the alien power which cramps its native energies, darkens its vision, and perverts its judgment of the truth. The true life of the spirit will, as in the theology of Plato, only begin when the unequal partnership is dissolved.[6]

The orthodox Stoic doctrine allowed a limited immortality, till the next great cosmic conflagration. But it was doubtful whether even this continued existence was real personal life, and with some Stoic doctors it was a privilege confined to the

[1] Sen. *Ep.* 57, § 7.
[2] *Ib.* 73, § 16; *Ep.* 83.
[3] Id. *De Prov.* iv. § 7, quos amat indurat, exercet.
[4] Id. *De Ben.* iv. 4; *De Ira*, ii. 27.
[5] Sen. *Ep.* 65, § 22; 102, § 26; *Ad Helv.* 11, § 7; *Ad Marc.* 24, § 5. Cf. Plat. *Phaed.* 83 C, D. Philostr. *Apoll. Tyan.* vi. 11; vii. 26.
[6] Plat. *Phaed.* 79 C; 81 A.

greater souls.[1] Like nearly all philosophers of this age, Seneca occasionally seems to admit the possibility of a return to antenatal nothingness at death. "Non potest miser esse qui nullus est" is a consolation often administered even by those who have the hope of something better than the peace of annihilation.[2] It was a consolation which might be a very real one to men living in the reign of Nero. Taken at the worst, death can only be dissolution, for the rivers of fire and the tortures of Tartarus are mere figments of poetic fancy. The mind trained in submission to universal law will not shrink from a fate which awaits the universe by fire or cataclysmal change. Its future fate can only be either to dwell calmly for ever among kindred souls, or to be reabsorbed into the general whole.[3] But in moments of spiritual exaltation, such an alternative does not satisfy Seneca. He has got far beyond the grim submission, or graceful contempt, of aristocratic suicide, or even the faith in a bounded immortality. He has a hope at times apparently more clear than any felt by the Platonic Socrates on the last evening in prison. Death is no longer a sleep, a blank peace following the futile agitations of life: it is the gateway to eternal peace. The brief sojourn in the body is the prelude to a longer and nobler life.[4] The hour, at which you shudder as the last, is really the birthday of eternity, when the mind, bursting from its fetters, will expatiate in all the joy of its freedom in the light, and have unrolled before it all the secrets and splendour of starry worlds, without a haunting shadow.[5] Nay, the vision is moralised almost in Christian fashion. The thought of eternity compels us to think of God as witness of every act, to remember that "decisive hour" when, with all veils and disguises removed, the verdict on our life will be pronounced. It also gives the hope of purging away for ever the taint of the flesh and entering on communion with the spirits of the blessed.[6] Thus as though

[1] Zeller, *Phil. der Griech.* iii. 1, p. 185.

[2] Sen. *Ad Marc.* c. 19, 20; cf. Plut. (?) *Consol. ad Apoll.* c. 15, εἰς τὴν αὐτὴν οὖν τάξιν οἱ τελευτήσαντες καθίστανται τῇ πρὸ τῆς γενέσεως: cf. *ib.* c. 34.

[3] Sen. *Ep.* 36; 71, § 12; *Ad Marc.* 19, § 4. Cf. Rohde, *Psyche*, ii. p. 328.

[4] Sen. *Ep.* 102, § 21.

[5] *Ep.* 120, § 14; 102, § 28, aliquando natura tibi arcana retegentur: discutietur ista caligo . . . nulla serenum umbra turbabit, cf. Rohde, *Psyche*, ii. p. 328, n. 4. Rohde, like Zeller, seems to me not to recognise sufficiently how far Seneca has departed from the old Stoicism.

[6] *Ep.* 26, § 5; *Ad Marc.* xxv.

with the Eternal eyes upon him, a man should shrink from all the baser and meaner side of his corporeal life, and so prepare himself for the great ordeal, and the beatitude of the life to come.

In the apocalypse of Seneca a new note is struck in pagan meditation on the immortality. We have left far behind the thought of the Manes haunting the ancestral tomb, and soothed in returning years by the jet of wine or the bunch of violets. We are no longer watching, with Pindar or Virgil, the spirits basking in Elysian meads and fanned by ocean breezes. We are far on the way to the City of God, *cujus fundamenta in montibus sanctis.* And indeed Seneca has probably travelled as far towards it as any one born in heathendom ever did. It is not wonderful that, in the fierce religious struggle of the fourth century, his moral enthusiasm, his view of this life as a probation for the next, his glowing vision of an almost Christian heaven, should have suggested an imaginary intercourse with St. Paul.[1]

What were the influences which really moulded his highest conception of the future state, how much was due to a pure and vigorous spiritual intuition, how much to Platonic and Pythagorean sources, we cannot pretend to say. In Seneca's most enraptured previsions of immortality, the very exuberance of the rhetoric seems to be the expression of intense personal feeling. But Seneca's was a very open and sensitive mind. One of his teachers was Sotion, who, like his master Sextius, was called a Pythagorean, and who, on true Pythagorean principles, taught Seneca to abstain from animal food.[2] We may be sure that no Pythagorean teacher of that age would fail to discuss with his pupil the problem of the future life. It is true that Seneca only once or twice alludes to the doctrine of a previous life, and he only mentions the Pythagorean school to record the fact that in his day it was without a head.[3] But that does not preclude the supposition that he may have felt its influence in the formative years of youth. And the Pythagoreans of the early empire were a highly eclectic school.

[1] See the apocryphal letters, p. 477, of Haase's ed. of Sen.; cf. Lightfoot, *S. Paul's Ep. to the Philippians*, p. 268 sqq. Zeller, *Phil. der Griech.* iii. 1, p. 637, n. 1; Baur, *Ch. Hist.* i. p. 16.

[2] Sen. *Ep.* 108, § 17; cf. Philostr. *Apoll. Tyan.* i. 7, 8.

[3] Sen. *Nat. Qu.* vii. 32, § 2, Pythagorica illa invidiosa turbae schola praeceptorem non invenit.

They still reproduced the spirit of their founder in mathematical symbolism, in the ideal of asceticism, in a pronounced religious tendency.[1] But they had absorbed much from Platonism, as well as from the Lyceum and the Porch. These mingled influences also account for the profound alterations which Stoicism had undergone in the mind of Seneca. And his contempt for the body or the flesh, and many of the phrases in which its cramping, lowering influences are described, savour of the Pythagorean and Platonist schools.

But Seneca is an inconsistent, though eloquent and powerful, expounder of that faith in personal immortality, with its moral consequences, which goes back through many ages to Plato, to Pythagoras, to the obscure apostles of the Orphic revelation, perhaps to Egypt.[2] The mythical Orpheus represents, in the field of religion and in the theory of life and death, an immense revolution in Greek thought and an enduring spirit which produced a profound effect down to the last years of paganism in the West.[3] With the names of Orpheus and Pythagoras are connected the assured faith in immortality, the conception of this life as only preparatory and secondary to the next, the need for purgation and expiation for deeds done in the body, the doctrine of transmigration and successive lives, possibly in animal forms. Orpheus was also the mythical founder of mysteries in whose secret lore the initiated were always supposed to receive some comforting assurance of a life to come.[4] A spokesman in one of Cicero's dialogues recalls with intense gratitude the light of hope and cheerfulness which the holy rites had shed for him both on life and death.[5] And Plutarch, on the death of their daughter, reminded his wife of the soothing words which they had together heard from the hierophant in the Dionysiac mysteries.[6] Long before their day Plato had often, on these high themes, sought a kind of high ecclesiastical sanction or suggestion for the tentative conclusions of dialectic.[7] The great name of Orpheus,

[1] Zeller, *Phil. der Griech.* iii. 2, p. 95.

[2] Herodot. ii. 123.

[3] Herodotus never mentions Orpheus, but speaks of τὰ Ὀρφικά, ii. 81; nor do the schol. on Homer allude to him (Lob. *Aglaoph.* i. p. 540; cf. *Aglaoph.* p. 255 sqq.). His existence was denied by Aristotle (Cic. *De Nat. Deor.* 1. 38, 108). Plato seems to be as assured of it as Iamblichus, *Cratyl.* 402; cf. Iambl. *Pythag.* 145, 243.

[4] Iambl. *Pythag.* 151; Lobeck, *Aglaoph.* i. p. 238.

[5] Cic. *De Leg.* ii. 14, 36, neque solum cum laetitia vivendi rationem accepimus, sed etiam cum spe meliore moriendi.

[6] Plut. *Cons. ad Ux.* c. 10.

[7] Plat. *Phaed.* 70 c; 69 c.

and the mystic lore of this esoteric faith, had indeed in Plato's day been sadly cheapened and degraded by a crowd of mercenary impostors.[1] And even the venerable rites of Eleusis may have contained an element of coarseness, descending from times when the processes of nature were regarded unveiled.[2] But philosophy and reason, which purged and elevated religion as a whole, did the same service for the mysteries, and Orphic and Pythagorean became almost convertible.[3] The systems represent a converging effort to solve those great questions which lie on the borderland of religion and philosophy, questions on which the speculative intellect is so often foiled, and has to fall back on the support of faith and religious intuition.[4] In an age which had forsaken curious speculation, whose whole interest was concentrated on the moral life, an age which longed for spiritual vision and supernatural support, an essentially religious philosophy like the new Pythagoreanism was sure to be a great power. Gathering up impartially whatever suited its main end from the ancient schools, maintaining a scrupulous reverence for all the devotion of the past, it shed over all a higher light, issuing, as its votaries believed, from the lands of the dawn.[5] Keeping a consecrated place for all the gods of popular tradition, linking men to the Infinite by a graduated hierarchy of spirits with their home in the stars, it rose to the conception of the One, pure, passionless Being to whom no bloody sacrifice is to be offered, who is to be worshipped best by silent adoration and a life of purity. And in cultivating this purity, the grossness of the body must be attenuated by a strict rule of life.[6] And though the Highest be so remote and so ethereal, He has not left us without messengers and interpreters to bridge the vast interval between us and the Infinite, by means of dream and vision and oracle. A world of strange daemonic life surrounds us, a world of spirits and heroic souls akin to ours.[7] For though we are immersed in the alien element of the flesh, yet our complex soul has a divine part, which may even here below have converse with the Divine. During its

[1] Plat. *Rep.* ii. 364 B.

[2] Cf. Gardner and Jevons, p. 268, who think the ceremonies never were indecent. Rohde, i. p. 289.

[3] Herodot. ii. 81; Iambl. *Pythag.* 151; Rohde, *Psyche*, ii. p. 103.

[4] Baur, *Ch. Hist.* ii. p. 178.

[5] Zeller, *Phil. der Griech.* iii. 2 p. 99.

[6] Philostr. *Apoll. Tyan.* i. 7, 8; cf. Sen. *Ep.* 108, §§ 17–20.

[7] Zeller, iii. 2, p. 122.

period of duress and probation, it may indeed become irremediably tainted by contact with matter. It may also, hearkening to the voice of philosophy, hold itself clear and pure from such defilement. When the mortal severance of the two natures comes, the divine part does not perish with its mouldering prison, but it may have a very different destiny in the ages to come, according to the manner of its earthly life. This life and the eternal state are linked in an inevitable moral sequence; as we sow, so shall we reap in successive lives. There is a Great Judgment in the unseen world, with momentous, age-long effects. The spirit which has refused to yield to the seductions of the flesh may, in the coming life, rise to empyrean heights beyond human imagination to picture. The soul which has been imbruted by its environment may have to pass a long ordeal of three thousand years, and then return to another sojourn in human form, or it may sink hopelessly to ever lower depths of degradation.

The biography of Apollonius of Tyana is, of course, in one sense a romance.[1] Yet its tales of miracle should hardly be allowed to obscure its value as a picture of the beliefs of that age. We cannot doubt that the Pythagorean apostle of the time of the Flavians went all over the Roman world, preaching his gospel of moral and ritual purity, kindling or satisfying the faith in the world of spirit, striving in a strange fashion to reconcile a mystic monotheism and devotion to a pure life of the soul with a scrupulous reverence for all the mythologies. It may, at first sight, appear strange that a mystic like Apollonius, of the Pythagorean school, should so seldom allude to the subject of immortality. The truth is that Apollonius was not a dogmatic preacher; he dealt little in theories. His chief business, as he conceived it, was with practical morality, and the reform or restoration of ritual where it had fallen into desuetude and decay.[2] Penetrated as he was with the faith in a spiritual world, he seems to assume as a postulate the eternity of the soul, and its incarnation for a brief space on earth. During its sojourn in the flesh, it is visited by visions from on high,

[1] Philostr. *Apoll. Tyan.* i. 2; cf. Zeller, iii. 2, p. 134, n.; Baur, *Ch. Hist.* ii. pp. 174, 206.

[2] Philostr. *Apoll. Tyan.* iv. 20; iii. 41; i. 11, 16; vi. 40.

and such revelations are vouchsafed in proportion to its ascetic purity.[1] What conception of the life to come Apollonius entertained we cannot say; but its reality to him was a self-evident truth. We are surrounded by the spirits of the departed, although we know it not. Sailing among the islands of the Aegean, he once gratified his disciples by the tale of his having met the shade of Achilles at his tomb in the Troad.[2] Men said that the hero was really dead, and in the old home of the Myrmidons, his worship was forgotten. But Apollonius, in a prayer which he had learnt from the sages on the Ganges, called upon the heroic shade to dispel all doubts by appearing at his call. At once an earthquake shook the tomb, and a fair youthful form was by his side of wondrous beauty and superhuman stature, clothed in a Thessalian mantle. His stature grew more majestic, and his beauty more glorious as Apollonius gazed. But the sage had no weak fears in the presence even of so august a spirit, and pressed him with questions which savour far more of antiquarian than spiritual interest. Was Helen really in Troy? Why does not Homer mention Palamedes? The hero resolved his doubts, sent a warning message to the Thessalians to restore his forgotten honours, and in a soft splendour vanished at the first cock-crow.[3]

The biography of Apollonius closes with a tale which throws a strong light on the spiritual cravings of that age. The sage firmly believed in transmigration and immortality, although he discouraged debate on these high themes.[4] After his death, the youth of Tyana were much occupied with solemn thoughts. But there was a sceptic among them who had vainly besought the departed philosopher to return from spiritland and dispel his doubts as to the future life. At last one day he fell asleep among his companions, and then suddenly started up as one demented, with the cry—"I believe thee." Then he told his friends that he had seen the spirit of the sage, that he had been actually among them, though they knew it not, chanting a marvellous song of life and death. It told of the escape of the soul from the mouldering frame and

[1] Philostr. *Apoll. Tyan.* ii. 37; vi. 11.
[2] *Ib.* iv. 16.
[3] *Ib.* iv. 16.
[4] *Ib.* viii. 31, περὶ ψυχῆς δέ, ὡς ἀθάνατος εἴη, ἐφιλοσόφει ἔτι διδάσκων μὲν ὅτι ἀληθὴς ὁ ὑπὲρ αὐτῆς λόγος, πολυπραγμονεῖν δὲ μὴ ξυγχωρῶν τὰ ὧδε μεγάλα.

of its swift flight to ethereal worlds. "Thou shalt know all when thou art no more; but while thou art yet among the living, why seek to pierce the mystery?"[1]

The new Platonist school, with Plutarch and Maximus at their head, were, in this age, the great apostles of the hope of immortality. Platonists in their theory of mind and God, Neo-Pythagorean in their faith in the openness of the human spirit at its best to supernatural influences, they felt the doctrine of the coming life to be axiomatic. It is true that the author of the *Consolation to Apollonius*, seems at times to waver, as Seneca did, between the idea of extinction at death and the hope of eternal beatitude.[2] This piece is full of pessimist thoughts of life, and embalms many a sad saying of the Greek poets on its shortness and its misery.[3] Bringing far more sorrow than joy, life may well be regarded as a mysterious punishment. That Thracian tribe which mourned at each birth as others do at death, had a true philosophy of man's estate. The great consolation is that, in the phrase of Heraclitus, death and life are one, we are dying every moment from our birth. Death is the great healer, in the words of Aeschylus, the deliverer from the curse of existence, whether it be an eternal sleep or a far journey into an unknown land. The prospect of blank nothingness offers no terrors; for the soul only returns to its original unconsciousness. But this was hardly a congenial mood to the author, and before the close, he falls back on the solace of mystic tradition or poetic vision, that, for the nobler sort, there is a place prepared in the ages to come, after the Great Judgment, when all souls, naked and stripped of all trappings and disguises, shall have to answer for the deeds done in the body.[4] The same faith is professed by Plutarch to his wife in the Consolation on the death of their little daughter, which took place while Plutarch was from home. The loss of a pure bright young soul, full of love and kindness to all, even to her lifeless toys, was evidently a heavy blow.[5] But Plutarch praises his wife's simple restraint and abstinence from the effusive parade of conventional mourning. All such displays seemed to him a rather vulgar intemperance

[1] Philostr. *Apoll. Tyan.* viii. 31, ἢ τί μετὰ ζῳοῖσιν ἐὼν περὶ τῶνδε ματεύεις;

[2] Plut. (?) *Consol. ad Apoll.* c. 34; cf. c. 15.

[3] *Ib.* c. 7 sqq.

[4] *Ib.* c. 36, τεθνεῶτας γὰρ δεῖ κρίνεσθαι κτλ.

[5] *Consol. ad Ux.* c. 3.

and self-indulgence.[1] And why grieve for one who is spared all grief? She had her little joys, and, knowing no other, she suffers no pain of loss. Yet Plutarch would not have his wife accept the cold consolation that death brings unconsciousness. He reminds her of the brighter, more cheering vision which they have enjoyed together as communicants in the Dionysiac mysteries. If the soul is undying, if it is of divine parentage and has a divine destiny, then the shortness of its imprisonment and exile is a blessing. The captive bird may come by use and wont actually to love its cage. And the worst misery of old age is not grey hairs and weakness, but a dull absorption in the carnal and forgetfulness of divine things. "Whom the gods love die young." By calling them back early, they save them from long wanderings.[2]

Plutarch's belief in immortality is a religious faith, a practical postulate. He nowhere discusses the bases of the belief in an exhaustive way. It is rather inseparable from his conception of God and His justice, and the relation of the human soul to God.[3] He admits that the prospect of reward or punishment in another world has but little influence on men's conduct.[4] Few believe in the tales of tortures of the damned. And those who do can soothe their fears, and purchase a gross immortality, by initiations and indulgences.[5] Yet it is impossible to doubt that to Plutarch the hope of the eternal life was a precious possession. He assails with force, and even asperity, the Epicurean school for their attempt to rob humanity of it, on the pretext of relieving men of a load of superstitious fears. They are like men on board a ship who, letting the passengers know that they have no pilot, console them with the further information that it does not matter, as they are bound to drive upon the rocks.[6] The great promise of Epicurus was to free men from the spectral terrors with which poetic fancy had filled the scenery of the under world. But in doing so, he invested death with a new horror infinitely worse than the fabled tortures of the damned. It was a subtle fallacy which taught that, as annihilation involves the extinction of consciousness, the lamented loss of the joys and vivid energy

1 *Consol. ad Ux.* c. 4, 6.

2 *Consol. ad Apoll.* c. 17–24.

3 *De Ser. Num. Vind.* c. 18 (561 A).

4 *Ib.* οὐδέν ἐστι πρὸς ἡμᾶς τοὺς ζῶντας ἀλλ' ἀπιστοῦνται καὶ λανθάνουσιν.

5 *Non p. Suav.* c. 26, 27.

6 *Ib.* c. 23 (1103).

of life was a mere imagination projected on a blank future where no regret could ever disturb the tranquillity of nothingness.[1] Plutarch took his stand on psychology. The passion for continued existence is, as a matter of fact, the most imperious in our nature. With the belief in immortality, Epicurus sweeps away the strongest and dearest hopes of the mass of men. This life is indeed full of pain and sorrow; yet men cling to it passionately, merely as life, in the darkest hours. And they are ready to brave the worst horrors of Cerberus and Chimaera for the chance of continued existence.[2] The privation of a dream of happiness in another world is a real loss, even though, when the grey day of nothingness dawns, the consciousness of loss be gone. Is it a light thing to tell the nobler spirits, the moral athletes, who have battled with evil all life long, that they have been contending for a visionary crown?[3] Is it nothing to the idealist who, amid all the obstructions of the life in the flesh, has been fostering his nobler powers, in the hope of eternal freedom and the full vision of truth, that that real life to which he fancied death was only the gateway is, after all, a mere illusion? Nor does Plutarch disdain to take account of that vivacity of love which in all ages has sought to soften the bitterness of parting by the hope of reunion and recognition in other worlds.[4]

The Consolation to Apollonius only refers briefly to the punishment of lawless wealth and power, as the complement to the reward of virtue.[5] But this aspect of immortality is dwelt on at length in the remarkable treatise on the Delays of the Divine Vengeance. The problem of hereditary guilt, and the punishment of the children for the sins of the fathers in this world, in view of the justice and benevolence of God, leads on to the thought of another tribunal which may terribly correct the injustices of time.[6] The doctrine of Divine providence and

[1] *Non p. Suav.* c. 30, 26.

[2] *Ib.* c. 27, δι' ἣν ὀλίγου δέω λέγειν πάντας καὶ πάσας εἶναι προθύμους τῷ Κερβέρῳ διαδάκνεσθαι ὅπως ἐν τῷ εἶναι διαμένωσι μηδ' ἀναιρεθῶσι.

[3] *Ib.* c. 28.

[4] *Ib.* c. 28, ἡλίκης ἑαυτοὺς χαρᾶς ἀποστεροῦσι . . . καὶ τὸν φίλον πατέρα καὶ τὴν φίλην μητέρα καί που γυναῖκα χρηστὴν ὄψεσθαι μὴ προσδοκῶντες μηδ' ἔχοντες ἐλπίδα τῆς ὁμιλίας ἐκείνης καὶ φιλοφροσύνης ἣν ἔχουσιν οἱ τὰ αὐτὰ Πυθαγόρᾳ καὶ Πλάτωνι δοξάζοντες.

[5] *Consol. ad Apoll.* c. 36.

[6] *De Ser. Num. Vind.* c. 16: cf. Gréard, *De la Morale de Plut.* p. 283; Oakesmith, *Rel. of Plut.* p. 111 sqq.

the doctrine of immortality stand or fall together.[1] God could not take so much care for ephemeral souls, blooming for a brief space and then withering away, as in the women's soon-fading gardens of Adonis.[2] Above all, Apollo would be the greatest deceiver, the god who has so often solemnly from the tripod ordered rites of expiation and posthumous honours to be paid to lofty souls departed.[3] Yet, like his great master Plato, Plutarch felt that the full assurance of the long dream of humanity lies beyond the veil—that we know not what we shall be. And, like the master, he invoked the apocalyptic power of the religious and poetic imagination to fortify the hesitating conclusions of the reason.

The visionary power and charm of the great master, whose reign was to be prolonged for ages after Plutarch's time, is seen, perhaps in a faint reflection, in Plutarch's mythical forecast of the future of the soul. Plato's psychology, his sharp opposition of the reason to the lower nature rooted in the flesh, his vision of the Eternal Goodness, his intensely moral conception of the responsibility of life on earth, its boundless possibilities of future unimpeded intuition, its possible eternal degradation through ages of cyclic change, all this, together with kindred elements, perhaps from the Semitic east, had left a profound effect on religious minds. The greatness of S. Augustine is nowhere more apparent than in his frank recognition of the spiritual grandeur of Plato. And that great spirit, so agile in dialectic subtlety, so sublime in its power of rising above the cramping limitations of our mortal life, is also, from its vivid poetic sympathy, most ready to aid weak ordinary souls to climb "the altar stairs." Never was pure detached intelligence wedded so harmoniously to glowing imagination, never was ethereal truth so clothed in the warm colouring and splendour of the world of sense. Where reason has strained its utmost strength to solve the eternal riddle, ecstatic vision and religious myth, transcending the limits of space and time, must be called in to lend their aid.

Plato and the Platonic Socrates are fully conscious that the conclusions of philosophic reason on a future state can be

[1] *De Ser. N. Vind.* v. c. 17, εἶς οὖν, ἔφην, λόγος ὁ τοῦ θεοῦ τὴν πρόνοιαν καὶ τὴν διαμονὴν τῆς ἀνθρωπίνης ψυχῆς βεβαιῶν, κτλ.

[2] *Ib.* c. 17 (560 F).

[3] *Ib.* c. 17, ad fin.

only tentative. And they often fall back on a divine doctrine, or tradition, or a mythopœic power by which poetic imagination peoples the dim regions of a world beyond the senses. The visions of Timarchus and Thespesius in Plutarch are, like the Nekuia of the *Phaedo* and of the *Republic*, an effort of the religious imagination to penetrate the darkness from which reason recoils. Nor is the effort strange in one who, along with the purest conception of an immaterial spirit, still believed in the efficacy of legend and material symbol to reveal the truth which they veiled.[1]

Thespesius of Soli, a man of evil life, once fell from a height, was taken up for dead, but revived again on the third day, on the eve of his funeral. He came back to the living an altered man, after a marvellous experience. His soul, on escaping from the body, was swept along a sea of light among the stars.[2] He saw other souls emerging in the form of fiery bubbles, which burst and gave forth a subtle form in the likeness of man.[3] Three or four he recognised, and would have spoken to them, but they seemed delirious or senseless, and shrank away from him, forming in the end little companies of their own, who swept along in wild disordered movements, uttering strange cries of wailing or terror. The soul of an old acquaintance then hailed him and became his guide, pointing out that the souls of the really dead cast no shadow, being perfectly pellucid, surrounded by light. Yet some of them are marked with scales and weals and blotches. Adrasteia is the inevitable judge of all, and, through three ministers, three great classes of criminals receive their proper doom. Some are punished swiftly on earth, another class meet with heavier judgment in the shades. The utterly incurable are ruthlessly pursued by the Erinnys, and finally plunged in a dark abyss, of which the horrors might not be told. The second class undergo a fierce purgatorial cleansing, in which some spirits have all their stains wiped out and become clear and lustrous. But where evil is more obstinate, and passion again and again asserts its power, the soul long retains a colour appropriate to its peculiar vice. The mean avaricious

[1] Rohde, *Psyche*, ii. pp. 275, 279; Jowett's *Plato*, i. p. 396; Pl. *Phaed.* 85 C, D; 60 B, C; 69 C; *Meno* 81 A; *Phaed.* 114 D, τὸ μὲν οὖν τοιαῦτα διισχυρίσασθαι οὕτως ἔχειν, οὐ πρέπει νοῦν ἔχοντι ἀνδρί, κτλ.

[2] Plut. *De Ser. Num. Vind.* c. 22 (563 C).

[3] *Ib.* εἶτα ῥηγνυμένης ἀτρέμα τῆς πομφόλυγος, ἐκβαίνειν τύπον ἐχούσας ἀνθρωποειδῆ, τὸν δ' ὄγκον εὐσταλεῖς κτλ.

soul is dark and squalid; the cruel is blood-red; the envious violet and livid. Short of the worst eternal torture, souls with insatiable craving for fleshly delights, gravitate to a birth into low animal forms.[1]

Thespesius and his guide are then swept on wings of light to other and less gloomy scenes. Over the chasm of Forgetfulness, clothed in its recesses with flowers and herbs which exhale a fragrant odour, the opening through which Dionysus had passed to his place among the gods, floated a cloud of spirits like birds, drinking in the fragrance with mirth and gladness. On again they passed, till they came to a crater which received the flow of many-coloured streams, snow-white or rainbow-hued,[2] and hard by was the oracle of Night and Selene, from which issue dreams and phantoms to wander among men. Then Thespesius was dazzled with the radiance which shot from the Delphic tripod upwards to the peaks of Parnassus; and, blinded by the radiance, he could only hear the shrill voice of a woman chanting a song which seemed to tell of the hour of his own death. The woman, his guide explained, was the Sibyl who dwells on the face of the moon. The sweep of the moon's onward course prevented him catching the Sibyl's words to the full, but he heard a prophecy of the desolation of Campania by the fires of Vesuvius, and the death of the emperor.

Other scenes of punishment follow, among which Thespesius saw his own father rising from the abyss, covered with weals and marks of torture which had been inflicted for a long-buried crime. Finally, the friendly guide vanished, and Thespesius was forced onwards by dread spectral forms to witness fresh scenes of torment. The hypocrite who had hidden his vices under a veil of decorum was forced, with infinite pain of contortion, to turn out his inmost soul. The avaricious were plunged by daemons by turns in three lakes, one of boiling gold, one of freezing lead, and one of hardest iron. But the worst fate of all was reserved for those whose sins had been visited on their innocent descendants upon earth, who pursued them with curses, or clung around them

[1] Plut. *De Ser. Num. Vind.* c. 22 (565).

[2] *Ib.* c. 22 (566), ἔδοξεν ἀφορᾶν κρατῆρα μέγαν, εἰς δὲ τοῦτον ἐμβάλλοντα ῥεύματα τὸ μὲν ἀφροῦ θαλάσσης ἢ χιόνων λαμπρότερον κτλ.

in clouds like bees or bats, keeping ever poignant the memory of transmitted guilt and suffering.[1]

The vision of Timarchus, in the piece on the Genius of Socrates, has a rather different motive from that which inspired the vision of Thespesius. Thespesius came back with a message as to the endless consequences of sin in worlds beyond the senses, and the far-reaching responsibilities of the life on earth. The experiences of Timarchus in the cave of Trophonius were intended to teach the doctrine of the existence, apart from the lower powers akin to fleshly nature, of the pure intelligence or daemon, which, coming from the Divine world, can catch its voices and transmit them to the mortal life here below. Timarchus made the descent into the cave of Trophonius and spent in its weird darkness two nights and a day, during which he saw a wondrous revelation of the spirit-world.[2] His higher part, escaping from the sutures of the head, emerged in pellucid ether. There was no trace of earthly scenery, but countless islands swept around him, gleaming with the shifting colours of lambent fire, amid tones coming from ethereal distances.[3] From a yawning abyss of surging darkness arose endless wailings and moans. An unseen guide explained to him the fourfold division of the universe and the boundaries of its provinces. High above all is the sphere of the One and the Invisible. Next in order is the region of pure mind, of which the Sun is lord. The third is the debatable land between pure intelligence and the sensible and mortal—the region of soul, whose mistress is the moon. Styx is the boundary between this lunar kingdom and the low world of matter, sin, and death. The three realms beneath the highest correspond to the three elements of our composite nature,—mind, soul, and body.[4] This mortal life is a temporary and unequal partnership of the Divine reason with the lower appetites, which have their roots in the flesh. It is an exile, an imprisonment; it is also a probation of the higher part of human nature, and its escape comes to it by a twofold death.

1 Plut. *De Ser. Num. Vind.* c. 22 (567 D), *πάντων δὲ πάσχειν ἔλεγεν οἰκτρότατα τὰς ἤδη δοκούσας ἀφεῖσθαι τῆς Δίκης, εἶτ' αὖθις συλλαμβανομένας· αὗται δ' ἦσαν ὧν εἴς τινας ἐκγόνους ἢ παῖδας ἡ ποινὴ περιῆλθεν κτλ.*

2 Cf. Pausan. ix. 39, § 5; Philostr. *Apoll. Tyan.* viii. 19; Plut. *De Gen. Socr.* c. 21, 22 (589, 590); cf. Gardner and Jevons, *Greek Antiq.* pp. 267–8.

3 Plut. *De Gen. Socr.* c. 22 (590), *ἀναβλέψας δὲ τὴν μὲν γῆν οὐδαμοῦ καθορᾶν, νήσους δὲ λαμπομένας μαλακῷ πυρί κτλ.*

4 *Ib.* (591).

The first, imperfect and incomplete, is the severance of soul from body in what men call death, the falling away of the gross wrappings of matter. This death is under the sway of Demeter. The second, under the care of Persephone, is a slower process, in which the ethereal reason, the true eternal personality of man, is finally released from association with the passionate and sensitive nature, which is akin to the bodily organism. After the first corporeal death, all souls wander for a time in the space between the moon and earth. In the vision of Timarchus, he saw over the chasm of darkness a host of stars with a curious variety of motion. Some shot up from the gulf with a straight decided impetus. Others wavered in deflexions to right or left, or, after an upward movement, plunged again into the abyss. These motions, as the invisible guide expounded, represent the various tendencies of souls, corresponding to the strength or weakness of the spiritual force within them. All souls have an element of the Divine reason, but it is variously blended with the baser elements in different natures. In some it becomes completely sunk and absorbed in the life of the senses. In others, the rational part holds itself above the lower bodily life, and maintains an almost separate existence. And yet there are natures in which the rational and irrational elements wage a long and indecisive conflict until, slowly, at last, the passions recognise their rightful master, and become obedient to the heavenly voice within. The debased and hopeless souls, rising for a moment after death, are repelled with fierce angry flashes by the moon, and fall back again to the world of sense and corruption, to undergo a second birth. The purer souls are received by her for a loftier destiny. In some, the pure spiritual part is finally released by the love of the Sun from the lower powers of the soul, which wither and fade away as the body does on earth. Others, still retaining the composite nature, though no longer tainted by the flesh, dwell in the moon as daemons, but often revisit the earth on various missions, to furnish inspiration to oracles and mysteries, to save men from crime or to punish, to help the struggling by land or sea. But even the daemons may fall from their high estate. If, in their duties of providence and succour, they show anger or favour or envy, they may be thrust down once more into the purgatory of material form.[1]

It may well be that the unsympathetic critic will regard such an imaginative invasion of the unseen as a freak of lawless fancy, hardly worth chronicling. And like all similar attempts, the apocalypse of Plutarch may easily be treated with an airy ridicule. To a more serious criticism, it seems vitiated by a radical inconsistency. Starting with the principle of the absolutely immaterial nature of the immortal part of man, it yet depicts its future existence in the warmest colours of the world of sense. Its struggles, its tortures, its beatitude, are described in terms which might seem fitting only to a corporeal nature. All this is true; and yet the answer which Plutarch would probably have made to any such cavils is very simple. How can you speak of pure disembodied spirit at all, how can you imagine it, save in the symbolism of ordinary speech? Refine and subtilise your language to the very uttermost, and it will still retain associations and reminiscences, however faint and distant, of the material world. Myth and symbol are necessary to any expression of human thought alike about God and the future of the soul. The Infinite Spirit and the future destiny of the finite, which is His child, are equally beyond the range of human sense and speech. When the human spirit has exhausted all its efforts of imagination to pierce the darkness of the world beyond the grave, it takes refuge in some religious system which claims to have a divine message and speaks in the tones of another world. The voice from eternity came to troubled heathendom from Egypt and the East.

[1] Plut. *De Fac. in Orb. Lun.* c. 30.

CHAPTER III

THE OLD ROMAN RELIGION

It is well known that, from the second Punic War to the revival of Augustus, old Roman religion was falling into decay. Yet sweeping assertions about the religious condition of any age must be taken with some reserve. They are often unsafe about a contemporary society; they must be still more so with regard to a society which is known to us almost entirely through the literary remains of a comparatively small cultivated class. Even among that limited circle, we can know only the opinions of a few, and hardly anything of its silent members, still less of the feelings of its women and dependents. A deep shadow rests on those remote granges and quiet country towns in Samnium or Lombardy where character remained untainted in the days of Nero or Domitian, and where the religion of Numa long defied the penal edicts of Theodosius and Honorius. Lucretius, whose mission it was to liberate men from the terrors of old Latin and Etrurian superstition, was not contending against an imaginary foe. The sombre enthusiasm which he throws into the conflict reveals the strength of the enemy. The grandmother of Atticus and Terentia, the wife of Cicero, were timorous devotees. Among the aristocratic augurs of Cicero's day there were firm believers in the sacred birds; and Lentulus, a confederate of Catiline, trusted implicitly in the oracles of the Sibyl.[1]

Still there can be no doubt that in the governing and thinking class of the last century of the Republic, scepticism and even open contempt for the old religion were rampant. Many causes were at work to produce this decadence of old Roman

[1] Boissier, *Rel. Rom.* i. p. 67.

faith. It was hardly possible for the cultivated Roman of the days of Scipio Aemilianus, or of Cicero and Caesar, who had fought and travelled in many lands, and studied their mythologies and philosophies, to acquiesce in the faith of the simple farmers of Latium, who founded the Ambarvalia and Lupercalia, who offered the entrails of a dog to Robigus[1] and milk to Pales and Silvanus, who worshipped Jupiter Feretrius under the mountain oak.[2] Since those far-off days, Latium had come under many influences, and added many new deities to her pantheon. The gods of Hellas had come to be identified with the gods of Rome, or to share their honours. Syncretism had been at work in Italy centuries before the days of Plutarch and Aristides. And the old Italian deities, who had only a shadowy personality, with no poetry of legend to invest them with human interest, melted into one another or into forms of alien mythology. Greek literature became familiar to the educated from the Hannibalic war, and a writer like Euripides, who had a great popularity, must have influenced many by the audacious skill with which he lowered the dignity and dimmed the radiance of the great figures of Greek legend. The comic stage improved upon the lesson. Early in the second century Ennius translated the Sacred Histories of Euhemerus, and familiarised his countrymen with a theory which reduced Jupiter and Saturn, Faunus and Hercules, to the stature of earthly kings and warriors. But Greek philosophy was the great solvent of faith. The systems of the New Academy and Epicurus were openly or insidiously hostile to religious belief. But they had not so long and powerful a reign over the Roman mind as Stoicism, and, although the earlier Stoicism extended a philosophic patronage to popular religion, it may be doubted whether it stimulated faith. There was indeed a certain affinity between Stoical doctrine and old Roman religion, as there was between Stoic morals and old Roman character. In resolving the gods by allegory and pseudo-scientific theory into various potencies of the great World-Soul, the follower of Zeno did not seem to do much violence to the vaguely personified abstractions of the old Latin creed. Above all, with the exception of Panaetius, the Stoic doctors did not throw doubt on the powers of divination and augury, so essential an element

[1] W. Fowler, *Rom. Festivals*, p. 89. [2] *Ib.* p. 229.

in the religion of Rome. The power to read the future was a natural corollary to the providence and benevolence of the gods.[1] Yet, although the Stoic might strive to discover the germ of truth, he did not conceal his contempt for the husk of mythology in which it was hidden, and for many of the practices of worship.[2]

Quintus Scaevola and Varro applied all the forces of subtle antiquarianism and reverence to sustain the ancestral faith. But they also drew the line sharply between the religion of philosophy and the religion of the State. And Varro went so far as to say that the popular religion was the creation of early statesmen,[3] and that if the work had to be done again, it might be done better in the light of philosophy. The Stoic in Cicero, as Seneca did after him, treated the tales of the gods as mere anile superstition.[4] It is probable that such was the tone, in their retired debates, of the remarkable circle which surrounded Scipio and Laelius. Panaetius, their philosophic guide, had less sympathy than any great Stoic with popular theology.[5] Polybius gave small place to Providence in human affairs, and regarded Roman religion as the device of statesmen to control the masses by mystery and terror.[6] Yet these men were enthusiastic champions of a system which they regarded as irrational, but which was consecrated by immemorial antiquity. Laelius defended the institutions of Numa in a speech of golden eloquence which moved the admiration of Cicero, just as Symmachus defended them five centuries later before the council of Valentinian.[7] The divorce between esoteric belief and official profession must have insidiously lowered the moral tone of those who were at once thinkers and statesmen. Such a false position struck some of the speakers in Cicero's theological dialogues, and it makes his own opinions an enigma.[8] The external and utilitarian attitude to

[1] Cic. *De Div.* i. 5, 9, existimo . . . si Dii sint, esse qui divinent; i. 38, 82. si sunt Dii, neque ante declarant hominibus quae futura sint, aut non diligunt homines, aut quid eventurum sit ignorant. This argument is attributed to Chrysippus and Diogenes in ii. 49, 101.

[2] Sen. *Frag.* 39 (Aug. *De Civ. D.* vi. 11). See Varro's opinion, *ib.* vi. 5.

[3] *De Civ. Dei*, vi. 4.

[4] Cic. *De Nat. D.* ii. 28, 70; cf. Sen. *Frag.* 39; cf. *Ep.* 95, 47.

[5] Cic. *De Div.* i. 3, 6.

[6] Polyb. vi. 56, καί μοι δοκεῖ τὸ παρὰ τοῖς ἄλλοις ἀνθρώποις ὀνειδιζόμενον τοῦτο συνέχειν τὰ Ῥωμαίων πράγματα, λέγω δὲ τὴν δεισιδαιμονίαν. ἐπὶ τοσοῦτον γὰρ ἐκτετραγῴδηται . . . ὥστε μὴ καταλιπεῖν ὑπερβολήν, κτλ.

[7] Cic. *De Nat. Deor.* iii. 17, 43, in illa aureola oratiuncula; cf. Sym. *Rel.* iii.

[8] Boissier, *Rel. Rom.* i. p. 60.

the State religion hardly secured even punctual or reverent conformity in the last age of the Republic. Divination and augury had become mere engines of political intrigue, and the aristocratic magistrate could hardly take the omens without a smile. Varro could not repress the fear that the old religion, on which he expended such a wealth of learning, might perish from mere negligence.[1] The knowledge of liturgical usage began to fade, and Varro had to recall the very names of forgotten gods. An ancient priesthood of the highest rank remained unfilled for seventy years.[2] Scores of the most venerable temples were allowed to fall into ruin,[3] and ancient brotherhoods like the Titii and Fratres Arvales are hardly heard of for generations before the reforms of the Augustan age.

It is not within the scope of this work to enter minutely into the subject of that great effort of reform or reaction. It is commonly said that the cool imperial statesman had chiefly political ends in view, and especially the aggrandisement and security of the principate. And certainly Ovid, who strove to interest his countrymen in the revival of their religion, does not display much seriousness in religion or morals. He treats as lightly the amours of Olympus as the intrigues of the Campus Martius and the Circus. Yet it may well have been that after the terrible orgies of civil strife through which the Roman world had passed, Augustus was the convinced representative of a repentant wish to return to the old paths. The Roman character, through all wild aberrations of a trying destiny, was an enduring type. And Augustus, if he may have indulged in impious revels in his youth, which recall the wanton freaks of Alcibiades,[4] had two great characteristics of the old Roman mind, formalism and superstition. He had an infinite faith in dreams and omens. He would begin no serious business on the Nones.[5] When he had to pronounce a funeral oration over his sister, Octavia, he had a curtain drawn before the corpse, lest the eyes of the pontiff might be polluted by the sight of death.[6] We may think that his

[1] Aug. *De Civ. D.* vi. 2 ; cf. Cic. *De Leg.* ii. 13, 33, dubium non est quin haec disciplina et ars augurum evanuerit jam et vetustate et negligentia.

[2] D. Cass. liv. 36 ; cf. W. Fowler's *Rom. Fest.* p. 343, Preller, *Rom. Mythol.* p. 24.

[3] Suet. *Octav.* c. 30.

[4] *Ib.* c. 70, coena δωδεκάθεος: cf. Thuc. vi. c. 28, § 1.

[5] Suet. *Octav.* c. 91, 92.

[6] D. Cass. liv. 35 *ad fin.*

religious revival was not inspired by real religious sentiment. Yet it is well to remind ourselves that old Roman religion, while it consecrated and solemnised the scenes and acts of human life, was essentially a formal religion; the *opus operatum* was the important thing. Its business was to avert the anger or win the favour of dim unearthly powers; it was not primarily to purify or elevate the soul. Above all, it was interwoven from the beginning with the whole fabric of society and the State. Four centuries after Augustus was in his grave, it was only by a violent wrench, which inflicted infinite torture even on pagan mystics of the Neoplatonist school, that Rome was severed from the gods who had been the guardians and partners of her career for twelve hundred years. The altar of Victory which Augustus had placed in the Senate-house, and before which twelve generations of senators after him offered their prayers for the chief of the State, the most sacred symbol of the pagan Empire, was only removed after a fierce, obstinate struggle.

The religious revival of Augustus may not have aroused any deep religious sentiment; that, as we shall see, was to come from a different source. But it gave a fresh life to the formal religion of the State, which maintained itself till within a few years before the invasion of Alaric. The title Augustus which the new emperor assumed was one which, to the Roman mind, associated him with the majesty of Jupiter and the sanctity of all holy places and solemn rites.[1] It was the beginning of that theocratic theory of monarchy which was to culminate, under the influence of Sun-worship, in the third century, and to propagate itself into ages far removed from the worship of Jupiter or the Sun. Although the counsels of Maecenas, recorded by Dion Cassius, may be apocryphal, Augustus acted in their spirit.[2] As triumvir he had raised a shrine to Isis,[3] as emperor he frowned on alien worships.[4] His mission was to restore the ancient religion of Latium. He burnt two thousand books of spurious augury, retaining only the Sibylline oracles.[5] He restored the ancient

[1] Ov. *Fasti*, i. 609, hic socium summo cum Jove nomen habet. Sancta vocant augusta patres; augusta vocantur Templa, sacerdotum rite dicata manu.

[2] D. Cass. lii. 36, τὸ μὲν θεῖον πάντῃ πάντως αὐτός τε σέβου καὶ τοὺς ἄλλους τιμᾶν ἀνάγκαζε.

[3] *Ib.* xlvii. 15 *ad fin.*

[4] *Ib.* liv. 6.

[5] Suet. *Octav.* c. 31.

temples, some of them, like those of Jupiter Feretrius and Juno Sospita, coeval with the Roman State, and encouraged his friends to do the same for other venerable monuments of devotion. The most lavish gifts of gold and jewels were dedicated in the Capitoline temples. The precision of ancient augury was restored. Ancient priesthoods which had been long vacant were filled up, and the sacred colleges were raised in dignity and wealth.[1] Special care was taken to recall the vestals to the chaste dignity from which they had fallen for a hundred years. Before taking his seat, each senator was required to make a prayer, with an offering of incense and wine before the altar. Three worships, specially connected with the fortunes of Augustus or his race,—those of Venus Genetrix, Mars Ultor, and the Palatine Apollo,—were revived with added splendour.[2] The emperor paid special attention to the ancient sacred colleges, such as the Salii and Arvales, which went back to days far earlier than the Republic. Amid all the cares of State, he attended their meetings punctually. The dangerous right of co-optation was quietly withdrawn, till the members in the end owed their appointment to the sacerdotal chief of the State.[3] The colleges became the most courtly and deferential supports of the prince's power. Prayers for his safety soon found a place in their antique litanies. It has been said with some truth that the Salii and Arvales seem to be thinking more of the emperors than of the gods. The colleges had a courtly memory for all anniversaries in the imperial family. The Arval brothers achieved the infamy of complimenting Nero on his return after the murder of Agrippina,[4] and made vows of equal fervour for all the emperors of the year 69.[5]

But it was through the chief pontificate that the emperors did most at once to fortify and dignify their secular power, and to prolong the reign of the old Latin religion. It was the highest religious dignity of ancient Rome. The college of which the emperor, as Pontifex Maximus, was head exercised a supreme and comprehensive control over the whole field of religion.[6] It was charged with the duty of maintaining

[1] D. Cass. li. 20.

[2] Boissier, *Rel. Rom.* i. 87.

[3] Momms. *Röm. Staatsr.* ii. p. 1024.

[4] *C.I.L.* vi. 2042; cf. 2444 and 2034; Boissier, *Rel. Rom.* i. p. 363.

[5] *C.I.L.* vi. 2051, 2.

[6] Momms. *Röm. Staatsr.* ii. p. 1022.

the ancestral purity and exactness of the national worship, and of repressing tendencies to innovation and the adoption of alien rites. It selected the virgins who guarded the eternal fire, and sat in judgment on erring vestals and their betrayers. It had special jurisdiction in questions of adoption, burial, and sacred sites.[1] From Augustus every emperor was also chief pontiff;[2] even the Christian princes from Constantine to Valentinian and Valens bear the honoured title in the inscriptions, and accepted the pontifical robes.[3] Thus the emperors strove in their religious attributes to connect themselves with the sacred tradition of Numa and the Roman kings. And, as time went on, the imperial house claimed a growing share in the pontifical honours. Nero, indeed, had been a member of all the sacred colleges as well as chief pontiff.[4] But down to the reign of Vespasian only one of the "Caesares" could belong to the sacred college. But his sons Titus and Domitian were co-opted to the pontificate and all the priestly colleges before his death.[5] From Hadrian the pontificate and all the highest sacerdotal honours were held by all designated successors of the emperor.[6] Antoninus Pius has the insignia of four priestly colleges on his coins.[7] M. Aurelius was one of the Salian brotherhood in his eighth year,[8] and was received into all the colleges at nineteen.[9] Commodus had reached the same sacred honours before he assumed the toga,[10] and in five years more was Pontifex Maximus. Thus deeply had the policy of Augustus sunk into the minds of his successors. It is little wonder that never in the great days of the Republic were the forms of ancient religion more scrupulously observed than in the reign of M. Aurelius.[11]

Private opinion after the Augustan revival greatly varied as to matters of faith. Men like the elder Pliny and Seneca scoffed at anthropomorphic religion. Men like Juvenal and Tacitus maintained a wavering attitude, with probably a receding faith. Others like Suetonius were rapacious collectors of every scrap of the miraculous. The emperors who succeeded

[1] Liv. i. 20.

[2] Habel, *De Pontif. Rom.* p. 45.

[3] *Or.* 1080, 1117; cf. Zosim. iv. 36; Amm. Marc. xvi. 10; Sym. *Ep.* x. 54.

[4] Habel, *De Pontif. Rom.* p. 13.

[5] *Ib.* pp. 16, 17, 62; *C.I.L.* vi. 932, 1984.

[6] Habel, p. 62.

[7] *Ib.* p. 24.

[8] Jul. Capitol. *M. Ant. Phil.* c. 4.

[9] *Ib.* c. 6.

[10] *Ib.* c. 16; Lamprid. *Com.* c. 12 (a. 175).

[11] Jul. Capitol. *M. Ant.* c. 13.

Augustus were, with the exception of Nero, loyal supporters and protectors of the religion of the State. Tiberius, although personally careless of religion, displayed a scrupulous respect for ancient usage in filling up the ancient priesthoods, and in guarding the Sibylline verses from interpolations.[1] He also frowned on the imported rites of Egypt.[2] Claudius, at once pedantic and superstitious, revived venerable rites of the days of Tullus Hostilius, and, when an ill-omened bird alighted on the temple of Jupiter, as supreme pontiff, the emperor pronounced the solemn form of expiation before the assembled people.[3] Nero, and the Neronian competitors for the Empire, in the fierce conflict which followed his death, were, indeed, often, though not always, careless of ancient rite, but they were all the slaves of superstition.[4] The Flavians and Antonines were religious conservatives of the spirit of Augustus. There is a monument to Vespasian of the year 78 A.D. as "the restorer of temples and public ceremonies."[5] The restoration of the Capitol, which had been burned down in the civil war, was one of the first tasks of his reign. And the ceremony made such an impression on the imagination of the youthful Tacitus, that he has recorded with studied care the stately and accurate ritual of olden time which was observed by the emperor.[6] Domitian carried on the restoration on even a more splendid scale; he was a devotee of Minerva, and a rigorous vindicator of old ascetic religious law.[7] The emperor Hadrian, whose character is an enigma of contrasts, to judge by his last famous *jeu d'esprit* on his death-bed, probably died a sceptic. Yet his biographer tells us that he was a careful guardian of the ancient ritual.[8] The archaistic fashion in literary taste, which had begun in the first century, and which culminated in Hadrian's reign, favoured and harmonised with a scrupulous observance of ancient forms in religion.[9] The genius of one too early taken away has done more than a legion of historic critics to picture for us the sad, dutiful piety of a spirit of the Antonine age, steeped in philosophies which

[1] Tac. *Ann.* iv. 16. Yet he is said to be *circa deos negligentior*, c. 69.

[2] *Ib.* c. 36.

[3] Suet. *Claud.* c. 22; Tac. *Ann.* xii. 8.

[4] Suet. *Otho*, c. 7, 8, 12; *Vitell.* c. 5, 11; Tac. *Hist.* i. 87.

[5] *Or.* 2364.

[6] Tac. *Hist.* iv. 53.

[7] Suet. *Dom.* c. 5, 15.

[8] Ael. Spart. *Hadr.* c. 22.

[9] *Ib.* 16, § 5; Plin. *Ep.* vi. 21, § 1; Macé, *Suétone*, p. 96; Martha, *Moralistes*, p. 184 sq.

made the passing moment of vivid artistic perception the great end of life, yet still instinct with the old Roman love of immemorial forms at the harvest gathering or the yearly offering to the dead members of the household.[1] The cheerless negation of Epicurus, and the equally withering theology of the Stoics, could not weaken in Roman hearts the spell of ancestral pieties which clustered round the vault near the grey old country house of the race, looking down on the Tyrrhene sea, or the awe of ancient grove or spring sacred to Silvanus and the Nymphs, or the calm, chastened joy in a ritual in which every act was dictated by a love of ceremonial cleanness and exactness, and redolent of an immemorial past. In such a household, and in such an atmosphere, the two great Antonines were reared. The first, who was before all else an honest country gentleman, fond of hunting, fishing, and the gladness of the vintage at Lorium, never failed to perform all due sacrifices unless he was ill. His coins bear the pictured legends of the infancy of Rome.[2] M. Aurelius was famous as a boy for his knowledge of Roman ritual. Enrolled in the college of the Salii in his eighth year, he performed all its sacred offices with perfect composure, reciting from memory, with no one to dictate the form, every word of the ancient liturgy which had in his generation become almost unintelligible.[3] In the terror of the Marcomannic invasion he delayed his departure for the seat of war to summon around him all the priests; he had the city purified in solemn, decorous fashion, not excluding even the rites of alien lands; and for seven days the images of the gods were feasted on their couches along all the streets.[4]

The emperors from Augustus found religion a potent ally of sovereignty, and the example of the master of the world was a great force. Yet it may well be doubted whether, in the matter of religious conservatism, the emperors were not rather following than leading public opinion. Gods were in those times being created by the score; apotheosis was in the air from the days of Nero to the days of the Severi. Petronius, with an exaggeration which has a certain foundation in fact, affirms that in Croton you could more readily light upon a god than on a man.[5] The

[1] Pater, *Marius*, chap. ii., xxvii.
[2] Jul. Capitol. *Ant. P.* c. 11.
[3] *Ib.* c. 4.
[4] *Ib.* c. 13.
[5] Petron. c. 17.

elder Pliny uses almost the same strength of language. The grumbler in Lucian indignantly complains of the fashion in which the ancient gods of Olympus are being overshadowed by the divine *parvenus* of every clime. And, as we shall presently see, the inscriptions reveal an immense propaganda of worships in tone and spirit apparently hostile to the old religion of the Latin race. Yet the inscriptions also show that the old gods had really little to fear from the new. A survey of the index to almost any volume of the Corpus will convince the student that the Trinity of the Capitol,—Jupiter, Juno, and Minerva,—that Hercules and Silvanus, the Nymphs, Semo Sancus and Dea Dia, Mars and Fortuna, so far from being neglected, were apparently more popular than ever.[1] In an age of growing monotheism the King of the gods was, of course, still supreme in his old ascendency. Jupiter is worshipped under many titles; he is often coupled or identified with some provincial deity of ancient fame.[2] But Jupiter is everywhere. The Lord of the thunder and the tempest has shrines on the high passes of the Apennines or the Alps,[3] and soldiers or travellers leave the memorials of their gratitude for his protection on perilous journeys.[4] The women of Campanian towns go in procession to implore him to send rain.[5] Antoninus Pius built a temple to Juno Sospita of Lanuvium, where the goddess had a sacred grove, and a worship of great antiquity.[6] The Quinquatria of Minerva were not only celebrated with special honour by Domitian, but by large and powerful classes who owned her divine patronage, physicians and artists, orators and poets.[7] Some of the old Latin deities seem to have even grown in popularity under the early Empire. Hercules, the god of plenty, strong truth, and good faith, whose legend is intertwined with the most venerable names in Roman story, has his altars and monuments everywhere.[8] Combining with his own native Latin character the poetic prestige of his brother of Greek legend, he became the symbol of world-

[1] *C.I.L.* iii. p. 1160 sqq.; xii. p. 924 sqq.; *Or. Henz.* iii.; *Ind.* pp. 25, 29, 30, 33.

[2] *C.I.L.* xii. 3070, 3077; 2383; iii. 2804, 5787; *Or. Henz.* 1244, 1245.

[3] Liv. xxi. 38, quem in summo sacratum vertice Poeninum montani appellant; *Or. Henz.* 231-6, 5028, 1271.

[4] *Or. Henz.* 1267, 1271.

[5] Petron. *Sat.* 44.

[6] Jul. Capitol. *Vit. Ant. P.* c. 8; Preller, *Rom. Myth.* p. 185.

[7] Suet. *Dom.* c. 4.

[8] *Or. Henz.* 1561, 1590; *C.I.L.* xii. 4316; iii. 1162.

wide conquest, and was associated in the end with the triumph of the "unconquered" Mithra. His image is stamped upon the coins of some of the emperors. Septimius Severus, Caracalla, and Diocletian took him for their great divine patron and ensample.[1] Silvanus, too, the god of the primeval forest, and, when the forest had receded, the god of the shepherd and the farmer, the guardian of boundaries, acquired a strange vogue in what was eminently an age of cities. One is apt, however, to forget sometimes that it was an age which had also a charming country life. A Roman cavalry officer in Britain has left a memorial of his gratitude to Silvanus for the capture of a wild boar of surpassing size and strength,[2] which had long defied the hunter. In one of the forest cantons of the Alps a procurator of the imperial estates inscribed his gratitude in a pretty set of verses to the god of the wilds, whose image was enshrined in the fork of a sacred ash.[3] It is the record of many a day passed in lonely forest tracks, coupled with a prayer to be restored safely to Italian fields and the gardens of Rome. The nymphs and river gods had all their old honours. Chapels and hostelries, in the days of Pliny, rose on the banks of the Clitumnus, where the votaries easily combined pleasure with religious duty. The nymphs receive votive thanks for the discovery of hidden springs, or for the reappearance of some fountain long dried up.[4] Aesculapius, who had been naturalised in Italy since the beginning of the third century B.C., sprang to a foremost place in the age of the Antonines. Whether it was "an age of valetudinarians," as has been said, may be doubtful; but it was an age eagerly in quest of the health which so often comes from the quiet mind. Whatever we may think of the powers of the old Olympians, there can be no doubt about the beneficent influence of the god of Epidaurus. He was summoned to Rome 300 years before Christ, and obtained a home in the island in the Tiber, where for ages he gave his succour in dreams. His worship spread far and wide, and was one of the last to succumb to the advance of the Church.[5]

The unassailable permanence of the old religion may perhaps

[1] Preller, p. 437.
[2] *Or. Henz.* 1603.
[3] *Ib.* 1613.
[4] *Ib.* 1632, 1634, 1637, 5758a.
[5] Preller, pp. 406–8; *Or.* 1580, 1581, 1572.

be still more vividly realised in the long unbroken life of sacred colleges, such as the Salii and the Fratres Arvales. The Arval brotherhood was probably the oldest sacred corporation of Latium, as its liturgy, preserved in the Acta from the reign of Augustus to that of Gordian, is the oldest specimen of the Latin language.[1] According to the legend, the first members were the twelve sons of Acca Larentia, the foster-mother of Romulus, and Romulus himself first held the dignity of master of the brotherhood.[2] Its patron goddess, Dea Dia,[3] was, as her very name suggests, one of those dim shadowy conceptions dear to old Roman awe, who was worshipped in the still solitude of ancient groves, on whose trunks no axe of iron might ever ring,[4] a power as elusive and multiform to picturing fancy as the secret forces which shot up the corn ear from the furrow. The whole tone of the antique ritual savours of a time when the Latin race was a tribe of farmers, believing with a simple faith that the yearly increase of their fields depended on the favour of secret unearthly powers. The meetings of the college took place on three days in May, the precise dates being fixed and solemnly announced by their master on the 3rd of January.[5] The festival began and ended in the master's house at Rome, the intermediate day being spent in a sacred grove on the right bank of the Tiber, about four miles from the city. There was much feasting, at which the brethren were attended by the Camilli, four sons of high-born senators. Corn of the new and the preceding year was touched and blessed; libations and incense were offered to the goddess, and all the rites were performed with many changes of costume, which were rigidly observed.[6] In the ceremonies which took place in the grove, an expiatory sacrifice of two porkers and a white cow was always offered, to atone for the use of any iron implement, or other infringement of the ancient rubric.[7] Fat lambs were offered in sacrifice to Dea Dia, and ancient earthen vessels of rude make, resembling those of the age of Numa, were adored upon the altar.[8] Ears of corn, plucked in some neighbouring field, were

[1] *Or. Henz.* 2270; cf. Wordsworth, *Specimens of Early Latin*, p. 158; *C.I.L.* vi. 2024 sqq.

[2] Preller, p. 293.

[3] Fowler, *Rom. Festivals*, p. 74, 275.

[4] *C.I.L.* vi. 2059, ob inlatum ferrum, etc.

[5] *Ib.* vi. 2040, 2041, 2043; Preller, p. 294; Oldenberg, *De Sacris Fr. Arv.* p. 5.

[6] Oldenberg, p. 9.

[7] *C.I.L.* vi. 2086.

[8] Boissier, i. p. 369; Oldenberg, p. 41.

blessed and passed from the hand of one member to another, and back again in reverse order, and, at last, in the closed temple, along with solemn dancing, the famous chant was intoned from ancient scrolls, the words of which had long become strange even to the antiquary. After another meal in the hall of the brotherhood, the members passed on to the circus and gave the signal for the races to begin.[1]

This ritual, so little heard of before the time of Augustus, is chiefly known to us from the Acta which have been recovered from the site of the ancient grove. The monuments of it extend from the reign of Augustus to the year 241 A.D.[2] Members of the highest aristocracy and princes of the imperial house appear on its lists. Its membership was a high distinction, and was sometimes conferred by the potent recommendation of the emperor.[3] The college evidently became a great support of the imperial power.

The emperors were elected *magistri* of the College, and we can read that Caligula, Nero, Vespasian, and Titus were present at its meetings. In the opening days of January the most solemn vows are made in old Roman fashion for the emperor's safety, to Jupiter, Juno, and Minerva, to Salus and Dea Dia, and they are duly paid by offerings of oxen with gilded horns.[4] So servile or so devoted to the throne was the brotherhood, that their prayers were offered with equal fervour for three emperors in the awful year 69 A.D.[5] The vows made for Galba in the first week of January were alertly transferred to the cause of Otho the day after Galba's murder.[6] The college met to sacrifice in honour of Otho's pontificate on the day (March 14) on which he set out to meet his doom in the battle on the Po. Thirteen days after his death, while the spring air was still tainted with the rotting heaps on the plain of Bedriacum, vows as fervent or as politic were registered for Vitellius. In the summer of the following year, the arrival of Vespasian in the capital was celebrated by the Arval brothers with sacrifices to Jupiter, Juno, Minerva and Fortuna Redux.[7]

The college, as a matter of course, paid due honour to the emperor's birthday and all important anniversaries in his

[1] Boissier, i. p. 374; Preller, p. 295.

[2] *C.I.L.* vi. 2023–2113.

[3] *Ib.* 2056, ex tabella missa Imp. Vesp. cooptamus, etc.

[4] *Ib.* 2024.

[5] *Ib.* 2051.

[6] Jan. 16, 69 A.D.

[7] *C.I.L.* vi. 2052.

family. It is interesting to see how for years the Neronian circle, the Othos and Vitellii, along with Valerii and Cornelii, appear in all the records of the college.[1] It was apparently devoted to Nero. The brothers celebrate his birthday and all the civic and sacerdotal honours heaped upon him.[2] They make vows for his wife Octavia, and soon after, for the safety of Poppaea in childbirth. The matricide dreaded to return from Campania after his unnatural crime, but his admirers knew well the abasement of the Roman aristocracy, and promised him an enthusiastic reception. The Arval brotherhood, which then included a Regulus and a Memmius, redeemed the promise, and voted costly sacrifices for his safe restoration to the capital.[3] They execrate the secret plots against his sacred person, and offer thanksgiving for the detection of the Pisonian conspiracy.[4]

The extant prayers and congratulations for the safety of Vespasian are much more quiet and restrained than those for his cruel son Domitian.[5] The public joy at Domitian's safe return from ambiguous victories in Germany or Dacia is faithfully re-echoed, and effusive supplications are recorded for his safety from all peril and for the eternity of the Empire whose bounds he has enlarged. There is a sincerer tone in the prayers, in the spring of 101, for the safe return of Trajan, when he was setting out for his first campaign on the Danube, and on his home-coming four years later.[6] The Arval records of Hadrian's reign are chiefly noteworthy for his letters to the college, recommending his friends for election.[7] In the reign of Antoninus Pius the Acta register those perfervid acclamations which meet us in the later Augustan histories:[8]—"O nos felices qui te Imperatorem videmus; Di te servent in perpetuo; juvenis triumphis, senex Imperator!" The young M. Aurelius is first mentioned in 155 A.D. Probably the sincerest utterance in the Arval liturgies is the petition for his safety, and that of L. Verus, from peril in the years when the Quadi and Marcomanni swept down through Rhaetia and the Julian Alps to the shores of the Adriatic.[9]

[1] *C.I.L.* vi. 2040, 2041.
[2] *Ib.* 2039.
[3] *Ib.* 2042.
[4] *Ib.* 2044; cf. 2029 (Caligula).
[5] *Ib.* 2064, 2067.
[6] *Ib.* 2074.
[7] *Ib.* 2078.
[8] *Ib.* 2086; cf. Flav. Vop. *Probus*, c. 12.
[9] *C.I.L.* vi. 2092.

It was thus that the antique ritual of a rustic brotherhood was converted into a potent support of the imperial power. No part of the Augustan revival was perhaps so successful. Probably few of the emperors, or of the aristocratic brothers who intoned the litany for the safety of the imperial house, had much faith in its efficacy. But the ceremony linked the principate with the most venerable traditions of Latium, and with Romulus the first master of the college. When we read the minute and formal record of these coarse sacrifices and rude, fantastic rites, with the chanting of prayers no longer understood, we are amazed at the prolongation for so many ages of religious ideas which the Roman mind might appear to have outgrown. Yet in such inquiries there is often a danger of treating society as a uniform mass, moving together along the same lines, and permeated through all its strata by the same influences. In another chapter we have shown that the masses were probably never so superstitious as in the second century. And the singular thing is that the influx of foreign religions, due to the wide conquests of Rome, never to the end seems to have shaken the supreme attachment of the people to their ancient gods. It is true that the drift towards monotheism was felt even among the crowd. But while the educated might find expression for that tendency in the adoration of Isis or the Sun, the dim monotheism of the people turned to the glorification of Jupiter. Dedications to him are the most numerous in all lands. He is often linked with other gods or all the gods,[1] but he is always supreme. And, while he is the lord of tempest and thunder,[2] he is also addressed by epithets which show that he is becoming a moral and spiritual power. On many a stone he appears as the governor and preserver of all things, monitor, guardian, and heavenly patron, highest and best of the heavenly hierarchy.[3] Yet it is equally clear that other gods are worshipped in the same spirit as of old. Roman religion was essentially practical. Prayer and vow were the means to win temporal blessings. The gods were expected, in return for worship, to be of use to the devotee. It is evident from the inscriptions that this conception of religion was as

[1] *C.I.L.* iii. 5788; *Or.* 1245, 1290.

[2] *Or.* 1238, Fulguratori, 1240, 1271, Jovi O. M. tempestatum potenti.

[3] *C.I.L.* iii. 1032, 1948, 1590; *Or.* 1269, 1248, 1225, 1269; *C.I.L.* xii. 1066.

prevalent in the age of the Antonines, or of the oriental princes, as it was under the Republic. The sailor still offers thanks for his preservation to Neptune and the gods of the sea.[1] The successful merchant still honours Mercury.[2] Minerva Memor receives thanks for succour in sickness. A lady of Placentia even pays her vows for the recovery of her hair.[3] The reappearance of a hidden spring is still attributed to the grace of the Nymphs.[4] And in many a temple the healing power of Aesculapius is acknowledged by grateful devotees.[5]

A more difficult problem is presented by the attitude of the cultivated class to the old mythologies. Since the days of Xenophanes and of Plato philosophy had revolted against the degradation of the Divine character by ancient legend. It had taught for ages the unity of the mysterious Power or Goodness which lies behind the shifting scene of sense. Moreover, philosophy for generations had deserted the heights of speculative inquiry, and addressed itself to the task of applying the spiritual truth which the schools had won to the problems of practical religion and human life. Alike in Cicero, in Seneca, in Plutarch, and M. Aurelius, there are conceptions of God and the worship due to Him, of prayer, of the relation of conduct to religion, which seem irreconcilable with conformity to the old religion of Rome. How could a man, nourished on such spiritual ideas and refined by a thousand years of growing culture, take part in a gross materialistic worship, and even gallantly defend it against all assailants?

The conformity of highly instructed minds to ancient systems which their reason has outgrown is not always to be explained by the easy imputation of dishonesty. And that explanation is even less admissible in ancient than in modern times. Roman religion did not demand any profession of faith in any theory of the unseen; all it required was ceremonial purity and exactness. And the Roman world was never scandalised by the spectacle of a notorious sceptic or libertine holding the office of chief pontiff. If a man were more scrupulous himself, philosophy, whether of the Porch or the Academy, came to his aid. It would tell him that frail

1 *Or.* 1335.
2 *Ib.* 1410.
3 *Ib.* 1428, 1429, restitutione facta sibi capillorum.
4 *Ib.* 1634.
5 *Ib.* 1572, 1576.

humanity, unable to comprehend the Infinite God, had parcelled out and detached his various powers and virtues, which it adored under material forms according to its varying needs.[1] Or it found a place for all the gods of heathendom, as ministering or mediating spirits in the vast abyss which separates us from the unapproachable and Infinite Spirit.[2] If the legends which had gathered around the popular gods offended a tender moral sense, men were taught that the apparent grossness was an allegorical husk, or a freak of poetic fancy which concealed a wholesome truth. Thus a pantheist or monotheist, who would never have created such a religious system for himself, was trained to cultivate a double self in matters of religion, to worship reverently with the crowd, and to believe with Zeno or with Plato.

The heathen champion in the dialogue of Minucius Felix maintains that, in the dimness and uncertainty of things, the safest course is to hold fast to the gods of our fathers.[3] The inclination of the sceptic was fortified by the conservative instinct of the Latin race and its love of precedent and precision of form. Moreover the religion of Numa was probably more than any other involved and intertwined with the whole life of the people. It penetrated the whole fabric of society; it consecrated and dignified every public function, and every act or incident of private life. To desert the ancient gods was to cut oneself off from Roman society, as the Christians were sternly made to feel. No established Church in modern Christendom has probably ever so succeeded in identifying itself with the national life in all its aspects. Alike under the Republic and under the Empire, religion was inseparable from patriotism. The imperial pontiff was bound to watch over the purity and continuity of the Latin rites. He might be a scoffer like Nero, or a spiritually-minded Stoic like M. Aurelius, an Isiac devotee like Commodus, or devoted to the Syrian worships like the Oriental princes of the third century. But he took his duties seriously. He would dance with the Salii,

[1] Plin. *H. N.* ii. 7, 5, fragilis et laboriosa mortalitas in partes ista digessit infirmitatis suae memor, ut portionibus coleret quisque quo maxime indigeret.

[2] *v.* supra, p. 425 sqq.

[3] Min. Fel. *Octav.* c. 6, quanto venerabilius ac melius antistitem veritatis majorum excipere disciplinam, religiones traditas colere, deos, quos a parentibus ante imbutus es timere quam nosse familiarius, adorare, etc.

or accept with gratitude the mastership of the Arval brotherhood, or order a *lectisternium* to ward off a pestilence or a menacing invasion. The imperial colleges still held their meetings on the eve of the revolution of Theodosius. Antiquarian nobles still discussed nice questions of ritual in the reign of Honorius. At the end of the fifth century the Lupercalia were still celebrated with coarse, half-savage rites which went back to the prehistoric times.[1] The imperial policy, founded by Augustus, no doubt inspired much of this conformity. But old Roman sentiment, the passion expressed with such moving eloquence by Symmachus, to feel himself in touch with a distant past[2] through a chain of unbroken continuity, was the great support of the State religion in the fourth century as in the first. Yet, among the great nobles who were its last champions—Flavianus, Praetextatus, or Volusianus—there was a spiritual craving for which the religion provided little satisfaction. They sought it in the rites and mysteries of Eastern lands which had little in common with the old Roman religious sentiment. In these alien rites they found a new religious atmosphere. The priest, set apart from the world, with his life-long obligations and the daily offices in the shrine, becomes in some way a minister to the spiritual life of his flock. Instead of cold ceremonial observance, ecstatic emotion is aroused, often to a degree which was perilous to character. Through a series of sacraments, with ascetic preparation for them, the votary rose under priestly guidance to some vision of the eternal world, with a new conception of sin; this life and the next were linked in a moral sequence, with tremendous issues of endless beatitude or endless degradation. In a temple of Magna Mater, Isis, or Mithra in the reign of Julian, we are far away from the worship of the Lares and the offering of a heifer to Dea Dia in the grove on the Tiber. We are travelling towards the spiritual mystery and sacramental consolations of the mediaeval Church.

[1] Virg. *Aen.* viii. 343; Ov. *Fasti*, ii. 267; Baronius, *Ann. Eccl.* viii. 60; Gibbon, c. 36; Fowler, *Rom. Fest.* p. 310.

[2] Sym. *Relat.* 3.

CHAPTER IV

MAGNA MATER

THE earliest invader from the East of the sober decorum of old Roman religion, and almost the last to succumb, was Magna Mater of Pessinus. There is no pagan cult which S. Augustine, and many of the Fathers before him, assail with such indignant contempt as hers.[1] And indeed it was long regarded with suspicion by old Romans of the cultivated class. For generations after her reception on the Palatine, no Roman was permitted to enter her official service. But there was something in that noisy and bloody ritual, and in the cruel, ascetic sacrifice of its devotees, which exercised an irresistible power over the imagination of the vulgar; and even Lucretius felt a certain imaginative awe of the tower-crowned figure drawn by lions and adored by the cities of many lands.[2] Varro, who probably had no great love for the un-Roman ritual, found a place for the Phrygian goddess in his théodicée.[3] Her baptism of blood in the taurobolium was a rite of such strange enthralling influence that it needed all the force of the Christian Empire to abolish it. And on many of the last inscriptions of the fourth century the greatest names in the Roman aristocracy leave the record of their cleansing in the curious phrase *renatus in aeternum*.[4] In his youth S. Augustine had seen processions of effeminate figures with dripping locks, painted faces, and soft womanish bearing, passing along the streets of Carthage, and begging alms of the crowd. His horror at the memory of the scene probably springs almost

1 Aug. *De Civ. Dei*, ii. 4; Tertull. *Apol.* 13; *Adv. Marc.* i. 13.

2 Lucret. ii. 600.

3 Aug. *De Civ. Dei*, vi. 8, vii. 24.

4 *C.I.L.* vi. 499, 504, 509, 510, 511, 512; xii. 1782, 1567; *Or.* 1899, 1890, 2335.

as much from the manly instincts of the Roman as from the detestation of the Christian moralist for a debasing superstition.[1]

But S. Augustine knew well the power of the superstition. For more than 600 years the Great Mother had been enthroned on the Palatine; for more than 300 years she had captivated the remotest provinces of the West.[2] In the terror of the Second Punic War, 204 B.C., she had been summoned by a solemn embassy from her original home at Pessinus in Galatia. In obedience to a sibylline command, the Roman youth with purest hands, together with the Roman matrons, had welcomed her at Ostia.[3] The ship which bore her up the Tiber,[4] when it grounded on a shoal, had been sent forward on its way, to vindicate her calumniated virtue, by the touch of a virgin of the Claudian house.[5] A decree of the Senate in 191 B.C. had given the strange goddess a home on the Palatine, hard by the shrine of Apollo; and the great Megalesian festival in April was founded.[6] But the foreign character of the cult was long maintained. It was a time when the passion for religious excitement was in the air, and when its excesses had to be restrained by all the forces of the State. No Roman was permitted to accept the Phrygian priesthood for a century after the coming of the Great Mother.[7] But towards the end of the Republic, the goddess had captured all imaginations, and her priests and symbols meet us in all the poets of the great age.[8] Augustus restored her temple; some of his freedmen were among her priests;[9] Livia is pictured with the crown of towers upon her brow.[10] Then came a long interval, till the death of Nero, during which the Phrygian goddess is hardly heard of.[11] With the accession of the Flavians the eastern cults finally entered on a long and unchallenged reign. Vespasian restored the temple of the Great Mother at Herculaneum, which had been thrown

[1] *De Civ. Dei*, ii. 4, 7, 8; vi. 7; vii. 24.

[2] *C.I.L.* ii. 179 (Spain, 108 p. Chr.); iii. 1100, 1443 (Dacia, p. Chr. 110); *Or. Henz.* 5839 (Portugal).

[3] Liv. 29, 10.

[4] *Or.* 1906, Navisalviae et matri D. (*v.* note).

[5] Ov. *Fasti*, iv. 305; Sen. *Frag.* 80; Suet. *Tib.* c. 2.

[6] Fowler, *Rom. Fest.* p. 70.

[7] Val. Max. vii. 7, 6; Goehler, *De Matr. Magn. Cultu*, p. 10.

[8] Lucret. ii. 600; Virg. *Aen.* ix. 620; x. 220; Ov. *A. Am.* i. 507; Prop. iii. 17, 35; cf. Preller, p. 484.

[9] *C.I.L.* vi. 496.

[10] Goehler, p. 12.

[11] Yet cf. D. Cass. lxi. 20, ἐκιθαρῴδησέ τε Ἄττιν ὁ Αὔγουστος.

down by an earthquake.[1] In the reign of Trajan her worship had penetrated to the Spanish peninsula,[2] and she is found, along with other Eastern deities, in the towns of the new province of Dacia.[3] The first glimpses of the taurobolium appear before the middle of the second century, and the goddess figures on the coins of Antoninus Pius.[4] A taurobolium for that emperor was offered "with intention" at Lyons in 160 A.D.,[5] and there are several dedications to Magna Mater in the same reign made by colleges of the *Dendrophori* at Ostia.[6] Tertullian tells how a high priest of Cybele vainly offered his blood for the safety of M. Aurelius, seven days after the Emperor had died in his quarters on the Danube.[7] It does not fall within the scope of our present inquiry to trace the immense popularity of the worship under the princes of the third century. That was the period of the great triumph of the spiritual powers of the East. At the end of the fourth century the Great Mother and Mithra were in the van of the pagan resistance to the religious revolution of Theodosius and his sons.[8]

The worship of Cybele, coming from the same regions as the Trojan ancestors of Rome, was at first a patrician cult.[9] Members of the proudest houses bore a part in welcoming her to a place in the Roman pantheon.[10] Yet, as we have seen, Romans were for generations forbidden to enrol themselves among her effeminate priesthood. By a curious contradiction of sentiment, people were fascinated by the ritual, while they despised the celebrants. The legend which was interpreted by Stoic and Neoplatonist as full of physical or metaphysical meanings,[11] had also elements of human interest which appealed to the masses, always eager for emotional excitement. The love of the Great Mother for a fair youth, his unfaithfulness, and penitential self-mutilation under the pine-tree; the passionate mourning for lost love, and then the restoration of the self-made victim, attended by a choir of priests for ever, who had made

[1] *C.I.L.* x. 1406. Imp. Vesp. templum M. M. terrae motu conlapsum restituit.

[2] *Ib.* ii. 179 (108 p. Chr.); cf. *Or. Henz.* 5839.

[3] *C.I.L.* iii. 1100, 1443.

[4] *Ib.* x. 1596 (Naples, p. Chr. 134).

[5] *Or. Henz.* 2322.

[6] Goehler, p. 15.

[7] Tertull. *Apol.* 25; D. Cass. lxxi. 33.

[8] *C.I.L.* vi. 501 (p. Chr. 383); 509, 511, 510, 500.

[9] Réville, p. 60; Ov. *Fasti*, iv. 251,

Cum Trojam Aeneas Italos portaret in agros,
Est dea sacriferas paene secuta rates.

[10] Ov. *l.c.* 293.

[11] Aug. *De Civ. Dei*, vi. 8; vii. 25; Jul. *Or.* v. p. 161 D.

the same cruel sacrifice[1]—all this, so alien to old Roman religious sentiment, triumphed over it in the end by novelty and tragic interest. The legend was developed into a drama, which, at the vernal festival of the goddess, was produced with striking, if not artistic, effect. On the first day the Dendrophori bore the sacred tree, wreathed with violets, to the temple. There was then a pause for a day, and, on the third, the priests, with frantic gestures and dishevelled hair, abandoned themselves to the wildest mourning, lacerating their arms and shoulders with wounds, from which the blood flowed in torrents. Severe fasting accompanied these self-inflicted tortures. Then came a complete change of sensation. On the day called Hilaria the votaries gave themselves up to ecstasies of joy, to celebrate the restoration of Attis. On the last day of the festival a solemn procession took its way to the brook Almon, to bathe the goddess in its waters.[2] The sacred stone, brought originally from her home in Asia, and the most sacred symbol of the worship, wrapped in robes, was borne upon a car with chants and music, and that gross, unabashed naturalism which so often shocks and surprises us in pagan ritual till we trace it to its source.

The government long treated the cult of Cybele as a foreign worship.[3] The title of its great festival is Greek. Yet before the close of the Republic, Romans are found enrolled in its priesthoods and sacred colleges, and long lists of these official votaries can be gathered from the inscriptions of the imperial period. The archigallus, or high priest, appears often on the Italian and provincial monuments. He is found at Merida, Capua, Ostia, and Lyons, in Numidia and Portugal.[4] He must have performed his part at many a taurobolium, crowned with laurel wreaths, wearing his mitre and ear-rings and armlets, with the image of Attis on his breast.[5] The names of the ordinary priests abound, from the freedman of the house of Augustus to the great nobles of the reign of Theodosius and Honorius.[6] The priesthood was sometimes held for life, or for a long term of years.

[1] There were many variations of the myth; *v.* Goehler, pp. 2, 3; Foucart *Assoc. Rel.* p. 89; Ov. *Fasti*, iv. 223.

[2] Réville, p. 64; Preller, p. 485.

[3] Fowler, *Rom. Festivals*, p. 70; cf. Foucart, *Assoc. Rel.* p. 88, for similar treatment at Athens.

[4] *C.I.L.* x. 3810; viii. 8203; xii. 1782; ii. 5260.

[5] *Ib.* xii. 1782; *Or. Henz.* 2325, 6031; Goehler, p. 40.

[6] Goehler, p. 12; *C.I.L.* vi. 511, 504, 500.

A priest at Salonae in Dalmatia had punctually performed the sacred offices for seventeen years.[1] Women were naturally admitted to the priesthood of a cult whose central interest was a woman's love and grief. Sometimes they are lowly freedwomen with Greek names, sometimes they bear the proudest names in the Roman aristocracy.[2] The Dendrophori, who on festive days bore the sacred tree, formed a religious college, and their record appears on many monuments of Italian and provincial towns—Como, Ostia, and Cumae, Caeserea (Afr.), Valentia, and Lyons.[3] Other colleges were the Cannophori and Cernophori, the keepers of the mystic symbols.[4] The chanters, drummers, and cymbal players were indispensable at great ceremonial scenes, such as the taurobolium,[5] and were arranged in graded ranks. Of a lower degree were the vergers and apparitors, who watched over the chapels of the goddess.[6] And, lastly, there were the simple worshippers, who also formed themselves into guilds, with all the usual officers of such corporations. This cult, like so many others, existed not only for ceremonial rite, but for fellowship and social exhilaration, and, through its many gradations of religious privilege, it must have drawn vast numbers into the sacred service in the times of the Empire.

But the pages of Apuleius, and other authorities, show us that, beside the official clergy and collegiate members, there were, as happens to all popular religions, a mass of unlicensed camp followers and mere disreputable vagrants, who used the name of the Great Mother to exploit the ignorant devotion and religious excitability of the rustic folk. The romance of Apuleius, as Dr. Mahaffy has suggested, is probably derived from earlier sources, and dressed up to titillate the prurient tastes of a degraded society.[7] Yet its pictures of country life in Thessaly, although they may not be always locally accurate, can hardly be purely imaginative. The scenes may not be always Thessalian, but that they are in the main true pictures of country life in the Antonine age may be proved from other authorities. Apuleius was too careful an artist to sever himself

[1] *C.I.L.* iii. 2920; xii. 1567.

[2] *Ib.* x. 6074; vi. 502, 508; *Or. Henz.* 7200 (Acte), 2330, 1902, 2371, 2319, 2325; *C.I.L.* xii. 4322, 4326.

[3] *Or. Henz.* 7336, 2322, 6031, 4109, 7197; *C.I.L.* viii. 9401.

[4] Goehler, p. 45.

[5] *C.I.L.* xii. 1782.

[6] *Or. Henz.* 2325, 2984.

[7] Mahaffy, *The Greek World under Roman Sway*, p. 295 sqq.

altogether from the actual life of his time. And what a picture it is! The air positively thrills with daemonic terror and power. Witches and lewd sorceresses abound; the solitary inn has its weird seductions; the lonely country cottage has its tragedy of lawless love or of chaste devotion to the dead. Brigands in mountain fastnesses divide their far-gathered spoil, and hold debate on plans of future lawless adventure. Mountain solitudes, and lonely villages or castles among the woods, are aroused by the yelping hounds, who start the boar from his lair, while the faithless traitor places his friend at its mercy. We meet the travelling cheese merchant, and the noble exile on his way to Zacynthus. We watch the raid on the banker's house at Thebes, and the peasants setting their dogs on the passing traveller; the insolence of the wandering legionary; the horrors of the slave prison, with its wasted, starved, and branded forms; the amours of buxom wives, and the comic concealment or discovery of lovers, in the manner of Boccaccio. It is only too certain that the vileness and superstition which Apuleius has depicted may easily find a parallel on the Roman stage, or in the pages of Martial.

In all this social panorama, romantic, amusing, or disgusting, there is no more repulsive, and probably no truer scene than that in which the wandering priests of the Syrian goddess appear. That deity, like many others of Eastern origin, was often identified with the Great Mother. Apuleius probably confounded them; the rites of their worships were often the same, and the picture in Apuleius may be taken to represent the orgies of many a wandering troop of professed devotees of the Great Mother in the age of the Antonines.[1] The leader is an old eunuch, with wild straggling locks—a man of the foulest morals, carrying about with him an image of the goddess, and levying alms from the superstition of the rustics. He is attended by a crew worthy of him, wretches defiled with all the worst vices of the ancient world, and shamelessly parading their degradation. But they combine a shrewd eye to business with this wild licence. They know all the arts to catch the fancy of the mob of clowns, whose grey dull lives and inbred superstition make them eager for any display which will intoxicate them with the novelty of a violent sensation. These

[1] Réville, *Rel. unter den Sev.* p. 65; Apul. *Met.* viii. 24 (*v.* Hildenbrand's notes).

people are on that level where lust and the passion for blood and suffering readily league themselves with religious excitement. After a night of moral horrors, the foul brotherhood go forth in various costume to win the largesses of the countryside. With painted cheeks and robes of white or yellow, crossed with purple stripes, their arms bared to the shoulder, and carrying swords or axes, they dance along wildly to the sound of the flute.[1] With obscene gesticulation and discordant shrieks they madly bite their arms or lacerate them with knives. One of the band, as if seized with special inspiration, heaving and panting under the foul afflatus, shrieks out the confession of some sin against the holy rites, and claims the penalty from his own hands.[2] With hard knotted scourge he belabours himself, while the blood flows in torrents. At last the cruel frenzy exhausts itself, and obtains its reward in the offerings of the spectators. Fine flour and cheese, milk and wine, coins of copper and silver, are eagerly showered upon the impostors, and as eagerly gathered in.[3] Surprised in frightful orgies of vice, the scoundrels have at last to retreat before the outraged moral sense of the villagers. They decamp during the night, and on the morrow once more find comfortable quarters in the house of a leading citizen who is devoted to the service of the gods, and blind to the imposture of their professing ministers.[4]

The episode in Apuleius suggests some curious questions as to the moral effect of these emotional cults. That in their early stages they had no elevating moral influence,—nay, that their votaries might combine a strict conformity to rite with great looseness of life,—is only too certain. The Delias and Cynthias of the poets, who kept the fasts of Isis, were assuredly not models of virtue. The assumption of the tonsure and linen habit by a debauchee like Commodus does not reassure us. Yet princes of high character in the second and the third centuries lent the countenance of imperial power to the worships of the East.[5] And the Mother of the Gods found her last and most gallant defenders among great nobles of high repute and sincere pagan piety in the last years of

[1] Apul. *Met.* viii. c. 27 (580); cf. Aug. *De Civ. Dei*, ii. 4.
[2] Apul. *Met.* viii. c. 28 (583).
[3] *Ib.* c. 28 (585).
[4] *Ib.* c. 30 (589).
[5] *C.I.L.* x. 1406; Lamprid. *Alex. Sev.* c. 37.

heathenism in the West. It was a strange transformation. Yet the problem is not perhaps insoluble. A religion may deteriorate as its authority over society becomes more assured with age. But, in times of moral renovation, and in the face of powerful spiritual rivalries, a religion may purge itself of the impurities of youth. Religious systems may also be elevated by the growing moral refinement of the society to which they minister. It is only thus that we can explain the undoubted fact that the Phrygian and Egyptian worships, originally tainted with the grossness of naturalism, became vehicles of a warm religious emotion, and provided a stimulus to a higher life. The idealism of humanity, by a strange alchemy, can marvellously transform the most unpromising materials. And he would make a grave mistake who should treat the Isis and Osiris, the Mater Deum or the Attis, of the reign of Augustus as representing the same ideals in the reign of Gratian. But these Eastern cults contained a germ, even in their earliest days, of their great future development and power. The old religion of Latium, along with much that was sound and grave and fortifying to character, was also hard and cold and ceremonial. It could mould and consecrate a militant and conquering state; it did little to satisfy the craving for moral regeneration or communion with a Higher Power. It could not appease the sense of error and frailty by ghostly comfort and sacramental absolution. It was, moreover, wanting in that warmth of interest and sympathy, linking the human and Divine, which has helped to make Christianity the religion of Western civilisation, and which in a feeble adumbration made the paganism of the East a momentary rival of the Church. These Eastern cults, often originating in gross symbolism of the alternations and recurring processes of nature,[1] often arousing a dangerous excitability and an unregulated emotion, yet contained the germ of a religious spirit far more akin to ours than the old austere Latin creed. A divine death and restoration, the alternation of joy and sorrow at a divine event, instinct with human interest, calming expiation and cleansing from the sins which burdened the conscience,—above all, the hope of a coming life, stamped on the imagination by symbol and spectacle,—these were the

[1] Firm. Matern. *De Err. Prof. Rel.* c. 2, 3.

elements which, operating on imperious religious yearnings, gave a fresh life to paganism, and prepared or deferred the victory of the Church. The religion of the Great Mother seems at first sight to offer the poorest promise of any moral message or spiritual support. It expressed at first the feelings of rude rustics at the recurring mortality and resurrection of material life in the order of the seasons. The element of human feeling which it contained was grossly expressed in bloody rites of mutilation. This cult was often defiled and disgraced by a crew of effeminate and lustful impostors. Yet the Thessalian villagers in Apuleius, who chased these vagabonds from their fields, evidently expected something better from them. They despised the foul hypocrites, but they did not cease to believe in their religion. The spiritual instinct of humanity triumphed, as it has so often done, over the vices of a historical system, extracted the good in it, rejected the evil, and made it an organ of some sort of spiritual life. Thus the Great Mother became the Mother of all, enthroned beside the Father of gods and men. She wears the chaste honours of the Virgin Goddess. Attis and her love for Attis are similarly transformed. In the syncretism of the age, which strove to gather up all the forces of heathenism and make them converge towards a spiritual unity, Magna Mater and Attis leagued their forces with the conquering Mithra.[1] In the taurobolium there was developed a ritual, in which, coarse and materialistic as it was, paganism made, in however imperfect form, its nearest approach to the religion of the Cross.

The greatest and most impressive rite in the worship of Cybele was the taurobolium. There was none which so excited the suspicion and indignation of the Christian apologists, from Tertullian to Prudentius, because in its ceremony of the cleansing blood, and in its supposed effects in moral regeneration and remission of sins, it seemed invented by the ingenuity of daemons to be a travesty of the sacrifice on Calvary.[2] It is

[1] Réville, p. 66; Goehler, p. 29; Cumont, *Mon. figurés de Mithra*, Introd. p. 333; *Or.* 2329, 2330, 1900; *C.I.L.* vi. 497, 500, 511; cf. *ib.* x. 1596, where the taurobolium is connected with Venus Coelesta (*sic*); Preller, p. 486.

[2] Tertull. *De Praescrip. Haeret.* 40; Firm. Matern. *De Err. Prof. Relig.* c.27, neminem aput idola profusus sanguis munit . . . polluit sanguis iste, non redimit. Tauribolium quid vel criobolium scelerata te sanguinis labe perfundit? S. Paulin. Nol. *Poem. Ult.* 112–117.

possible that the last champions of the ancient cults may have had some such defiant purpose when they inscribed, in the record of their cleansing, the words "*in aeternum renatus*." But in its origin there can be no doubt that the rite was purely heathen. Its appearance in the Phrygian ceremonial is comparatively late. The worship of Magna Mater was essentially an orgiastic cult, and theologically arid. But the syncretism of the second and third centuries came to its support. And the worships of Persia, Syria, and Phrygia were ready to coalesce, and to borrow from one another symbols and doctrines which gave satisfaction to the spiritual wants of the time. The taurobolium, with its ideas of cleansing and immortality, passed in the Antonine age from the worship of Anaitis of Cappadocia to the worship of Magna Mater, and gave the Great Mother a new hold upon the religious consciousness. In the earlier votive tablets the name of the rite is *tauropolium*. Anaitis had been identified with the Artemis Tauropolus of Brauron, whose legend, by popular etymology, came to be identified, as Milesian exploration spread in the Euxine, with the cult of the cruel goddess of the Tauric Chersonese.[1] And by another etymological freak and the change of a letter, we arrive at the bull-slaughtering rite of the later Empire. Whether the taurobolium ever became part of the service of Mithra is a disputed point.[2] Certainly the syncretistic tendency of the age, the fact that the most popular Mithraist symbol was the slaying of the mystic bull, and the record of the taurobolium on so many inscriptions dedicated to Mithra, would prepare us for the conclusion that the rite was in the end common to the Persian and the Phrygian deities. Whatever may be the truth on this point, the two worships, in the last ages of heathenism in the West, were close allies. Attis tended more and more to become a solar deity in the age which culminated in the sun-worship of Julian.[3] Heliolatry, the last refuge of monotheism in heathendom, which refused to accept the religion of Galilee, swept all the great worships of strong vitality into its system,

[1] Cumont, Introd. pp. 236, 333; Herodot. iv. 103; Eur. *Iph. T.* 1455; Strab. v. 3, § 12, p. 240.

[2] Cumont, p. 334; Gasquet, *Culte de Mithra*, p. 75; Cumont, Introd. p. 334, n. 5; Réville, *Rel. unter den Sev.* p. 93, takes an opposite view.

[3] Donsbach, *Die raümliche Verbreitung des Mithrasdienstes*, pp. 8, 9.

softened their differences, accentuated their similarities, by every effort of fancy, false science, or reckless etymology, and in the end, "Sol invictus" and Mithra were left masters of the field. But Magna Mater, however originally unworthy, shared in the victory. If she could lend the support of an accredited clergy, recognised for ages by the State, and the impressive rite of the bloody baptism, Mithra, on the other hand, had a moral and spiritual message, an assurance of a future life, and an enthralling force of mystic and sacramental communion, which made his alliance even more valuable. The Great Mother, indeed, admitted women to the ranks of her clergy, while the rites of Mithra probably excluded them.[1] And thus a Fabia Aconia Paulina, while her husband, Vettius Agorius Praetextatus, could inscribe himself "pater patrum," had no Mithraist grade which she could place beside her consecration to Hecate and the Eleusinian goddesses.[2] But the pair were united in the sacrament of the taurobolium. And the Great Mother probably never had purer or sincerer devotees.

When the taurobolium was first introduced into the West is uncertain.[3] The earliest monument belongs to A.D. 134 in the reign of Hadrian, when the ceremony seems to be connected with the Celestial Venus. The most famous inscription, which connects the rite with the Great Mother, is of the year 160 A.D., when one L. Aemilius Carpus, an Augustalis, and a member of the college of the Dendrophori at Lyons, had the ceremony performed "for the safety" of Antoninus Pius and the imperial house.[4] The rite was celebrated at the command of the goddess, or on the inspired advice of the priest.[5] It took place generally in early spring, and was often prolonged over three or four days.[6] It was a costly rite, and the expense was sometimes borne by the community, who made an offertory for the purpose.[7] The ceremony was superintended by the xvviri, and attended by a great concourse of the people, with the magistrates at their

[1] This is rendered doubtful by Porphyr. *De Abstin.* iv. 16, *ὡς τοὺς μὲν μετέχοντας τῶν αὐτῶν ὀργίων μύστας λέοντας καλεῖν (εἰώθασιν). τὰς δὲ γυναῖκας ὑαίνας* (altered by Felicianus to *λεαίνας*); cf Gasquet, p. 98.

[2] *C.I.L.* vi. 1778, 9.

[3] Goehler, p. 55; *C.I.L.* x. 1596; (Puteoli, p. Chr. 134; taurobol. Veneris Caelestae (*sic*).

[4] *Or.* 2382; Goehler, p. 55; cf. *C.I.L.* viii. 8203.

[5] *Or.* 2327, ex jussu ipsius; *C.I.L.* xii. 1782, ex vaticinatione Archigalli; cf. xii. 4321, 4323.

[6] *C.I.L.* xii. 1782.

[7] *Ib.* xii. 4321 (*stipe collata*); at private expense, xii. 1568.

head. It is needless to describe again the scene, so well known from the verses of Prudentius, in which the consecrated bull is with solemn forms slaughtered on a high-raised platform, and bathes with the streams of his blood the votary placed in a trench below.[1] The rite was believed to impart some sort of strength and purification, the effect of which lasted for twenty years, when the sacrament was often renewed. It was, as we have seen, sometimes performed "with intention," for the reigning emperor and his house,[2] and furnishes another example of the manner in which religion was employed to buttress the power of the Caesars. A considerable number of monuments in Italy and the provinces commemorate, in a phrase perhaps borrowed from the Church, the gratitude of one "born again to eternal life." It is probable that the coarse ritual often expressed only an external and materialistic conception of religious influence. On the other hand, following upon, or closely connected with initiation into the mysteries of Mithra, it may easily have become a symbol of moral and spiritual truth, or at any rate a record of moral aspiration.

For, indeed, in the syncretism and monotheistic drift of the age, the more powerful worships lost the hardness of their original lines and tended to absorption and assimilation. There was little strife or repulsion among these cults; they borrowed freely legends and ritual practice from one another; even characteristic insignia were interchanged. The legend and tone of the Cybele worship naturally linked her with others sprung from the same region, such as the Syrian goddess, Celestial Venus, and Bellona.[3] Fanaticism, self-mutilation, expiation by blood, were the common bond between them. The fierce goddess of Cappadocia, who had visited Sulla in a dream, was probably first introduced to Roman devotion in his time. Her dark-robed priests and priestesses were familiar figures in the Augustan age, gashing themselves like the Galli of Magna Mater, catching the blood in shields, and dashing it over their train of followers who believed in its powers of expiation. But Magna Mater, as her name promises, assumed a milder character, and was identified sometimes with Maia,

[1] *Peristeph.* x. 1011; cf. Duruy, v. p. 743.

[2] *C.I.L.* xii. 1311, 251, 1822, 4332; *Or.* 2332.

[3] Goehler, p. 34; Réville, p. 66; Preller, p. 488; Cumont, Introd. p. 333.

Ops, and Minerva; sometimes with Demeter, Bona Dea, and Fauna, as Attis was identified with Hercules.[1] In the last age the great goddess became the universal Mother, full of tenderness and grace, and giving peace through her cleansing rites. Hers is, along with the cults of Isis and Mithra, which will next claim our attention, an example of the process of Divine evolution, by which, in the painful progress of humanity, the crude efforts of religious symbolism are purged and elevated. It is an example of the way in which the human spirit, refusing to break with its past, sometimes succeeds, if only for a time, in putting new wine into old bottles.

[1] Goehler, p. 29.

CHAPTER V

ISIS AND SERAPIS

THE worship of Isis and Serapis, reckoning from the day when it established itself in the port of Athens, had a reign of more than seven centuries over the peoples of Europe. Its influence in the western provinces of the Empire and in the capital may be roughly said to cover a period of 500 years. It was not, indeed, the old native worship of the valley of the Nile which won such an empire over cultivated intellects from Chaeronea to the Thames. The ancient Egyptian worship underwent vast transformations in the crucible of all creeds at Alexandria. It was captured and utilised for political purposes by the Ptolemies.[1] It was linked with the most spiritual forces of Hellenic piety at Eleusis and Delphi;[2] it was transformed by the subtle syncretism of later Greek philosophy; and, through the secretaries of embassies, and the Egyptian slaves and merchants who poured into the ports of southern Italy in the second century B.C., it stole or forced itself into the chapels of great houses at Rome, till, in the end, emperors were proud to receive its tonsure, to walk in the processions, and to build and adorn Egyptian temples.[3]

The Isiac worship had conquered the Greek world before it became a power in Italy. In the fourth century B.C. traders from the Nile had their temple of Isis at the Peiraeus;[4] in the third century the worship had been admitted within the walls of Athens.[5] About the same time the goddess had found a

[1] Lafaye, *Culte des divinités d'Alexandrie*, p. 15; Plut. *De Is. et Osir.* c. 28.

[2] Plut. *De Is. et Osir.* c. 35, addressed to Clea, who was high in the worship of Dionysus, and "hereditarily devoted to Osiris."

[3] Lamprid. *Com. Ant.* c. 9; Spart. *Sev.* c. 17; Réville, *Rel. unter den Sev.* p. 58.

[4] Foucart, *Assoc. Religieuses*, p. 83.

[5] Lafaye, pp. 27–32; Paus. i. 18, § 4.

home at Ceos, and Delos, at Smyrna and Halicarnassus, and on the coasts of Thrace.[1] She was a familiar deity at Orchomenus and Chaeronea for generations before Plutarch found in her legends a congenial field for the exposition of his concordat between philosophy and myth. Nor need we wonder at his choice of the Egyptian cults. For the Isis and Osiris of Greek and Italian lands were very different objects of devotion from the gods who bore those names in Egyptian legend.[2] From the seventh century B.C. Greeks from the Asiatic coast had been securely settled at the mouth of the Nile.[3] Greek mercenaries had served in the Egyptian armies in the southern deserts; and Greek half-breeds had long amused and cajoled travellers from Miletus or Halicarnassus, as interpreters and guides to the scenes of immemorial interest. When Herodotus visited the country, the identity of Greek and Egyptian gods was a long accepted fact.[4] From the fifth century B.C. the Egyptian Trinity of Isis, Osiris, and Horus had found counterparts in Demeter, Dionysus, and Apollo. The campaign of the Athenian fleet in 460 probably hastened and confirmed the process of syncretism,[5] and crowds of travellers, steeped in Orphic and Pythagorean mysticism, returned from the valley of the Nile to spread the doctrine of a common faith. After the foundation of Alexandria the theory became a propaganda. The first Ptolemy strove to unite the two races under his sway by an eclecticism of which Alexandria was the focus for seven centuries. He found skilful allies in Manetho, the Egyptian priest who had written a treatise on the inner meaning of the myths, and in Timotheus, a scion of the Eumolpidae of Eleusis.[6] The Orphic and Dionysiac mysticism was leagued with the Isiac worship. The legend of Egypt was recast. A new deity was introduced, who was destined to have a great future in all lands under the Roman sway. The origin of Serapis is still a mystery[7] and the latest critic may have to acquiesce in the confused or

[1] Lafaye, p. 38.

[2] *v.* Plut. *De Is. et Osir.* c. 53, τὸ τῆς φύσεως θῆλυ, c. 52, οὐχ ἑτέραν τῆς σελήνης: c. 38, οὕτως Ἴσιδος σῶμα γῆν ἔχουσι καὶ νομίζουσιν, οὐ πάσαν, ἀλλ' ἧς ὁ Νεῖλος ἐπιβαίνει σπερμαίνων: cf. c. 32; c. 56, Ὄσιριν ὡς ἀρχήν, τὴν δὲ Ἶσιν ὡς ὑποδοχήν, τὸν δὲ Ὧρον ὡς ἀποτέλεσμα: cf. Herodot. ii. 156; Apul. *Met.* xi. c. 7, matrem siderum, parentem temporum, orbisque totius dominam blando mulcentes affamine.

[3] Herodot. ii. 154.

[4] *Ib.* 156; cf. Plew, *De Sarapide*, p. 23 sqq.

[5] Thuc. i. 104.

[6] Lafaye, p. 15 sqq.

[7] Plew, *De Sarapide*, p. 10 sqq.

balanced judgment of Tacitus.[1] Egyptian archaeologists claimed him as indigenous at Rhacotis or Memphis, and construed his name as a compound of Osiris and that of his earthly incarnation, the bull Apis.[2] The more popular tale was that the first Ptolemy, after repeated visions of the night, sent envoys to bring him from Sinope, where he was identified with Pluto, god of the under world. Other traditions connected him with Seleucia in Cappadocia, or with Babylon.[3] It may be that a false etymology, confounding a hill near Memphis with the name of Sinope, was the source of the tale in Tacitus.[4] However this may be, Serapis takes the place of Osiris; they never appear together in inscriptions. The infant Horus received the Greek sounding name Harpocrates, and Serapis, Isis, and Harpocrates became the Egyptian Trinity for Graeco-Roman Society. Anubis, the minister of the Trinity, was easily identified with Hermes, "the conductor of souls" in Greek legend.

Syncretism and mysticism were great forces at Eleusis, from which Ptolemy's adviser Timotheus came. And there all interest centred in the future life, and in preparation for it by sacerdotal ritual and moral discipline. The Orphic and Pythagorean mysticism which traced itself to Egypt or the remoter East, returned to its sources, to aid in moulding the cults of Egypt into a worship for the world. A crowd of ingenious theologians set to work, by means of physical explanation, wild etymology, and fanciful analogies, to complete the syncretism. And the final results of their efforts, preserved in the famous treatise of Plutarch on Isis, is a trinitarian monotheism, with an original dualism of the good and evil principles.[5] But the idea of God, although limited in one sense by the recognition of a co-ordinate evil power, tends on the other to become more all-embracing. Serapis is constantly linked with Jupiter and Sol Invictus in the inscriptions.[6] In the orations of Aristides he becomes the centre of the universe.[7] Isis of the "myriad names" tends to absorb all other deities,

[1] Tac. *Hist.* iv. 84.

[2] Plew, *De Sarapide*, p. 15; Preller, p. 478.

[3] Plew, *De Sarapide*, p. 6.

[4] Lafaye, p. 17.

[5] Plut. *De Is. et Osir.* c. 45, 49.

[6] *Or.* 1890 sqq.; *C.I.L.* viii. 1005; iii. 4560, 3.

[7] Aristid. *Or. Sac.* viii. 53, καὶ ταμίας ὢν τοῦ βιωσίμου κατὰ τοῦτ' ἂν δικαίως ἅπαντα περιειληφέναι νομίζοιτο . . . ὁ δὲ ὥσπερ κορυφαῖος πάντων ἀρχὰς καὶ πέρατα ἔχει. Cf. Baumgart, *Aristides als Repräsentant der Soph. Rhet.* p. 90 sqq.

and was addressed by her votaries as "Thou who art all."[1] The Isis of the dream of Lucius in Apuleius is the universal mother, creator of all things, queen of the world of shades, first of the inhabitants of heaven, in whom all gods have their unchanging type.[2] She is also pre-eminently the power who can cleanse and comfort, and impart the hope of the life everlasting.

The Isiac worship arrived in Italy probably through the ports of Campania. Puteoli, in particular, was the great entrepôt for the trade with Alexandria. Foreign merchants, sailors, and slaves were arriving there every day, and, in the century between 204 and 100 B.C., more than ten embassies passed between the Ptolemies and the Roman Senate, with a crowd of secretaries and servants attached to them.[3] There was probably a temple of Serapis at Puteoli as early as 150 B.C., and the old temple of Isis at Pompeii, which was thrown down by the earthquake of 63 A.D., may probably be referred to the year 105 B.C.[4] But the erection of temples must have been preceded by a period of less formal and more obscure worship, and we may perhaps conclude that Isis had established herself in Southern Italy, at all events early in the second century B.C. Thus, although it was generations before the worship won its way, in the face of fierce persecution, to an assured place at Rome, its first appearance coincides with the decay of the old religion, the religious excitement in the beginning of the second century B.C., and the immense popular craving for a more emotional form of worship.

The years at the end of the third and the beginning of the second century B.C. were in Italy years of strange religious excitement. In 204 the great goddess was brought from Pessinus.[5] In 186 the decree for the suppression of the Bacchanalian scandal was passed.[6] Magna Graecia and Etruria were the first points assailed by the invasion of the orgiastic rites. But they soon crept into the capital, with results which alarmed and shocked old Roman sentiment. At first, an appearance of asceticism disguised the danger. But the rites soon gave an opportunity for the wildest licence and for

[1] *Or.* 1871, tibi quae es omnia.
[2] Apul. *Met.* xi. 7.
[3] Lafaye, p. 43.
[4] Id. p. 40; Mau, *Pompeii,* p. 163.
[5] Liv. xxix. 10; Goehler, *De Matris Magnae Cultu,* p. 7.
[6] Liv. xxxix. 19.

political intrigue. 7000 men and women were found to be implicated, in one way or another, in the movement.[1] Within five years after the great scandal, the apocryphal books of Numa were unearthed in the grounds of Cn. Terentius on the Janiculum. The forgery was soon detected, and they were burnt publicly in the Comitium by the praetor L. Petilius.[2] But it was a suspicious circumstance that the rolls were of Egyptian papyrus, which had been till then unknown to the Roman world, and that they contained the dogmas of a Pythagorean lore which was equally strange. It is almost certain that, in the same years in which the Dionysiac fanaticism arrived at Ostia, the Egyptian cults had been brought by merchants and sailors to Puteoli. Osiris and Dionysus had long been identified by the Alexandrian theologians; both were the patrons of mystic rites which, in their form and essence, had much in common, and the Pythagorean system, combining so many influences of philosophy and religion in the East and West, was the natural sponsor of the new worships. It was perhaps some eclectic Alexandrian, half Platonist, half Buddhist, devoted to the Isiac worship, yet ready to connect it with the Dionysiac legends of Delphi, Cithaeron, and Eleusis, who penned the secret scrolls, and buried them in the garden on the Janiculum. The movement was setting in which, so often repulsed by the force of government and conservative feeling, was destined to have enormous influence over the last three centuries of paganism in the West.

It has been plausibly suggested that the ease and completeness with which the Bacchanalian movement was suppressed in 184 B.C. was due to the diversion of religious interest to the Egyptian mysteries. The cult of Isis had indeed very various attractions for different minds. But for the masses, slaves, freedmen, and poor working people, its great fascination lay in the pomp of its ritual, and the passionate emotion aroused by the mourning for the dead Osiris, and his joyful restoration. It is this aspect of the worship which is assailed and ridiculed by the Christian apologists of the reign of Alexander Severus and of the reign of Constantine.[3] The goddess, one of whose

[1] Preller, *Myth. Rom.* p. 473.

[2] Plin. *H. N.* xiii. 27; Liv. xl. 29; Momms. *Rom. Hist.* ii. p. 402; Lafaye, p. 41.

[3] Tertull. *Adv. Marc.* i. 13; Firm. Mat. *De Err. Prof. Rel.* 2, § 7, cur plangitis fruges terrae et crescentia lugetis semina?

special functions was the care of mothers in childbirth, appealed especially to female sensibility. As in the cult of Magna Mater, women had a prominent place in her services and processions, and records of these sacred dignities appear on the monuments of great Roman ladies down to the end of the Western Empire. The history of the Isiac cult at Rome from Sulla to Nero is really the history of a great popular religious movement in conflict with a reactionary conservatism, of cosmopolitan feeling arrayed against old Roman sentiment.

It is significant of the popularity of Isis that the reactionary Sulla, who restored the election of chief pontiff to the sacred college, was forced to recognise the Isiac guild of the Pastophori in 80 B.C.[1] Four times in the decade 58–48 B.C., the fierce struggle was renewed between the government and those who wished to place Isis beside the ancient gods; and in the year 50 B.C. the consul, when unable to find a workman to lay hands upon her shrine, had to unrobe and use the axe himself.[2] The victory of conservatism was only temporary and apparent. Within five years from the renewed fierce demolition of 48 B.C.,[3] the white robe and tonsure and the mask of Anubis must have been a common sight in the streets, when the aedile M. Volusius, one of those proscribed by the triumvirs, was able to make his escape easily in this disguise.[4] The influence of Cleopatra over Julius Caesar overcame his own prejudices and probably hastened the triumph of the popular cult. The triumvirs had to conciliate public feeling by erecting a temple of Isis in 42 B.C.[5] Priestesses and devotees of Isis are henceforth found among the freedwomen of great houses and the mistresses of men of letters of the Augustan age.[6] And, although the reaction following upon the battle of Actium, in which the gods of Latium and the Nile were arrayed against one another,[7] banished Isis for a time beyond the pomoerium,[8] the devotion of the masses to

[1] Apul. *Met.* xi. c. 30, Collegii vetustissimi et sub illis Sullae temporibus conditi, etc.

[2] Tertull. *Apol.* 6; *Ad Nat.* i. 10; prohibitos Capitolio Varro commemorat eorumque aras a senatu dejectas nonnisi per vim popularium restructas, Val. Max. i. 3, 4; cf. Lewald, *De Peregr. Rel. ap. Rom.* p. 10.

[3] D. Cass. xlii. 26.

[4] Lafaye, p. 47; Val. Max. vii. 3, 8; cf. App. *B. C.* iv. 47.

[5] D. Cass. xliii. 27; xlvii. 15.

[6] Catull. x. 26; Tibull. i. 3, 23; Propert. ii. 33.

[7] *Aen.* viii. 698.

[8] D. Cass. liii. 2, τὰ μὲν ἱερὰ τὰ Αἰγύπτια οὐκ ἐσεδέξατο εἴσω τοῦ πωμηρίου; cf. liv. 6.

her seems never to have slackened, and her tonsured, white stoled priests were to be seen everywhere. In the reign of Tiberius a serious blow fell on the Eastern worships. According to Josephus, a great lady named Paulina, was, with the collusion of the priest, seduced in an Isiac temple by a libertine lover in the guise of Anubis, and the crime was sternly punished by the emperor.[1] Tacitus and Suetonius seem to be ignorant of this particular scandal, but they record the wholesale banishment to Sardinia of persons of the freedmen class, who were infected with Judaic or Egyptian superstition. In the grotto of Cagliari there is to be seen the record of an obscure romance and tragedy which may have been connected with this persecution. Atilia Pomptilla, who bore also the significant name of Benedicta, in some great calamity had followed her husband Cassius Philippus into exile. Their union had lasted for two-and-forty years when the husband was stricken with disease in that deadly climate. Like another Alcestis, Atilia by her vows and devotion offered her life for his. The husband repaid the debt in these inscriptions, and the pair lie united in death under the sculptured serpent of the goddess whom they probably worshipped.[2]

Thenceforth under the emperors Isis met with but little opposition. Claudius struck hard at the Jewish and Druidic rites, but on the other hand he was ready to transport those of Eleusis to Rome.[3] He was probably equally tolerant to the rites of Egypt. And in his reign dedications were made to Isis by freedmen of great consular houses.[4] Nero despised all religions except that of the Syrian goddess; yet Isis had probably little to fear from a prince who had been touched by the charm and mystery of the East, and who at the last would have accepted the prefecture of Egypt.[5] Otho was, however, the first Roman emperor who openly took part in the Egyptian rites.[6] The Flavians had all come under the spell of Eastern superstition. Vespasian had had a solitary vigil in the

[1] Lafaye, p. 55, discredits the tale of the seduction, which is given by Josephus alone, *B. Jud.* xviii. 3; cf. Tac. *Ann.* ii. 85; Suet. *Tib.* 36.

[2] *C.I.L.* x. 2, 7563 sqq.

[3] Suet. *Claud.* 25; cf. D. Cass. lx. 6.

[4] *C.I.L.* vi. 353.

[5] Tac. *Ann.* xv. 36; cf. Suet. *Nero*, 40, 47, varia agitavit, an vel Aegypti praefecturam concedi sibi oraret, etc.

[6] Suet. *Otho*, 12.

temple of Serapis; in obedience to a dream from the god he had consented to perform miracles of healing.[1] In the fierce civil strife of 69 A.D., when the Capitol was stormed and burnt by the Vitellians, the service of Isis was actually going on, and Domitian, disguised in her sacred vestments, escaped among the crowd of priests and acolytes.[2] He repaid the debt by rebuilding the temple of Isis in the Campus Martius, in 92 A.D., on a magnificent scale.[3] The sarcasms of Juvenal on the "shaven, linen-clad herd," and the pious austerities of female worshippers of Isis, reveal the powerful hold which the goddess had obtained in his day, even on the frivolous and self-indulgent. Hadrian, of course, had the gods of the Nile in the Canopus of his cosmopolitan villa at Tibur.[4] Commodus walked in procession with shaven head and an image of Anubis in his arms.[5] The triumph of Isis in the Antonine age was complete.

The Serapeum at Alexandria was to the Egyptian cult what the Temple was to the religion of Israel.[6] And the world-wide trade and far-spreading influence of what was then the second city in the Empire might have given a wide diffusion even to a religion less adapted to satisfy the spiritual wants of the time. Slaves and freedmen were always the most ardent adherents and apostles of foreign rites. Names of persons of this class appear on many monuments as holders of Isiac office or liberal benefactors. A little brotherhood of household slaves at Valentia in Spain were united in the worship.[7] Petty traders from Alexandria swarmed in the ports of the Mediterranean, and especially in those of Campania, and near the Nolan gate of Pompeii the humble tombs of a little colony of these emigrants have been discovered.[8] The sailors and officers of the corn fleets from Africa also helped to spread the fame of Isis and Osiris. In the reign of Septimius Severus, their chief officer, C. Valerius Serenus, was neocorus of Serapis.[9] Alexandria also sent forth a crowd of artists, philosophers, and savants to the West. Several men of Egyptian origin filled high places in the imperial household,

[1] Suet. *Vesp.* iv. v. vii.; Tac. *Hist.* iv. 81.
[2] Tac. *Hist.* iii. 74; cf. Suet. *Domit.* i.
[3] Lafaye, p. 61, n. 8.
[4] Boissier, *Prom. Archaeol.* p. 238; Spart. *Hadr.* c. 26.
[5] Lamprid. *Commod.* 9.
[6] Gibbon, c. 28; Amm. Marc. xxii. 16.
[7] *C.I.L.* ii. 6004.
[8] Lafaye, p. 157.
[9] *Ib.* p. 158.

as librarians or secretaries in the first and second centuries. Chaeremon, who had been librarian at Alexandria, and who had composed a theological treatise on Isis and Osiris, became Nero's tutor.[1] Chaeremon's pupil, Dionysius, was librarian and imperial secretary in the reign of Trajan. And Julius Vestinus, who held these offices under Hadrian, is described in an inscription as chief pontiff of Egypt and Alexandria, —a combination of dignities which probably enabled him to throw his powerful protection around the Isiac rites at Rome.[2] An influence so securely seated on the Palatine was sure to extend to the remotest parts of the Empire. If Isis could defy all the force of the Republican Government, what might she not do when emperors were enrolled in her priesthood, and imperial ministers, in correspondence with every prefecture from Britain to the Euphrates, were steeped in her mystic lore?

Already in Nero's reign, Lucan could speak of Isis and Osiris as not only welcomed in the shrines of Rome, but as deities of all the world.[3] Plutarch and Lucian, from very different points of view, are witnesses to the same world-wide movement. The judgment will be confirmed by even a casual inspection of the religious records of the inscriptions. Although Isis and Serapis were not peculiarly soldiers' gods, like Mithra and Bellona, yet they had many votaries among the legions on distant frontiers. A legate of the Legion Tertia Augusta, who was probably of Egyptian birth, introduced the rites into the camp of Lambesi, and a temple to Isis and Serapis was built by the labour of many pious hands among his soldiers.[4] Serapis appears often on the African monuments, sometimes leagued or identified with Jupiter or Pluto.[5] In Dacia and Pannonia the cults of Egypt were probably not as popular as that of Mithra, but they have left traces in all the great centres of population.[6] In several inscriptions[7] Isis is called

[1] Lafaye, p. 157.

[2] *C.I.G.* 5900, Ἀρχιερεῖ Ἀλεξανδρείας καὶ Αἰγύπτου πάσης καὶ ἐπιστάτῃ τοῦ Μουσείου καὶ ἐπὶ τῶν ἐν Ῥώμῃ βιβλιοθηκῶν . . . ἐπιστολεῖ τοῦ αὐτοῦ αὐτοκράτορος: cf. Macé, *Suétone*, pp. 92, 116.

[3] Lucan, *Phars.* viii. 831, nos in templa tuam Romana accepimus Isin; ix. 158, jam numen gentibus Isin.

[4] *C.I.L.* viii. 2630; cf. Cagnat, *L'Armée Rom. d'Afr.* p. 423. See other dedications by officers in *Or. Henz.* 5836, 7.

[5] *C.I.L.* viii. 2629, 1002, 4, 5.

[6] *Ib.* iii. 881, 2, 1428, 1590, 1342, 4015; *Or. Henz.* 5838.

[7] *C.I.L.* iii. 4809; *Or. Henz.* 2035, 5833.

by a native name such as Noreia, and we find on others the instructive blending of the strata of four mythologies. Tacitus thought he had discovered the counterpart of Isis in the forests of Germany.[1] She is certainly found in Holland, and at Cologne.[2] Officers of the sixth Legion worshipped her at York.[3] French antiquaries have followed the traces of the Egyptian gods in nearly all the old places of importance in their own country, at Fréjus, Nîmes, and Arles, at Lyons, Clermont, and Soissons.[4] Shrines of Isis have been explored in Switzerland and at the German spas.[5] The scenes which were so common at Rome or Pompeii or Corinth, the procession of shaven, white-robed priests and acolytes, marching to the sound of chants and barbaric music, with the sacred images and symbols of a worship which had been cradled on the Nile ages before the time of Romulus, and transmuted by the eclectic subtlety of Platonic theologians into a cosmopolitan religion, were reproduced in remote villages on the edge of the Sahara and the Atlantic, in the valleys of the Alps or the Yorkshire dales.

What was the secret of this power and fascination in the religion of a race whose cult of the dog and cat had so often moved the ridicule of the satirist and comic poet? No single answer can be given to that question. The great power of Isis "of myriad names" was that, transfigured by Greek influences, she appealed to many orders of intellect, and satisfied many religious needs or fancies. To the philosopher her legends furnished abundant material for the conciliation of religion and pseudo-science, for the translation of myth into ancient cosmic theory, or for the absorption of troublesome mythologies into a system which perhaps tended more than any other, except that of Mithra, to the Platonic idea of the unity of God. The mystic who dreamt of an ecstasy of divine communion, in which the limits of sense and personality might be left behind in a vague rapture of imaginative emotion, found in the spectacle of her inner shrine a strange power far surpassing the most transporting effects of Eleusis. Women especially saw in the divine mother and mourner a glorified

[1] Tac. *Germ.* 9.

[2] *Or. Henz.* 1897.

[3] *Ib.* 5836.

[4] Lafaye, p. 162. For an interesting dedication for the support of the worship at Nîmes *v.* *C.I.L.* xii. 3058.

[5] *Or. Henz.* 457; cf. Tac. *Hist.* i. 67, in modum municipii exstructus locus, amoeno salubrium aquarum usu frequens.

type of their sex, in all its troubles and its tenderness, such as their daughters in coming ages were destined to find in the Virgin Mother.[1] The ascetic impulse, which has seldom been far from the deepest religious feeling, derived comfort and the sense of atonement in penitential abstinence and preparation for the holy mysteries. The common mass, who are affected chiefly by the externals of a religion, had their wants amply gratified in the pomp and solemnity of morning sacrifice and vespers, in those many-coloured processions, such as that which bore in spring-time the sacred vessel to the shore, with the sound of hymn and litany.[2] And in an age when men were everywhere banding themselves together in clubs and colleges for mutual help and comfort, the sacred guilds of Isis had evidently an immense influence. That evil, as in nearly all heathen worships, often lurked under her solemn forms cannot be denied, though there was also groundless calumny.[3] Yet there must have been some strange power in a religion which could for a moment lift a sensualist imagination like that of Apuleius almost to the height and purity of Eckhart and Tauler.[4]

The triumph of Isis and Serapis in the Western world is an instructive episode in the history of religion. It is, like that of Mithra, a curious example of the union of conservative feeling with a purifying and transforming influence of the growing moral sense. A religion has a double strength and fascination which has a venerable past behind it. The ancient symbolism may be the creation of an age of gross conceptions of the Divine, it may be even grotesque and repulsive, at first sight, to the more refined spiritual sense of an advanced moral culture. Yet the religious instinct will always strive to maintain its continuity with the past, however it may transfigure the legacy of ruder ages. Just as Christian theologians long found anticipations of the Gospel among patriarchs and warrior kings of Israel, so pagan theologians like Plutarch or Aristides could discover in the cults of Egypt all their highest cosmic theories, and satisfaction for all their spiritual wants.[5] With unwavering faith, Plutarch and his

[1] Lafaye, p. 160; Réville, *Rel. unter den Sev.* p. 53; *C.I.L.* ii. 3386, Isis puellaris.
[2] Apul. *Met.* xi. c. 11.
[3] Lafaye, p. 160, 1.
[4] *Met.* xi. c. 24.
[5] Plut. *De Is. et Osir.* c. 78; Aristid. *Or. Sac.* viii. 52, 53.

kind believed that under all the coarse mythic fancy of early ages there was veiled a profound insight into the secrets of nature and the spiritual needs of humanity. The land of the Nile, with its charm of immemorial antiquity, was long believed to have been the cradle of all that was best and deepest in the philosophic or religious thought of Hellas. The gods of the classic pantheon were identified with the gods of Egypt.[1] Pythagoras and the Orphic mystics had derived their inspiration from the same source.[2] The conquests of Alexander and the foundation of Alexandria had drawn to a focus the philosophical or the religious ideas of East and West, of India, Palestine, Persia, and Greece. At Alexandria were blended and transformed all the philosophies and mythologies by the subtle dialectic of Greece. The animal cult of Egypt, indeed, was always a stumbling-block to Greek and Roman.[3] It moved the contempt and ridicule of comedian and satirist.[4] It was an easy mark for the sneers of the crowd. Yet even the divinised dog or ibis could find skilful, if not convinced, defenders among the Greek eclectics, who lent all the forces of Hellenic ingenuity to the cause of antiquarianism in religion.[5] Their native mythology was not without traces of zoolatry. Their own god of healing, who became so popular in all lands, was always connected in art and legend with the serpent. The serpent of the Acropolis, which daily ate the holy wafer, was the immemorial companion of the tutelary goddess of Athens.[6] Had not Zeus, in his many amours, found an easy access to the fair victims of his love in animal forms? The Divine virtues are only faintly imaged in animals which have their uses in the world. If all religion is only symbolism, why should not the multiform beneficence of the unseen Powers be expressed in the form of creatures who give their service and companionship to man, as fitly as in lifeless bronze or marble?

But although men might try to reconcile theology even to a worship of animal forms, it was by very different spiritual influences that Isis and Serapis won the devotion of the

[1] Herodot. ii. c. 50.

[2] *Ib.* c. 81; Iambl. *De Pythag. Vit.* § 151, cf. § 14; Porph. *Pythag.* § 6; Plut. *De Is. et Osir.* c. 10.

[3] Philostr. *Apollon. Tyan.* vi. 19; D. Chrys. *Or.* xii. § 68.

[4] Juv. xv. 3; cf. Cic. *De Nat. Deor.* iii. 15; *Tuscul.* v. 27.

[5] Plut. *De Is. et Osir.* cc. 72–74.

[6] Herodot. viii. c. 41.

rustics of remote villages in Spain and Britain. The dog-headed Anubis might perhaps be borne in processions.[1] The forms of sacred animals might be portrayed, along with those of Io and Andromeda, on the frescoes of Herculaneum or Pompeii.[2] But the monuments of the Western provinces are, as a rule, singularly free from the grossness of early Egyptian zoolatry.[3] And there is hardly a hint of it in the famous picture of the initiation of Lucius in the *Metamorphoses* of Apuleius. In that fascinating scene, Isis is the universal mother, Nature, queen of the worlds of light and darkness, the eternal type of all lesser divinities. And on inscriptions she appears as the Power who "is all in all."[4] Whatever her special functions may be, goddess of the spring, or of the sailor on the sea, guardian of women in the pangs of motherhood, the "Queen of peace,"[5] guide and saviour of souls in the passage to the world beyond the tomb, she remains the Supreme Power, invoked by many names, with virtues and graces as various as her names. And Serapis, in the later theology, is not the president of any provincial territory in the universe. He is not the lord of sea or earth or air only; he is lord of all the elements, the dispenser of all good, the master of human life. It is thus that Aristides hails him after his rescue from the perils of the sea.[6] But although Serapis in many a monument is enthroned beside Jupiter, Queen Isis is also supreme in the world both of the living and the dead.

Yet, although there is a very decided tendency to monotheism in the Alexandrian religion, a tendency which appealed strongly to minds like Plutarch, it did not succeed in altogether breaking with polytheism and its attendant superstitions. The attempted alliance of religion and philosophy was far from complete. Philosophy, indeed, had substituted abstract theory for the poetry of legend. It struggled hard to assert the essential unity of the Divine nature. And Plutarch, in his treatise on Isis, declares that God is one and the same in all lands under whatever names He may be worshipped.[7] But the

[1] Apul. *Met.* xi. c. 11, attollens canis cervices arduas Anubis; cf. Juv. vi. 534; Plut. *De Is.* c. 44; Tertull. *Apol.* 6; *Ad Nat.* ii. 8.

[2] Mau, *Pompeii*, p. 175.

[3] Lafaye, p. 106, 7.

[4] *Or.* 1871.

[5] On a Dacian inscription, *C.I.L.* iii. 1590, Placidae Reginae.

[6] Baumgart, *Ael. Aristides Repräsent. der Soph. Rhet. des zweit. Jahr.* p. 91; cf. Hadrian's letter to Servianus, Vopisc. *Vit. Saturn.* c. 8.

[7] Plut. *De Is.* c. 66, 79.

treatise shows at the same time how vague and unsettled still was the theology of Alexandria, and how hard it found the task of wedding Platonism to the haunting tradition of old idolatry. Physics, metaphysics, etymology, are all employed with infinite ingenuity to recover the secret meaning which it is assumed that ancient wisdom had veiled under the forms of legend. But arbitrary fancy plays far too large a part in these random guesses, and system there is none, to bridge the gulf between the Platonist eclectic and the superstitious masses. Isis worship was in practice linked with all the reigning superstitions, with divination, magic, astrology, oneiromancy. Manetho, who was one of the founders of the worship of Serapis, wrote a treatise for the Greek world on the influence of the stars on human destiny.[1] Egyptian astrologists were always in great demand. The emperors Otho and M. Aurelius carried them in their train.[2] Many Roman ladies in sickness would not take food or medicine till the safe hour had been determined by inspecting the Petosiris.[3] The Isiac devotee was an enthusiastic believer in dreams sent by his favourite deities. On many inscriptions the record may be read of these warnings of the night.[4] In the syncretism of the time, Serapis came to be identified with the Greek god of healing, and patients sleeping in Egyptian temples received in dreams inspired prescriptions for their maladies.[5] Sometimes the deity vouchsafed to confer miraculous powers of cure on a worshipper. The sceptical good sense of Vespasian was persuaded by medical courtiers at Alexandria to try the effect of his touch on the blind and paralytic, who had a divine monition to seek the aid of the emperor.[6] The cultivated Aristides had a firm faith in these heaven-sent messages He even believed that Serapis could call back the dead to life.[7]

Yet Aristides, in his prose hymn to Serapis, gives us a glimpse of the better side of that religion. After all, the superstitions which clustered round it were the universal

[1] Lafaye, p. 101.

[2] Tac. *Hist.* i. 23; D. Cass. lxxi. 8, *καὶ γάρ τοι λόγος ἔχει Ἀρνοῦφίν τινα μάγον Αἰγύπτιον συνόντα τῷ Μάρκῳ κτλ.*

[3] Juv. vi. 580.

[4] *Or.* 1882, ex visu; *C.I.L.* vi. 346, 572; v. 484.

[5] Cic. *De Div.* i. 58, 132; Diod. i. 25; Aristid. *Or. Sacr.* iii. p. 319 (Jebb).

[6] Tac. *Hist.* iv. 81, monitu Serapidis, etc.

[7] Lafaye, p. 104; Aristid. *Or. Sacr.* viii. 55.

beliefs of the age, prevalent among the most cultivated and the most ignorant. The question for the modern student is whether these Alexandrian worships provided real spiritual sustenance for their devotees. And, in spite of many appearances to the contrary, the impartial inquirer must come to the conclusion that the cult of the Egyptian deities, through its inner monotheism, its ideal of ascetic purity, its vision of a great judgment and a life to come, was a real advance on the popular religion of old Greece and Rome. Isis and Serapis, along with Mithra, were preparing the Western world for the religion which was to appease the long travail of humanity by a more perfect vision of the Divine. It is impossible for a modern man to realise the emotion which might be excited by a symbolism like that of Demeter, or Mithra, or Isis, with its roots in a gross heathen past. But no reader of Apuleius, Plutarch, or Philostratus should fail to realise the surging spiritual energy which, in the second and third centuries, was seeking for expression and appeasement. It struck into strange devious tracks, and often was deluded by phantasms of old superstition glorified by a new spirit. But let us remember the enduring strength of hereditary piety and ancient association, and, under its influence, the magical skill of the religious consciousness to maintain the link between widely severed generations, by purifying the grossness of the past and transforming things absurd and offensive into consecrated vehicles of high spiritual sentiment. No one, who has read in Apuleius the initiation of Lucius in the Isiac mysteries, can doubt that the effect on the votary was profound and elevating. Pious artistic skill was not wanting to heighten emotion in Isis worship, as it is not disdained in our Christian churches. But the prayer of thanksgiving offered by Lucius might, *mutatis mutandis,* be uttered by a new convert at a camp-meeting, or a Breton peasant after her first communion. It is the devout expression of the deep elementary religious feelings of awe and gratitude, humility and joy, boundless hope and trust. In the same tone, Aristides sings his prose canticle to Serapis. There is not a memory of the brute gods of the Nile. The Alexandrian god is now the equal or counterpart of Zeus, the lord of life and death, who cares for mortal men, who comforts, relieves, sustains. He is indeed a most awful power, yet one full of loving-kindness, tenderness, and mercy.[1] In Plutarch we reach perhaps an even more spiritual height. Osiris, who in old legend represented the Nile, or the coarse fructifying powers of nature, passes into the Eternal Love and Beauty, pure, passionless, remote from any region of change or death, unapproachable in His ethereal splendour, save, as in moments of inspired musing, we may faintly touch Him as in a dream.

In the *Metamorphoses* of Apuleius, the goddess who appears in a vision to Lucius promises that, when his mortal course is run, he shall find her illumining the Stygian gloom. And, next to the maternal love with which she embraced her votaries in this life, the great attraction of her cult was the promise of a blessed future, through sacramental grace, which she offered for the world to come. Serapis, too, is from the beginning a god of the under world, a "guide of souls," as he is also their judge at the Great Assize.[2] The Orphic lore, the mysteries of the Eleusinian goddesses and Dionysus, had for ages taught a dim doctrine of immortality, under the veil of legend, through the scenic effects of their dramatic mysteries. They first revealed to the Greek race that the life to come was the true life, for which the present was only a purgatorial preparation. They taught, in whatever rude fashion, that future beatitude could only be secured by a purification from the stains of time.[3] The doctrine may have been drawn from Egypt, and Egypt once more gave it fresh meaning and force. The Alexandrian worship came with a deeper faith and more impressive ritual, with dreams and monitory visions, with a mystic lore, and the ascetic preparation for the holy mysteries, with the final scene in the inner sanctuary, when the votary seemed borne far beyond the limits of space and time into ethereal distances.[4] The soul might, indeed, have to pass through many bodies and mortal lives before it reached the life eternal. But the motto of the Isiac faith, inscribed on many tombs, was εὐψύχει, "be of good courage,"

[1] Aristid. *Or. Sacr.* viii. 54, φιλανθρωπότατος γὰρ θεῶν καὶ φοβερώτατος αὐτός, κτλ.

[2] *Ib.* viii. 54, σωτὴρ αὐτὸς καὶ ψυχοπομπός, ἄγων εἰς φῶς καὶ πάλιν δεχόμενος κτλ.; Plew, *De Sarapide*, p. 30.

[3] Rohde, *Psyche*, ii. p. 126; cf. i. 286; Lobeck, *Aglaoph.* i. p. 239; Hardie, *Lectures on Classical Subjects*, pp. 56, 57. The Orphici laid more stress on the moral aspect of immortality than the priests of Eleusis did.

[4] Apul. *Met.* xi. c. 22.

"may Osiris give the water of refreshment."[1] Everywhere the lotus, image of immortality, in its calix opening at every dawn, appears on symbols of the worship. And Harpocrates, the god who has triumphed over death, appears as the child issuing from the mystic flower. The Roman practice of burning the dead might seem to separate for ever the fate of the body from the spirit, although it is really a question of more or less rapid resolution of the mortal frame into its original elements. But, as we have seen, the man of the early Empire became more and more anxious to preserve undisturbed the "handful of white dust" rescued from the pyre, and would invoke the wrath of Isis against the desecrator.[2] The great object of many of the colleges was to secure their humble members a niche in the *columbarium.* The Alexandrine faith in immortality, by the grace of Isis and Serapis, probably did not inquire too curiously into the manner of the resurrection.

Undoubtedly another secret of the popularity of the Egyptian worships lay in their impressive ritual, the separation of their clergy from the world, and in the comradeship of the guilds in which their votaries were enrolled. Apuleius has left us, in the initiation of Lucius at Cenchreae, and again at Rome, a priceless picture of the Isiac ritual. Everything in the ceremonial tends to kindle pious enthusiasm. Sophocles and Pindar had extolled the blessedness of those who had seen the mystic vision.[3] The experience of Lucius would seem to confirm the testimony of the Greek poets. When the goddess has promised him deliverance from brutish form, and pledged him to strict obedience, Lucius is inspired with the utmost ardour to join in "the holy warfare." He takes up his abode in the sacred precincts, he begs to be admitted to full communion. But the venerable pontiff requires him to await the sign of the divine will. Lucius continues in fasting and prayer till the sign at last comes; when it comes he hastens to the morning sacrifice. The scrolls, covered with symbols of ancient Egypt, are brought in, and then, before a crowd of the faithful, he is plunged in the sacred font. Returning to the temple, as he lies prostrate

[1] *C.I.G.* 6562, δοίη σοι ὁ Ὄσιρις τὸ ψυχρὸν ὕδωρ: cf. Plew, *De Sarap.* p. 31.

[2] *Or.* 1879.

[3] Pind. *Fr.*137 (Christ); Soph. *Fr.*753—ὡς τρὶς ὄλβιοι κεῖνοι βροτῶν οἳ ταῦτα δερχθέντες τέλη μόλωσ' ἐς Ἅιδου. Cf. *O.C.* 1051.

before the image of the goddess in prayer, he has whispered to him "the unutterable words." Ten days more are spent in strictest retreat and abstinence from pleasures of the flesh; and then came the crowning rite, the solemn vigil in the inner sanctuary. There, as at Eleusis, a vivid drama of a divine death and resurrection probably passed before his eyes, in flashing radiance and awful visions, amid gloom and the tones of weird music. But the tale of what he saw and heard could never be fully unfolded to mortal ear.

There indeed are some sordid and suspicious traits in the history of this worship. As in the case of the taurobolium,[1] the mysteries of Isis and Serapis could not be enjoyed without a considerable outlay. And Lucius found a difficulty in meeting the expense.[2] But, whether in heathendom or Christendom, a regular priesthood and an elaborate ritual cannot be supported without the offerings of the faithful. There has probably never been a religion in which the charge of venality has not been levelled against the priests. But Lucius finds here no stumbling-block. No material offering can repay the goodness and love of the goddess. He feels towards her not only reverence and gratitude, but the love of a son to a Divine mother. Ascetic isolation has produced the natural result of imaginative ecstasy and mystic exaltation. The long, quiet hours of rapt devotion before the sacred figure in the stillness of the shrine, the spectral visions of the supreme hour of revelation, made a profound impression on a soul which was deeply tainted by other visions of old-world sin.

The daily ritual of Isis, which seems to have been as regular and complicated as that of the Catholic Church, produced an immense effect on the Roman mind. Every day there were two solemn offices, at which white-robed, tonsured priests, with acolytes and assistants of every degree, officiated.[3] The morning litany and sacrifice was an impressive service. The crowd of worshippers thronged the space before the chapel at the early dawn. The priest, ascending by a hidden stair, drew apart the veil of the sanctuary,[4] and offered the holy image

[1] *C.I.L.* xii. 4321, ex stipe collata.

[2] Apul. *Met.* xi. c. 28 (813), veste ipsa mea quamvis parvula distracta sufficientem corrasi summulum; cf. Tertull. *Apol.* 13.

[3] Tibull. i. 3, 31, bisque die, resoluta comas, tibi dicere laudes Insignis turba debeat in Pharia.

[4] Apul. *Met.* xi. c. 20 (795), velis candentibus reductis.

to their adoration. He then made the round of the altars, reciting the litany, and sprinkling the holy water "from the secret spring." At two o'clock in the afternoon the passers by could hear from the temple in the Campus Martius the chant of vespers.[1] A fresco of Herculaneum gives us a picture of the service. It is the adoration of the holy water, representing in symbol the fructifying and deathless power of Osiris. A priest, standing before the holy place, raises breast high a sacred urn for the adoration of the crowd. The sacrifice is smoking on the altar, and two choirs are chanting to the accompaniment of the seistron and the flute.[2] Another fresco from Herculaneum exhibits a bearded, dark-skinned figure, crowned with the lotus, in the attitude of dancing before a throng of spectators to the sound of music. It is plausibly conjectured that we have here a pantomimic representation of the passion of Osiris and its joyful close.[3] There was much solemn pomp and striking scenic effect in this public ceremonial. But it is clear from Apuleius, that an important part of worship was also long silent meditation before the image of the goddess. The poets speak of devotees seated thus before the altar, and in the temple at Pompeii a bench has been found which, from its position, was probably occupied by such silent worshippers.[4]

The great festivals of the Egyptian worship were the blessing of the sacred vessel on the fifth of March, and the celebration of the quest and finding of Osiris in November. The anniversary of the death and rising again of the god was strictly observed by large numbers, especially among women. Pagan and Christian writers have alike ridiculed the theatrical grief and joy for a god so often found, so often lost.[5] The death of Osiris at the hands of Typhon, the rending of the divine form, and the dispersion of the lacerated remains, were passionately lamented in sympathy with the mourning Isis. With effusive grief the devotees beat their breasts and lacerated their arms, and followed in eager search. When on the

[1] Mart. x. 48, 1, nunciat octavam Phariae sua turba juvencae.

[2] Mau, *Pompeii*, pp. 171, 172.

[3] Lafaye, p. 115; *Catal.* No. 222.

[4] Mau, p. 171; Apul. *Met.* xi. c. 17 (791), intuitans deae specimen pristinos casus meos recordabar; Mart. ii. 14, 8.

[5] Lafaye, p. 126; Plut. *De Is. et Osir.* c. 39, *διὸ μηνὸς Ἀθὺρ ἀφανισθῆναι τὸν Ὄσιριν λέγουσιν, κτλ*: Juv. viii. 29; vi. 534; Ov. *Metam.* ix. 692, nunquamque satis quaesitus Osiris; Lucan, viii. 831, et quem tu plangens hominem testaris Osirim; Min. Fel. c. 21.

third day the god had been found and restored, the joyful event was hailed with extravagant gladness, and celebrated by a banquet of the initiated. For some of these holy days the rubrics prescribed a long preparation of fasting and ascetic restraint. But that a general strictness of life was not required of the Isiac votary, at least under the early Empire, may be inferred from the fact that the frail Cynthias and Delias in Propertius and Tibullus were among the most regular in ritual observance.[1] The festival of the holy vessel of Isis, which marked the opening of navigation, and received the benediction of the goddess, was, in the early Empire, observed with solemn pomp and enthusiasm by the coast towns of the Mediterranean. A brilliantly vivid description of such a scene at Cenchreae has been left by Apuleius. It was a great popular carnival, in which a long procession, masquerading in the most fantastic and various costumes, conducted the sacred ship to the shore. Women in white robes scattered flowers and perfumes along the way. A throng of both sexes bore torches and tapers, to symbolise the reign of the Mother of the stars. The music of flute and pipe meanwhile filled the air with sacred symphonies, and a band of youths in snow-white vestments chanted a hymn. Wave upon wave came the throng of those who had been admitted to full communion, all clad in linen, and the men marked with the tonsure. They were followed by the priests, each bearing some symbol of the many powers and virtues of the goddess, the boat-shaped lamp, the "altars of succour," the palm of gold, the wand of Mercury. In a pix were borne the holy mysteries, and, last of all, the most venerable symbol, a small urn of shining gold and adorned in subtle workmanship with figures of Egyptian legend.[2] This holy vase, containing the water of the sacred river, which was an emanation from Osiris,[3] closed the procession. Arrived at the margin of the sea, the chief priest consecrated the sacred vessel with solemn form and litany, and named it with the holy name. Adorned with gold and citrus wood and pictures of old legend, it spread its white sails to the breeze, and bore

[1] Ov. *Am.* i. 8, 74; iii. 9, 30; Prop. ii. 33, 3; Tibull. i. 3, 23.

[2] Apul. *Met.* xi. c. 11 (774-78); Réville, *Rel. unter den Sev.* p. 56.

[3] Plut. *De Is. et Osir.* c. 38, Νεῖλον Ὀσίριδος ἀπορροὴν . . . ἔχουσι.

into the distance the vows and offerings of the faithful for the safety of those upon the deep.

The oriental religions of the imperial period were distinguished from the native religion of Latium by the possession of a numerous and highly organised priesthood, and an intensely sacerdotal spirit.[1] In an age of growing religious faith, this characteristic gave them enormous power. The priest became a necessary medium of intercourse with God. It is also one of the many traits in the later paganism, which prepared and softened the transition to the reign of the mediaeval Church. It would be tedious and unprofitable to enumerate the various grades of the Isiac priesthood. There were high priests of conspicuous dignity, who were also called *prophetae*.[2] But ordinary priests could perform many of their functions.[3] There were interpreters of dreams, dressers and keepers of the sacred wardrobe of the goddess,[4] whose duties must have been onerous, if we may judge from the list of robes and jewels and sacred furniture preserved in inscriptions or recovered from the ruins of Isiac shrines.[5] It has been remarked that the roaming Visigoths in southern Gaul must have had a rare spoil if they had the fortune to light on one of the great temples of Isis. The scribe of the Pastophori, in Apuleius, is also an important officer. He summons the sacred convocation, and recites the "bidding prayer" for the Emperor and all subjects, in their several places and stations.[6] Music took a large part in the ritual; there was hymn-singing to the sound of flutes, harp, and cymbal; and the chanters and paeanists of Serapis formed an order by themselves.[7] The prayer which Lucius offers to the goddess, in Apuleius, has been arranged as a metrical litany.[8] Women often appear in inscriptions and in our texts as priestesses, and had a prominent place in all solemn ritual.[9] And it is evident that, with all its sacerdotalism, the worship gave full recognition to devout wor-

[1] Réville, p. 54; Lafaye, p. 130 sqq.

[2] *C.I.G.* 6006; Apul. *Met.* ii. c. 28 (159), propheta primarius, xi. c. 17 (788), sacerdos maximus. *Or. Henz.* 2305, C. Ruf. Volusianus pater ierofanta profata Isidos; 1878, 6666; *C.I.L.* x. 6445; xii. 410.

[3] Lafaye, p. 133.

[4] *C.I.L.* xii. 3061, Ornatrix fani Nemausi.

[5] Lafaye, p. 135.

[6] Apul. *Met.* xi. c. 17 (789).

[7] *Ib.* c. 9 (772), dicati Serapi tibicines.

[8] Lafaye, p. 138, n. 4.

[9] *Or. Henz.* 2355, 6385, 2309.

shippers of every degree and sex. All who are devoted to the service have their place and function. The initiated might even wear the tonsure in the ordinary lay life. To do this, indeed, needed some courage, in the face of Roman ridicule. But the religious were, from the earliest times in Greece and Italy, associated for mutual support in sacred guilds, designated by various names, Isiaci or Pastophori or Anubiaci. In the third century B.C., such societies are found in Ceos and Peiraeus.[1] On the walls of Pompeii they have left their appeals to the electors to vote on behalf of candidates for the aedileship.[2] They were organised on the usual lines of the ancient colleges, divided into decuries, with a director and a treasurer, a "father" or a "mother," or a patron at their head.[3] The Isiac guilds must have had a powerful influence in the diffusion of the religion of Alexandria. But they also were probably one cause of the suspicion so long entertained for that worship by the Republican government, and they only asserted their full strength in the second century, when the colleges in general received the tacit sanction of the emperors. That the emperors felt little fear of these foreign sacred corporations became clear when an emperor actually took the tonsure of Isis.[4]

The Isiac system was energetic and self-assertive, but it can hardly be called dangerous or revolutionary. It threw many of the old gods into the shade, but its syncretism also found a place for many of them. Its inner monotheism, after the fashion of those days, had open arms of charity for all the ancient gods. One of the priests of Isis might be called Iacchagogus or Mithra;[5] statues of Dionysus and Venus and Priapus stood in the court of the Isium at Pompeii.[6] The Isis of Apuleius proclaims her identity with nearly all the great powers of classical legend, and gathers them into herself. But Isis identifies only to conquer and absorb. And her priesthood formed an aggressive and powerful caste. The sacerdotal colleges of the Latin religion were never, except in

[1] Foucart, *Assoc. Religieuses*, p. 117; *Inscr.* 66, 240.

[2] Mau, p. 478, Cn. Helv. Sabinum aed. Isiaci rogant.

[3] Foucart, pp. 25–30; *Or. Henz.* 6029, 2313, mater sacrorum; *C.I.L.* vi. 2277; *Or.* 2308, patrono Sacr. Isidis; Apul. *Met.* xi. c. 30 (817).

[4] Lamprid. *Commod.* c. 9.

[5] Apul. *Met.* xi. c. 22 (800).

[6] Lafaye, pp. 189, 190; Mau, p. 169.

the case of the Vestals, separated from ordinary life. The highest pontificate was held by busy laymen, by consuls or emperors or great soldiers. After the performance of his part in some great rite, the Roman priest returned to his civic place and duties. And in Greece, in the third and second centuries B.C., even the Isiac priesthood was held only for a year, or even for a month; and the sacred processions at one time needed the authorisation of the local council at Samos.[1] But when we come to the days of Apuleius, all this is changed. The chief priest at Cenchreae is evidently a great ecclesiastic, bearing the sacred Eastern name of Mithra.[2] He has given up ordinary civic life, and has probably abandoned his Greek name to take a new name "in religion." Every day two solemn services at least have to be performed in the temple, besides the private direction of souls, which had evidently become a regular part of the priestly functions. Attached to the great temples, and close to the altar, there is a "clergy house" where the ministers are lodged. It is called the Pastophorion, and its chambers have been traced in the débris of the temple at Pompeii.[3] One of these presbyteries was the scene of the seduction which convulsed the religious world in the reign of Tiberius, and which sent so many pious exiles to the solitudes of Sardinia. The ministers of Isis and Serapis are marked off by the tonsure and the Isiac habit, which meet us in the pages of poets from Tibullus to Juvenal,[4] and in the frescoes of Pompeii and Herculaneum. The abstinence, which was required as a preparation for communion in ordinary votaries, was a lifelong obligation on the priest. The use of woollen garments, of wine, pork, fish, and certain vegetables, was absolutely forbidden to them.[5] Chastity was essential in the celebrant of the holy mysteries, and even Tertullian holds up the priests of Isis as a reproachful example of continence to professing followers of Christ. The priesthood is no longer a secondary concern; it absorbs a man's

[1] Lafaye, p. 149.

[2] Apul. *Met.* xi. c. 22 (800), Mithram illum suum sacerdotem praecipuum, divino quodam stellarum consortio ut aiebat mihi conjunctum, sacrorum ministrum decernit.

[3] Lafaye, pp. 151, 186; Mau, *Pompeii*, p. 174.

[4] Tibull. i. 3, 30; Mart. xii. 29; Juv. vi. 526; Suet. *Otho*, 12.

[5] Plut. *De Is.* c. 4, 8, 32.

whole life, sets him apart within the sanctuary as the dispenser of sacred privileges, with the awful power of revealing the mystery of eternity, and preparing souls to meet the great ordeal.

It does not need much imagination to understand the fascination of Isis and Serapis foı a people who had outgrown a severe and sober, but an uninspiring faith. They came to the West at the crisis of a great spiritual and political revolution, with the charm of foreign mystery and the immemorial antiquity of a land whose annals ran back to ages long before Rome and Athens were even villages. But with antique charm, the religion combined the moral and spiritual ideas of generations which had outgrown the gross symbolism of Nature worship. The annual festivals might preserve the memory of the myth, which in its grossness and brutal tragedy once pictured the fructifying influence of the mysterious river on the lands which awaited his visitations, or the waning force of vegetative power and solar warmth. But Serapis, the new god of the Ptolemies, became the lord of life and death, the guide and saviour of souls, the great judge of all in the other world, an awful power, yet more inclined to mercy than to judgment.[1] And Isis rose to equally boundless sway, and one of greater tenderness. Powers above and powers below alike wait on her will: she treads Tartarus under her feet, and yet she embraces all, and specially the weak and miserable, in the arms of her charity.[2] Above all, she has the secret of the unseen world, and can lighten for her worshipper the Stygian gloom. But the Isiac, like the Orphic revelation, while it gave a blessed promise for the life to come, attached grave conditions to the pledge. In this brief time of probation, the soul must prepare itself under ghostly guidance for the great trial. Sacrament and mystery lent their aid to fortify the worshipper in the face of death, but, to derive their full virtue, he must exercise himself in temperance, abjure the pleasures of the senses, and purify himself for the vision of God.[3] The sacred ritual of the Egyptian might captivate the senses and imagination by its pomp and music, its steaming altars, and many-coloured symbolism. But in the stillness of the sanctuary the worshipper was trained to find his moments

[1] Aristid. *Or. Sacr.* xiii. p. 54. [2] Apul. *Met.* xi. c. 24. [3] *Ib.*

of purest and most exalted devotion in silent meditation before the Queen of heaven and the shades. The lonely, the weak, and the desolate found in the holy guilds succour and consolation, with a place in the ritual of her solemn seasons, which bound each to each in the love of a Divine Mother.

CHAPTER VI

THE RELIGION OF MITHRA

Of all the oriental religions which attracted the devotion of the West in the last three centuries of the Empire, that of Mithra was the most powerful. It is also the system which for various reasons has the greatest interest for the modern student. It is perhaps the highest and most striking example of the last efforts of paganism to reconcile itself to the great moral and spiritual movement which was setting steadily, and with growing momentum, towards purer conceptions of God, of man's relations to Him, and of the life to come. It is also the greatest effort of syncretism to absorb, without extinguishing, the gods of the classic pantheon in a cult which was almost monotheistic, to transform old forms of nature worship and cosmic symbolism into a system which should provide at once some form of moral discipline and real satisfaction for spiritual wants. In this effort, Mithraism was not so much impeded by a heritage of coarse legend as the worships of Pessinus and Alexandria. It was indeed sprung from the same order of religious thought as they. It could never detach itself from its source as a cult of the powers of nature.[1] But the worship of the Sun, with which Mithra was inseparably connected, was the purest and most natural form of devotion, if elemental powers were to be worshipped at all. And heathendom tended more and more under the Empire to fix its devotion on the source of all light and life. The Sun was to Plato the highest material symbol of the Infinite Good. Neo-Pythagoreanism and Neo-Platonism regarded him as the sacred

[1] Cumont, *Monuments Relatifs aux Mystères de Mithra*, Intr. pp. 309, 310.

image of the power beyond human ken.[1] "Before religion," it has been said, "had reached the point of proclaiming that God must be sought in the realm of the ideal and the absolute, outside the world of sense, the one rational and scientific cult, was that of the Sun."[2] Heliolatry also harmonised with absolutism in the State, as the old Persian kings and their imitators, the emperors of the third century, clearly perceived. The great temple of the Sun, which Aurelian, the son of a priestess of the deity, founded in the Campus Martius, with its high pontiffs and stately ritual, did honour not only to the great lord of the heavenly spheres, but to the monarch who was the august image of his power upon earth and who was endued with his special grace.[3] The power of Mithra in the fourth century lay in the fact that, while it was tender and tolerant to the old national worships, and never broke with the inner spirit of heathenism, it created an all-embracing system which rose above all national barriers, which satisfied the philosophic thought of the age in its mysticism, and gave comfort and a hope of immortality through its sacraments.

Mithra was one of the most ancient and venerable objects of pagan devotion, as he was one of the last to be dethroned. In faint outline he can be traced to the cradle of the Aryan race.[4] In the Vedas he is a god of light, and, as the god of truth, who hates all falsehood, he has the germ of that moral character which grew into a great force in the last age of his worship in the West. In the Avestas, the sacred books of the religion of Iran, which, however late their redaction, still enshrine a very ancient creed, Mithra has the same well-defined personality. He is the radiant god who seems to emerge from the rocky summits of eastern mountains at dawn, who careers through heaven with a team of four white horses; yet he is not sun or moon or any star, but a spirit of light, ever wakeful, watching with a thousand eyes, whom nothing can escape and nothing deceive.[5] And so, while he gives warmth and increase to the earth, and health and wealth to men, he is also from the beginning a moral power. He confers wisdom

[1] Zeller, *Phil. der Griech.* iii. 2, p. 101; cf. Macrob. *Sat.* i. 17; Philostr. *Apoll. Tyan.* ii. 38; vi. 10, § 1; M. Aurel. xi. 27.

[2] Cumont, Intr. p. 336; Dieterich, *Eine Mithrasliturgie*, p. 197.

[3] Flav. Vop. *Aurelian*, c. 36, 39.

[4] Cumont, Intr. p. 223 sq.; Gasquet, *Le Culte de Mithra*, p. 16 sq.

[5] Cumont, Intr. p. 225.

and honour and a clear conscience and concord. He wages a truceless war with the evil powers of darkness, and guards his faithful soldiers against the craft of the enemy. He is the friend and consoler of the poor; he is the mediator between earth and heaven; he is the lord of the world to come.[1] But his place in the Zoroastrian hierarchy was not always equally high. At one time he was only one of the *yazatas*, who were created by the supreme Ormuzd.[2] But Mithra has still the attributes of guardian and saviour; he is approached with sacrifice, libation, ablution, and litany, as in the latest days of his power in the West. And again a higher place is given to him; he is the vicegerent of the remote, ineffable Ormuzd, the mediator through whom the supreme power crushes evil demons, and wages war with Ahriman; he is invoked in the same prayers side by side with the Supreme. The Great Kings, especially the later, regard Mithra as their special guardian, swear by him in their most solemn oaths,[3] and call upon him in the hour of battle. If he was the god of the humble and afflicted, he was also the god of the prince and warrior noble, and so we shall find him at the end.

The Persian conquest of Babylon had lasting effects on the religion of Mithra. There he encountered a sacerdotal system which had its roots in an immemorial civilisation. The conquerors, as so often happens, were to some extent subdued by the vanquished.[4] Syncretism set in; the deities of the two races were reconciled and identified. The magical arts and the astrolatry of the valley of the Euphrates imposed themselves on the purer Mazdean faith, and never relaxed their hold, although they failed to check its development as a moral system. Ormuzd was confounded with Bel, Mithra with Shamash or the Sun-god. The astral and solar lore, the faith in mystic numbers, which had been cultivated in Babylonia through many generations, took its place in the theology of Mithra, and they have left their mark in many a chapel on the Danube and the Rhine. Yet Mithra, identified with the Sun at Babylon, was never absorbed in the cult of the solar deity in the West.[5] On many of the later

[1] Gasquet, p. 20.

[2] Cumont, Intr. p. 226 sqq.

[3] Xen. *Cyrop.* vii. 5, 53; *Oecon.* iv. § 24.

[4] Cumont, Intr. p. 231; Gasquet, p. 21 sqq.

[5] Donsbach, *Die räumliche Verbreitung des Mithrasdientes*, p. 5.

inscriptions Mithra and the Sun are mentioned side by side as equals and allies. Yet the connection of Mithra with Babylon is never forgotten either by Greeks or Romans. Claudian connects him with the mysteries of Bel.[1] The priest who, with many weird rites, in a waste sunless spot beside the Tigris, conducts Menippus to the underworld, wears the dress of Media, and bears the name Mithrobarzanes.[2]

With the destruction of the Persian empire and the diffusion of Magian influence in Asia Minor, the worship arrived at its last stage before entering on the conquest of the West. The monarchs of Pontus, Armenia, Cappadocia, and Commagene, who claimed descent from the Achaemenids, were politic or enthusiastic votaries of the religious traditions of Iran.[3] While they reverenced Ormuzd and Anaitis, Mithra was their special patron, as he was to Artaxerxes.[4] Mithra's name appears constantly in the names of royal houses, such as Mithradates and Mithrobarzanes. The inscription on the tomb of Antiochus of Commagene, who boasted of his descent from Darius the son of Hystaspes, records the endowment of solemn Persian rites, and combines the names of Ormuzd and Zeus, of Apollo and Mithra.[5] In the submergence of national barriers which followed the fall of the Persian monarchy, and under the influence of Greek philosophy, that process of syncretism began in Asia Minor which was destined to produce such momentous results in the third and fourth centuries. But the Mazdean faith, strong in its associations with the ancient sources of spiritual enlightenment in the East, never succumbed to the western paganism. The classical gods might be admitted to the Mazdean heaven; Zeus might be confounded with Ormuzd; Anaitis might find an analogue in Artemis Tauropolus. But the ancient name of Mithra was never profaned in the liturgy by any translation.[6] It was chiefly perhaps in Phrygia and Lydia that alien worships produced a lasting effect in modifying the Persian theology. The pure morality of the Mithraist creed might seem to have little in common with the orgies of the devotees of Attis and the Great Mother. But religious sentiment has a miraculous power both to

[1] *De Laud. Stilich.* i. 62.
[2] Luc. *Menippus*, cc. 6–9.
[3] Cumont, Intr. p. 232.
[4] *v.* Cumont, *Inscr. Orient.* i. 2, 3.
[5] Id. *Inscr. Grecques*, i.
[6] Cumont, Intr. p. 236.

reject and to transmute. The costume and Phrygian cap of Attis appear on all the monuments of Mithra to the end. And, although it is a subject of debate, the taurobolium, that baptism of blood which was the most impressive rite of the later paganism, was, in all probability, early borrowed by Mithra from the ritual of Phrygia.[1] The pine, the emblem of immortality, which is so prominent in the scenes of mourning for Attis,[2] also has a place in the sculptured remains of the Persian chapels. And the title Menotyrannus, a title of Attis, which is given to the Persian god on many slabs, recalls his passage through the same region.[3] But Greek art had a more powerful and enduring effect on the future of Mithra than any of these accretions. Probably the ancient Persian faith recoiled from any material image of its divine powers,[4] although here also Assyria may have corrupted its purity. But when Hellenic imagination began to play around the Mazdean gods, the result was certain. The victorious Mithra was clothed with human form, and his legend was fixed for ever by some nameless Pergamene artist, who drew his inspiration from the "steer-slaying Victory" of Athens.[5] The group in which the youthful hero, his mantle blown back by the wind, with a Phrygian cap upon his head, kneels on the shoulder of the bull, as he buries his poniard in its throat, was for four centuries reproduced in countless chapels from the mouth of the Danube to the Solway. That symbolic scene, conveying so many meanings in its hieratic rigidity, became to the pious Mithraist what the image of the Divine Figure on the Cross has been for so many centuries to the devout Catholic.

The revelation of the spread of Mithra worship in the Roman Empire is one of the greatest triumphs of modern archaeology. Only faint notices of the cult are found in Herodotus, Xenophon, and Strabo.[6] Quintus Curtius knew the Persian god as the soldier's special patron, inspiring courage in battle.[7] From the verses in the *Thebaid* of Statius we

[1] Gasquet, pp. 31 and 75; Réville, *Rel. unter den Sev.* p. 93; Goehler, *De Matris Mag. Cultu*, p. 55; but cf. Cumont, Intr. pp. 334-5.

[2] Gasquet, p. 31.

[3] *C.I.L.* vi. 508, 511; cf. Cumont, Intr. p. 235.

[4] Strab. xv. 3, § 13 (732), Πέρσαι τοίνυν ἀγάλματα μὲν καὶ βωμοὺς οὐχ ἱδρύονται . . . τιμῶσι δὲ καὶ Ἥλιον ὃν καλοῦσι Μίθραν, κτλ.

[5] Cumont, Intr. pp. 181, 237.

[6] Herod. i. 131; Xen. *Cyrop.* vii. 5, 53; Strab. *l.c.*

[7] Q. Curt. iv. 13, § 48.

may conclude that he knew something of the service in Mithra's grottoes, and that he had seen the figure of the "bull slaying" god.[1] Plutarch knows Mithra as the mediator between Ormuzd and Ahriman.[2] Lucian had probably seen the rites in his native Samosata; he knew the figure with the candys and tiara, and, from the sneer at the god's ignorance of Greek, he may perhaps have heard the old Mazdean litany.[3] But he had probably little notion of the hold which Mithra had already obtained on the farthest regions of the West. Still less had he any prevision of his great destiny in the third and fourth centuries. Literature, down to the Antonine age, teaches us little of the character and strength of the worship. Without votive inscriptions and the many ruins of his chapels, along with the indignant, yet anxious, invective of the Christian apologists, we should never have known how near the Persian god came to justifying his title of the "Unconquered."

It is impossible to fix the precise date when the worship of Mithra first crossed the Aegean. The silence of inscriptions must not indeed be taken as proving that he had no devotees in Italy before the Flavian age. A famous passage in Plutarch's life of Pompey would seem to refer the first appearance of the worship in the West to the conquest of the pirates of Cilicia by Pompey, in 70 B.C.[4] A religion of the alien and the slave may well have been long domiciled in Italy before it attracted general notice. And there may have been humble worshippers of Mithra at Rome or Puteoli even in the days of Julius Caesar. The Mithraist inscription of the time of Tiberius is now admitted to be a forgery.[5] But from his reign may probably be dated the first serious inroads of the cult. Under Tiberius, Cappadocia was incorporated in the Empire, and Pontus under Nero; Commagene, the home of Jupiter Dolichenus, who was a firm ally of Mithra, was finally absorbed in the reign of Vespasian.[6] The official organisation of these districts, and the constant intercourse established between central Asia Minor and the capital, must have opened many channels for the importation of new forms

[1] Stat. *Theb.* i. 717; cf. Cumont, *Textes*, p. 47.

[2] Plut. *De Is. et Osir.* c. 46.

[3] Luc. *Deor. Concil.* c. 9; *Menippus*, c. 6 sqq.; *Jup. Trag.* c. 8.

[4] Plut. *Pomp.* c. 24.

[5] *Or. Henz.* 5844.

[6] Cumont, Intr. p. 243, n. 3; Tac. *Ann.* ii. 42; D. Cass. lvii. 17; Suet. *Vesp.* c. 8.

of devotion from the East. Almost in the very year in which Statius was penning his verses about Mithra in the *Thebaid*, a freedman of the Flavian house erected a tablet to the god on the Esquiline,[1] and soldiers of the East carried his mysteries to the camps on the Danube. The 15th Legion, which had fought under Corbulo against the Parthians, and taken part in the conquest of Palestine in 70 A.D., in the first years of the reign of Vespasian, established the worship of Mithra at Carnuntum in Pannonia, which became henceforth the sacred city of Mithra in the West.[2] In 102 A.D. a marble group was dedicated by the slave of a praetorian prefect of Trajan.[3] It is probable that at Ostia we have records of the cult from the year 162.[4] The Mithraeum, found under the church of S. Clement at Rome, has yielded an inscription of the last years of Antoninus Pius. That emperor erected a temple to Mithra at Ostia.[5] Rome and Ostia were probably the earliest points in Italy invaded by the Persian worship. All the conditions were favourable to an early and rapid propagation of the cult in the capital of the world. Soldiers from the East would be serving in the garrison, or settled after their release from service. Eastern slaves swarmed in all the great houses, including that of the emperor. A large proportion of the dedications are made by men of servile origin, and the very name of the dedicator would often be enough to indicate his nationality. More than 100 inscriptions, more than 75 pieces of Mithraist sculpture, with the ruins of many chapels of the god, attest his powerful influence at Rome.[6] Ostia which, since the reconstruction of Trajan, had overshadowed Puteoli, was hospitable to all alien rites.[7] The port had at least four temples of Mithra in the second century, and it is significant of the alliance between the two worships, that a Mithraeum there was built close to a shrine of the Great Mother,[8] and that members of the college of the Dendrophori sometimes made offerings and dedications to Mithra.[9]

[1] *C.I.L.* vi. 732. On the date of the *Thebaid*, cf. Teuffel, *Rom. Lit.* § 316, n. 3.

[2] Cumont, Intr. p. 253; cf. Tac. *Ann.* xiii. 35.

[3] *C.I.L.* vi. 718, A.D. 102.

[4] Cumont, Intr. p. 265, *Inscr.* No. 133.

[5] Réville, p. 81.

[6] Cumont, Intr. p. 274, n. 6.

[7] *Ib.* p. 275; Donsbach, pp. 15–17.

[8] Cumont, p. 265, n. 4; cf. p. 333.

[9] Id. *Inscr.*; *C.I.L.* vi. 510; *Or. Henz.* 6040.

The remains at Ostia disclose some other indications of the prevailing syncretism. The Roman Sylvanus has a niche in one Mithraeum, and, in another, Saturn and Jupiter, Mars, Mercury and Venus, are figured beside the purely Eastern symbols of the planets and the signs of the zodiac.[1]

The inner secret of that rapid propaganda we shall never fully know. But we can discover with tolerable certainty the kind of people who carried the gospel of Mithra to the most remote parts of the western world. The soldiers were his most zealous missionaries.[2] Drafted from Cappadocia or Commagene, and quartered, far from his home, in a camp on the Danube or in the Black Forest, the legionary clung to the worship of his native East, and was eager to admit his comrades to fellowship in its rites. The appearance of Mithraism in certain places can be traced directly to the quartering of a legion which had been recruited from the countries which were the original home of the worship. Officers of eastern birth on promotion passed into other corps, and extended the influence of the East.[3] Centurions retiring from active service became apostles of the movement in the places where they settled. Syrian merchants, who were still found at Orleans in the time of the Merovingians, with all the fanaticism of their race popularised their native worships in the ports of Italy, Gaul, along the coasts of the Adriatic, and among the centres of commerce on the Danube or the Rhine.[4] The civil servants of the emperor, clerks and commissaries of every degree, procurators and agents of great estates, who were often men of servile origin, have left many traces of their zeal in spreading the Persian worship both throughout Italy and in countries north of the Alps.[5] The slave class probably did as much for the glory of Mithra as any other.[6] It was largely drawn from Cappadocia, Pontus, and Phrygia, those regions where the religion of Mithra had taken deep root before it passed into Europe. And, like the Christian, the religion of Mithra was, at the outset of its career, a religion of the poor and humble. It was only in the second century that it achieved the conquest of the court and the educated classes. It was probably through slaves that

1 Donsbach, p. 17.
2 Cumont, Intr. p. 246 sq.
3 *Ib.* p. 258, n. 8; cf. *Or. Henz.* 5855, 1916, 1917, 1922.
4 Cumont, Intr. p. 263.
5 *C.I.L.* iii. 3960, 4797, 5620, 4802; vi. 721.
6 Cumont, Intr. p. 265.

it found its way into remote corners of Apulia, Lucania, or Etruria.[1]

The stages in the spread of the Mithraist rites throughout Italy cannot be clearly traced. But in the second century the cult was established not only in Campania, Capreae, and Ischia, but in lonely country places in Southern Italy.[2] It had spread to a circle of towns around Rome—Lanuvium, Alba, Velitrae, Labici, and Praeneste.[3] Borne by traders, imperial officers or slaves, it followed the line of the great roads to the north. Thus we can trace its march along the Via Cassia through Etruria, at Volsinii, Arretium, and Florence.[4] It arrived at Pisa probably by sea. Along the Flaminian Way, it may be followed through Interamna, Spoletium, and Sentinum to Bononia. At Nersae, in the Aequian territory, the cult must have been of some antiquity in 172 A.D.[5] For, in that year the treasurer of the town, a man probably of the slave class, restored a chapel which had fallen into ruins. The roll of the patrons of a Mithraist society at Sentinum has come down to us, with the names of slaves or freedmen among its members.[6] In Gallia Cisalpina the traces of Mithra are less frequent. Milan, already growing to its great destiny in the fourth century, and Aquileia, are the chief seats of the Persian cult. Aquileia has yielded a large number of inscriptions. From its situation at the mouth of the Po, as the great *entrepôt* for the trade between the Adriatic and the Danubian provinces, it must have powerfully stimulated the diffusion of the worship.[7] It is curious, however, that the passes of the Alps have yielded richer booty to the investigator in this field than the plains of Lombardy. In the mountain valleys leading to Rhaetia and Noricum, as well as in those above the Italian lakes, many relics of this far-spreading religion have been given to the light.[8] A temple of Mithra has been discovered near Trent, in the valley of the Adige. In the Tyrol and Carinthia sacred grottoes, buried among woods and rocks, have disclosed bas-reliefs, sculptured with the traditionary figures of

[1] Cf. Cumont, *Inscr.* 150, sagaris actor; cf. the list of the Cultores Mithrae, *C.I.L.* xi. 5737.

[2] Cumont, Intr. p. 268; Donsbach, p. 19.

[3] Cumont, Intr. p. 268.

[4] Donsbach, p. 19.

[5] *C.I.L.* ix. 4109, 4110.

[6] *Ib.* xi. 5737.

[7] Donsbach, p. 20; Cumont, Intr. p. 266.

[8] Cumont, Intr. p. 269.

Persian legend. They were probably frequented by the faithful down to the reign of Valentinian.[1] Throughout Noricum and Pannonia imperial functionaries or agents of private enterprise, procurators, clerks of the treasury, custom-house officers, or eastern freedmen and slaves, have left many traces of their devotion to the Persian god.[2] Thus, everywhere along the great roads which radiated from Aquileia to the markets or strong places upon the Danube, the votary of Mithra would find in the days of the Antonines many a shrine, stately or humble, where he could refresh his piety by the way.

The Greek provinces have yielded but few memorials of the worship of Mithra. But, from the mouth of the Danube to the north of England his triumphant march can be traced, with only a break here and there. He follows the line of the rivers or the great roads, through the frontier camps or the centres of Roman commerce. Firmly seated at Tomi and the ports of the Black Sea, Mithra has not left many traces, so far as exploration has gone, in Thrace and Macedonia.[3] Nor have the Moesias as yet contributed many monuments, although at Troesmis and Oescus, along the great military road, bas-reliefs and inscriptions have been brought to light.[4] Next to Pannonia and the territory of the Upper Rhine, Dacia was the province where Mithraism seems to have reached its greatest popularity in Europe.[5] In the year 107, after six desolating and often doubtful campaigns, Dacia was resettled and organised by Trajan.[6] Its depopulated fields were colonised with immense masses of men from all parts of the Roman world. Probably there has seldom been such a *colluvies gentium* assembled. And, among these alien settlers, there were many from Edessa, Palmyra, and those regions of the East where Mithra or his kindred deities had their earliest and most fervent worshippers.[7] In the capital of the province, Sarmizegetusa, an excavated Mithraeum has afforded fifty bas-reliefs and inscriptions.[8] The colony of Apulum can show the remains of at least four temples. And Potaissa and other places, with names strange to English ears, have enriched the museums.

[1] Cumont, *Mon.* 237, 239; *Inscr.* 408.

[2] *C.I.L.* iii. 3480, 3479, 4796, 4797, 5121.

[3] Donsbach, p. 21.

[4] Cumont, Intr. p. 249; Donsbach, p. 22.

[5] Cumont, Intr. p. 250.

[6] Eutrop. viii. 6.

[7] Cumont, Intr. p. 247, n. 6.

[8] *Ib.* p. 251, n. 3.

Pannonia abounds with interesting remains of Mithra, not only in the great seats of Roman power on the Danube, but in places far in the interior. And in this province can be distinctly traced not only the progress of the military propaganda, but the dates, with approximate accuracy, when the mysteries of Mithra were first introduced.[1] Aquincum and Carnuntum were the chief seats of the Persian worship on the Danube. In the former town, the god had at least five chapels in the third century. There were at least four in the territory of Carnuntum, one of them being closely connected with that of the allied deity, Jupiter Dolichenus of Commagene.[2] The original votaries of the reign of Vespasian had been contented with a rude grotto, partially formed by the configuration of the rocks, the intervals being filled in with masonry.[3] This structure in the third century was replaced by a more stately edifice at the expense of a Roman knight.[4] There can be little doubt that the spread of Mithraism in Pannonia was chiefly the work of two Legions, the II. Adjutrix and XV. Apollinaris, both largely recruited from Commagene or Cappadocia.[5] The bricks of a Mithraeum at Carnuntum bear the stamp of the 15th Legion, and the inscriptions contain several dedications by soldiers of the two corps.[6] The 15th Legion, which was quartered on the Danube in 71 or 72, had fought under Corbulo against the Parthians, and had borne a part in suppressing the Jewish revolt of 70 A.D. We may be sure that the gaps in its ranks were filled by eastern recruits.[7] The soldiers of other corps, such as the Legions XIII and XIV, Geminae Martiae, caught the religious enthusiasm, and took part in the erection of buildings and in monumental offerings.[8] It was probably through officers, transferred from the Danube, that the worship was introduced into the camp of Lambesi in Numidia. There is a tablet of the third century to Mithra in that camp, dedicated by a prefect of the 3rd Legion, who was born at Carnuntum.[9] In Noricum and Rhaetia, the military propaganda seems to have been less vigorous than in

[1] Cumont, Intr. pp. 252, 3.

[2] Id. *Mon.* No. 228; Intr. p. 253.

[3] Id. *Mon.* No. 225; Intr. p. 253.

[4] Id. *Inscr.* No. 368.

[5] Mommsen, *Rom. Prov.* ii. p. 63, n.

[6] *C.I.L.* iii. 4418, 4416; Donsbach, p. 25.

[7] Tac. *Ann.* 13, 35, habiti per Galatiam Cappadociamque dilectus.

[8] Cumont, *Mon.* No. 225.

[9] *C.I.L.* viii. 2675; Cagnat, p. 189.

Pannonia. But a corner of the former province was once guarded by a corps from Commagene, which has left traces of its presence in the name of a town on the Danube and in some monuments to Mithra.[1] In Rhaetia his remains are singularly scanty.[2] But when we come to the *Agri Decumates* and the region of the Upper Rhine, we find ourselves in a district once more teeming with relics of Mithra. Not only has this region given to the light the largest number of his chapels,[3] but the bas-reliefs found in their ruins surpass all others in their dimensions and the completeness of their symbolism. The tauroctonus group of Osterburken is regarded as the masterpiece of Mithraist art in its complex variety and the vivid and masterly skill of the execution.[4] Many of the German inscriptions to Mithra are offered by simple citizens. But, from the number dedicated by soldiers also, Cumont may be right in tracing the diffusion of the worship once more to military zeal. It is true, the legions quartered in Germany did not contain any considerable number of recruits from the East. But they were in constant communication with the camps upon the Danube, where oriental influences were strong. It is significant that the earliest inscription to Mithra yet found in Germany, of the year A.D. 148, is that of a centurion of the 8th Legion, which was quartered in Moesia from 47 till 69, and which during that time had frequent communications with the East. The legion was in 70 removed from Moesia to Upper Germany.[5] It is probable that, however it was introduced, the worship of Mithra may have found its way into the valley of the Neckar, and even to the Lower Rhine, before the end of the first century. Coins of Trajan have been found in the temple at Friedberg;[6] a series of coins from Vespasian to M. Aurelius has been recovered from a temple in the neighbourhood of Cologne.[7] From Cologne the line of conquest may be followed to Boulogne, the station of the British fleet. Thence the cult passed easily to London, which, in the time of Tacitus, was a centre of great commercial

[1] *C.I.L.* iii. 5650; Cumont, *Inscr.* No. 416; *Mon.* No. 238; cf. Donsbach, p. 26.

[2] Cumont, Intr. p. 255; Donsbach, p. 27.

[3] For the number and the sites *v.* Donsbach, p. 27.

[4] Cumont, *Mon.* No. 351.

[5] Id. *Inscr.* No. 423; Intr. p. 256, n. 2.

[6] Id. *Mon.* No. 248 (p. 359).

[7] *Ib.* No. 265 (p. 388).

activity.[1] The legions probably carried the worship to the great camps of Caerleon, Chester and York. At all the guard-posts of the great rampart of Hadrian, there were chapels of the eastern god, and the inscriptions show that the officers at this remote outpost of the Empire maintained a warm devotion to the religion of their native East.[2]

The regions of the western world on which Mithra, from whatever causes, seems to have made least impression were Western Gaul, Spain, and North Africa.[3] Syrian merchants, slaves, or soldiers, had established the worship at Lyons, Arles, and Narbonne. But Elusa is the only place in Aquitaine where traces of it have been found. In Spain, the legionaries carried it only to a few remote frontier posts in Asturia or Gallicia.[4] The African garrisons, recruited largely from the surrounding country, remained true to their native deities, and the few inscriptions to Mithra at great military strongholds, like Lambesi, are probably due to the devotion of some of the higher officers, who had been transferred to these distant quarters from Syria or the Danube.[5]

If we try to explain the fascination of this religion of central Asia for western minds, we must seek it partly in its theological system, partly in its ritual and clerical organisation, still more in its clear promise of a life beyond the grave. In these characteristics, Mithraism differed profoundly from Graeco-Roman paganism, and seemed, in the eyes of the Christian apologists, to be a deceptive imitation of the rites and doctrines of the Christian Church. Inspired with the tendency or ambition to gather many races into its fold, Mithraism was a compound of the influences of very different ages, and offered many footholds for the faith or superstition of the lands which it traversed in its march. It drew, from points widely severed in time and place, doctrine or symbolism or rite, from the ancient lands of the Aryan race, from the mountain homes of the Persians, from Babylon and Phrygia and Commagene, from the philosophy of Greece, and the mythologies of all the peoples among whom it came. Yet it

[1] Tac. *Ann.* 14, 33, Londinium . . . copia negotiatorum maxime celebre.

[2] Cumont, *Inscr.* Nos. 471–490; Donsbach, p. 29.

[3] Id. Intr. p. 259 n.

[4] *Ib.* p. 260; Donsbach, p. 30.

[5] Cumont, *l.c.*; cf. Cagnat, *L'Arm. rom. d'Afr.* p. 353, on the history and composition of the Legio III. Augusta.

never to the end ceased to be a Persian cult. In the Divine Comedy of Lucian, as it may be called, Mithra, even when he is admitted to Olympus, cannot speak in Greek.[1] His name is never disguised or translated. On many of his inscriptions the names of the old Mazdean pantheon, such as Ahriman, the power of evil, still figure.[2] The mystic beasts which are always present in the sacred scene of the tauroctonus, the lion, the dog, the snake, the scorpion, had all a hieratic meaning in Persian theology.[3] The cave, which was the immemorial sanctuary of the worship, amid all the mystic meanings attached to it by later Neo-Platonist speculation, carried the mind back to Zoroastrian symbolism.[4] The *petra genetrix*, which is figured on so many sacred slabs on the Danube and in Upper Germany, goes back to the very cradle of the worship.[5] The young god, emerging from the spires of rock, round which a serpent coils itself, is the first radiance of the upspringing sun, as on high, lonely peaks it flashes and broadens to the dawn. The great elemental powers, sun and moon, ocean, the winds and seasons, are generally grouped around the central piece, in forms borrowed from classic art.[6] Fire and water are always present; no chapel was without its fountain.[7] And the tradition of the astral lore of the Euphrates can be seen in the signs of the zodiac which encompass the sacred scene of mystic sacrifice in the chapels on the Upper Rhine.[8] The very letters of the name of Mithra, expanded into Meithras, according to S. Jerome, like the mystic word Abraxas, yielded to ingenious calculation the exact number of days in the year.[9] It is difficult for us to conceive how these frigid astronomical fancies should form a part in a religious system which undoubtedly from the beginning had a profound moral effect on its adherents. Yet it is well to remember that there was a time when the mystery of the stellar spaces, and the grandeur and beneficence of the sun, were the most awful and impressive things in human

[1] Luc. *Deor. Concil.* c. 9.

[2] Réville, p. 87.

[3] Cumont, Intr. p. 190; Gasquet, p. 70.

[4] Cumont, Intr. p. 56; Gasquet, p. 36.

[5] Cumont, *Inscr.* 441, 444; *Mon.* 213, 245, 252.

[6] *Ib.* 251 (p. 365); Intr. p. 92; cf. Herod. i. 131.

[7] Cumont, *Mon.* 246 (p. 348).

[8] Id. Intr. p. 109; *Mon.* 246, 247, 248, 251, 273.

[9] Donsbach, p. 6; Gasquet, p. 24; Dieterich, *Mithrasliturgie*, p. 146; S. Hieron. *Com. in Amos*, v. 9, 10.

experience. The cold scrutiny of the telescope has long since robbed the heavenly orbs of their mystic power over human destiny. Yet even now, a man who has not been imbued with the influence of modern science, may, on some calm, starlit summer night, travel back in imagination to the dreams of the early star-gazers on the Ganges or the Euphrates, and fancy that, in the far solitary splendour and ordered movement of those eternal fires, which shine so serene and pitiless on this small point in the universe, there may be forces to guide or signs to predict the course of mortal destiny. Nor was it an altogether unworthy dream, which floated before the minds of so many generations, that in those liquid depths of space, where, in the infinite distance, the radiance of widely-severed constellations blends into a luminous haze, might be the eternal abode of spirits who, after their sojourn in the flesh, have purged themselves of earthly taint.[1]

The relative influence of Babylon and ancient Iran in moulding the theology of Mithraism, has long been a subject of controversy. The opposing schools, represented by Lajard and Windischmann,[2] have been discredited or reconciled by saner methods of criticism, and wider archaeological knowledge. It is now seen that while Babylonia has left a deep impress on the creed of Mithra, yet the original Aryan or Persian elements still maintained their ascendency. Mithra, in his long journey, came under many influences; and he absorbed many alien ideas from the cults and art of the many lands through which he travelled. His tolerance, indeed, was one great secret of his power. But, while he absorbed, he assimilated and transmuted. He remained the god of Persia, while he gathered into his creed mystic elements that might appease the spiritual cravings of the western world.[3] His system came to represent the best theological expression of the long movement of pagan mysticism, which, beginning with the mythic names of Orpheus and Pythagoras, organised in the classic mysteries, elevated and glorified by the genius of Plato, ended, if it has ended, in the Neo-Platonic movement which offered a last resistance to the Christian church. The central ideas of that

[1] Macrob. *Som. Scip.* i. 15, § 10 sqq.

[2] Cumont, Intr. pp. 71, 72.

[3] Cf. Dieterich, *Mithrasliturgie*, pp. 150, 165, 202; Cumont, Intr. pp. 331, 336.

theory of life and death were presented to the neophyte in the mysteries of Mithra, and one of the last expounders of the Platonic creed, in the reign of Theodosius, had probably been initiated in one of the last chapels of the worship.[1] In that vision of human destiny, of the descent and ascent of the human soul, the old Orphic doctrine is united with the star-lore of the Euphrates. Travelling towards its future prison-house in the flesh, the spirit which leaves the presence of Ormuzd descends by the gate of Cancer, through the spheres of the seven planets, and in each acquires a new faculty appropriate to its earthly state. The Mithraist discipline and sacraments prepare it for the ascent after death. When the soul at last leaves its mortal prison, it has to submit to a great judgment in the presence of Mithra, and if it pass the ordeal, it may then return through the seven spheres, at each stage divesting itself of those passions or earthly powers, which it had taken on for a time in its downward journey.[2] Finally, through the remote gate of Capricorn, its sublimated essence will pass back again to ecstatic union with the Supreme. It is thus that the East and West, Orphic mysteries and Chaldaean astrology, combined to satisfy the craving for a moral faith and the vision of another world.

The religion of Mithra probably achieved its highest victory through an ethical theology, typified and made concrete to the average worshipper by an elaborate symbolism in rite and sculptured scene. But it had also a cosmic theology. Mithra, in virtue of his moral power, became in the end the central figure. But in nearly all his chapels can be discovered a divine hierarchy, in which, for ages, he did not hold the foremost rank. The highest place is given to Infinite Time, without sex or passions, or properly without even a name, although in order to bring him within the vulgar ken, he may be called Cronus or Saturn and imaged in stone as a lion, wrapped in the coils of a snake.[3] He is the author of life and death; he carries the keys of heaven, and, in his limitless sway, he is identified with the unbending power of Fate. Like other cosmic systems of the East,

[1] Gasquet, p. 104; cf. Macrob. *Som. Scip.* i. 12; Macrob. *Sat.* i. 17; cf. Lobeck, *Aglaoph.* ii. 933; Rohde, *Psyche*, ii. pp. 121, 402.

[2] Cumont, Intr. pp. 308, 309; cf. Macrob. *Som. Scip.* i. 12.

[3] Cumont, Intr. p. 294; *ib.* p. 75. But cf. Gasquet, p. 41.

the Mazdean explained the universe by a succession of emanations from the Infinite First Cause.[1] From his own essence, Cronus engendered Earth and Heaven, whom mythologers may call Jupiter and Juno, and they in turn give life to Ocean. Jupiter, as in classical mythology, succeeded to the power of Cronus, and gave to the world the Olympian deities, along with Fortune, Themis, and the Fates. In the hemisphere of gloom and evil, another order was engendered by Infinite Time, which is represented by Ahriman, or, in the fancy of more western lands, by Pluto and Hecate. The evil spirits, who are their progeny, like the Titans of Greek legend, have tried to storm Olympus, and been hurled back to the under world.[2] There they still retain their power to plague and corrupt the race of men; but, by means of incantation, and sacrifice, their malice may be turned aside. In this daemonology Mithraism joined hands with the new Platonism, of which Plutarch, as we have seen, was one of the earliest apostles, and the affinity between them continued to the last age of paganism.[3] But it was in its divinisation of the elemental powers and heavenly bodies that this religion probably obtained its most powerful hold on an age profoundly fatalist and superstitious. The strife of the four elements figures under animal symbolism on innumerable sculptures of the chapels of Mithra, around the image of the bull-slaying God.[4] The divine fire which sparkles in the stars, and diffuses the warmth of life in animal or plant, blazed perpetually on the altar of the crypt.[5] The sun and moon are seldom missing from these slabs. In the great masterpiece of Mithraic art at Osterburken, the two deities occupy opposite corners of the tablet.[6] The sun-god, with a cloak floating from his right shoulder, is urging his four-horse team up the steep of heaven, and over the car floats Phosphorus, as a naked boy, bearing a torch in each hand. On the opposite side, Selene, crowned with the crescent and erect in her car, is urging her team of oxen downwards towards the gloom. On another piece, also found in the heart of Germany, there is an impressive scene, in which Mithra and the Sun, arrayed in eastern costume, stand side by side over a

[1] Cumont, Intr. p. 295.
[2] *Ib.* p. 296.
[3] *Ib.* p. 301.
[4] Id. *Mon.* 251 (p. 365).
[5] Id. Intr. p. 297.
[6] Id. *Mon.* 246 (p. 349).

huge slaughtered bull. The sun god is handing to Mithra a bunch of grapes, which he receives with a gesture of admiration.[1]

The most popular, and the least wholesome, element, which Mithraism borrowed from Babylon, was the belief in planetary influence. The seven planets became the arbiters of human destiny, and their number acquired a hieratic significance.[2] The days of the week and the seven principal metals were consecrated to them. The various grades of initiation into the mysteries of Mithra found a correspondence in the intervals of the seven spheres.[3] The soul, in descending to its earthly tenement for a season, passes through their successive realms, and assumes appropriate faculties in each, just as, on its release and ascension, it divests itself of them, one by one, as it returns to the region of ethereal purity. But the astral doctrine, introduced into the system of Iran from Chaldaea, was a dangerous addition to the creed. It was a fatal heritage from ages of benumbing superstition, and, while it gave an immense impetus to the progress of the solar cult, it counterbalanced, and, to some extent, neutralised its more spiritual and salutary doctrines.[4] A co-ordinate evil power, side by side with the beneficent Creator and Preserver, and his revealer and mediator, a host of daemons, tempting to sin, as well as visiting men with calamity, an iron Fate at the centre of the Universe, whose inevitable decrees are at once indicated and executed by the position and motions of the planets—all this gloomy doctrine lay like a nightmare on the human mind for many ages, and gave birth to all sorts of evil arts to discover or avert or direct the pitiless forces which controlled the fate of man. This is the dark side of Mithra worship, and, in this evil tradition from Babylon, which partially overlaid the purer creed of Persia, we may find some explanation of the strange blending of dark superstition with moral earnestness which characterised the reaction of Julian, the votary of the Sun, and the patron of Maximus.

But, although the deification of the great elemental powers and the mingled charm and terror of astrology gave the religion of Mithra a powerful hold on the West, there were

[1] Cumont, *Mon.* 251 (p. 365).
[2] Id. Intr. p. 300; Gasquet, p. 62.
[3] Cumont, Intr. p. 316; cf. Gasquet, pp. 94, 95.
[4] Cumont, Intr. p. 301.

other and nobler elements in his system which cannot escape the candid enquirer. The old unmoral, external paganism no longer satisfied the spiritual wants of all men in the second century. It is true the day will probably never come when the religion of many will not begin and end in solemn, stately rite, consecrated to the imagination by ancient use, and captivating the sense by scrupulously ordered ceremonial. The ritualist and the puritan conception of worship will probably always exist side by side, for they represent two opposite conceptions of religion which can never entirely blend. And certainly in the days of M. Aurelius the placid satisfaction in a sumptuous sacrifice, at which every word of the ancient litany was rendered to the letter, was still profoundly felt by many, even by the philosophic emperor himself. But there were other ideas in the air. Men heard from wandering preachers that God required other offerings than the "blood of bulls and the ashes of a heifer," that the true worship was in the sacrifice of a purified spirit.[1] Platonist and Pythagorean, even when they might reverently handle the ancient symbolism of ritual, were teaching that communion with the Infinite Father was only possible to a soul emancipated from the tyranny of sense. Moreover, as we have seen, the new Platonism was striving to create some mediatorial power between the world of sense and the Infinite Spirit, transcending all old materialistic fancies of the Divine.[2] This Platonic daemonology, indeed, from the Christian point of view, was a very crude and imperfect attempt to bridge the gulf. And it had the graver fault that it was really a revival of the old mythology. Yet it was also an attempted reformation. It was an effort to introduce a moral influence into paganism. It was an effort to substitute for physical and naturalistic conceptions a moral theory of the government of the world. That was surely an immense advance in religious history, and foreshadowed the great revolution which was to launch the western world on a new spiritual career. The hosts of sister spirits, whom Maximus of Tyre imagines as surrounding and sustaining the life of men, involved in the darkness and sorrow of time, are

[1] Cf. Denis, *Idées Morales*, etc. ii. p. 248 sq. ; cf. Burgmann, *Seneca's Theologie*, p. 37 ; Sen. *Ep.* 95, 50 ; 31, § 11 ; Philostr. *Apoll. Tyan.* v. 25 ; Max. Tyr. *Diss.* viii. ; xiv. § 7, 8 ; xvi. § 9.

[2] *v.* supra, p. 426.

a conception strange to the old paganism. And the need of mediatorial sympathy, of a sympathetic link, however slight, with the dim, awful Power, ever receding into more remote and mysterious distances, was also connected with the need of some assurance, or fainter hope, of a life beyond the tomb. To that hope the old classical paganism afforded only slight and shadowy nutriment. Yet, from hundreds of sepulchral inscriptions the yearning, often darkened by a doubt, appeals with pathetic force. Apart, in fact, from the crowd of mere antiquarian formalists and lovers of spectacle, there were, we believe, a great mass who longed for some channel through which they might have the faintest touch of sympathy with the Infinite Spirit; for some promise, however veiled in enigmatic symbolism, that this poor, puzzling ineffectual life should not close impotently at death.

In all the Mazdean pantheon, it has been remarked, Mithra was the only divine figure that profoundly affected the religious imagination of Europe. Who can dare at this distance to pierce the mystery? But we may conjecture that the ascendency is partly due to his place as mediator in the Persian hierarchy, partly to the legends, emblazoned on so many slabs, of his miraculous and Herculean triumphs; but still more to the moral and sacramental support, and the sure hope of immortal life which he offered to his faithful worshippers. Mithra came as a deliverer from powers of evil and as a mediator between man and the remote Ormuzd. He bears the latter office in a double sense. In the cosmic system, as lord of light, he is also lord of the space between the heavenly ether and the mists of earth. As a solar deity, he is the central point among the planetary orbs.[1] In the ubiquitous group of the slaughtered bull, Mithra stands between the two Dadophori, Cautes and Cautopates, who form with him a sort of Trinity, and are said to be incarnations of him.[2] One of these figures in Mithraic sculpture always bears a torch erect, the other a torch turned downwards to the earth. They may have a double significance. They may figure the ascending light of dawn, and the last radiance of day as it sinks below the horizon. They may be taken to image the growth of solar strength to its midsummer triumphs, and its slow decline towards fading

[1] Cumont, Intr. p. 303. [2] *Ib.* pp. 207, 208.

autumn and the cold of winter. Or again, they may shadow forth the wider and more momentous processes of universal death and resurgent life. But Mithra also became a mediator in the moral sense, standing between Ormuzd and Ahriman, the powers of good and evil, as Plutarch conceives him.[1] He is the ever victorious champion, who defies and overthrows the malignant demons that beset the life of man; who, above all, gives the victory over the last foe of humanity.

The legend of Mithra in hymn or litany is almost entirely lost. But antiquarian ingenuity and cultivated sympathy have plausibly recovered some of its meanings from the many sculptural remains of his chapels. On the great monuments of Virunum, Mauls, Neuenheim, and Osterburken, can be seen the successive scenes of the hero's career. They begin with his miraculous birth from the "mother rock," which was familiar to Justin Martyr, S. Jerome, and many of the Fathers.[2] The dedications *petrae genetrici* abound along the Danube, and the sacred stone was an object of adoration in many chapels.[3] A youthful form, his head crowned with a Phrygian cap, a dagger in one hand, and a torch in the other, is pictured emerging from an opening rock, around which sometimes a serpent is coiled. Shepherds from the neighbouring mountain gaze in wonder at the divine birth, and presently come nearer to adore the youthful hero, and offer him the firstlings of their flocks and fields.[4] And again, a naked boy is seen screening himself from the violence of the wind in the shelter of a fig tree; he eats of its fruit and makes himself a garment from the leaves.[5] In another scene, the sacred figure appears in full eastern costume, armed with a bow from which he launches an arrow against a rock rising in front of him.[6] From the spot where the arrow strikes the stone, a fountain gushes forth, and the water is eagerly caught in his upturned palms by a form kneeling below. Then follow the famous scenes of the chase and slaughter of the mystic bull. At first the beast is seen borne in a skiff over an expanse of waters. Soon afterwards

[1] Plut. *De Is. et Osir.* c. 46.

[2] Firm. Matern. c. 20, alterius profani sacramenti signum est θεὸς ἐκ πέτρας, etc. Cf. S. Hieron. *Adv. Jov.* i. § 7; Just. Mart. *Dial. c. Tryph.* c. 70; Prud. *Cathem.* v. 9; Cumont, *Mon.* 199, 207.

[3] Id. Intr. p. 160.

[4] *Ib.* p. 162; *Mon.* 204.

[5] Id. Intr. p. 164.

[6] *Ib.* p. 165; *Mon.* 204 (p. 318), 235 (p. 338).

he is grazing quietly in a meadow, when Mithra comes upon the scene. In one monument the hero is carrying the bull upon his shoulders; in others he is borne upon the animal's back, grasping it by the horns. Or again, the bull is seen in full career with the hero's arms thrown around his neck. At last the bull succumbs to his rider's courage, and is dragged by the hind-legs, which are drawn over his captor's shoulders, into a cavern where the famous slaughter was enacted.[1] The young god, his mantle floating on the wind, kneels on the shoulder of the fallen beast, draws back its head with his left hand, while with the other he buries his dagger in its neck.[2] Below this scene are invariably sculptured the scorpion, the faithful dog, and the serpent lapping the flowing blood. The two Dadophori, silent representatives of the worlds of light and gloom, one on each side, are always calm watchers of the mystic scene. But the destruction of the bull was not a mere spectacle of death. It was followed by a miracle of fresh springing life and fertility, and, here and there, on the slabs are seen ears of corn shooting from the tail of the dying beast, or young plants and flowers springing up around.[3] His blood gives birth to the vine which yields the sacred juice consecrated in the mysteries. Thus, in spite of the scorpion and the serpent, symbols of the evil powers, who seek to wither and sterilise the sources of vitality, life is ever rising again from the body of death.[4]

Mithra's mysterious reconciliation with the Sun is figured in other groups.[5] Mithra, as usual, in eastern costume, has, kneeling before him, a youthful figure either naked or lightly clad. The god touches the head of the suppliant with some mysterious symbol, and the subject of the rite raises his hands in prayer. The mystic symbol is removed, and Mithra sets a radiant crown on the suppliant's head. This reconciliation of the two deities is a favourite subject. In the sculpture of Osterburken, they ratify their pact with solemn gestures before an altar. Their restored harmony is commemorated in even

[1] Cumont, Intr. p. 167 sq.; *Mon.* 253, 192, 204, 221.

[2] See the finest extant specimen from Osterburken; Cumont, *Mon.* 246; cf. the one at Heddernheim, *Mon.* 251.

[3] Cumont, Intr. p. 186 sq.; *Mon.* 104, 246.

[4] Gasquet, p. 70.

[5] Cumont, *Mon.* 191 (p. 312); 203 (p. 317); 242 (p. 342); 246 (p. 350); Intr. p. 172.

more solemn fashion. In one monument the two are reclining on a couch at a solemn agape, with a table before them bearing the sacred bread, which is marked with the cross, and both are in the act of raising the cup in their right hands.[1]

The legend of Mithra, thus faintly and doubtfully reconstructed from the sacred sculptures, in the absence of express tradition, must probably for ever remain somewhat of an enigma. It has been, since the third century, the battle-ground of ingenious interpreters. To enumerate and discuss these theories, many of them now discredited by archaeological research, is far beyond the scope of this work. It is clear that from the early Chaldaean magi, who, to some extent, imposed their system on Iranian legend, down to the Neo-Platonists, the god and his attendants were treated as the symbols of cosmic theory. The birth from the rock was the light of dawn breaking over serrated crests of eastern hills.[2] The cave, which was always piously perpetuated in the latest Mithraist architecture, was the solid vault of heaven, and the openings pierced in its roof were the stars shining through the celestial dome.[3] The fountain which rose in every chapel, the fire on the altar, the animals surrounding the bull, represent the powers of nature in their changes and conflict. The young archer, causing water to spring from the rock by a shot from his bow, marks the miraculous cessation of prehistoric dearth, as the bull leaping from a skiff perhaps commemorates a primaeval deluge. The slaying of the bull, the central scene of all, may go back to the exploits of the heroic pioneers of settled life, a Hercules or a Theseus, who tamed the savage wilderness to the uses of man. It had many meanings to different ages. To one occupied with the processes of nature, it may have symbolised the withering of the vegetative freshness of the world in mid-summer heats, yet with a promise of a coming spring. To another it may have meant a victory over evil spirits and powers of darkness.[4] Or it may, in the last days, have been the prototype of that sacramental cleansing which gave assurance of immortal life, and which seemed to the Fathers the mockery of a Diviner Sacrifice.

[1] Cumont, Intr. p. 175.
[2] Réville, p. 83.
[3] *Ib.* p. 89.
[4] Gasquet, p. 77.

There can be no doubt that Mithra and his exploits, in response to a great need, came to have a moral and spiritual meaning. From the earliest times, he is the mediator between good and evil powers; ever young, vigorous, and victorious in his struggles, the champion of truth and purity, the protector of the weak, the ever vigilant foe of the hosts of daemons who swarm round the life of man, the conqueror of death. His religion, in spite of its astrology, was not one of fatalist reverie; it was a religion of struggle and combat. In this aspect it was congenial to the virile Roman temperament, and, above all, to the temperament of the Roman soldier, at once the most superstitious and the most strenuous of men.[1] Who can tell what inspiration the young heroic figure, wearing an air of triumphant vigour even on the rudest slabs,[2] may have breathed into a worn old veteran, who kept ceaseless watch against the Germans in some lonely post on the Danube, when he spent a brief hour in the splendour of the brilliantly lighted crypt, and joined in the old Mazdean litany? Before him was the sacred group of the Tauroctonus, full of so many meanings to many lands and ages, but which, to his eyes, probably shed the light of victory over the perilous combats of time, and gave assurance of a larger hope. Suddenly, by the touch of an unseen hand, the plaque revolved,[3] and he had before him the solemn agape of the two deities in which they celebrated the peaceful close of their mystic conflict. And he went away, assured that his hero god was now enthroned on high, and watching over his faithful soldiers upon earth.[4] At the same time, he had seen around him the sacred symbols or images of all the great forces of nature, and of the fires of heaven which, in their motions and their effluences, could bring bane or happiness to men below. In the chapels of Mithra, all nature became divine and sacred, the bubbling spring, the fire on the cottage hearth, the wind that levelled the pine tree or bore the sailor on his voyage, the great eternal lights that brought seed-time and harvest and parted day from night, the ever-welling vital force in opening leaf and springing corn-ear, and birth of young creatures, triumphing in regular round over the

[1] Gasquet, p. 108.
[2] Cumont, *Mon.* 31, 35, 43.
[3] *Ib.* 251 (p. 364).
[4] Id. Intr. pp. 308, 309.

malignant forces which seem for a time to threaten decay and corruption. The "Unconquered Mithra" is thus the god of light and hope in this world and the next.[1]

The ancient world was craving for a promise of immortality. Mithraism strove to nurse the hope, but, like the contemporaneous Platonism and the more ancient Orphic lore, it linked it with moral responsibility and grave consequences. Votaries were taught that the soul descended by graduated fall from the Most High to dwell for a season in the prison of the flesh.[2] After death there is a great judgment, to decide the future destiny of each soul, according to the life which had been led on earth.[3] Spirits which have defiled themselves during life are dragged down by Ahriman and his evil angels, and may be consigned to torture, or may sink into endless debasement. The pure, who have been fortified by the holy mysteries, will mount upwards through the seven spheres, at each stage parting with some of their lower elements, till, at last, the subtilised essential spirit reaches the empyrean, and is received by Mithra into the eternal light.

But the conflict between good and evil, even on this earth, will not last for ever. There will be a second coming of Mithra, which is to be presaged by great plagues. The dead will arise from their tombs to meet him. The mystic bull will again be slain, and his blood, mingled with the juice of the sacred Haoma, will be drunk by the just, and impart to them the gift of eternal life.[4] Fire from heaven will finally devour all that is evil. Thus the slaughter of the bull, which is the image of the succession of decay and fructifying power in physical nature, is also the symbol and guarantee of a final victory over evil and death. And, typifying such lofty and consolatory truths, it naturally met the eye of the worshipper in every chapel. It was also natural that the taurobolium, which was originally a rite of the Great Mother, should be absorbed, like so many alien rites and ideas, by the religion which was the great triumph of syncretism. The baptism of blood was, indeed, a formal cleansing from impurity of the flesh; but it was also cleansing in a higher sense. The inscrip-

[1] Cumont, Intr. p. 297.

[2] Dieterich, *Mithrasliturgie*, p. 197; Cumont, Intr. p. 309.

[3] *Ib.* p. 308 sqq.

[4] *Ib.* p. 310.

tions of the fourth century, which commemorate the blessing of the holy rite, often close with the words *in aeternum renatus.*[1] How far the phrase expressed a moral resurrection, how far it records the sure hope of another life, we cannot presume to say. Whether borrowed from Christian sources or not, it breathes an aspiration strangely different from the tone of old Roman religion, even at its best. There may have been a good deal of ritualism in the cleansing of Mithra. Yet Mithra was, from the beginning, a distinctly moral power, and his worship was apparently untainted by the licence which made other heathen worships schools of cruelty and lust. His connection, indeed, with some of them, must at times have led his votaries into more than doubtful company; Sabazius and Magna Mater were dangerous allies.[2] Yet, on the whole, it has been concluded that Mithraism was a gospel of truth and purity, although the purity was often a matter of merely ceremonial purification and abstinence.

The day is far distant when the mass of men will be capable of the austere mystic vision, which relies little on external ceremonies of worship. Certainly the last ages of paganism in the West were not ripe for any such reserved spirituality. And the religions which captivated the ages that preceded the triumph of the Catholic Church, while they strove to satisfy the deeper needs of the spirit, were more intensely sacerdotal, and more highly organised than the old religions of Greece and Rome. Probably no small part of their strength lay in sacramental mystery, and an occult sacred lore which was the monopoly of a class set apart from the world.[3] Our knowledge of the Mithraic priesthood is unfortunately scanty, and the ancient liturgy has perished.[4] But inscriptions mention an *ordo sacerdotum*; and Tertullian speaks of a "high pontiff of Mithra" and of holy virgins and persons vowed to continence in his service.[5] The priestly functions were certainly more constant and exacting than those of the old priestly colleges of Greece and Rome. There were

[1] Réville, p. 150; cf. *C.I.L.* vi. 510; *Or. Henz.* 2352.

[2] *Or. Henz.* 6042; Gasquet, p. 112, on the inscription of Vincentius, priest of Sabazius, who was buried by the side of Aurelius, a priest of Mithra; cf. Réville, p. 92; Renan, *M. Aurèle*, pp. 578–9, n. 1.

[3] Cumont, Intr. pp. 299, 323.

[4] *Ib.* p. 313; cf. Dieterich, *Mithrasliturgie*, pp. 25, 26.

[5] Tert. *De Praescrip. Haeret.* c. 40; cf. *C.I.L.* vi. 2151, Ordo sacerdotum Mag. suo; xiv. 403; xiv. 65.

solemn sacraments and complicated rites of initiation to be performed. Three times a day, at dawn, noon, and evening, the litany to the Sun was recited.[1] Daily sacrifice was offered at the altars of various gods, with chanting and music. The climax of the solemn office was probably marked by the sounding of a bell.[2] And turning on a pivot, the sacred slab in the apse displayed, for the adoration of the faithful, the scene of the holy feast of Mithra and the Sun after their reconciliation. The seventh day of the week was sacred to the Sun, the sixteenth of each month to Mithra, and the 25th of December, as marking the sun's entrance on a new course of triumph, was the great festival of Mithra's sacred year.[3]

Initiation in the mysteries, after many rites of cleansing and trial, was the crowning privilege of the Mithraist believer. The gradation of spiritual rank, and the secrecy which bound the votaries to one another in a sacred freemasonry, were a certain source of power. S. Jerome alone has preserved for us the seven grades through which the neophyte rose to full communion. They were Corax, Cryphius, Miles, Leo, Perses, Heliodromus, and Pater.[4] What their origin was who shall say? They may correspond to the seven planets, and mark the various stages of the descent of the soul into flesh, and its rise again to the presence of God. According to Porphyry, the first three stages were merely preliminary to complete initiation. Only the Lions were full and real communicants,[5] and the title Leo certainly appears oftenest on inscriptions. The dignity Pater Patrum, or Pater Patratus, was much coveted, and conferred a real authority over the brethren, with an official title to their reverence.[6] The admission to each successive grade was accompanied by symbolic ceremonies, as when the Miles put aside the crown twice tendered to him, saying that Mithra was his only crown.[7] The veil of the Cryphius, and the Phrygian bonnet of the Perses, have a significance or a history which needs no comment. Admission

[1] Cumont, Intr. p. 325.

[2] *Ib.* p. 325; cf. Lafaye, *Div. d'Alexandrie*, p. 138; flutes and bells have been found among débris of chapels, Cum. *Mon.* 253 (p. 380); Intr. p. 68.

[3] Gasquet, p. 125.

[4] S. Hieron. *Ep.* 107, § 2; Gasquet, pp. 91, 2; 96; Cumont, Intr. p. 315; Réville, p. 97.

[5] *De Abstin.* iv. 16. Porphyry connects the degrees with ideas of metempsychosis, *τὴν κοινότητα ἡμῶν τὴν πρὸς τὰ ζῷα αἰνιττόμενοι, κτλ.*

[6] Gasquet, p. 101; Réville, p. 97.

[7] Tert. *De Corona*, xv.

to full communion was preceded by austerities and ordeals which were made the subject of exaggeration and slander. The neophyte, blindfold and bound, was obliged to pass through flame. It was said that he had to take part in a simulated murder with a blood-dripping sword. On the sculpture of Heddernheim a figure is seen standing deep in snow. These ceremonies probably went back to the scenes and ages in which mutilations in honour of Bellona and Magna Mater took their rise. They may also have been a lesson, or a test of apathy and moral courage.[1] But the tales of murder and torture connected with these rites have probably no better foundation than similar slanders about the early Christian mysteries.[2]

The votaries of Mithra, like those of Isis and other eastern deities, formed themselves into guilds which were organised on the model of ordinary sodalities and colleges. As funerary societies, or under the shelter of Magna Mater, they escaped persecution. They had their roll of members, their council of decurions, their masters and curators.[3] And, like the secular colleges, they depended to a great extent, for the erection of chapels and the endowment of their services, on the generosity of their wealthier members and patrons.[4] One man might give the site of a chapel, another a marble altar; a poor slave might contribute out of his *peculium* a lamp or little image to adorn the walls of the crypt.[5]

One undoubted cause of the success of Mithra in the West was the spirit of fraternity and charity which was fostered in his guilds. The hopeless obscurity and depression of the plebeian and servile classes had some alleviation in companies where, for the moment, the poor and lowly-born found himself on an equality with his social superiors. Plebeians and the slaves had a great part in the propagation of the eastern worships, and especially that of the God of Light.[6] In his

[1] Cumont, Intr. p. 322.

[2] Lamprid. *Commodus Ant.* c. 9, sacra Mithriaca homicidio vero polluit, cum illic aliquid ad speciem timoris, vel dici vel fingi soleat; Gasquet, p. 90.

[3] Cumont, Intr. p. 326. For the organisation of the societies of Magna Mater *v.* Foucart, *Associations Religieuses*, p. 20 sqq. Cf. *C.I.L.* vi. 717; vi. 734; vi. 3728; xiv. 286; *Or. Henz.* 6042 (Sentinum).

[4] *Or. Henz.* 6042; on the doubt, however, as to the meaning of *patroni* in this inscription *v. Henz.* note; and Cumont, Intr. p. 327, n. 4.

[5] Cumont, *l.c.*

[6] *Ib.* p. 264. Cf. dedications by slaves or liberti, *Inscr.* 67, 245, 175, 53, 410, 47, 178, 292.

mysteries and guilds the highest dignities were open to them.[1] Moreover, from the size of the chapels it is clear that the congregations were generally small, so that the members of lower social importance were not lost in a crowd.[2] Growing numbers were accommodated, not by enlarging, but by multiplying the shrines.

In the sacraments of Mithra, Tertullian and other Apologists perceived a diabolic parody of the usages of the Church.[3] The *acceptio* of the neophytes, the *sacramentum,* in which they were pledged to secrecy and holy service, the sign or brand made on the brow of the Miles, the ablutions or baptism with holy water, as in the rites of Isis, whatever their origin, could not fail, in an age of death-struggle for supremacy, to arouse the suspicions and fears of the champions of the Church.[4] Finally, the consecrated bread and mingled water and wine, which were only offered to the higher grades, may well have seemed the last and worst profanation of the most solemn Christian rite. The draught from the mystic cup, originally the juice of Haoma, was supposed to have supernatural effects. It imparted not only health and prosperity and wisdom, but also the power to conquer the spirits of evil and darkness, and a secret virtue which might elude the grasp of death.[5]

The temples in which these rites took place repeated for ages the same original type. Mithra and his cave are inseparable ideas, and the name *spelaeum, antrum,* or *specus,* remained to the end the regular designation of his chapels.[6] In country places, grottoes or recesses on the side of a rocky hill might supply a natural oratory of the ancient type.[7] But, in the centre of great towns, the skill of the architect had to simulate the rude structure of the original cavern. Entering through an open portico, the worshipper found himself in an antechapel, through which he passed into another chamber which was called the *apparatorium,* where the priests and neophytes arrayed themselves in their robes or masques before the holy

[1] Cf. *Or. Henz.* 6042 ; Cumont, Intr. p. 327, n. 4.

[2] For the dimensions of one at Rome *v.* Cumont, *Mon.* 19 (p. 205).

[3] Tert. *De Pr. Haeret.* c. 40.

[4] Gasquet, p. 84 ; Cumont, Intr. p. 318.

[5] Gasquet, pp. 81, 82 ; Cumont, Intr. p. 320.

[6] Just. Mart. c. 78 ; Porphyr. *De Antro Nymph.* c. 5 ; Tertull. *De Cor.* xv. ; S. Hieron. *Ep.* 57, 107.

[7] Cumont, Intr. p. 57 ; *Mon.* 237.

rites.[1] Thence they descended by stairs to the level of the cave-like crypt, which was the true sanctuary. On each side there ran a bench of stone, on which was ranged the company of the initiated.[2] The central aisle led up to the apse, against the walls of which was set the sculptured scene of the slaying of the bull, surrounded by the symbolic figures and emblems of Chaldaean star-lore, with altars in front.[3] This was the holiest place, and, from some remains, it would seem to have been railed in, like the chancel of one of our churches.[4] The neophyte, as he approached, must have been impressed by a dazzling scene. On either side the congregation knelt in prayer. Countless lamps shed their brilliant light on the forms of ancient Hellenic gods, or on the images of the mighty powers of earth or ether[5]—above all, on the sacred scene which was the memorial of the might of the "unconquered." The ancient rhythmic litany was chanted to the sound of music; the lights came and went in startling alternations of splendour and gloom. The draught of the sacred cup seemed to ravish the sense. And the votary, as in the Isiac vision in Apuleius, for a moment seemed borne beyond the bounds of space and time into mystic distances.[6]

The Persian cult owed much of its success to imperial and aristocratic favour. The last pagan emperor of the West, the last generation of the pagan aristocracy, were devotees of the Sun-god. It is a curious thing that even under the early Empire Mithraism seems never to have suffered from the suspicion and persecution with which other alien worships had to contend.[7] Its close league with the cult of the Great Mother, which, since the second century B.C., had been an established institution, may have saved Mithra from official mistrust. He also emerged into prominence in the age in which imperial jealousy of guilds and colleges was visibly relaxing its precautions.[8] A more satisfying explanation may perhaps be found in the sympathy of the Flavian dynasty[9] and the

[1] Cumont, Intr. p. 59. Cf. *C.I.L.* iii. 1096, cryptam cum porticibus et apparatorio et exedra, etc.; iii. 3960.

[2] Cumont, Intr. p. 61; *v.* the sketch of the Mithraeum under the Church of S. Clement, at Rome, Cumont, Mon. 19.

[3] Id. *Mon.* 19.

[4] Id. Intr. p. 64.

[5] Twenty-six lamps were found in one Mithraeum, Cumont, *Mon.* 250 (p. 362). For the classical gods, cf. *Mon.* 221 (p. 326), 235, 246 (p. 349).

[6] Apul. *Met.* xi. c. 22.

[7] Cumont, Intr. p. 279 sqq.

[8] *v.* supra, p. 254.

[9] Suet. *Vesp.* iv. v. vii.; *Tit.* v.; *Domit.* i. xiv.; cf. Renan, *Les Évangiles*, p. 226 sq.; *L'Antéchrist*, p. 491.

princes of the third century for the religious ideas of the East, and in the manifest support which heliolatry lent to growing absolutism and the worship of the Caesars.

The apotheosis of the emperors began even in the time of the first Caesar, who rose to the highest divine honours before his death. But it was long a fluctuating and hesitating creed. The provinces, and particularly the cities of Asia Minor,[1] were more eager to decree temples and divine honours to the lord of the world than even the common people of Italy. The superstitious masses and the soldiery, indeed, were equal to any enthusiasm of flattery and superstition. But the cultivated upper class, in spite of the effusive compliance of court poets,[2] having but little belief in any Divine Powers, were not likely to yield an easy faith to the godhead of a Claudius or a Nero.[3] The emperors themselves, belonging to this class, and often sharing its fastidious scepticism, for a time judiciously restrained a too exuberant devotion to their person.[4] The influence of Herod may have filled the lunatic imagination of Caligula with dreams of an eastern despotism and the superhuman dignity of kings.[5] Nero, who had visions of a new monarchy with its seat on eastern hills, may have rejoiced in being adored by Tiridates as the equal of Mithra.[6] But the politic Augustus, while he permitted the foundation of temples and priestly orders in his honour throughout the provinces, and even in Italian towns, along with the divinity of Rome, obstinately refused to have shrines erected to him in the capital.[7] Tiberius pursued the same policy, which was congenial to his cold, realistic temperament. Vespasian, although eastern superstition had a certain charm for him, jested on his death-bed about his own claims to divinity.[8] It was reserved for his son Domitian to be the first emperor who claimed the salutation of "Dominus et Deus" in his lifetime.[9] The best of the early emperors aspired to full divine honours only when their career on earth had closed.

[1] D. Cass. xliii. 14; Tac. *Ann.* iv. 15; vi. 18.

[2] Mart. ix. 4.

[3] Sen. *Lud. De Morte Claud.* c. 12; cf. Boissier, *Rel. Rom.* i. p. 193.

[4] Suet. *Aug.* c. lii.

[5] Id. *Calig.* c. xxii.; Meriv. vi. pp. 4–9.

[6] D. Cass. lxiii. 5, *ἦλθον πρός σε τὸν ἐμὸν θεὸν προσκυνήσων σε ὡς καὶ τὸν Μίθραν.*

[7] Suet. *Aug.* lii.; D. Cass. li. 20; lxvii. 13; Boissier, *Rel. Rom.* i. p. 163.

[8] Id. *Vesp.* c. xxiii. vae, inquit, puto, deus fio.

[9] Id. *Domit.* c. xiii.

Many historic causes made their posthumous elevation to divine rank seem not unnatural. The cult of the Manes, or good spirits of departed friends and ancestors, prepared the Roman mind to adore the memory of the father of the State. The legendary kings of the Latin race—Saturnus, Faunus, Picus, Latinus—were worshipped as *Di indigetes*;[1] Romulus had vanished in a tempest and been carried up to heaven to join the company of the gods. The hero-worship of the Greeks, which raised to semi-divine state after death those who had done great deeds of service to mankind, who had founded cities, or manifested splendid gifts of mind or body, influenced the imagination of a people who had long sat at the feet of Greece. Greek cities raised altars to Rome and to Roman generals who had enslaved them.[2] When the Senate decreed divine honours to a dead emperor, he became *divus*, not *deus*, at least to the cultivated class, and *divus* is a title which even modern sentiment might accord to men who have borne a great and shining part in a world-wide system of administration. The Spartan women were said to call great warriors, men who won their admiration by gallantry, "divine."[3] To the masses the dead emperor no doubt became a veritable god, as the image of M. Aurelius two centuries after his death was found among the *penates* of every pious family in the West.[4] But the philosophic man of the world might also honestly accept the imperial apotheosis by the decree of the Senate, in the sense that another figure had been added to the rare company of those who have been lifted by fortune or merit far above their fellows, and have filled a great space in the life of humanity. People, who for generations erected shrines to the minion of Hadrian, might easily believe in the claims of the Antonine emperors to a place among the gods.

The influence of Egypt and Persia lent its force to stimulate native and original tendencies to king-worship, and to develop the principate of Augustus into the theocratic despotism of Aurelian and Diocletian. The eastern peoples were always eager to lavish on the emperors the adoration which they had been used to offer to their native princes. The ancient

[1] Virg. *Georg.* i. 498; Warde Fowler, *Rom. Festivals*, p. 258.

[2] Plut. *Flamin.* c. 16; cf. Herod. v. 47; Thuc. v. 11.

[3] Plato, *Meno*, 99 D.

[4] Capitol. *M. Aurel.* c. 18.

Pharaohs had been revered as incarnations of the deity and gods upon earth.[1] The Ptolemies inherited and utilised so useful a superstition. These ideas spread into Italy with the diffusion of the Isiac cult among the upper class, and through the influence of travellers and envoys who kept up a fruitful intercourse between Alexandria and Rome. But Egypt went rather too far for the western mind in its apotheosis of kings.[2] A more potent and congenial influence came from the lands of the remoter East. The Persians prostrated themselves before their monarchs, but they did not actually adore them as gods. They reverenced the daemon, or, in Roman phrase, the "genius Caesaris," without worshipping the monarch himself.[3] The king was supposed to be enlightened, inspired, and guarded by a heavenly grace; his brow was crowned by a divine aureole. Yet he was not the equal of God. But the majesty and fortune of kings was something divine and supernatural; they reigned by special grace and had a divine protection. The dynasties who succeeded to the great heritage of the East exploited these ideas to the full, and the most solemn oath was by the Fortune of the King.[4] The superstition of Chaldaea, which connected all human destiny with the orbs of heaven, exercised a profound influence for many centuries both in the East and West. And the Sun, the monarch of the heavens, often identified with Mithra, was regarded as the special patron of kings, enduing them with irresistible power, and guarding their lofty destiny. These ideas spread easily from Pontus and Commagene into the western world. In eastern cities, Caligula and Nero had altars raised to them as solar deities,[5] and Tiridates offered to Nero the adoration due to Mithra.[6] The enigmatical goddess Fortuna, who seems to have had early associations with the Sun,[7] gained fresh strength from the ideas of the divinised destiny of eastern monarchs. According to Plutarch, Tyche left the regions of Assyria and Persia to make her home on the Palatine.[8] The

[1] Boissier, *Rel. Rom.* i. 125; Cumont, Intr. p. 283 sqq.

[2] Amm. Marc. xv. 1, 3.

[3] Athen. vi. 252, *τράπεζαν παρετίθει χωρὶς ὀνομάζων τῷ δαίμονι τῷ βασιλέως.*

[4] Cumont, Intr. p. 286.

[5] *Ib.* p. 290, n. 2.

[6] D. Cass. lxiii. 5, *καὶ ἦλθον πρός σε τὸν ἐμὸν θεόν, προσκυνήσων σε ὡς καὶ τὸν Μίθραν.*

[7] W. Fowler, *Roman Festivals*, p. 169.

[8] Plut. *De Fort. Rom.* iv. *οὕτως ἡ τύχη καταλιποῦσα Πέρσας καὶ Ἀσσυρίους . . . τῷ δὲ Παλατίῳ προσερχομένη, κτλ.*

republican "Fortune of the Roman People" naturally passed into the "Fortuna Augusti," which appears on the imperial coins from the reign of Vespasian. In the age of the Antonines, the image of the goddess in gold always stood in the prince's bed-chamber, and was transferred at the hour of his death to his successor.[1] With the reign of Commodus, who was himself initiated both in the Isiac and Mithraic mysteries, begins the temporary triumph of the oriental cults, which was to reach its height in the reign of Julian. The absence of full materials for the history of the third century,[2] a century crowded with great events, and pregnant with great spiritual movements, should perhaps impose greater caution in tracing the development of imperial power than some writers have always observed. Yet there can be little doubt that the monarchy of the West tended to become a theocratic despotism, and that Persian Sun-worship had a large share in this development. There was always a sober sense in the West which rebelled against the oriental apotheosis of the prince.[3] Yet the iterated adulation, so often recorded faithfully in the Augustan History, reveals an extraordinary abasement of the upper class before the person of the emperor.[3] The emperors never, indeed, claimed like the Sassanids to be "brothers or sons of the Sun and Moon."[4] But in their official style and insignia there were many approaches to the divine claims of the monarchs of the East. The title *invictus*, sacred to Mithra and the Sun, was assumed by Commodus, and borne by his successors.[5] The still more imposing title of "eternal," springing from the same origin, came into vogue in the third century, and appears in the edicts of the last shadowy emperors of the fifth. From the reign of Nero, the imperial crown with darting rays, symbolised the solar ancestry of the prince. Gallienus used to go forth crowned in this manner, and with gold dust in his hair, and raised a colossal statue of himself in the garb of the Sun.[6] The coins of Aurelian, who built the great temple of the Sun from the spoils of Palmyra, bear the legend "deo et domino nato."[7] The West probably never took

[1] Capitol. *Ant. P.* c. 12.
[2] Cf. Vop. *Prob.* c. i. § 3.
[3] Cf. Amm. Marc. xv. 1, 3.
[4] Amm. Marc. xxiii. 6, 5, unde reges ejusdem gentis praetumidi appellari se patiuntur Solis fratres et Lunae.
[5] D. Cass. lxxii. 15, 5.
[6] Treb. Poll. *Gallien.* 16, 18, crinibus suis auri scobem aspersit, etc.
[7] Cumont, Intr. p. 291, n. 5.

these assumptions so literally as the East. But metaphor and imagery tended to become a real faith. The centre of the great religion which was to be the last stronghold of paganism, was the prototype of the emperor in the starry world, and his protector on earth. And the solar grace which surrounded the prince found an easy explanation in the mystic philosophy of the soul's descent which had been absorbed by Mithraism. In coming to earth from the empyrean, the future lord of the world received a special gift of grace and power from the great luminary which is the source of light and life. The religion of the Sun thus tended to become a great spiritual support of an absolutism which was more and more modelling itself on the royalty of the East. The cult of the Sun, which was established in such splendour in 273 A.D. by Aurelian, must have had a great effect in preparing for the oriental claims of monarchy from the reign of Diocletian. Thirty years after the foundation of the stately shrine on the Esquiline, and only twenty years before the conversion of Constantine, all the princes of the imperial house, Jovii Herculii, Augusti, Caesares, as an inscription tells, united to restore a temple of Mithra at Carnuntum, his holy city on the Danube.[1] But the days of Mithra as the god of kings were numbered. After the establishment of the Christian Empire, he had a brief illusory triumph in the reign of Julian, and again in the short-lived effort of reaction led by Eugenius and Nicomachus Flavianus, which had a tragic close in the battle on the Frigidus. Yet his mystic theology was the theme of debate among Roman nobles, trained in the philosophy of Alexandria, long after his last chapels had been buried in ruins; and his worship lingered in secluded valleys of the Alps or the Vosges into the fifth century.[2] The theocratic claim of monarchy, to which Mithra lent his support for so many generations, was destined, in its symbols and phrases, to have a long reign.

M. Renan has hazarded the opinion that, if the Christian Church had been stricken with some mortal weakness, Mithraism might have become the religion of the western world. And, indeed, its marvellously rapid diffusion in Italy and the

[1] Cumont, *Inscr.* No. 367.

[2] Macrob. *Sat.* i. 17; Cumont, Intr. p. 348. The Mithraeum of Sarreburg seems to have been frequented till 395 A.D.

provinces along the Danube and the Rhine, in the second and third centuries, might well have inspired the hope of such a splendid destiny. Although it was primarily a kingly and military creed, it appealed in the end to all classes, by many various attractions. Springing from remote regions of the East, it seemed instinctively to seize the opportunity offered by a marvellous political unity, along with anarchy in morals and religion, to satisfy the imperious needs of a world eager for spiritual light and hope, but distracted among the endless claimants for its devotion. Philosophy had long tried and was still trying to find a spiritual synthesis, and to draw from old mythologies a support for life and conduct. Might not religion succeed where philosophy had failed? Or rather, might not religion gather up into itself the forces of philosophy, and transmute and glorify them in a great concrete symbol? Might not the claims of the past be harmonised with the higher intuitions of a more instructed age, and the countless cults embraced within the circuit of the Roman power be reconciled with the supreme reverence for one central divine figure, as the liberties of an Alpine canton, like those of a great city of Asia, were sheltered under the unchallenged supremacy of Rome? Mithra made the effort, and for the time he succeeded. In his progress to what seemed an almost assured victory, he swept into his orbit the Greek and Latin and Phrygian gods—nay, even the gods of Celtic cantons.[1] They all found a place in his crypts, beside his own sacred image and the Persian deities of his original home. Their altars were ranged around his chapels, and were duly visited by his priests. Yet, though the Persian deity might seem very cosmopolitan and liberal in his indulgence to parochial devotion, he never abated his own lofty claims, and he never forgot his ancestry. While he might ally himself with Magna Mater and Jupiter Dolichenus, he coldly repulsed any association with Isis and Serapis, who were his rivals for oecumenical sway. The old hostility between the worships of Persia and Egypt was only softened in the internecine conflict of both with a more powerful foe. It is only in the last stone records that a votary of Mithra is found combining a devotion to Isis.[2] The claims of the Sun-god to spiritual primacy are

[1] Cumont, Intr. p. 332, n. 3.

[2] *C.I.L.* vi. 504, 846; C. Volusianus was perhaps Praef. Urb. in 365 or Consul in 314.

expounded in the orations of Julian and the dissertations of Praetextatus in the *Saturnalia* of Macrobius. Monotheism in the pagan world was not, indeed, a new thing. It goes back to the philosophers of Ionia and Elea, to Aeschylus and Plato. Nor was syncretism unknown to earlier ages. The Greeks of the days of Herodotus identified the gods of Egypt with their own, as Julius Caesar and Tacitus identified Gallic and German deities with those of the Roman pantheon.[1] But the monotheistic syncretism of Mithra was a broader and more sweeping movement. Local and national gods represented single aspects of nature. Mithra was seated at the centre on which all nature depends. If nature-worship was to justify itself in the eyes of philosophic reason, men must rise to the adoration of the Sun-king, the head of a great hierarchy of divine forces, by means of which he acts and diffuses his inexhaustible energy throughout the universe. And such is the claim made for him by Praetextatus, in the *Saturnalia* of Macrobius, who was a high adept in the mysteries of Mithra.

But the world needed more than a great physical force to assuage its cravings; it demanded a moral God, Who could raise before the eyes of men a moral ideal, and support them in striving to attain it; One Who could guide and comfort in the struggles of life, and in the darkness of its close, Who could prepare the trembling soul for the great ordeal, in which the deeds done in the body are sifted on the verge of the eternal world. In fulfilling his part, Mithra could rely on his own early character as a god of truth and righteousness, a mediator between the powers of good and evil: he had also the experience of the classic mysteries, stretching back to the legendary Orpheus, which, in whatever crude, shadowy symbolism, had taught for ten centuries the doctrine of a moral sequence between this life and the next. The descent of the soul into gross material form, and its possible ascent again, if duly fortified, to ethereal worlds, was common to Mithra and the Orphic and Pythagorean systems. Such a system on one side sad and pessimist, on another was full of the energy of hope. And Mithraism combined the two. It was a religion of strenuous effort and warfare, with the prospect of high rewards in some far-off eternal life.

[1] Herod. ii 48, 50; Caes. *B.G.* vi. 17; Tac. *Germ.* c. 9.

It is little wonder that the Fathers, from the second century, saw in Mithra the most formidable foe of Christ. Indeed, the resemblances between the two religions, some of them superficial, others of a deeper kind, were very striking. How far some of these were due to a common stock of ideas in East and West, how far they were the result of conscious borrowing and mutual imitation, seems to be an insoluble problem. The most learned student of the cult of Mithra is the most cautious in his conclusions on the subject.[1] On the one hand, the two religions, in outlying regions of the Empire, long followed different lines of dispersion. Christianity from its origin in the religion of Israel, spread at first among the cities on the Mediterranean, chiefly where there were colonies of Jews.[2] On the other hand, outside Italy, Mithraism, which was propagated by soldiers and imperial officers, followed the line of the camps and centres of commerce chiefly along the great rivers of the northern frontier. Yet at Ostia and Rome and elsewhere, the two eastern religions must have been early brought face to face. In the syncretism of that age, the age of Gnosticism, rites and doctrines passed easily from one system to another. Mithra certainly absorbed much from kindred worships of Asia Minor, from Hellenic mysteries, and from Alexandrian philosophy. It is equally certain that the Church did not disdain a policy of accommodation, along with the consecration of altars of Christ in the old shrines of paganism. The cult of local heroes was transferred to saints and martyrs. Converts found it hard to part with consecrated phrases and forms of devotion, and might address Jesus in epithets sacred to the Sun. Some Christians in the fifth century still saluted the rising sun with a prayer.[3]

Futile attempts have been made to find parallels to Biblical narrative or symbolism in the faint and faded legend of Mithra recovered from his monuments, the miraculous birth, the sacred rock, the adoration of the shepherds, the grotto,—above all, in the mystic sacrifice of the bull, which seemed to occupy the same space in Mithraic devotion as the Sacrifice on Calvary. But one great weakness of Mithraism lay precisely here—that, in place of the narrative of a Divine life, instinct

[1] Cumont, Intr. pp. 341, 2. [2] *Ib.* p. 339.
[3] *Ib.* p. 341; cf. Gasquet, p. 118 sqq.

with human sympathy, it had only to offer the cold symbolism of a cosmic legend. In their offices and sacramental system the two religions had a more real affinity. Mithra had his baptism and confirmation of new disciples, his ablutions, ascetic preparation for the sacred mysteries, and holy feasts of the consecrated bread and wine, where the mystic draught gave purity and life to soul and body, and was the passport to a life in God. The sacerdotal and liturgical character of his worship, with its striking symbolism, using to the full the emotional effects of lights and music and sacred pomp, offered to souls, who were ripe for a diviner faith, some of that magical charm which was to be exerted over so many ages by the Catholic Church. There are, however, deeper and more fundamental resemblances between the faiths of Mithra and of Christ, and it was to these that the Persian cult owed its great superiority to classical mythology and the official Roman paganism. It responded to a great spiritual movement, of which it is one great object of this book to show the sweep and direction. Formal devotion and ascetic discipline were linked with lofty doctrines as to the origin of the human spirit and an immortal destiny, depending on conduct, as well as sacramental grace, through Mithra the mediator. While the vulgar may have rested in the external charm and power of the worship, there were others who drank in a more spiritual creed expounded to us by one of the last Neo-Platonic votaries of the Sun-God. It told of a fall of the soul into the duress of the body, for a brief period of probation, of a resurrection and great judgment, of a final ascent and beatitude in the life in God, or of endless exile from His presence.[1]

And yet the two systems were separated by an impassable gulf, and Mithra had associations which could not save him from the fate of Jupiter and Demeter, of Hecate and Isis. It is true that his fate was hastened by hostile forces and causes external to religion. Many of his shrines in the Danubian provinces, and along the upper Rhine, were desolated and buried in ruins by the hordes of invaders in the third century.[2] And in the fourth century, the fiercest assaults of the Christian Empire were directed against the worship which was thought to be the patron of magic arts, and a device of the Evil One to travesty and defy the Religion of the

[1] Macrob. *Som. Scip.* i. 13.

[2] Cumont, Intr. p. 344.

Cross.[1] But material force, however fiercely and decisively exerted, although it hastened the doom of the Persian god, only anticipated an inevitable defeat.

A certain severity in Mithraism, which marked it off honourably from other worships of the East, also weakened it as a popular and enduring force. The absence of the feminine charm in its legend, while it saved it from the sensual taint of other heathen systems, deprived it of a fascination for the softer and more emotional side of human nature.[2] Although women may, perhaps, have not been altogether excluded from his mysteries,[3] still Mithra did not welcome them with the warm sympathy which gave Demeter and Magna Mater and Isis so firm a hold on the imagination of women for many generations. The Mater Dolorosa has in all ages been an enthralling power. The legend of the Tauroctonus was a religion for strenuous men. And even its symbolism, with all its strange spell, seems to lack depth and warmth for human nature as a whole. It would indeed be rash to set limits to the power of pious sentiment to transfigure and vivify the most unspiritual materials. And the slaughtered bull in the apse of every chapel of Mithra may have aroused in the end visions and mystic emotion which had passed far beyond the sphere of astral symbolism.

Yet such spiritual interpretation of ancient myth is only for the few, who find in a worship what they bring. For the gross masses, the symbolism of natural processes, however majestic, could never have won that marvellous power which has made a single Divine, yet human, life the inexhaustible source of spiritual strength for all the future. With all his heroic effort to make himself a moral and spiritual force, Mithra remained inextricably linked with the nature-worships of the past. And, with such associations, even the God of light could not be lord of the spiritual future of humanity. Mithraism, with all its strange moral force, with all its charm of antiquity and sacramental rite, with all its charity and tolerance, had within it the germs of a sure mortality. In its tolerance lay precisely its great weakness. The Christian Church might, in S. Augustine's phrase, "spoil the Egyptians," it might borrow

[1] S. Hieron. *Ep.* 107 (Ad Laetam).
[2] Gasquet, p. 134.
[3] Cumont, Intr. p. 329; Porphyr. *De Abstin.* iv. 36; cf. Gasquet, p. 98.

and adapt rites and symbols from pagan temples, or ideas from Greek philosophy.[1] But in borrowing, it transfigured them. In all that was essential, the Church would hold no truce with paganism. "Break the idols and consecrate the temples" was the motto of the great Pontiff. But Mithra was ready to shelter the idols under his purer faith. The images of Jupiter and Venus, of Mars and Hecate, of the local deities of Dacia and Upper Germany, find a place in his chapels beside the antique symbols of the Persian faith.[2] And thus, in spite of a lofty moral mysticism, Mithra was loaded with the heritage of the heathen past. A man admitted to his highest ministry might also worship at the old altars of Greece and Rome. The last hierophant of Eleusis was a high-priest of Mithra.[3] Human nature and religious sentiment are so complex that men of the sincere monotheistic faith of Symmachus, Praetextatus, and Macrobius, have left the almost boastful record of an all-embracing laxity of tolerance on their tombs.[4] On many of these slabs you may read that the man who has been a "father" in the mysteries of Mithra, who has been "born again" in the taurobolium, is also a priest of Hecate, the goddess of dark arts and baleful spirits of the night.[5] Through the astral fatalism of Babylon, Mithra was inseparably connected with the darkest superstitions of East or West,[6] which covered all sorts of secret crime and perfidy, which lent themselves to seduction, conspiracy, and murder, which involved the denial of a moral Providence of the world. Many a pious devotee of Mithra and Hecate would have recoiled, as much as we do, from the last results of his superstition. Such people probably wished only to gain another ally in facing the terrors of the unseen world. Yet there can be little doubt that the majestic supremacy of Mithra, through its old connection with Babylon, sheltered some of the most degrading impostures of superstition.

So rooted is religious sentiment in reverence for the past, for what our fathers have loved and venerated, that men will long tolerate, or even wistfully cherish, sacred forms and ideas which their moral sense has outgrown. Down to the last years

[1] Hatch, *Hibbert Lectures*, pp. 49, 135, 292.

[2] Cumont, Intr. p. 334.

[3] Gasquet, p. 137.

[4] *C.I.L.* vi. 500, 504, 511, 1779.

[5] Maury, *La Magie*, p. 54.

[6] *Ib.* p. 146.

of the fourth century, the Persian worship was defended with defiant zeal by members of the proudest Roman houses. In their philosophic gatherings in the reign of Honorius, they found in Sun-worship the sum and climax of the pagan devotion of the past.[1] Many a pious old priest of Mithra, in the reign of Gratian, was probably filled with wonder and sorrow when he saw a Gracchus and his retinue break into the sanctuary and tear down the venerable symbols from the wall of the apse.[2] He deemed himself the prophet of a pure immemorial faith, as pure as that of Galilee. He was probably a man of irreproachable morals, with even a certain ascetic sanctity, unspotted by the world. He treasured the secret lore of the mysterious East, which sped the departing soul with the last comforting sacraments on its flight to ethereal worlds. But he could not see, or he could not regret, that every day when he said his liturgy, as he made the round of the altars, he was lending the authority of a purer faith to other worships which had affrighted or debauched and enervated the Roman world for forty generations. He could not see that the attempt to wed a high spiritual ideal with nature-worship was doomed to failure. The masses around him remained in their grossness and darkness. And on that very day, it may be, one of his aristocratic disciples, high in the ranks of Mithra's sacred guilds, was attending a priestly college which was charged with the guardianship of gross and savage rites running back to Evander, or he was consulting a Jewish witch, or a Babylonian diviner, on the meaning of some sinister omen, or he may have been sending down into the arena, with cold proud satisfaction, a band of gallant fighters from the Thames or the Danube, to butcher one another for the pleasure of the rabble of Rome. Mithra, the Unconquered, the god of many lands and dynasties from the dawn of history, was a fascinating power. But, at his best, he belonged to the order which was vanishing.

[1] Macrob. *Sat.* i. 17, § 4. [2] S. Hieron. *Ep.* 107, § 2.

INDEX

THE END

Samuel Dill

Samuel Dill was born in County Down, Ireland, in 1844. After serving as a tutor at Oxford, he became Professor of Greek in Queen's College, Belfast. Dublin and Edinburgh universities awarded him honorary degrees and Oxford named him an Honorary Fellow. He died in 1924. He is the author of *Roman Society in the Last Century of the Western Empire,* and *Roman Society in Gaul in the Merovingian Age.*

MERIDIAN BOOKS

Philosophy

BABBITT, IRVING *Rousseau and Romanticism.* M3
BOSANQUET, BERNARD *A History of Aesthetic.* MG36
BURKE, KENNETH *A Grammar of Motives* and *A Rhetoric of Motives.* M143
BURNET, JOHN *Early Greek Philosophy.* MG30
CLIVE, GEOFFREY *The Romantic Enlightenment.* M85
COHEN, MORRIS R. *A Preface to Logic.* M32
GUARDINI, ROMANO *The Death of Socrates.* M138
HERBERG, WILL (ED.) *The Writings of Martin Buber.* M29
HUME, DAVID *A Treatise of Human Nature, Book I: Of the Understanding.* M139
HUXLEY, ALDOUS *The Perennial Philosophy.* M144
JAMES, WILLIAM *Essays on Faith and Morals.* M130
JAMES, WILLIAM *Pragmatism.* M16
KAUFMANN, WALTER (ED.) *Existentialism from Dostoevsky to Sartre.* M39
KAUFMANN, WALTER *Nietzsche.* M25
KONVITZ, MILTON R., AND KENNEDY, GAIL (EDS.) *The American Pragmatists.* M105
MARITAIN, JACQUES *Creative Intuition in Art and Poetry.* M8
MARSAK, LEONARD (ED.) *French Philosophers from Descartes to Sartre.* MG40
MILL, JOHN STUART *Utilitarianism, On Liberty, Essay on Bentham.* M140
MOLNAR, THOMAS *The Decline of the Intellectual.* M128
MONTESQUIEU *The Persian Letters.* M104
ORTEGA Y GASSET, JOSÉ *On Love.* M84
ROSS, W. D. *Aristotle.* M65
RUSSELL, BERTRAND *An Outline of Philosophy.* M97
SALOMON, ALBERT *In Praise of Enlightenment.* M137
TAYLOR, A. E. *Plato: The Man and His Work.* MG7
VIGNAUX, PAUL *Philosophy in the Middle Ages.* M81
WOLFSON, HARRY AUSTRYN *The Philosophy of Spinoza.* MG16
ZELLER, EDWARD *Outlines of the History of Greek Philosophy.* M9
ZIMMER, HEINRICH *Philosophies of India.* MG6

MERIDIAN BOOKS

Art, Architecture, and Music

BARZUN, JACQUES *Berlioz and His Century.* M30

BERENSON, BERNARD *The Italian Painters of the Renaissance.* M40

BIKEL, THEODORE *Folksongs and Footnotes.* MG27

FRY, ROGER *Vision and Design.* M33

GILSON, ETIENNE *Painting and Reality.* M79

HUXLEY, ALDOUS *On Art and Artists.* M99

KAUFMANN, EDGAR, AND RAEBURN, BEN (EDS.) *Frank Lloyd Wright: Writings and Buildings.* MG22

NOSS, LUTHER (ED.) *Christian Hymns.* LA38

PACK, ROBERT, AND LELASH, MARJORIE (TRS.) *Mozart's Librettos.* M80

PANOFSKY, ERWIN *Gothic Architecture and Scholasticism.* M44

PATER, WALTER *The Renaissance.* M124

PHILIPSON, MORRIS (ED.) *Aesthetics Today.* M112

READ, HERBERT *The Grass Roots of Art.* M108

READ, HERBERT *The Philosophy of Modern Art.* M7

SMITH, G. E. KIDDER *The New Architecture of Europe.* MG33

STEINBERG, SAUL *The Catalogue.* M147

TOVEY, DONALD FRANCIS *The Forms of Music.* M36

TOVEY, DONALD FRANCIS *The Main Stream of Music and Other Essays.* M74

Meridian Books are published by The World Publishing Company, Cleveland and New York. For a free Meridian catalogue write to Dept. AM, Meridian Books, 119 West 57th Street, N.Y.